LATIN *FOR THE* NEW MILLENNIUM

STUDENT TEXT

LEVEL 3

LATIN FOR THE NEW MILLENNIUM
Series Information

LEVEL ONE

Student Text (2008)

Student Workbook (2008)

Teacher's Manual (2008)

Teacher's Manual for Student Workbook (2008)

ENRICHMENT TEXTS

From Romulus to Romulus Augustulus:
Roman History for the New Millennium (2008)

The Original Dysfunctional Family:
Basic Classical Mythology for the New Millennium (2008)

LEVEL TWO

Student Text (2009)

Student Workbook (2009)

Teacher's Manual (2009)

Teacher's Manual for Student Workbook (2009)

ENRICHMENT TEXTS

From Rome to Reformation:
Early European History for the New Millennium (2009)

The Clay-footed SuperHeroes:
Mythology Tales for the New Millennium (2009)

LEVEL THREE

Student Text (2012)

Teacher's Manual (2012)

ENRICHMENT TEXTS

Latin III: Select Latin Enrichment Readings (2012)

ELECTRONIC RESOURCES

www.lnm.bolchazy.com

www.bolchazy.com/eBooks.htm

Quia Question Bank

LATIN *FOR THE* NEW MILLENNIUM

STUDENT TEXT

LEVEL 3

Edited by Helena Dettmer and LeaAnn A. Osburn

Bolchazy-Carducci Publishers, Inc.
Mundelein, Illinois USA

Series Editor: LeaAnn A. Osburn

Volume Editor: Donald E. Sprague

Contributing Editors: Bridget Buchholz, Laurel De Vries, Laurie Haight Keenan,
   Karen Lee Singh, Peter Sipes, John Traupman

Cartography: Mapping Specialists

Indexing: Michael Hendry

Proofreading: Gary K. Varney

Cover Illustration: The Pantheon, Rome © 2012 Shutterstock Images, LLC

Other Illustrations: Photo Credits appear on pp. 609–610

Latin for the New Millennium
Student Text, Level 3

Helena Dettmer and LeaAnn A. Osburn, Editors

AP is a registered trademark of the College Entrance Examination Board, which was
not involved in the production of, and does not endorse this product.

Reprint with corrections, 2014

Bolchazy-Carducci Publishers, Inc.
1570 Baskin Road
Mundelein, Illinois 60060
www.bolchazy.com

Printed in Canada
2014
by Friesens

ISBN 978-0-86516-760-5

Library of Congress Cataloging-in-Publication Data

Latin for the new millennium : student text level 3 / edited by LeaAnn Osburn and
Helena Dettmer.
    pages. cm.
 Includes bibliographical references and index.
 ISBN 978-0-86516-760-5 (hardbound : alk. paper) 1. Latin language--Readers. 2.
Latin literature--History and criticism. I. Osburn, LeaAnn A. II. Dettmer, Helena.
 PA2095.L345 2012
 478.6'421--dc23
                                                                    2012013762

CONTENTS

PART1: AUTHORS OF THE LATE REPUBLIC

PART 2: AUTHORS OF THE AUGUSTAN AGE

PART 3: AUTHORS FROM THE POST-ANTIQUE ERA

LIST OF MAPS

FOREWORD

Skeptics may scoff at the idea that another volume of Latin readings is needed in intermediate level classrooms, but even the most dubious will be swayed by the latest addition to the *Latin for the New Millennium* series. This Level 3 text strives to address all the deficiencies teachers encounter with other transitional volumes and offers instead a comprehensive introduction to a series of authors with every support—lexical, grammatical, historical—that the reading neophyte could need.

Most pleasing is the inclusion of all six of the authors so often read in the schools—Caesar, Cicero, Catullus, Vergil, Horace, and Ovid. Too often teachers are forced to choose readers for one or two authors to the exclusion of others. As a result some students have no exposure either to prose or to poetry in meters other than dactylic hexameter. But this volume allows students to experience a variety of both prose and poetic styles. The inclusion of a chapter devoted to post-antique Latin continues the series' commitment to reminding teachers and students alike that there is an abundance of engaging and elegant Latin texts spanning the last millennium and more, which we can and should be enjoying. The decision to incorporate letters of Erasmus, who was at the center of the humanist movement of the fifteenth and sixteenth centuries, opens for students a window into the scholarly community of his time, in which Erasmus and his friends and associates were remarkably interconnected. The inclusion of pieces by Petrarch and John Parke on Vergil and Horace, respectively, nicely brings the reader back to the classical sources from which the movement began.

The selections from each author are modest, which is precisely what is suitable for students reading their first extended, unadapted Latin. There is a nice variety in the readings from Cicero, drawn from the *Prō Archiā*, *In Catilīnam* I, and *De amicitiā*. All of the passages from Caesar and several of those from Vergil appear also on the AP syllabus, giving students who read them in an intermediate course and then go on to AP a leg up on the required reading, but more important, exposure to those authors in a less harried, more supportive setting. Beginning the *Aeneid* or *Dē bellō Gallicō* again will be like revisiting an old friend.

Equally as important as the variety of authors is the superb context that this text provides through several historical essays and introductions, not only to each author but also to each reading selection. Many readers ask Latin students to deal with texts in a virtual vacuum, with very little idea of the author's motivation or the audience for which each selection was composed. Instructors are left to fill in knowledge gaps. This volume not only sets the scene for each passage but then, in the passage notes and in the "Take Note" sections, provides cultural details that relate directly to customs and practices mentioned in the reading. All of these resources give students the means to apply top-down reading strategies to the text, anticipating what may be said and relating it to what they already know—a critical skill for fluent readers to develop.

Of great assistance to the student is the markup of the first selection for each classical author. Variations in font and the use of underlining and spacing all facilitate the breaking of the text into intelligible chunks and highlight the syntactical structure of the Latin. In addition, words that are missing by ellipsis are included in parentheses, as a way to acclimate the reader to the compressed nature of the language. Of particular importance is the inclusion of the passage again toward the end of the section without any markup, so that students can envision for themselves the structure of the Latin and the necessary repetition of elements for understanding. Special attention has been given to the first selections from Cicero, whose periodic style can be so befuddling for inexperienced readers. The editors have applied the "pass-through" system, adding a clause at a time and indenting clauses to indicate subordination and illuminate structure and meaning. All these supports lead the student to develop a sensitivity to arrangement and style.

The editors of this Level 3 text know their students well; notes in other readers that do not appear immediately adjacent to a text too frequently remain unconsulted; and so here vocabulary and notes for each section of the selection appear beneath and opposite the Latin. The notes are thorough without being wordy or overwhelming, as can happen with overly zealous commentators.

All of these elements discussed so far (context, notes, etc.) can be found in varying degrees in a number of readers, albeit generally not executed nearly as well as in this volume. But this text truly excels in the materials that follow each chunk of a reading, beginning with comprehension questions and exercises.

The first exercise after each passage draws students to a bottom-up assessment of the Latin, enhancing skills that enable them to understand the details of a passage, adding to the more global assessment of meaning that top-down strategies provide. Here students must capture the nitty-gritty details of the grammar, parsing words and analyzing structures. Then most selections are followed by at least one "Language Fact"—a category used to introduce new grammar in the *Latin for the New Millennium* Level 1 and Level 2 texts. In this volume the "Fact" concerns a syntactical element that is employed in the selection just read and serves as a review for students, and so rather than suffer through a stilted and dull review of grammar undertaken at the beginning of the course, students will refresh and strengthen their knowledge of syntax organically, as they encounter it in their reading. Each of the "Language Facts" is immediately reinforced by an exercise whose content is drawn from the preceding and previous reading selections. The outcome is thus twofold: the students' attention is drawn to the syntactical form at the same time as their understanding of the reading is enhanced—a magnificent combination.

The text eschews traditional vocabulary lists; instead the editors have chosen to include sections entitled "Vocabulary Building," with such varied content as names of peoples and rivers, synonyms and antonyms, roots, prefixes and suffixes, and idioms. Other familiar features from the earlier Level 1 and 2 texts are "Study Tips" and "By the Ways," which point out sticky grammatical points, unusual features of Latin grammar or vocabulary, rhetorical and poetic devices, and other intriguing bits of information.

Finally, and perhaps most important for teachers of AP and any instructor who wants students to be able to do literary analysis of Latin texts, an essay assignment is included for each reading selection, in which students are asked to write a response that is supported by direct citation of the Latin text. This kind of assignment prepares students not only for the demands of the AP Latin curriculum, but for critical writing across many disciplines, where analysis of source material is vital to a successful argument.

While this is the third volume of the *Latin for the New Millennium* series, using a number of familiar elements from the earlier levels, it can quite happily be used as a beginning reader in any intermediate Latin classroom, following the completion of any introductory text or series. The editors are to be applauded for assembling a well-conceived, remarkably complete, and thoroughly usable resource.

JACQUELINE M. CARLON
Associate Professor of Classics
University of Massachusetts at Boston

PREFACE

Latin for the New Millennium, Level 3, will help you learn how to read unadapted passages of Latin with ease and understanding. There are seven chapters in this book. The first six chapters include passages from Caesar, Catullus, Cicero, Vergil, Horace, and Ovid. The seventh chapter contains passages from Erasmus and his correspondents as well as a reading from Petrarch about Vergil and a poem praising Horace by an early American Latin poet, John Parke.

Latin for the New Millennium, Level 3, is indebted to Bolchazy-Carducci Publishers' primary author texts for high school, its Workbook Series, and its LEGAMUS Transitional Reader Series, *Latin for the New Millennium*, Level 1 and Level 2, as well as to several other titles. The solid pedagogy, excellent scholarship, and success of these texts have been an inspiration to the development of *Latin for the New Millennium*, Level 3. Please consult the Acknowledgements pp. xx–xxii for a complete listing of these texts.

CHAPTER COMPONENTS

READING PASSAGES, VOCABULARY, AND NOTES

In *Latin for the New Millennium*, Level 3, each reading section begins with a Latin passage taken from a Latin author. The first passage in each section is designed to ease you into reading the style of the author. You may find certain words underlined, in different fonts, or in parentheses. Directions before the passage will explain how to use these special aids. The same reading passage will be repeated without adaptations after the adapted passage. For most authors the remaining reading passages in each chapter will not feature these aids. You will find in the Cicero chapter, however, that the aids continue for the first five reading passages owing to the style of his Latin.

Each reading passage is followed by notes that include vocabulary entries, translation aids, grammatical and syntactical features, historical and cultural material, and suggestions on ways to interpret and analyze the Latin. The editors have endeavored to incorporate every new vocabulary word and grammatical/syntactical item found in the reading selection in order to assist you with reading the Latin passage. In addition, grammatical/syntactical explanations and vocabulary entries may refer to words and topics already seen in *Latin for the New Millennium*, Levels 1 and 2. If the word has a different meaning or nuance or can be easily forgotten, if the topic contains new information or is often confused or not remembered, or if the editors felt that there was sufficient reason, the word or topic is included again. Translations can be easily recognized in the notes because they are surrounded by quotation marks. A new figure of speech is defined in a By the Way, which also explains how the figure enhances the line or passage. Figures of speech already introduced in a By the Way are usually indicated in the notes. It is your responsibility to determine how the figure of speech enriches the line or passages in which it is included.

COMPREHENSION QUESTIONS

Comprehension questions follow the vocabulary and notes for each reading passage and are designed to help you determine how well you understood the passage. Some comprehension questions ask you to "cite the Latin." For these questions you should find the Latin words in the passage that illustrate the answer you have given in English. Citing the Latin is an important skill to master since you will be required to do this in the answers you write to essay questions and on some standardized examinations.

VOCABULARY BUILDERS

Latin for the New Millennium, Level 3, does not ask you to master specific vocabulary words as you were asked to do in the Vocabulary to Learn sections of the Levels 1 and 2 books. Yet one of the goals of Latin 3 is to increase your vocabulary and thereby your ability to read Latin. To this end, a Vocabulary Builder in which you will find information and sometimes exercises on ways to build your vocabulary will follow many of the Latin passages. This will include learning Latin synonyms and antonyms, mastering an author's idioms, using derivative study to aid your vocabulary development, and studying prefixes, suffixes, and Latin word families.

SHORT ANSWER QUESTIONS—EXERCISE 1

Understanding Latin grammar and syntax underpins your ability to read and comprehend Latin accurately. The short answer questions that follow each reading passage focus on the case, number, and use of nouns; the tense, voice, mood, person, and number of verbs; the use of subjunctive verbs; the degree of adjectives and adverbs, the word(s) that an adjective modifies; and the tense, voice, and use of infinitives and participles. In this book when you are asked for the "form" of a Latin word, you are being instructed to identify the word as an infinitive, participle, or imperative.

LANGUAGE FACTS AND EXERCISES

As in *Latin for the New Millennium*, Levels 1 and 2, the Language Fact section provides information on grammar or syntax that you have already seen in the reading passage. Sometimes the information will be new to you and, therefore, something that you need to master; at other times, the information will be a review of a topic presented earlier in the book or in Levels 1 or 2. Sometimes a new piece of information is added to what is being reviewed.

The exercise(s) that follows the Language Fact section is designed to help you practice the Language Fact. You will often see in this exercise(s) phrases and sentences that will seem familiar to you since many of these have been taken from or adapted from current or past reading passages.

ESSAY QUESTIONS

The ability to express yourself in writing is a skill that is necessary for state and standardized tests, for university courses, and for the world of work. An essay question about each reading passage is included in *Latin for the New Millennium*, Level 3. It is helpful to think through or to jot down the points you intend to make in your essay before you begin writing. When writing about a piece of literature, it is necessary to support what you say with quotations (called citations) from the passage in the original language and with a translation of the citation.

SCANSION EXERCISES

In Latin poetry, it is essential to know which vowels are long and which ones are short. For a fuller discussion of Latin meter and scansion, see Appendix B. You will be asked to scan several lines of Latin poetry at the end of each reading passage of Catullus, Vergil, Horace, and Ovid.

ADDITIONAL FEATURES

MEMORĀBILE DICTŪ

In the *Memorābile Dictū* section at the beginning of each chapter, a Latin quote from the chapter's author is given and an explanation of the significance of this saying is presented. Learning this quote will increase your understanding of the thoughts and ideas of the author.

STUDY TIPS

The same Study Tip icon that was used in *Latin for the New Millennium*, Levels 1 and 2, will notify you of something to study or of a way to learn the information. Sometimes rhymes or mnemonic devices are given as learning aids.

BY THE WAY

The By the Way icon that you saw in *Latin for the New Millennium*, Levels 1 and 2, called your attention to additional information of note. This By the Way icon serves the same function in *Latin for the New Millennium*, Level 3, but also introduces new figures of speech (these special terms are identified in SMALL capital letters) and explains how these figures enhance the Latin under discussion. Smaller points of grammar and syntax are also sometimes explained in a By the Way instead of in the Language Fact sections, which focus on larger topics.

REMINDER

Latin for the New Millennium, Level 3, introduces many grammatical and syntactical topics along with numerous figures of speech. In order to assist you with this new information, a Reminder icon will be used to signal that information is being repeated. A Reminder is usually given only once, although occasionally an additional Reminder is given when the information was presented much earlier in the text. Sometimes, too, you will be reminded about a grammatical or syntactical topic in the information on the given line in the Notes. If you realize that there is something you need to refresh in your mind and there is no Reminder, you should consult the index to find the page on which the topic was first presented.

TAKE NOTE

As in *Latin for the New Millennium*, Level 2, a Take Note icon following the notes and vocabulary for a reading alerts you to additional information related to the reading passage. These help you build your Latin reading skills and your understanding of the literature and the culture that produced it.

HISTORICAL ESSAYS

Latin literature should be read and interpreted within the historical context that influenced the writers of that time. For this reason *Latin for the New Millennium*, Level 3, offers two historical overviews so that you can better understand the times of turbulence and transition in the first century BCE and at the start of the first century CE, an age that produced the six extraordinary authors whose remarkable writings are presented in this book. The last chapter of this book contains selections from medieval and Renaissance writers of Latin and continues the theme, presented in *Latin for the New Millennium*, Level 2, of the importance of medieval and later Latin literature that has spanned the millennia.

ACKNOWLEDGEMENTS

The editors would like to thank a number of people who have offered us help through personal comments and written suggestions as well as those authors without whose works of scholarship this volume would not have been finished in a timely manner, including the following:

Our volume editor, Donald Sprague, for all his suggestions and comments from the inception of this project.

Judy Armstrong, Bridget Buchholz, Jody Cull, Laurel De Vries, Laurie Haight Keenan, and Adam Velez, all of Bolchazy-Carducci Publishers, without whose contributions this volume would have been delayed.

John Traupman for doing the marking of macrons in the first manuscript.

Peter Sipes for his work on the glossary and checking macrons.

Karen Lee Singh and Donald E. Sprague for their valuable work on Chapter 7.

The College of Liberal Arts and Sciences at the University of Iowa for generously providing funds for Billie Cotterman and Jackie Jones, graduate students at the University of Iowa, to augment the vocabulary for several authors and for Joshua Langseth, another graduate student at the University of Iowa, to assist in closely proofreading the text.

Rosemary Moore for writing the historical overviews "The Last Century of the Roman Republic" and "Augustus and the Principate" and for reviewing the "Timeline of the Catilinarian Conspiracy" and the "Introduction to Cicero."

Terence Tunberg for his essay "Why Post-antique Latin?" in Part 3.

Chris Craig for sending us a copy of his article on teaching the *In Catilīnam*.

John Finamore, Craig Gibson, Carin Green, Peter Green, and Jack Holtsmark, faculty of the Classics Department at the University of Iowa, both current and past, with whom on a few occasions we conferred on difficult points of grammar and translation.

Laurie Haight Keenan, Bridget Buchholz, Laurel De Vries, and Gary Varney for their careful proofreading and Michael Hendry for his index.

Elisa Denja and Rose Williams whose many phone conversations with us have brought issues involved in the pedagogy of this volume into clearer focus.

All the consultants on this volume for their pertinent comments that have improved this work, including Jill Crooker, Sherwin Little, Sherrilyn Martin, Kelly Northrup, Mary Pendergraft, Rebecca Wick, Rose Williams, and Philip Woodruff as well as the consultant pilot teachers Sherry Jankowski and Nicholas Young.

All the authors whose books (please see list below), previously published by Bolchazy-Carducci Publishers, have formed sections of this book, including Ronnie Ancona, Henry Bender, Barbara Weiden Boyd, Katherine Bradley, Jane Crawford, Denise Davis-Henry, Sheila Dickison, G. Facer, Phyllis Young Forsyth, Karl Frerichs, Judith Hayes, Mark Haynes, Charbra Adams Jestin, Leo Kaiser, Phyllis Katz, Kenneth Kitchell, Milena Minkova, Hans-Friedrich Mueller, David J. Murphy, Debra Nousek, Caroline Perkins, Patsy Ricks, Judith Sebesta, Thomas Sienkewicz, Karrie Singh, Sean Smith, Terence Tunberg, and Rose Williams.

And, especially, Marie and Lou Bolchazy for their vision that this was a truly needed work.

HELENA DETTMER and LEAANN OSBURN
2012

WORKS CONSULTED, ADAPTED, AND REVISED

The first set of titles are those Bolchazy-Carducci texts that were adapted and revised for *Latin for the New Millennium*, Level 3. The editors significantly adapted these texts and developed the many student-friendly supplementary materials like the "Vocabulary Builders," "By the Ways," "Study Tips," and "Reminders" that are incorporated into this text. Helena Dettmer wrote the introductions for the Catullus and Cicero chapters. Following these titles is a list of other sources consulted in the development of the text.

CAESAR

Mueller, Hans-Friedrich. *Caesar: Selections from His Commentarii on De Bello Gallico.* Mundelein, IL: Bolchazy-Carducci Publishers, 2012.

Williams, Rose, and Debra. L. Nousek. *A Caesar Workbook.* Mundelein, IL: Bolchazy-Carducci Publishers, 2012.

———. *A Caesar Workbook Teacher's Manual.* Mundelein, IL: Bolchazy-Carducci Publishers, 2012.

Williams, Rose, and Hans-Friedrich Mueller. *Caesar: A Legamus Transitional Reader.* Mundelein, IL: Bolchazy-Carducci Publishers, 2012.

———. *Caesar: A Legamus Transitional Reader Teacher's Guide.* Mundelein, IL: Bolchazy-Carducci Publishers, 2012.

CATULLUS

Bender, Henry V., and Phyllis Young Forsyth. *Catullus Expanded Edition.* Wauconda, IL: Bolchazy-Carducci Publishers, 2008.

———. *Catullus Expanded Edition Teacher's Guide.* Wauconda, IL: Bolchazy-Carducci Publishers, 2007.

Dettmer, Helena, LeaAnn Osburn, and Ronnie Ancona. *A Catullus Workbook.* Wauconda, IL: Bolchazy-Carducci Publishers, 2006.

————. *A Catullus Workbook Teacher's Manual.* Wauconda, IL: Bolchazy-Carducci Publishers, 2006.

Kitchell, Kenneth F., and Sean Smith. *Catullus: A Legamus Transitional Reader.* Wauconda, IL: Bolchazy-Carducci Publishers, 2008.

Smith, Sean. *Catullus: A Legamus Transitional Reader Teacher's Guide.* Mundelein, IL: Bolchazy-Carducci Publishers, 2010.

CICERO

Dickison, Sheila K., and Patsy Rodden Ricks. *Cicero De Amicitia Selections.* Wauconda, IL: Bolchazy-Carducci Publishers, 2006.

————. *Cicero De Amicitia Selections Teacher's Guide.* Wauconda, IL: Bolchazy-Carducci Publishers, 2006.

Frerichs, Karl. *Cicero's First Catilinarian Oration.* Wauconda, IL: Bolchazy-Carducci Publishers, 1997.

Hayes, Judith, and Jane Webb Crawford. *A Cicero Workbook.* Wauconda, IL: Bolchazy-Carducci Publishers, 2007.

————. *A Cicero Workbook Teacher's Manual.* Wauconda, IL: Bolchazy-Carducci Publishers, 2007.

Haynes, Mark, and Judith Lynn Sebesta. *Cicero: A Legamus Transitional Reader.* Mundelein, IL: Bolchazy-Carducci Publishers, 2010.

————. *Cicero: A Legamus Transitional Reader Teacher's Guide.* Mundelein, IL: Bolchazy-Carducci Publishers, 2010.

HORACE

Ancona, Ronnie. *Horace Selected Odes and Satire 1.9.* 2nd ed. Wauconda, IL: Bolchazy-Carducci Publishers, 2005.

————. *Horace Selected Odes and Satire 1.9, Teacher's Guide.* 2nd ed. Wauconda, IL: Bolchazy-Carducci Publishers, 2005.

Ancona, Ronnie, and David J. Murphy. *A Horace Workbook.* Wauconda, IL: Bolchazy-Carducci Publishers, 2005.

————. *A Horace Workbook Teacher's Manual.* Wauconda, IL: Bolchazy-Carducci Publishers, 2006.

————. *Horace: A Legamus Transitional Reader.* Wauconda, IL: Bolchazy-Carducci Publishers, 2005.

Murphy, David J. *Horace: A Legamus Transitional Reader Teacher's Guide.* Mundelein, IL: Bolchazy-Carducci Publishers, 2010.

OVID

Jestin, Charbra A., and Phyllis. B. Katz. *An Ovid Workbook*. Wauconda, IL: Bolchazy-Carducci Publishers, 2006.

———. *An Ovid Worbook Teacher's Manual*. Wauconda, IL: Bolchazy-Carducci Publishers, 2010.

———. *Ovid: Amores, Metamorphoses Selections*. 2nd ed. Wauconda, IL: Bolchazy-Carducci Publishers, 2000.

Perkins, Caroline, and Denise Davis-Henry. *Ovid: A Legamus Transitional Reader*. Wauconda, IL: Bolchazy-Carducci Publishers, 2009.

———. *Ovid: A Legamus Transitional Reader Teacher's Guide*. Wauconda, IL: Bolchazy-Carducci Publishers, 2009.

POST-ANTIQUE LATIN

Facer, G. S. *Erasmus and His Times*. 1951. Reprinted ed. Bristol, England: Bristol Classical Press, and Wauconda, IL: Bolchazy-Carducci Publishers, 1988.

Godfrey, Aaron W. *Medieval Mosaic: A Book of Medieval Latin Readings*. Wauconda, IL: Bolchazy-Carducci Publishers, 2003.

Kaiser, Leo M. *Early American Latin Verse*. Wauconda, IL: Bolchazy-Carducci Publishers, 1984.

VERGIL

Boyd, Barbara Weiden. *Vergil's Aeneid: Selections from Books 1, 2, 4, 6, 10, & 12*. Wauconda, IL: Bolchazy-Carducci Publishers, 2002.

———. *Vergil's Aeneid: Selections from Books 1, 2, 4, 6, 10, & 12 Teacher's Guide*. Wauconda, IL: Bolchazy-Carducci Publishers, 2002.

Boyd, Barbara Weiden, and Katherine Bradley. *A Vergil Workbook*. 2nd ed. Mundelein, IL: Bolchazy-Carducci Publishers, 2012.

———. *A Vergil Workbook Teacher's Manual*. 2nd ed. Mundelein, IL: Bolchazy-Carducci Publishers, 2012.

Osburn, LeaAnn, and Karrie Lee Singh. *Vergil: A Legamus Transitional Reader Teacher's Guide*. Mundelein, IL: Bolchazy-Carducci Publishers, 2010.

Sienkewicz, Thomas J., and LeaAnn Osburn. *Vergil: A Legamus Transitional Reader*. Wauconda, IL: Bolchazy-Carducci Publishers, 2004.

GRAMMATICAL APPENDIX

The following text formed the basis for Appendix D: Grammatical Forms, Paradigms, and Syntax, Appendix E: Supplementary Grammar, Morphology, and Syntax, and the Latin to English Glossary:

Minkova, Milena, and Terence Tunberg. *Latin for the New Millennium*, Level 2. Mundelein, IL: Bolchazy-Carducci Publishers, 2009.

HELENA DETTMER

BA Indiana University; PhD University of Michigan

Professor of Classics and Associate Dean for Undergraduate Programs in the College of Liberal Arts and Sciences at the University of Iowa

Dettmer received the University of Iowa's 2012 Lola Lopes Award for Undergraduate Student Advocacy. A former Mellon Fellow at Duke University, a recipient of the Iowa May Brodbeck Humanities Fellowship, an Iowa Faculty Scholar, an Iowa collegiate fellow, and past president of the Classical Association of the Middle West and South, Dettmer has authored *Horace: A Study in Structure* (1983) and *Love by the Numbers: Form and Meaning in the Poetry of Catullus* (1997). She is coauthor of *A Workbook to Ayers' English Words from Latin and Greek Elements* (1986), in its second printing and used widely in vocabulary-building courses around the country, as well as *A Catullus Workbook* (2006) and its *Teacher's Manual* (2006), which she coauthored with LeaAnn Osburn. Her current project is a book-length study examining the poetic structure of Ovid's *Amores*.

LEAANN A. OSBURN

BA Monmouth College, Illinois; MA Loyola University Chicago

Teacher Emerita, Barrington High School, Barrington, Illinois

LeaAnn A. Osburn received an American Classical League *Emerita* Award in 2012, served as both vice president and president of the Illinois Classical Conference, and received the ICC Lifetime Achievement Award in 2008. Osburn received the Illinois Latin Teacher of the Year Award (1989), the Illinois Lt. Governor's Award (1990), and the CAMWS Good Teacher Award (1996). She coauthored *A Catullus Workbook* (2006) and *Teacher's Manual* (2006) with Helena Dettmer, *Vergil: A Legamus Transitional Reader* (2004) with Thomas J. Sienkewicz, and *Vergil: A Legamus Transitional Reader Teacher's Guide* (2010) with Karen Lee Singh. Osburn served as the series editor for *Latin for the New Millennium*, Levels 1 and 2.

EDITORS, CONSULTANTS, PILOT TEACHERS

VOLUME EDITOR AND CONTRIBUTOR

DONALD E. SPRAGUE

BA Williams College, Massachusetts; MPS Loyola University Chicago

Donald Sprague also studied at the Intercollegiate Center for Classical Studies in Rome. He taught Latin and Greek, founded the Honors Program, established a summer study tour of Italy and Greece, and served as an administrator for many years at Loyola Academy, Wilmette, Illinois. He regularly develops and leads adult tours of classical sites. He served as treasurer of the Illinois Classical Conference for fourteen years and two terms as president of the Chicago Classical Club. In 1990, Sprague received the Illinois Latin Teacher of the Year award and the Illinois Lt. Governor's Award. He was a 2011 finalist for Adjunct Professor of the Year at Kennedy-King College. Sprague contributed to Chapter 7 of this volume.

CONTRIBUTORS

KAREN LEE SINGH

BA, MA, and PhD University of Wisconsin at Madison

Karen Lee Singh taught at the University of Wisconsin and retired from Florida State University in 2006 where she also taught in the Florida State University School. Singh was three times named the N.H.S. Teacher of the Year, and received the DeMolay Teacher of the Year for Tallahassee (1980), the Florida Latin Teacher of the Year (1985), and The Irwing Wershow Award for Lifetime Achievement (1999). She has regularly been invited to present workshops and papers to classics groups. Singh served as president of the Florida Foreign Language Association and first vice president of the Classical Association of Florida. She contributed two chapters to Paul MacKendrick's *The Philosophical Books of Cicero* (1989). Singh served on the AP Development Committee and on the National Committee on Standards for Teaching Latin and Greek. Singh served as contributor to and editor of Chapter 7.

ROSEMARY MOORE

BA Harvard; PhD University of Michigan

Prior to joining the faculty at the University of Iowa in 2003, Rosemary Moore served as a visiting professor at St. Olaf College. She has taught a range of courses including Roman History, The Hellenistic World and Rome, Food in Ancient Society, Ancient Warfare, and Ancient Sports and Leisure. Her publications and presentations have focused on such topics as Roman generalship, military history, Crassus at Carrhae, the art of command, and related topics. In 2007, Moore was honored to serve as the recipient of a Blegen Research Fellowship and, in that capacity, to teach two courses at Vassar College. Moore wrote two of the historical overview essays in this volume.

TERENCE TUNBERG

BA, MA University of Southern California; PhD University of Toronto

Terence Tunberg is a professor of classics at the University of Kentucky. He has also taught in Belgium and Canada. He is a specialist in Latin composition, and an expert in the history of the approaches to writing Latin prose from antiquity to early modern times. His works include an edition of a collection of medieval Latin speeches, commentaries on Latin works, and numerous studies of the history of imitation in Latin writing. In addition, for more than a decade he has offered summer seminars designed to introduce people to the use of spoken Latin.

Tunberg coauthored *Latin for the New Millennium*, Levels 1 and 2, with Milena Minkova. Tunberg composed the introductory essay for the post-antique section.

CONSULTANTS

JILL CROOKER

BA University of Illinois; MS Ed Nazareth College of Rochester, New York

Jill Crooker taught Latin for many years at Pittsford-Mendon High School in Pittsford, New York. She has served as the College Board Advisor to AP Latin Test Development Committee and in 1996 received the Morton E. Spillenger Award for Distinguished Leadership to the Classical Association of the Empire State. In 2003 she received the ACL *Merita* Award and in 2006 an *Ovatio* from the Classical Association of the Atlantic States. She served as the chair of the Latin Review Committee for New York's Latin for the 21st Century Core Curriculum. Crooker has also served as president of the Classical Association of the Empire State.

SHERWIN LITTLE

BA University of Cincinnati; MA University of Colorado

Sherwin Little has taught Latin from sixth grade through Latin AP at Indian Hill Exempted Village School District since 1983. Little has received an *Ovatio* and the Good Teacher Award from Classical Association of the Middle West and South and the Hildesheim Vase Award from the Ohio Classical Conference in 1986 and 2007. Little holds National Board Certification in World Languages Other than English and has been both vice president and president of the American Classical League as well as director of ACL's Teacher Placement Service.

SHERRILYN MARTIN

BA Wilson College; MA, PhD University of Cincinnati

Sherrilyn Martin began teaching at Keith Country Day School, Rockford, Illinois, in 1970. She has taught all levels of Latin at both the middle and upper school level and Greek I and II for the upper school. Martin was named Illinois Latin Teacher of the Year in 1993, was a recipient of a Lt. Governor's Award for Foreign Language Teaching in 2001, and was named a Claes Nobel Teacher of Distinction in 2007. She is a past president of the Illinois Classical Conference and is active in the Rockford Society of the Archaeological Institute of America. Martin spent a year in independent study at the University of Thessaloniki, Greece.

KELLY NORTHRUP

BA/BS Ursinus College, New York; MAT Indiana University

Following a brief stint as a visiting instructor at Knox College, Kelly Northrup has taught Latin at all levels from seventh grade to AP at the Webb School, Bell Buckle, Tennessee, since 2007. In 2006 she was awarded one of the five Student Teacher of the Year Awards at Indiana University, and in 2007 she received the Amy High Scholarship to study at Papal Latinist Fr. Reginald Foster's *Aestiva Romae Latinitas* (Summer Latin in Rome) program. At Ursinus she was valedictorian and inducted into Phi Beta Kappa. She is a frequent contributor to the *LNM* Teachers' Lounge and an *LNM* webinar presenter.

MARY PENDERGRAFT

AB, PhD University of North Carolina, Chapel Hill

After teaching at UNC-Greensboro and Duke University, Mary Pendergraft began teaching classics full-time at Wake Forest. She is a former president of the North Carolina Classical Association and participated in the focus group that wrote the North Carolina Standard Course of Study for Latin. Pendergraft is a 2011 recipient of an American Classical League *Merita* Award.

JOHN TRAUPMAN

BA Moravian College, Pennsylvania; PhD Princeton

John Traupman taught at St. Joseph's University in Philadelphia from 1951 until retirement in 1989. He taught in the Graduate School at Villanova University from 1958 to 1963. Honors include St. Joseph University's Distinguished Teaching Award and a Faculty Merit Award for Research, two awards recognizing his professional service from the Classical Association of the Atlantic States, the Pennsylvania Department of Education's Certificate of Appreciation, and the Comenius Award from the Moravian Alumni Association.

Traupman has served as president of the Philadelphia Classical Society, the Pennsylvania Classical Association, and the Classical Association of the Atlantic States. He was a consultant for the Pennsylvania Department of Education, classics department chair at St. Joseph's for thirty-two years, and a member of ACTFL's Board of Reviewers for National Standards in Foreign Language. Traupman's most popular books are the *New College Latin and English Dictionary* (1994) and *Conversational Latin for Oral Proficiency* (2006).

REBECCA WICK

BA University of Scranton; MA Loyola University Chicago

Rebecca Wick has taught classical languages on the high school level since 1988 in Wilmette, Illinois. She taught all four levels of Latin (including AP Vergil and Catullus/Horace) at Regina Dominican High School for nine years. In 1997, she moved to Loyola Academy where she has taught both Latin and Greek. As an undergraduate, Wick spent a year abroad at Ireland's University College Cork. She also did graduate work at the American School of Classical Studies in Athens. Wick has also run the Athens Marathon. She has served as president and vice president of the Illinois Classical Conference and as president of the Chicago Classical Club.

ROSE WILLIAMS

BA Baylor University, Texas; MA University of North Carolina, Chapel Hill

Rose Williams has written a number of books for high school Latin students. Her most recent Latin text is *A Beginning Christian Latin Reader: De Bonis Cogitationibus*; other recent titles include the four enrichment texts for *Latin for the New Millennium: From Romulus to Romulus Augustulus, The Original Dysfunctional Family, The Clay-footed SuperHeroes*, and *From Rome to Reformation*. Williams has taught at both high school and college levels. She has done postgraduate work in Latin and the Humanities at the University of Dallas and the University of Texas at Arlington. On a Rockefeller Grant she did research at Oxford's Bodleian Library and the University of Pisa.

PHILIP WOODRUFF

BA, MA Loyola University Chicago; MS Secondary Education Northwestern University

Philip Woodruff has been a secondary school Latin teacher for twenty-five years. At Lake Forest High School, Lake Forest, Illinois, since 1991, he has taught Latin I through AP courses along with occasional Classical Greek students. Woodruff served for five years as the department chair for the World Languages Department at Lake Forest. He has served as a peer editor for textbooks and has recently been active with translating articles for the Leonard Euler Archive.

CONSULTANT PILOT TEACHERS

SHERRY JANKOWSKI

BA, MA Ed Virginia Tech

Sherry Jankowski has taught Latin I, II, III, IV, AP and Ancient Greek in Maryland and in Las Vegas, Nevada. As an undergraduate, she studied at the Intercollegiate Center for Classical Studies in Rome. In addition, she has served as the Nevada Junior Classical League State Chair for three years and was named a Master Teacher by The Meadows School in 2010.

NICHOLAS YOUNG

BA, MA Wayne State University

Nicholas Young has been a classroom teacher for over forty years, the last twenty of which have been at University of Detroit Jesuit High School in Detroit, Michigan. He is also an instructor at the University of Detroit Mercy. He has done studies at the American School of Classical Studies in Athens, in Latin with Fr. Reginaldus Foster in Rome, and archaeological field work in Tuscany through Wayne State and Northern Kentucky State University. He was state chair for Michigan Junior Classical League for ten years and has served two terms as president of the Michigan Classical Conference. Currently, he serves as president of the Detroit Classical Association. He was awarded the 2010 Glenn Knudswig Award from the University of Michigan as Teacher of the Year. He is the author of several articles and the book *Instant Answers*.

INTRODUCTION

Latin for the New Millennium, Level 3, introduces you to six authors of the classical period, Caesar, Catullus, Cicero, Vergil, Horace, and Ovid, and several authors from later centuries. Why should you devote so much effort to reading the works of these authors in the original Latin texts? Reading Latin literature in translation will allow you to understand the thoughts of the ancient authors—thoughts that have shaped the culture of our world—but reading the same authors in Latin allows you to see the subtleties and nuances of language and word order that often cannot be captured in a translation. Examples illustrating this point follow.

In Poem 5 Catullus invites Lesbia to enjoy life and to love; Lesbia is the focal point of the "living" and "loving" as is suggested by her occupying the center of the line.

> *Vīvāmus, mea Lesbia, atque amēmus*
> "Let us live, my Lesbia, and let us love"

He next requests that she discount the rumors of rather stern old men. The repetition of "s" in lines 2–3 subtly suggests the sound of the whispers of those very individuals who would disapprove of his and Lesbia's love; all such rumors are to be valued at one cent:

> *rūmōrēsque senum sevēriōrum*
> *omnēs ūnius aestimēmus assis!*
>
> "and all rumors of rather stern old men
> let us assess at one cent!"

We can replicate the "s" sound in English to a certain extent, but it is difficult to do so in the sustained way that Catullus accomplishes in his poem.

To reinforce his point that Lesbia should embrace love, Catullus reminds her of life's brevity by juxtaposing the renewal of nature against the inevitability of death for humankind (*nōbis, . . . nox est perpetua ūna dormienda*, lines 5–6). The repeated "re–" (which, as a prefix means "back" or "again") in line 4, a repetition that cannot be achieved in our English translation, calls to mind nature's cycles:

> *sōlēs occidere et redīre possunt;*
> "suns are able to set and to return;"

Play on sound and syllables as well as the word order all contribute to the impact of Catullus's poem.

In Book 2 of the *Aeneid* lines 524 and following, Vergil describes how Achilles's son Pyrrhus first kills one of Priam's sons in front of Priam and his wife and then kills Priam himself. The Latin passage cited below paints a heartrending picture of Priam trembling (*trementem*) from rage and old age and slipping repeatedly—for this is what the participle *lāpsantem* suggests—in the copious blood of his son:

> *(Pyrrhus) . . . altāria ad ipsa (Priamum) trementem*
> *trāxit et in multō lāpsantem sanguine nātī,*
> *implicuitque comam laevā, dextrāque coruscum*
> *extulit ac laterī capulō tenus abdidit ēnsem.*
>
> (*Aeneid* 2.550–553)

> "Pyrrhus drew to the altar itself Priam trembling
> and slipping in the copious blood of his son,
> and he entwined Priam's hair with his left hand and
> unsheathed with his right hand the gleaming sword and
> buried it in Priam's side up to the hilt."

Notice that Vergil has, in fact, located Priam in the middle of the pool of blood, with *lāpsantem*, which refers to Priam, framed by *multō* and *sanguine* (line 551). This example shows how the flexibility of the Latin language enables Vergil to exploit word order to enhance the meaning of the text.

In the *First Catilinarian* (5.11), Cicero effusively gives thanks to the immortal gods and to Jupiter Stator, in whose temple the Senate is meeting, for allowing Cicero to escape so many times from the dangers posed by Catiline:

> *Magna dīs immortālibus habenda est atque huic ipsī Iovī Statōrī, antīquissimō custōdī huius urbis, grātia, quod hanc tam taetram, tam horribilem tamque īnfestam reī pūblicae pestem totiēns iam effūgimus.*

> "Great gratitude must be given to the immortal gods and to this very Jupiter Stator (Cicero refers to a statue of the god in the temple), the most ancient guardian of this city, because we now have so often escaped this disease so foul, so fear-inspiring, and so dangerous to the state."

In this passage Cicero emphasizes the word "gratitude" by placing *grātia* at the end of its clause and separating the word from *magna*, the adjective at the beginning of the clause that modifies it, with the result that "great gratitude" frames the entire main clause. English cannot replicate this effect because, unlike Latin, its word order is less flexible. The *quod* clause also is notable because Cicero uses a metaphor of disease here to refer to Catiline. Catiline is a *pestis*, an infectious and contagious disease that is physically offensive (*taeter* can refer to the smell that accompanies illness), fear-inspiring (*horribilem*), and dangerous (*īnfestus*). It is difficult to capture this metaphor in translation and at the same time make clear that *pestis* signifies Catiline.

Julius Caesar begins his *Dē bellō Gallicō* by explaining why the Helvetians decided to invade Gaul. Orgetorix, the richest and most noble of the Helvetians, had great ambitions to expand their territory. As Orgetorix sets plans in place for the emigration of the Helvetians from their lands, he decides to invite the leaders of the Sequanians and the Aeduans to participate in his scheme to conquer all Gaul:

Perfacile factū esse illīs probat cōnāta perficere, proptereā quod ipse suae cīvitātis imperium obtentūrus esset.

"He demonstrates to them that to bring about the undertakings is very easy to do because he himself would obtain the command of his own state."

The language that Caesar uses to reflect Orgetorix's conversation with these leaders focuses on the doability of his idea by repeating the base for "to do" in *perfacile, factū,* and *perficere*. It is impossible to render this wordplay in English.

In *Odes* 1.5, the first love poem of the *Odes* 1–3, Horace uses word order to focus the first line on the subject of his poem; a chiastic arrangement of nouns and adjectives (an ABBA order of words that is very difficult to achieve in English), a slender boy and many roses, frames Pyrrha (*tē*): *Quis multā gracilis tē puer in rosā*. The Latin here provides a word picture of what is actually happening in the poem, because the close proximity of the *puer* to the *puella* in line 1 is reinforced in line 2 where the *puer* is described as "pressing" her (*urget*):

> *Quis multā gracilis tē puer in rosā*
> *perfūsus liquidīs urget odōribus*
>   *grātō, Pyrrha, sub antrō?*

"What slender youth, drenched with liquid perfumes, presses you amid many a rose, Pyrrha, under [the shelter of] a pleasant grotto?"

Several lines later (6–8) Horace uses a metaphor of the sea to describe Pyrrha's fickle character: *aspera / nigrīs aequora ventīs / ēmīrābitur.* "[Her suitor] will wonder at the seas [now] rough with black winds." The Latin also can be translated as "[her suitor] will wonder at seas [now] black with harsh winds" if both adjectives are interpreted as "transferred epithets"; that is, the adjective agrees in sense, but not in gender and form, with another noun. And so *nigris* could be taken with *aequora* and *aspera* with *ventīs*. Chances are Horace intended both interpretations, which in English, unlike Latin, are impossible to reproduce simultaneously.

Ovid uses word order in his story of Pyramus and Thisbe for a different effect. In predicting the death of the two lovers, he writes at *Metamorphōsēs* 4.108: *"ūna duōs" inquit "nox perdet amantēs"* ("one night will destroy two lovers"). The interlocked order of nouns and adjectives (an ABAB order of words) closely intertwines the single night and the two lovers in a way that English cannot reproduce; what is more, the striking antithesis between the juxtaposed numerals "one" and "two" cannot be replicated in English.

Reading the literature and thoughts of the ancients will broaden your education and sensitize you particularly to classical allusions and sources. For example, in reading the story of the star-crossed lovers, Pyramus and Thisbe, in the chapter on Ovid, you will recognize that this story very likely forms the source for one of Shakespeare's greatest and most celebrated tragedies, *Romeo and Juliet*. Similarly, Ovid's tale of Pygmalion inspired works of literature and art, including the well-known musical *My Fair Lady*. In the chapter on Catullus, you will discover that poetry of the classical period can transcend time and seem as fresh and spontaneous as when it was written over two thousand years ago. From Vergil's *Aeneid* you will learn that literary heroes suffer much personal loss and have to overcome seemingly insurmountable obstacles; the same qualities characterize heroes in current literary works such as the Harry Potter series, in which J.K. Rowling brilliantly recycles classical myth to suit the purposes and needs of her epic tale. Cicero's *Dē amīcitiā* reminds us of the universality of friendship and how essential interpersonal relationships are to humankind. Caesar's commentaries on the Gallic War, the only surviving historical document from the first century BCE to focus on this part of the world, provide us with a firsthand account of the culture and civilization of Gaul, Germany, and Britain. For some, seeing the continuity between the past and present western cultures offers one of the principal attractions for studying the classical world.

SIGNS AND ABBREVIATIONS

Take note of these signs and abbreviations as they are regularly used in the vocabulary and other notes in the text.

‡ = indicates a **Take Note** that follows the line notes for a given reading

(1) = first conjugation

abl. = ablative

acc. = accusative

adj. = adjective

adv. = adverb

Cat. = *Catilīnam*

cf. = Latin, *confer*; English, "compare"

comp. = comparative

conj. = conjunction

dat. = dative

e.g. = Latin, *exemplī grātiā*; English, "for the sake of an example," usually reduced to "for example"

f. = feminine

ff. = and following

gen. = genitive

i.e. = Latin, *id est*; English, "that is"

impers. = impersonal

indeclin. = indeclinable

inf. = infinitive

interj. = interjection

lit. = literally

m. = masculine

Met. = *Metamorphōsēs*

n. = neuter

nom. = nominative

num. = numerical

p. = page

pass. = passive

pl. = plural

pp. = pages

prep. = preposition

sg. = singular

voc. = vocative

LATIN-SPEAKING WORLD

BRITANNIA

Oxonium
Cantabrigia
Londīnium
Roffa
Dubrī

Fretum Gallicum

Roterodamum

Gandavum
Sānctus Audumarus
Bolōnia
Camaracum

GERMĀNIA

Saltus
Teutoburgiēnsis

Rhēnus

EURŌPA

Sēquana

GALLIA

Lutetia Parīsiōrum

Basilēa

ĀTLANTICUS
ŌCEANUS

A L P Ē S   M O N T Ē S

Genavā

Rhodanus

Sirmiō
Verōna
Venetiae
Patavium
Mantua
Mutina
Bonōnia
Rubicō

ILLYRICUM

Augusta
Taurinōrum

PRŌVINCIA

Faesulae

Lūca

ETRŪRIA

ITALIA

Mare (H)Ādriāticum

Massilia

Tiberis

LATIUM

Sulmo

PỸRĒNAEĪ MONTĒS

CORSICA

Ostia
Rōma
Alba Longa
Lavinium

Arpīnum
Formiae

APŪLIA

Brundisiu

HISPĀNIA

Neāpolis

Venusia

LŪCĀNIA

Tarentum

CAMPĀNIA

SARDINIA

Mare Tyrrhēnum

*Mare
Īonium*

HISPĀNIA
ULTERIOR

SICILIA

Carthāgō

GAETŪLIA

NUMIDIA

M a r e

*Syrtis
Minor*

MAURĪTĀNIA

Ā F R I C A

*Syrtis
Major*

CAUCASUS

Pontus Euxīnus

DĀCIA

Tomis

Dānuvius

PARTHIA

BĪTHȲNIA

PONTUS

ASIA

THRĀCIA

IACEDONIA

Philippī

Carrhae

Trōia/Īlium

ASIA MINOR

LESBOS

AEOLIA

SYRIA

EMESA

ĪRUS

Pharsālus

Antiochīa

ctium

Cyrrhaesis

GRAECIA

Babylōn

Athēnae

PAROS

Paphos

CȲPRUS

Sidon

CRĒTA

I n t e r n u m

ARABIA

Alexandrēa

AEGYPTUS

LIBȲA

PART 1

Authors of the Late Republic

- **GAIUS JULIUS CAESAR**
- **GAIUS VALERIUS CATULLUS**
- **MARCUS TULLIUS CICERO**

THE LAST CENTURY OF THE ROMAN REPUBLIC

The Roman Republic was founded on the principle of collegial rule. Power was divided among many assemblies and magistrates. Except for the dictatorship, no magistracy was held by only one man. This was intended to prevent tyranny. Collegial rule also allowed the powerful Roman elite to satisfy their ambitions while serving the state. It was in the best interest of this class to share power. If any one man became too powerful, it would prevent other families from exercising their right to participate. For many years this system worked well.

THE GROWTH OF ROMAN TERRITORIES DURING THE SECOND CENTURY BCE

But the situation changed in the second century BCE. This was a time of incredible yet disruptive growth for Rome. Roman commitments overseas made it routine for politicians to govern far from Rome, with their armies away from Italy for years at a time. It was impractical for the old system of annual commands to work when campaigns took years to conclude. Yet the longer a commander remained with his army, the more loyal they were to him. At the same time, because many high-ranking politicians abused their power, especially in the provinces, the relationship between Romans and non-Romans grew strained.

In Rome and Italy, the number of slaves Romans held increased substantially. They were often employed on the very large Roman farms that developed during this period. As a result, the population of the city of Rome grew significantly as Romans and Italians left the countryside behind.

During this period questions began to be raised about the declining number and quality of men qualified for service in the Roman army. Unlike today's US military, the Roman army had a minimum property qualification. Those who did not meet it were unable to enlist. Presumably, increasing the number of men qualified to serve would result in better armies.

TIBERIUS GRACCHUS

As a newly elected tribune (*tribūnus plēbis*) of the people in 133 BCE, Tiberius Gracchus attempted to address this problem of a need for more men with the appropriate property qualifications to serve in the militia with a plan to distribute publicly owned land to Roman citizens. A number of politicians supported this proposal. But it was also controversial. Many wealthy citizens, including senators, were using far more than the (long-ignored) legal allotment. More disturbing were the extraordinary actions Tiberius Gracchus took to ensure the bill would pass. He sidestepped the Senate and took his bill directly to the Popular Assembly. When another tribune vetoed the submission of his bill, Tiberius tried to expel him from the office of tribune. These actions were ultimately perceived by many of the Roman elite as a threat to state security. When Gracchus stood for election for an unprecedented consecutive term, serious rioting began in Rome, and he and many of his supporters lost their lives. Even though the land redistribution bill was enacted, the events surrounding Tiberius Gracchus's term set a dangerous example.

POPULĀRĒS AND *OPTIMĀTĒS*

Later Roman politicians, following the example of Tiberius Gracchus, exploited the office of tribune. They were labeled *populārēs*—men who relied on popular support for political influence. Circumventing the traditional position of the Senate as advisors for legislation and providers of funds, *populārēs* appealed directly to the assemblies themselves. Politicians who wished to keep the Senate at the center of influence were called *optimātēs*.

Though weaker, the Roman Senate and elite remained very influential. Roman society was traditional and conservative, and the nobility still dominated politics. Even *populāris* politicians came from this elite group. Still, the tribuneship was used to force through legislation that the Senate would oppose. Though their methods polarized the political world, their bills often addressed real needs such as distributing land to veteran soldiers and stabilizing the cost of grain.

GAIUS GRACCHUS

Nine years after the death of his older brother, Gaius Gracchus served as tribune (123–122 BCE). His legislation was designed to appeal to a number of groups: the urban poor, the *equitēs*, and military veterans. He had laws passed that sold grain at half-price to the urban poor, that transferred the courts that dealt with cases of corruption by provincial governors from the Senate to the *equitēs*, and that created land holdings for veterans outside of Italy. Gaius's unsuccessful attempt to be elected as tribune for a third consecutive year resulted in a riot. To deal with these protestors, the *senātūs cōnsultum ultimum*, the "final decree of the Senate," was passed, which empowered the consuls to do what was necessary to protect and preserve the state. As a result of this decree, Gaius and three thousand of his supporters were killed. By circumventing the Senate and taking legislation directly to the people, the Gracchi brothers had set a dangerous precedent that would be followed by other politicians determined to have their way by whatever means possible.

GAIUS MARIUS

Populāris methods also allowed men outside the Roman nobility, such as Gaius Marius, to become influential. Marius was a talented general, and his victories made him so popular that he was elected to the consulship for an unprecedented five consecutive terms (107–101 BCE). One of Marius's most consequential initiatives was that he opened the army to all Roman citizens, regardless of whether they owned property or not. Marius chose to enlist men from all classes because he needed recruits, and they clearly fought loyally and well. But, unlike today's professional military, Roman soldiers did not receive any benefits beyond the small stipend they were paid and whatever rewards their general granted them. Marius and many generals to follow knew it was beneficial to reward these men with land. Yet the Senate generally did not support such legislation because it would grant the general too much influence. Senatorial opposition to the generals' proposals caused soldiers to value their loyalty to their commander more than to the Roman Senate and to the state itself.

CORNELIUS SULLA

Sulla had distinguished himself as a commander during the Social War. This was a rebellion of Rome's allies that ended by granting Italians Roman citizenship. Sulla's success contributed to his election as consul in 88 BCE. He anticipated winning even more glory in the command he was assigned against Mithridates VI, king of Pontus (today, northern Turkey). But Marius, an enemy of Sulla, also desired this command. While Sulla was away fighting some of the last resistance from the Social War, Marius and his ally Cinna had a motion passed that granted Marius the command against Mithridates instead. When the news reached Sulla, he persuaded his soldiers to march with him and took Rome by force. He then proceeded east to fight Mithridates.

During Sulla's absence, Rome was in chaos. Although Cinna and Marius were driven from the city, they recaptured it with their soldiers. Both men then rid Rome of their political enemies. Their actions, however, would be no match for the ruthlessness that Sulla would show on his return to Rome in 82 BCE. By this time both Marius and Cinna were dead, Marius of natural causes and Cinna at the hands of mutinous soldiers. Sulla again took Rome by force at the battle of the Colline Gate. He was aided in his efforts to attain supremacy by Crassus and the future Pompey the Great.

Sulla's reign was truly one of terror. He published a list of enemies who were stripped of citizenship and whose property was to be confiscated by the state. The proscription list essentially placed a bounty on the heads of thousands of citizens, justified or not, and provided a way to reward Sulla's supporters while also eradicating his opponents. He also had a law passed that made him dictator for an indefinite period of time. Despite using the traditional magistracy of the dictatorship, Sulla distorted its original intent, which was to guide the city during an emergency not to exceed a period of six months. This office, which Sulla held for two years (82–80), gave him the authority to do as he wished.

SULLA'S REFORMS

Sulla's government reforms were extensive. In general, he tried to restore order by limiting potential abuses of Roman magistracies. These reforms included increasing the numbers of certain magistracies so that provincial service would be limited to one year at a time. He also restricted the powers of the tribune in two important ways: tribunes would have to receive senatorial approval before submitting a bill to the popular assembly, and tribunes could hold no other magistracy. By doubling the size of the Senate, he favored his supporters and diluted the opposition.

In 80 BCE Sulla resigned all power and retired to his villa in Campania. He died soon afterward, probably due to complications from a life of heavy drinking. He left a terrible legacy. Despite his attempts to stabilize Roman government, his ruthlessness and violence set a precedent that others would follow. Sulla also made clear just how powerful a politician could be with an army supporting him.

THE RISE OF POMPEY THE GREAT

Shortly after Sulla's death in 78 BCE, civil unrest occurred again. In Spain the anti-Sullan governor Sertorius led an army of exiled Romans and Spanish tribesmen in revolt. Their resistance was serious enough that the Senate sent Pompey and his legions to Spain to quell the rebellion though he was a private citizen. Pompey's appointment was even more remarkable because he had not yet been elected to any Roman magistracy. He had, however, made himself prominent as a commander supporting Sulla in the 80s, and he remained influential despite his youth. Pompey and Metellus, governor of the province Farther Spain (*Hispānia Ulterior*), coordinated efforts against Sertorius, who was assassinated in 74 and whose army was finally defeated in 72.

WARS AGAINST MITHRIDATES AND SPARTACUS

At the same time Rome was fighting two other wars: the one was against Mithridates, to be concluded in 72, and the other was a local war, against Spartacus. Spartacus was a Thracian gladiator and slave who in 73 led an uprising against Rome. His army defeated several Roman armies but was eventually conquered by Roman forces led by the praetor Crassus who, like Pompey, was given *imperium*, the right of command, with special privileges and extensive resources. Though necessity demanded such arrangements, the Romans were right to suspect the potential for abuse of power that these extraordinary commands provided.

The decade ended peacefully with all major wars against Rome concluded. As consuls for 70 BCE, Pompey and Crassus revoked many of Sulla's reforms, including restrictions on tribunes. But this peace would not last because problems contributing to political instability had not really been resolved. A greater willingness to resort to violence to advance one's agenda and the disregard for self-restraint and tradition were Sulla's true legacies to the state.

POMPEY GIVEN *IMPERIUM*

In 67 BCE Pompey was again called upon to serve the state. Piracy had risen in the Mediterranean following on yet another war with Mithridates, a war that had resumed in 69. Pompey was asked to deal with the pirates. He was given *imperium* with powers that gave him greater authority than any of the (more senior) Roman governors in that region. He concluded the war in less than three months, and his allies in Rome extended his *imperium* to the war against Mithridates. Both of these commands were granted by the motions of tribunes and passed despite strong opposition within the Senate.

THE RISE OF JULIUS CAESAR AND MARCUS TULLIUS CICERO

Around this period Julius Caesar began to rise to prominence. He was a member of a very old, patrician Roman family that traced its origins back to Aeneas and Romulus but had not been important for some time. Politically he clearly was aligned with *populāris* interests and methods. In addition, he was a nephew (by marriage) of Marius and throughout his political career demonstrated his opposition to Sulla. Caesar first became well known during the aedileship he held in 65 BCE. Aediles were responsible for running state festivals. Ambitious politicians wishing to become widely known spent huge amounts of money on lavish entertainments. Caesar went into great debt doing this. Though his generous spending paid off by his being elected to a praetorship and then to *Pontifex Maximus* (the highest office in Roman state religion, which was principally concerned with preserving "peace with the gods," the *pāx deōrum*), at the same time he won a reputation for outrageous behavior. He was, for example, suspected of supporting Catiline, whose conspiracy against Rome was uncovered by Cicero, one of the consuls of 63 BCE.

Cicero's background, philosophy, and political style were about as different from Caesar's as can be imagined. He became known through the eloquence and courage he demonstrated in court, first defending a man victimized by Sulla's proscriptions, Sextus Roscius of Ameria, and then prosecuting the corrupt governor of Sicily, Verres. Another speech that brought Cicero fame was his defense of Archias, a poet and mentor, who was accused of assuming Roman citizenship illegally.

Cicero strongly believed in the ideals of the Republic. This is clear in his opposition to Catiline. Catiline had been frustrated in two unsuccessful campaigns for the consulship, and in 63 BCE Cicero uncovered his plan to overthrow the state. He and many of his supporters withdrew from Rome after Cicero dramatically revealed his plans during a Senate meeting in the first of four speeches he wrote against him. The first Catilinarian oration is a model of Roman rhetorical style. Catiline later died in battle against a Roman army. A number of prominent Romans were implicated in the conspiracy and were executed by Cicero, who had been authorized to do whatever was necessary to preserve the state through the passage of the *senātūs cōnsultum ultimum*.

THE FIRST TRIUMVIRATE

By the end of the 60s BCE, Pompey and Crassus had become political outsiders unable to get the legislation they each favored passed in the Senate. They joined Caesar in a political arrangement often referred to as the First Triumvirate. Pompey and Crassus would support Caesar for the consulship, and Caesar would ensure that their legislation was passed.

By the time of Caesar's election to the consulship for 59 BCE, this political arrangement was common knowledge. The optimate faction tried to block it by arranging for Marcus Bibulus to be elected as Caesar's consular colleague. But Caesar ensured that Bibulus was publically humiliated early in their term. Bibulus withdrew to his house for the remainder of the year and occupied himself declaring unfavorable omens, which would invalidate all of Caesar's actions as consul. But Caesar ignored these, passed his allies'

This marble bust idealizes Caesar's facial features but does recreate his receding hairline. Tradition holds that Caesar was fond of wearing a wreath so as to hide his baldness.

legislation, and was given the command over Cisalpine and Transalpine Gaul. Pompey, Crassus, and Caesar continued to work together. Caesar and Pompey strengthened their ties when Pompey married Caesar's daughter.

Caesar very quickly ensured that Rome was drawn into war with Gallic tribes after he took his command in Gaul in 58 BCE. He, Crassus, and Pompey would meet in 56 at Luca, a small town just outside Roman territory, to negotiate continuing the triumvirate. Caesar would keep his command of the Gallic provinces, Crassus would receive Syria, and Pompey would govern the Spanish provinces.

During this period Cicero was driven into exile on the pretext of his having used the *senātūs cōnsultum ultimum* to execute Romans without due process. The real reason was that the tribune Clodius Pulcher was exacting revenge for humiliating testimony Cicero gave against him years earlier. Cicero would be obligated to support Pompey, Caesar, and Crassus because they allowed him to return to Rome. Around this time Catullus wrote invective poems against some politicians, such as Caesar and Pompey, and ironical or unflattering poems to others, such as Cicero.

The "First Triumvirate" would begin to dissolve soon after 56 BCE. Caesar's daughter Julia died in 54, and Pompey would soon marry the daughter of a prominent optimate. Crassus would die during the Roman defeat at Carrhae in 53. Due to rioting, elections for 52 could not be held, and Pompey was appointed sole consul with the support of the optimates. The situation suggested that Pompey now was allied with the optimates.

CAESAR IN GAUL AND HIS RETURN TO ROME

Caesar's command in Gaul was incredibly successful. There he wrote *Dē bellō Gallicō,* where he reported on the wars he fought, as well as the customs and religion of the Gallic tribes, in elegant, concise language. With his victory at Alesia in 52 BCE, Transalpine Gaul was made peaceful and Roman influence there grew steadily from the 50s onward. The wars made Caesar tremendously wealthy and even more popular with the Roman people. However, his political opponents grew still more hostile.

Caesar's political survival depended on being able to move directly from his governorship to an elected magistracy. Otherwise, he would be open to prosecution by his political enemies. But special legislative action would be required for this to happen—contenders for political office had to declare their candidacies in person at Rome. This would require Caesar to lay down his *imperium,* the power of command. As the end to Caesar's governorship drew closer, debate over his candidacy grew more heated. Caesar was ordered by the Senate to surrender his legions while Pompey was allowed to retain his. When Caesar refused to obey, the Senate declared him a public enemy. In 49 BCE he led his army into Italy, crossing the Rubicon River, the formal boundary between Cisalpine Gaul and Roman territory. Civil war had begun again.

THE DEATH OF POMPEY AND THE ASSASSINATION OF JULIUS CAESAR

As Caesar marched on Rome, Pompey and his supporters withdrew to the Eastern provinces. Caesar soon won a decisive victory over Pompey at Pharsalus in 48 BCE. Pompey fled to Egypt, where he was murdered by men hoping to win Caesar's favor. Caesar's victory over his opponents was final by 46.

Rome would not be at peace for long. Although Caesar elected not to follow the example of Sulla by proscribing and executing his enemies, the extending of *clēmentia* ("mercy") to his opponents and allowing them to live, made these individuals resentful, for they now felt obligated to him. In addition, little could be done politically without his approval. Finally, in February 44 BCE, he declared himself *dictātor perpetuō*, "dictator for life." In addition, he was voted his own priest as if he were a god. One month later, on the Ides of March, Caesar was assassinated by a well-coordinated conspiracy made up of Caesar's old enemies as well as his supporters.

Caesar's assassins hoped that the Republic would be restored after Caesar's death. But this was naïve. The recent past had shown that controlling Rome depended on controlling the urban population and army. The next generation would consist of civil wars. The eventual victor, Caesar's heir Octavian, would claim that he restored the Republic, while in reality, he ruled alone.

ROSEMARY MOORE
The University of Iowa

GAIUS JULIUS CAESAR

Demonstrative Adjectives and Pronouns; Relative Pronouns; Adjectives with Genitive in –īus and Dative in –ī; Participles Including Gerunds and Gerundives; Gerunds and Gerundives in Purpose Constructions; Subjunctive Purpose Clauses and Indirect Commands; Ablative Absolutes; The Active Periphrastic; Indirect Statements; The Passive Periphrastic, Review of Gerund and Gerundive Uses

Asyndeton, Ellipsis, Hendiadys, Litotes, Polysyndeton, Alliteration

A series of nine panels by Andrea Mantegna (1431–1506) celebrates the triumphs of Caesar. Inspired by written accounts of Caesar's processions and by his study of Roman artifacts, Mantegna painted the panels for Francesco Gonzaga, the Duke of Mantua. This panel depicts the standard-bearers and tuba players, two key components in the Roman army's communications.

MEMORĀBILE DICTŪ

Gallia est omnis dīvīsa in partēs trēs.

"Gaul as a whole is divided into three parts." (Caesar *Dē bellō Gallicō* 1.1)

With this simple, geographical description, Julius Caesar begins his seven books of commentaries concerning an extended war against Gaul that results in the Gallic peoples becoming Roman and their descendants speaking a Latin-derived language.

INTRODUCTION TO CAESAR

Gaius Julius Caesar (100–44 BCE) is one of the most fascinating and significant figures in all of Roman history. Renowned as a leading politician, an extraordinarily successful general, and an accomplished orator, he also was an author of the first rank. Caesar had a decisive and long-lasting impact on Rome's political institutions despite the fact that his life was cut short by assassination. Today his career still inspires both emulation and loathing, with its influence traceable in such founding documents as our own Constitution of the United States.

THE ROMAN REPUBLIC DURING CAESAR'S FORMATIVE YEARS

The Roman Republic was in a state of upheaval during Caesar's formative years. Two names from this period stand out: Marius (157–86 BCE) and Sulla (138–79 BCE). Marius reformed the Roman army to include the lower classes; he held an unprecedented seven consulships; and his politics tended to support more popular leaders against the interests of the conservative aristocracy. Caesar had familial ties to Marius because Marius was married to Caesar's aunt Julia. Sulla was Marius's former lieutenant, a great general in his own right, and dictator in Rome when Caesar was in his teens. Sulla won supreme authority in Rome by marching on the city with his army. He then reorganized the Roman constitution with two principal goals in mind: first, to restore the authority of the Roman Senate, which was dominated by the conservative aristocracy, and, second, to suppress the tribunes of the people, who often rallied Rome's common people to support legislation opposed by the conservative aristocracy. Politicians who used the Senate to pass legislation and tried to limit the power of the tribunes were called *optimātēs*, "the best men"; conversely, politicians who used the people's assemblies and tribunes to pass legislation, instead of going through the Senate, were called *populārēs*, "men of the people." Neither group represented a political party, but rather a style of politics and a loose set of alliances with like-minded colleagues. Sulla was aligned with the *optimātēs*, Marius with the *populārēs*, as was Caesar. Sulla's initial plan for political renewal also included proscriptions, which entailed writing the names of political enemies on lists that would be posted in public. Proscribed men were hunted down and killed. Those who did the hunting and killing earned a right to a portion of the proscribed man's estate.

Like Caesar, Pompey the Great (although he had not yet earned the title) was young at this time; he profited from Sulla's proscriptions, earning him the nickname "teenage butcher" (*adulēscentulus carnifex*). Caesar, on the other hand, because of his connection to Marius as well as his refusal to divorce a wife whose *populāris* family was hostile to Sulla, barely escaped proscription. Eventually he had to travel to the East until things became safer in Rome. While in the East Caesar served in the entourage of a Roman official and participated in battle where he earned the "civic crown" by saving the life of a fellow citizen. Around this time pirates reputedly kidnapped Caesar. After the ransom was collected and paid, the former hostage led an expedition to catch his captors, personally overseeing their crucifixion. Caesar then traveled to Rhodes to study Greek rhetoric with Apollonius Molon, the same outstanding teacher of rhetoric with whom Cicero studied. Although Caesar was not as accomplished an orator as Cicero, he nevertheless was a very fine speaker.

POLITICS

Caesar's early career included numerous military and civil posts, in addition to his military experience and work as a prosecutor in Rome's courts. In 65 BCE he was elected to the aedileship. His year in this office was notable for his staging of extravagant games, which was necessary for winning the favor of the voting public. In 63 BCE Caesar was elected *Pontifex Maximus*, the highest office in Roman religion. To secure Rome's chief priesthood, he reputedly borrowed huge sums of money for the purpose of bribing the voters. Individuals from prominent families sought election to a number of priesthoods because of the close connection between religion and politics. The government at Rome at this time was hopelessly corrupt, a situation that Caesar exploited. He had, in fact, borrowed so much money that his creditors went to court to prevent his departure for Spain, the province he was to govern in 61 BCE. Crassus, the richest man in Rome, had to personally guarantee Caesar's debts before he was allowed to depart.

THE FIRST TRIUMVIRATE

With the profits Caesar made governing in Spain by conducting warfare with rebellious tribes (generals and soldiers shared in the profits derived from war), he paid off his enormous debt and prepared to run for election to the consulship. In this campaign he was able to enlist the aid of Pompey the Great and Crassus. These two senior politicians were enemies, but Caesar reconciled them and brokered a three-way alliance that would be mutually beneficial. (The triumvirate was formed against a mutual enemy, Cato and the *optimātēs*.) The alliance, which they called "friendship" (*amīcitia*), is frequently referred to as the "first triumvirate." This term implies an official commission sanctioned by the state, which it was not. Even if its public impact was profound, their *amīcitia* was, from a legal point of view, private. Caesar strengthened his relationship with Pompey by offering his daughter Julia in marriage to him. After his election to the consulship in 59 BCE, Caesar used constitutionally dubious methods to pass legislation that would benefit his "friends," such as physically preventing his fellow-consul Marcus Bibulus from participating so that he could not veto the proceedings. Hence, the year of 59 BCE was referred to sarcastically by contemporaries as the consulship of Julius and Caesar, instead of the consulship of Bibulus and Caesar.

Caesar received a proconsulship of Illyricum (located on the Adriatic coast opposite northern Italy) and the two Gauls, which consisted of Cisalpine Gaul (northern Italy) and Transalpine Gaul (the Mediterranean coast of what is now France) for a period of five years. After he became involved in the conquest of the remainder of Gaul (roughly corresponding to what is now France), Caesar realized that it would take him longer than the original five-year commission to accomplish the task. He renewed his alliance with Crassus and Pompey in 56 BCE and completed the conquest of Gaul by 50 BCE. In the process Caesar flooded Roman markets with slaves, acquired fabulous wealth, dispensed many political favors, and won the fierce devotion of his soldiers.

Caesar's campaigns in Gaul established his reputation as an exceptional military commander. The Roman army was a highly organized institution. Caesar's tactical skills and the technological superiority of the Roman army were key components in his success. A group of reenactors demonstrates the Roman *testūdō*, which facilitated the army's offensive maneuvers.

THE END OF THE FIRST TRIUMVIRATE

Roman politics had in the meantime entered into a critical phase. In 54 BCE Julia, Caesar's daughter and Pompey's wife, died in childbirth. In 53 BCE, leading a large contingent of Roman soldiers against Parthia, Crassus was defeated and died in battle. Parthia ruled a territory roughly equivalent to what is now Iraq and Iran. The defeat was humiliating for Rome. After the deaths of Julia and Crassus, Pompey began drifting into a closer alliance with leaders in the Roman Senate who were opposed to Caesar. Before their political alliance fell apart, Caesar had been promised by Pompey that he could celebrate a triumph, a military victory parade, in Rome as well as run for a second consulship *in absentiā* without giving up his proconsular *imperium*. Instead, after winning Pompey over to their side, leading senators felt powerful enough to ruin Caesar's career, which, constitutionally speaking, they were entitled to do. They ordered

Caesar to lay down his command while at the same time allowing Pompey to retain his. When Caesar refused to obey, the Senate declared him a public enemy. Caesar then marched his army into Rome's territory in the middle of winter in early January 49 BCE. According to the Roman historian Suetonius, as he crossed the Rubicon River in northern Italy, Caesar proclaimed *iacta ālea est* ("the die has been cast") to indicate that there was no turning back. The Rubicon represented the boundary between the Cisalpine province and Roman territory, and thus to cross the Rubicon with an army was considered an act of treason. Today people both quote the Latin expression and refer to "one's Rubicon" to communicate the notion of a significant decision that cannot be reversed.

Pompey and the Senate appear to have been taken by surprise by Caesar's boldness. Many fled to Greece. Caesar secured Italy and then moved operations to Greece where he defeated Pompey at Pharsalus in 48 BCE. Pompey fled to Egypt (still independent under the Ptolemies) where he was assassinated. Caesar arrived in Egypt too late to engage Pompey, but he became involved in a local dispute over who had the right to rule in Egypt. Caesar supported Cleopatra over her brother. Because he arrived with so few soldiers, Caesar was at times in real danger, but eventually he prevailed. After settling affairs in Egypt, where he became romantically involved with Cleopatra, Caesar moved on to the East where in 47 BCE he penned his famous report from the battle of Zela: *vēnī, vīdī, vīcī* ("I came, I saw, I conquered"). But the civil war was not over yet. He had to fight senatorial armies in North Africa (46 BCE) and then in Spain (45 BCE).

THE ASSASSINATION OF JULIUS CAESAR

After a bitter civil war Caesar was faced with the task of reestablishing constitutional government. He had in the interim been named "dictator for life" (*dictātor perpetuō* [*tempore*]). The dictatorship was convenient because it allowed Caesar to hold office continuously without the necessity of annual election. The rest of the machinery of government ran as usual, but Caesar determined who held positions of importance such as the consulship.

However, Caesar did not possess sole rule for long. During his short-lived administration he attempted to settle economic affairs by relieving, but not abolishing, debt. This satisfied neither debtors nor creditors. He also reformed the Roman calendar by increasing the number of days of the year from 355 to 365 with a regular leap year every four years. With only modest adjustments later made by Pope Gregory XIII of the sixteenth century, we still use Caesar's calendar today. It seems fitting, therefore, that because of Caesar's significant reform of the calendar, one month of our year bears his name, the month of July.

After his victory in the civil war, Caesar, unlike Sulla, preferred to forgive rather than proscribe his enemies, reckoning that people who owed their very lives to him would demonstrate future gratitude. This policy contributed to Caesar's early demise. Many of those whom he forgave joined the successful conspiracy to assassinate him because they could not tolerate the notion of Caesar as a dictator for life. The conspirators struck during a meeting of the Senate on March 15th (the Ides), 44 BCE—the eve of Caesar's planned departure for Parthia where he hoped to avenge Crassus's humiliating defeat.

Guillaume Lethiere (c. 1780–1832) communicates the mayhem of the crowd as the Roman people
come to view the body of the dead Caesar displayed at the Senate house.

CAESAR'S LEGACY

After Caesar's murder, another round of civil war erupted, but not before the Senate declared
that Caesar was a god. In his will Caesar had adopted his great-nephew, Gaius Octavius (the son
of his sister's daughter), who assumed Caesar's name, as did every subsequent Roman emperor.
Caesar's name eventually passed into other languages with the meaning of "emperor," such as
kaiser in German and *czar* in Russian. Caesar worship would be transformed into emperor worship, and this worship of the emperors after they died and while they lived became an important
element of Roman administrative policy during the empire. This element of Roman religion
eventually involved the Roman government in conflict with Jews and early Christians.

But Caesar's legacy goes beyond his calendar, his divinity, and his name. The people of Gaul
became Roman, and their descendants today speak a Latin-derived language. Caesar's example
of a single individual assuming ultimate power has attracted imitators for thousands of years. In
North America fear of such would-be imitators inspired the framers of the US Constitution to
create a complex system of checks and balances to prevent any single individual from usurping
supreme constitutional authority on Caesar's model.

Caesar is in every respect a pivotal historical figure. His career marks the end of the Roman
Republic, and his dictatorship served as the prelude to a constitutional reorganization that inau-
gurated the Roman Empire under his adoptive great-nephew Octavian (who became Augustus).
We still reckon time by Caesar's reformed calendar, and our constitution continues to protect us
from those who might otherwise try to imitate him.

CAESAR AS AN AUTHOR

Caesar's literary fame rests on his surviving "commentaries" on the Gallic and Civil Wars: *Commentāriī dē bellō Gallicō* and *Commentāriī dē bellō cīvilī*. Caesar composed the first seven books of the Gallic War. Aulus Hirtius supplemented the work after Caesar's death, contributing an eighth book. Caesar also wrote the three books of the *Civil War*. These books were supplemented as well with books (authorship uncertain) on events in Egypt (the *Alexandrian War*), North Africa (the *African War*), and Spain (the *Spanish War*). Caesar also wrote many works that do not survive, including a work on Latin grammar. In light of the great number of exceptions to grammatical rules found in other authors, the loss of this work is a bitter one given Caesar's fondness for clean and clear prose.

What were *commentāriī*? Roman governors and generals wrote official reports, which they sent to the Senate. Caesar's actual reports to the Senate are not what we read today. We read reports modeled on the style of those reports. Why would Caesar have chosen a genre that imitated such reports? Caesar was the politician who during his consulship first published "minutes" or "proceedings of the Senate" (*acta Senātūs*), much to the resentment of the conservative aristocracy, who preferred to settle matters among themselves without public scrutiny. When Caesar departed for Gaul, he probably chose *commentāriī* as a genre to publicize his accomplishments among as wide a public as possible in a format that made it appear as if he were sharing his official reports to the Senate with all Roman citizens. Caesar was also absent from Rome for nine years. His "dispatches" on the Gallic War would have been devoured by a public eager for news and would have been promoted by Caesar's political allies. Similarly, Caesar's "reports" on the civil war were likely crucial in presenting Caesar's side in this bitterly divisive conflict. When were these books published? How were they published? Did they appear serially or as a complete work? Were there revisions along the way? The answers to all these questions remain disputed. We do have testimony, however, that although the genre was in general conceived of as providing the raw materials for historians, Caesar's *commentāriī* were considered so polished that they dissuaded competitors from attempting to rewrite his accounts, especially of his Gallic campaigns.

Caesar's style has often been praised for its distinctive qualities. He tells his stories logically, clearly, and without obscure Latin vocabulary. If readers compare his prose to his contemporary Cicero or to the later historian Livy, they will soon perceive why Caesar's style is called "plain." His sentences, artfully constructed though they are, do not become involved in the complex syntax of subordinate and relative clauses (a style called "periodic"). His use of rhetorical devices is more subtle. He writes as a dispassionate observer, as opposed to the outraged orator or the emotional and moralizing historian.

Caesar also writes about himself in the third person. His intent in doing so has been the subject of scholarly debate. His writing in the third instead of the first person may have to do with his original audience at Rome: a public eagerly listening to reports about the progress of the Gallic war. Texts were often read aloud to larger groups who gathered to listen. If we compare, "When Caesar was informed of this, he decided to . . ." to the sentence "When I heard this, I reckoned I should . . . ," we can observe that the third person would seem more natural in reporting the great general's accomplishments in the wilds of Gaul to a large, diverse audience. Even upper-class "readers" frequently employed slaves to read texts to them out loud. If Caesar were not writing letters to people personally, the first person would have been jarring. Why would Caesar be speaking to them directly, especially if they were in a group, and he was so far away in Gaul? With the help of the third person, the focus of the reports was more squarely on Caesar's actions rather than his authorship, and their plain and unemotional style lent them a seeming objectivity.

Caesar's *commentāriī* have persuaded many readers over thousands of years with this seemingly objective authority. A cursory glance, however, at the bitterly partisan times in which they were written quickly reveals what was at stake for Caesar: his reputation, his public career, and even his life, as the subsequent civil war and Caesar's murder amply demonstrate.

GAUL

Britannia
Tamesis
Londinium
Cantiī
Portus
Dubris
Belgae
Nervii
Germānī

Rhēnus

Sequana
Matrona
Dānuvius
Boiī

Venetī
Lutetia
Parīsiōrum

Liger
Alesia
Latōbrigī
Tulingī
Norēia

Avāricum
Bibracte
Sēquanī
Rauraci
Helvētiī

Gallia
Celtica
Aeduī
Arar
ĀTLANTICUS
ŌCEANUS
Gergovia
Lacus
Lemannus
Allobrogēs
Genāva
A L P Ē S   M O N T Ē S
Illyricum

Gallia
Cisalpīna
Mare (H)Ādriāticum

Garumna
Aquītānī
Rhodanus
Rubico

P Ȳ R Ē N A E Ī   M O N T Ē S
Gallia Transalpīna/
Gallia Narbōnēnsis
Massilia
Tiberis
Narbō
Rōma

Hispānia

Mare   Internum

© 2012 Bolchazy-Carducci Publishers, Inc.

READING 1

In the passage below, you will find certain words in a different font, some words underlined, and other words in parentheses. The words in a different font are the words in a relative clause, including the relative pronoun, and the underlined words are the antecedents of relative pronouns. This method will help you determine what the main clause of each sentence is.

In Latin prose and poetry, the reader often needs to "understand" or supply words that are not in the Latin text. Words to be understood are in parentheses in the text below. When one or more words are needed to complete the thought in one of two or more clauses, this is called ELLIPSIS *and is quite common in Latin.*

Later in this chapter, the same passage of Latin will be seen again without the use of words in different fonts and in parentheses.

In Chapter 1 of Book 1 of his *Commentaries*, Caesar comments on the valor of the Belgians and Helvetians. The geographical description of Gaul that he provides does not include the Roman province of Transalpine Gaul (modern Provence) in the southeastern part. This province was already under the control of Rome and was one of the provinces he was assigned as governor, in addition to Cisalpine Gaul and Illyricum.

GAUL AND ITS INHABITANTS

CAESAR *DĒ BELLŌ GALLICŌ* 1.1

1   Gallia est omnis dīvīsa in <u>partēs</u> trēs, *quārum ūnam (partem) incolunt Belgae, aliam (partem incolunt) Aquītānī, (et) tertiam (partem incolunt) (<u>eī</u>) quī ipsōrum linguā Celtae, nostrā (linguā) Gallī appellantur.*

NOTES AND VOCABULARY

Line 1:   **Gallia, -ae,** f. Gaul; Gaul or the territories known today as France and northern Italy. From the Roman perspective, the Alps divided Gaul on "this side (*cis*) of the Alps" (*Gallia Cisalpīna*) from the Gaul that was "across (*trāns*) the Alps" (*Gallia Trānsalpīna*). Another Gaul was the area beyond the Alps, but along the Mediterranean, which the Romans frequently called *Prōvincia* or "the Province."‡

omnis, omne all; *omnis* modifies *Gallia*; translate "Gaul as a whole"; that is, if one looks at the entire territory, one finds three major ethnic groups among which it has been "distributed."

dīvidō, dīvidere, dīvīsī, dīvīsum to divide; *dīvīsa* is the perfect passive participle serving as a predicate adjective; with *est,* translate "is divided."

pars, partis, f. part

trēs, tria three; note that here the numeral follows, instead of precedes, the noun it modifies for emphasis.

ūnus, -a, -um one

incolō, incolere, incoluī to inhabit, dwell in, live in; when transitive (taking a direct object) as here, translate "inhabit." In line 8, where *incolō* is intransitive, translate "dwell" or "live."

Belgae, -ārum, m. pl. the Belgians; the Belgians are located in northern Gaul along the English Channel.

alius, alia, aliud another, other

STUDY TIP

The genitive, both singular and plural, of the relative pronoun *quī, quae, quod* is most commonly translated "whose." Sometimes, however, English usage dictates that the genitive be translated "of which."

Line 2:

Aquītānī, -ōrum, m. pl. the Aquitanians; the Aquitanians are located on the Atlantic coast above the Pyrenees, the mountains that separate the Spanish peninsula from Gaul.

tertius, -a, -um third

is, ea, id this, that, he, she, it; translate "those." *eī* is the antecedent of *quī,* and Caesar, like many Roman authors, omits this antecedent. Note that the *eī,* which needs to be supplied, forms the subject of the understood *incolunt.*

ipse, -a, -um himself, herself, itself, themselves; *ipsōrum linguā* literally translates "by the language of them themselves" but a smoother translation is "by their own language."

lingua, -ae, f. language

BY THE WAY

Note the omission of *et* between the second and third in a series. The omission of a connective such as *et* or *-que* is called ASYNDETON (from the Greek meaning "lack of connection") and often occurs in Latin literature. The ASYNDETON enhances the brevity of this sentence. In this passage ASYNDETON occurs again in line 3 (before *lēgibus*), in line 14 (before *vergit*), and in line 15 (before *spectant*).

Line 3:

Celtae, -ārum, m. pl. the Celts

noster, nostra, nostrum our

Gallī, -ōrum, m. pl. Gauls; people from the Celtic territories of northern Italy as well as from Transalpine Gaul.

appellō (1) to name, call

STUDY TIP

Predicate nominatives and predicate adjectives rename, define, or describe the subject of the sentence. They are in the nominative case and are seen with a form of the verb *sum* or with other intransitive verbs such as those that mean "appear," "be made," "become," and "be named." In line 3, the verb *appellantur,* "are named," sets up the predicate nominatives *Celtae* and *Gallī.*

CAESAR *DĒ BELLŌ GALLICŌ* 1.1, CONTINUED

Hī omnēs linguā, īnstitūtīs, (et) lēgibus inter

sē differunt. Gallōs ab Aquītānīs Garumna flūmen (dīvidit), (Gallōs) ā Belgīs Matrona

5   (flūmen) et Sēquana (flūmen) dīvidit. Hōrum omnium fortissimī sunt Belgae, proptereā

quod ā cultū atque hūmānitāte prōvinciae longissimē absunt, minimēque ad eōs

mercātōrēs saepe commeant atque <u>ea</u> *quae ad effēminandōs animōs pertinent*

important. Proximī sunt <u>Germānīs</u>, *quī trāns Rhēnum incolunt, quibuscum*

continenter bellum gerunt. Quā dē causā Helvētiī quoque reliquōs Gallōs virtūte

10   praecēdunt, quod ferē cōtīdiānīs proeliīs cum Germānīs contendunt, cum aut suīs finibus

NOTES AND VOCABULARY

Line 3:   **hic, haec, hoc** this

            īnstitūtum, -ī, n. custom, habit

            lēx, lēgis, f. law

            inter, *prep. + acc.* among, between; translate "from one another."

STUDY TIP

An ablative of respect shows "in respect to" what something is or is done. In line 3, *linguā, īnstitūtīs, lēgibus* are ablatives of respect; translate "in language, . . ."

Line 4:   **suī, sibi, sē, sē** himself, herself, themselves

            differō, differre, distulī, dīlātum to differ

            Garumna, -ae, m. the Garonne River; *flūmen* agrees with *Garumna* in case because the words

                are in apposition.‡

            Matrona, -ae, m. the Marne River.‡

Line 5:   **Sēquana, -ae,** m. the Seine River; the *Matrona* and *Sēquana* are the dual subject of a singular

                verb because Caesar considered the two rivers as functioning as one boundary.‡

Lines 5–6: **proptereā quod:** *lit.,* "on account of which"; translate "because."

Line 6:   **cultus, cultūs,** m. culture, civilization‡

            hūmānitās, hūmānitātis, f. refinement, human feeling, civilization

            longissimē, *superlative adv.* farthest

            absum, abesse, āfuī, āfutūrus to be away, be absent

            minimē, *superlative adv.* least

Line 7:   **mercātor, mercātōris,** m. merchant; note that *mercātōrēs* serves as the subject and is not being

                modified by *eōs.* The prepositional phrase *ad eōs* is placed before the subject for emphasis.

            commeō (1) to come and go

            atque, *conj.* and, and also

            effēminō (1) to weaken, make effeminate; translate *ad effēminandōs animōs* "to weakening

                courage." The verb *pertineō* governs *ad* + *acc.* and thus *ad effēminandōs animōs* is not a

                gerundive of purpose, although it seems like one at first glance.

animus, -ī, m. will, spirit, judgment, courage

pertineō, pertinēre, pertinuī (+ *ad* + *acc.*) to extend (to), pertain to, reach (to)

STUDY TIP

Adjectives like *proximus* (line 8), and others that mean "dear, near, kind, friendly" and the like, take the dative and, in English, are often followed by "to" or "for." In line 8 the dative is *Germānīs*.

Line 8: **importō** (1) to bring or carry in

proximus, -a, -um nearest, last, next, nearest

trāns, *prep.* + *acc.* across

Rhēnus, -ī, m. the Rhine river

quibuscum = *cum quibus*

Line 9: **continenter,** *adv.* constantly, continuously

bellum, -ī, n. war

gerō, gerere, gessī, gestum to wage, carry on

quā dē causā translate "for this reason."

Helvētiī, -ōrum, m. pl. the Helvetians; a people who lived in the territory corresponding to modern Switzerland.

quoque, *adv.* also

reliquus, -a, -um the rest of

virtūs, virtūtis, f. courage, manliness

Line 10: **praecēdō, praecēdere, praecessī, praecessum** to surpass, precede

ferē, *adv.* almost

cōtīdiānus, -a, -um daily

proelium, -ī, n. battle

contendō, contendere, contendī, contentum to struggle, fight

Lines 10–11: **aut . . . aut:** either . . . or

suus, -a, -um his, her, its, their; this adjective refers to the subject of the sentence only, no matter which word it modifies, which in this case is the Helvetians.

fīnis, fīnis, m. end, *pl.* boundaries, territory; *fīnibus*: ablative of separation; translate "from."

STUDY TIP

Cum can be either a preposition meaning "with" or a conjunction meaning "when, since, although." The preposition *cum* takes the ablative while the conjunction *cum* takes a verb. The presence of an ablative or a verb in the vicinity of *cum* will help you determine the word's function, and, therefore, which meaning to use. As a preposition, *cum* typically precedes the noun it governs but is usually joined to first and second-person pronouns (e.g., *tēcum*, *mēcum*), to the reflexive pronoun (*sēcum*), and to interrogative and relative pronouns (as in line 8). As a conjunction, as in line 10, *cum* signifies "time when" and takes the indicative mood.

CAESAR *DĒ BELLŌ GALLICŌ* 1.1, CONTINUED

eōs prohibent aut ipsī in eōrum fīnibus bellum gerunt. Eōrum ūna <u>pars</u>, ***quam Gallōs obtinēre dictum est***, initium capit ā flūmine Rhodanō, continētur Garumnā flūmine, Ōceanō, (et) fīnibus Belgārum, attingit etiam ab Sēquanīs et Helvētiīs flūmen Rhēnum, (et) vergit ad septentriōnēs. Belgae ab extrēmīs Galliae fīnibus oriuntur, pertinent ad
15 īnferiōrem partem flūminis Rhēnī, (et) spectant in septentriōnem et orientem sōlem. Aquītānia ā Garumnā flūmine ad Pȳrēnaeōs montēs et eam <u>partem</u> Ōceanī ***quae est ad Hispāniam*** pertinet; spectat inter occāsum sōlis et septentriōnēs.

NOTES AND VOCABULARY

Line 11: **prohibeō, prohibēre, prohibuī, prohibitum** to keep off, restrain, prevent

ūna pars: refers to the country or territory; translate "one part of their *(eōrum)* territory."

Line 12: **obtineō, obtinēre, obtinuī, obtentum** to hold, obtain

dīcō, dīcere, dīxī, dictum to say; in *quam Gallōs obtinēre dictum est, quam* is the object of *obtinēre; Gallōs* is the accusative subject of *obtinēre;* translate "which it has been said the Gauls hold."

initium, -ī, n. beginning

capiō, capere, cēpī, captum to take, seize

Rhodanus, -ī, m. the Rhone River; the Rhone flows from Lake Geneva in Switzerland to the Mediterranean.

contineō, continēre, continuī, contentum to contain, keep, hem in, bound by

Line 13: **attingō, attingere, attigī, attāctum** to touch, reach, border (on)

etiam, *adv.* also

ab Sēquanīs et Helvētiīs: translate "on the side of the Sequanians and Helvetians." The Sequani were a tribe of eastern Gaul.

Line 14: **vergō, vergere** to slope, lie

septentriō, septentriōnis, m. the seven stars comprising the Big Dipper; north

extrēmus, -a, -um farthest

orior, orīrī, ortus sum to rise, arise, originate

pertinent ad: translate "extend to."

STUDY TIP

Remember that deponent verbs like *orior* in line 14, although passive in form, translate actively in all indicative and subjunctive tenses.

Line 15: **īnferior, īnferius** lower

Rhēnus, -ī, m. the Rhine river

spectō (1) to look at; translate as "face" (when the verb indicates a specific direction).

in, *prep. + acc.* into, toward

sōl, sōlis, m. sun; *orientis sōlis* means "the rising sun"; translate "the east."

Line 16:   **ad,** *prep. +* *acc.* to, toward, near

Line 17:   **occāsus, occāsūs,** m. setting, fall; *occāsum sōlis* means "the setting of the sun"; translate "the West."

TAKE NOTE

1. The province of *Gallia Narbōnēnsis* was organized about 120 BCE. Its chief cities were *Massilia* (Marseilles), an old Greek free city, and the capital, *Narbō* (Narbonne), a Roman colony. The Romans called this part of Gaul closest to Italy on the northwestern side *Prōvincia,* or the "Province." Today the French call it Provence.

2. The names of rivers in Latin are usually masculine, including those that belong to the first declension such as the *Garumna, Matrona,* and *Sēquana.* The Garonne River forms the boundary between Aquitania and the Gaul Caesar calls Celtic. The Seine River flows across northern Gaul and with the Marne River forms a boundary with the Belgians.

3. In line 6, *cultus* indicates the outward characteristics of civilization (dress, habits of life, etc.); *hūmānitās,* the moral characteristics (refinement of thought and feeling, education, etc.).

COMPREHENSION QUESTIONS

1. Name in both Latin and English the three parts of Gaul that Caesar outlines.

2. Which of these three parts is the bravest and why, according to Caesar?

3. Why are the Helvetians more courageous than the Gauls?

▶ EXERCISE 1

1. In line 1, what Latin word is the antecedent of *quārum*?

2. In lines 1–2, what three Latin words modify the understood noun *partem*?

3. In line 2, what is the case and use of *ipsōrum*?

4. What is the case and use of *linguā* in line 2?

5. In line 3, what is the tense, voice, and mood of *appellantur*?

6. In line 4, to what does *sē* refer?

7. What is the case and use of *Aquītānīs* in line 4?

8. In lines 4–5, what are the Latin subjects of *dīvidit*?

9. What is the case and degree of *fortissimī* in line 5?

10. What is the case and use of *cultū* in line 6?

11. What is the subject of *commeant* in line 7?

12. What is the antecedent of *quī* in line 8?

13. What is the case and use of *virtūte* in line 9?

14. In line 10, what is the subject of *praecēdunt?*

15. In line 10, what is the case and use of *proeliīs?*

16. In line 11, to whom does *eōs* refer?

17. What is the antecedent of *quam* in line 11?

18. In line 12, what is the tense, voice, and mood of *dictum est?*

19. In lines 12–14, *ūna pars* is the subject of what four verbs?

VOCABULARY BUILDER

It is easier to read passages of *Dē bellō Gallicō* if you know the geographical terms for the peoples and places Caesar is discussing. Here are terms that will help you read Caesar's Latin text. Which of these can you find on the map on p. 17?

PEOPLE

Gallī, -ōrum, m. pl. the Gauls

Belgae, -ārum, m. pl. the Belgians

Aquītānī, -ōrum, m. pl. the Aquitanians

Germānī, -ōrum, m. pl. the Germans

Helvētiī, -ōrum, m. pl. the Helvetians

Sēquanī, -ōrum, m. pl. the Sequanians

Hispānī, -ōrum, m. pl. the Spaniards

Celtae, -ārum, m. pl. the Celts

Aeduī, -ōrum, m. pl. the Aeduans

PLACES

Gallia, -ae, f. Gaul

Belgica, -ae, f. Belgium

Aquītānia, -ae, f. Aquitania

Germānia, -ae, f. Germany

Helvētia, -ae, f. Helvetia

Hispānia, -ae, f. Spain

Gallia Celtica, -ae, f. Celtic Gaul (as opposed to the Roman provinces of Gaul)

RIVERS

Garumna, -ae, m. the Garonne river

Matrona, -ae, m. the Marne river

Sēquana, -ae m. the Seine river

Rhēnus, -ī, m. the Rhine river

Rhodanus, -ī, m. the Rhone river

Using the Latin glossary to help you, what are the Latin adjectives that correspond to the peoples listed above? Be careful since there are a few difficult ones in the list of people.

Example: Gallī, -ōrum, m. pl. the Gauls   Gallus, -a, -um Gallic

LANGUAGE FACT

DEMONSTRATIVE ADJECTIVES AND PRONOUNS

- **hic, haec, hoc** (See p. 508 in Appendix D for the paradigm of *hic*.)

    The adjective forms of **hic**, meaning "this" or "these," can modify a noun or serve as pronouns meaning "he, she, it, they."

. . . ab *hōc* cultū atque hūmānitāte longissimē absunt. "They are very far away from **this** civilization and refinement."	**ADJECTIVE**
Hī omnēs linguā, īnstitūtīs, lēgibus inter sē differunt. (Caesar *Dē bellō Gallicō* 1.1.3–4) "All **these [men]** differ from one another in language, customs, and laws."	**PRONOUN**
Hōs ab Aquītānīs Garumna flūmen dīvidit. "The Garonne river divides **them** from the Aquitanians."	**PRONOUN**

- **ille, illa, illud** (See p. 508 in Appendix D for the paradigm of *ille*.)

    As an adjective, **ille** means "that" or "those" but as a pronoun means "he, she, it, they."

. . . pertinent ad *illam* partem flūminis Rhēnī. "They stretch to **that** part of the Rhine river."	**ADJECTIVE**
Proximī sunt *illīs*, quī trāns Rhēnum incolunt. "They are next to **those [men]** who live across the Rhine."	**PRONOUN**
Helvētiī quoque reliquōs *illōs* virtūte praecēdunt. "The Helvetians also surpass the rest of **them** in courage."	**PRONOUN**

- **is, ea, id** (See p. 507 in Appendix D for the paradigm of *is*.)

    The adjective forms of **is, ea, id** when serving as pronouns mean "he, she, it," but as adjectives can also be translated as "this, these, that, those."

Aquītānia ā Garumnā flūmine ad. . . . *eam* partem Oceanī . . . pertinet. (Caesar *Dē bellō Gallicō* 1.1.16–17) "Aquitania stretches from the Garonne river to **that** part of the Ocean."	**ADJECTIVE**
. . . suīs fīnibus *eōs* prohibent. (Caesar *Dē bellō Gallicō* 1.1.10–11) "They keep **them** from their borders."	**PRONOUN**
. . . *ea* quae ad effēminandōs animōs pertinent important. (Caesar *Dē bellō Gallicō* 1.1.7–8) "They bring in **those [things]** which pertain to weakening courage."	**PRONOUN**

BY THE WAY

The demonstrative pronouns *hic* and *ille* may be used as a pair to refer to people or things that have already been mentioned. In these instances, *hic* means "latter" (to remember: think of "hook and ladder") and *ille* means "former."

▶ EXERCISE 2

Identify the demonstrative pronoun/adjective in each sentence, indicate whether it is being used as a pronoun or an adjective, and translate the entire sentence.

1. Hōrum omnium fortissimī sunt Belgae.

2. Illī Belgae ab extrēmīs Galliae fīnibus oriuntur.

3. Eōrum ūna pars, quam Gallī obtinent, initium capit ā flūmine Rhodanō.

4. Suīs fīnibus hunc prohibent.

5. Aquītānia ab eō flūmine ad Pȳrēnaeōs montēs pertinet.

6. Hanc partem incolunt Belgae, illam Aquītānī, et eam Gallī.

7. In eōrum fīnibus bellum gerunt.

8. Ferē cōtīdiānīs proeliīs cum illīs contendunt.

9. Haec pars initium capit ā Rhodanō flūmine.

10. Illī Germānī quibuscum continenter Belgae bellum gerunt incolunt trāns Rhēnum.

LANGUAGE FACT

RELATIVE PRONOUNS

quī, quae, quod (See p. 509 in Appendix D for the paradigm of *quī*.)

The relative pronoun *quī, quae, quod* "who, whose, whom, which, that" connects its own clause to a word in another clause. This word in the other clause is called the antecedent. A relative clause governs either an indicative or a subjunctive verb. Indicative verbs are used here. (See pp. 179–180 and 542–543 for relative clauses with subjunctive verbs.) The relative pronoun takes its number and gender from its antecedent, but takes its case from its function in the clause that it introduces.

Look at these examples in which the antecedent is underlined and the relative clause is in bold.

> *Aquītānia ā Garumnā flūmine ad . . . eam <u>partem</u> Ōceanī **quae est ad Hispāniam pertinet**.* (Caesar *Dē bellō Gallicō* 1.1.16–17)
> "Aquitania stretches from the Garonne river to that part of the Ocean **which is near Spain**."

> *Proximī sunt <u>Germānīs</u>, **quī trāns Rhēnum incolunt.***
> (Caesar *Dē bellō Gallicō* 1.1.8)
> "They are nearest to the Germans **who live across the Rhine**."

> _Ea_ **quae ad effēminandōs animōs pertinent** important.
> (Caesar _Dē bellō Gallicō_ 1.1.7–8)
> "They bring in those things **which pertain to weakening [their] courage**."

STUDY TIP

Sometimes the antecedent of a relative clause is an understood form of _hic, is,_ or _ille_ as in the example below.

> ... tertiam (partem incolunt) **quī ipsōrum linguā Celtae, nostrā Gallī appellantur** (Caesar _Dē bellō Gallicō_ 1.1.2–3)
> "Those **who are called the Celts by their language, by ours the Gauls,** inhabit the third part."

BY THE WAY

When a form of the relative pronoun is found at the beginning of a Latin sentence, it is sometimes being used to link the sentence to a noun or idea in the previous sentence. This use is called the "connecting _quī_" and is translated by the corresponding form in English of _is, hic,_ or _ille_.

> **Quī** in fīnibus Gallōrum bellum gerunt.
> "**They** wage war on the borders of the Gauls."

> **Quā** dē causā Helvētiī quoque reliquōs Gallōs virtūte praecēdunt.
> (Caesar _Dē bellō Gallicō_ 1.1.9–10)
> "For **this** reason the Helvetians also surpass the remaining Gauls in courage."

▶ EXERCISE 3

Translate.

1. Gallia est omnis dīvīsa in partēs trēs, quārum ūnam partem incolunt Belgae.
2. Ūna pars, quae initium capit ā Rhodanō, continētur Garumnā flūmine.
3. Quī ā cultū atque humānitāte prōvinciae longissimē absunt fortissimī sunt.
4. Matrona, Sēquana, Garumna quae sunt tria flūmina in Galliā, sunt longissimī.
5. Quī linguā, īnstitūtīs, lēgibus inter sē differunt.
6. Belgae quōrum mīlitēs sunt fortissimī multīs proeliīs cum Germānīs contendunt.
7. Mīlitēs eīs grātiās agunt ab quibus cibus ad castra importātur.
8. Belgae ab extrēmīs fīnibus quī sunt in Galliā oriuntur.

READING 1 REDUX

You are now ready to read the passage exactly as Caesar wrote it. For this reason the words in parentheses, the special fonts, and the underlined words are no longer used. You have already seen notes in the first version of this passage, and you may refer to those notes if you need to. Additional notes for this passage are given below the text.

1   [1] Gallia est omnis dīvīsa in partēs trēs, quārum ūnam incolunt Belgae, aliam Aquītānī, tertiam quī ipsōrum linguā Celtae, nostrā Gallī appellantur. Hī omnēs linguā, īnstitūtīs, lēgibus inter sē differunt. Gallōs ab Aquītānīs Garumna flūmen, ā Belgīs Matrona et Sēquana dīvidit. Hōrum omnium fortissimī sunt Belgae, proptereā quod ā cultū atque

5   hūmānitāte prōvinciae longissimē absunt, minimēque ad eōs mercātōrēs saepe commeant atque ea quae ad effēminandōs animōs pertinent important, proximīque sunt Germānīs, quī trāns Rhēnum incolunt, quibuscum continenter bellum gerunt. Quā dē causā Helvētiī quoque reliquōs Gallōs virtūte praecēdunt, quod ferē cōtīdiānīs proeliīs cum Germānīs contendunt, cum aut suīs fīnibus eōs prohibent aut ipsī in eōrum fīnibus bellum gerunt.

10   Eōrum ūna pars, quam Gallōs obtinēre dictum est, initium capit ā flūmine Rhodanō, continētur Garumnā flūmine, Ōceanō, fīnibus Belgārum, attingit etiam ab Sēquanīs et Helvētiīs flūmen Rhēnum, vergit ad septentriōnēs. Belgae ab extrēmīs Galliae fīnibus oriuntur, pertinent ad īnferiōrem partem flūminis Rhēnī, spectant in septentriōnem et orientem sōlem. Aquitānia ā Garumnā flūmine ad Pȳrēnaeōs montēs et eam partem

15   Ōceanī quae est ad Hispāniam pertinet; spectat inter occāsum sōlis et septentriōnēs.

NOTES AND VOCABULARY

Line 1:   Note how *partem* is to be understood from the word *partēs* earlier in the sentence with both *aliam* and *tertiam*.

BY THE WAY

It is called ELLIPSIS when one or more words are needed to complete the thought in one or more clauses. See p. 194 for more detailed information on ELLIPSIS.

Line 2:   Notice that *linguā* is to be understood with *nostrā* from the previous phrase. This is another example of ELLIPSIS.

Line 9:   *suīs fīnibus* is an example of an ablative of separation, which in some instances features the preposition *ā, ab* and in other instances does not.

Helvetia is the name Switzerland still uses on its currency and its stamps. The god Mercury, recognized by his special cap, is an artifact from the days when Chur was a Roman foundation. This stamp issued in 1986 celebrates the 2,000-year anniversary of the city's founding.

ESSAY

Caesar discusses the factors that he believes contribute to the bravery, first of the Belgians and then of the Helvetians. In a short essay identify these factors. Point out and explain the significance of the factor that he mentions in the case of the Belgians but not of the Helvetians.

What does this omission indicate?

Support your assertions with references to the Latin text. All Latin words must be copied or their line numbers provided, AND they must be translated or paraphrased closely enough that it is clear that you understand the Latin. Direct your answer to the question; do not merely summarize the passage. Please write your essay on a separate piece of paper.

READING 2

The rest of the Caesar passages in this book will no longer feature the words in parentheses, the underlined words, and the use of special fonts. Use the notes below the passage to help you.

Orgetorix, the most noble and richest of the Helvetians, has great ambitions both for himself and for his people. The Helvetians are by nature bellicose, but geographical limitations hinder their ability to engage in warfare or to expand their boundaries as their population grows.

THE CONSPIRACY OF ORGETORIX

CAESAR *DĒ BELLŌ GALLICŌ* 1.2

1   [2] Apud Helvētiōs longē nōbilissimus fuit et dītissimus Orgetorīx. Is M. Messālā et M.
    Pīsōne cōnsulibus, rēgnī cupiditāte inductus coniūrātiōnem nōbilitātis fēcit, et cīvitātī
    persuāsit ut dē fīnibus suīs cum omnibus copiīs exīrent: perfacile esse, cum virtūte
    omnibus praestārent, tōtīus Galliae imperiō potīrī. Id hōc facilius eīs persuāsit, quod
5   undique locī nātūrā Helvētiī continentur: ūnā ex parte flūmine Rhēnō, lātissimō atque
    altissimō, quī agrum Helvētium ā Germānīs dīvidit; alterā ex parte monte Iūrā altissimō,
    quī est inter Sēquanōs et Helvētiōs; tertiā lacū Lemannō et flūmine Rhodanō, quō
    prōvinciam nostram ab Helvētiīs dīvidit.

NOTES AND VOCABULARY

Line 1:   **apud,** *prep. + acc.* among
             longē, *adv.* by far
             nōbilis, nōbile remarkable, noble
             dītissimus, -a, -um richest, wealthiest
             is: "he" refers to Orgetorix.‡

Lines 1–2:   **M. Messālā et M. Pīsōne cōnsulibus:** this ablative absolute is the standard Roman format
             for indicating a year, here 61 BCE. The literal translation is "with M. Messala and M. Piso
             being the consuls," but is commonly translated "in the consulship of M. Messala and M.
             Piso." In 61 BCE Caesar was *quaestor* in Spain, and this was three years before his first
             campaign in Gaul.

Line 2:   **rēgnum, -ī,** n. kingly government, royal power, kingdom
             cupiditās, cupiditātis, f. desire, eagerness, ambition
             indūcō, indūcere, indūxī, inductum to induce
             coniūrātiō, coniūrātiōnis, f. plot, conspiracy
             nōbilitās, nōbilitātis, f. the nobility, the nobles
             cīvitās, cīvitātis, f. state, body of citizens, community

BY THE WAY

Certain verbs govern a dative object. In this book, this type of verb has the notation (+ *dat.*) after the principal parts in the vocabulary entry. Verbs of pleasing, trusting, believing, persuading, resisting, commanding, obeying, serving, and sparing generally take a dative object.

Line 3:
persuādeō, persuādēre, persuāsī, persuāsum (+ *dat.*) to persuade; *persuādeō* and other similar verbs can be followed by *ut* + a subjunctive clause, a grammatical construction called an indirect command. English often uses an infinitive in this situation; translate "he persuaded the body of citizens to . . . ." (For more information on this topic, see p. 48.)

fīnis, fīnis, m. end, limit, *pl.* territory

cōpia, -ae, f. supply, abundance, resource, possession

exeō, exīre, exīvī, exitum to go out, march out; note how Caesar picks up the implied notion of "citizens" from *cīvitātī* in line 2, by using the plural in *exīrent, praestārent,* and *eīs* in lines 3–4.

perfacilis, perfacile very easy; understand an implied verb of saying with *perfacile esse;* translate "[saying] it would be very easy . . . ."

cum, *conj.*: here means "since," and for this reason takes the subjunctive.

virtūs, virtūtis, f. courage; *virtūte* is an ablative of respect; translate "in courage."

Line 4:
praestō, praestāre, praestitī, praestitum (+ *dat.*) to excel, outdo

tōtus, -a, -um whole, entire, all; *tōtīus* is genitive singular modifying *Galliae.*

imperium, imperiī, n. supreme authority

potior, potīrī, potītus sum (+ *gen.* or + *abl.*) to gain possession of, obtain; the infinitive *potīrī* is dependent on *perfacile.*

id: direct object of *persuāsit;* here *id* refers to the idea in the *ut* clause in the preceding sentence, that the Helvetians should leave their land.

hōc: ablative of cause; translate "for this reason."

facilis, facile easy; *facilius* is a comparative adverb. Translate *facilius* "the more easily."

quod, *conj.* because

Line 5:
undique, *adv.* on all sides, everywhere

contineō, continēre, continuī, contentum to contain, keep, hem in

pars, partis, f. part, side; *ūnā ex parte* means "on one side"; *alterā ex parte* "on another side" (i.e., "second"); and *tertiā [ex parte]* "on the third side."

flūmen, flūminis, n. river

lātus, -a, -um wide

Line 6:
altus, -a, -um high, deep, tall

ager, agrī, m. land, territory

alter, altera, alterum another, one (of two); second

Iūra, -ae, m. a chain of mountains, north of the Alps, extending from the Rhine to the Rhone; translate *monte* "mountain range."

Line 7:
Sēquanī, -ōrum, m. pl. the Sequanians

tertius, -a, -um third; understand *ex parte* after *tertiā.*

lacus, lacūs, m. lake

Lemannus, -ī, m. (Lake) Geneva

Rhodanus, -ī, m. the Rhone river

CAESAR *DĒ BELLŌ GALLICŌ* 1.2, CONTINUED

Hīs rēbus fīēbat ut et minus lātē vagārentur
et minus facile fīnitimīs bellum īnferre possent; quā ex parte hominēs bellandī cupidī

10   magnō dolōre adficiēbantur. Prō multitūdine autem hominum et prō glōriā bellī atque
fortitūdinis angustōs sē fīnēs habēre arbitrābantur, quī in longitūdinem mīlia passuum
CCXL, in lātitūdinem CLXXX patēbant.

NOTES AND VOCABULARY

BY THE WAY

The ablative is used to express cause when that cause is a property or characteristic of
the subject of the main verb. When the cause is external to the subject, the prepositions
propter or *ob* are preferred. These two examples illustrate the two ways to show cause:

Fortitūdine tuā dīcēbāris esse fortis.
"Because of your courage you were said to be brave."

Propter fortitūdinem tuam cōnsulēs tē laudāvērunt.
"Because of your courage the consuls praised you."

Line 8:	**hīs rēbus:** ablative of cause; translate "because of these things."
	fīō, fierī, factus sum to be made, be done, happen, become; here *fīō* is being used impersonally and should be translated "it happened"; when *fīō* is used impersonally, it usually is followed by a result clause introduced by *ut* or *ut nōn*.
	minus, *adv.* less
	vagor (1) to wander, roam
Lines 8–9:	**et . . . et:** both . . . and
Line 9:	**fīnitimus, -a, -um** neighboring; *as a noun,* neighbor
	bellum īnferō, īnferre, intulī, illātum to make or wage war
	quā ex parte: for this reason
	hominēs: in apposition to the subject of *adficiēbantur*
	bellō (1) to wage war, fight; *bellandī* is a genitive gerund dependent on *cupidī*; translate "of making war."
	cupidus, -a, -um (+ *gen.*) longing for, fond of
Line 10:	**dolor, dolōris,** m. pain, grief, resentment
	adficiō, adficere, adfēcī, adfectum to influence, afflict, impair
	prō, *prep.* + *abl.* for, in proportion to
	autem, *conj.* but, however, moreover‡

BY THE WAY

In lines 10–11, the phrase *bellī atque fortitūdinis* offers an example of HENDIADYS, a rhetorical figure of speech in which two nouns linked by a conjunction express one idea. The HENDIADYS enhances the thought here by giving equal emphasis to bravery and war.

Line 11:   **fortitūdō, fortitūdinis,** f. bravery, courage; translate *bellī atque fortitūdinis* "bravery in war."
angustus, -a, -um narrow, close
arbitror (1) to decide, judge, consider
longitūdō, longitūdinis, f. length
mīlia, mīlium, n. pl. thousands
passus, passūs, m. step; *mīlia passuum* = a thousand steps, i.e., a (Roman) mile

BY THE WAY

The word *mīlle*, "thousand," is an indeclinable adjective and singular only. Thus the nominative phrase *mīlle virī* means "a thousand men" just as the nominative phrase *mīlle passūs* means "mile." To write "two thousand men" in Latin, the plural noun for thousands, *mīlia, mīlium,* n. must be used. A partitive genitive (genitive of the whole) follows this noun. Thus the nominative phrase is *duo mīlia virōrum*. Likewise, in the phrase *duo mīlia passuum*, meaning "two miles," *passuum* is in the genitive plural.

Line 12:   **lātitūdō, lātitūdinis,** f. width, breadth
pateō, patēre, patuī to extend, stretch out

STUDY TIP

Be careful to distinguish between *passus, passūs,* m. "step, pace" and *passus,* a principal part from *patior, patī, passus sum* "to permit, allow."

TAKE NOTE

1. Popular government ruled most Gallic states. Orgetorix is planning a coup d'etat of the nobility to bring back royal government.

2. The conjunction *autem* is postpositive, which means that it is not placed first in a Latin sentence or clause.

COMPREHENSION QUESTIONS

1. What did Orgetorix persuade his citizens to do?

2. With whom did Orgetorix make a conspiracy?

3. Name the three geographical features that surrounded the Helvetians. Cite the Latin.

4. Why were the Helvetians afflicted with grief? Cite the Latin.

▶ EXERCISE 1

1. In line 1, what degree and case are the adjectives *nōbilissimus* and *dītissimus*?

2. In line 2, what is the case and use of *cupiditāte*?

3. What is the case and use of *cīvitātī* in line 2?

4. What is the case and use of *copiīs* in line 3?

5. In what tense and mood is *exīrent* in line 3?

6. What is the case and use of *omnibus* in line 4?

7. What is the case and use of *nātūrā* in line 5?

8. What is the antecedent of *quī* (line 6)?

9. What is the case and use of *lacū* in line 7?

10. In line 8, what part of speech is *lātē*?

11. In line 9, what is the case and use of *fīnitimīs*?

12. What is the mood and tense of *possent* in line 9?

13. In line 10, what is the case and use of *dolōre*?

14. What is the case and use of *sē* in line 11?

LANGUAGE FACT

ADJECTIVES WITH GENITIVE IN *–ĪUS* AND DATIVE IN *–Ī*

Certain first and second declension adjectives have an *–īus* ending in the genitive singular in all genders and an *–ī* ending in the dative singular in all genders.

> ... **tōtīus** Galliae imperiō potīrī (Caesar Dē bellō Gallicō 1.2.4).
> "to gain possession of the command of **all** Gaul."

> **Ūnī** fīnitimae cīvitātī bellum īnferre poterant.
> "They were able to make war against **one** neighboring state."

The complete paradigm of an adjective that follows this pattern can be found in Appendix D. The nine adjectives that show *–īus* in the genitive singular and *–ī* in the dative singular follow.

> tōtus, -a, -um – whole, entire, all
> sōlus, -a, -um – alone, only
> ūllus, -a, -um – any
> nūllus, -a, -um – no, none
> uter, utra, utrum – who, which (of two)
> neuter, neutra, neutrum – neither
> alius, alia, aliud – another, other
> alter, altera, alterum – the other (of two)
> ūnus, -a, -um – one (singular only)

BY THE WAY

In addition to these nine adjectives, certain pronouns (see p. 122) such as *ille, ipse,* and *is* have an *–īus* ending in the genitive and an *–ī* ending in the dative.

STUDY TIP

As noted on p. 249 of *Latin for the New Millennium*, Level 2, these nine adjectives, sometimes called the "naughty nine," can be remembered by learning the phrase ŪNUS NAUTA, in which each letter in bold is the beginning letter of one of the naughty nine.

Ūnus – one
Neuter – neither
Uter – who, which
Sōlus – alone, only

Nūllus – no, none
Alter – the other
Ūllus – any
Tōtus – whole, entire, all
Alius – another, other

This photograph of Lake Geneva, the ancient *Lacus Lemannus,* and the surrounding Alps assists the reader in visualizing the topographical challenges the Helvetians faced in trying to emigrate westward.

▶ EXERCISE 2

Identify the naughty nine adjective in each sentence and identify its case and use. Then translate the entire sentence.

1. Orgetorīx sōlus erat fortissimus Helvētiōrum.

2. Coniūrātiōnem tōtīus nōbilitātis fēcit.

3. Virtūte nūllī Rōmānō exercituī praestant.

4. Aliīs cīvibus persuāsit ut dē finibus suīs exīrent.

5. Lātitūdō ūnīus flūminis agrum Helvētium ā Germānīs dīvidit.

6. Alterā ex parte altissimō monte dīviditur.

7. Minus facile ūllīs finitimīs bellum īnferre poterant.

LANGUAGE FACT

PARTICIPLES INCLUDING GERUNDS AND GERUNDIVES

Let's review what the more common participles look like and how to translate them. Remember that a participle is a **verbal adjective** and thus it agrees in gender, number, and case with the noun that it modifies. The forms of all these participles can be seen in Appendix D on pp. 505–506.

- The Prese**nt** Active Participle is a third declension adjective. Its ablative singular can end in either *–e* or *–ī*. Remember that **–ns** and **–nt–** are the clues to recognizing the prese**nt** participle.

  Virtūte omnibus praestāns . . .   **REGULAR VERB**
  "Surpassing all in courage . . ."

- The Perfect Passive Participle, the fourth principal part of most verbs, is declined like *bonus, -a, -um*. The most literal translation of the first sentence below, "having been influenced," preserves the sense of "perfect" (having) and "passive" (been) but can be awkward. The perfect passive participle of deponent verbs translates actively, as in the second example, "having gained possession."

  rēgnī cupiditāte inductus . . .   **REGULAR VERB**
      (Caesar *Dē bellō Gallicō* 1.2.2)
  "Influenced by a desire for [of] the kingdom . . ."

  Potītī alterīus cīvitātis, Helvētiī dēlectantur.   **DEPONENT VERB**
  "Having gained possession of another state,
      the Helvetians are pleased."

STUDY TIP

The participles of deponent verbs are formed in the same way as the participles of regular verbs. Remember that deponent verbs have three principal parts that correspond to the first, second, and fourth principal parts of regular verbs.

- The Future Active Participle, also formed from the fourth principal part of most verbs but with –**ūr**– before the case ending, is also declined like *bonus, -a, -um*.

  > *Cīvitātī persuāsūrus ut dē suīs fīnibus . . .*   **REGULAR VERB**
  >   *exīrent, . . .*
  > "About to persuade the body of citizens to
  >   leave their territory . . . "

- The Geru**nd**ive, sometimes called the future passive participle, is formed from the present stem with –**nd**– before the case endings and is declined like *bonus, -a, -um*. The gerundive can be used in two ways: (1) with the meaning of the gerund (translate "___ing"). When the geru**nd**ive is used with the meaning of a gerund, it agrees with its noun in gender, number, and case or (2) to express necessity or obligation (to be introduced later; see p. 74).

  > *Indūcendā nōbilitāte, coniūrātiōnem fēcit.*   **GERUNDIVE** (Use 1)
  > "By influencing the nobility, he made a
  >   conspiracy."

- The Gerund, in form, is the neuter singular of the gerundive without a nominative case. The infinitive supplies the nominative case. Unlike the gerundive and the other participles in this section, the gerund is a **verbal noun.** It is more common to see the gerundive with an object in the same case expressed as the gerundive, as in the example above, but sometimes, as in the second example below, the gerund is seen with an object in the appropriate case.

  > *Quā ex parte hominēs bellandī cupidī . . .*   **GERUND**
  >   (Caesar *Dē bellō Gallicō* 1.2.9)
  > "For this reason, men desirous of waging
  >   war . . . "
  >
  > *Indūcendō nōbilitātem, coniūrātiōnem fēcit.*   **GERUND** (with an object)
  > "By influencing the nobility, he made a
  >   conspiracy."

 STUDY TIP

Although the present participle as well as the gerund and gerundive often translate into English with "–ing," otherwise they are not alike. The present active participle is a verbal adjective and modifies a noun. The gerund is a verbal noun. The gerundive takes on the function of a gerund.

▶ EXERCISE 3

Identify the participle, gerund, or gerundive in each sentence. Translate the entire sentence.

1. Minus lātē vagandō, minus facile fīnitimīs bellum īnferre poterant.

2. Cupidus coniūrātiōnis faciendae, facile nōbilitātī persuāsit.

3. Dīvīsī ā Germānīs montibus et flūminibus, Helvētiī erant fortissimī.

4. Bellandō, tōtīus Galliae imperiō potītur.

5. Vagātī trāns flūmen longē ab cīvitāte, magnō dolōre adficiēbantur.

6. Arbitrantēs angustōs sē fīnēs habēre, Helvētiī fīnitimīs bellum intulērunt.

7. Undique locī nātūrā contentī, Helvētiī minus facile ex suīs fīnibus exīvērunt.

8. Inductūrus nōbilitātem, Orgetorīx dīxit mīlitēs esse fortissimōs.

ESSAY

In section 2 of Book 1, Caesar provides an explanation for the factors that led up to the Gallic Wars. Discuss how Orgetorix's ambitions, the character of the Helvetians, and the geography of the place all play a part in the decision of the Helvetians to emigrate from the land they hold.

Support your assertions with references to the Latin text throughout the passage above. All Latin words must be copied or their line numbers provided, AND they must be translated or paraphrased closely enough that it is clear that you understand the Latin. Direct your answer to the question; do not merely summarize the passage. Please write your essay on a separate piece of paper.

Constructed to commemorate his victory over Dacia, Trajan's Column provides a variety of scenes from Roman military life. The soldiers in these relief panels engage in such activities as fighting, carrying the standards, seeking provisions, sailing, and building. Visual evidence such as this enables us to reconstruct the army of Caesar's day.

READING 3

The Helvetians begin their preparations to invade Gaul. In the meantime, Orgetorix persuades Casticus, a chieftain of the Sequanians, and Dumnorix, a chieftain of the Aeduans, to join him in creating a Gallic triumvirate, in order to seize power of all Gaul.

PREPARATIONS TO LEAVE

CAESAR *DĒ BELLŌ GALLICŌ* 1.3

1   [3] Hīs rēbus adductī et auctōritāte Orgetorīgis permōtī, cōnstituērunt ea quae ad
    proficīscendum pertinērent comparāre, iūmentōrum et carrōrum quam maximum
    numerum coemere, sēmentēs quam maximās facere ut in itinere cōpia frūmentī
    suppeteret, cum proximīs cīvitātibus pācem et amīcitiam cōnfirmāre. Ad eās rēs
5   cōnficiendās biennium sibi satis esse dūxērunt: in tertium annum profectiōnem lēge
    cōnfirmant. Ad eās rēs cōnficiendās Orgetorīx dēligitur. Is sibi lēgātiōnem ad cīvitātēs
    suscēpit.

NOTES AND VOCABULARY

Line 1:   **addūcō, addūcere, addūxī, adductum** to influence, sway
          auctōritās, auctōritātis, f. authority
          permoveō, permovēre, permōvī, permōtum to stir up, influence
          cōnstituō, cōnstituere, cōnstituī, cōnstitūtum to organize, set up, decide
Line 2:   **proficīscor, proficīscī, profectus sum** to set out, depart
          pertineō, pertinēre, pertinuī (+ *ad* + *acc.*) to extend (to), pertain to, reach (to); note that
              here, as with *ad effēminandōs animōs* in 1.1, line 6, the preposition *ad* does not introduce
              purpose, but should be taken closely with the verb *pertineō.*
          comparō (1) to prepare
          iūmentum, -ī, n. beast of burden, mule, pack animal
          carrus, -ī, m. cart, wagon
          maximus, -a, -um largest, greatest

STUDY TIP

When *quam* is used with a superlative adjective or adverb, the phrase means "as . . . as possible." Note that the superlative adjective or adverb is not translated with its superlative meaning but with its positive meaning. Translate *quam maximum numerum* in lines 2–3 "as great a number as possible."

Line 3: **coemō, coemere, coëmī, coëmptum** to buy up, purchase

sēmentis, sēmentis, f. the sowing, planting; translate *facere sēmentēs* "to grow crops."

copia, -ae, f. supply, abundance; *in plural*, resources, possessions, wealth, troops; note that not all instances of *cōpia* in the plural mean "troops," as, for example, *cōpiīs* in line 14 of section 3 below, which signifies "resources" or "possessions."

Line 4: **suppetō, suppetere, suppetīvī, suppetītum** to be available

proximus, -a, -um nearby, neighboring

cīvitās, cīvitātis, f. state, citizenship

cōnfirmō (1) to establish, strengthen, affirm

Line 5: **cōnficiō, cōnficere, cōnfēcī, cōnfectum** to accomplish, make ready

biennium, -ī, n. two-year period, two years; *biennium* is the accusative subject of the indirect statement that is dependent on *dūxērunt* in line 5.

sibi: a dative of reference, which frequently occurs with a form of *sum* joined with a noun or adverbial phrase. The reflexive pronoun looks back to the subject of the sentence or clause. Translate "for them."

dūcō, dūcere, dūxī, ductum to consider

tertius, -a, -um third; *in* + the accusative may express intent; translate "for the third year."

profectiō, profectiōnis, f. departure

lēx, lēgis, f. law

STUDY TIP

Be careful to distinguish among these look-alike words.

dēligō, dēligere, dēlēgī, dēlēctum to pick, choose
dēligō (1) to fasten, bind
dīligō, dīligere, dīlēxī, dīlēctum to choose, esteem, love

Line 6: **dēligō, dēligere, dēlēgī, delēctum** to pick, choose‡

lēgātiō, lēgātiōnis, f. embassy, mission

Line 7: **suscipiō, suscipere, suscēpī, susceptum** to undertake, take up

In eō itinere persuādet Casticō Catamantaloedis fīliō Sēquanō, cūius pater rēgnum in Sēquanīs multōs annōs obtinuerat et ā senātū populī Rōmānī amīcus appellātus erat, ut rēgnum in cīvitāte suā occupāret, quod pater ante habuerat; itemque

10 Dumnorīgī Aeduō frātrī Dīviciācī, quī eō tempore prīncipātum in cīvitāte obtinēbat ac maximē plēbī acceptus erat, ut idem cōnārētur persuādet eīque fīliam suam in mātrimōnium dat.

NOTES AND VOCABULARY

Line 7: **persuādeō, persuādēre, persuāsī, persuāsum** (+ *dat.*) to persuade‡

Casticō Catamantaloedis fīliō Sēquanō: translate "Casticus, the son of Catamantaloedes, the Sequanian."

STUDY TIP

An appositive is a noun that gives more information about another noun. The appositive and the noun to which it refers are in the same case and often are the same gender and number. In line 7, for example, *fīliō*, dative with *persuādet*, is in apposition with *Casticō*.

Line 8: **rēgnum, -ī,** n. kingship, kingdom, dominion, sovereignty, rule, authority

multōs annōs: accusative of duration of time; translate "for many years."

populī Rōmānī amīcus: it was a great honor to be called "a friend of the Roman people"; the Roman Senate conferred this title on certain foreign states or individuals to establish an informal alliance with them.

Line 9: **appellō** (1) to call (by name); to name

ante, *adv.* previously, before

item, *adv.* likewise

Line 10: **Aeduus, -a, -um** Aeduan, of the Aeduī‡

Dīviciācus, -ī, m. Diviciacus

Dumnorīgī Aeduō frātrī Dīviciācī: translate "to Dumnorix the Aeduan, the brother of Diviciacus." The Aeduans are one of the most powerful of Gallic tribes; Diviciacus, Dumnorix's brother, the chief of the Aeduans, was friendly to the Romans.

prīncipātus, -ūs, m. rule, leadership, chief command

cīvitās, cīvitātis, f. state, clan

ac, *conj.* and, and moreover

Line 11: **maximē,** *adv.* especially, very

plēbs, plēbis, f. the common people, the masses; *plēbī* is dative case because it is governed by the adjective *acceptus*, meaning "acceptable."

īdem, eadem, idem the same, the same one/thing

cōnor (1) to try, attempt

Lines 11–12: **in mātrimōnium dō, dare, dedī, datum** to give in matrimony, to marry‡

As part of his Roman Forum renovations, Julius Caesar founded a new forum near the site of the Curia. Its chief feature was the Temple of Venus Genetrix, which celebrated the Julio-Claudian lineage that extended back to Aeneas, the legendary Trojan founder of Rome and son of Venus, and to Mars, the legendary father of the twins Romulus and Remus. Augustus completed the construction of the Forum of Julius Caesar.

CAESAR *DĒ BELLŌ GALLICŌ* 1.3, CONTINUED

        Perfacile factū esse illīs probat cōnāta perficere, proptereā quod ipse suae cīvitātis imperium obtentūrus esset: nōn esse dubium quīn tōtīus Galliae plūrimum Helvētiī possent; sē suīs cōpiīs suōque exercitū illīs rēgna conciliātūrum cōnfirmat.

15   Hāc ōrātiōne adductī inter sē fidem et iūs iūrandum dant et rēgnō occupātō per trēs potentissimōs ac firmissimōs populōs tōtīus Galliae sēsē potīrī posse spērant.

NOTES AND VOCABULARY

Line 12:   **perfacile factū esse:** translate this indirect statement "that it was very easy to do."

            probō (1) to prove, show

            perfacile . . . perficere: *probat* introduces the indirect statement, with *cōnāta perficere* (infinitive with an object) serving as the subject of *esse. Perfacile* is modifying the neuter infinitive *perficere* and is taking a second supine, *factū*, to complete its meaning. Note that three of the seven words derive from the base *fac–, fact–* (*per-ficere, per-facile,* and *factū*).

            cōnātum, cōnātī, n. attempt

            proptereā quod: translate "because."

            ipse, ipsa, ipsum, *intensive pronoun* -self

STUDY TIP

The noun or pronoun that the intensive *ipse, ipsa, ipsum* modifies often must be understood. The understood word can usually be determined by considering the gender, number, and case of *ipse*. In lines 12–13, since *ipse* is masculine, singular, nominative, the pronoun to be understood is "he" and *ipse . . . obtentūrus esset* translates "he himself was about to obtain."

Line 13:   **imperium, -ī,** n. absolute authority, command

            dubius, -a, -um doubtful

            quīn (= *quī* + negative *nē*), *adv.* but that; after negative expressions of doubt, the relative adverb *quīn* regularly is used to introduce a subjunctive clause.

            nōn esse dubium quīn: the indirect statement is dependent on "he said," words which must be understood. Translate "he said that there was no doubt but that . . . ."

Lines 13–14:   **plūrimum . . . possent:** to be the most powerful

Line 14:   **cōpiīs:** translate "resources."

            exercitus, exercitūs, m. army

            illīs: a dative indirect object referring to Casticus and Dumnorix‡

            conciliō (1) to unite, win over

Line 15:   **ōrātiō, ōrātiōnis,** f. speech, oration

            fidēs, fideī, f. promise, pledge, trust

            iūs iūrandum, iūris iūrandī, n. oath ("a binding code or formula that must be sworn to"); the idiom *iūs iūrandum* generally is considered as a single word.

            inter sē . . . dant: to exchange (*lit.,* "to give among themselves")‡

Line 16:   **potēns, potentis** powerful

firmus, -a, -um strong

potior, potīrī, potītus sum to gain possession of; *potior* may take its object in the genitive case although it usually governs the ablative case.

spērō (1) to hope (for); Casticus, Dumnorix and Orgetorix serve as the subject of *spērant*. Note that a future infinitive generally follows verbs of hoping. The verb *possum*, however, lacks a future infinitive, and so Caesar uses the present tense instead.

TAKE NOTE

1. In this passage are several historical presents: *cōnfirmō* in lines 6 and 14, *dēligō* in line 6, *persuādeō* in lines 7 and 11, *dō* in lines 12 and 15, *probō* in line 12, and *spērō* in line 16. Their purpose is to enliven the narrative. Historical presents should be translated into English as a past tense. In the sequence of tenses, these verbs may be followed by either a primary or a secondary tense verb. The verb *persuādet* in lines 7 and 11 is followed by verbs in the secondary tense (*occupāret* and *cōnārētur*).

2. In English a term that describes groups such as the Aeduans, Sequanians, etc. might be "clan" or "tribe." There were about sixty of these groups in Gaul whose territory had no local name, but was known only by that of the clan, which was sovereign and wholly independent, except for voluntary alliances.

3. Note that the repetition of the reflexive pronoun and adjective (*sē suīs . . . suōque*) in line 14 emphasizes the key role that Orgetorix envisions himself playing in the proposed triumvirate.

COMPREHENSION QUESTIONS

1. What preparations did the Helvetians decide to make in order to be ready to leave?

2. How long did the Helvetians think it would take to complete the preparations?

3. Why did Orgetorix send an embassy to Casticus and Dumnorix? Cite the Latin.

4. According to Caesar, who was called a friend of the Roman people?

5. To whom does Orgetorix marry his daughter?

▶ EXERCISE 1

1. In line 1, what is the case and use of *hīs rēbus*?

2. What is the tense, voice, and form of *adductī* in line 1?

3. In lines 2–4, what four infinitives are dependent on *cōnstituērunt*?

4. In line 4, what is the tense, voice, and mood of *suppeteret*?

5. In line 5, what is the case and use of *biennium*?

6. What is the case and use of *lēge* in line 5?

7. In line 7, what is the case and use of *Casticō*?

8. What is the case and use of *annōs* in line 8?

9. In line 8, what is the case and use of *senātū*?

10. What is the case and use of *Dumnorīgī* in line 10?

11. In line 10, what is the case and use of *tempore*?

12. In line 13, what is the tense, voice, and form of *obtentūrus*?

13. In line 14, what is the case and use of *sē*?

14. What is the case and use of *fidem* in line 15?

15. What is the case and use of *rēgnō* in line 15?

16. In line 16, what is the tense, voice, form, and use of *posse*?

VOCABULARY BUILDER

The Latin preposition *per* means "through." When *per-* is used as a prefix on a Latin word, however, it often gives that Latin word the meaning of "very" or "thoroughly." Thus, while *mōtus, -a, -um* means "moved," *permōtus, -a, -um* (line 1) means "thoroughly moved" in an emotional sense. Likewise, *facilis* means "easy" but *perfacilis* (line 12) means "very easy." In other instances the prefix *per-* retains its meaning of "through." For example, *percurrō* means "to run through."

What does each word in the following pairs of words mean? Use the glossary for help.

magnus	permagnus
paucī	perpaucī
volō (1)	pervolō
labor, labī	perlabor
vagor	pervagor
saepe	persaepe
turbō	perturbō
gravis	pergravis
iūcundus	periūcundus
invītus	perinvītus

LANGUAGE FACT

GERUNDS AND GERUNDIVES IN PURPOSE CONSTRUCTIONS

One way to show purpose in Latin is through the use of gerunds and gerundives with *ad, causā*, and *grātiā*. *Ad* with an accusative gerund or gerundive is seen the most often in Latin. *Causā* or *grātiā* follow a genitive gerund or gerundive. Consider the following examples.

- **Gerund in a Purpose Construction**

    ***Ad proficīscendum** iūmentōrum et carrōrum numerum coēmērunt.*
    "They bought a number of mules and cart **for the purpose of setting out**."

Excēdendī causā, *multa parāvērunt.*
"**For the sake of leaving**, they prepared many things."

Celeriter **adveniendī grātiā**, *sēcum multa nōn tulērunt.*
"**For the sake of arriving** quickly, they did not bring many things with them."

- **Gerundive in a Purpose Construction**

  Ad eās rēs cōnficiendās *Orgetorīx dēligitur.* (Caesar *Dē bellō Gallicō* 1.3.6)
  "Orgetorix is chosen **to accomplish these things**."

  Persuādendārum cīvitātum causā, *is lēgātiōnem ad eās suscēpit.*
  "**For the sake of persuading the states**, he undertook an embassy to them."

  Pācis faciendae *cum proximīs cīvitātibus* **grātiā**, *amīcitiam celeriter cōnfirmant.*
  "**For the sake of making peace** with the nearest states, they establish
    friendship quickly."

▶ EXERCISE 2

Translate the sentences. Identify the gerund or gerundive purpose construction in each sentence.

1. Fīliae adducendae causā, Orgetorīx Dumnorīgem esse bonum virum dīxit.

2. Ad obtinendum rēgnum, dīxit patrem Rōmānī populī esse amīcum.

3. Fugiendī grātiā, nēmō sēmentēs fēcit.

4. Obtinendī cibī causā, in agrīs labōrāvērunt.

5. Ad loquendum pūblicē, Orgetorīx ōrātiōnem parāvit.

6. Proficīscendī causā, numerum carrōrum iūmentōrumque coēmērunt.

LANGUAGE FACT

SUBJUNCTIVE PURPOSE CLAUSES AND INDIRECT COMMANDS

- **Purpose Clauses**

The most commonly used **purpose** construction in Latin is the *ut/nē* subjunctive purpose clause. Subjunctive purpose clauses translate in several ways—"so that," "in order to," or "to." Consider the following examples.

  Cōnstituērunt . . . **ut** *in itinere cōpia frūmentī* **suppeteret** *. . . .*
    (Caesar *Dē bellō Gallicō* 1.3.1–4)
  "They decided . . . **so that** a supply of grain **might be on hand** on
    the journey . . . ."

  Pecūniam ferunt . . . **ut** *numerum carrōrum* **emant**.
  "They bring money . . . **in order to buy** a number of carts."

*Orgetorīx dēligitur **ut** eās rēs **cōnficiat**.*
"Orgetorix is chosen **to accomplish** these things."

*Multa perfēcērunt . . . **nē** hostis cīvitātis imperium **obtinēret**.*
"They did many things . . . **so that** the enemy **might not obtain**
    the rule of the state."

- **Indirect Commands**

An indirect command is similar to a purpose clause in many ways. Like purpose clauses, the clause contains an action not yet completed and the same *ut/nē* subjunctive construction is used. Verbs of requesting, commanding, and persuading introduce the subjunctive clause in an indirect command. Consider the following examples.

*In eō itinere persuādet Casticō . . . **ut** rēgnum in cīvitāte suā **occupāret** . . . .*
    (Caesar *Dē bellō Gallicō* 1.3.7–9)
"On that journey he persuaded Casticus to occupy the kingdom in
    his own state . . . ."

*Dumnorīgem hortātus est **ut** idem **cōnārētur**.*
"He encouraged Dumnorix to try the same thing."

*Ab Helvētiīs quaerit **ut** ex suīs fīnibus **proficīscantur**.*
"He asks the Helvetians to leave their territory."

*Suīs imperāvit **nē pugnārent**.*
"He commanded his own men not to fight."

Both purpose clauses and indirect commands like other subjunctive clauses follow the sequence of tenses. (See pp. 546–547 in Appendix D.)

Although the *ut* in purpose clauses may be translated as "to" or "so that," the *ut* in indirect commands can only be translated as "to."

BY THE WAY

As noted on p. 98 of *Latin for the New Millennium*, Level 2, the verb *iubeō* takes an accusative and infinitive construction instead of an indirect command.

▶ EXERCISE 3

Translate the entire sentence. Identify whether a purpose clause or an indirect command is in the sentence.

1. Orgetorīx hāc ōrātiōne eōs hortātus est ut inter sē fidem darent.

2. Cōnstituērunt iūmenta et carrōs coemere ut proficīscerentur.

3. Orgetorīx rogat eōs ut in tertium annum profectiōnem lēge cōnfirment.

4. Dē fīnibus suīs Orgetorīx profectus est ut Casticō Sēquanō et Dumnorīgī Aeduō persuādēret.

5. Eōs monuit ut suae cīvitātis imperium obtentūrus esset.

6. Sēmentēs quam maximās faciunt nē in itinere cōpiā frūmentī careant.

7. Rogat Casticum ut rēgnum in cīvitāte suā capiat.

8. Biennium sibi satis esse dūxērunt ut eās rēs cōnficerent.

9. Is sibi lēgātiōnem ad cīvitātēs suscēpit ut illīs persuādēret.

10. Orgetorīx dēligitur ut Helvētiōs dē fīnibus cum omnibus cōpiīs ēdūcat.

ESSAY

In this passage we see how Orgetorix intends to use the dissatisfaction of Helvetians and others for his own ends. Discuss Orgetorix's ultimate goal, the allies he chose, why he probably chose them, what he wanted them to do, and what he promised that he himself would do. How does Orgetorix's alliance with Casticus and Dumnorix resemble Caesar's alliance with Pompey and Crassus? Refer to the historical review "The Last Century of the Roman Republic" and the "Introduction to Caesar" to prepare your answer.

Support your assertions about the Latin passage with references to the Latin text. All Latin words must be copied or their line numbers provided, AND they must be translated or paraphrased closely enough that it is clear that you understand the Latin. Direct your answer to the question; do not merely summarize the passage. Please write your essay on a separate piece of paper.

READING 4

The Helvetians find out about the Gallic triumvirate that was created in secret, with the result that Orgetorix commits suicide. Despite the loss of their leader, the Helvetians decide to emigrate, and they burn to the ground their towns, villages, and private buildings in order to ensure commitment to the plan.

THE DEATH OF ORGETORIX

CAESAR *DĒ BELLŌ GALLICŌ* 1.4–5

1   [4] Ea rēs est Helvētiīs per indicium ēnūntiāta. Mōribus suīs Orgetorīgem ex vinculīs
causam dīcere coēgērunt. Damnātum poenam sequī oportēbat ut ignī cremārētur. Diē
cōnstitūtā causae dictiōnis Orgetorīx ad iūdicium omnem suam familiam, ad hominum
mīlia decem, undique coēgit, et omnēs clientēs obaerātōsque suōs, quōrum magnum
5   numerum habēbat, eōdem condūxit: per eōs nē causam dīceret sē ēripuit.

NOTES AND VOCABULARY

Line 1:   **ea rēs:** translate "this conspiracy."‡

indicium, -ī, n. proof or evidence (given against someone), disclosure; *per indicium = per indicēs,* "through informers"

ēnūntiō (1) to reveal, express, say

mōs, mōris, m. custom; translate *mōribus suīs* "according to their customs."

vinculum, -ī, n. chain, pl. prison; translate *ex vinculīs* "in chains."

STUDY TIP

Be careful to distinguish among these four words with the *mor–* base.

mōs, mōris, m. custom	THIRD DECLENSION NOUN
mora, -ae, f. delay	FIRST DECLENSION NOUN
moror, morārī, morātus sum to delay	FIRST CONJUGATION DEPONENT VERB
morior, morī, mortuus sum to die	THIRD –*IO* CONJUGATION DEPONENT VERB

Line 2:   **causam dīcō, dīcere, dīxī, dictum** to plead a case

cōgō, cōgere, coēgī, coāctum to force, compel, bring together, collect; with a complementary infinitive (line 2) translate "to force, compel"; otherwise, translate "bring together, collect" (line 4).

damnō (1) to condemn; here the participle *damnātum* has conditional force; translate "if condemned."

poena, -ae, f. punishment, penalty

sequor, sequī, secūtus sum to follow, come next

oportet, oportēre, oportuit, *impersonal* it is necessary, it is proper

BY THE WAY

To translate *oportēbat . . . damnātum* in English, follow this word order: *oportēbat poenam sequī damnātum (hominem).* The verb *oportēbat* is taking an indirect statement, with *poenam* serving as the subject of the infinitive *sequī; hōminem,* "understood" and modified by *damnātum,* serves as the object of *sequī.* The *ut* clause is in apposition to *poenam.*

ignī: the *i*-stem third declension noun *ignis* often ends in *–ī* in the ablative singular in both prose and poetry, although it sometimes has *–e* in the ablative as well.‡

cremō (1) to burn, to burn alive

Line 3:   **cōnstituō, cōnstituere, cōnstituī, cōnstitūtum** to determine, arrange, establish, appoint; translate *diē cōnstitūtā* "on the day appointed." This is an ablative of time with a perfect passive participle modifying "day." The feminine gender of "day" refers to a fixed day.

dictiō, dictiōnis, f. speaking; with *causae* "pleading of a case"

iūdicium, -ī, n. court, trial, judgment

familia, -ae, f. translate here, "slave."

ad, *prep. + acc.* to, toward, near; with numbers translate "about."

hominum: partitive genitive with *mīlia*

Line 4:   **undique,** *adv.* everywhere, on all sides, from all directions

obaerātus, -ī, m. debtor

Line 5:   **eōdem,** *adv.* to the same place

condūcō, condūcere, condūxī, conductum to assemble

nē . . . ēripuit: translate "he avoided pleading his case" (*lit.,* "he escaped so that he did not plead his case").

sē ēripiō, ēripere, ēripuī, ēreptum to escape

CAESAR *DĒ BELLŌ GALLICŌ* 1.4–5, CONTINUED

5   Cum cīvitās

ob eam rem incitāta armīs iūs suum exsequī cōnārētur, multitūdinemque hōminum
ex agrīs magistrātūs cōgerent, Orgetorīx mortuus est; neque abest suspiciō, ut Helvētiī
arbitrantur, quīn ipse sibi mortem cōnscīverit.

NOTES AND VOCABULARY

Line 5:   **cum:** translate "while."

Line 6:   **incitō** (1) to incite, stir up

              iūs, iūris, n. law, justice

              exsequor, exsequī, exsecūtus sum to carry out, perform, enforce

              cōnor, cōnārī, cōnātus sum to try, attempt

Line 7:   **ex agrīs:** translate "from the countryside."

              magistrātus, magistrātūs, m. official, magistrate

              absum, abesse, āfuī, āfutūrum to be absent, missing; *neque abest suspiciō* is roughly
                  equivalent in meaning to *nōn dubium est*, and thus introduces a *quīn* subjunctive clause as in
                  1.3.13–14.

              suspiciō, -ōnis, f. suspicion, mistrust

              ut, utī so that, that, as, when

Line 8:   **arbitror, arbitrārī, arbitrātus sum** to think, decide, judge, consider

              cōnscīscō, cōnscīscere, cōnscīvī, cōnscītum to decide on; with *sibi*, to inflict on oneself

BY THE WAY

The phrase *neque abest suspiciō* is an example of a figure of speech called LITOTES in
which something is understated for emphasis or IRONY. LITOTES is frequently created
by using a double negative. LITOTES here emphasizes that there was some suspicion
that Orgetorix committed suicide.

STUDY TIP

When *ut* introduces an indicative clause as here in line 7, *ut Helvētiī arbitrantur, ut*
means "as." An alternate form of *ut* is *utī* (line 15), which should not be confused with
ūtī, the infinitive of *ūtor*, "to use."

52 • Latin for the New Millennium

HELVETIAN ESCAPE ROUTES

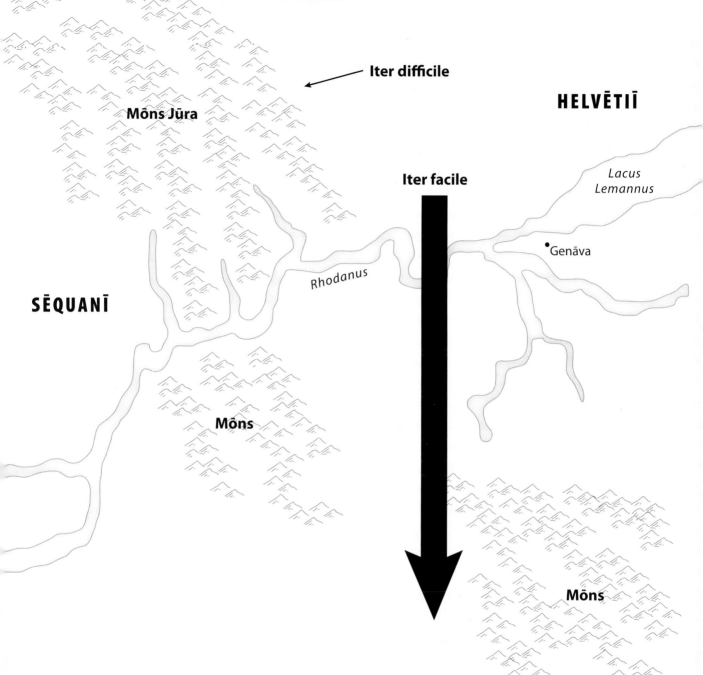

Iter difficile

Mōns Jūra

HELVĒTIĪ

Iter facile

Lacus
Lemannus

•Genāva

SĒQUANĪ

Rhodanus

Mōns

Mōns

ALLOBROGĒS

CAESAR *DĒ BELLŌ GALLICŌ* 1.4–5, CONTINUED

[5] Post eius mortem nihilō minus Helvētiī id quod cōnstituerant facere cōnantur, ut ē

10 fīnibus suīs exeant. Ubi iam sē ad eam rem parātōs esse arbitrātī sunt, oppida sua omnia, numerō ad duodecim, vīcōs ad quadringentōs, reliqua prīvāta aedificia incendunt; frūmentum omne, praeterquam quod sēcum portātūrī erant, combūrunt, ut domum reditiōnis spē sublātā parātiōrēs ad omnia perīcula subeunda essent; trium mēnsum molita cibāria sibi quemque domō efferre iubent. Persuādent Rauracīs et Tulingīs et

15 Latōbrigīs fīnitimīs suīs, utī eōdem ūsī cōnsiliō, oppidīs suīs vīcīsque exustīs ūnā cum eīs proficīscantur, Boiōsque quī trāns Rhēnum incoluerant et in agrum Nōricum trānsierant Nōrēiamque oppugnārant, receptōs ad sē sociōs sibi ascīscunt.

NOTES AND VOCABULARY

Line 9: **nihilum, -ī,** n. nothing; *nihilō minus* nevertheless

Line 10: **exeō, exīre, exīvī, exitum** to go out, escape; *ut exeant* is a substantive clause of result, in apposition to *id quod cōnstituerant.*

ubi, *conj.* when, where

oppidum, -ī, n. town; the *oppida* are strongholds, while the *vīcī* are groups of houses that comprise a village.

Line 11: **vīcus, -ī,** m. village

quadringentī, -ae, -a four hundred

aedificium, -ī, n. building

incendō, incendere, incendī, incēnsum to burn, set on fire

Line 12: **praeterquam quod:** translate "except what" or "apart from what."

combūrō, combūrere, combussī, combustum to burn up, ruin

domum: accusative of motion, place to which

Line 13: **reditiō, reditiōnis,** f. return; *reditiō,* an infrequently used noun in Latin, has a verbal sense here of "returning."

spēs, speī, f. hope, expectation

tollō, tollere, sustulī, sublātum to remove

subeō, subīre, subīvī, subitum to enter, approach, undergo; *ad . . . subeunda* is a gerundive of purpose.

mēnsis, mēnsis, m. month; *mēnsis* is one of several *i*-stem nouns that admit two forms in the genitive plural, both *mēnsum* and *mēnsium.*

BY THE WAY

The preposition *ā, ab* is omitted from a place from which, and *ad, in* are omitted from place to which when the object of the preposition is the name of a city, a town, a small island, *domus,* or *rūs. Domus* is an irregular noun in that some of its forms are from the fourth declension and some from the second declension. (See the complete paradigm of *domus* on p. 497 in Appendix D.)

Line 14:   **molitus, -a, -um** milled, ground

cibāria, cibāriōrum, n. pl. food, an allowance of food; *molita cibāria* ("ground food") = "meal."

domus, domūs, f. home; *domō* is an ablative of place from which with the preposition *ā, ab* omitted.

efferō, efferre, extulī, ēlātum to carry out, bring out

BY THE WAY

The three datives in lines 14–15, joined by the repeated *et* (*Rauracīs et Tulingīs et Latobrigīs*) illustrate the rhetorical figure of POLYSYNDETON, which repeats many connectives in close succession, where one or more could be omitted (from the Greek *poly* = "many" and *syndeton* = "connection"). The repeated "and" focuses equally on all three peoples and lengthens the list of groups joining the Helvetians in their quest for more land.

Line 15:   **utī:** alternate form of *ut*

īdem, eadem, idem the same

ūtor, ūtī, ūsus sum (+ *abl.*) to use

cōnsilium, -ī, n. plan

vīcus, vīcī, m. village

exūrō, exūrere, exussī, exustum to burn down, destroy

ūnā, *adv.* together

Line 16:   **proficīscor, proficīscī, profectus sum** to set out, depart

Boiī, Boiōrum, m. pl. Boii, a Celtic tribe in southern Germany and Cisalpine Gaul

incolō, incolere, incoluī to live in, inhabit

Nōricus, -a, -um Noric; *agrum Nōricum* corresponds, in general, with the western part of Austria south of the Danube, between Bavaria and Hungary; now eastern Bavaria and upper Austria.

trānseō, trānsīre, trānsiī, trānsitum to cross

Line 17:   **Nōrēia, -ae,** f. principal town of the Norici

oppugnō (1) to attack; *oppugnārant* = *oppugnāverant*.

receptōs ad sē sociōs sibi ascīscunt: translate "they take the Boii as allies to themselves (*sociōs sibi ascīscunt*) who had found refuge in them (*receptōs ad sē*)."

sē . . . recipiō, recipere, recēpī, receptum (+*ad* + *acc.*) to withdraw, escape to, find refuge in; the reason that Caesar adds the detail about the Boii is that these people join the Helvetians in their emigration and fight with them against Caesar.

ascīscō, ascīscere, ascīvī, ascītum to take to as an ally

BY THE WAY

The final sentence of section 5 contains a striking example of ALLITERATION, a rhetorical figure in which consonants (usually initial) are repeated in a series of two or more words: *sē sociōs sibi a-scī-scunt*; the alliterative final four words of this section are intended to call attention to the point that the Helvetians took on the Boii as allies.

TAKE NOTE

1. The generic word *rēs* is constantly used in Caesar, where in English we should use more specific words such as "occurrence," "movement," "exploit," "misfortune," "undertaking," "fact," "supplies," etc., according to the context. No word in Latin admits such a variety of meanings as *rēs*. In this respect it is similar to the generic usage of the English word "things." The student must always determine by the context the most suitable word to employ in translating *rēs*.

2. Certain *i*-stem nouns that have the same number of syllables in the nominative and genitive singular (except those in which the nominative singular ends in –*es* and the genitive singular in –*is*) are called pure *i*-stems. The term "mixed *i*-stem" is used to describe masculine and feminine nouns that show regular third declension endings in the singular and *i*-stem endings in the plural. For a fuller explanation of endings on pure and mixed *i*-stems, see Appendix D.

COMPREHENSION QUESTIONS

1. What punishment would Orgetorix undergo if convicted?

2. What happened when Orgetorix summoned his slaves and clients to listen at his trial?

3. How did the Helvetians believe that Orgetorix died? Cite the Latin.

4. What did the Helvetians burn when they thought they were ready to leave their territory?

5. What did the Helvetians persuade their neighbors to do?

▶ EXERCISE 1

1. In line 1, what is the case and use of *Orgetorīgem*?

2. In line 2, what is the tense and form of *sequī*?

3. What is the tense, mood, and voice of *cremārētur* in line 2?

4. What Latin word does *omnem* (line 3) modify?

5. In line 5, what is the tense, voice, and mood of *dīceret*?

6. What is the tense and form of *exsequī* in line 6?

7. What is the tense and mood of *cōnārētur* in line 6?

8. What is the case and use of *agrīs* in line 7?

9. What is the case and use of *magistrātūs* in line 7?

10. In line 7, what is the case and use of *suspiciō*?

11. In line 8, what is the tense, voice, and mood of *cōnscīverit*?

12. What is the case and use of *mortem* in line 9?

13. What Latin word is the antecedent of *quod* in line 9?

14. What is the tense, voice, and mood of *cōnstituerant* in line 9?

15. What is the tense, voice, and mood of *exeant* in line 10?

16. In line 11, what is the case and use of *numerō*?

17. In line 12, what is the case and use of *frūmentum*?

18. What is the tense, voice, and form of *portātūrī* in line 12?

19. What is the tense, voice, and form of *sublāta* in line 13?

20. In line 13, what is the case and degree of *parātiōrēs*?

21. In line 14, what is the case and use of *domō*?

22. In line 14, what is the tense, voice, and form of *efferre*?

23. What is the case and use of *fīnitimīs* in line 15?

24. What type of clause does *utī* in line 15 introduce?

25. In line 16, what is the tense and mood of *proficīscantur*?

26. What Latin word is the antecedent of *quī* in line 16?

27. In line 16, what is the tense and voice of *incoluerant*?

28. What is the case and use of *agrum* in line 16?

VOCABULARY BUILDER

Latin, like many languages, contains idioms. An idiom is a phrase that has a unique meaning when the words in the phrase are used together. Recognizing idioms and knowing their meaning will increase your Latin vocabulary and help you read with more ease. Here is a list of Latin idioms that Caesar uses in the readings in this book. (The asterisked citations refer to the Latin reading on p. 28.)

> bellum gerō, gerere, gessī, gestum to wage war
> > (Caesar *Dē bellō Gallicō* 1.1.7 and 9*)
>
> oriēns sōl, orientis sōlis, m. the rising sun, the East
> > (Caesar *Dē bellō Gallicō* 1.1.14*)
>
> occāsus sōlis, occāsūs sōlis, m. the setting of the sun, the West
> > (Caesar *Dē bellō Gallicō* 1.1.15*)
>
> bellum īnferō, īnferre, intulī, inlātum to make war on
> > (Caesar *Dē bellō Gallicō* 1.2.9)
>
> plūrimum possum, posse, potuī to be very powerful
> > (Caesar *Dē bellō Gallicō* 1.3.13–14)
>
> iūs iūrandum, iūris iūrandī, n. oath
> > (Caesar *Dē bellō Gallicō* 1.3.15)

quam + superlative adjective/adverb as . . . as possible
(Caesar *Dē bellō Gallicō* 1.3.2–3)

quam + superlative adjective + possum as . . . as possible.
(Caesar *Dē bellō Gallicō* 1.7.13 and 14)

dō, dare, dedī, datum inter sē to exchange
(Caesar *Dē bellō Gallicō* 1.3.15)

causam dīcō, dīcere, dīxī, dictum to plead a case
(Caesar *Dē bellō Gallicō* 1.4.2)

sē ēripiō, ēripere, ēripuī, ēreptum to escape
(Caesar *Dē bellō Gallicō* 1.4.5)

certiōrem/ēs faciō, facere, fēcī, factum to inform
(Caesar *Dē bellō Gallicō* 1.7.16)

sibi esse in animō to be his/her/its/their intention
(Caesar *Dē bellō Gallicō* 1.7.18)

(in) memoriā teneō, tenēre, tenuī, tentum to remember
(Caesar *Dē bellō Gallicō* 1.7.20)

LANGUAGE FACT

ABLATIVE ABSOLUTES

The ablative absolute construction is comprised of a noun or pronoun in the ablative case along with a participle or, in some cases, another noun or adjective in the ablative. The ablative absolute phrase is connected with the main sentence in thought but not grammatically. The literal translation of an ablative absolute is generally awkward in English, and so it is better to use a temporal, conditional, causal, or concessive clause. Consider the following sentences.

*Frūmentum . . . combūrunt, ut **domum***
***reditiōnis spē sublātā** parātiōrēs . . . essent.*
(Caesar *Dē bellō Gallicō* 1.5.12–13)

"They burn the grain so that **with the
hope of returning home having been
removed**, they might be more prepared."

LITERAL
TRANSLATION

"They burn the grain so that **after hope
of returning home had been removed**,
they might be more prepared."

TEMPORAL
TRANSLATION

There may be instances in which a temporal or causal interpretation will both make sense. The next sentence illustrates this point. The context usually will guide which interpretation makes the best sense.

Familiā et clientibus ad iūdicium conductīs,
  Orgetorīx sē ēripuit.

"**With his slaves and clients having been assembled for the trial**, Orgetorix escaped."	LITERAL TRANSLATION
"**Since his slaves and clients had been assembled for the trial**, Orgetorix escaped."	CAUSAL TRANSLATION
"**When his slaves and clients had been assembled for the trial**, Orgetorix escaped."	TEMPORAL TRANSLATION

Orgetorīge mortuō, tamen sē parātōs esse
  arbitrātī sunt.

"**With Orgetorix dead**, nevertheless they thought that they were prepared."	LITERAL TRANSLATION
"**Although Orgetorix was dead,** nevertheless they thought that they were prepared."	CONCESSIVE TRANSLATION

There may also be cases in which a temporal or causal or conditional interpretation will make sense. The next sentence illustrates this point. The context usually will guide which interpretation makes the best sense.

Helvētiīs ex suīs fīnibus exeuntibus, finitimī
  quoque proficīscuntur.

"**With the Helvetians leaving their territory**, their neighbors also set out."	LITERAL TRANSLATION
"**If the Helvetians leave their territory,** their neighbors also set out."	CONDITIONAL TRANSLATION
"**(At the time) when the Helvetians are leaving their territory,** their neighbors also set out."	TEMPORAL TRANSLATION
"**Since the Helvetians are leaving their territory,** their neighbors also set out."	CAUSAL TRANSLATION

STUDY TIP

Perfect passive participles translate time before the main verb. Present participles translate the same time as the main verb. If an adjective or another noun completes the ablative absolute, generally a form of the English verb "to be" is used in the same time as the main verb.

▶ EXERCISE 2

Translate the sentences with a temporal, causal, concessive, or conditional translation.

1. Orgetorīge duce, ea rēs Helvētiīs ēnūntiāta est.

2. Cibō ēlātō domō, sē parātōs esse arbitrātī sunt.

3. Oppidīs exustīs, persuādent fīnitimīs ut sēcum proficīscantur.

4. Orgetorīge ex vinculīs causam dīcere coāctō, omnis familia ad iūdicium vēnit.

5. Magistrātibus multitūdinem hominum ex agrīs cōgentibus, tamen Orgetorīx mortuus est.

LANGUAGE FACT

THE ACTIVE PERIPHRASTIC

The future active participle, which is the fourth principal part of the verb with the addition of the syllable –ur– before the case ending, is most often used in Latin with a form of *sum*. This is called the active periphrastic.

The tense of the form of *sum* gives the active periphrastic its tense. Consider the following examples.

> *Frūmentum omne, praeterquam quod sēcum **portātūrī erant**, combūrunt....*
> (Caesar *Dē bellō Gallicō* 1.4.12)
> "They burn all the grain, except what **they were about (or intended) to carry** with them...."

> *Eam rem Helvētiīs per indicium **ēnūntiātūrus est**.*
> "**He is going to announce** this thing to the Helvetians through a disclosure."

BY THE WAY

The word "periphrastic" is derived from the Greek preposition "peri" (περί), which means "around," and from the Greek noun "phrasis" (φράσις), which means "speech." The English word "circumlocution" has a similar derivation but from Latin instead of from Greek. In Latin *circum* means "around" and *loquor, loquī, locūtus sum* means "to speak."

BY THE WAY

The active periphrastic is used to speak of things pending or intended in the present, past, or future.

▶ EXERCISE 3

Fill in the blank with the future active participle of the verb in parentheses in order to form an active periphrastic. Then translate these sentences.

1. Magnum numerum clientum eōdem _____ erat. (condūcō)

2. Orgetorīx causam _____ fuerat. (dīcō)

3. Helvētiī Orgetorīgem _____ sunt. (cremō)

4. Multitūdinem hominum ex agrīs magistrātūs _____ sunt. (cōgō)

5. Fēminae ē fīnibus suīs _____ erunt. (exeō)

ESSAY

In a short essay identify which preparations the Helvetians made for setting out from home *en masse* and discuss why the Helvetians made the preparations they did.

Support your assertions about the Latin passage with references to the Latin text in lines 9–17 above. All Latin words must be copied or their line numbers provided, AND they must be translated or paraphrased closely enough that it is clear that you understand the Latin. Direct your answer to the question; do not merely summarize the passage. Please write your essay on a separate piece of paper.

READING 5

In emigrating from their lands, the Helvetians decide to take the route that goes through the Roman province. When Caesar discovers their plans, he rushes from Rome to the Allobrogian city of Geneva, where a bridge leads from the Helvetian territory to that of the Allobrogians, whom the Romans have recently subdued. When the Helvetians ask Caesar for permission to cross through Transalpine Gaul, he responds that he needs time to consider their request. His true motive is that he needs time to levy troops to support his efforts to oppose the Helvetians.

CAESAR'S RESPONSE TO THE HELVETIANS

CAESAR *DĒ BELLŌ GALLICŌ* 1.6–7

1   [6] Erant omnīnō itinera duo, quibus itineribus domō exīre possent: ūnum per Sēquanōs, angustum et difficile, inter montem Iūram et flūmen Rhodanum, vix quā singulī carrī dūcerentur; mōns autem altissimus impendēbat, ut facile perpaucī prohibēre possent: alterum per prōvinciam nostram, multō facilius atque expedītius, proptereā quod inter

5   fīnēs Helvētiōrum et Allobrogum, quī nuper pācātī erant, Rhodanus fluit, isque nōn nūllīs locīs vadō trānsitur. Extrēmum oppidum Allobrogum est proximumque Helvētiōrum fīnibus Genāva.

NOTES AND VOCABULARY

Line 1:   **omnīnō,** *adv.* in all, altogether

        iter, itineris, n. translate *itinera* "routes."

        quibus . . . possent: *possent* is a subjunctive in a relative clause of characteristic; this type of clause provides characteristics or qualities of an antecedent that are not defined.

        ūnum: refers to *iter*.

        Sēquanī, -ōrum, m. pl. the Sequani or Sequanians, a Gallic people who occupied the upper river basin of the Arar (Saône), the valley of the Doubs and the Jura Mountains, their territory corresponding to Franche-Comté and part of Burgundy.

Line 2:   **angustus, -a, -um** narrow

        vix, *adv.* scarcely, barely

        singulī, -ae, -a one at a time, individual

Lines 2–3: **vix quā singulī carrī dūcerentur:** another relative clause of characteristic

Line 3:   **autem,** *conj.* but, however

        impendeō, impendēre to overhang, loom over; the understood object of *impendēbat* is *iter*.

        perpaucī, -ae, -a very few

        prohibeō, prohibēre, prohibuī, prohibitum to defend, keep away; the understood object is "them." Note the ALLITERATION.

Line 4: **alter, altera, alterum** other; *alterum* refers to *iter*.

multō facilius: literally the phrase means "easier by much." Translate "much easier." *Multō* is an ablative of degree of difference.

expedītus, -a, -um unobstructed, convenient

BY THE WAY

With comparatives or expressions that suggest a comparison, the amount of difference is expressed by an ablative (e.g., *paulō ante* "before by a little" = "a little before").

Line 5: **Allobrogēs, Allobrogum,** m. pl. the Allobroges, a Celtic tribe of ancient Gaul, located between the Rhône River and the Lake of Geneva in what later became Savoy, Dauphiné, and Vivarais.

nūper, *adv.* lately, recently

pācō (1) to pacify; the Allobrogians recently had been subjugated again by the Romans.

is: translate "that" (i.e., river) or "it."

nōn nūllīs: *lit.,* "not none"; translate "some"; an example of LITOTES.

Line 6: **vadum, -ī,** n. ford

trānseō, trānsīre, trānsiī/trānsīvī, trānsitum to cross, go across

extrēmus, -a, -um outermost, farthest

proximus, -a, -um (+ *dat.*) closest; next to

Line 7: **Genāva, -ae,** f. Geneva, a city located on Lake Geneva, at the point where the Rhone passes from it. Note how the word "Geneva" occurs last in the sentence for emphasis, and also to reflect the notion of "farthest," for the word is placed as far as possible from *extrēmum*.

CAESAR *DĒ BELLŌ GALLICŌ* 1.6–7, CONTINUED

Ex eō oppidō pōns ad Helvētiōs pertinet. Allobrogibus sēsē vel persuāsūrōs, quod nōndum bonō animō in populum Rōmānum vidērentur, exīstimābant vel vī coāctūrōs ut per suōs fīnēs eōs īre patērentur. Omnibus rēbus ad profectiōnem

10   comparātīs, diem dīcunt, quā diē ad rīpam Rhodanī omnēs conveniant. Is diēs erat a.d. V. Kal. Aprīl. L. Pīsōne, A. Gabīniō cōnsulibus.

NOTES AND VOCABULARY

Line 7:   **pōns, pontis,** m. bridge

Lines 7–9:   **vel . . . vel:** either . . . or

STUDY TIP
The Latin verb *videō, vidēre, vīdī, vīsum* "to see" when used in the passive voice often means "to seem" as seen in line 8 above.

Line 8:   **nōndum,** *adv.* not yet

bonō animō: ablative of description; translate the phrase "well disposed."

exīstimō (1) to judge, suppose, think‡

Lines 8–9:   **exīstimābant . . . coāctūrōs:** supply *eōs* = *Allobrogēs* as the object of *coāctūrōs.*

STUDY TIP
In the singular, only three forms of *vīs* regularly appear: *vīs* (nominative), *vim* (accusative), and *vī* (ablative). The forms in the plural are these: *vīrēs, vīrium, vīribus, vīrīs (or vīrēs), vīribus.* Be careful to distinguish between *vīs,* second person singular present tense of *volō, velle, voluī* "to wish" and *vīs,* nominative singular "strength." Also, don't confuse the plural forms of *vīs* (e.g., *vīrēs, vīrium, vīribus, vīrīs [or vīrēs], vīribus*) with the forms of *vir, virī,* m. "man." It should be noted that *vīs,* second person singular of *volō,* and *vīs,* nominative singular of the noun, both have a macron over the "i" and so are identical in form.

Line 9:   **vīs, vim, vī,** f. force, violence

cōgō, cōgere, coēgī, coāctum to force, compel, bring together, collect

ut per suōs fīnēs eōs: note that in the *ut* clause *suōs* refers to the subject of the clause, the Allobrogians, while *eōs* refers to the Helvetians.

patior, patī, passus sum to allow, permit

profectiō, profectiōnis, f. departure

Line 10:   **comparō** (1) to prepare, plan

diem dīcere: to assign a day

rīpa, -ae, f. riverbank

quā diē . . . conveniant: relative clause of purpose

Lines 10–11:   **a.d. V. Kal. Aprīl:** March 28th; see Take Note on p. 69.‡

Line 11:   **L. Pīsōne, A. Gabīniō cōnsulibus:** this ablative absolute is usually translated "in the consulship of L. Piso and A. Gabinius."

STUDY TIP

Be careful to distinguish among these four similar-looking verbs.

   patior, patī, passus sum to allow, permit (as in line 9)

   pateō, patēre, patuī to be open, lie open

   partior, partīrī, partītus sum to divide

   potior, potīrī, potītus sum (+ *gen.* or *abl.*) to gain possession of

The *imāginifer* "standard-bearer" (also known as the *signifer*) played an important role in Roman army communications. Each maniple (120 soldiers) had its own *signifer* who carried the legion's standards (*signa*) to indicate where the group was to assemble. He also used the standards to rally the troops. The tombstone of Aurelius Diogenes, at the Grosvenor Museum in Chester, England, identifies him as *imaginifer* in its inscription and with a representation of the standards. Caesar made two invasions of Britain but it took until the time of Claudius to subdue the Britons.

CAESAR *DĒ BELLŌ GALLICŌ* 1.6–7, CONTINUED

[7] Caesarī cum id nūntiātum esset, eōs per prōvinciam nostram iter facere cōnārī, matūrat ab urbe proficīscī et quam maximīs potest itineribus in Galliam ulteriōrem contendit, et ad Genāvam pervenit. Prōvinciae tōtī quam maximum potest mīlitum
15 numerum imperat (erat omnīnō in Galliā ulteriōre legiō ūna), pontem quī erat ad Genāvam, iubet rescindī. Ubi dē eius adventū Helvētiī certiōrēs factī sunt, lēgātōs ad eum mittunt nōbilissimōs cīvitātis, cūius lēgātiōnis Nammēius et Verucloetius prīncipem locum obtinēbant, quī dīcerent sibi esse in animō sine ūllō maleficiō iter per prōvinciam facere, proptereā quod aliud iter habērent nūllum: rogāre ut eius voluntāte id sibi facere liceat.

NOTES AND VOCABULARY

Line 12: **id nūntiātum esset, eōs per prōvinciam nostram iter facere cōnārī:** translate *id* "this fact," which is explained by its appositive *eōs ... cōnārī*. Caesar was in Rome, on the point of leaving for the province of Gaul, when he learned the news of the Helvetians' plans.

Line 13: **mātūrō** (1) to hasten, hurry

quam maximīs potest itineribus: translate "by the greatest possible marches" = "as quickly as possible."

ulterior, ulteriōris farther; *Gallia Ulterior* or Transalpine Gaul.

REMINDER

As noted on pp. 57–58, to signify the highest degree possible, Latin uses *quam* + the superlative, or *quam* + the superlative + a form of *possum*.

Line 14: **contendō, contendere, contendī, contentum** to aim for, march, hasten

perveniō, pervenīre, pervēnī, perventum to reach, come to

tōtus, -a, -um whole, entire. Remember that *tōtus* is one of the "naughty nine" that have *-īus* in the genitive singular and *-ī* in the dative singular.

Line 15: **imperō** (1) to requisition from, demand from

legiō, legiōnis, f. legion

STUDY TIP

Be careful to distinguish among these military terms that Caesar often uses in his writings.

> lēgātus, -ī, m. deputy, ambassador, envoy
>
> lēgātiō, lēgātiōnis, f. embassy, commission; the post of deputy or subordinate commander under a commander-in-chief
>
> legiō, legiōnis, f. legion

The terms *lēgātus* and *lēgātiō* are derived from *lēgō* (1) "to appoint a person, to make a deputy," which itself is derived from *lēx, lēgis,* f. "law." The word *legiō* is derived from *legō, legere, lēgī, lēctum,* "to choose," since the legion originally was composed of a chosen body of men (before the time of Marius).

Line 16: **iubeō, iubēre, iussī, iussum** to order

rescindō, rescindere, rescidī, rescissum to cut down

adventus, adventūs, m. approach

certiōrem faciō, facere, fēcī, factum to inform

lēgātus, -ī, m. deputy, ambassador, envoy; *lēgātōs* is in apposition to *virōs,* which should be supplied as the direct object of *mittunt.* Translate "as envoys."

Line 17: **lēgātiō, lēgātiōnis,** f. embassy, the post of deputy or subordinate commander under a commander-in-chief

prīnceps, prīncipis first, foremost, leading

Line 18: **quī dīcerent:** a relative clause of purpose after a verb of motion

sibi esse in animō: translate "they intended"; *sibi* is a dative of reference.

maleficium, -ī, n. crime, offense; mischief, harm

Line 19: **proptereā . . . habērent:** this subordinate clause has its verb in the subjunctive because it expresses the thought of someone other than the speaker.

voluntās, voluntātis, f. will, approval, desire; consent; translate *ad voluntātem; dē, ex voluntāte;* or just *voluntāte,* "according to the will, with the consent, at the desire of (anyone)."

licet, licēre, licuit, *impersonal* (+ *dat.* + *inf.*) it is permitted

rogāre . . . liceat: *sē* must be supplied as the accusative subject of *rogāre. Sē rogāre* is dependent on *quī dīcerent;* the indirect statement is, in turn, introducing an indirect command, *ut . . . liceat.*

CAESAR *DĒ BELLŌ GALLICŌ* 1.6–7, CONTINUED

20   Caesar, quod memoriā tenēbat L. Cassium cōnsulem occīsum exercitumque eius ab

     Helvētiīs pulsum et sub iugum missum, concēdendum nōn putābat; neque hominēs

     inimīcō animō, datā facultāte per prōvinciam itineris faciendī, temperātūrōs ab iniūriā

     et maleficiō exīstimābat. Tamen, ut spatium intercēdere posset dum mīlitēs quōs

     imperāverat convenīrent, lēgātīs respondit diem sē ad dēlīberandum sūmptūrum: sī quid

25   vellent, ad Īd. Aprīl. reverterentur.

NOTES AND VOCABULARY

Line 20:   **memoriā teneō, tenēre, tenuī, tentum** to remember, keep in mind

        occīdō, occīdere, occīdī, occīsum to kill; *esse* needs to be supplied with *occīsum, pulsum,*
          missum, and *concēdendum.*

        exercitus, exercitūs, m. army

Line 21:   **pellō, pellere, pepulī, pulsum** to push, drive back, rout

        iugum, -ī, n. yoke‡

        concēdō, concēdere, concessī, concessum to grant, give up; translate impersonally
          "permission ought to be granted."

        putō (1) to think, consider, judge‡

Line 22:   **inimīcus, -a, -um** hostile, unfriendly

        facultās, facultātis, f. opportunity, capacity; translate *datā facultāte* as though the phrase
          were the first part of a condition: "if opportunity . . . should have been given . . . ."

        temperō (1) to refrain, control

        iniūria, -ae, f. injustice, harm

Line 23:   **spatium, -ī,** n. interval, time, space

        intercēdō, intercēdere, intercessī, intercessum to pass

        dum: translate "until."

Line 24:   **imperāverat:** translate "had requisitioned."

        diēs, diēī, m. indefinite here; translate "time."

        dēlīberō (1) to think over, to consider carefully, deliberate

        sūmō, sūmere, sumpsī, sūmptum to take, use

        sī quid: translate "if . . . anything."

Line 25:   **ad Īd. Aprīl:** translate "on April 13th."

STUDY TIP

After the words *sī, nisi, num,* or *nē,* the Latin words *quis* and *quid* stand for *aliquis* and
aliquid. A mnemonic device to help you remember this is as follows: "after *sī, nisi,
num,* and *nē,* all the *ali*'s fall away." In some versions "fall away" is replaced by "take
a holiday."

TAKE NOTE

1. The Roman calendar had three main days. The day before each of these three days was referred to by the word *prīdiē*, "the day before." All other dates were given by counting backward from these main days; the Romans included the first and last day in their reckoning. The abbreviation a.d. (*ante diem*) with a Roman numeral indicates how many days to count backward.

> Kalendae, "the Kalends," referred to the first day of the month;

> Nōnae, "the Nones," referred to the fifth or seventh of the month; and

> Īdūs, "the Ides," referred to the thirteenth or fifteenth of the month.

Thus in lines 10–11 of the Latin passage above, Caesar writes *a.d. V. Kal. Aprīl.* This means *ante diem* V (Roman numeral five) or five days before the Kalends (Kal., the first) of April. By counting backward from the Kalends (first of April), to March 31st, to March 30th, to March 29th, and to March 28th, one arrives at the corresponding date in our calendar.

2. To be sent under a yoke (of spears) was an act of humiliation for the soldiers of a defeated army because they had to bend their heads as they passed under the yoke and they were mocked by the opposing army. The English word "subjugate" derives from this practice.

3. The verb *putō* (1) "to think" is used in line 21; *exīstimō* (1) "to think" is seen in lines 8 and 23. In Caesar 1.4–5, line 8 the deponent verb *arbitror* (1) "to think" was used. These verbs are synonyms and are frequently employed to set up an indirect statement.

COMPREHENSION QUESTIONS

1. Name the two routes that the Helvetians could choose to follow when leaving their own territory.

2. What did the Helvetians think that they could either force or persuade the Allobroges to do? Cite the Latin.

3. Why did Caesar hasten to leave Rome and go to Geneva?

4. What other two actions did Caesar take when he heard the news?

5. What was the Helvetian response to Caesar?

6. Why did Caesar stall in giving the Helvetians an answer? Cite the Latin.

▶ EXERCISE 1

1. In line 1, what Latin word is the antecedent of *quibus*?

2. What is the case and use of *domō* in line 1?

3. In line 3, what is the tense, voice, and mood of *dūcerentur*?

4. In line 3, what part of speech is *facile*?

5. In line 3, what Latin word is the subject of *possent*?

6. In line 4, what part of speech and degree is *facilius*?

7. What is the case and use of *vadō* in line 6?

8. What is the case and use of *Genāva* in line 7?

9. To what Latin word does *eō oppidō* in line 7 refer?

10. In line 9, what is the case and use of *vī*?

11. In line 9, what is the tense, voice, mood, and use of *patērentur*?

12. What is the case and use of *omnibus rēbus* in line 9?

13. What is the case and use of *quā diē* in line 10?

14. What is the case and use of *L. Pīsōne, A. Gabīniō cōnsulibus* in line 11?

15. In line 12 what is the tense, voice, and mood of *nūntiātum esset*?

16. What is the case and use of *eōs* in line 12?

17. In line 13, what is the tense, form, and use of *proficīscī*?

18. In line 14, what is the case and use of *prōvinciae tōtī*?

19. In line 15, what is the case and use of *pontem*?

20. What is the tense, voice, and form of *rescindī* in line 16?

21. In line 16, to whom does *eius* refer?

22. What is the tense, voice, and mood of *dīcerent* in line 18?

23. In line 18, what is the case and use of *iter*?

24. In line 19, what Latin word does *nūllum* modify?

25. What is the tense, voice, and mood of *liceat* in line 19?

26. In line 20, what is the tense, voice, and form of *occīsum*?

27. In line 21, what is the case and use of *Helvētiīs*?

28. What is the case and use of *inimīcō animō* in line 22?

29. In line 22, what is the case and form of *faciendī*?

30. What is the tense, voice, mood, and use of *posset* in line 23?

31. In line 24, what is the case and use of *lēgātīs*?

32. In line 24, what type of construction is *ad dēlīberandum*?

33. In line 25, what is the tense, voice, and mood of *vellent*?

VOCABULARY BUILDER

In 1.6–7 of Caesar's *Dē bellō Gallicō* as well as in other sections of his work and in the works of many authors, one can see how a familiar Latin word is the root of one or more other Latin words. Noting this relationship is a way to help you remember what these similar looking words mean. Look at these word groups.

Familiar Latin Word	Related Latin Word
proficīscor, proficīscī, profectus sum to depart (line 13)	profectiō, profectiōnis, f. departure (line 9)
facilis, facile easy (line 4)	facultās, facultātis, f. ability, ease, opportunity (line 22)
volō, velle, voluī to wish, will (line 25)	voluntās, voluntātis, f. will, consent (line 19)
faciō, facere, fēcī, factum to do (line 16) + malus, -a, -um bad, evil	maleficium, -ī, n. evil deed, crime (line 18)
pāx, pācis, f. peace	pācō (1) to pacify, make peace (line 5)
adveniō, advenīre, advēnī, adventum to come to, arrive	adventus, adventūs, m. arrival, approach (line 16)

▶ EXERCISE 2

Give the English meaning for these words and list the simple or uncompounded Latin word with its English meaning from which the words derive.

1. pervēnit (line 14)

2. exīre (line 1)

3. trānsitur (line 6)

4. omnīnō (line 1)

5. expedītius (line 4)

6. reverterentur (line 25)

7. coāctūrōs (line 9)

8. comparātīs (line 10)

LANGUAGE FACT

INDIRECT STATEMENTS

Direct statements are someone's exact words or thoughts. Indirect statements (sometimes called indirect discourse or *ōrātiō oblīqua*) indirectly communicate these words or thoughts. An indirect statement depends upon a verb of saying, thinking, telling, etc. (often called the main verb) to tell the speaker's words indirectly.

Per prōvinciam nostram iter faciunt.	**DIRECT STATEMENT**
"They were making a journey through our province."	
*Id nūntiātum est **eōs** per prōvinciam nostram iter **facere**.*	**INDIRECT STATEMENT**
"It was announced **that** they were making a journey through our province."	

The **subject of the indirect statement** is in the **accusative** case and the **verb** is an **infinitive**. To review the forms of Latin infinitives, see Appendix D on pp. 551–552. In English the word "that" is often used to introduce the indirect statement. However, the Latin sentence does not contain a word for "that."

STUDY TIP

If the subject of the indirect statement is the same as the subject of the main clause, a reflexive pronoun must be used in the indirect statement. Consider these two sentences. In example 1, the person who is taking a day to think it over is the same person as the one who spoke to the envoys. In example 2, the person thinking it over is a different person than the one speaking to the envoys.

Example 1:
Lēgātīs respondit diem sē ad dēlīberandum sūmptūrum.
    (Caesar *Dē bellō Gallicō* 1.7.24)
"He replied to the envoys that he would take time to think it over."

Example 2:
Lēgātīs respondit diem eum ad dēlīberandum sūmptūrum.
"He replied to the envoys that he (a different person from the one replying) would take time to think it over."

The tense of the infinitive tells the reader/listener when the action of the indirect statement is happening in relationship to the action of the verb of saying, telling, thinking, and the like.

> **Present infinitives** indicate action happening at the **same time** as the action of the main clause.
>
> **Perfect infinitives** show action happening **before** the action of the main clause.
>
> **Future infinitives** denote action happening **after** the action of the main clause.

Angustōs sē fīnēs habēre arbitrābantur.
  (Caesar *Dē bellō Gallicō* 1.2.11)
"They thought that they had narrow
  borders."

**PRESENT ACTIVE
INFINITIVE
SAME TIME**

*Sē suīs cōpiīs rēgna conciliāvisse
  cōnfirmāvit.*
"He confirmed that he had won over the
  kingdoms by [means of] his troops."

**PERFECT ACTIVE
INFINITIVE
TIME BEFORE**

*Caesar . . . memoriā tenēbat L. Cassium
  cōnsulem occīsum [esse] . . . .*
  (Caesar *Dē bellō Gallicō* 1.7.20)
"Caesar remembered that Lucius Cassius
  the consul had been killed . . . ."

**PERFECT PASSIVE
INFINITIVE**

TIME BEFORE

STUDY TIP

In the perfect passive infinitive and in the future active infinitive, *esse* is often a word to
be understood. Look immediately above and below this study tip for examples.

*Lēgātīs respondit diem sē ad dēlīberandum
  sūmptūrum [esse].*
  (Caesar *Dē bellō Gallicō* 1.7.24)
"He responded to the envoys that he
  would take time to think it over."

**FUTURE ACTIVE
INFINITIVE**

TIME AFTER

STUDY TIP

When a future infinitive is used in an indirect statement after a past tense main verb,
the future infinitive can be translated into English with the word "would" or with another way of expressing the future, such as "was going to."

▶ EXERCISE 3

Identify the tense and time of the infinitive in each sentence. Then translate the entire sentence.

1. Allobrogibus sēsē persuāsūrōs exīstimābant.

2. Iam sē ad eam rem parātōs esse arbitrātī sunt.

3. Sē eōs vī coāctūrōs dīcunt.

4. Biennium sibi satis esse exīstimāvērunt.

5. Dīcunt sē in animō habēre sine ūllō maleficiō iter per prōvinciam facere.

6. Omnēs rēs ad profectiōnem comparātās scīvērunt.

7. Sēsē tōtīus Galliae imperium obtinēre posse spērant.

8. Eōs temperātūrōs ab iniūriā et maleficiō putābat.

9. Helvētiī certiōrēs factī sunt eum lēgātōs nōbilissimōs lēgisse.

LANGUAGE FACT

THE PASSIVE PERIPHRASTIC, REVIEW OF GERUND AND GERUNDIVE USES

- **The Passive Periphrastic**

Sometimes the gerundive (the future passive participle ending in -*ndus*) is used as an adjective. *Vir laudandus*, for example, is translated literally as "a man to be praised," less literally as "a man deserving of praise." More often, however, Latin uses the gerundive plus the verb *esse* to indicate necessity or obligation. This is called the "passive periphrastic." The tense of *sum* indicates the time of the passive periphrastic. The gerundive in a passive periphrastic is ordinarily in the nominative case in agreement with the subject of the sentence. The agent—the person who performs the action—is expressed by the dative; accordingly, this dative is referred to as "the dative of agent." The literal translation of a passive periphrastic is in the passive voice, but a translation into more natural English requires changing the passive voice to the active.

Omnia ad profectiōnem Helvētiīs comparanda sunt.

"All things must be prepared by the Helvetians for departure." **LITERAL TRANSLATION**

"The Helvetians must prepare all things for departure." **MORE NATURAL TRANSLATION**

Singulī carrī virīs dūcendī erunt.

"The carts will have to be led one at a time by the men." **LITERAL TRANSLATION**

"The men will have to lead the carts one at a time." **MORE NATURAL TRANSLATION**

When a passive periphrastic occurs in an indirect statement, the form of *sum* may need to be understood, and the gerundive is in the accusative case in agreement with the indirect statement's accusative subject, which is sometimes also a word to be understood.

Concēdendum [esse] [sibi] nōn putābat.
(Caesar *Dē bellō Gallicō* 1.7.21)

"He did not think that it must be yielded by him." **LITERAL TRANSLATION**

"He did not think that he must yield." **MORE NATURAL TRANSLATION**

- **Review of Gerund and Gerundive Uses**

The gerund and gerundive, both of which use the –*nd*– form of the verb, have several uses and translations. Be careful to distinguish among these uses, some of which have been introduced previously in this book.

Uses of the Gerund

Proficīscendō celeriter, ad Genāvam pervēnit.	**VERBAL NOUN**
"By setting out quickly, he arrived at Geneva."	**TRANSLATION = –ing**
Ad proficīscendum carrōs coēmit.	**PURPOSE CONSTRUCTION**
"He bought up wagons in order to set out."	**TRANSLATION = in order to, to, for the sake of**

Uses of the Gerundive

Caesar, imperātor virtūte metuendus . . .	**VERBAL ADJECTIVE**
"Caesar, a commander to be feared because of (his) courage . . . "	**TRANSLATION = "to be . . . "**
Caesar hostis vincendī cupidus erat.	**VERBAL ADJECTIVE**
"Caesar was desirous of defeating (eager to defeat) the enemy."	**TRANSLATION = –ing**
Rērum cōnficiendārum causā, Orgetorīx dēligitur.	**PURPOSE CONSTRUCTION**
"Orgetorix is chosen for the sake of completing things."	**TRANSLATION = in order to, to, for the sake of**
Iter per prōvinciam nōn faciendum est.	**PASSIVE PERIPHRASTIC**
"A journey must not be made through the province."	**TRANSLATION = must be, had to be, will have to be**

▶ EXERCISE 4

Describe the use of the gerund or gerundive in each sentence. There may be more than one gerund/gerundive in a sentence. Translate the entire sentence.

1. Dīxit Allobrogēs vī cōgendōs esse.

2. Omnēs rēs conficiendae erunt.

3. Hostēs concēdendō nōn vincet.

4. Ad faciendum iter per prōvinciam, numerus carrōrum coemendus est.

5. Nammēius et Verucloetius prīncipis locī obtinendī cupidī erant.

6. Pōns rescindendus erat.

7. Conveniendī eōdem tempore grātiā, lēgātīs respondit diem sē ad dēlīberandum sūmptūrum.

8. Caesar sibi concēdendum nōn putābat.

ESSAY

In this passage the Helvetians ask Caesar for permission to cross through the Roman province, promising they will do no mischief. In lines 20–25, Caesar gives his thoughts on and his reaction to the Helvetian request. In a short essay, discuss the factors Caesar weighed when considering the request, his publicly stated reason(s) for delay, and his private and practical reason(s). Comment on his ability as a leader as evidenced in this process of decision.

Support your assertions about the Latin passage with references to the Latin in lines 20–25 of the text. All Latin words must be copied or their line numbers provided, AND they must be translated or paraphrased closely enough that it is clear that you understand the Latin. Direct your answer to the question; do not merely summarize the passage. Please write your essay on a separate piece of paper.

CHANGE

GAIUS VALERIUS CATULLUS

Complementary Infinitives and Infinitives with Impersonal Verbs; Partitive Genitive; Diminutives; *Cum* Clauses; Imperatives and Prohibitions; Conditional Sentences; Positive, Comparative, and Superlative Adjectives and Adverbs; Genitive and Dative Pronouns

Chiasmus, Sibilance, Anaphora, Apostrophe, Rhetorical Question, Hyperbaton, Onomatopoeia, Transferred Epithet

Antonio Zucchi (1726–1795) depicts the poetic tradition of Cupid inspiring the Greek poet Sappho in his painting "Sappho Taking Notes from Love." Catullus highly esteemed the poetry of Sappho and emulated her work in his own love poetry.

MEMORĀBILE DICTŪ

Vīvāmus, mea Lesbia, atque amēmus.

"Let us live and love, my Lesbia." (Catullus 5.1)

In this often quoted line, Catullus links living and loving, and later in the poem he recommends a life of love since humans are ultimately mortal.

INTRODUCTION TO CATULLUS

Gaius Valerius Catullus is considered one of Rome's most beloved and influential poets. The time during which he lived, however, was tumultuous, characterized by the aftermath of Sulla's dictatorship (82–79 BCE), by the slave revolt of Spartacus (73–71 BCE), by the conspiracy of Catiline to overthrow the state (63 BCE), and by the jockeying for power by three ambitious and ruthless men, Crassus, Caesar, and Pompey, in the years 70 BCE and following. Periods of civil unrest often generate great literary works, and the collection of Catullus's poetry is no exception. This body of literature represents some of the most original and brilliant poetry of the time, and it was considered a classic already by the early 40s and late 30s BCE when Vergil and Horace began writing poetry.

CATULLUS'S LIFE

Catullus was born around 84 BCE and died in Rome some thirty years later, around 54–52 BCE. He was born in Verona, Italy, to a wealthy and prominent family. According to Suetonius (first century CE), Catullus's father entertained Julius Caesar at his home in Verona. Like other young men from well-to-do provincial families, Catullus was sent to Rome to receive an education that would lead to a career in law and/or politics. From his poetry we learn that Catullus served on the staff of the praetorian governor Gaius Memmius who was assigned the province of Bithynia (57–56 BCE), which in modern times approximates the territory now occupied by north central Turkey. Although Catullus's year abroad in Bithynia was financially disappointing, his assignment to this province apparently afforded him the opportunity to visit the grave of his brother who had died and was buried in the vicinity of ancient Troy.

LESBIA

Catullus wrote poems on many topics, including love, friendship, poetry, marriage, his own and his friends' experiences in the provinces, and social mores. His poems also contain sometimes bitter attacks on rivals for the affections of a beloved, on friends who betray him, on political figures, on social upstarts, and on inferior poets. But he is most well known for the series of love poems about a woman whom he refers to as "Lesbia." Most critics believe that the Lesbia poems are based on a real-life experience.

The name Lesbia alludes to the Greek lyric poetess Sappho of Lesbos, whose love poetry influenced Catullus. The name is intended to suggest a woman possessing the irresistible combination of great intelligence and passion. Almost certainly "Lesbia" is a pseudonym for the very aristocratic Clodia, wife of Quintus Caecilius Metellus Celer (who held the consulship shortly before his death in 59 BCE) and the older sister of the notorious Clodius Pulcher, one of whose more risqué exploits involved disguising himself as a woman in order to infiltrate the exclusively female religious festival of the *Bona Dea* in 62 BCE. The love affair proved to be tempestuous because Catullus the lover expected fidelity from his lady while Lesbia's/Clodia's apparently flirtatious character attracted the attention of a number of admirers. One of these admirers was Marcus Caelius Rufus, who betrayed his friend Catullus by becoming involved with Lesbia/Clodia (this is hinted at in Poem 77). Cicero provides us with a picture of this fascinating woman in the *Prō Caeliō* (56 BCE), where he ruthlessly maligns Clodia's character. In his speech on Caelius's behalf, Cicero defends his protégé from several charges, one of which was plotting to poison Clodia, and argues that the entire trial was motivated by Clodia's deep resentment that her lover broke off the affair with her.

It is important to recognize that Catullus the poet has created a character "Catullus" who is the central figure in his poetry. This character is called the poet's "persona" and can be witty, charming, playful, romantic, arrogant, foul-mouthed, whining, and verbally abusive. The infatuation of this character with Lesbia has great importance for the poetry because the intense and obsessive quality of his love for her serves as a predominant theme that integrates the entire collection.

From a Roman perspective, Catullus's relationship with Lesbia was unusual because he describes his love for her as transcending the physical. As a result, Catullus struggles to express the unique quality of this love and resorts to using vocabulary that characterizes male friendship and social/political networks among Rome's male elite (e.g., *foedus, fidēs, amīcitia*).

THE NEOTERICS

During the middle of the first century, a literary revolution took place in republican Rome. Catullus and like-minded poets of his generation discovered in Alexandrian literature of the third century BCE (for example, the poet Callimachus) literary values that were relevant and adaptable to their own literary ideals. Like their Alexandrian predecessors, these poets were interested in experimenting with meter, language, content, style, and genre. They preferred short poems over long, discursive epics and personal poetry over that concerned with the public sphere. They embraced the qualities of originality, erudition, and refinement, infusing Latin poetry with new life by introducing to it the language of the man on the street. Conversational language having to do with charm and wit and their opposite notions (*lepidus/illepidus, venustus/invenustus, ēlegāns/inēlegāns, urbānus/inurbānus,* and *salsus/insulsus*) often is featured in poems having to do with social correctness. Diminutives, also characteristic of informal language, permeate the poetry, adding to the effect Catullus is trying to achieve, whether it is wit, irony, sarcasm, sadness, or affection. Cicero refers to these individuals as the "neoterics" or "new poets."

The poetry is lively and entertaining, and the characters Catullus introduces are unforgettable, from Suffenus who is sophisticated until he sets his hand to composing poetry—then he is more rustic than the rustic countryside—to Rufus, who has a bad case of body odor, to Egnatius, who is so socially inept he grins all the time, including on the wrong occasions. The principal topics of love and friendship transcend time; the poetry seems as relevant and original today as when Catullus composed it over two thousand years ago.

CATULLUS'S *LIBELLUS*

The poetry of Catullus made its way into the Middle Ages by the slimmest of threads. A single manuscript of the poetry came to light in Verona near the start of the 14th century; fortunately several copies of this manuscript were made before the original disappeared as mysteriously as it had appeared. The extant collection consists of three major parts: the polymetra (1–60), short poems that are composed in a variety of meters, but mostly in hendecasyllables; the long poems (61–68b), which form the centerpiece of the collection, unified by the theme of marriage; and the elegiac epigrams (69–116), short poems written in elegiac couplets.

The question of whether the order of the poems reflects the hand of Catullus or that of a posthumous editor has been the subject of intense debate. Some scholars are now of the opinion that Catullus organized all (and not just part) of the transmitted text because the organization resembles that in later collections of Latin poetry, where ring patterns of thematically paired poems emerge as the unifying principle. Just as Catullus experimented with form, meter, and content in the individual poems, so the organization of the collection on the basis of length, meter, and, to a certain extent, theme seems experimental, the result, perhaps, of Catullus's deciding to assemble and integrate his best work in a single body of poetry. Verbal repetition often signals relationships between thematically related poems. For instance Poems 49 and 58 are linked by the nearly identical phrases *Romulī nepōtum* (49.1) and *Remī nepōtēs* (58.5), which, in turn, suggest a link between the poems' recipients, Cicero and Caelius (who almost certainly is the same person as Cicero's protégé, M. Caelius Rufus). Recognition of these relationships serves to enhance the interpretation of individual poems. For example, Poems 107 and 109 both deal with the theme of reconciliation of Catullus and Lesbia. While Poem 107 describes Catullus's ecstatic happiness that he and Lesbia are a couple again, Poem 109 reacts to this totally unexpected development, with Catullus having doubts that his lady is capable of making a permanent and exclusive commitment to him alone. The correspondence of Poem 109 to 107, therefore, tempers the rapturous joy of the first of the two poems.

CATULLUS'S LEGACY

Catullus appears to be "the first poet in Greek or Latin who decided to write about a particular love-affair in depth in a related collection of poems" (R. O. A. M. Lyne, *The Latin Love Poets* [Oxford, 1980] 21). This innovation inspired later writers of Latin love poetry (Propertius, Tibullus, and Ovid). Roughly one-fourth of the short poems in the collection (both the polymetrics and elegiacs), together with the long poem 68b, chronicle the on-again, off-again love affair between Lesbia and Catullus in his persona as infatuated lover. This series contains some of Catullus's most memorable and remarkable literary pieces that are so engaging that we share in the lover's desire, joy, anguish, anger, frustration, and despair. It seems appropriate, therefore, that Catullus principally is celebrated as a poet of love.

Our English word "paper" is derived from the Latin *papyrus*, which refers to the parchment-like material made from the papyrus plant, which grew abundantly in the Nile river delta. Pliny the Elder describes the process of making paper in his *Historia Natūrālis* 13.74–82. This image is helpful in visualizing the *libellus* Catullus discusses in his dedicatory poem (see p. 82).

READING 1

In Latin prose and poetry, the reader often needs to "understand" or supply words that are not in the Latin text. Words to be understood are in parentheses in the text below. Different fonts point out words that belong together.

In Poem 1 Catullus dedicates his new book of poems to Cornelius Nepos, whom you met in *Latin for the New Millennium*, Chapter 8 of Level 1 (see p. 123) and then you met him in each chapter of Level 2, where you read selections from his biography of Cicero's confidant and friend Atticus. Like Catullus, Atticus's contemporary Cornelius Nepos (110–24 BCE) hailed from Cisalpine Gaul. Catullus compliments his friend in this poem by describing his and Nepos's literary achievements in similar terms.

THE DEDICATION OF CATULLUS'S *LIBELLUS*

CATULLUS *CARMEN* 1

Meter: Hendecasyllable (for the meter see Appendix B.)

1   Cui dōnō (hunc) *lepidum novum libellum*

        āridā modo *pūmice expolītum?*

        Cornēlī, tibi: namque tū solēbās

        meās esse aliquid putāre *nūgās*

5   iam tum, cum (tū) **ausus es** ūnus Ītalōrum

        omne aevum *tribus* explicāre *cartīs*

        doctīs, Iuppiter, et *labōriōsīs.*

        quārē habē tibi quidquid hoc (est) libellī

        quālecumque; quod, ō patrōna virgō,

10   plūs *ūnō* maneat perenne *saeclō.*

NOTES AND VOCABULARY

Line 1:   **cui:** the dative of *quis,* meaning "to whom"

          dōnō (1) to give

          lepidus, -a, -um charming, delightful

          libellus, -ī, m. little book; *libellus* is the diminutive of *liber, librī,* m. book; see the Language
             Fact later in this chapter on p. 89.

Line 2:   **āridus, -a, -um** dry

          modo, *adv.* just now, recently‡

          pūmex, pumicis, f. pumice stone‡

          expoliō, expolīre, expolīvī, expolītum to polish

Line 3: **Cornelī:** refers to Cornelius Nepos.‡

namque, *conj.* for; *namque* is an emphatic form of *nam*.

soleō, solēre, solitus sum (semi-deponent) to be accustomed

Line 4: **aliquid:** something; i.e., something noteworthy

putō (1) to think; *putāre meās nūgās esse*: indirect statement, "to think that my trifles were."

nūgae, -ārum, f. pl. trifles

Line 5: **cum,** *conj.* when

audeō, audēre, ausus sum (semi-deponent) to dare

ūnus = *sōlus*

Ītalus, -a, -um Italian

STUDY TIP

Semi-deponent verbs have active forms and active meanings in the present, imperfect, and future tenses but in the perfect tenses the forms are passive with active meanings. Some examples of semi-deponent verbs are *audeō, audēre, ausus sum* "to dare"; *gaudeō, gaudēre, gāvīsus sum* "to rejoice"; and *soleō, solēre, solitus sum* "to be accustomed."

Line 6: **aevum, -ī,** n. age, history, time

trēs, tria three

explicō (1) to explain

carta, -ae, f. a sheet of papyrus; here, "volume"

Line 7: **doctus, -a, -um** learned, knowledgeable

Iuppiter: translate this nominative of exclamation "by Jove!"

labōriōsus, -a, -um full of (involving) work

BY THE WAY

Quārē can be written as one word or as two, *quā rē*. As an interrogative, *quārē* means "how?" or "why?" As a relative, *quārē* means "therefore, on which account." In line 8, however, it is a simple adverb meaning "therefore."

Line 8: **quārē,** *adv.* therefore

tibi: a reflexive pronoun; translate "have this book for yourself."

quisquis, quidquid whoever, whatever

Line 9: **quāliscumque, quālecumque** of whatever sort

patrōna, -ae, f. patroness, protectress

virgō: indirect reference to the muse; translate "maiden."

Line 10: **perennis, perenne** lasting a long time, eternal

saeculum, -ī, n. age, generation; *saeclum* is the syncopated form of *saeculum*.

ūnō . . . saeclō: this phrase is an ablative of comparison to be taken with *plūs*, "more than one generation."

maneat: a subjunctive expressing a wish, sometimes called the "optative subjunctive." Translate "May it . . ." (See Appendix D, p. 540, for more information on this topic.)

TAKE NOTE

1. In the time when Catullus was writing, a Roman book manuscript was rolled up and stored, and unrolled to be read. To make up a roll, papyrus was soaked and cut into strips, which were then joined together to create one sheet of varying length. The sheets were then joined together to produce a roll, and the sheets were polished with pumice to provide a smooth writing surface. When stored, a Roman book resembled a roll of wallpaper. Pumice also was used to smooth the ends of a roll of papyrus, which is what Catullus refers to in line 2.

2. Be careful to distinguish the adverb *modo* that means "just now, recently, only" from *modō,* the ablative singular of *modus, -ī,* m. "manner, method." You can tell the difference only by the final long vowel. When the adverb *modo* is seen twice in a sentence, the pair means "sometimes . . . sometimes" or "now . . . now" or "at one time . . . at another time." The phrase *non modo . . . sed etiam* means "not only . . . but also."

3. Cornelius Nepos was born in a small town in northern Italy near Verona, the birthplace of Catullus and home of Shakespeare's legendary couple, Romeo and Juliet. According to Catullus, Cornelius's work (entitled *Chronica),* like his own collection of poetry, is characterized by innovation and literary achievement. In addition, Catullus indicates that Nepos's history of three volumes exhibits *doctrīna* "learning," a quality highly esteemed by Catullus and his fellow poets. The excessively flattering praise in lines 5–7 lends a humorous touch to Catullus's tribute, which correlates with the poet's modesty regarding his own accomplishment.

COMPREHENSION QUESTIONS

1. Make a list of phrases and words that Catullus uses to describe his book. Provide the Latin and their English equivalents.

2. If these words describe not only the physical book but also the poems it contains, what is Catullus telling us about his poetry?

3. Why would Catullus use words like *nūgae* that might indicate that the poems were unimportant?

▶ EXERCISE 1

1. In line 2, what Latin word does *āridā* modify?

2. In line 2, what case is *expolītum* and why?

3. What case is *Cornēlī* in line 3?

4. What word is complementary to *solēbās* in lines 3–4?

5. Translate *ausus es* (line 5).

6. In line 6, what case and use is *tribus cartīs*?

7. What Latin word does *labōriōsīs* (line 7) modify?

VOCABULARY BUILDER

Here are some English derivatives based on words in Poem 1. From what Latin word in the poem is each derived? Give the Latin vocabulary entry and the English meaning for each word.

1. perennial

2. novice

3. putative

4. arid

5. secular

6. explicate

7. laborious

8. patron

LANGUAGE FACT

COMPLEMENTARY INFINITIVES AND INFINITIVES WITH IMPERSONAL VERBS

- **Complementary Infinitives**

  A complementary infinitive completes the meaning of another verb in the sentence. Complementary infinitives do not take an accusative subject. Consider these examples.

  > *namque tū solēbās . . . putāre* (Catullus 1.3–4)
  > "for you were accustomed to think . . ."

  > *cum ausus es . . . explicāre* (Catullus 1.5–6)
  > "when you dared to explain . . ."

- **Infinitives with Impersonal Verbs**

  Many impersonal verbs also govern an infinitive. The person doing the action in these phrases is sometimes in the dative case and other times in the accusative.

  > *Nōn libet mihi scrībere magnum librum.*
  > "It does not please me to write a large book."

  > *Oportet mē scrībere doctum libellum.*
  > "It is necessary for me to write a learned little book."

Here is a list of some of the verbs that take complementary infinitives and impersonal expressions that govern an infinitive.

Verbs Governing a Complementary Infinitive	Impersonal Verbs Governing an Infinitive
possum, posse, potuī to be able, can	libet (+ *dat.*) it is pleasing
audeō, audēre, ausus sum to dare	placet (+ *dat.*) it is pleasing
soleō, solēre, solitus sum to be accustomed	visum est (+ *dat.*) it seemed
coepī, coepisse to have begun	oportet (+ *acc.*) it is necessary
dubitō (1) to hesitate	pudet (+ *acc.*) it shames
dēbeō, dēbēre, dēbuī, dēbitum to ought	licet (+ *dat.* or *acc.*) it is allowed, permitted
dēsinō, dēsinere, dēsiī, dēsitum to cease	necesse est (+ *dat.* or *acc.*) it is necessary

▶ EXERCISE 2

Translate. Identify whether each sentence contains a complementary infinitive, an infinitive with an impersonal verb, or an infinitive in an indirect statement (see pp. 72–73 in the Caesar chapter of this book).

1. Cornēlī, dubitāsne meās esse aliquid putāre nūgās?

2. Necesse est mē omne aevum tribus explicāre cartīs.

3. Placet mihi scrībere lepidum novum libellum.

4. Sciō meum libellum āridā modo pūmice expolītum esse.

5. Licet tibi habēre quidquid hoc est libellī.

6. Meus libellus plūs ūnō manēre perenne saeclō potest.

7. Cornēlius exīstimāvit sē omne aevum tribus cartīs explicātūrum esse.

LANGUAGE FACT

PARTITIVE GENITIVE

Most genitive case nouns translate with the word "of." Sometimes there is a better or more natural way to translate genitive nouns. The partitive genitive expresses the "whole" of which a "part" is being described.

> *optima pars libellī ...*
> "the best part of the little book"

> *quidquid hoc libellī ...* (Catullus 1.8)
> "whatever this (is) of a little book"   **LITERAL TRANSLATION**
> "this little book, such as it is"   **MORE NATURAL**
>   **TRANSLATION**

▶ EXERCISE 3

Fill in the blank with the genitive of the phrase requested. Give a literal and then a more natural translation of each sentence.

Example: quantum est hominum beātiōrum (hominēs beātiōrēs)
literal: how much there is of rather blessed people
natural: however many happy people there are

1. quantum est _____ (hominēs doctiōrēs)
2. quidquid est _____ (nūgae)
3. tantum _____ (pecūnia) habēs
4. aliquid _____ (bonum)
5. nihil _____ (novum)

READING 1 REDUX

You are now ready to read the poem exactly as Catullus wrote it. For this reason, the words in parentheses and the special use of fonts are no longer used. You have already seen notes in the first version of this poem and you may refer to those notes if you need to. Additional notes are given below the text.

CATULLUS *CARMEN* 1

1   Cui dōnō lepidum novum libellum
     āridā modo pūmice expolītum?
     Cornēlī, tibi: namque tū solēbās
     meās esse aliquid putāre nūgās
5   iam tum, cum ausus es ūnus Ītalōrum
     omne aevum tribus explicāre cartīs
     doctīs, Iuppiter, et labōriōsīs.
     quārē habē tibi quidquid hoc libellī
     quālecumque; quod, <ō> patrōna virgō,
10 plūs ūnō maneat perenne saeclō.

NOTES AND VOCABULARY

Line 1:   Poem 1 is the only formal introductory poem contained in the collection. This poem may have been intended to serve as an introduction to the entire work. If so, the diminutive *libellus* does not reflect the size of the collection ("a small book"), but rather reflects the modest tone characteristic of the poem as a whole with regard to Catullus's achievement.

Lines 1–2: **lepidum novum. . . expolītum:** these adjectives apply to the external appearance of the book as well as to the poetry contained within the book.

Line 3:   **Cornēlī:** Cornelius Nepos's *Chronica*, the three-volume history referred to in this line, is not extant. Cornelius was friends not only with Catullus and Cicero but also with Atticus.

Line 8:   **habē tibi:** an abrupt, colloquial phrase with legalistic overtones suggesting the transfer of real property: essentially Catullus says, "Take it in 'as-is' condition."

Line 9:   The symbol < > is supplied by editors and indicates there is a missing word, syllable, or phrase in the text. Here we know that there has been an omission of a word or syllable as the line is hendecasyllabic (having eleven syllables) but has only ten syllables. The text can easily be restored by the addition of "**ō.**"

           <ō> patrōna virgō: Note that Catullus does not ask the Muse for inspiration, a request one would expect in an introductory poem, but rather asks her to assure the immortality of the work.

LANGUAGE FACT

DIMINUTIVES

Many languages have special forms that indicate something is a smaller version of something else. Diminutives often imply affection and "cuteness" as well.

So in Spanish *perro* is "dog" but *perrito* is "puppy," and you might affectionately call your father *papito* instead of *papá*. We have diminutives in English too. A "piglet" could never be confused with a "pig," and if you had an hour, you might finish reading a "booklet" but never a "book." Other examples in English include kitchenette, gosling (a lot smaller than a goose!), and diskette.

Catullus likes and often coins diminutives. Their meaning is usually clear if you know the word from which they derive.

STUDY TIP

Latin diminutives tend to have the letter "l" in their endings, e.g., *-lus, -lum, -ella.*

▶ EXERCISE 4

Fill in the following chart. All the words are used by Catullus in his other poems.

Diminutive	Meaning	Latin Word from Which It Is Derived
libellus	"little book"	liber, book
ocellus	_____	oculus, eye
frīgidulus, -a, -um	_____	frīgidus, cold
labellum	_____	labrum, lip
flōsculus	_____	flōs, flower
misellus, -a, -um	_____	miser, wretched, lovesick
amīculus	_____	amīcus, friend
versiculus	_____	versus, a verse, line of poetry

ESSAY

Use your answers to the first two comprehension questions on p. 84 to help you write this essay.

Discuss what qualities characterize good literature based on the information presented in Poem 1.

Support your assertions with references drawn from throughout the poem. All Latin words must be copied or their line numbers provided, AND they must be translated or paraphrased closely enough so that it is clear you understand the Latin. Direct your answer to the question; do not merely summarize the passage. Please write your essay on a separate piece of paper.

SCANSION

Name the meter and scan the following lines.

iam tum, cum ausus es ūnus Ītalōrum

omne aevum tribus explicāre cartīs

doctīs, Iuppiter, et labōriōsīs.

A mosaic of one of the Evangelists (the authors of the Gospels of the Christian New Testament) demonstrates the continuity of Roman influence in the Byzantine world. The Evangelist is dressed in a Roman toga and sandals. He has unrolled his papyrus with its Greek script. Catullus's collection of poems would have been written on a similar papyrus scroll.

READING 2

The rest of the Catullus poems in this book will no longer feature the words in parentheses and the use of special fonts. Use the notes below the poem to help you.

Although he writes on a variety of subjects, Catullus is particularly celebrated as a poet of love. The course of love rarely runs smoothly, and Catullus's love affair with a woman he calls "Lesbia" is no exception, for Poem 5 is one of the few happy love poems in his collection of poetry. As was indicated in the Introduction (p. 78), the name Lesbia represents a literary nod to Catullus's Greek antecedent Sappho of Lesbos, a poetess much admired in antiquity as a writer of lyric and love poetry.

In Poem 5 Catullus invites his sweetheart Lesbia to enjoy life and to surrender to love. He reinforces this call to action by telling her to discount the gossip of old men and to be mindful of life's brevity. The thousands of kisses that Catullus requests from Lesbia represent his response to human mortality and death's finality. The notion that "love is the answer" has a pleasantly modern ring.

A THOUSAND AND MORE KISSES

CATULLUS *CARMEN* 5

Meter: Hendecasyllable

1 Vīvāmus, mea Lesbia, atque amēmus,

   rūmōrēsque senum sevēriōrum

   omnēs ūnius aestimēmus assis!

   sōlēs occidere et redīre possunt;

5 nōbīs, cum semel occidit brevis lūx,

   nox est perpetua ūna dormienda.

NOTES AND VOCABULARY

Line 1:   **vīvō, vīvere, vīxī, vīctum** to live, to enjoy life; *vīvāmus* is in the present subjunctive. It is a volitive subjunctive and translates "let us live." At the end of this line *amēmus* is likewise a volitive subjunctive. In the phrase *Lesbia atque amēmus,* notice how the first elision between *Lesbia* and *atque* and the second elision between *atque* and *amēmus* connect Lesbia with the theme of love. (For more information on elision, see p. 480 in Appendix B.)

BY THE WAY

Note how the verbs *vīvāmus* and *amēmus* in line 1 frame *mea Lesbia.* This ABBA order of words is a figure of speech called CHIASMUS, a term derived from the Greek letter of the alphabet *chi, χ.* The point of the CHIASTIC arrangement here is to associate Lesbia closely with Catullus's summons to live and to love.

Line 2: **senex, senis,** m. old man

sevērus, -a, -um strict, austere

BY THE WAY

The figure of speech that uses the repeated "s" sound is called SIBILANCE. In lines 2–3, its purpose is to suggest the whispering of gossipy, critical old men who are opposed to the love affairs of youth. (Cf. *Aeneid* 2.209, where the repeated sound of "s" suggests the hissing of the waves.)

Line 3: **aestimō** (1) to assess; line 3 carries over the sound of "s" from line 2, with every word in this line ending in the letter "s."

as, assis, m. a copper coin, penny; translate *ūnius . . . assis* "at one *as*"; genitive of value. The "i" of *ūnius*, which is long, is shortened here for the sake of the meter.‡ Note that the initial syllable of *aes-timō* contains the Latin word *aes, aeris,* n. "copper" and so correlates well with *as,* which signifies a copper coin. The *as* was the coin of least value to the Romans.

Line 4: **sōl, sōlis,** m. sun

occidō, occidere, occidī, occāsum to fall, set

redeō, redīre, rediī, reditum to rise, return

Line 5: **nōbīs,** "by us," dative of agent with the passive periphrastic *est . . . dormienda* in line 6.

semel, *adv.* once

brevis, breve brief, short

lūx, lūcis, f. light, life

Line 6: **nox:** this monosyllabic word is juxtaposed with the last word of the previous line, *lūx.* In lines 4–6 Catullus uses the motifs of light and darkness to illustrate the theme of the brevity of life. The monosyllabic *nox* in line 6, following directly on the monosyllabic *lūx* of line 5, is suggestive of the swiftness with which the light of life passes and disappears into the darkness of death.

perpetuus, -a, -um everlasting

est . . . dormienda: this is a passive periphrastic and translates literally "must be slept."

CATULLUS *CARMEN* 5, CONTINUED

> dā mī bāsia mīlle, deinde centum,
>
> dein mīlle altera, dein secunda centum,
>
> deinde ūsque altera mīlle, deinde centum.
>
> 10   dein, cum mīlia multa fēcerīmus,
>
> conturbābimus illa, nē sciāmus,
>
> aut nē quis malus invidēre possit,
>
> cum tantum sciat esse bāsiōrum.

NOTES AND VOCABULARY

Line 7:   **dā:** the present imperative from *dō, dare, dedī, datum*, to give

             bāsium, -ī, n. kiss; the noun *basium* makes its first attested appearance in Latin literature in Poem 5.

             deinde, *adv.* then

BY THE WAY

Note how *deinde* and its contracted synonym *dein* are repeated at the beginning of the next six phrases. This is an example of ANAPHORA, a figure of speech in which a word(s) is repeated for emphasis at the beginning of a series of phrases or clauses. By using ANAPHORA here, Catullus is reinforcing his invitation to Lesbia to love.

Line 8:   **alter, altera, alterum** another

Line 9:   **ūsque,** *adv.* continuously

Line 10:   **fēcerīmus:** the financial sense of *faciō* is "to reach a total"; the verb is future perfect indicative, but the *–i* is long to fit the meter.

Line 11:   **conturbō** (1) to mix up, jumble; *conturbāre*, "to throw one's accounts into confusion" is a technical term for "fraudulent bankruptcy with concealment of assets."

REMINDER

As noted in the Caesar chapter of this book on p. 68, remember that after *sī, nisi, num, and nē* the *ali*'s fall away or take a holiday.

Line 12:   **nē quis:** translate "so that not anyone."

             invideō, invidēre, invīdī, invīsum to cast an evil eye (upon), envy

Line 13:   **tantum, -ī,** n. so much, this much

             cum tantum sciat esse: indirect statement; translate "when he knows that there are so many."

             bāsiōrum: partitive genitive with *tantum*

TAKE NOTE

The genitive is used to indicate general worth with verbs of estimating and buying. Many different neuter singular adjectives and a few nouns indicate worth in the genitive, such as *tantī* ("of so much"), *parvī* ("of small worth"), *magnī* ("of great worth"), *naucī* ("of a trifle"), and *floccī* ("of the value of a lock of wool"). This is called the genitive of indefinite value (and sometimes the genitive of price) but is not to be confused with the ablative of price which denotes a specific price (see Appendix E on p. 560). A few examples of the genitive of indefinite value, such as the one you saw in line 3, follow.

> *Floccī nōn faciō hōs hominēs.*
> "I don't care a straw (i.e., the value of a lock of wool) for these people."

> *Quantī cōnstat hic ager?*
> "How much (i.e., of how much) does this field cost?"

> *Parvī aestimō hunc librum.*
> "I consider this book of little worth."

COMPREHENSION QUESTIONS

1. How much does Catullus say the rumors of old men are worth? Cite the Latin.

2. What does Catullus mean when he says that they must sleep for one continuous night?

3. What does Catullus think will happen when they have kissed so many times?

▶ EXERCISE 1

1. In line 1, what case and use is *Lesbia*?

2. Translate *senum sevēriōrum* (line 2).

3. What tense and mood is *aestimēmus* in line 3?

4. In line 5, what type of clause does *cum* introduce?

5. From what word is *mī* (line 7) the shortened form?

6. To what word does *altera* in line 9 refer?

7. In line 11, what is the mood, tense, and use of *sciāmus*?

8. What case and use is *tantum* in line 13?

LANGUAGE FACT

CUM CLAUSES

- ### *Cum* Temporal Clauses

Look at these examples of *cum* clauses, most of which you just read in Poem 5.

> *cum semel occidit brevis lūx, nox est . . . dormienda.* (Catullus 5.5–6)
> "When once the short light has set, the night must be slept."

> *cum mīlia multa fēcerīmus, conturbābimus illa.* (Catullus 5.10–11)
> "When we will have made many thousands, we will confuse them."

> *cum rūmōrēs senum ūnīus aestimāverāmus assis, laetī erāmus.*
> "Whenever we estimated the rumors of the old men at one cent, we were happy."

> *nē quis malus invidēre possit cum tantum sciat esse bāsiōrum.* (Catullus 5.12–13)
> "So that nobody evil can envy . . . when he knows that there are so many kisses."

In each of these sentences *cum* introduces a temporal clause and means "when" or "whenever." The first two examples contain indicative verbs because a pure time relationship exists between the *cum* clause and the main verb. In the third example, since an indicative pluperfect verb is used in the clause, *cum* means "whenever." The fourth example, however, contains the subjunctive verb *sciat;* this shows that the *cum* clause indicates the circumstances under which the main verb occurs. (For more information on *cum* circumstantial clauses, see pp. 454–455.)

- ### *Cum* Causal Clauses

Now consider this sentence.

> *Cum amārēmus, multa mīlia bāsiōrum dedimus.*
> "Since we were in love, we gave many thousands of kisses."

A *cum* causal clause contains a subjunctive verb and translates with "since."

- ### *Cum* Concessive Clauses

> *Cum sōlēs occiderent, tamen redīre poterant.*
> "Although the suns set, nevertheless they were able to return."

A *cum* concessive clause also contains a subjunctive verb and translates with "although." In the main clause of sentence that contains a *cum* concessive clause, the word *tamen* will be present or will be implied.

▶ EXERCISE 2

Identify the type of *cum* clause and translate the entire sentence.

1. Cum amāverāmus, vīvimus.

2. Cum hic sit lepidus, habē tibi meum libellum.

3. Tū solēbās meās esse aliquid putāre nūgās iam tum, cum ausus es ūnus Italōrum omne ae-vum tribus explicāre cartīs.

4. Cum essent multī rūmōrēs senum sevēriōrum, omnēs tamen ūnīus aestimāvimus assis.

5. Cum semel occiderit lūx, nox erit.

6. Reliquōs Gallōs virtūte praecēdunt, quod ferē cōtīdiānīs proeliīs cum Germānīs contend-unt, cum aut suīs fīnibus eōs prohibent aut ipsī in eōrum fīnibus bellum gerunt.

7. Cīvitātī persuāsit ut dē fīnibus suīs cum omnibus copiīs exīret: perfacile esse, cum virtūte omnibus praestāret, tōtīus Galliae imperiō potīrī.

8. Caesarī cum id nuntiātum esset, eōs per prōvinciam nostram iter facere cōnārī, mātūrat ab urbe proficīscī.

ESSAY

In this poem what course of action does Catullus exhort Lesbia to adopt? How does he reinforce his message to her? In a brief essay discuss what Catullus wants Lesbia to do and how he reinforces his message to her.

Support your assertions with references drawn from throughout the poem. All Latin words must be copied or their line numbers provided, AND they must be translated or paraphrased closely enough so that it is clear you understand the Latin. Direct your answer to the question; do not merely summarize the passage. Please write your essay on a separate piece of paper.

SCANSION

Name the meter and scan the following lines.

deinde ūsque altera mīlle, deinde centum.

dein, cum mīlia multa fēcerīmus,

conturbābimus illa, nē sciāmus

READING 3

Offering a fresh approach to the theme of the jilted lover, Poem 8 dramatizes a conflict between Catullus's rational persona, the poet, and his irrational self, the lover, who is having difficulty accepting the fact that the relationship with Lesbia (the unnamed *puella*) is over. Repeated language conveys intense emotion and serves to define the structure of the poem. Poem 8, a mini-masterpiece, is remarkable because each line forms a complete unit of thought. The pause at the end of each line may be seen as contributing to the emotions of sadness and anguish.

FAREWELL, GIRL

CATULLUS *CARMEN* 8
Meter: Limping Iambics

1   Miser Catulle, dēsinās ineptīre,

       et quod vidēs perīsse perditum dūcās.

       fulsēre quondam candidī tibi sōlēs,

       cum ventitābās quō puella dūcēbat

5   amāta nōbīs quantum amābitur nūlla.

       ibi illa multa cum iocōsa fīēbant,

       quae tū volēbās nec puella nōlēbat,

       fulsēre vērē candidī tibi sōlēs.

NOTES AND VOCABULARY

Line 1:   **miser, misera, miserum** unhappy, lovesick

      Catulle: the poem begins with a self-address, with Catullus the rational poet addressing Catullus the irrational lover.

      dēsinō, dēsinere, dēsiī, dēsitum to cease, stop; *dēsinās* is a volitive subjunctive being used with the sense of an imperative. For example, "you should stop" is equivalent to "stop."

      ineptiō, ineptīre to make a fool of oneself

STUDY TIP
Verbs that mean "cease, stop" such as *dēsinō* take a complementary infinitive in Latin, but in English the complementary infinitive should be translated with –ing. Thus *dēsinās ineptīre* in line 1 translates "stop playing the fool."

Line 2: **quod vidēs:** this phrase serves as the subject of *perisse*.

pereō, perīre, periī, peritum to perish, die; *perisse* is the contracted form of *periisse*.

perdō, perdere, perdidī, perditum to destroy, lose; *perditum* = *perditum esse*

dūcō, dūcere, dūxī, ductum to lead, consider; *dūcās* is a volitive subjunctive being used with the sense of an imperative; the verb introduces an indirect statement, *perditum [esse]*. Note how Catullus uses *dūcās* in line 2 with the meaning "consider," but in line 4 *dūcēbat* is used with the more ordinary meaning of "lead."

Line 3: **fulgeō, fulgēre, fulsī** to shine; in poetry, third person plural perfect active verbs can appear in a contracted form in which *-ērunt* is replaced with *-ēre* and so here *fulsēre* = *fulsērunt*.

quondam, *adv.* once, formerly

candidus, -a, -um bright, radiant

tibi: the second "i" in *tibi* is consistently long in Poem 8 for the sake of the meter.

sōl, sōlis, *m.* sun; note how the "suns" recall those of Poem 5.

Line 4: **ventitō** (1) to go or come frequently; the verbal ending *-itō* implies repetition. *Ventitō* is derived from *veniō*.

quō, *adv.* where

Line 5: **nōbīs:** dative of agent with *amāta*; *nōbīs* here may be a "true" plural, referring to both the irrational and rational Catullus, instead of a poetic plural that refers to just one person or thing. The dative of agent occurs often in poetry where prose would use the ablative of agent.

quantum, *adv.* as much as

Line 6: **ibi,** *adv.* then, there

iocōsus, -a, -um joking, playful

fīō, fierī, factus sum to happen, take place

Line 7: **volō, velle, voluī** to wish, want, be willing

nōlō, nōlle, nōluī to not wish, not want, be unwilling

nec . . . nōlēbat: observe the LITOTES in "she was not unwilling."

REMINDER

As noted in the Caesar chapter of this book on p. 52, LITOTES is an understatement that expresses an affirmative by negating its opposite (e.g., not unlucky = lucky). A double negative frequently characterizes this figure of speech.

Line 8: **vērē,** *adv.* truly

fulsēre . . . sōlēs: line 8 is nearly identical to line 3; the repeated lines act as a frame for this section on the lover's past happiness.

CATULLUS *CARMEN* 8, CONTINUED

nunc iam illa nōn volt: tū quoque inpotē<ns nōlī>,

10   nec quae fugit sectāre, nec miser vīve,

sed obstinātā mente perfer, obdūrā.

valē, puella. iam Catullus obdūrat,

nec tē requīret nec rogābit invītam.

at tū dolēbis, cum rogāberis nūlla.

15   scelesta, vae tē! quae tibi manet vīta?

quis nunc tē adībit? cui vidēberis bella?

quem nunc amābis? cūius esse dīcēris?

quem bāsiābis? cui labella mordēbis?

at tū, Catulle, dēstinātus obdūrā.

NOTES AND VOCABULARY

Line 9:   **nunc iam:** translate "now at this time."

illa: construe as nominative singular, referring to Lesbia.

nōn volt: "to be unwilling"; *volt* is the archaic form of *vult*.

inpotēns, inpotentis powerless, weak; the adjective is best construed here as a substantive in the vocative. Translate "weak one," "weakling."

Line 10:   **quae:** note that *eam*, "her" (referring to Catullus's *puella*), is to be understood as the antecedent of *quae*; the relative clause *quae fūgit* functions as the direct object of *sectāre*.

fugiō, fugere, fūgī, fugitum to flee

sector, sectārī, sectātus sum to follow, pursue; *sectāre* is a present imperative, not an infinitive.

STUDY TIP

Deponent verbs do not have a present active infinitive, and so a deponent verb form that looks like an infinitive is either a singular present imperative or the alternate form of a second person singular in the present tense.

Line 11:   **obstinātus, -a, -um** resolute, determined

mēns, mentis, *f.* mind

perferō, perferre, pertulī, perlātum to endure, put up with

obdūrō (1) to persist

BY THE WAY

In line 12, the word *puella* is an example of APOSTROPHE; in this figure of speech there is a sudden shift in addressee to some person or personified object, absent or present. The APOSTROPHE, combined with the farewell to his sweetheart, is intended to strengthen Catullus's resolve to be firm and not to weaken as he attempts to accept the fact that the affair is over.

Line 13:   **requīrō, requīrere, requīsīvī/requīsiī, requīsītum** to seek
             invītus, -a, -um unwilling
Line 14:   **doleō, dolēre, doluī, dolitum** to grieve, be sorry
             nūlla: used in an adverbial sense here, equivalent to "not."
Line 15:   **scelestus, -a, -um** wretched, unfortunate
             vae, *interj.* (+ *dat.* or *acc.*) alas, woe to!

BY THE WAY

In line 15, *quae . . . vīta?* begins a series of RHETORICAL QUESTIONS, a figure of speech in which a question is asked but an answer is not expected. The RHETORICAL QUESTIONS here reflect Catullus's agitated state as he recalls erotic moments in his love affair with Lesbia. He is really projecting how his own life will be without Lesbia rather than what her life will be without him.

Line 16:   **adeō, adīre, ad(i)ī, aditum** to approach
             vidēberis: passive forms of *videō* often are translated as "seem."
             bellus, -a, -um pretty
Line 17:   **dīcēris:** in third conjugation verbs, a long "e" indicates the future passive.
Line 18:   **bāsiō** (1) to kiss. The reference to kisses recalls Poem 5.
             cui: translate "whose"
             labellum, -ī, n. little lip; diminutive from *labrum, -ī,* n. lip
             mordeō, mordēre, momordī, morsum to bite
Line 19   **dēstinātus, -a, -um** determined

BY THE WAY

Verbal repetition characterizes Poem 8, with even *vīta* in line 15 echoing *in-vītam* in line 13, and *la-bella* in line 18 echoing *bella* in line 16. The repetition enhances the intense emotion of the heartbroken lover. Because of all the repeated language in the poem, it seems likely that Catullus intended the reader to make the connection between these unrelated words.

TAKE NOTE

Catullus the lover is so devastated by his lady's rejection that he cannot bring himself to mention or call her by name, and so refers to her as *puella* or *illa*.

COMPREHENSION QUESTIONS

1. What does Catullus think he has lost?

2. What does Catullus tell himself to do in this poem? Cite the Latin.

3. Lines 13–19 contain several second person pronouns and several verbs in the second person singular. To whom do these refer? List the pronouns and verbs in Latin, along with their line numbers.

▶ EXERCISE 1

1. In line 1, what word does *miser* modify?

2. What is the tense, voice, and form of *perīsse* in line 2?

3. In line 5, what is the case and use of *nūlla*?

4. What part of speech is *cum* in line 6?

5. In line 8, what word does *candidī* modify?

6. What word does *obstinātā* modify in line 11?

7. In line 17, translate *cūius*.

8. In line 18, what is the case and use of *cui*?

9. In line 18, what is the case and use of *labella*?

VOCABULARY BUILDER

In poem 8, Catullus uses a number of synonyms and antonyms. Knowing Latin synonyms and antonyms will help you build a larger Latin vocabulary. Give the vocabulary entry information for each word and its English meaning.

SYNONYMS

perferō (line 11)/obdūrō (line 11)

requīrō (line 13)/rogō (line 13)

miser (line 1, 10)/scelestus (line 15)

ANTONYMS

volō (line 7)/nōlō (line 9)

dūcō (line 4)/sector (line 10)

pereō (line 2)/vīvō (line 10)

adeō (line 16)/fugiō (line 10)

LANGUAGE FACT

IMPERATIVES AND PROHIBITIONS

Catullus expresses commands in several ways in Poem 8. His doing so provides the opportunity to review the whole spectrum of giving commands in Latin.

- **Positive Imperatives**

The most common command is the present active positive imperative, which in the singular usually consists of the present stem of the verb while the plural adds the ending *–te*.

Obdūrā! (Catullus 8.19)	"Endure!"
Vidēte!	"See!"

The present passive positive imperative looks like an infinitive in the singular, so be careful not to confuse the two. In the plural the passive imperative ends in *–minī*. Deponent verbs use the present passive imperatives. Remember that deponent verbs are active in their English meaning.

Dūcēre!	"Be led!"
Rogāminī!	"Be asked!"
Sectāre! (Catullus 8.10)	"Follow!"
Sequiminī!	"Follow!"

The present subjunctive in the active and the passive (called a volitive subjunctive) can convey the sense of an imperative.

Dēsinās!	(You should) "stop!"
Requīrāminī!	(You should) "be asked!"

- **Prohibitions (Negative Imperatives)**

The imperative of *nōlō* with an infinitive forms a negative command.

Nōlī mox venīre.	"Be unwilling to come soon." = "Don't come soon!"
Nōlīte ineptīre.	"Don't be foolish!"

Cavē + subjunctive

Cavē sīs.	"Beware of being." = "Don't be!"
Cavēte perferātis	"Don't endure!"

Nē + perfect subjunctive

When the perfect subjunctive is used, translate it as a present imperative.

Nē id fēceris!	"Don't do that!"
Nē rogāveritis!	"Don't ask!"

And, sometimes, in poetry, *nē* + the present imperative expresses a negative command.

Nē obdūrā!	"Don't endure!"
Nē fulgēte!	"Don't shine!"

▶ EXERCISE 2

Translate the following and identify the form of the imperative verb, the prohibition, or the equivalent. These are all based on Catullus's actual words.

1. Miser Catulle, dēsinās ineptīre!
2. Obstinātā mente, obdūrā!
3. Cavē conturbēs illa bāsia!
4. Nē nōbīs invidēte!
5. Dā mī bāsia mīlle!
6. Libellum expolī!

ESSAY

Poem 8 is characterized by striking verbal repetition. In a short essay identify the repeated language and discuss how it is used by Catullus to organize his poem.

Support your assertions with references drawn from throughout the poem. All Latin words must be copied or their line numbers provided, AND they must be translated or paraphrased closely enough so that it is clear you understand the Latin. Direct your answer to the question; do not merely summarize the passage. Please write your essay on a separate piece of paper.

SCANSION

Name the meter and scan the following lines.

nunc iam illa nōn volt: tū quoque inpotē<ns nōlī>,

nec quae fugit sectāre, nec miser vīve,

sed obstinātā mente perfer, obdūrā.

This Roman villa on the island of Sirmio overlooks Lake Garda in northern Italy. Because Catullus wrote about his beloved Sirmio, through the centuries people have called the villa Catullus's.

READING 4

Poem 13 combines an invitation to a dinner party with the theme of male friendship. In his invitation to Fabullus, Catullus inverts the idea of serving as host by suggesting that his good friend cater the dinner party himself, while Catullus volunteers to supply extraordinary perfume. This delightful poem ends on a humorous and surprising note.

AN INVITATION TO FABULLUS

CATULLUS *CARMEN* 13

Meter: Hendecasyllable

1   Cēnābis bene, mī Fabulle, apud mē

      paucīs, sī tibi dī favent, diēbus,

      sī tēcum attuleris bonam atque magnam

      cēnam, nōn sine candidā puellā

5   et vīnō et sale et omnibus cachinnīs.

      haec sī, inquam, attuleris, venuste noster,

      cēnābis bene; nam tuī Catullī

      plēnus sacculus est arāneārum.

      sed contrā accipiēs merōs amōrēs

10   seu quid suāvius ēlegantiusve est:

      nam unguentum dabō, quod meae puellae

      dōnārunt Venerēs Cupīdinēsque,

      quod tū cum olfaciēs, deōs rogābis,

      tōtum ut tē faciant, Fabulle, nāsum.

NOTES AND VOCABULARY

Line 1:   **cēnō** (1) to dine

        mī: the vocative singular form of *meus, -a, -um* in the masculine

        Fabullus, -ī, m. Fabullus, friend of Catullus

        apud, *prep. + acc.* at the house of

Line 2:   **dī** = *deī*

        paucīs . . . diēbus: translate "in, within a few days"; ablative of time within which‡

        faveō, favēre, fāvī, fautum (+ *dat.*) to favor

BY THE WAY

The separation of words that belong together, like *paucīs . . . diēbus* in line 2, is an example of a rhetorical figure called HYPERBATON. Another example of this figure occurs at the end of the poem with *tōtum . . . nāsum*. The purpose of the HYPERBATON in both instances is to enhance the humor of the poem.

Line 3:   **adferō, adferre, attulī, allātum** to bring

Line 4:   **cēna, cēnae,** f. dinner

        candidus, -a, -um beautiful, gorgeous, shining

Line 5:   **sāl, salis,** m. salt, (figurative) wit; *sal* is used in both the literal and figurative sense here.

        Note the POLYSYNDETON.

        cachinnus, -ī, m. loud laughter

Line 6:   **inquam, inquit** to say

        venustus, -a, -um charming; this word connects Fabullus with Venus of line 12, whose gift Fabullus will receive.

        noster: translate in the singular "my."

Lines 6–7:   Note how *attuleris* and *cēnābis* from lines 1 and 3 are repeated here.

Line 8:   **plēnus, -a, -um** full

        sacculus, -ī, m. little bag, wallet, purse

        arānea, -ae, f. spider's web

Line 9:   **contrā,** *adv.* in return

        accipiō, accipere, accēpī, acceptum to receive

        merus, -a, -um pure, unmixed; usually used of wine; in a poem that is a dinner invitation, the reader would have expected the word *merus* to modify a word for wine. But here Catullus uses *merus* to describe *amor.*

Line 10:   **seu,** or if; here: *quid = aliquid*

        suāvis, suāve pleasant

        ēlegāns, ēlegantis elegant

Line 11:   **unguentum, -ī,** n. ointment, perfume

Line 12:   **dōnārunt** = *dōnāvērunt*

Line 13:   **quod:** this is an example of the connecting use of the relative pronoun. *Quod* refers to *unguentum* and can be translated "it."

        olfaciō, olfacere, olfēcī, olfactum, to smell

        rogō (1) to ask

Line 14:   **tōtus, -a, -um** whole, all; *tōtum* most likely should be understood with *nāsum* (although it is possible to take the adjective with *tē*). The arrangement of the words would thus mirror the context of the line with Fabullus *(te . . . , Fabulle)* enveloped by his entire nose.

        nāsus, -ī, m. nose

TAKE NOTE

In line 2 of this poem the phrase *paucīs diēbus* provides an example of an ablative of time within which. The ablative (occasionally with the Latin preposition *in* but more often with no preposition) indicates time when (using ordinal numbers) or within which (using cardinal numbers). Time when is translated into English with the words "on, at" while time within which is translated with "in, within." Neither of these **ablative uses** is to be confused with the **accusative** of duration of time, which translates with the English preposition "for."

Examples:

Tertiō diē terram cōnspexērunt. "On the third day they observed land."	TIME WHEN
Tribus diēbus omnem cibum cōnsūmpsērunt. "Within three days they consumed all the food."	TIME WITHIN WHICH
Multōs annōs cum Germanīs pugnāvērunt. "They fought with the Germans for many years."	DURATION OF TIME

COMPREHENSION QUESTIONS

1. What five items does Catullus ask Fabullus to bring to dinner? Cite the Latin.

2. Why is Catullus unable to provide these five items?

3. What is the source of the perfume?

▶ EXERCISE 1

1. In line 1, translate *apud mē*.

2. What case is *puellā* in line 4?

3. In line 6, what is the mood and tense of *inquam*?

4. In line 7, what is the case and use of *Catullī*?

5. What is the mood and tense of *accipiēs* in line 9?

6. What grammatical form is *suāvius* in line 10?

7. In line 11, what is the antecedent of *quod*?

8. In line 13, what part of speech is *cum*?

9. What is the mood, tense, and use of *faciant* in line 14?

LANGUAGE FACT

CONDITIONAL SENTENCES

There are two conditional sentences in Poem 13.

> *Cēnābis bene . . . sī tibi dī favent . . .* (Catullus 13.1–2)
> "You will dine well . . . if the gods favor you . . . "

> *haec sī, . . . attuleris . . . cēnābis bene . . .* (Catullus 13.6–7)
> "If you will have brought these things, you will dine well . . . "

There are more types of conditional sentences than the two seen in Poem 13. Let's review the entire scope of conditional sentences.

- **Simple Conditions**

  Simple Present Conditions using the present indicative tense in both the "if" and the "then" clauses state factual conditions about the present.

  > *Sī tibi dī favent, cēnās bene.*
  > "If the gods favor you, you dine well."

  Simple Past Conditions using the past indicative tense in both clauses state factual conditions about the past.

  > *Sī tibi dī fāvērunt, cēnāvistī bene.*
  > "If the gods favored you, you dined well."

- **Future Conditions**

  Future More Vivid Conditions (FMV) using the future or the future perfect in the "if" clause and the future in the "then" clause state conditions about the future that are factual and very straightforward. Futures in the "if" clause often are translated as though they were present tense.

  > *Sī tēcum attuleris cēnam, cēnābis bene.*
  > "If you will bring (*lit.,* "will have brought") dinner with you, you will dine well."

  Future Less Vivid Conditions (FLV) using the present subjunctive in both clauses are sometimes called "should/would" conditions because of the way they are translated into English. They are also called "future less vivid" conditions because they refer to the future without any assurance of the statement's certainty. We will use the term Future Less Vivid Condition.

  > *Sī tēcum afferās cēnam, cēnēs bene.*
  > "If you should bring dinner with you, you would dine well."

- **Contrary to Fact Conditions**

  Present Contrary to Fact Conditions (CTF) using the imperfect subjunctive in both clauses state conditions about the present that are not true or factual—therefore, contrary to fact.

  > *Sī deōs rogārēs, tē facerent nāsum.*
  > "If you were to ask the gods, they would make you a nose."

  Past Contrary to Fact Conditions (CTF) using the pluperfect subjunctive in both clauses state conditions about the past that are not true or factual.

  > *Sī deōs rogāvissēs, tē fēcissent nāsum.*
  > "If you had asked the gods, they would have made you a nose."

Use this chart to help you identify and translate these conditions.

	If Clause	Translation	Main Clause	Translation
Simple Present	Present Indicative	English Present	Present Indicative	English Present
Simple Past	Past Indicative	English Past	Past Indicative	English Past
FMV	Future or Future Perfect Indicative	will or will (shall) have or English Present	Future Indicative	will (shall)
FLV	Present Subjunctive	should	Present Subjunctive	would
CTF Present	Imperfect Subjunctive	were to	Imperfect Subjunctive	would
CTF Past	Pluperfect Subjunctive	had	Pluperfect Subjunctive	would have

▶ EXERCISE 2

Identify the tense and mood of all the verbs. Identify the type of condition and translate:

1. Sī mihi multa bāsia dederis, illa conturbābimus.

2. Nisi tū meās nūgās esse aliquid putāvissēs, illum libellum lepidum nōn tibi dedissem.

3. Sī sōl occidit, nox erat.

4. Sī vīnum ferrēs, cēnārēs bene.

5. Sī ventitēs quō puella dūcit, fulgeant candidī tibi sōlēs.

6. Sī vīvis, amās.

7. Sī explicārēs omne aevum tribus cartīs, bene scrīberēs.

8. Sī plēnus sacculus fuisset arāneārum, cēnam nōn afferre potuissēs.

9. Sī rūmōrēs senum sevēriōrum audiāmus, omnēs ūnīus aestimēmus assis.

10. Haec sī attuleris, unguentum dabō.

ESSAY

Wit characterizes Catullus 13. Identify and discuss several humorous elements in the poem.

Support your assertions with references drawn from the poem. All Latin words must be copied or their line numbers provided, AND they must be translated or paraphrased closely enough so that it is clear you understand the Latin. Direct your answer to the question; do not merely summarize the passage. Please write your essay on a separate piece of paper.

SCANSION

Name the meter and scan the following lines.

sī tēcum attuleris bonam atque magnam

cēnam, nōn sine candidā puellā

et vīnō et sale et omnibus cachinnīs.

READING 5

In Poem 49 Catullus expresses thanks to Marcus Tullius Cicero, Rome's greatest lawyer. The occasion of the poem—the reason for Catullus's gratitude—is shrouded in mystery. Nevertheless, the hyperbolic expression of gratitude, the formality of Catullus's addressing Cicero by both his *praenōmen* and *nōmen*, the five superlative adjectives that occur within the space of seven lines, which mimic Cicero's own style, Catullus's description of himself as "the worst poet of all," and the double meaning of the phrase *optimus omnium patrōnus* strongly suggest that the poem has ironic undertones.

A THANK YOU

CATULLUS *CARMEN* 49

Meter: Hendecasyllable

1   Disertissime Rōmulī nepōtum,

     quot sunt quotque fuēre, Mārce Tullī,

     quotque post aliīs erunt in annīs,

     grātiās tibi maximās Catullus

5   agit pessimus omnium poēta,

     tantō pessimus omnium poēta,

     quantō tū optimus omnium patrōnus.

NOTES AND VOCABULARY

Line 1:   **disertus, -a, -um** articulate, eloquent

          Rōmulus, -ī, m. Romulus, the traditional founder of Rome

          nepōs, nepōtis, m. descendant; the phrase *Rōmulī nepōtum* refers to the Romans at the time that Catullus was writing.

Line 2:   **quot,** *adv.* how many; note the ANAPHORA in the repetition of *quot* in lines 2–3.

          fuēre = *fuērunt*

Line 3:   **post:** used as an adverb here, with the meaning of "hereafter, in the future."

          alius, alia, aliud other

Lines 4–5: **grātiās . . . agit:** give thanks, thank

Line 6–7: **tantō . . . quantō:** by as much as . . . so much

Line 7:   **patrōnus, -ī,** m. lawyer, patron

          optimus omnium patrōnus: In addition to the meaning "best lawyer of all [lawyers]," the phrase can be interpreted to mean "best lawyer of all [men]," with the less than flattering implication that Cicero was willing to defend anyone, even those individuals he had previously prosecuted, such as the scoundrel Vatinius, who was a loyal supporter of Caesar.

COMPREHENSION QUESTIONS

1. To whom is Catullus referring with the phrase *disertissime Rōmulī nepōtum*?

2. To whom is Catullus referring with the phrase *pessimus . . . poēta*?

3. To whom is Catullus referring with the phrase *optimus . . . patrōnus*?

▶ EXERCISE 1

1. In line 1, what is the case and degree of *disertissime*?

2. What is the case and use of *nepōtum* in line 1?

3. In line 3, what is the tense and mood of *erunt*?

4. What is the case and use of *tibi* in line 4?

5. In line 5, what is the case and number of *omnium*?

LANGUAGE FACT

POSITIVE, COMPARATIVE, AND SUPERLATIVE ADJECTIVES AND ADVERBS

Poem 49 contains several examples of superlative adjectives or adverbs: *disertissime* (line 1), *maximās* (line 4), *pessimus* (lines 5, 6), and *optimus* (line 7). Let's review these as well as positive and comparative adjectives and adverbs that you have seen in other places in this book. (Complete paradigms of positive, comparative, and superlative adjectives can be found in Appendix D on pp. 498–503)

- **Positive Adjectives** may belong to the first and second declension (e.g., *longus, -a, -um*) OR to the third declension (e.g., *fortis, forte*).

> *ūnum per Sēquanōs,* **angustum** *et* **difficile** (Caesar *Dē bellō Gallicō* 1.6.1–2)
> "one [route] through the Sequanians, **narrow** and **difficult**"

- **Comparative Adjectives** belong to the third declension only and are formed by adding *–ior* in the nominative singular, masculine and feminine, and *–ius* in the nominative singular neuter to the base of the positive adjective. The *–ior* form of the comparative adjective is also the base of the comparative adjective, and to this base third declension endings are added. (A complete paradigm of comparative adjectives is given in Appendix D on pp. 500–501.) Here are some sample comparative forms.

> **Candidior** *sōl fulget.*
> "A bright**er** sun is shining."

> *. . .* **parātiōrēs** *ad omnia perīcula subeunda essent.* (Caesar *Dē bellō Gallicō* 1.5.13)
> "They were **more prepared** to undergo all dangers."

> *. . . seu quid* **suāvius ēlegantius**ve *est* (Catullus 13.10)
> ". . . whether anything is **more pleasant** or **more elegant**"

- **Superlative Adjectives** belong to the first and second declension only and feature three types of endings attached to the base of the positive adjective.

-issimus, -issima, -issimum is added to the base of most adjectives.

> ***nōbilissimus*** *fuit et* ***dītissimus*** *Orgetorīx* (Caesar *Dē bellō Gallicō* 1.2.1)
> "the **most noble** and **richest** was Orgetorix."

-rimus, -rima, -rimum is added to the masculine nominative singular of adjectives ending in *–r*.

> ***Miserrimus*** *Catullus dēsinit ineptīre.*
> "The **very sad** Catullus stops playing the fool."

-limus, -lima, -limum is added to the base of six adjectives: *facilis, difficilis, similis, dissimilis, humilis,* and *gracilis.*

> ***Humillimus*** *Catullus libellum Cornēliō dat.*
> "The **most humble** Catullus gives his little book to Cornelius."

STUDY TIP

If you want to make a situation **better**, you should strive to **ameliorate** the circumstances. A **minor** is less than (i.e., **smaller** than) the legal age while a **major** in the army has a **greater** rank than a private. An **optimist** thinks that things will turn out for the **best** while a **pessimist** thinks everything will happen for the **worst**. The **maximum** refers to the **largest** amount while the **minimum** refers to the **smallest** amount. These derivatives will help you remember some of the irregular comparative and superlative adjectives.

- **Positive Adverbs** end in *–ē* if they are formed from first and second declension adjectives but end in *–iter*, *–ter*, or *–nter* if formed from a third declension adjective.

> *Fulsēre* ***vērē*** *candidī tibi sōlēs* (after Catullus 8.8)
> "The bright suns **truly** shone for you."

> *Sōlēs occidere et redīre celeriter possunt.* (after Catullus 5.4)
> "Suns can set and return **quickly**."

- **Comparative Adverbs** end in *–ius* and look the same as the neuter singular comparative adjective.

> *Id hōc* ***facilius*** *eīs persuāsit* (Caesar *Dē bellō Gallicō* 1.2.4)
> "For this reason, he persuaded it the **more easily** to them."

- **Superlative Adverbs** feature the ending *-ē* attached to the base of the superlative adjective.

> *Catullus disert**issimē** scrībit.*
> "Catullus writes **most eloquently**."

> *Tū celer**rimē** dolēbis, cum nōn rogāberis.*
> "You will be sorry **very quickly** when you are not asked."

> *Catullus libellum facil**limē** amīcō dat.*
> "Catullus gives his little book **very easily** to his friend."

A small group of adjectives and adverbs have irregular positive, comparative, and superlative forms.

Irregular Comparative and Superlative Adjectives

bonus, -a, -um good	*melior, melius* better	*optimus, -a, -um* best
malus, -a, -um bad	*peior, peius* worse	*pessimus, -a, -um* worst
magnus, -a, -um large, great	*maior, maius* larger, greater	*maximus, -a, -um* largest, greatest
parvus, -a, -um small	*minor, minus* smaller	*minimus, minima, minimum* smallest
multus, -a, -um much, many	*plūs, plūris* more	*plūrimus, plūrima, plūrimum* most

Irregular Comparative and Superlative Adverbs

bene well	*melius* better	*optimē* best
male badly	*peius* worse	*pessimē* worst
magnopere largely, greatly	*maius* more largely, more greatly	*maximē* very largely, very greatly
parum not enough, too little	*minus* less	*minimē* least
multum much	*plūs* more	*plūrimum* most

▶ EXERCISE 2

Translate the following sentences. These sentences are based on Catullus's poems.

1. Catullus Cornēliō optimum libellum dat.
2. Miserrimus Catullus obdūrat.
3. Deōs rogābis ut tē faciant, Fabulle, maximum nāsum.
4. Catullus Cicerōnī grātiās plūrimās agit.

5. Ad cēnam venīre nōlī sine candidiōre puellā et meliōre sale et plūrimīs cachinnīs.

6. Cum semel occidit brevissima lūx, nox est perpetua ūna dormienda.

7. Cornēlius omne aevum doctissimē explicāvit.

8. Vīvēmus atque amābimus simillimē.

9. Contrā suāviōrēs amōrēs accipiēs.

10. Fer tēcum meliōrem atque maiōrem cēnam.

ESSAY

Compare and contrast the content, style, and tone of Poems 1 and 49, in which Catullus expresses gratitude to Cornelius Nepos and Cicero.

Support your assertions with references drawn from throughout the poem. All Latin words must be copied or their line numbers provided, AND they must be translated or paraphrased closely enough so that it is clear you understand the Latin. Direct your answer to the question; do not merely summarize the passage. Please write your essay on a separate piece of paper.

SCANSION

Name the meter and scan the following lines.

quotque post aliīs erunt in annīs,

grātiās tibi maximās Catullus

The German sculptor Gustav Seitz (1906–1969) entitled his bronze portrait of a seated Sappho "A Young Resting Sappho." The statue sits in the park between the Culture Hall and the Music School of Wiesloch, Germany.

READING 6

A free translation of a Greek poem written by Sappho, Poem 51 describes the intense physical sensations Catullus experiences (apparently) the first time he catches sight of Lesbia. The poem appears to be a retrospective on this romantic experience, as is suggested by lines 13–16, which do not derive from Sappho's poem. Here Catullus chides himself for having too much leisure time on his hands, which enables him to dwell obsessively on his passionate and self-destructive love for Lesbia.

LOVE FOR LESBIA

CATULLUS *CARMEN* 51

Meter: Sapphic stanza

1   Ille mī pār esse deō vidētur,

     ille, sī fās est, superāre dīvōs,

     quī sedēns adversus identidem tē

         spectat et audit

5   dulce rīdentem, miserō quod omnīs

     ēripit sēnsūs mihi: nam simul tē,

     Lesbia, aspexī, nihil est super mī

     * * * * * * * * * * * *

NOTES AND VOCABULARY

Line 1:   **ille:** translate "that man."

        mī: the shortened form of *mihi*

        pār, paris equal; adjectives meaning "near, dear, kind, friendly, pleasing, similar, suitable, equal" and their synonyms and antonyms take the dative and are often followed by "to," which suggests the dative.

        vidētur: remember that passive forms of *videō* often mean "seem."

Line 2:   **fās,** *indeclin.,* right according to divine law

        superō (1) to surpass, overcome

Line 3:   **adversus, -a, -um** opposite, facing

        identidem, *adv.* repeatedly, again and again

Line 5:   **dulce,** *adv.* sweetly

        rīdeō, rīdēre, rīsī, rīsum to laugh, smile

        miserō: modifies *mihi* in line 6.

        quod: translate "a thing which"; the *quod* clause is in apposition to the description in lines 1–5.

        omnīs: *omnīs* is equivalent to *omnēs* and thus modifies *sēnsūs*; the *-īs* of *omnīs* is an alternate accusative plural ending often found in poetry.

Line 6: **ēripiō, ēripere, ērēpī, ēreptum** to snatch away, take away

sēnsus, sēnsūs, m. sense, feeling

mihi: dative of separation

nam simul: for as soon as

Line 7: **aspiciō, aspicere, aspexī, aspectum** to catch sight of, observe

est super = *superest* from *supersum, superesse, superfuī, superfutūrum* to remain, survive

Line 8: The asterisks indicate that an entire line is missing from the poem. Some critics supply *vōcis in ōre* for what has been omitted, taking *vōcis* as a partitive genitive with *nihil*.

The island of Lesbos, where Sappho was born, is in the northeastern part of the Aegean Sea not far from the coast of Turkey. The island attracts visitors keen to visit its harbors, villages, beaches, and vineyards. The wine produced on Lesbos, particularly in the area around Mithymna, was celebrated by the Augustan poets for its fine quality. Vergil mentions it in his *Georgics* and Ovid in the *Ars amātōria* while Horace cites it four times, twice in the *Odes* and twice in the *Sermōnēs*. This photo shows the town of Molivos with its Byzantine citadel that serves as the administrative center for this area.

CATULLUS *CARMEN* 51, CONTINUED

> lingua sed torpet, tenuis sub artūs
> 10 flamma dēmānat, sonitū suōpte
> tintinant aurēs, geminā teguntur
> lūmina nocte.
>
> ōtium, Catulle, tibi molestum est:
> ōtiō exsultās nimiumque gestīs:
> 15 ōtium et rēgēs prius et beātās
> perdidit urbēs.

NOTES AND VOCABULARY

Line 9: **torpeō, torpēre, torpuī** to be numb, be stiff
      tenuis, tenue thin, slender
      artus, artūs, m. joint, limb

Lines 9–12: Note the ASYNDETON.

Line 10: **dēmānō** (1) to flow down
      sonitus, sonitūs, m. sound
      suōpte: emphatic form of *suus* = *suō* + *opte*; note the SIBILANCE.

BY THE WAY

In line 11, the sound of *tintinō* suggests the actual sound of ringing. This figure of speech is called ONOMATOPOEIA. The "t-" sound in **t**in**t**inan**t**, coupled with that in soni**t**ū suōp**t**e, enhances the ONOMATOPOEIA.

Line 11: **tintinō** (1) to ring
      auris, auris, f. ear
      geminus, -a, -um twin, both
      tegō, tegere, tēxī, tēctum to cover

Line 12: **lūmen, lūminis,** n. light; here, "eye"

BY THE WAY

Although *geminā* (line 11) is in the ablative case and thus agrees with and modifies *nocte* in line 12, it should be taken with *lūmina* (line 12). This is an example of a figure of speech called a TRANSFERRED EPITHET. The effect is to emphasize the notion of night/death by making this image quite vivid.

BY THE WAY

The poem ends, as it began, with ANAPHORA: *ille . . . ille, . . . quī* (lines 1–3) and *ōtium, . . . ōtiō . . . ōtium* (lines 13–15).

Line 13:   **ōtium, -ī,** n. free time, leisure

               molestus, -a, -um troublesome, irksome

Line 14:   **ōtiō:** ablative to be taken with *exsultās*

               exsultō (1) to revel in

               nimium, *adv.* too much

               gestiō, gestīre, gestīvī, gestītum to exult, desire eagerly

Line 15:   **prius,** *adv.* beforehand, previously

               beātus, -a, -um prosperous

Line 16:   **perdō, perdere, perdidī, perditum** to destroy

COMPREHENSION QUESTIONS

1. According to stanza one of this poem, why is Catullus jealous of "that man?"

2. What four sensations does Catullus experience, according to stanza three?

3. What is Catullus's opinion of *ōtium* according to stanza four? Cite the Latin.

▶ EXERCISE 1

1. In line 1, what is the case of *mī*?

2. What is the case and use of *deō* in line 1?

3. To what verb is *superāre* in line 2 complementary?

4. In line 3, what is the case, number, and form of *sedēns*?

5. What word does *rīdentem* in line 5 modify?

6. In line 5, what word does *miserō* modify?

7. In line 6, what is the case and use of *sēnsūs*?

8. What is the case and use of *Lesbia* in line 7?

9. In line 9, what case is *tenuis,* and what word does it modify?

10. What word does *geminā* in line 11 modify?

11. In line 12, what is the case and use of *nocte*?

12. What is the case and use of *Catulle* in line 13?

13. In line 15, what is the case and use of *ōtium*?

14. What word does *beātās* in line 15 modify?

LANGUAGE FACT

GENITIVE AND DATIVE PRONOUNS

Catullus often uses pronouns. Many of the forms are immediately clear since they have the forms of regular adjectives. Forms such as *quās, quōrum, nostrōrum, ipsās,* or *hōs* are easily identified, and complete paradigms of these pronouns can be found in Appendix D. The genitive and dative singular, however, are frequently irregular.

Singular First and Second Person Personal Pronouns

	Gen. Sg.	Dat. Sg.
I (ego)	meī	mihi (sometimes shortened to "mī") (lines 1, 6, 7)
you (tū)	tuī	tibi (line 13)

BY THE WAY

The genitive singular of first and second person pronouns (singular and plural) is NOT used to show possession but is used for partitive genitives (genitive of the whole) and objective genitives. The adjectives *meus, tuus, suus, noster,* and *vester* show possession. See p. 386 for more about possession.

There is a large group of pronouns, like the "naughty nine" adjectives (see p. 35–36), where

- the genitive singular ends in *–īus.*
- the dative singular ends in *–ī.*

These irregular forms are important to know because they occur so frequently in Latin. Here are some common singular pronouns in the genitive and dative case. Note that these forms are the same for all three genders.

	Gen. Sg.	Dat. Sg.
he, she, it/this, that (is, ea, id)	eius	eī
this/he, she, it (hic, haec, hoc)	huius	huic
that/he, she, it (ille, illa, illud)	illīus	illī
who (quī, quae, quod)	cūius	cui
each (quisque, quaeque, quidque)	cūiusque	cuique
same (īdem, eadem, idem)	eiusdem	eīdem
-self (ipse, ipsa, ipsum)	ipsīus	ipsī

▶ EXERCISE 2

Translate each sentence in which a pronoun takes the place of the bold noun.

1. Ille vir fortis esse **puellae** vidētur. (That man appears/seems to be brave to the girl.)

    a. Ille vir fortis esse mihi vidētur. That man appears to be brave to me.
    b. Ille vir fortis esse tibi vidētur.
    c. Ille vir fortis esse huic (fēminae) vidētur.
    d. Ille vir fortis esse illī (virō) vidētur.

2. Libellus **Catullī** lepidus est. (Catullus's little book is charming.)

    a. Cūius libellus lepidus est?
    b. Libellus eius lepidus est.
    c. Libellus illīus lepidus est.
    d. Libellus huius lepidus est.

Now try it the other way around. Put the pronoun into the correct form to parallel the sample sentence.

3. Ōtium **Catullō** molestum est. (Leisure is troublesome for Catullus.)

    a. To whom is leisure troublesome? cui
    b. to this (person)
    c. to him
    d. to you
    e. to me

4. Fulsēre quondam candidī **tibi** sōlēs.

    a. For whom did the suns shine bright?
    b. for this (man)
    c. for that (woman)
    d. for that (man)
    e. for each (person)

ESSAY

In Poem 51 Catullus describes the sensations of a person in love. In a short essay analyze the ways in which he refers to the senses to indicate a lover's emotional state.

Support your assertions with references drawn from throughout the poem. All Latin words must be copied or their line numbers provided, AND they must be translated or paraphrased closely enough so that it is clear you understand the Latin. Direct your answer to the question; do not merely summarize the passage. Please write your essay on a separate piece of paper.

SCANSION

Name the meter and scan the following lines.

lingua sed torpet, tenuis sub artūs

flamma dēmānat, sonitū suōpte

tintinant aurēs, geminā teguntur

   lūmina nocte.

CHAPTER 3

MARCUS TULLIUS CICERO

Result Clauses; Comparison; Contraction of *–vi–* and *–ve–*; The Alternate Ending *–re*; Relative Clauses of Purpose and Characteristic; Parallelism, Ellipsis (Gapping), and Words To Be Understood; The Volitive Use of the Present Subjunctive; Correlatives

Irony, Hyperbole, Metonymy, Tricolon, Preterition, Metaphor, Personification, Oxymoron, Simile, Climax, Crescendo, Synecdoche

Sallust's account of the Catilinarian conspiracy highlights the significant role Fulvia played as informer to Cicero. Nicolas-André Monsiau (1754–1837) captures Fulvia's fateful nocturnal visit to Cicero.

MEMORĀBILE DICTŪ

Ō tempora, Ō mōrēs!

"O the times, O the customs!" (Cicero *In Catilīnam* I 1.2)

At the high point of his political career Cicero wrote this emotional outcry against the patrician Lucius Sergius Catilina who was plotting the overthrow of the Roman Republic. This famous phrase is quoted even today to communicate a disturbing state of affairs.

INTRODUCTION TO CICERO

Marcus Tullius Cicero is one of the late Roman Republic's most prolific and influential writers and intellectuals. Roughly seventy-five percent of the extant body of literature from the period 90–43 BCE comes from his pen. Cicero wrote speeches, poetry, and rhetorical, philosophical, and political essays. Additionally, he left a wealth of letters that reveal his innermost thoughts, feelings, and motivations. Written largely in the last few years of Cicero's life, these surviving letters shed light on his personal life and family, on Roman society of his day, and on this tumultuous and significant period of Roman history in which he actively participated. Titus Pomponius Atticus, Cicero's closest and dearest friend and his literary advisor, was the recipient of many of these letters.

Generally regarded as Rome's greatest orator, Cicero also is recognized as one of her most important philosophers. He developed a Latin prose vocabulary to transmit Greek philosophical ideas to a Roman readership, with his treatises providing a window into the many schools of Greek thought. As a young man, Cicero avidly studied Greek philosophy, since he viewed this discipline as complementary to rhetoric. His essays on philosophical subjects proved to be influential on European thought from antiquity through the nineteenth century.

CICERO'S LIFE

Cicero (his cognomen means "chickpea") was born to a wealthy equestrian family on the third of January 106 BCE in Arpinum, a small town sixty miles southeast of Rome. Cicero had one sibling, a younger brother named Quintus, to whom he was very close. His father apparently had ambitions for his two sons, for he took them to Rome to further their education. Cicero studied first with the well-known orator Lucius Licinius Crassus and then with the distinguished lawyer and former consul Quintus Mucius Scaevola the Augur. Courts and assemblies served as the classrooms for young men interested in law and politics, and so Cicero learned by observation from other Roman orators and statesmen. Cicero studied, too, with the Greek poet Archias, whom he would later successfully defend in 62 BCE against the charges that Archias gained Roman citizenship through false pretenses.

From his experience serving in the Social War between the Romans and Italians (89–88 BCE), Cicero discovered he was not well suited to life in the military. Interestingly, his brother was a good soldier; Quintus served Julius Caesar in his Gallic campaigns. Cicero's talent rested with his rhetorical abilities, which he continued to develop and perfect. Consequently, by 80 BCE he was more than ready to take on an important criminal case. Sextus Roscius of Ameria was falsely accused of murdering his father during the Sullan proscriptions in order that Chrysogonus, Sulla's henchman and former slave, could procure the murdered man's sizeable estate for a small sum of money. In successfully defending Roscius, Cicero showed great finesse and political savvy in accusing Chrysogonus and his accomplices of the murder and other atrocities involved in the proscriptions while not casting blame on Sulla. Following this criminal proceeding, Cicero spent two years abroad in order to restore his health.

CICERO'S EARLY CAREER AND THE *CURSUS HONŌRUM*

After returning to Rome in 77 BCE, Cicero was elected to one of twenty quaestorships for 76; the quaestorship was the first in a sequence of offices (the *cursus honōrum*) that led to the consulship. The importance of this office for Cicero was that he became the first in his family to serve in the Roman Senate; in other words, he was a *novus homō*. Cicero was assigned a quaestorship in Sicily, where he showed himself to be a fair and honest administrator. His moral integrity paid big dividends for his career several years later (70 BCE) when the Sicilians sought him out to represent them in prosecuting the unscrupulous Verres, a former governor of Sicily, for extortion. The information Cicero gathered during his whirlwind tour of Sicily prior to the trial proved to be so damaging that, after the first day in court, Verres elected to go into exile, recognizing that he would be convicted. Cicero was now regarded as Rome's leading lawyer because of his brilliant tactics in this court case and because he defeated Quintus Hortensius Hortalus, the former leading lawyer in Rome.

Cicero was elected to the office of aedile for 69 BCE and to that of praetor for 66. During his praetorship the tribune Gaius Manlius proposed a bill that would give unrestricted authority of the war against Mithridates to Pompey. Pompey, a brilliant military commander, had recently and swiftly rid the Mediterranean of pirates. Cicero made his first political speech in support of this bill; his intent was to secure the backing of Pompey for his upcoming bid for the consulship.

CICERO THE CONSUL

The pinnacle of Cicero's political career was his election to the consulship for 63 BCE—an extraordinary achievement for one not born to the ruling elite—for during this year Cicero successfully foiled a plot against the state. A patrician unsuccessful in his recent campaign for the consulship, Lucius Sergius Catilina had collected a group of other disgruntled and heavily indebted individuals and raised an army with the goal of overthrowing the government. On being made aware of the conspiracy, the Senate passed the *senātūs cōnsultum ultimum* ("the ultimate decree"), which empowered the consuls to do whatever was necessary to protect the state. The failed attempt on his life compelled Cicero to convene the Senate, and, to his surprise, Catiline attended. Thereupon he delivered a brilliant speech that provided many details of the conspiracy (*In L. Catilīnam ōrātiō prīma*) and resulted in the desired effect of persuading Catiline to depart from Rome. Catiline joined the insurgents raising an army in Etruria, a region located in west-central Italy, where he was later killed by Roman troops. The five conspirators remaining in Rome to carry out Catiline's plans for revolution were captured and executed without a trial. The decision to put to death Roman citizens without due process would later result in Cicero's exile.

THE FIRST TRIUMVIRATE AND CICERO'S EXILE

Cicero's extraordinary success in the political sphere was short-lived. By 60 BCE Caesar, Pompey, and Crassus formed a political alliance (which generally is referred to as the "first triumvirate") in order to advance their individual political goals. Cicero declined Caesar's repeated invitations to join this coalition as a fourth member because of his commitment to the traditional form of Roman government. The members of this alliance came to view Cicero as a threat. As a result, in 58 BCE the tribune Clodius Pulcher, an unscrupulous adherent of Caesar and enemy of Cicero because of Cicero's testimony against Clodius in the *Bona Dea* scandal, proposed a law that would banish anyone who had executed Roman citizens without a trial. The law, which passed, would be applied retroactively. In order to avoid prosecution, Cicero set off for exile voluntarily where he remained for a year and a half. When he was recalled to Rome in 57 BCE, he resumed his career as a lawyer; he did not, however, participate in politics because of the continued dominance of the triumvirs.

Thomas Worthington Whittredge, an American painter of the Hudson Valley School who enjoyed painting expansive landscapes, spent time on the continent as did many artists of his day. In the Alban Hills outside Rome he painted this picture of the theatre in Tusculum. Cicero owned a country villa in the hills of Tusculum and composed his Tusculan Disputations there.

Because the triumvirs enabled his recall from exile, Cicero felt an obligation to repay the debt. This obligation involved supporting legislation before the Senate that was proposed by the triumvirs as well as defending a few individuals Cicero had previously attacked and personally loathed such as Vatinius, a strong supporter of Caesar. It is likely that Catullus is referring to Cicero's political dexterity in his only poem directed to Cicero where the poet describes him as "the best lawyer of all," that is, "the best lawyer of anyone and everyone" (Poem 49, p. 112).

The political alliance among Caesar, Pompey, and Crassus began to disintegrate in 54 BCE after the death of Caesar's daughter Julia who was married to Pompey. Her death was followed by that of Crassus at the hands of the Parthians the very next year. Rejecting Caesar's offer of marriage to a grandniece, Pompey re-established his allegiance with the conservative Roman senators. Pompey's decision paved the way for a power struggle between him and Caesar, which led inevitably to civil war by 49 BCE. Cicero tried to remain neutral. Out of a sense of personal loyalty to Pompey, who had worked tirelessly for his recall from exile, Cicero eventually left Italy and traveled to Greece to join Pompey and his supporters. Caesar defeated Pompey in a decisive battle that took place at Pharsalus in Thessaly, Greece, in 48 BCE. Pompey then fled to Egypt, hoping to enlist assistance but instead was slain on his arrival on the orders of the brother of Cleopatra. Cicero did not participate in combat because he was ill. In due course he made his way back to Italy where he and other followers of Pompey were pardoned by Caesar.

THE FINAL YEARS OF CICERO'S LIFE

Between his return to Italy in 47 and the end of his life in 43 BCE, Cicero devoted much of his time to studying and writing about philosophy. The death of his beloved daughter Tullia in 45 increased his interest in philosophy, to which he turned for comfort as he tried to deal with this almost unbearable loss. *Dē amīcitiā* ("On Friendship"), *Dē senectūte* ("On Old Age"), and *Dē officiīs* ("On Duties"), to name a few of his most important essays, were written during this period.

The assassination of Caesar in 44 BCE resulted in another struggle for power. The central players included Marc Antony, who was consul at the time of Caesar's death, Marcus Aemilius Lepidus, one of Caesar's staunchest supporters and his second-in-command, and Octavian, Caesar's grand-nephew, adopted son, and chief heir. During this pivotal period in Roman history, Cicero, ever hopeful that the Republic could be restored, emerged as one of the leading statesmen. His strategy was to pit Antony, who was supported by Lepidus, against Octavian, a youth of a mere 18 years of age, whose ambition and abilities Cicero underestimated. In a series of speeches known as *The Philippics* (derived from the title of the Greek orator Demosthenes's oppositional speeches against Philip II of Macedon), Cicero attacked Antony, accusing him of being an enemy of the state, at the same time that he strongly advocated for the republican cause.

Ultimately Antony, Lepidus, and Octavian met and came to an agreement to share power. They created a second triumvirate, which was legally sanctioned by the Roman assembly. One of their first acts as co-dictators was to draw up a proscription, a list of political enemies. These individuals would be executed and their property confiscated because the triumvirs were in need of financial resources. In light of Cicero's fourteen speeches that attacked Antony, it is not surprising that he appeared on the list of the proscribed. Attempting to escape from Italy to Macedonia, he was overtaken by Antony's soldiers at his villa at Formiae (modern-day Formia, located halfway between Rome and Naples). Cicero courageously offered his neck to his executioner who also cut off his hands. His head and hands were put on display up over the rostra, the speaker's platform, in the Roman Forum as a warning to anyone who might oppose the members of the Second Triumvirate.

Such was the tragic end of a most brilliant orator and lawyer, a leading intellectual of his time, and a dedicated statesman who had served his country well during the course of his entire life.

CICERO'S ITALY

Lūca
Faesulae
Rubicō
Mare (H)Àdriàticum
Tiberis
Rōma
LATIUM
Arpinum
Formiae
Via Appia
Neāpolis
Tarentum
Brundisium
Rudiae
Hēraclēa
Mare Tyrrhēnum
MAGNA GRAECIA
Locrī
Rhēgium
SICILIA

© 2012 Bolchazy-Carducci Publishers,

INTRODUCTION TO CICERO'S *PRŌ ARCHIĀ POĒTĀ*

AULUS LICINIUS ARCHIAS

Born at Antioch, Syria, in 119 BCE, Archias earned a reputation for his gift of poetic improvisation. Arriving in Rome in 102, he gained the favor of the ruling elite who loved Greek literature. Prominent among these, the Luculli were instrumental in helping Archias acquire Roman citizenship in 89.

In 62 BCE a prosecutor named Grattius (otherwise unknown) accused Archias of claiming citizenship illegally. His real purpose, apparently, was to embarrass and disgrace Lucius Licinius Lucullus, whose family had been Archias's patron since he arrived in Rome forty years earlier. Had Archias been found guilty of the charge of being an "illegal alien," he would have been expelled from Rome. Expulsion would have been a hardship for Archias since he was totally dependent on the patronage of the Luculli for his livelihood.

Cicero agreed to defend Archias in order to assist his former teacher and to gain favor with Lucullus. After easily refuting Grattius's charge that there was no proof Archias had ever been given citizenship in Heraclea, Cicero focused the rest of the speech on how literary study supports the public welfare and how Archias had extended the glory of Rome through his poetry.

Over the centuries the *Prō Archiā* has been read by countless generations of Latin students because of the emphasis Cicero places on the importance of poetry and literature (i.e., the humanities) for the life of the mind.

CICERO AND ORATORY

Romans valued highly the ability to persuade since they saw the processes of debate and persuasion essential to maintaining a republic. Training was based to a large extent on Greek practices and oratorical theory, and many elite Romans hired Greek rhetoricians (teachers of debate and public speaking) to teach in schools or as private tutors. Romans beginning a public career would frequent law courts, assemblies, and other gatherings to observe and learn from individuals making speeches so that they could gain experience in politics and legal matters.

In Cicero's time, there were two main styles of oratory, Attic and Asiatic, the latter being the more prevalent. Cicero commented that the Asiatic style was more suitable for a young orator as it is characterized by a rapid flow of speech with much verbal embellishment, including similes, metaphors, and other figures of speech. This style tended toward pompousness and wordiness. By contrast, the Attic style was characterized by energy, restraint, taste, and refinement rather than showiness.

Cicero studied both styles and then developed one of his own. Up to his time, Roman orators, whichever style they favored, arranged their ideas by having their sentences form a series of independent clauses (parataxis). An example of parataxis can be illustrated by this sentence of Cicero's first speech against Catiline, with its series of of independent clauses: *immō verō etiam in senātum venit, fit pūblicī cōnsilī particeps, notat et dēsignat oculīs ad caedem ūnum quemque nostrum.* "No, indeed he (Catiline) even comes into the Senate, he becomes a participant in public debate, he notes and designates each one of us for slaughter." Subordinated clauses and ideas (hypotaxis), however, are more typical in Cicero's speeches, as, for example, this sentence from the *Prō Archiā*, which, in addition to the main clause, contains a *cum* clause and an ablative absolute: *Hāc tantā celebritāte fāmae cum esset iam absentibus nōtus, Rōmam vēnit Mariō cōnsule et Catulō.* "When because of this so great a reputation of fame he (Archias) was well known even to those absent (i.e., those he had never met), he came to Rome when Marius and Catulus were consuls." Cicero's innovative style excited his audiences: Longinus (*On the Sublime* 12.4) likened Cicero's style to a wildfire that rolls on and on, devouring everything in its path.

The Roman Forum as the center of the city's activities—financial, judicial, legislative, religious—drew a variety of everyday citizens to its various buildings. Most of the buildings that remain are of imperial vintage. While Cicero would not recognize some of the Forum buildings in today's archaeological site, he would probably acclimate quite quickly. To the left, this photo looks through the Temple of Saturn raised on its podium. Beyond the six columns lies the covered area of the Lapis Niger and beyond it the Basilica Aemilia. Compare the remains with the plan of the Forum on p. 204. This view emphasizes the west side of the Forum with the Basilica Julia in the foreground. Beyond the basilica are three columns from the Temple of Castor and Pollux and farther along one can make out the round white Temple of Vesta. The Temple of Saturn dedicated in 498 BCE served as the state treasury. Its present form reflects post-fire rebuilding in 283 CE and 400 CE of the temple built by L. Munatius Plancus, one of Caesar's legates in the Gallic War, in 42 BCE. The Basilica Julia begun by Julius Caesar and completed by Augustus housed the courts that heard civil cases. The Temple of Castor and Pollux was rebuilt by Augustus and Tiberius. To its east stood the Arch of Augustus commemorating the victory at Actium and a second triple arch celebrating the recapturing of standards from the Parthians.

READING 1

We will use a method of reading called a "pass through." In this method you will first read the main clause of each sentence, and then in two subsequent readings of each sentence more information will be added through subordinate clauses or phrases so that you can always see the relationship of those subordinate ideas to the main clause.

ARCHIAS AND ANTIOCH

CICERO *PRŌ ARCHIĀ POĒTĀ*, SENTENCES 1–3 (*PRŌ ARCHIĀ 4.2–4*)

Cicero traces Archias's early interest and ability in writing. This interest was a consequence not only of Archias's innate talent, but of his birthplace, Antioch, a city on the crossroads between the West and the East that abounded in scholars and ideas.

BY THE WAY

Roman Law Courts

Most civil suits, such as this one, were presented first to a *praetor*. Both plaintiff and defendant presented their sides of the suit, and if the *praetor* decided that the suit followed all the technicalities, he might hear it himself or assign a judge (*iūdex*). If the defendant was found guilty, he had thirty days to pay any damages, etc. A defendant could either plead his own case or have a professional lawyer, such as Cicero, do so. A law enacted in 204 BCE forbade lawyers to accept payment for their work. Conveniently perhaps for Cicero, the *praetor* hearing Archias's case was his younger brother Quintus.

INITIAL PASS THROUGH FOR THE FIRST SENTENCE

First, you will read the short main clause of the first sentence of the first selection.

Nam, Archiās contulit sē ad scrībendī studium.

NOTES AND VOCABULARY

Line 1:   **nam,** *conj.* for

        cōnferō, cōnferre, contulī, collātum (+ *sē*) to apply oneself

        scrībendī: translate this gerund "of writing."

        studium, -ī, n. study, zeal

SECOND PASS THROUGH

In this pass through reading, a second clause has been added. Note that the additional clause is in a different font to distinguish it from the main clause read in the initial pass through.

> Nam, Archiās **ut prīmum excessit ex puerīs atque ab eīs artibus**
> contulit sē ad scrībendī studium.

STUDY TIP

Although *prīmum* generally means "first," when combined with *ut* the phrase *ut prīmum* means "as soon as," and its clause contains an indicative verb. And *prīmō* means "at first."

NOTES AND VOCABULARY

Line 1:   **nam,** *conj.* for

ut prīmum: as soon as

excēdō, excēdere, excessī, excessum to go away, depart

puer, -ī, m. boy, boyhood; although this word usually means "boy," Cicero is using the plural here to refer to "childish things, boyhood."

ars, artis, f. art, skill; here (plural) liberal arts, humanities

STUDY TIP

Just as *tulī* is the third principal part of *ferō*, so *contulī* is the third principal part of *cōnferō*.

Line 2:   **cōnferō, cōnferre, contulī, collātum** (+ *se*) to apply oneself

scrībendī: translate this gerund "of writing"

studium, -ī, n. study, zeal

THIRD PASS THROUGH

This section adds the remaining subordinate clause to the first sentence in the passage. This added relative clause is underlined so that you can more easily distinguish it from what you have already read. Be sure to read through the entire sentence from the beginning to the end so that you see the relationship of the two subordinate clauses both to each other and to the main clause that you read in the first pass through.

Nam, ut prīmum ex puerīs excessit Archiās atque ab eīs artibus,

<u>quibus aetās puerīlis ad hūmānitātem īnfōrmārī solet</u>, sē ad scrībendī

studium contulit.

NOTES AND VOCABULARY

Line 1:   **nam,** *conj.* for

ut prīmum: as soon as

puer, -ī, m. boy, boyhood; although this word usually means "boy," Cicero is using the plural here to refer to "childish things, boyhood."

excēdō, excēdere, excessī, excessum to go away, depart

ars, artis, f. art, skill; here (plural) liberal arts, humanities; *eīs* looks forward to the relative pronoun *quibus*; translate *ab eīs artibus* "from those [studies of the] liberal arts."

Line 2:   **aetās, aetātis,** f. age, time of life

puerīlis, puerīle boyish, childish, puerile

hūmānitās, hūmānitātis, f. culture; translate *ad hūmānitātem* "with a view to culture."

īnfōrmō (1) to shape, conform

soleō, solēre, solitus sum (+ complementary infinitive) to be accustomed

scrībendī: translate this gerund "of writing"

Line 3:   **studium, -ī,** n. study, zeal

cōnferō, cōnferre, contulī, collātum (+ *sē*) to apply oneself

INITIAL PASS THROUGH FOR THE SECOND SENTENCE

Now we will read the short main clause of the second sentence of the first selection. In Latin prose and poetry, as you have seen, the reader often needs to "understand" or supply words that are not in the Latin text. Words to be understood are in parentheses in the text below.

(Archiās) celeriter antecellere omnibus ingeniī glōriā coepit.

NOTES AND VOCABULARY

Line 1:   **celeriter,** *adv.* quickly

antecellō, antecellere (no perfect system) to surpass, distinguish oneself before; *antecellere* takes a dative of person and an ablative of the thing surpassed. Translate "to surpass all with the fame."

ingenium, -ī, n. ability, talent

glōria, -ae, f. fame; the word *glōria* had a different connotation for the Romans. For them, it meant particularly "fame, renown; praise or honor given to a person by others," rather than the notion of "adoration" or "magnificence."

coepī, coepisse, coeptum (+ complementary infinitive, no present system) to have begun

BY THE WAY

The verb *coepī* is called a defective verb. It does not have a traditional first and second principal part. Instead, the first part *coepī* is the perfect first person singular, and *coepisse* is the perfect infinitive. This means that the verb *coepī* is missing a present system, which is supplied by other Latin verbs such as *incipiō*, and should be translated, as the form indicates, in one of the perfect tenses. The verb *antecellō* is also a defective verb since it does not have a third or fourth principal part and thus is lacking a perfect system. Its present system translates as its form indicates.

SECOND PASS THROUGH

In this pass through reading, a second clause has been added. Note that the clause added is in a different font to distinguish it from the main clause read in the initial pass through.

Prīmum Antiochīae—nam ibi nātus est locō nōbilī—(Archiās) coepit
    celeriter antecellere omnibus ingeniī glōriā.

NOTES AND VOCABULARY

Line 1:   **prīmum,** *adv.* first

Antiochīa, -ae, f. Antioch; the most important city for the Romans in the province of Syria, Antioch is located in modern-day Turkey. Translate "at Antioch." (This is the locative case.)

nāscor, nāscī, nātus sum to be born; may be followed by an ablative of origin/source.

locus, -ī, m. place, position in society; family

nam . . . nōbilī: Cicero adds this parenthetical remark to "casually" bring in the fact that Archias, though not born a Roman, was of distinguished birth. "For he was born there of noble parentage." It is possible to interpret *locō nōbilī* also as referring to Antioch, "for he was born there from a noble place."

coepī, coepisse, coeptum (+ complementary infinitive; no present system) to have begun

Line 2:   **celeriter,** *adv.* quickly

antecellō, antecellere (no perfect system) to surpass, distinguish oneself before

ingenium, -ī, n. ability, talent

glōria, -ae, f. fame

REMINDER

In the Caesar chapter of this book on p. 54, it was noted that with the names of towns, small islands, *domus,* or *rūs,* the preposition is to be understood in an "ablative of place from which" or an "accusative of place to which."

STUDY TIP

The preposition also is to be understood to express "place where" with the name of a town, small island, *domus,* or *rūs*. In these instances the noun is placed in the locative case. In the first and second declensions, the locative singular noun looks like a genitive singular noun (e.g., *Rōmae,* "at Rome"). In the plural and in other declensions, the locative looks like the ablative case (e.g., *Carthāgine,* "at Carthage"; *Athēnīs,* "at Athens"). And so the locative singular of the city of Antioch is *Antiochīae*; this form is identical to the genitive singular of the same noun. The locative case of *domus* and *rūs* is *domī* and *rūrī* or *rūre.*

THIRD PASS THROUGH

This section adds the remaining bit of information to the second sentence in the passage. This long phrase describing Antioch is underlined so that you can more easily distinguish it from what you have already read. Different fonts point out words that belong together.

Prīmum Antiochīae—nam ibi nātus est locō nōbilī—***celebrī*** <u>quondam</u>
<u>***urbe*** et ***cōpiōsā*** atque ērudītissimīs hominibus līberālissimīsque</u>
<u>studiīs ***adfluentī,***</u> (Archiās) celeriter antecellere omnibus ingeniī glōriā
coepit.

NOTES AND VOCABULARY

Line 1:   **prīmum,** *adv.* first

     Antiochīa, -ae, f. Antioch; the most important city for the Romans in the province of Syria, Antioch is located in modern-day Turkey. Translate "at Antioch." (This is the locative case.)

     nāscor, nāscī, nātus sum to be born; may be followed by an ablative of origin/source.

     locus, -ī, m. place, position in society; family

     nam . . . nōbilī: Cicero adds this parenthetical remark to "casually" bring in the fact that Archias, though not born a Roman, was of distinguished birth. "For he was born there of noble parentage." It is possible to interpret *locō nōbilī* also as referring to Antioch, "for he was born there from a noble place."

     celeber, celebris, celebre busy, populous

     quondam, *adv.* formerly, at one time

Line 2:   **urbs, urbis,** f. city; *urbe* is in apposition to *Antiochīae* (Antioch is the city). Cicero uses *urbe* to resume his thought about Antioch after the preceding parenthetical remark. The phrase *in urbe* usually is used in apposition to a locative; here the *in* is to be understood.

     cōpiōsus, -a, -um abundant, well supplied

     ērudītus, -a, -um learned, scholarly

     homō, hominis, m. man

     līberālis, līberāle of the liberal arts

Lines 2–3:   **atque ērudītissimīs . . . adfluentī:** The two ablative phrases *ērudītissimīs hominibus* and *līberālissimīs studiīs* are dependent on the present participle *adfluentī.* Translate "and overflowing with very learned men and very liberal studies."

Line 3:   **adfluō, adfluere, adflūxī, adflūxum** to abound, overflow with

     celeriter, *adv.* quickly

     antecellō, antecellere (no perfect system) to surpass, distinguish oneself before

     ingenium, -ī, n. ability, talent

     glōria, -ae, f. fame

Line 4:   **coepī, coepisse, coeptus sum** (+ complementary infinitive; no present system) to have begun

INITIAL PASS THROUGH FOR THE THIRD SENTENCE

Now we will read the main clause of the final sentence of the first selection. Different fonts point out words that belong together.

Post in **cēterīs** Asiae *partibus* cūnctāque Graeciā eius adventūs

celebrābantur.

NOTES AND VOCABULARY

Line 1: **post,** *adv.* afterward, subsequently

cēterī, -ae, -a the rest of, the other, the remaining

Asia, -ae, f. Asia Minor; *Asiae* is genitive singular, not locative. Note that in this prepositional phrase the genitive (here, *Asiae*) is bracketed by an ablative object *partibus* and the preposition *in*.

pars, partis, f. part, section

cūnctus, -a, -um all, all together; notice that the *–que* of *cūnctāque* connects the two objects of the preposition *in* in this long prepositional phrase that indicates where Archias's arrivals were attended.

Graecia, -ae, f. Greece

eius = his (i.e., Archias's)

adventus, adventūs, m. arrival

Line 2: **celebrō** (1) to attend in large numbers

BY THE WAY

In line 1, *Graeciā* is in the ablative case and is the second object of the preposition *in*. The noun is not in the locative case because Greece is a country, not a town or small island. See Study Tip on p. 138.

SECOND PASS THROUGH

In this pass through reading, a second clause has been added. Note that the additional clause is in a different font to distinguish it from the main clause read in the initial pass through.

Post in cēterīs Asiae partibus cūnctāque Graeciā sīc eius adventūs

celebrābantur,

> *ut fāmam ingeniī exspectātiō hominis (superāret).*

NOTES AND VOCABULARY

Line 1:   **post,** *adv.* afterward, subsequently

    cēterī, -ae, -a the rest of, the other, the remaining

    Asia, -ae, f. Asia Minor

    pars, partis, f. part, section

    cūnctus, -a, -um all, all together

    Graecia, -ae, f. Greece

    sīc, *adv.* so, to such an extent, so much; notice how the presence of *sīc* signals the result clause that begins with *ut.*

    eius = his (i.e., Archias's)

    adventus, adventūs, m. arrival

Line 2:   **celebrō** (1) to attend in large numbers

Line 3:   **ut,** *conj.* that

    fāma, -ae, f. fame, reputation

    ingenium, -ī, n. ability, talent; this is a genitive dependent on *fāmam.*

    exspectātiō, exspectātiōnis, f. expectation, anticipation; be sure to make *exspectātiō* the subject of *superāret.*

    homō, hominis, m. man

    superō (1) to surpass, exceed

THIRD PASS THROUGH

This section adds a second result clause to show the extent to which Archias's arrivals were celebrated. All the words added in this pass through have been underlined. Words to be understood are in parentheses in the text below.

Post in cēterīs Asiae partibus cūnctāque Graeciā sīc eius adventūs

celebrābantur,

ut fāmam ingeniī exspectātiō hominis (superāret),

(et)

(ut) exspectātiōnem ipsīus adventus admīrātiōque superāret.

NOTES AND VOCABULARY

Line 1:   **post,** *adv.* afterward, subsequently

cēterī, -ae, -a the rest of, the other, the remaining

Asia, -ae, f. Asia Minor

pars, partis, f. part, section

cūnctus, -a, -um all, all together

Graecia, -ae, f. Greece

sīc, *adv.* so, to such an extent, so much; notice how the presence of *sīc* signals the result clause that begins with *ut.*

eius = his (i.e., Archias's)

adventus, adventūs, m. arrival

Line 2:   **celebrō** (1) to attend in large numbers

Line 3:   **ut,** *conj.* that

fāma, -ae, f. fame, reputation

ingenium, -ī, n. ability, talent; this is a genitive dependent on *fāmam.*

exspectātiō, exspectātiōnis, f. expectation, anticipation; be sure to make *exspectātiō* the subject of *superāret.*

homō, hominis, m. man

superō (1) to surpass, exceed

Line 4:   **exspectātiō, exspectātiōnis,** f. expectation, anticipation

ipse, ipsa, ipsum –self; *ipse* is an intensive, not a reflexive, and thus need not refer to the subject. This genitive form refers to Archias. Translate "of Archias himself."

adventus, adventūs, m. arrival

admīrātiō, admīrātiōnis, f. admiration, astonishment

superō (1) to surpass, exceed; this singular verb has two nominatives as its subject (*adventus admīrātiōque*). If two abstract nouns are considered a single whole, they often will take a singular verb.

COMPREHENSION QUESTIONS

1. What did Archias study as soon as he finished his boyhood studies? Cite the Latin.

2. Where was Archias born?

3. How does Cicero characterize Antioch? Cite the Latin.

4. In addition to other places in Asia, where else was Archias's arrival a cause of great expectation?

▶ EXERCISE 1

The line numbers that are referenced in this exercise can be found on p. 146.

1. In line 1, what is the subject of *excessit*?

2. Identify the case and use of *quibus* in line 2.

3. Identify the tense, voice, form, and use of *īnfōrmārī* (line 2).

4. What is the subject of *solet* (line 2)?

5. In line 3, what is the tense and form of *nātus est*?

6. What does *celeriter* (line 5) modify?

7. Identify the case and use of *omnibus* in line 6.

8. In line 6, identify the case and use of *ingeniī*.

9. Identify the case and use of *glōriā* (line 6).

10. What is the case and use of *adventūs* in line 7?

11. In lines 7–8, what are the subjects of *superāret*?

12. What does *–que* (line 8) connect?

VOCABULARY BUILDER

In Latin, as in many languages, some basic words become the root of other words. Consider in English the words "free, freely, freedom." All three of these words are based on the root word "free," but represent different parts of speech: "free" is an adjective or a verb, "freely" is an adverb, and "freedom" is a noun. Such word families are found in Latin as well.

celeber, celebris, celebre busy, populous (line 4)	adjective
celebrō (1) to attend in large numbers, praise (line 7)	verb
celebritās, celebritātis, f. crowded conditions	noun

If you can see that the same root occurs in each word, it is easier to remember the meanings of each one.

While the splendid city of Antioch, Archias's hometown, has been destroyed over the years, the Roman road that survives near Tall Aqibrin is a reminder of that once vibrant city. The Roman road system facilitated trade and travel and a cosmopolitan culture in which Romans studied in Greece and scholars like Archias settled in Italy.

STUDY TIP

Be careful to distinguish between Latin words with the root *celebr–* and words with the root *celer–* such as *celeriter* in line 5 (p. 146). Note the relationship among the following three words.

> celer, celeris, celere quick, swift
> celerō (1) to make quick
> celeritās, celeritātis, f. quickness, speed

LANGUAGE FACT

RESULT CLAUSES

Result clauses usually are preceded by a "tip-off" word that indicates a result of the action of the main clause is coming. Consider these sentences.

> ... *sīc eius adventūs celebrābantur, ut fāmam ingeniī exspectātiō ... superāret.* (Cicero *Prō Archiā*, lines 7–8 [p. 146])
> "... his arrivals were **so** praised **that** the expectation of his talent exceeded his reputation."

*Archiās poēta **tantus** erat **ut** multī audīre eum venīrent.*
"Archias was **so great** a poet **that** many came to hear him."

Notice how the "tip-off" words *sīc* and *tantus* anticipate the *ut* + subjunctive of the result clause. Here is a list of the most common adverbs and adjectives used to signal a result clause in Cicero.

ita	so, thus, to such an extent, in such a way
sīc	so, thus, in this way
tantus, -a, -um	so great, so large, such
tam	so, so much, in such a degree
adeō	so, so much, to such a degree
tot	so many

A careful reader will note that when these words have a meaning such as "so much, such, to such an extent, so great," etc., a result of some sort is likely to follow. Sometimes a verb without one of these signal words can anticipate a result clause if its meaning is "to bring about (in such a way), to accomplish, to effect," etc. The verb *faciō* along with its compounds (*cōnficiō, efficiō, perficiō,* etc.) and impersonal verbs such as *accidit, ēvenit,* and *contingit* are often used in this way. These clauses are called explicative clauses or noun clauses of result. Result clauses must have a verb in the subjunctive after the *ut*. If the subordinate clause is negative, the *ut* does not change. A *nōn* is simply added to the clause.

▶ EXERCISE 2

Translate the following sentences as you keep in mind the information about result clauses reviewed above.

1. Archiās ita contulit sē ad scrībendī studium ut omnibus ingeniī glōriā antecelleret.

2. Antiochīa erat tam cōpiōsa ērudītissimīs hominibus ut esset celeberrima.

3. Archiās fuit tam doctus ut multōs ingeniō superāret.

4. Tot hominēs Antiochīam adveniunt ut urbs sit celeberrima.

5. Sīc Archiae adventūs celebrantur, ut exspectātiōnem ipsīus adventus admīrātiōque superāret.

STUDY TIP

If you notice the present infinitive forms *esse* and *posse* inside the verbs *esset* and *posset*, it will be easy to remember that they are imperfect subjunctive forms. Likewise, if you see the present active infinitive form of any verb with a personal ending attached to it, you will be looking at an imperfect subjunctive form.

READING 1 REDUX

You are now ready to read this passage exactly as Cicero wrote it. For this reason, the words in parentheses, the underlined words, and the special fonts are no longer used. You have already seen notes in the first version of these lines and you may refer to those notes if you need to. Additional notes are given below the text.

CICERO, *PRŌ ARCHIĀ POĒTĀ*, SENTENCES 1–3

1   Nam, ut prīmum ex puerīs excessit Archiās atque ab eīs artibus,
     quibus aetās puerīlis ad hūmānitātem īnfōrmārī solet, sē ad scrībendī
     studium contulit, prīmum Antiochīae—nam ibi nātus est locō
     nōbilī—celebrī quondam urbe et cōpiōsā atque ērudītissimīs
5   hominibus līberālissimīsque studiīs adfluentī, celeriter antecellere
     omnibus ingeniī glōriā coepit. Post in cēterīs Asiae partibus cūnctāque
     Graeciā sīc eius adventūs celebrābantur, ut fāmam ingeniī exspectātiō
     hominis, exspectātiōnem ipsīus adventūs admīrātiōque superāret.

NOTES AND VOCABULARY

Line 2:   **scrībendī:** "of writing"; notice how the genitive *scrībendī* is "nested" in the middle of the prepositional phrase *ad studium*. Note also the ALLITERATION in *solet, sē ad scrībendī studium.*

STUDY TIP

Do not confuse the idiom *sē cōnferō, cōnferre, contulī, conlātum ad* "to devote oneself **to**, apply oneself **to**" with the idiom *sē cōnferō, cōnferre, contulī, conlātum* "to betake oneself," i.e., "to go."

Line 5:   Note the repetition of the sound *celer-* in the juxtaposed *celeriter antecellere*, which suggests that Cicero may have selected the infrequently used verb *antecellō* to achieve this effect.

Line 6:   **post:** notice how the adverb *post* at the beginning of the second sentence parallels *prīmum* in line 3 ("first at Antioch . . . afterward in parts of Asia . . .") indicating that Archias's reputation is growing.

Lines 7–8:   **fāmam . . . hominis:** owing to the parallel structure of the two clauses, there is an ELLIPSIS of *superāret*. Compare the English sentence: "He went to his car, I to the library." Note the ASYNDETON in both the English and the Latin sentence.

REMINDER

As noted in the Caesar chapter on p. 28 and later on p. 194 respectively, when the reader must understand one or more words in order to make the thought in one or more clauses complete, this is called ELLIPSIS; when conjunctions must be supplied, this is called ASYNDETON. Both ELLIPSIS and ASYNDETON can be seen in lines 7–8.

ESSAY

Give three specific pieces of information that Cicero gives about the city of Antioch. Explain why he would want to include all of this detail about a city so far from Rome.

Support your assertions with references drawn from the Latin passage. All Latin words must be copied or their line numbers provided, AND they must be translated or paraphrased closely enough so that it is clear you understand the Latin. It is your responsibility to convince your reader that you are basing your conclusions on the Latin text and not merely on a general recollection of the passage. Direct your answer to the question; do not merely summarize the passage. Please write your essay on a separate piece of paper.

READING 2

The initial pass throughs of the first two sentences in this reading, in contrast to sentences 1–3 of the first reading, contain more information in the main clauses. The sentences here, therefore, are more straightforward in nature since Cicero uses less hypotaxis ("subordination") and more parataxis ("coordination") to organize his ideas. Since the Greeks developed the theory of the art of speaking (rhetoric), the Romans (and we, too, still) used Greek rhetorical terms. Again, different fonts point out words that belong together.

Cicero proceeds to describe how Archias came to Italy, how his talents gained him fame in various cities, and how his reputation even preceded his arrival in Rome.

ARCHIAS'S REPUTATION

CICERO *PRŌ ARCHIĀ POĒTĀ*, SENTENCES 4–6 (*PRŌ ARCHIĀ* 5.1–3)

INITIAL PASS THROUGH FOR THE FIRST SENTENCE

BY THE WAY

Hypotaxis signifies an arrangement of clauses that emphasizes subordination; the word comes from the Greek prefix *hypo* (underneath) and *taxis* (arrangement). Parataxis comes from the Greek prefix *para* (alongside) and *taxis* (arrangement) and indicates that two or more sentences are placed side-by-side in order to give equal weight to each of them. Through parataxis Cicero looks at Italy, Latium, and Rome in the sentence that follows, to show that Greek literature was equally important in each geographical area.

Erat ***Italia*** tum **plēna** Graecārum artium ac disciplīnārum,

    studiaque **haec** et in Latiō colēbantur

      et hīc Rōmae propter tranquillitātem reī pūblicae nōn neglegēbantur.

NOTES AND VOCABULARY

Line 1:   **tum,** *adv.* at that time, then

               plēnus, -a, -um (+ *gen.*) full of

               Graecus, -a, -um Greek, of Greece

               ars, artis, f. art, skill

               ac, *conj.* and; *ac* is a contracted form of *atque* and equivalent to *et.*

               disciplīna, -ae, f. learning, instruction, science

Line 2:   **studium, -ī,** n. study, literary occupation

               et, *adv.* also

               Latium, -ī, n. Latium; the region around Rome

               colō, colere, coluī, cultum to cultivate, revere

BY THE WAY

The three independent clauses (*erat, colēbantur,* and *neglegēbantur*) are connected by the *-que* of *studiaque* and the *et* of *et hīc*; the *et* preceding the phrase *in Latiō* is an adverb meaning "also."

Line 3:
> **hīc,** *adv.* here
>
> **Rōmae:** locative case; translate "in Rome."
>
> **propter** (*prep. + acc.*) on account of
>
> **tranquillitās, tranquillitātis,** f. peace
>
> **rēs, reī,** f. thing
>
> **pūblicus, -a, -um** belonging to the state, public
>
> **neglegō, neglegere, neglēxī, neglēctum** to neglect

STUDY TIP

When *rēs* is modified by the adjective *pūblica* (from *pūblicus, -a, -um*), this phrase takes on the meaning "state." The English word "republic" is derived from this phrase.

SECOND PASS THROUGH FOR THE FIRST SENTENCE

In this second pass through, you will find a subordinate clause added. Note that the additional clause is in a different font to distinguish it from the clause read in the initial pass through.

Words to be understood are in parentheses in the text below.

> Erat Italia tum plēna Graecārum artium ac disciplīnārum,
>
> studiaque haec et in Latiō ***vehementius tum*** colēbantur
>
> ***quam nunc īsdem in oppidīs (coluntur)***
>
> et hīc Rōmae propter tranquillitātem reī pūblicae nōn neglegēbantur.

NOTES AND VOCABULARY

Line 1:
    tum, *adv.* at that time, then

    plēnus, -a, -um (+ *gen.*) full of

    Graecus, -a, -um Greek, of Greece

    ars, artis, f. art, skill

    ac, *conj.* and; *ac* is a contracted form of *atque* and equivalent to *et.*

    disciplīna, -ae, f. learning, instruction, science

Line 2:
    studium, -ī, n. study, literary occupation

    et, *adv.* also

    Latium, -ī, n. Latium; the region around Rome

    vehemēns, vehementis earnest, enthusiastic; the comparative form *vehementius,* "more earnestly/enthusiastically," is a "tip off" for the reader that the *quam* that follows means "than."

    tum: this second *tum* correlates with *nunc* "then . . . now."

    colō, colere, coluī, cultum to cultivate, revere

Line 3:
    quam, *adv.* than

    nunc, *adv.* now

    īdem, eadem, idem same; *īsdem* is the contracted form of the ablative plural *eīsdem.*

    oppidum, -ī, n. town

Line 4:
    hīc, *adv.* here

    Rōmae: locative case; translate "in Rome."

    propter (*prep.* + *acc.*) on account of

    tranquillitās, tranquillitātis, f. peace

    rēs, reī, f. thing

    pūblicus, -a, -um belonging to the state, public

    neglegō, neglegere, neglēxī, neglēctum to neglect

INITIAL PASS THROUGH FOR THE SECOND SENTENCE

In this initial pass through, you will find two independent clauses connected by et *that will indicate first what the inhabitants of several towns gave to Archias and then what all men thought of him. Words to be understood are in parentheses in the text below. The syllable –ve– in parentheses shows the uncontracted form of the Latin word.*

Itaque hunc et Tarentīnī et Locrēnsēs et Rēgīnī et Neāpolitānī cīvitāte

cēterīsque praemiīs dōnā(vē)runt,

et omnēs (virī) (Archiam) (esse) cognitiōne atque hospitiō dignum

exīstimā(vē)runt.

NOTES AND VOCABULARY

Line 1: **itaque,** *adv.* and so

hunc: notice that *hunc,* referring to Archias, stands first in the sentence for emphasis and is the direct object of *dōnāvērunt.* Translate "him."

Tarentīnī, -ōrum, m. pl. inhabitants of Tarentum, the Tarentines

Locrēnsēs, -um, m. pl. inhabitants of the town of Locri, the Locrians

Rēgīnī, -ōrum, m. pl. inhabitants of the town of Regium, the Regians

Neāpolitānī, -ōrum, m. pl. inhabitants of the town of Naples, the Neapolitans

cīvitās, cīvitātis, f. citizenship

Line 2: **cēterī, -ae, -a** other

praemium, -ī, n. reward, gift

dōnō (1) (+ *acc.* of person and/or + *abl.* of thing) to reward, to gift with; *dōnārunt* is the contracted form of *dōnāvērunt.*

Line 3: **Archiam . . . dignum:** this indirect statement, dependent on *exīstimā(vē)runt,* tells us what *omnēs (virī)* thought.

cognitiō, cognitiōnis, f. acquaintance

hospitium, -ī, n. hospitality

Line 4: **exīstimō** (1) to think, suppose; *exīstimārunt* is the contracted form of *exīstimāvērunt.*

SECOND PASS THROUGH FOR THE SECOND SENTENCE

In this pass through, a relative clause that indicates more about the men who thought Archias worthy of recognition and hospitality has been added. Note that the additional clause is in a different font to distinguish it from the main clause read in the initial pass through. Words to be understood are in parentheses in the text below.

Itaque hunc et Tarentīnī et Locrēnsēs et Rēgīnī et Neāpolitānī cīvitāte

cēterīsque praemiīs dōnā(vē)runt,

et omnēs (virī), *quī aliquid dē ingeniīs poterant iūdicāre,* (Archiam)

(esse) cognitiōne atque hospitiō dignum exīstimā(vē)runt.

NOTES AND VOCABULARY

Line 1: **itaque,** *adv.* and so

hunc: notice that *hunc,* referring to Archias, stands first in the sentence for emphasis and is the direct object of *dōnāvērunt.* Translate "him."

Tarentīnī, -ōrum, m. pl. inhabitants of Tarentum, the Tarentines

Locrēnsēs, -um, m. pl. inhabitants of the town of Locri, the Locrians

Rēgīnī, -ōrum, m. pl. inhabitants of the town of Regium, the Regians

Neāpolitānī, -ōrum, m. pl. inhabitants of the town of Naples, the Neapolitans

cīvitās, cīvitātis, f. citizenship

Line 2: **cēterī, -ae, -a** other

praemium, -ī, n. reward, gift

dōnō (1) (+ *abl.*) to reward, to gift with; *dōnārunt* is the contracted form of *dōnāvērunt.*

Line 3: **aliquis, aliquid** anyone, anything

ingenium, -ī, n. genius, natural talent

iūdicō (1) to judge

Lines 3–4: **(Archiam) ... dignum:** this indirect statement dependent on *exīstimā(vē)runt* indicates what *omnēs (virī)* thought.

Line 4: **cognitiō, cognitiōnis,** f. acquaintance

hospitium, -ī, n. hospitality

exīstimō (1) to think, suppose; *exīstimārunt* is the contracted form of *exīstimāvērunt.*

PASS THROUGH FOR THE FINAL SENTENCE

Since the final sentence of this reading is shorter than the rest, the entire sentence is given in one reading. The two subordinate clauses are in a different font to distinguish them from the main clause. Note that the conjunction cum *has been postponed until the fifth place in the subordinate clause; by placing the phrase* hāc tantā celebritāte fāmae *first, Cicero is emphasizing Archias's reputation.*

Hāc tantā celebritāte fāmae cum esset iam absentibus nōtus, Rōmam

vēnit *Mariō cōnsule et Catulō.*

NOTES AND VOCABULARY

Line 1:   **tantus, -a, -um** such great, so great

celebritās, celebritātis, f. reputation, crowded conditions; *hāc tantā celebritāte* is an ablative of cause, "because of . . . ."

fāma, -ae, f. fame

cum, *conj.* when

iam, *adv.* already

absēns, absentis absent; this participle is treated as a noun here. You may have learned this as a substantive use of the participle. Translate "to those he had never met." Literally it is "to those being absent."

nōtus, -a, -um well-known, familiar

Rōmam: accusative of place to which with *ad* understood

Line 2:   **cōnsul, cōnsulis,** m. consul, the highest political office in Rome

REMINDER

Mariō cōnsule et Catulō in line 2 is an ablative absolute. Since Latin does not have a present participle for the verb "to be," we supply "being" in a literal translation of the ablative absolute. As we have seen in the Caesar readings, Romans used this reference to the consuls as a means of communicating the year in which an event took place. For more on the ablative absolute, see pp. 58–59 in the Caesar chapter of this book.

BY THE WAY

Don't confuse the poet Catullus with the consul Catulus.

COMPREHENSION QUESTIONS

1. What was cultivated in Italy and not neglected in Rome? Cite the Latin.

2. Who gave Archias rewards?

3. Who thought that they should become acquainted with Archias? Cite the Latin.

4. When did Archias come to Rome?

▶ EXERCISE 1

The line numbers that are referenced in this exercise can be found on p. 158.

1. In line 1, what word does *plēna* modify?

2. Identify the case and use of *artium* in line 1.

3. What does *haec* (line 2) modify?

4. Identify the case and use of *oppidīs* in line 3.

5. In line 3, what part of speech is *hīc*?

6. What is the case of *Rōmae* (line 3)?

7. In line 3, identify the case and use of *tranquillitātem*.

8. What is the subject of *neglegēbantur* (line 4)?

9. To whom does *hunc* in line 4 refer?

10. Of what verb is *hunc* (line 4) the object?

11. Find the four subjects of *dōnārunt* (line 5).

12. In line 5, identify the case and use of *omnēs*.

13. In line 6, identify the case and use of *aliquid*.

14. Identify the tense, voice, form, and use of *iūdicāre* in line 6.

15. In line 6, identify the case and use of *cognitiōne* and *hospitiō*.

16. What is the tense and voice of *exīstimārunt* in line 7?

17. In line 7, what is the case and use of *celebritāte*?

18. In line 8, what is the case and use of *Rōmam*?

19. Who/what is the subject of *vēnit* (line 8)?

VOCABULARY BUILDER

Knowing synonyms and antonyms is an effective way to increase your Latin vocabulary. Here are some synonyms from the two selections you have just read from Cicero's *Prō Archiā poetā*.

cūnctus, -a, -um	omnis, omne	all
superō (1)	antecellō, antecellere	to surpass
rēs pūblica, reī pūblicae, f.	cīvitās, cīvitātis, f.	state
ac, atque	et	and

Here are a few other words used by Cicero in the last two sections. Can you recall what Latin synonym for each of these was used by either Caesar or Catullus?

exīstimō (1)
cūnctus, -a, -um/omnis, omne
cēterī, -ae, -a
ac, atque, *conj.*/et, *conj.*
excēdō, excedere, excessī, excessum

LANGUAGE FACT

COMPARISON

Like result clauses that we looked at in the last section, certain other words, phrases, and clauses have their own "tip-off" words. For example, in the sentence "Catiline tried to interrupt him, but Cicero spoke louder . . . ," we can expect that one possible conclusion is a clause of comparison such as "than Catiline could."

When we see comparative adverbs and adjectives (for example, *celerius* adverb; *celerior, celerius* adjective), we may reasonably expect a comparison ("than") to come next. The comparative form (adverb or adjective) is a "tip-off" that a comparison may be coming next.

There are two principal ways to compare things in Latin.

- If you are comparing two nouns, you may use the ablative of comparison:

    Archiās est senior Cicerōne.
    "Archias is older than Cicero."

- More common in comparisons, however, is the use of *quam*, "than":

    Archiās est senior quam Cicerō (est).
    "Archias is older than Cicero (is)."

As the example above shows, the *quam* comparison is actually a clause, though often the verb in the second clause must be understood because it is the same as the main verb. This is another example of ELLIPSIS (see p. 194). Note that in English all comparisons are in the form of a clause and usually one that is characterized by ELLIPSIS. For example:

> Archias talks faster than Cicero (talks).
> Archias writes poetry more easily than Cicero (writes poetry).

Here are some more examples in Latin of ELLIPSIS with the verb in the comparison understood.

> *Artēs līberālēs vehementius colēbantur in Graeciā quam in Latiō (colēbantur).*
> "The liberal arts were more enthusiastically pursued in Greece than (they were pursued) in Latium."
>
> *Cicerō plūs temporis līberālibus artibus dat quam aliī hominēs (dant).*
> "Cicero gives more time to the liberal arts than other men (give)."

▶ EXERCISE 2

Translate the following sentences as you keep in mind the information about comparison as reviewed above.

1. Graecae artēs ac disciplīnae vehementius hīc colēbantur quam illīs in oppidīs.

2. Populī in Magnā Graeciā hunc maiōribus praemiīs dōnāvērunt quam aliae cīvitātēs.

3. Archiās erat dignior cēterīs cīvibus.

4. Nam Archiās facilius contulit sē ad scrībendī studium quam aliī.

5. Archiās erat nōtior multīs aliīs.

6. Catullus unguentum suāvius elegantiusque dābit quam Fabullus.

7. Cicerō fuit disertior multīs patrōnīs Rōmānīs.

8. Orgetorīx fuit nōbilior aliīs Helvētiīs.

9. In eō itinere persuādet Casticō facilius quam Dumnorīgī.

10. Parātiōrēs ad omnia perīcula subeunda erant quam vīcīnī.

LANGUAGE FACT

CONTRACTION OF –VI– AND –VE–

In the perfect system (the perfect, pluperfect, and future perfect tenses), verbs of four syllables or more may be contracted by removing the –vi– or –ve– of the form. Contraction is often called syncopation. Here are some examples of sentences that contain a contracted verb form.

Hunc . . . cēterīsque praemiīs dōnārunt.
    (Cicero *Prō Archiā*, lines 4–5)
"They awarded him with other gifts."

dōnārunt = dōnāvērunt

Hunc cognitiōne atque hospitiō dignum
    exīstimāstī.
    (based on Cicero *Prō Archiā*, lines 6–7)
"You thought that he was worthy of
    acquaintance and hospitality."

exīstimāstī = exīstimāvistī

REMINDER

Remember also, as was discussed in Poem 8 of the Catullus chapter of this book on p. 99, that verbs ending in –ērunt can be contracted to feature the ending –ēre.

▶ EXERCISE 3

Use the information about contraction to complete this exercise.

For each of the following syncopated forms, give the unsyncopated form and translate the word into English.

Example

Syncopated Form	Unsyncopated Form	English Meaning
iūdicārant	iūdicāverant	they had judged

1. exīstimārint

2. celebrāstī

3. superārunt

4. neglēxēre

5. dōnārit

6. īnfōrmāstis

7. contulēre

READING 2 REDUX

You are now ready to read this passage exactly as Cicero wrote it. For this reason, the words in parentheses, the underlined words, and the special fonts are no longer used. You have already seen vocabulary and notes in the first version of these lines and you may refer to those notes if you need to. Additional notes for these lines are given below the text.

CICERO *PRŌ ARCHIĀ POĒTĀ*, SENTENCES 4–6

1   Erat Italia tum plēna Graecārum artium ac disciplīnārum, studiaque
    haec et in Latiō vehementius tum colēbantur quam nunc īsdem
    in oppidīs et hīc Rōmae propter tranquillitātem reī pūblicae nōn
    neglegēbantur. Itaque hunc et Tarentīnī et Locrēnsēs et Rēgīnī et

5   Neāpolitānī cīvitāte cēterīsque praemiīs dōnārunt, et omnēs, quī
    aliquid dē ingeniīs poterant iūdicāre, cognitiōne atque hospitiō
    dignum exīstimārunt. Hāc tantā celebritāte fāmae cum esset iam
    absentibus nōtus, Rōmam vēnit Mariō cōnsule et Catulō.

NOTES AND VOCABULARY

Line 1:   **artium ac disciplīnārum:** compare our phrase "arts and sciences."

Lines 2–3:   **īsdem in oppidīs:** note the typical arrangement of adjective, preposition, noun. Compare the phrase *magnā cum laude*.

Lines 3–4:   **nōn neglegēbantur:** Note how the LITOTES in this phrase has the effect of reinforcing the fact that in Rome in 102 BCE the liberal arts really were pursued with great vigor.

Lines 4–5:   **Tarentīnī . . . Neāpolitānī:** Tarentum, Locri, Regium, and Naples are all located in the southern part of Italy known at that time as Magna Graecia. It should come as no surprise that a Greek poet would find his first welcome to Italy in the region where most of the inhabitants spoke Greek as their first language. Note the POLYSYNDETON.

Line 7:   **cum esset:** notice that in the actual text Cicero chooses to place the circumstantial conjunction *cum* ("when") after the ablative of cause phrase (*Hāc tantā celebritāte fāmae cum*). Usually the conjunction *cum* is the first or at least the second word in the clause. By postponing *cum*, Cicero may be manipulating the arrangement of the language to reflect the meaning that Archias's fame preceded him.

Line 8:   **Mariō cōnsule et Catulō:** i.e., 102 BCE. Gaius Marius, the famous general, married Julia, the aunt of Julius Caesar. Quintus Lutatius Catulus was also a distant blood relative of Julius Caesar and married a Julia.

ESSAY

In this passage Cicero includes a number of geographical references, beginning in line 1 with *Italia*. In a short essay, discuss the different geographical locations he cites and his purpose in referring to them.

Support your assertions with references drawn from the Latin passage. All Latin words must be copied or their line numbers provided, AND they must be translated or paraphrased closely enough so that it is clear you understand the Latin. Direct your answer to the question; do not merely summarize the passage. Please write your essay on a separate piece of paper.

INTRODUCTION TO CICERO'S *IN CATILĪNAM* I

Catiline (Lūcius Sergius Catilīna) was born around the year 108 BCE to one of the oldest patrician families in Rome, a distinguished family, however, that had fallen into poverty. Despite the fact that a member of his aristocratic family had not achieved the highest office, the consulship, in several hundred years, Catiline successfully advanced through the *cursus honōrum* until his propraetorship in the province of Africa in 67–66 BCE. Embassies from Africa came to Rome as early as 66 BCE to complain of Catiline's administration. As a result of being prosecuted for provincial extortion in 65 BCE—a charge for which he was acquitted—Catiline could not run for the consulship until 64. Because he no longer had the backing of Crassus and Caesar, Catiline lost his bid for election this year to Cicero and Gaius Antonius Hybrida. After suffering defeat again in the election of 63 BCE, Catiline gathered the disaffected and disgruntled senators, knights, and Sullan veterans in a conspiracy to overthrow the state. Cicero was well informed regarding Catiline's activities as a result of spies and thus was able to frustrate him at every turn. On the day after Catiline's failed attempt to assassinate him, Cicero called a meeting of the Senate in the temple of Jupiter Stator, which was easier to fortify than the Curia, where he delivered the *In L. Catilīnam ōrātiō prīma*. The purpose of this speech was to persuade the senators of the danger that Catiline posed and to persuade Catiline to depart from Rome, taking his followers with him.

The Roman Senate house known as the Curia stands proudly in the Forum. Fortuitously, the building was converted to a Christian church and then decommissioned and restored to its present look in the twentieth century. This building is also known as the Curia Julia because Augustus built it according to Julius Caesar's plan. After a fire, Diocletian restored it following the same plan. Today's building lacks the beautiful marble panels that would have covered the brick. The Senate did not always meet in the Curia as on the occasion when Cicero denounced Catiline. Julius Caesar was on his way to the Theater of Pompey, where the Senate was meeting instead of in the Curia, on the Ides of March.

TIMELINE OF THE CATILINARIAN CONSPIRACY

October 19 of 63 BCE	Cicero convenes a meeting of the Senate to present evidence that Manlius is planning an insurrection in Faesulae, a town in Etruria.
October 20	Quintus Arrius offers more specific evidence to the Senate of the danger posed by Manlius, who is arming a legion in Etruria.
October 21	Senate passes *senātūs cōnsultum ultimum*.
October 27	Open revolt at Faesulae instigated by Manlius.
November 6	Catiline and his fellow conspirators meet at Laeca's house.
November 7	Assassination attempt on Cicero's life.
November 8	Cicero calls a meeting of the Senate in the temple of Jupiter Stator and accuses Catiline in his *First Catilinarian*.
Evening of November 8	Catiline and some of his adherents leave Rome.
November 9	Cicero delivers *Second Catilinarian*, in which he justifies his actions of the day before.
Mid-November	Senate declares Catiline and Manlius enemies of the state.
End of November	Allobrogians come to Rome and indicate that they were approached by Catiline; they agree to act as spies.
December 2	Allobrogians supply letters indicating that Catiline has approached them.
December 3	Cicero brings the five chief conspirators who remained in Rome to the Senate; the conspirators are cross-examined and placed under house arrest.
December 5	The conspirators who were arrested are executed.
Early January of 62 BCE	Cicero's consular colleague Antonius pursues and defeats Catiline's small army in a battle near Pistoria, where Catiline is killed.

READING 3

Now that you have been introduced to Cicero's style of writing, the pass through method will no longer be used. Words to be understood are still in parentheses and when necessary, different fonts will continue to be used to point out words that go together. Use the notes below to help you with reading this text.

Cicero convenes a meeting of the Senate at the temple of Jupiter Stator for the purpose of accusing Catiline of conspiracy.

CICERO'S ACCUSATIONS AGAINST CATILINE

CICERO *IN CATILĪNAM* I I.1–2

M. Tullī Cicerōnis

In L. Catilīnam Ōrātiō Prīma

Habita In Senātū

1 **[1]** [1] Quō ūsque tandem abūtēre, Catilīna, patientiā nostrā? Quam diū etiam furor iste tuus nōs ēlūdet? *Quem* ad *fīnem* sēsē *effrēnāta* iactābit *audācia?* Nihilne tē nocturnum praesidium Palātī, nihil urbis vigiliae, nihil timor populī, nihil concursus bonōrum omnium (virōrum), nihil **hic mūnītissimus** habendī senātūs **locus,** nihil hōrum

5 (virōrum) ōra vultūsque mōvērunt?

NOTES AND VOCABULARY

Title: **In L. Catilīnam:** *In* with a person in the accusative means "against" or "versus." If this were a court, Cicero would be the prosecutor and Catiline the defendant.

L. = *Lūcium*, but translate using the nominative, *Lūcius.* In Latin, every name declines, just as every other noun does, but in an English translation the nominative form is always used.

Habita: translate with *ōrātiō.* The standard Latin idiom for "to give a speech" is *ōrātiōnem habēre.*

In Senātū: translate "in a meeting of the Senate," or "before the Senate." This does not indicate the actual place of the meeting. The Senate usually met in the Curia, but for reasons Cicero later explains, this meeting was held in the temple of Jupiter Stator.

Line 1:   **quō ūsque tandem:** "How long, tell me, . . ." (*lit.,* "how far at length")

abūtor, abūtī, abūsus sum (+ *abl.*) to abuse; *abūtēre* is second person, future, indicative. The verb *ūtor* and its compounds govern a word in the ablative case (here, *patientiā*). Note that Cicero begins with six RHETORICAL QUESTIONS, three short and three long.

quam diū: "for how long a time"

etiam, *adv.* still

furor, furōris, m. madness

iste, ista, istud that of yours, this

Line 2:	**ēlūdō, ēlūdere, ēlūsī, ēlūsum** to mock
	quem ad fīnem: "how long" or "to what end"
	effrēnātus, a, -um unbridled, unrestrained
	iactō (1) to show (himself/herself/itself) off
	audācia, -ae, f. boldness, recklessness
	nihilne: "in no way at all . . . ?"‡
	tē: the direct object of *mōvērunt* (line 5)
	nocturnus, -a, -um of the night, nocturnal
Line 3:	**praesidium, -ī,** n. defense, guard, garrison,
	Palātium, -ī, n. the Palatine (the hill immediately south of the Forum)
	vigilia, -ae, f. night watch
	timor, timōris, m. fear
	concursus, concursūs, m. gathering
Lines 3–4:	**bonōrum omnium:** translate "of all good men." *Bonōrum* is an example of an adjective being used as a substantive (see p. 241 in the Vergil chapter of this book).
Line 4:	**mūnītissimus, -a, -um,** *superlative adj.* most fortified
	habendī senātūs: genitive case with *locus. Habendī* is a gerundive modifying *senātūs.* Note the CHIASMUS.
	hōrum: like *bonōrum* in line 7, *hōrum* is being used substantively. Translate "of these men."
Line 5:	**ōs, ōris,** n. mouth, face
	vultus, vultūs, m. face, expression
	ōra vultūsque: translate "the expressions on their faces." Note the HENDIADYS.

REMINDER

As noted p. 33 in the Caesar chapter of this book, HENDIADYS is a figure of speech in which two nouns connected by the conjunction "and" are used to express one idea that usually would be expressed by a noun modified by an adjective or a genitive.

5   Patēre tua cōnsilia nōn sentīs, **cōnstrictam** iam hōrum omnium (virōrum) scientiā tenērī **coniūrātiōnem** tuam nōn vidēs? Quid proximā (nocte), quid superiōre nocte ēgeris, ubi fueris, quōs convocāveris, quid cōnsilī cēperis, quem nostrum ignōrāre arbitrāris?

    [2] Ō tempora, Ō mōrēs! Senātus haec intellegit, cōnsul (haec) videt; hic (vir) tamen vīvit.

10   Vīvit? immō vērō etiam in senātum venit, fit pūblicī cōnsilī particeps, notat et dēsignat oculīs ad caedem ūnum quemque nostrum. Nōs autem, fortēs virī, satis facere reī pūblicae vidēmur, sī istīus (virī) furōrem ac tēla vītāmus.

NOTES AND VOCABULARY

Line 5:   **pateō, patēre, patuī** to lie out in the open, be obvious. *Patēre* is an infinitive in indirect statement after *sentīs*.

              cōnsilium, -ī, n. plan, debate

              sentiō, sentīre, sēnsī, sēnsum to notice, perceive

              cōnstringō, cōnstringere, cōnstrīnxī, cōnstrictum to bind, restrain

Lines 5–6:   **cōnstrictam . . . tenērī coniūrātiōnem tuam nōn vidēs:** in this indirect statement dependent upon *nōn vidēs*, Cicero uses a participle (*cōnstrictam*) and a passive infinitive (*tenērī*) where English would use two verbs joined by a conjunction. Translate "restrained and held (back)."

Line 6:   **hōrum:** again being used substantively.

              scientia, -ae, f. knowledge

              coniūrātiō, coniūratiōnis, f. conspiracy

Lines 6–8:   Five indirect questions (*quid proximā . . . quid cōnsilī*) are followed by the direct question (*quem nostrum ignōrāre arbitrāris?*). Translate the five indirect questions and the one direct question in the same order as they are written in Latin.

              proximus, -a, -um, *superlative adj.* last

              proximā . . . superiōre: refers to November 7th and 6th respectively.

Line 7:   **superior, superius,** *comp. adj.* before last

              agō, agere, ēgī, āctum to do

              convocō (1) to call together

              cōnsilium capere to adopt a plan

Lines 7–8:   **quid cōnsilī . . . quem nostrum:** *cōnsilī* and *nostrum* are both partitive genitives—the genitive plural *nostrum* is used with partitive genitives while *nostrī* is used with an objective genitive. Note that the phrase *quem nostrum* ("whom of us") retains the genitive idea in English, while *quid cōnsilī* ("what plan") does not.

Line 8:   **ignōrō** (1) to be unaware of; fail to recognize

Line 9:   **ō tempora, ō mōrēs:** accusatives of exclamation. In English, some would say "What's the world coming to?"‡

              mōs, mōris, m. habit, custom

              haec: neuter plural direct object of *intellegit.* Translate "these things" since *haec* is being used substantively.

intellegō, intellegere, intellēxī, intellēctum to understand, perceive

hic: translate as "this man." *Hic* is being used substantively and refers to Catiline.

tamen, *adv.* still, nevertheless

Line 10:   **immō,** *adv.* no, rather

fīō, fierī, factus sum *irregular pass.* to be made, become

particeps, participis, m. (+ *gen.*) participant in

notō (1) to mark

dēsignō (1) to indicate, assign

Line 11:   <u>**caedes, caedis,**</u> f. slaughter, murder

ūnum quemque nostrum: translate "each and everyone of us."

fortēs virī: Cicero must have uttered these words with strong IRONY.

satis + facere: to do enough, satisfy

BY THE WAY

IRONY is a figure of speech in which one thing is said but the opposite is meant. Cicero uses IRONY to mock both himself and the members of the Senate by suggesting that enough is not being done for the Republic by merely avoiding the madness and weapons of Catiline.

REMINDER

As noted in the Caesar chapter of this book on p. 64, the passive of *videō* (*vidēmur*, line 12) often means "seem."

Line 12:   **istīus:** being used substantively, translate "of that man."

ac (= *atque*), *conj.* and also

tēlum, -ī, n. weapon, spear, javelin

vītō (1) to avoid

STUDY TIP

Don't confuse the verb *vītō*, "to avoid" with the noun *vīta*, "life" or with the verb *vīvō, vīvere, vīxī, vīctum,* "to live."

TAKE NOTE

1. Cicero repeats the word *nihil* six times in lines 2–4. In a similar fashion Catullus used ANAPHORA by repeating forms of the word *deinde* six times in Poem 5 (lines 7–10).

    > . . . deinde centum,
    > dein mīlle altera, dein secunda centum,
    > deinde ūsque altera mīlle, deīnde centum.
    > dein, cum mīlia multa fēcerīmus,

    Here, as in Catullus's poem, the repetition reflects the intense emotion of the speaker.

2. Exclamations, like the one in line 9, are expressed in the accusative case, and verbs, if expressed, are in the infinitive form. Less frequently an exclamation is in the nominative case. Consider these three examples.

Ō, mē fortūnātam! "Oh, fortunate me!"	ACCUSATIVE OF EXCLAMATION
Mēne in tālem locum dēscendere!? "What! I go down into a place like that!?"	ACCUSATIVE OF EXCLAMATION WITH INFINITIVE
Ō dī immortālēs! "Oh immortal gods!"	NOMINATIVE OF EXCLAMATION

COMPREHENSION QUESTIONS

1. What does Cicero accuse Catiline of abusing?

2. List the six things that Cicero says do not seem to affect Catiline. Cite the Latin.

3. Of what does Cicero say that the Senate and the consul are aware?

4. What does Cicero indicate that Catiline is doing with his eyes?

5. And what does Cicero say that the "brave men" are doing?

▶ EXERCISE 1

1. What case is *patientiā* in line 1 and why?

2. What case and use is *praesidium* in line 3?

3. What case and use is *vigiliae* in line 3?

4. What grammatical form and case is *habendī* in line 4?

5. What case and use is *coniūrātiōnem* in line 6?

6. What mood and tense is *ēgeris* in line 7?

7. What case and use is *tempora* in line 9?

8. What case and use is *oculīs* in line 11?

VOCABULARY BUILDER

Like Caesar, Cicero uses a number of idioms in his writings. The following idioms can be found in the Cicero passages in this book, and knowing these will help you read Cicero.

sē cōnferō ad to devote oneself to, apply oneself to	(Cicero *Prō Archiā* 4.2.2–3)
ut prīmum as soon as	(Cicero, *Prō Archiā* 4.2.1)
ōrātiōnem habeō, habēre, habuī, habitum to give a speech	(Cicero *In Cat.* I)
cōnsilium capiō, capere, cēpī, captum to adopt a plan	(Cicero *In Cat.* I 1.1.7)
satis faciō, facere, fēcī, factum to satisfy	(Cicero *In Cat.* I 1.2.11)
orbis terrae, orbis terrae, m. world	(Cicero *In Cat.* I 4.9.10)
patrēs cōnscrīptī, patrum cōnscrīptōrum, m. pl. senators	(Cicero *In Cat.* I 4.9.8)
rēs pūblica, reī pūblicae, f. republic	(Cicero *In Cat.* I 4.9.7)
quae cum ita sint since these things are so	(Cicero *In Cat.* I 5.10.1)
nesciō, nescīre, nescīvī, nescītum + quis, quid to not know some, someone, something	(Cicero *In Cat.* I 13.31.2)

LANGUAGE FACT

THE ALTERNATE ENDING *–RE*

The alternate second person passive ending for *–ris* is *–re*. Although possible in the present and imperfect tenses, the alternate ending *–re* is most often seen in the future tense. In the future tense of the third conjugation, the *ē* preceding the second person passive ending is long by nature while in the present tense the *e* is short.

> *Quō ūsque tandem abūtēre, Catilīna, patientiā nostrā?* (Cicero *In Cat.* I 1.1.1)
> "How long finally will you abuse our patience, Catiline?"

STUDY TIP

When you see a Latin word that ends in *–ere*, be careful to distinguish among words that look alike.

The first and second forms immediately below occur frequently in Latin literature.

- dēfendere = to defend, present active infinitive; this form is the most common of the five and will appear in a sentence with a conjugated verb.

- dēfendēre = they defended, syncopated form for *dēfendērunt;* this form occurs regularly in poetry. The long *ē* in *–ēre* distinguishes the form from the infinitive.

The other forms, all in the passive indicative, do not occur as often, but you should be aware of them.

- dēfendere = you are defended, the present passive with the alternate ending *–re* for *–ris*.
- dēfendēre = you will be defended, the future passive with the alternate ending *–re* for *–ris* (note the macron over the penultimate *–e*).
- dēfendere = be defended, passive imperative; this form is quite rare.

▶ EXERCISE 2

Decide what form each word is and translate. There may be more than one correct answer.

Example:

dēsignābēre   future passive second singular   you will be pointed out

1. ēlūsere
2. capiere
3. arbitrābāre
4. habēre
5. fuēre
6. vēnēre
7. vītābēre
8. ēgēre
9. tenēre
10. sēnsēre

ESSAY

Give examples of repeated language and expressions in *In Cat.* I 1 and then discuss how the repetition contributes to the effect Cicero is trying to achieve.

Support your assertions with references drawn from the Latin passage. All Latin words must be copied or their line numbers provided, AND they must be translated or paraphrased closely enough so that it is clear you understand the Latin. Direct your answer to the question; do not merely summarize the passage. Please write your essay on a separate piece of paper.

The portrait bust of Cicero depicts him in his later years with receding hairline and wrinkled neck. The sculptor communicates Cicero's seriousness of purpose by means of a furrowed brow and the set of the jaw.

READING 4

Words to be understood are still in parentheses and different fonts point out words that go together. Use the notes below the passage to help you.

In this passage Cicero indicates that he was aware, shortly after the meeting of the conspirators at Laeca's house, of Catiline's plans and the duties he assigned to the co-conspirators, which included Cicero's own assassination. Cicero urges Catiline to leave the city and to proceed to his and Manlius's camp at Faesulae, taking with him as many followers as possible who still remain in Rome.

REVEALING CATILINE'S PLANS

CICERO *IN CATILĪNAM* I 4.8–10; 5.10–11

1 [4] [8] Recognōsce tandem mēcum noctem illam superiōrem; iam intellegēs **multō** mē vigilāre **ācrius** ad salūtem (reī pūblicae) quam tē (vigilāre) ad perniciem reī pūblicae. Dīcō tē priōre nocte vēnisse inter falcāriōs—nōn agam obscūrē—in M. Laecae domum; (dīcō) convēnisse eōdem **complūrīs** eiusdem āmentiae scelerisque **sociōs.** Num negāre audēs?

5 Quid tacēs? Convincam (tē), sī negās. Videō enim esse hīc in senātū quōsdam (virōs) quī tēcum ūnā fuērunt.

NOTES AND VOCABULARY

Line 1:   **recognōscō, recognōscere, recognōvī, recognitum** to recall, recount, review

   tandem, *adv.* at length, finally

   noctem illam superiōrem: translate "that night before last" (November 6th).

   iam, *adv.* now, already, + *future tense* soon

   multō: ablative of degree of difference with *ācrius.* Translate *multō ācrius* "much more keenly."

Line 2:   **vigilō** (1) to be attentive

   ācrius, *comp. adv.* more keenly

   salus, salūtis, f. safety

   perniciēs, perniciēī, f. destruction, ruin

   reī pūblicae: take with both *salūtem* and *perniciem.*

Line 3:   **prior, prius,** *comp. adj.* before last

   falcāriī, falcāriōrum, m. pl. Scythe Makers' Street (a neighborhood in Rome); translate *inter falcāriōs* "to the Scythe Makers' Street."

   agam: = *loquar*

   M. Laecae: = *Mārcī Laecae.* Little is known about Marcus Porcius Laeca beyond the fact that he was of senatorial rank and a participant in the Catilinarian conspiracy.

Line 4:   **convēnisse:** infinitive in indirect statement/discourse dependent on *dīcō* in line 2.

eōdem, *adv.* in the same place

complūrēs, complūra several, many; the long vowel "ī" in *complūrīs* shows that the word is the alternate accusative plural form for *complūrēs*.

āmentia, -ae, f. madness, folly

scelus, sceleris, n. crime

āmentiae scelerisque: "criminal madness." This HENDIADYS gives the noun *sceleris* the force of an adjective modifying *āmentia*.

num, *interrogative adv.* expects a negative answer; translate using this formula "subject doesn't . . . , does subject?"

negō (1) to deny; if the transitive verb *negāre* does not have an expressed object, one needs to be supplied. Translate *negāre* "to deny this."

audeō, audēre, ausus sum, *semi-deponent*, to dare, be bold

STUDY TIP

Do not confuse *audeō* "to dare" with *audiō* "to hear" or *adeō, adv.* "even, in fact, so, thus."

Line 5:   **quid** = *cūr*

taceō, tacēre, tacuī, tacitum to be quiet, silent

convincō, convincere, convīcī, convictum to prove wrong

enim, *conj.* for, indeed, in fact

hīc, *adv.* here

quīdam, quaedam, quoddam (quiddam), *indef. pron./adj.* certain, some

Line 6:   **ūnā,** *adv.* together

STUDY TIP

Hīc with a macron means "here." *Hic* without a macron is a form of *hic, haec, hoc,* a demonstrative adjective or pronoun meaning "this, he, she, it." When macrons are given in a text, it is easy to see the difference between the two forms of *hic*. When macrons are not given, context will determine the meaning.

CICERO *IN CATILĪNAM* I 4.8–10; 5.10–11, CONTINUED

[9] Ō dī immortālēs! Ubīnam gentium sumus? Quam rem pūblicam habēmus? In quā urbe vīvimus? Hīc, hīc sunt in nostrō numerō, patrēs cōnscrīptī, in **hōc** orbis terrae **sanctissimō gravissimō**que **cōnsiliō,** (eī) quī dē **nostrō** omnium **interitū,** quī dē

10 (exitiō) huius urbis atque adeō dē orbis terrārum exitiō cōgitent. Hōs (virōs) **ego** videō **cōnsul** et dē rē pūblicā (hōs) sententiam rogō, et quōs ferrō trucīdārī oportēbat, eōs nōndum (meā) vōce vulnerō!

NOTES AND VOCABULARY

Line 7:   **dī:** nom./voc. pl. from *deus, deī,* m.; *dī* is a nominative of exclamation.

        ubīnam gentium: although *gentium* is gen. pl., translate "where in the world."

        quam rem pūblicam: this may be translated "what type of state."

Lines 7–8: **in quā urbe:** this may also be translated "in what type of city"; note the three RHETORICAL QUESTIONS in these lines.

Line 8:   **patrēs cōnscrīptī:** translate "senators" (*lit.,* "enrolled fathers").

        orbis, orbis, m. circle, ring; translate *orbis terrae* "the world."

Line 9:   **sanctus, -a, -um** consecrated, inviolable, pure

        gravis, grave serious, weighty

        cōnsilium, -ī, n. meeting (of the Senate)

        dē, *prep. + abl.* from, about, concerning

        interitus, interitūs, m. ruin, death, destruction; *nostrō omnium interitū = interitū omnium nostrum*

BY THE WAY

Note the HYPERBOLE (a figure of speech in which something is exaggerated for effect) in lines 9 and 10. Cicero uses HYPERBOLE here to reinforce and emphasize his opinion on the gravity and danger of the situation posed by Catiline and his adherents.

Line 10:   **exitium, -ī,** n. ruin, destruction

        adeō, *adv.* even, in fact, so, thus

Line 11:   **sententia, -ae,** f. thought, opinion

        rogō (1) to ask; the two accusatives (called a double accusative) in *(hōs) sententiam rogō* can be translated "I ask these men (for) their opinion."

        ferrum, -ī, n. iron; by METONYMY, sword

        trucīdō (1) to slaughter, butcher

        quōs . . . oportēbat: The antecedent of *quōs* is the *eōs* at the end of line 11. For the sake of simplicity, translate the relative clause immediately after its antecedent. The present infinitive with a past tense of *oportet* is translated often in English as though it were a perfect infinitive. Translate "whom it was necessary to have been slaughtered with a sword."

Line 12:   **nōndum,** *adv.* not yet
             vulnerō (1) to harm

BY THE WAY

METONYMY is a figure of speech in which one word is used for another with which it is closely associated. The METONYMY of *ferrum* ("iron") for "sword" here complements a very strong verb for "killing"; *trucīdō* signifies "slaughtering" or "butchering." Cicero's desire "to slaughter with iron" the members of the Catilinarian conspiracy effectively reflects his anger against those who threaten the Republic.

An interior view of the Curia reveals the stunning *opus sectile* flooring that is comprised of cut pieces of variously colored marble imported from locations throughout the empire. The lower portion of the brick walls shows that the walls were originally covered with marble. Today, the Curia hosts special archaeological and art historical exhibits and houses a number of sculptural panels and statues from the Forum.

CICERO *IN CATILĪNAM* I 4.8–10; 5.10–11, CONTINUED

Fuistī igitur apud Laecam illā nocte, Catilīna, distribuistī partēs Italiae, statuistī quō
quemque proficīscī placēret, dēlēgistī quōs Rōmae relinquerēs, quōs tēcum ēdūcerēs,
15 discrīpsistī urbis partēs ad incendia, cōnfirmāstī **tē *ipsum*** iam esse exitūrum, dīxistī
paulum tibi esse etiam nunc morae, quod ego vīverem. Repertī sunt duo equitēs Rōmānī
quī tē istā cūrā līberārent et sē illā ipsā nocte paulō ante lūcem mē in meō lectō
interfectūrōs esse pollicērentur.

[10] ***Haec*** ego ***omnia*** vixdum etiam coetū vestrō dimissō comperī; domum meam
20 maiōribus praesidiīs mūnīvī atque firmāvī, exclūsī eōs quōs tū ad mē salūtātum māne
mīserās, cum illī ipsī vēnissent quōs ego iam multīs ac summīs virīs ad mē id temporis
ventūrōs esse praedīxeram.

[5] [10] Quae cum ita sint, Catilīna, perge quō coepistī: ēgredere aliquandō ex urbe;

NOTES AND VOCABULARY

Line 13:   **igitur,** *conj.* therefore, then

apud, *prep. + acc. of person* at the house of

distribuō, distribuere, distribuī, distribūtum to divide, assign

statuō, statuere, statuī, statūtum to decide

Lines 13–15:   **distribuistī . . . dīxistī:** notice that Cicero uses no conjunctions to connect the independent
verbs.

Lines 13–14:   **quō . . . placēret:** *quō* introduces an indirect question ("where . . ."; *lit.,* "to where" or "to what
place").

Line 14:   **quemque proficīscī placēret:** *tibi* is to be understood with *placēret,* and *quemque* is the
subject of the infinitive *proficīscī;* translate "it pleased [you] that each set out."

placet, placēre, placuit, *impers. verb* it pleases, is pleasing

dēligō, dēligere, dēlēgī, dēlēctum to choose

Line 15:   **discrībō, discrībere, discrīpsī, discrīptum** to distribute, assign

incendium, -ī, n. fire; *pl.* arson

exeō, exīre, exiī, exitum to go out, leave

Line 16:   **paulum, -ī,** n. a little bit

mora, -ae, f. delay; translate *morae* "cause for delay." *Morae* is a genitive of the whole (also
called the partitive genitive) with *paulum.*

quod: translate "the fact that."

reperiō, reperīre, repperī, repertum to find

eques, equitis, m. knight, member of the equestrian order; according to Sallust's *Bellum
Catilīnae,* section 28, the two knights were C. Cornelius and L. Vargunteius.

Line 17:   **istā cūrā:** ablative of separation after *līberārent*; translate "from that care."

sē: accusative subject of indirect discourse/statement dependent on *pollicērentur*.

paulō, *adv.* shortly before, a little while ago

lectus, -ī, m. bed, couch

Lines 17–18:   **quī . . . pollicērentur:** "who would free (*līberārent*) . . . and (who) would promise (*pollicērentur*) . . ." is a relative clause of purpose.

Line 19:   **vixdum,** *adv.* hardly yet, barely

coetus, coetūs, m. meeting, gathering

dīmittō, dīmittere, dīmīsī, dīmissum to adjourn, dismiss

comperiō, comperīre, comperī, compertum to find out, discover

Line 20:   **mūniō, mūnīre, mūnīvī, mūnītum** to fortify

firmō (1) to strengthen

exclūdō, exclūdere, exclūsī, exclūsum to shut out

salūtō (1) to greet, pay respects to; translate *salūtātum* "to greet," which is an accusative supine expressing purpose (see p. 180 and p. 547). Cicero here is alluding to the *salūtātiō*, the morning greeting a group of clients gave to their patron in his home.

māne, *adv.* early in the morning

Lines 20–21:   **eōs quōs . . . illī ipsī . . . quōs:** the same *equitēs* mentioned in line 16

Line 21:   **quōs:** accusative subject of the indirect statement dependent on *praedīxeram* (line 22)

multīs . . . virīs: dative indirect objects with *praedīxeram*

summus, -a, -um highest, distinguished

id temporis = *eō tempore*

Line 22:   **ventūrōs esse:** future active infinitive in the indirect statement dependent on *praedīxeram*

praedīcō, praedīcere, praedīxī, praedictum to foretell, predict

STUDY TIP

The three words for "where" correspond to "place to which," "place where," and "place from which."

quō – to where, to which

ubi – where

unde – from where

Line 23:   **quae cum ita sint:** "since these things are so," or "under these circumstances." In this phrase the connecting relative *quae* is equivalent to *haec* ("these things"), and refers to the facts stated in the previous section. *Cum* means "since"; it is the causal use of this conjunction that takes a subjunctive verb, here *sint*.

pergō, pergere, perrēxī, perrēctum to keep on, proceed, go forward‡

quō: translate "where." *Quō* is used instead of *ubi* with a verb of motion. Literally, *quō* means "to where," or the rather archaic English word "whither," e.g., "Whither goest thou?"

ēgredior, ēgredī, ēgressus sum to go out, leave

aliquandō, *adv.* at some time, at last

CICERO *IN CATILĪNAM* I 4.8–10; 5.10–11, CONTINUED

patent portae; proficīscere. Nimium diū tē imperātōrem tua illa Manliāna castra

25 dēsīderant. Ēdūc tēcum etiam omnīs tuōs, sī minus, quam plūrimōs; purgā urbem.
Magnō mē **metū** līberāveris, modo inter mē atque tē mūrus intersit. Nōbīscum versārī
iam diūtius nōn potes; nōn feram, nōn patiar, nōn sinam.

[11] **Magna** dīs immortālibus **habenda est** atque huic ipsī Iovī Statōrī, antīquissimō

custōdī huius urbis, **grātia,** quod *hanc* tam *taetram,* tam *horribilem* tamque *īnfestam*

30 reī pūblicae *pestem* totiēns iam effūgimus.

NOTES AND VOCABULARY

Line 24: **pateō, patēre, patuī** to be open

proficīscor, proficīscī, profectus sum to depart

nimium, *adv.* too, too much

imperātor, imperātōris, m. leader, general

Manliānus, -a, -um of Manlius

tua . . . castra: Cicero has turned Manlius's name into an adjective, a change that may sound
pretentious in English: Marlon's book = the Marlonian book. *Illa* here refers to the camp at
Faesulae, so "up there" is about as close to Cicero's effect as English can come: "Your and
Manlius's camp up there."

REMINDER

As you read on p. 65 in the Caesar chapter of this book, be careful to distinguish among
these four verbs that look quite similar but have very different meanings.

partior, partīrī, partītus sum to divide

pateō, patēre, patuī to be open

patior, patī, passus sum to allow, bear, suffer

potior, potīrī, potītus sum (+ *abl.* or + *gen.*) to gain possession of

Line 25: **dēsīderō** (1) to long for, miss

omnīs: this is the alternate accusative plural for *omnēs.*

minus, *comp. adv.* not; less

purgō (1) to cleanse, purify

REMINDER

As you learned on p. 40 and p. 57 in the Caesar chapter of this book, *quam* with the
superlative signifies "as . . . as possible." So, *quam plūrimōs* (in line 25) means "as many
as possible" in English.

STUDY TIP

The word *quam* can be used in various ways in Latin and can have different meanings.

quam – which, that (*acc. sing.* of the relative pronoun *quī, quae, quod*)

quam – which? what? (*acc. sing.* of the interrogative adjective *quī, quae, quod*)

quam – how (used in exclamations)

quam + superlative adjective/adverb – as . . . as possible

quam + noun after a comparative – than

Line 26: **metus, metūs,** m. fear, anxiety; note the ALLITERATION.

modo: = *dum modo, conj.* so long as, provided that; *modo* (*dum modo*) sets up a proviso clause that takes a subjunctive verb, here *intersit.*

mūrus, -ī, m. wall

versor (1) to live

Line 27: **diūtius,** *comp. adv.* longer; translate *iam diūtius nōn* "no longer" or "not anymore."

nōn feram . . . sinam: These words are not exactly synonymous, although each can have the meaning "to permit."

sinō, sinere, sīvī, situm to permit, allow

BY THE WAY

In line 27, *nōn feram . . . sinam*, note the TRICOLON, a figure of speech in which three words, phrases, or clauses are arranged in a particular order, often using ANAPHORA to mark off the set of three. Here, the three verbs are set in a row, each one beginning with the word *nōn*. The TRICOLON here, in which Cicero essentially says the same thing three times, effectively communicates his unwavering position that Catiline must leave Rome.

Lines 28–29: **magna . . . grātia:** Cicero has separated the adjective *magna* from the noun *grātia* in order to emphasize his gratitude. Here *magna* and *grātia* bracket the datives *dīs immortālibus* and *huic ipsī Iovī Statōrī, antīquissimō custōdī* as well as the verb *habenda est*. Note the HYPERBATON.

habenda est . . . grātia: *grātia* is the subject of the passive periphrastic verb *habenda est.* Translate *habenda est* "must be given."

dīs: dat./abl. pl. of *deus, deī,* m.

Stator, Statōris, m. the Stayer, Supporter (a name given to Jupiter)

Line 29: **custōs, custōdis,** m./f. guardian

taeter, taetra, taetrum loathsome, foul

īnfestus, -a, -um hostile, dangerous (+ *dat.*)

Line 30: **pestis, pestis,** f. plague, destruction

totiēns, *adv.* so many times

iam: with perfect tense as here, *iam* means "already"; with the present tense "now"; with the future tense "soon."

effūgimus: use the present perfect in English; translate "we have escaped."

TAKE NOTE

1. *Pergō* = *per* + *regō*. This information accounts for *perrēxī* and *perrēctum* in the third and fourth principal parts of the verb. *Regō* can mean "to direct the course of"; hence, *pergō* means to "direct one's course through, to go."

COMPREHENSION QUESTIONS

1. What two events does Cicero ask Catiline to recall? Cite the Latin.
2. What group of individuals does Cicero say are inside the Senate?
3. What seven things does Cicero say Catiline did at Laeca's house the night before last?
4. What were the two Roman knights supposed to do?
5. When did Cicero say he found out about what had happened at the meeting at Laeca's house? Cite the Latin.
6. What did Cicero do after he found out what had happened at the meeting?
7. What does Cicero say that he will not endure?

▶ EXERCISE 1

1. In line 1, what case and use is *mē* in the word *mēcum*?
2. What is the case and use of *mē* at the end of line 1?
3. In line 3, what is the case and use of *nocte*?
4. In line 3, what is the tense, voice, form, and use of *vēnisse*?
5. In line 5, what is the tense and mood of *convincam*?
6. In line 7, what is the case and use of *gentium*?
7. In line 8, what is the case and use of *patrēs cōnscrīptī*?
8. In line 9, what is the case and degree of *gravissimō*?
9. What is the tense, voice, and form of *trucīdārī* in line 11?
10. In line 12, what is the case and use of *vōce*?
11. In line 14, what is the tense, mood, and use of *placēret*?
12. In line 14, what is the case and use of *Rōmae*?
13. In line 15, what is the tense, voice, form, and use of *esse exitūrum*?
14. What is the case and use of *sē* in line 17?
15. What is the case and use of *haec* in line 19?
16. In line 20, what is the case and degree of *maiōribus*?
17. In line 21, what is the tense, voice, and mood of *mīserās*?

18. What is the tense, mood, and use of *vēnissent* in line 21?

19. What tense and form is *ēgredere* in line 23?

20. In line 26, what case and use is *metū*?

21. What noun does *taetram* (line 29) modify?

VOCABULARY BUILDER

When Cicero needs to repeat a thought, he often uses synonyms. Consider the groups of verbs below. What do the verbs in each group mean in English, and how are they similar in meaning?

Group A	Group B
pergō	ēgredior
eō	excēdō
sē cōnferō	exeō
	proficīscor

What do the words in this group mean? Are they synonyms?

existimō
cōgitō
putō
arbitror

LANGUAGE FACT

RELATIVE CLAUSES OF PURPOSE AND CHARACTERISTIC

Relative clauses are introduced by the relative pronoun *quī, quae, quod*.

If the information in the relative clause is descriptive, explanatory, or factual, the clause takes an indicative verb. See p. 26 for more examples of this type of relative clause.

> *Exclūsī eōs quōs tū ad mē . . . māne mīserās.* (Cicero *In Cat.* I 4.10.20–21)
> "I shut out those whom you had sent to me early in the morning."

If the clause includes more than simple description, the subjunctive may be used. Here are two types of relative clauses that take a subjunctive verb.

- **Relative Clauses of Purpose**

  Relative clauses of purpose explain the purpose why something was done, and frequently mean the same thing as purpose clauses with *ut/nē*.

  > *Repertī sunt duo equitēs Rōmānī quī tē istā cūrā līberārent.*
  >   (Cicero *In Cat.* I 4.9.16–17)
  > "Two Roman knights were found to free you from that care."
  >   (*lit.*, "who were to free you from that care.")

- **Relative Clauses of Characteristic**

Sometimes considered almost the equivalent of result clauses, these clauses describe a characteristic or quality of the antecedent that often is indefinite, negative, or modified by *sōlus* or *ūnus*.

> *Hīc, hīc sunt in nostrō numerō . . . quī dē huius urbis atque*
> *adeō dē orbis terrārum exitiō cōgitent.*
> (Cicero *In Cat.* I 4.9.8–10)
> "Here, here there are in our number those who think
> about the destruction of this city and even about the
> destruction of the world."

BY THE WAY

In line 20 of the text the supine *salūtātum* is used. A supine ending in *–m*, used after a verb of motion, is another way to express purpose in addition to gerunds and gerundives, relative purpose clauses, and *ut/nē* purpose clauses.

▶ EXERCISE 2

Translate these sentences and identify whether each sentence contains an explanatory, purpose, or characteristic relative clause.

1. In hōc orbis terrae sanctissimō gravissimōque cōnsiliō sunt quī dē nostrō omnium interitū cōgitent.

2. Nōndum vōce vulnerō illōs virōs quī ferrō trucīdārī dēbent.

3. Virī Rōmānī repertī sunt quī mē interficerent.

4. Hīc in senātū sunt eī quī dē cōnsulis exitiō cōgitent.

5. Virōs mīsī quī meam domum firmārent et mūnīrent.

6. Helvētiī Orgetorīgem quī eās rēs cōnficiat dēligunt.

7. Belgae quī ā cultū atque hūmānitāte prōvinciae longissimē absunt hōrum omnium fortissimī sunt.

8. Nam unguentum dabō quod meae puellae dōnārunt Venerēs Cupīdinēsque.

ESSAY

How does Cicero attempt to convince the members of the Senate without hard proof that Catiline is conspiring against the State?

Support your assertions with references drawn from the Latin passage. All Latin words must be copied or their line numbers provided, AND they must be translated or paraphrased closely enough so that it is clear you understand the Latin. Direct your answer to the question; do not merely summarize the passage. Please write your essay on a separate piece of paper.

Taken from the Palatine Hill, this photograph provides a comprehensive view of the Roman Forum from the House of the Vestals in the foreground, across the Forum to the Basilica Aemilia, to the Curia. The House of the Vestal Virgins is a large rectangular complex with an open courtyard, in the Roman fashion, at its center. Its foundations date from the time of the Republic, but it was rebuilt following the fire of 64 CE. At its edge, the white circular building is the Temple to Vesta. To the front of the temple are the brick remains of the Temple to the Deified Julius Caesar. The Basilica Aemilia frames the eastern edge of the Forum and it abuts the Senate House or Curia. The current brick building would have originally boasted polished marble coverings. When Cicero delivered his speeches denouncing Catiline, the Senate was meeting at the Temple of Jupiter Stator as it could be more readily defended.

READING 5

Beginning with this section, different fonts will no longer be used to highlight words that belong together. Words to be understood will continue to appear in parentheses in the Latin text. Check the notes for help with these types of issues.

Is it important to bear in mind that many senators learned about the conspiracy for the first time during the emergency meeting of the Senate when Cicero delivered the *First Catilinarian.* Cicero is claiming that the senators informed of the plot were afraid to let the others know they should be afraid. This claim is a ploy on Cicero's part.

In section 6 Cicero enumerates shameful deeds and crimes that he attributes to Catiline; the text below provides the culmination of the list of Catiline's misdeeds, his attempted assassination of Cicero both as consul-elect and as consul.

In section 7 the predominant theme is fear of Catiline. The senators both shun and fear him; the citizens fear him; and the common parent of all, the *patria* (personified here), fears him and, as a result of that fear, urges him to depart from Rome.

ALLEGED ATTEMPTS TO KILL CICERO; THE PERSONIFIED *PATRIA* SPEAKS

CICERO *IN CATILĪNAM* I 6.15–16; 7.16–18

1   **[6] [15]** . . . Ac iam illa omittō neque enim sunt aut obscūra, aut nōn multa (ā tē) commissa
posteā quotiēns tū mē dēsignātum (cōnsulem interficere cōnātus es), quotiēns vērō
cōnsulem interficere cōnātus es! Quot ego tuās petītiōnēs ita coniectās ut vītārī posse
nōn vidērentur parvā quādam dēclīnātiōne et, ut āiunt, corpore effūgī! Nihil agis, nihil
5   assequeris, neque tamen cōnārī ac velle dēsistis.

NOTES AND VOCABULARY

Line 1:   **omittō, omittere, omīsī, omissum** to leave out, pass over; note the PRETERITION.

neque . . . aut obscūra, aut nōn multa: equivalent to *et nōta et multa.*

obscūrus, -a, -um covered, concealed

nōn multa: translate "a few." This is a good example of LITOTES.

committō, committere, commīsī, commissum to commit

BY THE WAY

To include precisely what a speaker indicates he will not discuss, as Cicero does in 6.15, is a figure of speech known as *praeteritiō* or PRETERITION. This rhetorical figure provides a way of drawing attention to something important the speaker claims he will disregard.

Line 2: **posteā,** *adv.* later on, afterward

quotiēns, *exclamation* how often

dēsignātus, -a, -um elect; with *cōnsulem* translate "consul-elect."

cōnor, cōnārī, cōnātus sum to try

Line 3: **quot,** *indeclin. adv.* how many

ego: the subject of *effūgī* in line 4.

petītiō, petītiōnis, f. blow, attack

coniciō, conicere, coniēcī, coniectum to throw together, hurl; *ita coniectās ut*: "thrown together in such a way that . . ." The result clause ends with *vidērentur.*

vītō (1) to avoid, evade

BY THE WAY

In lines 3–4, *petītiōnēs . . . effūgī,* Cicero is using a fencing METAPHOR (a figure of speech in which a comparison is made without using the words "like" or "as") for how he escaped Catiline's attempts to kill him. *Petītiōnēs* are the thrusts, and the phrase *parvā quādam dēclīnātiōne et . . . corpore,* "with some little twist of the body," taken with *petītiōnēs,* suggests a dodge or sidestep. By inserting *ut aiunt,* Cicero is in effect apologizing for his using the METAPHOR, as if such a figure were not appropriate for such an important political speech. The fencing METAPHOR aptly suggests a "duel" of sorts that has been ongoing between Catiline and Cicero in which the senior consul has successfully escaped death by the thrust of a sharp blade (as, for example, the plot to kill him in his bed).

REMINDER

As noted on p. 52 in the Caesar chapter of this book, remember that *ut* with an indicative verb means "as," but as you have seen with purpose clauses and result clauses with a subjunctive verb it also means "so that, that."

Line 4: **dēclīnātiō, dēclīnātiōnis,** f. a bending; sidestep; note the HENDIADYS found in *dēclīnātiōne et . . . corpore.*

āiō, āis, āit, āiunt, *defective verb* to say

Line 5: **assequor, assequī, assecūtus sum** to accomplish, gain

REMINDER

As you saw on p. 98 in the Catullus chapter of this book, the verb *dēsistō* takes a complementary infinitive, which is translated with "–ing" instead of the more usual "to." Example: *dēsistēs excēdere* translates "you will stop leaving," not "you will stop to leave."

CICERO *IN CATILĪNAM* I 6.15–16; 7.16–18, CONTINUED

5   [16] Quotiēns iam tibi extorta est ista sīca

dē manibus, quotiēns excidit cāsū aliquō et ēlāpsa est! Quae quidem quibus abs tē initiāta

sacrīs ac dēvōta sit nesciō, quod eam necesse putās esse in cōnsulis corpore dēfīgere.

NOTES AND VOCABULARY

Line 5:   **tibi:** a dative of reference ("your") with *manibus* in line 6

               extorqueō, extorquēre, extorsī, extortum to wrest away, take by force

               sīca, -ae, f. dagger

STUDY TIP

Do not confuse these words that look very similar.

       casa, -ae, f. hut, cottage

       cāsus, cāsūs, m. chance, mishap, misfortune

       causa, -ae, f. reason

Line 6:   **excidō, excidere, excidī** to fall out, fall

               cāsus, cāsūs, m. chance, mishap, misfortune‡

               ēlābor, ēlābī, ēlāpsus sum to slip away, escape

               quae quidem quibus: note the ALLITERATION. The *quae* is a connecting relative with
                   its antecedent being *sīca*. *Quidem* is adverbial in force, meaning "indeed." The *quibus*
                   introduces an indirect question after the main verb *nesciō* and agrees with *sacrīs*. In English
                   word order, the sentence would read: *quidem nesciō quibus sacrīs ea (sīca) initiāta ac dēvōta sit*
                   abs tē.

               initiō (1) to initiate, consecrate

Line 7:   **dēvoveō, dēvovere, dēvōvī, dēvōtum** to devote, consecrate

               quod: translate "for this reason that."

               necesse, *indeclin. adj.* with *esse; necesse . . . esse:* "it is necessary"; indirect statement with *putās*

               dēfīgō, dēfīgere, dēfīxī, dēfīxum to plunge

Cicero informs the Senate of Manlius's plans to foment a rebellion using the old Etruscan settlement of Faesula as his staging grounds. Modern day Fiesole, set on a hill like many Etruscan towns, is quite close to Florence. Fiesole has maintained the archaeological site of Roman Faesula including the remains depicted as well as a theatre.

CICERO *IN CATILĪNAM* I 6.15–16; 7.16–18, CONTINUED

1   [**7**] Nunc vērō quae tua est ista vīta? Sīc enim iam tēcum loquar, nōn ut odiō permōtus esse videar, quō dēbeō (permōtus esse), sed ut misericordiā (permōtus esse videar) quae tibi nūlla (misericordia) dēbētur. Vēnistī paulō ante in senātum: quis tē ex hāc tantā frequentiā (salūtāvit), tot ex tuīs amīcīs ac necessāriīs salūtāvit? Sī hoc post hominum

5   memoriam contigit nēminī, vōcis exspectās contumēliam, cum sīs gravissimō iūdiciō taciturnitātis oppressus? Quid? Quod adventū tuō ista subsellia vacuēfacta sunt, quod omnēs cōnsulārēs, quī tibi persaepe ad caedem cōnstitūtī fuērunt, simul atque assēdistī, partem istam subselliōrum nūdam atque inānem relīquērunt, quō tandem animō tibi ferendum (esse) putās?

NOTES AND VOCABULARY

Line 1:   **loquor, loquī, locūtus sum** to speak, talk

         odium, -ī, n. hate, grudge

         permoveō, permovēre, permōvī, permōtum to arouse; *permōtus esse* is a perfect passive infinitive that is complementary to *videar.*

STUDY TIP

If the verb *dēbeō* takes an infinitive, it means "ought," which in today's speech usually is expressed by "should." If *dēbeō* does not govern an infinitive, it means "owe."

Line 2:   **dēbeō, dēbēre, dēbuī, dēbitum** to owe, ought

         misericordia, -ae, f. compassion, pity; *ut misericordiā* is elliptical for *ut misericordiā permōtus esse videar.*

Lines 2–3:   **quae . . . nūlla:** translate "none of which." By using *nulla* instead of *nōn*, Cicero gives emphasis to the fact that Catiline deserves no pity at all.

Line 3:   **paulō ante,** *adv.* a little while ago, shortly before

Line 4:   **frequentia, -ae,** f. crowd

         tot, *indeclin. num. adj.* so many, in such numbers

         necessārius, -ī, m. relative, client

         post: an expression of time; translate "within."

Line 5:   **contingō, contingere, contigī, contāctum** (+ *dat.*) to happen to

         nēmō, nēminī, nēminem no one, nobody; in classical Latin, *nēmō* is defective in the genitive and ablative cases, where *nullīus* is used for the genitive and *nullō/nullā* for the ablative.

         vōcis: translate "spoken" with *contumēliam* (*lit.*, "of the voice").

         contumēlia, -ae, f. reproach, insult

         iūdicium, -ī, n. judgment, sentence

Line 6:	**taciturnitās, taciturnitātis,** f. silence
	adventus, adventūs, m. approach, arrival
	subsellium, -ī, n. seat, bench
	vacuēfaciō, vacuēfacere, vacuēfēcī, vacuēfactum to make empty, vacate
Lines 6–9:	**quid? . . . putās?:** The two *quod* clauses are the subjects of *ferendum* (sc. *esse*) in line 9. The main verb, then, is the *putās* of line 9. There are (at least) two approaches to translation: (1) break up the three clauses into independent questions and translate the *Quid? Quod* as "what of the fact that" and the following *quod* likewise; or (2) start by translating the main clause and then translate the *quod* clauses, i.e., "Then, with what disposition do you think you ought to bear the fact that . . . ?"
Line 7:	**cōnsulāris, cōnsulāre** of consular rank, consular
	tibi: dative of agent with a perfect passive participle (i.e., *cōnstitūtī*), similar to the dative of agent in a passive periphrastic.
	persaepe, *adv.* very often
	cōnstituō, cōnstituere, cōnstituī, cōnstitūtum to designate; the form *cōnstitūtī fuērunt* is not in most grammar books since the usual perfect passive is *cōnstitūtī sunt*. Cicero may have liked the rhythm of this form better, but there is difference in meaning as well. The combination of the perfect form of *esse* and perfect participle as a predicate adjective emphasizes the completion of the action. In other words, Catiline designated certain Roman citizens for death many times already, but he failed to have them killed; thus, he presumably no longer poses that sort of threat.
	simul atque, *conj.* as soon as
	assīdō, assīdere, assēdī to sit down
Line 8:	**nūdus, -a, -um** bare
	inānis, ināne empty
Line 9:	**ferō, ferre, tulī, lātum** to endure; *ferendum* with the omission of the infinitive *esse* is a passive periphrastic within an indirect statement. Translate *ferendum esse* "it must be endured."

10 [17] Servī mēhercule meī sī mē istō pactō metuerent ut tē metuunt omnēs cīvēs tuī, (mihi) domum meam relinquendam (esse) putārem: tū tibi urbem (relinquendam esse) nōn arbitrāris? Et sī mē meīs cīvibus iniūriā suspectum tam graviter atque offēnsum vidērem, carēre mē aspectū cīvium quam īnfestīs omnium oculīs cōnspicī māllem: tū, cum cōnscientiā scelerum tuōrum agnōscās odium omnium iūstum et iam diū tibi dēbitum,

15 dubitās quōrum mentēs sēnsūsque vulnerās, eōrum aspectum praesentiamque vītāre? Sī tē parentēs timērent atque ōdissent tuī neque eōs ūllā ratiōne plācāre possēs, ut opīnor, ab eōrum oculīs aliquō concēderes. Nunc tē patria, quae commūnis est parēns omnium nostrum, ōdit ac metuit et iam diū nihil tē iūdicat nisi dē parricīdiō suō cōgitāre: huius tū neque auctōritātem verēbēre nec iūdicium sequēre nec vim pertimēscēs?

NOTES AND VOCABULARY

Line 10:   **mēhercule,** *interjection* by Hercules!

sī, *conj.* if; *sī* begins a contrary to fact present conditional sentence; translate "if my slaves feared . . . " (which they do not).

istō pactō: translate "in that way."

metuō, metuere, metuī to fear, be afraid of

Line 11:   **relinquō, relinquere, relīquī, relictum** to leave; *domum meam relinquendam* is an indirect statement dependent on *putārem*. With *relinquendam,* understand the missing infinitive *esse. Relinquendam esse* is a passive periphrastic within the indirect statement. Translate this phrase "that my house must be abandoned."

tibi: dative of agent with *relinquendam esse,* which must be understood here.

Line 12:   **arbitror, arbitrārī, arbitrātus esse** to think; this synonym of *putō* sets up a second indirect statement with *relinquendam esse* left out by ELLIPSIS. *Tū . . . arbitrāris* is parallel in thought to *(mihi) . . . putārem.*

sī . . . vidērem: a present contrary to fact condition; *vidērem* sets up the indirect statement that begins with the accusative subject *mē* and the understood infinitive (*esse*) that is completed by *offēnsum.*

meīs cīvibus: a dative of agent with the participle *suspectum.*

iniūriā: translate "wrongly, unjustly."

suspectus, -a, -um suspected

offēnsus, -a, -um disliked, offensive

Line 13:   **careō, carēre, caruī** (+ *abl.*) to be without, go without

aspectus, aspectūs, m. seeing, sight, view

quam: translate "rather than," because of the implied comparison in *māllem.*

īnfestus, -a, -um hostile, dangerous

cōnspiciō, cōnspicere, cōnspexī, cōnspectum to look at

mālō, mālle, māluī to prefer

cum: when, since, although; here *cum* introduces a concessive clause and so translate "although."

Line 14: **cōnscientiā:** ablative of means. To the Romans, *cōnscientiā* meant "common knowledge" and did not imply the modern sense of "guilty conscience."

agnōscō, agnōscere, agnōvī, agnitum to recognize, acknowledge

iūstus, -a, -um just, right

Line 15: **dubitō** (1) to hesitate, doubt; translate *dubitās* "do you hesitate." When *dubitō* takes an infinitive, it usually means "to hesitate."

quōrum . . . eōrum: in English the antecedent (here *eōrum*) usually precedes the relative pronoun (here *quōrum*), but in Latin the relative clause often precedes the antecedent. Translate the main clause first and then the relative clause.

praesentia, -ae, f. presence

Line 16: **ōdī, ōdisse,** *defective verb used only in the perfect tenses* to hate; the verb is perfect in form, but translated as if present tense. *Ōdī* means "I hate."

ūllus, -a, -um any

ratiō, ratiōnis, f. way, manner

plācō (1) to soothe, appease

opīnor (1) to suppose

Line 17: **aliquō,** *adv.* to somewhere, somewhere

concēdō, concēdere, concessī, concessum to retreat

nunc, *adv.* now; translate "as it is now."

Line 18: **tē . . . cōgitāre:** *tē* is the subject of *cōgitāre* in indirect statement.

iūdicō (1) to decide, judge

nisi except

parricīdium, -ī, n. murder, parricide

huius: refers to *patria* (line 17). A common use of *hic, haec, hoc* is to connect two sentences and thus show that there is a common theme in both.

Line 19: **vereor, verērī, veritus sum** to fear, respect; *verēbēre* is second person, future, deponent.

pertimēscō, pertimēscere, pertimuī to become alarmed at, fear

BY THE WAY

The use of the word *parricīdium* in line 18 is particularly appropriate here since Cicero is personifying the fatherland, describing it as the common parent of all. PERSONI-FICATION is a figure of speech in which human qualities are attributed to inanimate objects. PROSOPOPEIA (the Greek term) in some instances is used as a synonym for PERSONIFICATION; in other instances it refers to the representation of an absent or deceased person as present and speaking. Here Cicero uses the personified fatherland to provide variety in reiterating a principal theme of the speech, that Catiline must leave Rome, and to appeal to the emotions of the senators as he tries to persuade them of the danger posed by Catiline.

20   [18] Quae tēcum, Catilīna, sīc agit et quōdam modō tacita loquitur: "Nūllum iam aliquot
annīs facinus exstitit nisi per tē, nūllum flāgitium (exstitit) sine tē; tibi ūnī multōrum
cīvium necēs (impūnītae fuērunt ac līberae), tibi vexātiō dīreptiōque sociōrum impūnīta
fuit ac lībera; tū nōn sōlum ad neglegendās lēgēs et quaestiōnēs vērum etiam ad
ēvertendās perfringendāsque (lēgēs et quaestiōnēs) valuistī. Superiōra illa, quamquam

25   ferenda nōn fuērunt, tamen ut potuī tulī; nunc vērō mē tōtam esse in metū propter ūnum
tē, quicquid increpuerit, Catilīnam timērī, nūllum vidērī contrā mē cōnsilium inīrī posse
quod ā tuō scelere abhorreat, nōn est ferendum. Quam ob rem discēde atque hunc mihi
timōrem ēripe; sī est vērus (timor), nē opprimar, sīn falsus (timor), ut tandem aliquandō
timēre dēsinam."

NOTES AND VOCABULARY

Line 20:   **quae:** Here *quae* is a connecting relative that refers to *patria* and is to be translated as "she."
Note the HYPERBOLE throughout the speech.

tēcum . . . agit: "pleads with you."‡

quōdam modō: after a manner, so to speak

taceō, tacēre, tacuī, tacitum to be silent, be quiet

aliquot, *indeclin. adj.* some, several

BY THE WAY

OXYMORON is a figure of speech that combines contradictory terms. In other words, although silent, the fatherland after a manner (*quōdam modō*) is speaking. Cicero may also be playing on the silence of the senators themselves. The OXYMORON draws attention to the PERSONIFICATION of the *patria*.

Line 21:   **annīs:** ablative of time within which

facinus, facinoris, n. deed, crime, outrage

exsistō, exsistere, exstitī to appear, arise

flāgitium, -ī, n. deed of shame, outrage, disgrace

tibi ūnī: "for you alone"

Line 22:   **nex, necis,** f. murder; *necēs . . . dīreptiōque: necēs* alludes to Catiline's involvement in the proscriptions of Sulla, 82 BCE; *vexātiō dīreptiōque* refer to Catiline's propraetorship in Africa, 67 BCE, after which he was tried for extorting the province.

vexātiō, vexātiōnis, f. harassing

dīreptiō, dīreptiōnis, f. plundering, pillaging

impūnītus, -a, -um unpunished, unchecked

Line 23:   **quaestiō, quaestiōnis,** f. trial, court

Line 24: **ēvertō, ēvertere, ēvertī, ēversum** to overthrow

perfringō, perfringere, perfrēgī, perfractum to break down

valeō, valēre, valuī, valitum to be strong, be able; *valēre ad:* translate "to succeed at."

superiōra, n. pl. the aforementioned, the foregoing

Line 25: **ferenda . . . fuērunt:** "ought to have . . . ." The past tense of a passive periphrastic is similar in translation to *oportēbat.*

ut potuī: translate "as best I could."

ferō, ferre, tulī, lātum to bear, tolerate

nunc vērō: "but now." The adverb *nunc* indicates that the fatherland is turning to the present situation, and *vērō* emphasizes the difference between now and the previous times.

Lines 25–27: This is a very difficult sentence. The infinitives with their accusative subjects, *mē esse, Catilīnam timērī,* and *cōnsilium vidērī* are serving as the subjects of the passive periphrastic *nōn est ferendum. Vidērī* ("seem"), in turn, governs the infinitive *posse,* whose meaning is completed by *inīrī. Quod . . . abhorreat* modifies *cōnsilium.* One might translate somewhat literally: "Now truly it must not be tolerated that I (the *patria*) . . . ."

Line 26: **increpō, increpāre, increpuī, increpitum** to rattle, sound, make a noise; *quicquid incrēpuerit* is an adverbial clause that literally means "at whatever made a noise"; translate "at every sound."

ineō, inīre, iniī, initum to enter into; to attempt

Line 27: **scelus, sceleris,** n. wickedness, crime

abhorreō, abhorrēre, abhorruī to be inconsistent with (+ *ab* + *abl.*)

ferendum: In Latin, when a verb is to be construed with two or more subjects separately, as here, the verb is in the singular. Compare lines 22–23: *tibi vexātiō dīreptiōque sociōrum impūnīta fuit ac lībera.*

quam ob rem: and for this reason, therefore (*lit.,* "on account of this thing"); *quam* is a connecting relative.

discēdō, discēdere, discessī, discessum to depart, leave

mihi: "from me." The dative of separation ("from") is used with a person instead of the ablative, the case that would be expected to indicate separation.

Line 28: **ēripiō, ēripere, ēripuī, ēreptum** to snatch away

vērus . . . falsus: both modify an implied *timor.*

vērus, -a, -um well-founded, justifiable, true

opprimō, opprimere, oppressī, oppressum to oppress, suppress, crush

sīn, *conj.* but if, if on the contrary

aliquandō, *adv.* at some time

Lines 28–29: **nē opprimar . . . ut . . . dēsinam:** both purpose clauses depend upon the main verb, *ēripe.*

Line 29: **dēsinō, dēsinere, dēsiī, dēsitum** to cease, stop

TAKE NOTE

1. The noun *cāsus, cāsūs,* m. "misfortune" comes from the fourth principal part of *cadō, cadere, cecidī, cāsum* "to fall, befall, happen." What befalls someone may be a mishap or misfortune. When a soldier falls in battle, he may die, and so "die" is another meaning of *cadō.* This verb should not be confused with *caedō, caedere, cecīdī, caesum* "to cut, kill." From *cadō* comes the compound verb *excidō, excidere, excidī* "to fall, fall out."

2. The verb *agō, agere, ēgī, āctum* has a general meaning of "do," but can also signify "drive, discuss, plead, live," and "spend," in addition to having many other meanings that depend on context.

COMPREHENSION QUESTIONS

1. List at least one thing that Cicero says he will leave out but then adds in. Cite the Latin.
2. What happened when Catiline first came into the Senate?
3. What happened when Catiline sat down? Cite the Latin.
4. What does Cicero suggest that Catiline should do since the citizens fear him?
5. What does Cicero say that Catiline recognizes due to the common knowledge of his crimes?
6. According to Cicero, what is the one thing the country says Catiline is thinking about?
7. According to the country, who has been committing all the crimes recently?
8. What does Cicero on behalf of the country ask Catiline to do at the end of this passage? Cite the Latin.

▶ EXERCISE 1
SECTION 6

1. In line 1, what is the case and use of *illa*?
2. In line 3, what is the tense and form of *vītārī*?
3. What tense is *assequeris* in line 5?
4. In line 5, what tense, voice, and mood is *extorta est*?
5. In line 6, what is the case and use of *cāsū*?

SECTION 7

1. In line 1, what is the tense and mood of *loquar*?
2. What is the case and use of *odiō* in line 1?
3. In line 2, what is the case and use of *quō*?
4. In line 4, what is the case and use of *frequentiā*?
5. What is the tense and mood of *contigit* in line 5?
6. In line 7, what is the case and use of *cōnsulārēs*?
7. In line 10, what is the tense and mood of *metuerent*?
8. What part of speech and degree is *graviter* in line 12?
9. In line 13, what is the tense, voice, and form of *cōnspicī*?
10. What is the tense and mood of *māllem* in line 13?
11. In line 14, what is the tense and mood of *agnōscās*?

12. In line 15, what is the case and use of *mentēs*?

13. In line 16, what is the case and use of *parentēs*?

14. What is the case and use of *ratiōne* in line 16?

15. What is the tense and voice of *pertimēscēs* in line 19?

16. *Nūllum* in line 21 modifies what word in the sentence?

17. In line 21, what case is *ūnī*?

18. In line 22, what is the case and use of *vexātiō*?

19. In line 27, what is the tense, voice, and form of *discēde*?

20. In line 28, what type of clause contains *opprimar*?

LANGUAGE FACT

PARALLELISM, ELLIPSIS (GAPPING), AND WORDS TO BE UNDERSTOOD

- **Parallel Expressions and Words**

  Parallel expressions are characteristic of Cicero's style of writing, in which he often uses periodic sentences. A periodic sentence is a long sentence in which the main idea is delayed until the end after a series of related thoughts. The balancing of nouns, adjectives, verbs, or whole clauses lends greater emphasis and complexity to the main thought. The "parallel expressions" may be adjectives modifying the same noun or adverbs modifying the same verb, or parallel prepositional phrases, infinitives, or even clauses. The words that exemplify parallelism are in bold font below.

Parallel Prepositional Phrases

> *Quis tē **ex hāc tantā frequentiā, tot ex tuīs amīcīs ac necessāriīs** salūtāvit?*
>   (Cicero *In Cat.* I 7.16.3–4)
> "Who greeted you **from this so great a crowd, from so many of your friends and clients?**"

Parallel Adjectives Modifying the Same Noun

> *Agnōscis **odium** omnium **iūstum** et iam diū tibi **dēbitum**.*
>   (based on Cicero *In Cat.* I 7.17.14)
> "You recognize that the **hatred** of all is **just** and already for a long time **owed** to you."

Parallel Clauses

> ***sī est vērus**, nē opprimar, **sīn falsus**, ut tandem aliquandō timēre dēsinam.* (Cicero *In Cat.* I 7.18.28–29)
> "**If it** (the fear) **is true**, so that I may not be oppressed, but **if false**, so that finally at sometime I may stop being afraid."

STUDY TIP

If you see in a Latin sentence the phrase *nōn sōlum . . . sed (vērum) etiam* ("not only . . . but also"), look for parallelism in the text.

> *tū **nōn sōlum ad neglegendās** lēgēs et quaestiōnēs **vērum etiam ad ēvertendās perfringendās**que valuistī.* (Cicero *In Cat.* I 7.18.23–24)
> "You succeeded **not only at neglecting** the laws and trials **but also at overthrowing and breaking** them down."

- ### Ellipsis

Ellipsis, defined earlier on p. 18 and p. 28, sometimes called gapping, is the absence of one or more common elements (i.e., word or phrase) in one of two or more clauses. The absent element is needed to complete the thought of one or more clauses in the sentence. Note in the following example that the parallelism of *ut odiō* with *ut misericordiā* sets up the Ellipsis of *permōtus esse videar*.

> *Tēcum loquar, nōn ut odiō permōtus esse videar, . . . ut misericordiā* (***permōtus esse videar***). (Cicero *In Cat.* I 7.16.1–2)
> "I will speak with you not so that I seem to have been moved by hatred, but (**so that I seem to have been moved**) by pity."

Since Ellipsis occurs in English as well as in Latin, it is necessary to supply the absent words only when the English translation requires it. In the example above it is not necessary to supply "so that I may seem to have been moved" since these words are to be understood by Ellipsis in English also. Now consider this example.

> *Quid proximā (**nocte ēgeris**), quid superiōre nocte ēgeris . . .* (Cicero *In Cat.* I 1.6–7)
> "What (**you did**) last (**night**), what you did the night before last . . ."

In this sentence it is necessary to supply in English the ellipsed words "you did" and "last" because without them the English does not make sense.

- ### Words to Be Understood

In sentences without more than one clause, there may also still be a word to be understood.

> *Quō tandem animō tibi ferendum (**esse**) putās?* (Cicero *In Cat.* I 7.16.8–9)
> "With what disposition, then, do you think that it must (**be**) endured by you?"

In the above example, the word to be supplied is *esse*. The words that most often need to be understood in Latin are forms of the verb "to be." Other words that are frequently absent are prepositions (especially in poetry). Look at this example.

> *Nam plēbēs paene servōrum habētur (**in**) locō.* (Caesar *Dē bellō Gallicō* 6.13)
> "For the plebeians are considered in place almost of slaves."

BY THE WAY

Sometimes PARALLELISM, ELLIPSIS, and a word(s) to be understood can all be seen in one sentence. In the example below, *esse* is a word to be understood, *relinquendam esse* is absent by ELLIPSIS, and the parallel expressions are *servī . . . meī* with *omnēs cīvēs*, *domum meam* with *urbem*, and *putārem* with *arbitrāris*.

> *Servī mehercule meī sī mē istō pactō metuerent ut tē metuunt omnēs*
> *cīvēs tuī, domum meam relinquendam* (**esse**) *putārem: tū tibi urbem*
> **(relinquendam esse)** *nōn arbitrāris?* (Cicero *In Cat.* I 7.17.10–12)
> "My slaves, by Hercules, if they were to fear me in that way as all
> your citizens fear you, I would think that my house must be left:
> do you not think that the city **must be left** by you?"

▶ EXERCISE 2

Translate each sentence; identify parallel expression(s), ellipsis, and words to be understood. There may be more than one identification to be made per sentence.

1. Servī mehercule meī nōn mē ōdērunt ut tē omnēs cīvēs.

2. Dubitās nōn sōlum eōrum aspectum sed etiam praesentiam vītāre?

3. Nūllum iam aliquot annīs facinus exstitit nisi per tē, nūllum flagitium sine tē.

4. Sī tē tuī parentēs timērent, domum tuam relinquendam arbitrārer.

5. Auctoritās sequenda et iūdicium pertimēscendum.

6. Simul atque assēdistī, omnēs cōnsulārēs nōn sōlum partem istam subselliōrum nūdam atque inānem reliquērunt vērum etiam discessērunt.

7. Quotiēns tū mē dēsignātum, quotiēns cōnsulem interficere cōnātus es.

8. Carēre mē aspectū cīvium quam īnfestīs omnium oculīs cōnspicī mālō.

9. Tibi multōrum cīvium necēs, tibi vexātiō dīreptiōque sociōrum impūnīta fuit ac lībera.

ESSAY

How does Cicero set the stage for the introduction of the *patria* through the themes of speech, silence, and fear, and what is his purpose in having the fatherland address Catiline?

Support your assertions with references drawn from the Latin passage. All Latin words must be copied or their line numbers provided, AND they must be translated or paraphrased closely enough so that it is clear you understand the Latin. Direct your answer to the question; do not merely summarize the passage. Please write your essay on a separate piece of paper.

READING 6

The last section of the speech contains Cicero's final appeal to Catiline to leave Rome, taking his followers with him. This is necessary for the continued health of the Republic. Cicero closes with an appeal to Jupiter Stator for protection.

The rest of the Cicero passages in this book will no longer feature words to be understood in parentheses. Use the notes below the passage to help you.

CICERO'S FINAL APPEAL TO CATILINE

CICERO *IN CATILĪNAM* I 13.31–33

1　**[13] [31]** Etenim iam diū, patrēs cōnscrīptī, in hīs perīculīs coniūrātiōnis insidiīsque versāmur, sed nesciō quō pactō omnium scelerum ac veteris furōris et audāciae mātūritās in nostrī cōnsulātūs tempus ērūpit. Hōc sī ex tantō latrōciniō iste ūnus tollētur, vidēbimur fortasse ad breve quoddam tempus cūrā et metū esse relevātī, perīculum autem residēbit

5　et erit inclūsum penitus in vēnīs atque in vīsceribus reī pūblicae. Ut saepe hominēs aegrī morbō gravī, cum aestū febrīque iactantur, sī aquam gelidam bibērunt, prīmō relevātī videntur, deinde multō gravius vehementiusque afflictantur, sīc hic morbus quī est in rē pūblicā relevātus istīus poenā vehementius reliquīs vīvīs ingravēscet.

NOTES AND VOCABULARY

Line 1:　**etenim,** *adv.* and indeed, and really

insidiae, -ārum, f. pl. ambush; trap, plot

Line 2:　**versor** (1) to live, dwell

nesciō quō pactō: although literally *nesciō quō pactō* means "I do not know how," the phrase was used so often that it came to mean "somehow."

vetus, veteris long-established, old

furor, furōris, m. madness, insanity

mātūritās, mātūritātis, f. ripeness, maturity

Line 3:　**in . . . tempus:** the accusative after *in*, here translated "into," when taken closely with *mātūritās* and *ērūpit*, seems to suggest that the conspiracy was destined to break out during Cicero's consulship.

cōnsulātus, cōnsulātūs, m. consulship

ērumpō, ērumpere, ērūpī, ēruptum to break out, rush out

latrōcinium, -ī, n. band of robbers

tollō, tollere, sustulī, sublātum to destroy, wipe out

Line 4:　**fortasse,** *adv.* perhaps

ad breve quoddam tempus: *ad* is used in some idiomatic expressions of time. Here translate *ad* "for."

relevō (1) to relieve, ease; *relevātī esse* is complementary to *vidēbimur* in line 3.

resideō, residēre, resēdī to stay behind, be left

Line 5:   **penitus,** *adv.* deep, deeply

vēna, -ae, f. vein, artery

vīscus, vīsceris, n. (*usually pl.*) internal organs, vitals

ut with the indicative verb *videntur* translates "as" and begins a SIMILE.

aeger, aegra, aegrum sick

BY THE WAY

A SIMILE is a figure of speech in which an analogy or comparison is made using a word for "like" or "as." The SIMILE of an illness in lines 5–8 (*ut . . . ingravēscet*) enables Cicero to elaborate on his PERSONIFICATION of the Republic from the previous sentence and to express metaphorically why Catiline must leave Rome and take all his supporters with him.

Line 6:   **morbus, -ī,** m. disease

cum: note that *cum* is a conjunction here and not a preposition.

aestus, aestūs, m. heat, glow; note the HENDIADYS in *aestū febrīque*. Translate "by or because of the heat of fever."

febris, febris, f. fever; *febrī* is the ablative of a third declension *i*-stem.

iactō (1) to throw about, hurl, torment

gelidus, -a, -um very cold, icy

bibō, bibere, bibī, bibitum to drink

prīmō, *adv.* at first, in the beginning

Line 7:   **afflictō** (1) to distress, torment

Line 8:   **istīus:** refers to Catiline

poenā: ablative of means with *relevātus*

reliquīs vīvīs: ablative absolute with conditional force. Translate as if *sī reliquī erunt vīvī*.

ingravēscō, ingravēscere, *defective verb* to worsen, become aggravated

[32] Quā rē sēcēdant improbī, sēcernant sē ā bonīs, ūnum in locum congregentur, mūrō
10 dēnique, quod saepe iam dīxī, sēcernantur ā nōbīs; dēsinant īnsidiārī domī suae cōnsulī,
circumstāre tribūnal praetōris urbānī, obsidēre cum gladiīs cūriam, malleolōs et facēs ad
īnflammandam urbem comparāre; sit dēnique īnscrīptum in fronte ūnīus cūiusque quid
dē rē pūblicā sentiat. Polliceor hoc vōbīs, patrēs cōnscrīptī, tantam in nōbīs cōnsulibus
fore dīligentiam, tantam in vōbīs auctōritātem, tantam in equitibus Rōmānīs virtūtem,
15 tantam in omnibus bonīs cōnsēnsiōnem ut Catilīnae profectiōne omnia patefacta,
illūstrāta, oppressa, vindicāta esse videātis.

NOTES AND VOCABULARY

Line 9:   **quā rē:** and for this reason, therefore

    sēcēdō, sēcēdere, sēcessī, sēcessum to withdraw, go away

    improbus, -a, -um wicked, base, shameless; with *improbī* understand *hominēs*.

    sēcernō, sēcernere, sēcrēvī, sēcrētum to separate, set apart

    congregō (1) to assemble

Line 10:   **quod:** translate "as" (*lit.,* "a thing which"). The relative pronoun *quod* must be referring to the whole situation suggested by *murō . . . sēcernantur* since the neuter *quod* cannot have the masculine *murus* as its antecedent.

    dēsinō, dēsinere, dēsiī, dēsitum to cease, stop; *dēsinant* must be understood with *īnsidiārī* (line 10), *circumstāre* (line 11), *obsīdere* (line 11), and *comparāre* (line 12). This is a good example of ELLIPSIS.

    insidior (1) (+ *dat.*) to lie in wait for, plot against

    domī suae: locative case; translate "in his home," i.e., Cicero's.

    cōnsulī: object of the verb *īnsidiārī* that takes a dative object.

Line 11:   **circumstāre . . . cūriam:** *circumstāre* is complementary to *dēsinant*; this tribunal and the Curia were in the Forum. Catiline's men had surrounded these places to intimidate those not involved in the conspiracy. In the following lines Cicero further suggests that an armed attack on the administrative center for Rome's government would be completely foolish.

    tribūnal, tribūnālis, n. platform

    urbānus, -a, -um of the city, urban

    obsīdeō, obsīdēre, obsēdī, obsessum to besiege; lie in wait for

    cūria, -ae, f. the Senate house

    malleolus, -ī, m. small hammer; firebrand; a *malleolus* was the ancient equivalent of a Molotov cocktail. In Rome, a *malleolus* was a hollowed-out wooden hammer filled with a loose cloth that had been soaked in sap. The cloth and sap were lit before being thrown.

    fax, facis, f. torch, firebrand

Line 12: **īnflammō** (1) to set on fire

comparō (1) to collect

īnscrībō, īnscrībere, īnscrīpsī, īnscrīptum to write upon

frōns, frontis, f. forehead; *in fronte* is an allusion to the branding on the forehead of runaway slaves, but here the mark would not necessarily be one of shame.

Lines 12–13: **quid . . . sentiat:** the indirect question is the subject of *sit . . . īnscrīptum*.

Lines 13–16: **polliceor . . . videātis:** Note the ALLITERATION, ANAPHORA, and CLIMAX.

BY THE WAY

The CLIMAX is the highpoint of an argument following a CRESCENDO in which words or phrases are gradually built in order of importance or intensity. The CLIMAX and CRESCENDO seem particularly appropriate at this point of the speech since Cicero is completing his address to the Roman senators before his final appeal to Catiline to leave the city and his prayer to Jupiter Stator for protection and retribution.

Line 14: **fore:** the contracted form of *futūram esse* in the indirect statement that is dependent on *polliceor*.

dīligentia, -ae, f. attention, energy

virtūs, virtūtis, f. courage

Line 15: **bonīs:** understand *hominibus* with *bonīs*.

cōnsēnsiō, cōnsēnsiōnis, f. agreement, unanimity

profectiō, profectiōnis, f. departure, a setting out

patefaciō, patefacere, patefēcī, patefactum to lay open; disclose

Line 16: **illūstrō** (1) to make clear

opprimō, opprimere, oppressī, oppressum to crush

vindicō (1) to punish

STUDY TIP

Carefully distinguish between *ōmen, ōminis,* n. sign, harbinger and *omnis, omne* all.

CICERO *IN CATILĪNAM* I 13.31–33, CONTINUED

[33] Hīsce ōminibus, Catilīna, cum summā reī pūblicae salūte, cum tuā peste ac perniciē cumque eōrum exitiō quī sē tēcum omnī scelere parricīdiōque iūnxērunt, proficīscere ad impium bellum ac nefārium. Tū, Iuppiter, quī īsdem quibus haec urbs
20 auspiciīs ā Rōmulō es cōnstitūtus, quem Statōrem huius urbis atque imperī vērē nōmināmus, hunc et huius sociōs ā tuīs cēterīsque templīs, ā tēctīs urbis ac moenibus, ā vītā fortūnīsque cīvium omnium arcēbis et hominēs bonōrum inimīcōs, hostēs patriae, latrōnēs Italiae, scelerum foedere inter sē ac nefāriā societāte coniūnctōs, aeternīs suppliciīs vīvōs mortuōsque mactābis.

NOTES AND VOCABULARY

Line 17:   **hīsce:** *–ce* is an intensive suffix added to forms of *hic, haec, hoc.*

ōmen, ōminis, n. sign, harbinger; *hīsce ōminibus* answers the question "how," i.e., translate "with." The omens to which Cicero refers are both the words of his speech and those of the prayer that follows.

summā reī pūblicae salūte: "the very existence of the state"

Lines 17–18:   **cum . . . cum . . . cumque eōrum exitiō:** "attended by." Technically these are ablatives of attendant circumstance. Take the repeated prepositional *cum* phrases after *proficīscere ad impium bellum ac nefārium.* By openly going to war, Catiline will serve the "highest welfare of the state."

Line 18:   **perniciēs, perniciēī,** f. destruction, ruin

exitium, -ī, n. destruction, ruin

parricīdium, -ī, n. murder, parricide

Line 19:   **impius, -a, -um** irreverent, wicked, shameless

nefārius, -a, -um unspeakable, wicked

Lines 19–24:   **tū . . . mactābis:** Cicero is addressing the statue of Jupiter Stator. Speeches in the Senate often closed with a prayer.

BY THE WAY

The pronoun or adjective *īdem, eadem, idem* followed by *ac* or a form of *quī* may signify "the same . . . as."

Lines 19–20:   **quī īsdem quibus . . . es cōnstitūtus:** Two highly elliptical clauses; translate as if they were written *quī es cōnstitūtus ā Rōmulō īsdem auspiciīs quibus haec urbs cōnstitūta est.* Translate *es cōnstitūtus* "were consecrated" and *īsdem . . . quibus* "same . . . as."

Line 20:   **auspicium, -ī,** n. sign, omen

cōnstituō, cōnstituere, cōnstituī, cōnstitūtum to worship, consecrate, establish

Stator, Statōris, m. the Stayer, the Supporter (a name given to Jupiter)

Line 21: **nōminō** (1) to name, call

tēctum, -ī, n. roof

moenia, moenium, n. pl. ramparts, walls of a city‡

BY THE WAY

SYNECDOCHE is a figure of speech in which a part of something is used to represent the whole, or the whole is used to represent a part. Here "the roof" is part of a house, and thus by SYNECDOCHE, *tēctum* (line 21), "roof," is used to mean "house." SYNECDOCHE allows writers to expand their vocabulary by using a variety of words for a specific object.

Line 22: **vītā:** translate in the plural, "lives."

Lines 22–24: **arcēbis ... mactābis:** Cicero's confidence in the outcome is reflected in the future indicative, rather than potential subjunctive.

arceō, arcēre, arcuī to keep (someone/something in the accusative) away from (*ab* + something/someone in the ablative)

inimīcus, -ī, m. enemy‡

hostis, hostis, m. enemy

hominēs ... mactābis: note that in lines 22–24 *hominēs* has three noun phrases in apposition, *bonōrum inimīcōs, hostēs patriae,* and *latrōnēs Italiae,* and is modified by the participle *coniūnctōs,* and the adjectives *vīvōs mortuōsque. Hominēs* is the direct object of *mactābis.*

Line 23: **latrō, latrōnis,** m. thief, robber

foedus, foederis, n. treaty, alliance, contract

societās, societātis, f. association

Line 24: **supplicium, -ī,** n. punishment, penalty

mactō (1) to afflict, vex

TAKE NOTE

1. The Latin words *mūrus, -ī,* m. and *moenia, moenium,* n. pl. are synonyms; both signify the walls of a city. *Pariēs, pariētis,* f., on the other hand, refers to a wall of a house or building.

2. The word *inimīcus* refers to a personal enemy while *hostis* connotes an enemy of the state or of the country.

COMPREHENSION QUESTIONS

1. According to Cicero, in the midst of what two things are he and the senators living? Cite the Latin.

2. Why does Cicero say that even if Catiline were destroyed it would not help?

3. What does Cicero say temporarily relieves the effect of fever?

4. What does Cicero say will grow worse even if Catiline is punished?

5. List at least one thing Cicero wants all the wicked people to do. Cite the Latin.

6. List at least one thing Cicero says Jupiter will do.

▶ EXERCISE 1

1. In line 1, what is the case and use of *patrēs cōnscrīptī*?

2. Name the condition in lines 3–5.

3. What is the case and use of *cūrā* in line 4?

4. What is the tense, voice, and form of *esse relevātī* in line 4?

5. What is the case and use of *aestū* in line 6?

6. In line 6, what is the tense, voice, and form of *relevātī*?

7. In line 7, what is the case and use of *multō*?

8. What part of speech and what degree is *gravius* in line 7?

9. In line 8, what is the case and use of *poenā*?

10. In line 9, what is the case and use of *bonīs*?

11. In lines 11–12, what is the grammatical construction of *ad inflammandam urbem*?

12. What is the tense and mood of *polliceor* in line 13?

13. What is the uncontracted form of *fore* in line 14?

14. In line 16, what is the tense, voice, and form of *vindicāta esse*?

15. In line 19, what is the tense and form of *proficīscere*?

16. In line 20, what is the tense, voice, and mood of *es cōnstitūtus*?

17. In line 20, what case is *imperī*?

VOCABULARY BUILDER

In Latin, as in most languages, there are many words that have similar meanings but not precisely the same connotation. For each pair of words below, explain the similarity and difference in meaning.

1. hostis   inimīcus

2. malleolus   fax

3. moenia   pariēs

4. tēctum   domus

5. rēs pūblica   patria

Other words in Latin are more synonymous to one another. What meaning does each pair below share?

1. supplicium   poena

2. perniciēs   exitium

3. patefaciō   illūstrō

4. improbus   nefārius

5. timeō   metuō

6. auspicium   ōmen

LANGUAGE FACT

THE VOLITIVE USE OF THE PRESENT SUBJUNCTIVE

In Catullus's Poem 8, the present subjunctive was briefly presented. It was noted that the present subjunctive in the second person singular and plural could convey the sense of an imperative.

> *Dēsinās*! "You should stop!"
> *Requīrāminī.* "You should be asked."

The examples you see above are a part of an independent use of the subjunctive called the volitive subjunctive, which in some books is called the jussive or hortatory subjunctive. Whatever name is used, the present subjunctive in this use is the primary verb in the sentence and indicates a milder command than the imperative does. In the second persons, the volitive subjunctive is translated with "should" or "may" but in the first and third persons is translated with "let."

> *Quā rē sēcēdant improbī . . . .* (Cicero *In Cat.* I 13.32.9)
> "Therefore let the wicked men withdraw . . . ."

> *Sēcernantur ā nōbīs!* (Cicero *In Cat.* I 13.32.10)
> "Let them be separated from us!"

Nē makes a volitive subjunctive verb negative.

BY THE WAY

You will also see the present subjunctive used in indirect questions, in purpose and result clauses, in indirect commands, and in other uses of the subjunctive. In all these types of clauses, the present subjunctive functions as a verb in a dependent clause and follows the sequence of tenses.

THE ROMAN FORUM

1 Tabulārium
2 Porticus Deōrum Consentium
3 Templum Concordiae
4 Templum Saturnī
5 Mīliārium Aureum
6 Umbilīcus Urbis
7 Rostra
8 Lapis Niger
9 Comitium
10 Cūria Hostīlia
11 Cūria Jūlia
12 Basilica Jūlia
13 Lacus Curtius
14 Fanum Jānī Geminī
15 Templum Castoris et Pollūcis
16 Porticus Gāiī et Lūciī
17 Basilica Aemilia
18 Arcus Augustī
19 Fanum et Lacus Jūturnae
20 Templum Dīvī Jūliī
21 Templum Vestae
22 Domus Vestālium
23 Domus Pontificis Maximī
24 Rēgia
25 "Templum Rōmulī"
26 mansiōnēs*
27 "Templum Jovis Statōris"

*from Republican era
NB: Quotation marks around a building indicate that its identity or location is not definitive.

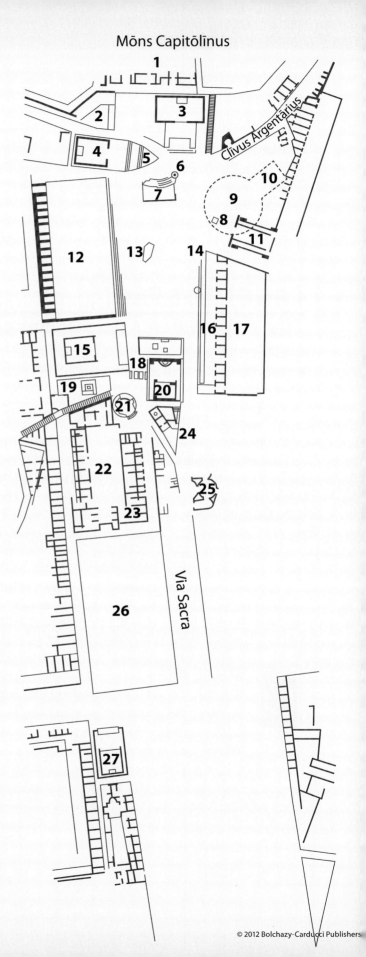

Mōns Capitōlīnus

Clivus Argentārius

Via Sacra

▶ EXERCISE 2

Translate the following sentences and indicate the use of the subjunctive in each sentence. There may be more than one subjunctive verb in a sentence.

1. Ūnum in locum congregentur.

2. Sit dēnique īnscrīptum in fronte ūnīus cūiusque quid dē rē pūblicā sentiat.

3. Tanta in nōbīs cōnsulibus dīligentia erit ut Catilīnae profectiōne omnia patefacta videātis.

4. Dēsinant circumstāre tribūnal praetōris urbānī.

5. Nē versēmur in hīs perīculīs.

6. Malleolōs et facēs comparat ut urbem īnflammet.

7. Tanta in equitibus Rōmānīs virtūs erit ut Catilīnā ex urbe ēgrediente omnia illūstrāta esse videantur.

8. Arceāmus latrōnēs ā tēctīs urbis ac moenibus.

ESSAY

In the conclusion of the *First Catilinarian*, Cicero reiterates key points from earlier in the speech. Identify two of these and explain how they relate to their occurrences in earlier passages.

Support your assertions with references drawn from the Latin passage. All Latin words must be copied or their line numbers provided, AND they must be translated or paraphrased closely enough so that it is clear you understand the Latin. Direct your answer to the question; do not merely summarize the passage. Please write your essay on a separate piece of paper.

READING 7

The *Dē amīcitiā* is one of several philosophical treatises that Cicero wrote shortly before his death in 43 BCE. This essay is dedicated to Atticus, Cicero's best and dearest friend, and it takes the form of a dialogue between Gaius Laelius and Quintus Mucius Scaevola (the Augur), Cicero's mentor. Scaevola and Marcus Fannius, who also is present during the discussion, are the sons-in-law of Laelius. This literary piece is set shortly after the death of Scipio Africanus Minor and showcases the great friendship between Laelius and Scipio. "Friendship" was a complex and important notion for the Romans, owing to the political implications of *amīcitia*. In this context, *amīcitia* referred to a political alliance that joined men in public life in a bond of mutual obligation.

In this passage Laelius describes the value and benefits of friendship, which is bestowed by the gods and is as essential to mankind as fire and water.

THE BENEFITS OF FRIENDSHIP

CICERO *DĒ AMĪCITIĀ* 5.20–6.22

1 [5] [20] . . . Quanta autem vīs amīcitiae sit ex hōc intellegī maximē potest, quod ex
   īnfīnītā societāte generis humānī, quam conciliāvit ipsa nātūra, ita contrācta rēs est et
   adducta in angustum ut omnis cāritās aut inter duōs aut inter paucōs iungerētur.

   [6] Est autem amīcitia nihil aliud nisi omnium dīvīnārum humānārumque rērum cum
5 benevolentiā et cāritāte cōnsēnsiō; quā quidem haud sciō an exceptā sapientiā nīl
   unquam melius hominī sit ā dīs immortālibus datum.

NOTES AND VOCABULARY

Line 1:   **quanta:** how great, as great; modifies *vīs.*
          vīs, vim, vī, f. force, strength, power (defective in the singular)
          quanta . . . sit: an indirect question dependent on *intellegī.*
          maximē, *superlative adv.*, very greatly, especially
          quod: that

REMINDER
As you read on p. 64 in the Caesar chapter of this book, the forms of the irregular and defective noun *vīs* are *vīs, vim, vī* in the singular and *vīrēs, vīrium, vīribus, vīrēs, vīribus* in the plural.

Line 2:   **īnfīnītus, -a, -um** infinite

societās, societātis, f. bond, society, connection

genus, generis, n. class, race

conciliō (1) form, unite, bring about

contrahō, contrahere, contrāxī, contrāctum to restrict, draw together, unite

rēs, reī, f. thing; stands here for *amīcitia*.

Line 3:   **adducta (est) in angustum:** reduced in measure, narrowed

ut . . . iungerētur: result clause. Translate as present tense.

cāritās, cāritātis, f. regard; love, affection

iungō, iungere, iūnxī, iūnctum to join

Line 4:   **nihil aliud:** translate "nothing else."

nisi, *conj.* except, unless, if not

omnium divīnārum humānārumque rērum: an objective genitive dependent on *cōnsēnsiō*

cum: translate "joined with."

BY THE WAY

As in lines 4–5, some nouns that indicate action, agency, or feeling govern another noun in the genitive case. This is called an objective genitive. Consider this sentence.

> *Priamus fuit rēgnātor Asiae.*
> "Priam was the ruler of Asia Minor."

The noun *rēgnātor* indicates the action of ruling; if the corresponding verb *regnō* were used instead, Asia Minor would be the direct object:

> *Priamus Asiam rēgnāvit.*
> "Priam ruled Asia Minor."

For this reason *Asiae* in the first example is called an **object**ive genitive.

Line 5:   **benevolentia, -ae,** f. goodwill, kindness, affection

cōnsēnsiō, cōnsēnsiōnis, f. an agreement, harmony; translate here "harmony of, agreement on."

quidem, *adv.* certainly, indeed, in fact

quā . . . an: *lit.,* "than which in fact I do not know whether." *Quā* is ablative of comparison referring to *amīcitia* in the previous sentence and dependent on *melius*; *quā* serves as a connecting relative and should be translated less literally as "this." Translate: "I do not know in fact whether anything better than this (friendship) . . . ."

Lines 5–6: **haud sciō . . . datum:** construe the sentence as *haud sciō an . . . nīl . . . melius . . . sit . . . datum.* *Sciō* sets up the indirect question beginning with *an*, which has *nīl*, modified by *melius*, as its subject.

excipiō, excipere, excēpī, exceptum to take out, except, take, capture; *exceptā sapientiā* is an ablative absolute.

nīl, *indeclin.* nothing; the second negative (*nīl*) is added for the purpose of emphasis and should be translated "anything." *Nīl* is the contracted form of *nihil*.

Line 6:   **sit . . . datum:** take *nīl* as the subject. The verb *sit* is present subjunctive in an indirect question dependent on *haud sciō an*.

CICERO *DĒ AMĪCITIĀ* 5.20–6.22, CONTINUED

Dīvitiās aliī praepōnunt, bonam
aliī valētūdinem, aliī potentiam, aliī honōrēs, multī etiam voluptātēs. Beluārum hoc
quidem extrēmum; illa autem superiōra cādūca et incerta, posita nōn tam in cōnsiliīs
nostrīs quam in fortūnae temeritāte. Quī autem in virtūte summum bonum pōnunt,
10   praeclārē illī quidem, sed haec ipsa virtus amīcitiam et gignit et continet, nec sine virtūte
amīcitia esse ūllō pactō potest.

[21] Iam virtūtem ex cōnsuetūdine vītae sermōnisque nostrī interpretēmur, nec eam,
ut quīdam doctī, verbōrum magnificentiā mētiāmur, virōsque bonōs eōs quī habentur
numerēmus, Paulōs, Catōnēs, Gallōs, Scīpiōnēs, Philōs: hīs commūnis vīta contenta est:
15   eōs autem omittāmus quī omnīnō nusquam reperiuntur. Tālēs igitur inter virōs amīcitia
tantās opportūnitātēs habet quantās vix queō dīcere.

NOTES AND VOCABULARY

Line 6:   **dīvitiae, -ārum,** f. riches

    praepōnō, praepōnere, praeposuī, praepositum to put before, prefer

Lines 6 –7:   **aliī . . . aliī . . . :** some . . . others; note the ANAPHORA and parallelism of *aliī* in these lines.

Line 7:   **valētūdō, valētūdinis,** f. health

    potentia, -ae, f. power

    voluptās, voluptātis, f. pleasure; sexual pleasure

    belua, beluae, f. beast; animal; *beluārum* is a genitive of characteristic; translate
        "characteristic of beasts."

Lines 7–8:   **beluārum . . . extrēmum:** supply *est.*

Line 8:   **extrēmum:** refers back to *voluptātēs.* Translate "this last thing."

    superior, superius, *comparative adv.* higher, former, above; *illa . . . superiōra,* n. pl. refers to all
        the desires mentioned above. Translate "those desires mentioned above."

    cādūcus, -a, -um frail, transitory, perishable. Supply *sunt.*

    posita: the perfect passive participle of *pōnō,* here modifying *illa.* With *in* + the ablative means
        "dependent on."

Lines 8–9:   **tam . . . quam** so . . . as

Line 9:   **temeritās, temeritātis,** f. whim; caprice

    quī = *eī quī:* "those who"

    virtūs, virtūtis, f. virtue, goodness

Line 10: **praeclārē** especially well, nobly, very well

praeclārē illī quidem: use the order *illī quidem* (plural verb understood) *praeclārē*; English would supply a verb like "do so" for the understood verb in the Latin. Note *quidem* follows the word it emphasizes. Translate "those who, however, place the highest good in virtue, those men in fact do so nobly."

gignō, gignere, genuī, genitum to give birth to, produce

continet: here translate "sustains, preserves."

Line 11: **ūllō pactō:** ablative of respect; translate "in any manner, at all."

REMINDER

As you learned in the Caesar chapter of this book on p. 20, the ablative noun showing in respect to what something exists or is done is called an ablative of respect.

Line 12: **cōnsuetūdō, cōnsuetūdinis,** f. custom, habit

sermō, sermōnis, f. speech, conversation

interpretor (1) to explain, interpret, understand, call; *interpretēmur* like *mētiāmur* (line 13), *numerēmus* (line 14), and *omittāmus* (line 15) is a volitive subjunctive.

eam: refers to *virtūtem*, the accusative object of *mētiāmur*.

Line 13: **doctus, -ī,** m. wise man, learned man

magnificentiā: ablative of means

mētior, mētīrī, mēnsus sum to measure, estimate, value

quī habentur: translate literally as "who are (so) considered," or "who are considered (good)."

Line 14: **numerō** (1) to count, number

Paulōs, Catōnēs, Gallōs, Scīpiōnēs, Philōs: take in apposition to *virōs bonōs*. Laelius mentions these men in the plural to stand for all men who exhibit the same strength of character as was found among them. Lucius Aemilius Paulus was a great general and the father of Scipio Aemilianus; Marcus Porcius Cato was known for his integrity and severity; Gaius Sulpicius Gallus was consul and a famous orator; Lucius Furius Philus was a friend of Laelius and the Scipios; Scipio Aemilianus was Laelius's dearest friend.

hīs commūnis vīta contenta est: ordinary life is satisfied with these (men); i.e., these men satisfy the ordinary standard for "good men"; *contenta* takes the ablative.

Line 15: **omittō, omittere, omīsī, omissum** to omit, pass over, pass by

omnīnō: "at all" with the negative. Cicero again refers to the perfect men Stoic philosophy describes. Cicero does not believe these men exist in reality.‡

nusquam, *adv.* nowhere

reperiō, reperīre, repperī, repertum to find

tālis, tāle, such; *tālēs:* modifies *virōs*

Line 16: **tantās opportūnitātēs . . . quantās:** translate "such great opportunities . . . as."

habet: here means "offers."

queō, quīre, quīvī (quiī), quitum to be able, can

dīcō, dīcere, dīxī, dictum to explain, describe

CICERO *DĒ AMĪCITIĀ* 5.20–6.22, CONTINUED

[22] Prīncipiō, quī potest esse vīta vītālis, ut ait Ennius, quae nōn in amīcī mūtuā
benevolentiā conquiēscat? Quid dulcius quam habēre quīcum omnia audeās sīc
loquī ut tēcum? Quī esset tantus frūctus in prosperīs rēbus, nisi habērēs quī illīs aequē
20   ac tū ipse gaudēret? Adversās vērō ferre difficile esset sine eō quī illās gravius
etiam quam tū ferret. Dēnique cēterae rēs quae expetuntur opportūnae sunt
singulae rēbus ferē singulīs; dīvitiae ut ūtāre; opēs ut colāre; honōrēs ut laudēre;
voluptātēs ut gaudeās; valētūdō ut dolōre careās et mūneribus fungāre corporis: amīcitia
rēs plūrimās continet.

NOTES AND VOCABULARY

Line 17:   **prīncipiō,** *adv.* in the first place

      quī: archaic or old ablative used as an adverb meaning "how."

      vītālis: "worth living"; nominative completion of *esse;* translate "How can a life be worth living?"

      aiō, ait, āiunt, *defective verb,* to say

      Ennius, -ī, m. Ennius, Roman poet‡

      amīcī: genitive singular dependent on *benevolentiā.*

      mūtuus, -a, -um mutual, reciprocal

Lines 17–18:   **quae . . . conquiēscat:** a relative clause of characteristic. Translate "of the kind that does not rest."

Line 18:   **quid dulcius:** supply *est.*

      quīcum: archaic form of *quōcum;* translate "[someone] with whom."

      audeās: subjunctive in a relative clause of characteristic; translate "with whom you would dare."

Line 19:   **quī:** as in line 17, *quī* means "how."

      esset . . . nisi habērēs: imperfect subjunctives in a contrary to fact condition. Translate "How would there be such great enjoyment in prosperous times, unless you were to have [someone] who might rejoice equally in them (your good times) as you yourself [do]?"

      quī: relative pronoun; supply "someone" as the antecedent.

      illīs: dative with *gaudēret; illīs* refers to *prosperīs rēbus.*

Lines 19–20:   **aequē ac:** equally . . . as, as much . . . as

Line 20:   **tū ipse:** *gaudērēs* is understood here.

      adversās: supply *rēs.*

      difficile esset: "it would be difficult." Understand the two subjunctive verbs (*esset* and *ferret*) as an implied contrary to fact condition, expressing a position similar to that of the previous sentence. (The thought is that it be would difficult to bear adverse circumstances if one did not have someone who bore these circumstances more strenuously than one did oneself. When one has a true friend, an alter ego, the implication is that it is not difficult to bear adversity.)‡

      illās: refers to *adversās.*

Line 21: **tū:** *ferres* is understood here.

cēterī, -ae, -a the rest of

expetō, expetere, expetīvī, expetītum to desire

Lines 21–22: **opportūnae sunt singulae rēbus ferē singulīs:** translate "are individually suited for the most part to individual matters"; i.e., men have certain desires for specific reasons. Latin uses the adjective *singulae* here where English uses an adverb. The word *rēbus* refers to these nouns: *dīvitiae . . . opēs . . . honōrēs . . . voluptātēs . . . valētūdō.*

Line 22: **rēbus . . . singulīs:** dative with *opportūnae*

ferē *adv.* for the most part, almost; usually

ūtāre . . . colāre . . . laudēre: the alternative form for the second singular subjunctive passive used in purpose clauses introduced by *ut.* Note that *ūtāre* is a deponent verb; the more common forms are *ūtāris . . . colāris . . . laudēris.*

ops, opis, f. power

colō, colere, coluī, cultum to honor, esteem

Line 23: **dolor, dolōris,** m. pain; *dolōre* is ablative with *cāreās.*

careō, carēre, caruī (+ *abl.*) to be without

mūnus, mūneris, n. gift; *mūneribus* is ablative with *fungāre.*

fungor, fungī, fūnctus sum (+ *abl.*) to use, perform, enjoy; *fungāre* is the alternative form for the second singular deponent present subjunctive of *fungor.*

Line 24: **plūrimus, -a, -um,** *superlative adj.* the most

contineō, continēre, continuī, contentum to embrace, sustain, preserve

The town of Larnaca, the ancient Citium of Cyprus, honors one of its famous sons with a statue in the town square. Zeno of Citium (335–263 BCE) moved to Athens where he studied philosophy. He developed his own school of philosophy known as Stoicism that taught that happiness comes from surrendering one's will to the divine reason that governs the universe. Zeno taught in the Stoa Poikile, the "Painted Stoa," near the agora in Athens. He and his followers gathered there to discuss logic, ethics, physics, and other philosophical topics. They were called "stoics" because of their meeting place, in the shade of the colonnaded stoa.

CICERO *DĒ AMĪCITIĀ* 5.20–6.22, CONTINUED

Quōquō tē verteris praestō est: nūllō locō exclūditur: nunquam
25 intempestīva, nunquam molesta est. Itaque nōn aquā, nōn ignī, ut āiunt, locīs plūribus
ūtimur quam amīcitiā. Neque ego nunc dē vulgārī aut dē mediocrī, quae tamen ipsa et
dēlectat et prōdest, sed dē vērā et perfectā loquor, quālis eōrum quī paucī nōminantur fuit.
Nam et secundās rēs splendidiōrēs facit amīcitia, et adversās partiēns commūnicānsque
leviōrēs.

NOTES AND VOCABULARY

Line 24:   **quōquō,** *adv. functioning as a conjunction,* wherever

vertō, vertere, vertī, versum to turn; *verteris* is the future perfect tense. Latin emphasizes
that this action will have taken place before the time of the main verb. *Tē* is the reflexive
object of *verteris.*

praestō, *adv.* ready at hand, present

nūllō locō: ablative of separation with *exclūditur.*

Lines 24–25:   **est . . . exclūditur . . . est:** understand *amīcitia* as the subject of these three verbs. Note the
ASYNDETON and ANAPHORA.

Line 25:   **intempestīvus, -a, -um** out of season

nunquam, *adv.* never

Line 25:   **molestus, -a, -um** bothersome, annoying

nōn aquā, nōn ignī, ut āiunt: fire and water were considered two essentials for life and
therefore proverbial ("as they say"). A court sentence forbidding someone from the use of
fire and water (*aquā et ignī interdīcere*) was the equivalent of a death sentence. In the phrase
nōn aquā, nōn ignī, repetition of the negative with these proverbial nouns, rather than the
verb, makes the point forcefully that friendship is of universal use.

plūs, plūris, n. more; for *locīs plūribus* supply *in.*

Lines 25–26:   **aquā . . . ignī . . . amīcitiā:** ablatives dependent on *ūtimur.*

STUDY TIP

Plūs, plūris, n. ("more") is a neuter pronoun in the singular. It often takes a partitive
genitive, also called a genitive of the whole. The phrase *plūs cibī,* "more food," provides
an example of this grammatical point. By contrast, the plural *plūrēs, plūra* ("more") is an
adjective and so agrees with its noun in number, gender, and case. Both the pronoun and
the adjective are the comparative degree of the adjective *multus, -a, -um.*

Line 26:   **quam** (+ *comparative*) than

vulgāris, vulgāre, common, ordinary; *vulgārī, mediocrī, vērā, perfectā*: all modify the
understood noun *amīcitiā.*

mediocris, mediocre ordinary

Line 27: **dēlectō** (1) to delight, please

prōsum, prōdesse, prōfuī to benefit (+ *dat.*)

vērus, -a, -um true

quālis, quāle such as, as; *quālis* refers to *amīcitia*.

quālis . . . fuit: *tālis* is understood in this sentence as being correlative to *quālis*; *tālis . . . quālis*, such . . . as; translate "such as was the friendship of those few who are mentioned." *Paucī* is incorporated into the relative clause when one might expect from English that it would be a genitive antecedent of *quī*.

Line 28: **secundus, -a, -um** favorable

splendidus, -a, -um splendid, magnificent

adversus, -a, -um adverse

partior, partīrī, partītus sum (and **partiō, partīre, partīvī, partītum**) to divide

commūnicō (1) to share; *partiēns commūnicānsque* are present active participles modifying *amīcitia*. Cicero here enunciates a lovely thought about the value of friendship: it doubles pleasures but relieves troubles by dividing them in half.

Lines 28–29: **splendidiōrēs . . . leviōrēs:** note the parallel construction in the two halves of this sentence (*facit secundās rēs splendidiōrēs . . . [facit] adversās [rēs] leviōrēs*).

Line 29: **levis, leve** light, easy, tolerable

TAKE NOTE

1. Stoicism is an ancient philosophy, founded by Zeno around the third century BCE, which its adherents viewed as a way of life. The Stoics believed that events in human lives are predetermined by fate. Humans possess free will, which, however, is limited to their reacting to predestined events. Stoics also believed that moral virtue determines human happiness, which further derives from inner peace and restricting desires. Stoicism was popular with the Romans because it fit with their view of life. The modern meaning of stoic, "impassive" or "characterized by calm fortitude," comes from the Stoic notion that humans should maintain emotional composure in good times and in bad.

2. Ennius, whom the Romans regarded as the father of Latin poetry, was born in 239 BCE. He wrote tragedies and the *Annālēs*, an epic poem of Rome from its mythical beginnings to his own time. Although only fragments of his works now remain, Roman writers such as Cicero, who frequently refers to him as "our own dear Ennius," often quote from his works. Cato the Elder brought him to Rome, and when he died in his seventies, he was buried in the Scipio family tomb.

3. In the two sentences in lines 19–21 Cicero uses contrary to fact conditions to make his case by asking what it would be like not to have a friend in certain circumstances. Contrary to fact conditions contain suppositions that imply they are not true. Consider, for example, the condition "if Cicero had not been informed of the plot against him, he would have been assassinated in his bed." He was, in fact, informed of the plot, and took measures so as not to be killed. These kinds of conditions here, therefore, are an emphatic way of stating that one needs a close friend to make prosperity more enjoyable, just as one needs such a friend to help bear adverse situations.

COMPREHENSION QUESTIONS

1. According to Cicero, friendship can be defined as the harmony of what? Cite the Latin.
2. What does virtue produce?
3. Cicero refers to men like Paulus, the Catos, Gallus, and the Scipios as examples of what?
4. According to Cicero, what did Ennius say?
5. How does friendship affect favorable times and adverse times? Cite the Latin.

▶ EXERCISE 1

1. In line 1, what is the case and use of *amīcitiae*?
2. Identify the use of the subjunctive illustrated in line 1 by *sit*.
3. What is the subject of *conciliāvit* (line 2)?
4. In line 4, what is the function of *nihil*?
5. Identify the case and use of *aliud* in line 4.
6. Identify the case and use of *cōnsēnsiō* in line 5.
7. What is the tense, voice, and mood of *sit datum* in line 6?
8. To what does *illa* in line 8 refer?
9. Identify the case and use of *fortūnae* in line 9.
10. What is the antecedent of *quī* (line 9)?
11. What does *haec* (line 10) modify?
12. What does *nostrī* in line 12 modify?
13. Identify the case and use of *Paulōs, Catōnēs, Gallōs, Scīpiōnēs, Philōs* (line 14).
14. What is the antecedent of *quī* (line 15)?
15. What does *tālēs* (line 15) modify?
16. In line 16, what is the use of *dīcere*?
17. What is the antecedent of *quae* in line 17?
18. Identify the form of *dulcius* in line 18.
19. Identify the tense and form of *loquī* in line 19.
20. In line 19, what is the subject of *esset*?
21. In line 19, to what does *illīs* refer?
22. Identify the tense and mood of *ūtāre* in line 22.
23. Identify the case and use of *locō* in line 24.
24. In line 25, what is the case and use of *ignī*?
25. In line 28, what is the form of *splendidiōrēs*?

This late fifteenth-century illuminated manuscript contained translations into French of Cicero's *Dē senectūte, On Old Age*, and his *Dē amīcitiā, On Friendship*, along with Martin of Braga's *Formulae Honestae Vitae, A Model for a Respectable Life*. Cicero in the left panel is seated at his desk writing *Dē senectūte* while the right panel depicts Cato the Elder on the left and to the right good friends Scipio and Laelius.

LANGUAGE FACT

CORRELATIVES

Correlatives are conjunctions and adverbs used in pairs to make parallel or balanced clauses. Most correlatives can be used alone with one meaning but when used with a paired word means something else.

Used Alone:		Used in Pairs or as Correlatives:	
et	and	et . . . et	both . . . and
aut	or	aut . . . aut	either . . . or
neque (nec)	nor, and . . . not	neque (nec) . . . neque (nec)	neither . . . nor
sīve	whether	sīve . . . sīve	whether . . . or
tantus	so great	tantus . . . quantus	as much . . . as
quantus	how great		
tam	so	tam . . . quam	so . . . as
quam	how		
tālis	such	tālis . . . quālis	such . . . as
quālis	of what sort		
tot	so many	tot . . . quot	so many . . . as
quot	how many		
totiēns	so often	totiēns . . . quotiēns	so often . . . as
quotiēns	how often		
cum	when	tum . . . cum	not only . . . but also
tum	then		

BY THE WAY

The two phrases *tum . . . cum* and *nōn sōlum . . . sed etiam* are synonymous. They both mean "not only . . . but also."

Examples:

- **Used Alone**

    Quanta *autem vīs amīcitiae sit ex hōc intellegī maximē potest.*
        (Cicero *Dē amīcitiā* 5.20.1)
    "It is especially able to be understood from this **how great**, moreover, the force of friendship is."

- **Used as Correlatives**

    *Inter virōs amīcitia **tantās** opportūnitātēs habet **quantās** vix queō dīcere.* (Cicero *Dē amīcitiā* 6.21.15–16)
    "Among men friendship has **as many** advantages **as** I am scarcely able to say."

▶ EXERCISE 2

Indicate which words are correlatives used in pairs or alone and translate the complete sentence.

1. Tālēs igitur inter virōs amīcitia magnam vim habet.

2. Illa autem posita sunt nōn tam in cōnsiliīs nostrīs quam in fortūnae temeritāte.

3. Haec ipsa virtūs amīcitiam et gignit et continet.

4. Omnis cāritās aut inter duōs aut inter paucōs iungitur.

5. Neque ego nunc dē vulgārī aut dē mediocrī amīcitiā loquor.

6. Tantus frūctus in prosperīs rēbus est.

7. Amīcitia et dēlectat et prōdest.

8. Tot sunt dīvitiae quot honōrēs.

9. Hominēs tum valētūdinem ut dolōre cāreant cum opēs ut colantur dēsīderant.

10. Totiēns rēs adversās tulimus.

ESSAY

Define the following words: *dīvitiae, opēs, honōrēs, voluptātēs, valētūdō*; give their benefits according to Cicero, and then discuss briefly the advantages of friendship.

Support your assertions with references drawn from the Latin passage. All Latin words must be copied or their line numbers provided, AND they must be translated or paraphrased closely enough so that it is clear you understand the Latin. Direct your answer to the question; do not merely summarize the passage. Please write your essay on a separate piece of paper.

PART 2

Authors of the Augustan Age

- **PUBLIUS VERGILIUS MARO**

- **QUINTUS HORATIUS FLACCUS**

- **PUBLIUS OVIDIUS NASO**

AUGUSTUS AND THE PRINCIPATE

The first century BCE was a tumultuous and transformational period in Roman history, as the historical overview of the Republic made clear. During this period the foundations and traditions of the Roman Republic started to crumble, to be replaced by what was essentially single-man rule. For the Romans, autocracy went against the very definition of *rēs pūblica*, which was based on the principle of rule by assemblies. That Augustus was able to establish himself as a single ruler and to retain such power was quite remarkable, especially since his adoptive father Julius Caesar was assassinated shortly after he was declared "dictator for life."

THE RESTRUCTURING OF THE ROMAN GOVERNMENT BY AUGUSTUS

A clear understanding of the ways in which Augustus restructured Roman government is essential to understanding how he was able to stay in power. He reshaped traditional Roman government to give the impression that nothing had changed—annual elections of magistrates continued, popular assemblies continued to be held—but he altered their substance and included special privileges for himself so that he held unparalleled power while preventing anyone else from following his example. It is important to note that at no time was Augustus ever referred to as "emperor" in the way that the word is defined today, and he was certainly never called "king" or "dictator."

This colossal statue of Augustus portrays a solemn ruler—his toga revealing a bare chest, the fasces, a symbol of authority in his left hand, and his head crowned with a laurel wreath. Now housed in the National Museum in Naples, the statue originally graced the Augusteum in Herculaneum where it was found in the course of excavations of the volcanic mud in the city.

Instead, his power was drawn from a number of traditional institutions and altered for his benefit. Augustus was granted command of the Roman military, which traditionally was assigned to the supreme republican magistrates, the consuls; in addition, he assumed the powers granted to the *tribūnus plēbis*, particularly the right to veto any government action, as well as their sacrosanctity, that is, special protection from any sort of harm. He did receive the title *imperātor*, "victorious general," from which the word "emperor" is derived, but the title referred to his command of the Roman army. Later in his reign, Augustus also became *Pontifex Maximus*, the most important figure in Roman state religion.

No man before Augustus had held all these powers simultaneously. Yet Augustus managed to persuade the Roman people that he had earned this unprecedented influence. It was his hard work that allowed the Republic to be restored, after all. Augustus was *prīnceps*, that is, "first among equals," the most influential and well-regarded Roman citizen, and no more. Understanding why Augustus chose to structure power in this way requires context: the fundamental values of Roman republican government and how these were weakened in the century or so prior to 27 BCE, the year in which Augustus claimed to have restored the *rēs pūblica*.

THE RISE OF AUGUSTUS

The eighteen-year-old Octavian (Gaius Octavius Thurinus) was Caesar's grandnephew. After Julius Caesar's assassination in 44 BCE, it was revealed in his will that he had adopted Octavian and made him his heir. The young man's name then became Gaius Julius Caesar Octavianus. He is generally referred to as Octavian by modern scholars until 27 BCE, when he received the title Augustus. The news that Octavian was Caesar's heir was certainly unexpected, and only added to the already unstable political situation after Caesar's assassination, since there was already substantial mistrust between Marc Antony, Caesar's consular colleague for 44 BCE, and the Senate. The members of the conspiracy against Caesar miscalculated how unpopular Caesar's assassination would be and were far more vulnerable than they had anticipated. Although Antony had the support of the people and of Caesar's legions, he knew that he would likely share Caesar's fate if he attempted to take power for himself. Neither Antony nor the Senate could predict how Octavian would change the political landscape once he came to Rome.

It was easy to underestimate Octavian. He was only eighteen years of age, and he lacked experience and a connection to the Roman nobility. Octavian's opponents also miscalculated how popular he would be with his adoptive father's armies as well as with the Roman people. Octavian soon showed, however, that he was nobody's fool and that he would not allow himself to be manipulated. Initially, Cicero and the Senate enlisted him and his army against Antony, who had been declared a public enemy and was being besieged in Mutina. There Octavian would join forces with the armies of the consuls Aulus Hirtius and Vibius Pansa elected for 43. Cicero's strategy seemed wise: Octavian would not only draw from Antony's potential supporters, he would also give the Senate some degree of support from the Roman people. In return, Octavian was made a senator, was given the rank of praetor, and received the right to stand for consul at a much younger age than was previously permitted. Cicero wrongly anticipated that Octavian would be satisfied with these many privileges and would be easy to control.

The siege at Mutina did not turn out well for the Senate. Antony escaped to Gaul, and both consuls opposing Antony died in battle. Still, Brutus and Cassius, leaders of the conspiracy against Caesar, had organized armies in the East, where each governed a province, and the Senate still had loyal and powerful men in the West. Octavian, however, first revealed his ambitions and abilities when given what he felt to be inadequate rewards for his service at Mutina: he marched his armies against Rome. His opponents either surrendered or fled. Octavian then had himself elected consul and gave his soldiers large cash rewards.

THE SECOND TRIUMVIRATE

His new name of Gaius Julius Caesar Octavianus continued to give Octavian an edge when negotiating with other Roman commanders. Though Antony and Marius Aemilius Lepidus, the new *Pontifex Maximus* and the man to whom Antony had eventually fled, commanded more soldiers, they decided to ally themselves with Caesar's heir rather than risk losing their armies to him. The three men then agreed to create a triumvirate that gave them supreme power over the state. This time the triumvirate was a formal arrangement, in contrast to the informal agreement that Caesar, Pompey, and Crassus had made. Octavian, Lepidus, and Antony divided up Roman territory among themselves and drew up a proscription list to get rid of political enemies and to raise money to pay soldiers. Among the first victims of the proscriptions was Cicero, who had made Antony a lasting enemy when he delivered a series of vitriolic speeches called the *Philippics*. These denunciations of Antony were filled with personal insults, as was common in Roman political speeches, and intended to prevent him from becoming too powerful. Not only did they influence greatly the Senate's decision to declare Antony a public enemy, but the humiliating and doubtlessly exaggerated content also made Antony eager for revenge. Before he could escape from Italy, Cicero was captured and executed, and Antony had Cicero's head and hands displayed up over the rostra in the Forum for all to see.

After Octavian and Antony secured sufficient funds for their armies, they headed east in pursuit of the leaders of the conspiracy to assassinate Caesar. In 42 BCE they defeated Brutus's and Cassius's armies in the battle of Philippi in

The sculptor presents an idealized and composed bust of Augustus's wife Livia Drusilla. The black basalt portrait is dated to 31 BCE, a momentous year when Augustus defeated Antony in the Battle of Actium to become sole ruler of Rome.

Greece, and Brutus and Cassius each committed suicide. Antony remained in the East and allowed Octavian to return to the much more turbulent situation in Italy. Against the odds, Octavan's influence continued to grow.

In 40 BCE the triumvirate met in Brundisium to reaffirm their agreement. At this time Octavian gave his sister Octavia in marriage to Antony to strengthen their alliance, and Lepidus, who was suspected of negotiating with the triumvirate's enemies, was reassigned less important provinces. Around this time, too, Octavian met and married the great love of his life, Livia Drusilla, who was equally devoted to him. Livia was well connected to the traditional Roman aristocracy and proved to be an astute political advisor to Octavian. She had two sons by a previous marriage, Tiberius and Drusus; Tiberius would eventually be chosen by Augustus to be his successor.

THE DISSOLUTION OF THE SECOND TRIUMVIRATE

After the treaty in Brundisium, Antony and Octavia stayed in Athens, for Antony was now in charge of the eastern part of the empire while Octavian was in charge of the western part. By 37 BCE Antony and Octavia's marriage started to become strained by Antony's resuming a romantic relationship that he had had with Cleopatra in 41 and that had resulted in his fathering twins. This new development provided Octavian with material to begin a propaganda war against Antony. Octavian was able to suggest more and more successfully that by Antony's remaining in the East and by his attachment to Cleopatra, he was letting himself become ruined by the corruption many Romans associated with the East.

In 32 BCE Octavian declared war against Antony after he formally divorced Octavia. With his childhood friend, the *eques* Agrippa, commanding his army and navy, he won a significant battle at Actium on September 31st. Cleopatra abandoned her forces when defeat was clear, and Antony chose to follow her back to Egypt rather than remain with his army, further evidence, according to Octavian, that Antony was no true Roman. The war, essentially over at Actium, was concluded in April of the following year. Antony committed suicide when he received the false report that Cleopatra was dead, and Cleopatra herself committed suicide soon afterward. The opposition was gone, and Rome now belonged to one man. Octavian's challenge would be finding a way to retain his power.

OCTAVIAN'S RETURN TO ROME

Octavian returned to Rome in 30. He held the consulship that year as well as the next, and shared the consulship and the censorship with his close companion Agrippa in 28. This was the first time Roman censors had been appointed in almost 40 years. During their term as censors, the roll of the Senate was drastically reduced, eventually reaching the traditional number of 600, and many public works were authorized. In addition, Octavian created new requirements for many magistracies and set a minimum property level for *equitēs* and senators. At the start of 27 BCE, he announced before the Senate that he was resigning all his offices, and declared the Republic restored.

OCTAVIAN GRANTED THE TITLE AUGUSTUS

In thanksgiving, the Senate granted Octavian the title of Augustus, "revered," an exceptional honor of great religious significance. From this point on, Octavian will be referred to by this title. In addition, he was given one of the foundations of his rule, a ten-year command over the provinces Gaul, Spain, Syria, and the newly annexed province of Egypt. This extensive command granted him control over almost all of the Roman legions in service at that point, and essentially made his power uncontestable. The remaining provinces were governed by senators. At Rome, Octavian was the *prīnceps*, the "leading citizen," a man of great influence but one who also respected the traditional role of the Senate to guide the state, for example, in overseeing state finances. He also increased the Senate's powers by granting it the right to make law. In this way its authority could never be overstepped by the popular assemblies or ambitious tribunes.

More generally Augustus ensured that the state was returned to its traditional routines. For example, regular elections were held, and many long ignored priesthoods were restored. The Romans did not separate government from religion. The prosperity of the state was dependent on the *pāx deōrum*, "harmony with the gods." By restoring traditional religious practices, Augustus hoped to bring Rome back into the favor of the gods who had helped it succeed earlier.

The *Āra Pācis* "Altar of Peace" built on the Campus Martius in Rome served as a tribute to Augustus's *pietas* and to his establishing what became known as the *Pāx Rōmāna*. The altar's sculptural reliefs include a religious procession in which one is able to identify some of Augustus's colleagues and perhaps himself robed as Pontifex Maximus.

GOVERNMENTAL REFORMS

For several years after 27 BCE, the new state appeared to run smoothly. But in 23 Augustus resigned the consulship after holding it for eleven consecutive terms. At this time he was granted *tribūnicia potestās*, that is, all the powers granted to the tribune of the people, including the right to propose and veto legislation, as well as sacrosanctity, making it a religious offense to harm him. In addition, his *imperium* was formally made greater, *maius*, than that of his senatorial colleagues. Though Augustus must have intended not to stand for the consulship again, he was forced to assume the appearance of greater authority after riots in 22 and after a serious political threat arose in 19. At this time the senator Egnatius Rufus attempted to run for the consulship immediately after holding the praetorship, in direct violation of Augustus's rules. The major addition to Augustus's powers by this point was consular power. For example, he was given the privilege of sitting in a third curule chair between the two regularly elected consuls. This compromise satisfied both the people and the Senate, and what reforms appear afterward have more to do with government organization.

Though Augustus preserved the appearance of senatorial prestige, he was careful to balance it by also showing favor to long-ignored constituencies: the *equitēs*, the Italians, and, to a lesser extent, freed slaves (*lībertīnī*). Augustus's close advisors Agrippa and Maecenas represented the

Freedmen Mazaeus and Mithridates dedicated a triple arched gateway to Augustus in gratitude for the attention he paid to their class, the *lībertīnī*. The monumental gateway leads into Ephesus, a major metropolis in Asia Minor, today's Turkey. In sponsoring such an impressive public building, its donors not only embellish the city but also show how successful they have been.

prominence of the *equitēs* and the Italians. Maecenas was especially important in encouraging Vergil and Horace to support Augustus and his programs through their poetry, thus ensuring Augustus's prestige among the nobility. *Equitēs* often served as army officers, procurators of certain provinces such as Egypt, or in positions essential to public order, such as having responsibility for the oversight of the grain dole. Freed slaves, also known as freedmen, might assume lower positions of authority within imperial administration. Unlike the aristocracy, men from these groups owed their primary loyalty to Augustus. Additionally, he limited how influential individual senators could become simply by ensuring that their periods as governor were short. If they commanded troops, it was usually as his subordinates.

Augustus maintained his popularity with the urban population by funding numerous festivals and entertainments. His *naumachia*, or mock naval battle, is an extreme example of his generosity. Augustus had a large basin custom built for the event, in which thousands of combatants and hundreds of full-size ships would participate. He even had an aqueduct, an expensive and highly engineered project in its own right, built to supply water for it. No other Roman would be capable of financing such a project, and therefore no other Roman could create so memorable an occasion. Augustus also paid for the grain dole, which distributed close to 1.5 bushels of wheat each to 150,000–200,000 citizen residents of Rome monthly.

Augustus also passed laws to strengthen the hierarchy that had always existed in Roman society. He separated senators from *equitēs* and the people from these classes at Roman spectacles, with men and women often placed separately in their own sections as well. In addition, he attempted to strengthen traditional family structures and encourage population growth. He made it mandatory, for example, for men to divorce adulterous wives. He promoted childbearing by penalizing aristocratic men for remaining bachelors. He also granted legal rights to women of any class who gave birth to at least three children. Other laws followed similar principles. Though it is debatable how effective these laws were, it is clear that Augustus's vision for restoring the Republic included returning to old Roman ways in private as well as public life.

REFORMS IN THE ARMY

When Augustus returned to Rome after Actium, he had demobilized about one half of the legions, leaving approximately 160,000 men in service. By 13 BCE, he established an army that was truly professional. Soldiers who enlisted would serve continuously for up to 25 years. Prior to this, the Roman army was organized as a militia, similar to today's US National Guard or Reserves—soldiers who served only in times of state need. Though Roman soldiers were paid a small sum for their service, previously they were never guaranteed retirement or additional benefits. Now Augustus provided his soldiers pay and retirement benefits. He made himself the supreme commander of almost the entire army so that the troops would be loyal to him.

Suetonius immortalized Augustus's quip that he had left what had been a city of brick, a city of marble. In his *Rēs Gestae*, he enumerates the renovations, reconstructions, and new building programs he oversaw in Rome. His Forum of Augustus with its Temple to Mars Ultor at its center showcased the accomplishments of the Julian clan and traced the clan's ancestry back to Romulus and Mars as well as Aeneas and Venus.

THE INCREASE IN ROMAN TERRITORY

Roman territory grew under the first half of Augustus's reign. He, Agrippa, and then the younger generations of the Julio-Claudian family campaigned frequently. For the most part, these campaigns were successful: Spain and Gaul grew more settled and several provinces were annexed in the Alps. German territory proved more difficult. Roman armies conquered the Rhine region and then advanced eastward. But Augustus miscalculated how secure Roman control past the Rhine was. In 9 CE three Roman legions led by Quintilius Varus were ambushed and destroyed at the Teutoberg Forest near modern Hamburg. The obliteration of these legions profoundly affected Augustus, who mourned their loss for several months. As a result of their defeat, Roman control of this area moved back to the Rhine, which, together with the Danube, would remain the frontier of Roman territory for most of the Principate.

The Roman east was governed directly by Roman provincial governors or procurators, or indirectly, by client kings. Client kings had long been part of Roman rule, but the territory they governed came to be annexed as provinces in a piecemeal fashion. Still, for much of Augustus's reign, the rulers of kingdoms such as Emesa (now central Syria) provided a useful buffer between Rome, inhabitants of the Arabian desert, and further east, Parthia. The client kingdoms of this region were annexed on the deaths of their rulers.

THE END OF AUGUSTUS'S RULE

One of the major questions during Augustus's rule was who would succeed him. Certainly it would have become obvious through time that he did not intend to return the state to true republican government. He appears to have decided about 23 BCE that power should be handed over to a relative, or at a minimum to a trusted friend. Augustus's first candidate was his nephew Marcellus, whom he married to his daughter Julia, and who was mentioned as the eventual ruler of Rome in book six of Vergil's *Aeneid*. Marcellus, however, died unexpectedly later that year. Soon Augustus married Julia to Agrippa, who had divorced his own wife at Augustus's request. Their first two sons, Gaius and Lucius, were adopted by Augustus, marking them as his intended successors. Unfortunately, both Gaius and Lucius died near the start of the new millennium. Augustus formally adopted Tiberius and the youngest son of Agrippa and Julia, Agrippa Postumus, who proved unsuitable for rule. As Augustus grew older, Tiberius took on more responsibilities, and by 13 CE held *imperium* and *tribūnicia potestās* with Augustus. When Augustus died in 14 CE, Tiberius was granted these powers without hesitation by the Senate.

The smooth transition of power from Augustus to Tiberius, as well as Augustus's long and peaceful reign, demonstrates how fundamentally and how successfully he transformed the Roman state. He matured in a period when politicians tore the state apart in pursuit of influence and honor and his own rise to power was marked by a certain ruthlessness. Yet when he defeated his last rival, he was able to use his exceptional political and organizational skills to construct a new system of government that permitted him to control the state stably while satisfying the ambitions of the traditional Roman elite. Like a true Roman, he created a government that maintained a sense of continuity with tradition but was modified with the necessary pragmatism characteristic of Roman ways. His system was the model for Roman imperial rule over the next two centuries.

Rosemary Moore
The University of Iowa

CHAPTER 4

PUBLIUS VERGILIUS MARO

Substantives (Adjectives Used as Nouns); Supines; Reflexive/Middle Voice; Patronymics and Other Names; Assimilation and Dative With Compound Verbs; Figures of Speech and Meaning; Alternate Endings and Syncopated Words

Epithet, Synchesis, Extended Simile, Tmesis, Hysteron Proteron, Anastrophe, Epanalepsis, Euphemism, Royal or Editorial "We"

A fifteenth-century illuminated manuscript of Vergil's *Aeneid* provides an overview of the Dido and Aeneas story. In the background are the ruins of defeated Troy, the story of which Aeneas will share with Dido. The harbor reveals Aeneas's fleet, suggesting the travails of Aeneas's journey. The seven birds in flight recall the favorable omen of Aeneas's fleet being reunited after the storm arranged by Juno. Dido welcomes Aeneas and his faithful companion Achates, who stands beside him.

MEMORĀBILE DICTŪ

"Ō fortūnātī, quōrum iam moenia surgunt!"
(Vergil *Aeneid* 1.437)

"O fortunate ones whose walls already are rising."

Vergil's hero, Aeneas, utters these words as he looks at the walls of Carthage. Aeneas undertakes his epic journey to find a city where he, his refugee Trojans, and his descendants can put down roots—roots that will become the ancestry of the Romans, according to Vergil.

INTRODUCTION TO VERGIL

VERGIL'S LIFE

Vergil (Publius Vergilius Maro) was born on October 15th, 70 BCE near the Italian town of Mantua in northern Italy. Mantua is located not very far from Catullus's hometown of Verona. Many of the details of the poet's life are uncertain. The ancient biographical tradition suggests that his father was rich enough to give his son an excellent education, first in Cremona and Milan and then in Rome. In the capital Vergil probably studied rhetoric and early Roman literature, including the works of the early second-century BCE Latin poet Ennius, who introduced the Greek hexameter to Latin poetry. Hexameter is the meter that Vergil used for all of his poetry.

The tumultuous years following the assassination of Julius Caesar in 44 BCE were difficult ones for all Romans, and Vergil was no exception. His father probably lost his property in the land confiscated for war veterans in 41 BCE. (The tradition that this property was later restored to the poet is unlikely.) Vergil himself refers to the loss of this farm in the *Eclogues*, his first collection of poems on pastoral themes, published in 37 BCE. During this period Vergil gained the attention of the wealthy Maecenas who became the poet's patron and who introduced him to his powerful friend Octavian, later the emperor Augustus. The *Eclogues* were followed by the *Georgics*, usually described as a didactic poem on farming, published in 30 BCE. However, there is little practical advice in the *Georgics*, which celebrate the joys of rural life. In this poem, dedicated to Maecenas, Vergil tells the sad story of Orpheus and Eurydice.

After completing the *Georgics*, Vergil spent the next ten years working on his masterpiece, the *Aeneid*. In 19 BCE Vergil began a tour of Greece and Asia, but while in Athens the poet was persuaded by the emperor Augustus to return to Italy with him. Vergil fell ill on the return voyage and died on September 20th, 19 BCE, in the Italian city of Brundisium. He was buried in Naples in a tomb with the following inscription, which he himself is said to have composed on his deathbed:

> *Mantua mē genuit, Calabrī rapuēre, tenet nunc*
> *Parthenopē; cecinī pascua rūra ducēs.*

> "Mantua bore me, the Calabrians (i.e., Brundsium) seized me, and now
> Naples holds me; I sang of pastures, fields, leaders."

Vergil left instructions that if the *Aeneid* remained unfinished at his death, the epic should be burned. Augustus did not allow the poet's wishes to be carried out. The unfinished state of the manuscript is reflected in partially complete hexameter lines, which appear here and there throughout the poem.

THE *AENEID*

The *Aeneid* is an epic, a long narrative poem centered on a hero. In the opening words of the poem, *arma virumque canō* ("Of the arms and man I sing"), Vergil indicates that his inspiration and model for his poetic work are the two epics of Homer. The first half of the *Aeneid*, which deals with the wanderings of Aeneas from the time he leaves Troy until he arrives in Italy, resembles Homer's *Odyssey* with its focus on the wanderings of Odysseus after the Trojan War. The second half of the

Aeneid, with its narratives of the many battles fought by Aeneas and his men to found a home in Latium, resembles the *Iliad*. Although the *Aeneid* uses Homer's poems as a model, the epic is thoroughly Roman in thought, mood, and message. Such imitation of earlier Greek authors was common in Latin literature. For example, Catullus Poem 51 is modeled on Sappho's *phainetai moi* (frag. 31 L.P.).

Other Greek and Latin literary works also influenced Vergil. The depiction of Medea in Apollonius of Rhodes's third-century BCE epic *Argonautica* is probably a source for Vergil's portrayal of Dido. The influence of Greek tragedy, especially dramas like Euripides's *Medea*, can also be seen in the *Aeneid*. Tragedies and epics (now lost) of the Latin poet Ennius probably played an important role in Vergil's development as a poet.

Although the events described in the *Aeneid* take place in the distant, mythic times of the Trojan War and its aftermath, Vergil expected his audience to interpret these events through Roman eyes and through contemporary events. The hero of Vergil's epic, the Trojan Aeneas, is destined to found a city in Italy from which the Roman people will descend. The success of Aeneas means the success of Rome. Aeneas's son Ascanius, also known as Ilus or Iulus, was believed to be the founder of the famous Julius *gēns* ("clan"), which includes Julius Caesar and his adopted son, the emperor Augustus. Thus the Julians could claim descent from the goddess Venus, Aeneas's mother.

Vergil stands guard on the south flank of the Los Angeles, California Public Library.

The events described in the *Aeneid*, then, look ahead to later events in the history of Rome. These events include the founding of the city by Romulus, the city's prolonged rivalry with Dido's city of Carthage in the Punic Wars (264–146 BCE), and events during the Civil Wars that followed the assassination of Julius Caesar in 44 BCE, including the naval battle of Actium (31 BCE), in which the forces of Octavian defeated those of Antony and Cleopatra. The Dido depicted in the *Aeneid* is, in fact, not only the queen of Carthage, Rome's later archenemy, but is intended to call to mind the dangerous Egyptian queen Cleopatra, whom Vergil and his contemporaries feared.

THE VALUE OF READING THE *AENEID* IN LATIN

Since many English translations of the *Aeneid* are available, why read the poem in Latin? A comparison of just one line of the *Aeneid* in four different English translations will provide an answer to this question. A translation of *forsan et haec ōlim meminisse iuvābit* in line 203 of Book 1 might be rendered literally as: "Perhaps even these things some day it will be pleasing to remember." Here are translations of the line taken from Dickinson, Copley, Fitzgerald, and Ruden:

> "One day you may look back on these memories as pleasant memories."
> (Dickinson, 1961)

> "Some day these memories, too, will bring a smile."
> (Copley, 1965)

> "Some day, perhaps, remembering even this will be a pleasure."
> (Fitzgerald, 1981)

> "Sometime you may recall today with pleasure."
> (Ruden, 2008)

One reason to read the *Aeneid* in Latin is that no single translation captures the full meaning of Vergil's original. In this line Vergil emphasizes the uncertainty of what the future may bring by placing *forsan* ("perhaps") as the first word in the line. Dickinson's translation places the emphasis instead on "one day." Likewise, Copley, Fitzgerald, and Ruden emphasize "some day/time." The uncertainty alluded to in "perhaps" is expressed by the word "may" in Dickinson's line. Copley's translation leaves out this word as does Ruden's. Fitzgerald does use the word "perhaps," but places it after "some day," and thereby reduces its impact.

By making the Latin word *iuvābit* the last word in the line, Vergil also stresses the idea that remembering these troubles will be pleasurable in the future. Dickinson uses the word "pleasant" to convey this idea but emphasizes instead "memories." Ruden also stresses "memories" with "you may recall." Ruden and Fitzgerald use the word "pleasure," place it last in the line of poetry, and thus come closest to Vergil's meaning. Copley, like Vergil, stresses the idea of pleasure in his line but translates *iuvābit* as "bring a smile," which is a much more colloquial phrase, and thus the grandeur of Vergil's line is lost. Dickinson, Copley, and Ruden omit "even" (*et*) from their translation, which is an important word here; this seems like a serious omission.

There are other reasons to read the *Aeneid* in Latin. No translation can produce the beauty of the sound and rhythm of Vergil's Latin. The flow of the dactylic hexameter meter can only be hinted at in English. Nuances, allusions, word play, and figures of speech are usually lost, for often they cannot be replicated in translation. In sum, by reading Vergil's *Aeneid* in Latin, the reader gains a greater understanding of the brilliance of this remarkable literary work composed by Rome's greatest poet.

EPIC

Vergil includes in his epic many of the following characteristics found in earlier classical epics, especially the *Iliad* and the *Odyssey*:

- *In mediās rēs*, or, beginning in the middle of the story. Vergil begins the *Aeneid* not at the beginning of the story, that is, in the Trojan War, but with a storm that drives Aeneas's fleet onto the coast of Africa, near Carthage.

- Flashback. If the story begins *in mediās rēs*, then the poet must, at some point, tell the story up to that point. Vergil does this in *Aeneid* 2–3, in which Aeneas tells Dido and her court everything that happened to him from the fall of Troy until his arrival in Carthage.

- Invocation. A prayer to the Muse, the goddess of inspiration. When the poet prays for poetic inspiration, he usually summarizes the plot of the epic. Invocations can also appear at important points in the narrative, such as the start of the second half of the epic (Book 7, lines 37 ff.).

- Catalogues or lists, such as the list of heroes and historical figures Aeneas meets in *Aeneid* 6.

- Divine machinery or the involvement of the gods in the plot. The roles of the goddesses Venus and Juno are particularly important in the *Aeneid*.

- Epithets or descriptive phrases used with the name of a hero, place, and the like; for example, *pius Aenēās* ("loyal Aeneas") and *miserrima Dīdō* ("very unhappy Dido").

- Similes or comparisons. Some of these are brief while others are longer and take on a life of their own.

- Descent into the Underworld. In *Aeneid* 6 Aeneas descends into the Underworld to see the ghost of his dead father Anchises. His father will show Aeneas the future city of Rome and reveal a moral code sanctioned by the gods.

- Dactylic Hexameter. This meter used by Homer and other Greek poets was introduced to Latin by the poet Ennius and became the standard meter for Roman epic poets. The meter is based on six feet (hexameter) consisting of dactyls ($-\smile\smile$) or spondees ($--$).

The pediment of this neoclassical temple facade provides the perfect perch
for the assembly of the Olympians with Jupiter at the center.

THE GODS

Gods play an important role in the *Aeneid*. Vergil often uses the gods to speed up the plot; for example, in Book 4 Venus and Juno collaborate to cause the thunderstorm and thereby provide the opportunity for Dido and Aeneas to act on their love. The principal Roman gods in the *Aeneid* include:

> Apollō, Apollinis, m. Apollo, god of prophecy and music
>
> Cerēs, Cereris, f. Ceres, goddess of grain
>
> Cupīdō, Cupīdinis, m. Cupid, also known as Amor, Amōris m. god of love
>
> Diāna, Diānae, f. Diana, goddess of the hunt
>
> Īris, Īr(id)is, f. Iris, goddess of the rainbow
>
> Iūnō, Iūnōnis, f. Juno, queen of the gods
>
> Iuppiter, Iovis, m. Jupiter, king of the gods
>
> Mercurius, Mercur(i)ī, m. Mercury, the messenger god
>
> Minerva, Minervae, f. Minerva, goddess of wisdom
>
> Neptūnus, Neptūnī, m. Neptune, god of the sea
>
> Plūto, Plūtōnis, m. Pluto, god of the Underworld
>
> Proserpina, Proserpinae, f. Proserpina, goddess of the Underworld
>
> Venus, Veneris, f. Venus, goddess of love
>
> Volcānus, Volcānī, m. Vulcan, god of fire

VERGIL'S INFLUENCE

From the time it was written in the late first century BCE, Vergil's *Aeneid* has maintained a continuing influence upon other authors and on Western and world cultures. Ovid's *Metamorphōsēs*, Lucan's *Pharsālia,* and other later Roman epics owe much of their language and structure to Vergil's epic. John Milton's *Paradise Lost* also contains many Vergilian characteristics. Rafael Landivar's *Rusticātīo Mexicāna*, an epic written about the New World in 1782, shows the influence of Vergil's *Aeneid.* J. R. R. Tolkien's *Fellowship of the Ring,* George Lucas's *Star Wars* series, and other twentieth-century adventure stories reveal a debt to Vergil in their heroic journeys and cosmic scale. Vergil's influence is even seen in Robert Frost's poem written for the inauguration of John F. Kennedy. And, of course, in the fourteenth century the Florentine Dante consciously expressed his debt to Vergil in the creation of his masterpiece the *Divine Comedy* by making Vergil his guide through hell.

Vergil's influence has been felt not only by poets and authors but also by the many people who have read his epic for the past two thousand years. Students who read the *Aeneid* in school today are following in the footsteps of ancient Roman students who studied the epic. The *Aeneid* became a school text almost immediately after its publication. The appeal of Vergil lies in the good adventure story well-told, the all too human hero Aeneas who struggles to fulfill his destiny, and the tension between personal sacrifice and creating an empire.

As Rose Williams, author of *The Labors of Aeneas, Vergil for Beginners,* and *Examining Vergil,* has stated, "Vergil's *Aeneid* forms a priceless part of the cultural heritage of Western civilization. Vergil's flowing, spirited *Aeneid* remains one of the greatest literary works of all time. This multi-dimensional tapestry of Vergil's work has grandeur, tragedy, beauty, and strength. Vergil's poetry expresses in powerful and beautiful language the humanity that we share with Aeneas."

READING 1

In Latin prose and poetry, the reader often needs to "understand" or supply words that are not in the Latin text. Words to be understood are in parentheses in the text below. Different fonts point out words that belong together.

The prologue of the *Aeneid* introduces the hero and provides a brief summary of the plot of the epic. The opening sentence (*Arma virumque canō*) indicates that the poem is about the wars and wanderings of a hero and the personal costs that the hero will endure in order to set the stage for the eventual foundation of Rome. Repeated references to the gods indicate the important part they will play in the story, especially Juno, whose hatred for Aeneas endures through almost the entire work. A prayer rounds off the first eleven lines, with the poet appealing to the Muse for assistance in telling the tale.

The ancient Romans believed that destiny (*fātum, -ī,* n. fate, destiny) and the will of the gods significantly affect human events. Thus Aeneas is driven by fate (*fātō profugus,* 1.2) and by the anger of Juno (*Iūnōnis ob īram,* 1.4) toward his destiny in Italy.

PROLOGUE AND INVOCATION

VERGIL *AENEID* 1.1–11

Meter: Dactylic Hexameter

1   Arma virumque canō, Trōiae quī prīmus ab ōrīs

       (ad) Italiam fātō profugus ***Lāvīn(i)a****que* vēnit

       lītora—multum ***ille*** (vir) et (in) terrīs ***iactātus*** et (in) altō

       vī super(ōr)um **saevae memorem Iūnōnis** ob **īram,**

NOTES AND VOCABULARY

Line 1:   **arma, armōrum,** n. pl. arms, the tools of war. "Arms," standing for the war itself, is an example of METONYMY.

            vir, virī, m. man; the name of this *virum* is Aeneas.

            canō, canere, cecinī, cantum to sing of, sing about; the direct objects of *canō* become the objects of the English preposition "about" or "of."

            ōra, -ae, f. shore; translate *Troiae* with *ōrīs,* "the shores of Troy."

Line 2:   **fātum, -ī,** n. fate, destiny; *fātō* is an ablative of means; translate "by fate."

            profugus, -a, -um exiled; *as noun,* an exile

            Lāvīn(i)a: the Lavinian shores refer to Italy's shores; *-que* connects *Lāvīna lītora* with *Italiam.*‡

STUDY TIP

Vergil uses many synonyms in the *Aeneid*. Note that in line 1 *ōra, ōrae,* f. means "shore," and in line 3 *lītus, lītoris,* n. "shore" is a synonym of *ōra*. Don't confuse *ōra, ōrae,* f. "shore" with *ōra,* the neuter nominative and accusative plural of *ōs, ōris,* n. "face, mouth."

Line 3:   **lītus, lītoris,** n. shore

multum, *adv.* much; a neuter accusative adjective sometimes, as here, is used in Latin as an adverb. Translate with *iactātus* "much."

ille: translate "that man" with the word "man" understood, or translate "he."

et . . . et: both . . . and

terra, -ae, f. land; Vergil uses the plural *terrīs* to emphasize the many different places where Aeneas suffered.

iactō (1) to toss

altum, -ī, n. the deep (sea)

Line 4:   **vīs,** f. force, strength; *vī* is an ablative of means; translate "by the force of."

superum: the contracted form of *superōrum. Superī* functions as a substantive here and should be translated "of the gods" or "of the gods above."

saevus, -a, -um cruel

memor, memoris mindful, unforgetting

ob, *prep.* + *acc.* on account of

īra, -ae, f. anger, wrath

STUDY TIP

Note that *ob* and *propter* are synonyms. Both mean "on account of," and both take their objects in the accusative case.

VERGIL *AENEID* 1.1–11, CONTINUED

5   multa quoque et (in) bellō (ille vir) passus, dum conderet urbem

īnferretque deōs Latiō—***genus*** unde ***Latīnum***

Albānīque ***patrēs*** atque altae moenia Rōmae (orta sunt).

(Ō) Mūsa, mihī causās memorā, **quō nūmine laesō**

quidve dolēns rēgīna de(ōr)um tot volvere cāsūs

10   ***īnsignem*** pietāte ***virum,*** (et) tot adīre labōrēs

impulerit. Tantaene animīs caelestibus īrae (sunt)?

NOTES AND VOCABULARY

Line 5:   **multus, -a, -um** much, many; translate the neuter plural accusative substantive *multa* "many things."

quoque, *adv.* also

patior, patī, passus sum to endure, suffer; the perfect passive participle of deponent verbs, here *passus*, translates "having" instead of "having been."

condō, condere, condidī, conditum to found, establish

Lines 5–6:   **dum conderet . . . īnferretque:** translate this subjunctive clause "until he could found . . . and bring to."

Line 6:   **īnferō, īnferre, intulī, illātum** to bring (into)

deōs: refers to the gods of Troy whose statues Aeneas brought to Italy.

Latium, -(i)ī, n. Latium, the area around Rome; translate "to Latium."

genus, generis, n. type, kind; race

unde, *adv.* from where; translate "from which."

Latīnus, -a, -um Latin, of Latium

BY THE WAY

In line 6, the dative *Latiō* is used instead of a place to which with *ad* + accusative. This dative, which occurs mainly in poetry and in later prose, is called the dative of direction or the dative of motion toward.

Line 7:   **Albānus, -a, -um** Alban; Rome is located in the Alban Hills.

altus, -a, -um high, deep; translate *altae moenia Romae,* "the high walls of Rome."

moenia, moenium, n. pl. walls (of a city)

orior, orīrī, ortus sum to arise; translate "are descended."

STUDY TIP

The adjective *altus, -a, -um* means "high" or "deep." The noun *altum, -ī*, n. means "the deep" or "the sea." A form of the noun *altum* appears in line 3 while the adjective *altus* occurs in line 7.

Line 8: **Mūsa, -ae,** f. Muse, goddess of the arts, especially the composition of poetry‡

memorō (1) to recall, call to mind, state

causa, -ae, f. reason

nūmen, nūminis, n. divinity; *quō nūmine laesō* is an ablative of cause or manner; translate "by which deity having been wounded." This indirect question and the following one explain why Juno is angry.

laedō, laedere, laesī, laesum to hurt, offend

Line 9: **doleō, dolēre, doluī, dolitum** to grieve (over), be angry (at); *quid* is the direct object of *dolēns*; translate *quidve dolēns* "or grieving over what."

tot, *adv.,* so many

volvō, volvere, volvī, volūtum to undergo; *volvere* depends on *impulerit* (line 11). The subject of the infinitive is *virum.*

cāsus, cāsūs, m. misfortune; *cāsus* is the direct object of *volvere.*

Line 10: **īnsignis, īnsigne** distinguished

pietās, pietātis, f. loyalty, sense of duty; *pietāte* is an ablative of respect; translate "in duty."‡

adeō, adīre, adīvī, aditum to approach

Line 11: **impellō, impellere, impulī, impulsum** to drive, force

tantus, -a, -um so great

animus, -ī, m. mind

caelestis, caeleste divine, heavenly

STUDY TIP

Another set of Latin synonyms appears in this passage. In line 11 the adjective *caelestis, caeleste,* if used as a noun, means the "heavenly gods." *Deus* (line 9) is the most frequently used Latin noun for "god." The substantive *superī, superōrum,* m. pl. (line 4) refers to the "gods above," and in line 8 *nūmen, nūminis,* n. means "divine power" or "god."

TAKE NOTE

1. Some manuscripts read *Lāvīna* in line 2 instead of *Lāvīnia* because of the meter. With an "i" in the penultimate position of the word, *Lavinia* must be scanned as though the "i" were a "y."

2. The poet's prayer to a Muse for inspiration is called "the invocation."

3. Unlike the English derivatives "piety" from *pietās* and "pious" from *pius,* which have religious connotations, the Latin word *pietās* means "duty to one's country, family, and gods" while *pius* means "dutiful" in the same three respects. The three parts of *pietās* are largely inseparable in the Roman mind. *Pius* is often used to describe Aeneas and serves as his EPITHET in the *Aeneid.*

BY THE WAY

An EPITHET is a word or phrase that characterizes a person or thing and that is often used to emphasize that attribute.

COMPREHENSION QUESTIONS

1. According to lines 1–2, from where did Aeneas depart and where did he arrive? Cite the Latin for these places.

2. What caused Aeneas to suffer so much during his travels?

3. What two things did Aeneas bring from Troy to Italy?

4. Write the Latin phrase that characterizes Aeneas in this passage. Translate the Latin phrase.

5. What is the Muse asked to explain?

▶ EXERCISE 1

1. What is the case, number, and use of *arma* in line 1?

2. What is the case, number, and use of *ōrīs* in line 1?

3. What is the tense and mood of *vēnit* in line 2?

4. In line 4, what case is *saevae* and what Latin word does it modify?

5. In line 5, what is the tense and mood of *conderet*?

6. In line 7, what is the case and use of *moenia*?

7. What is the case and use of *Mūsa* in line 8?

8. In line 9, what tense, voice, and form is *dolēns*?

9. What is the case and use of *labōrēs* in line 10?

10. What is the case and use of *animīs* in line 11?

VOCABULARY BUILDER

Many of these people and places will be mentioned in the *Aeneid*. Although these Latin words look somewhat similar, it is important to be able to distinguish one from another.

Latin Word	English Translation	Explanation
Latium, -ī, n.	Latium	The region of Italy where the Latin people lived.
lingua Latīna, -ae, f.	the Latin language or Latin	The language spoken in Latium.
Latīnus, -ī, m.	Latinus	The name of Latium's king who became Aeneas's father-in-law later in the epic.
Latīnus, -a, -um	Latin	The adjective used to describe Latinus's people and places near Latium.
Rōma, -ae, f.	Rome	The city that was later founded in Latium near Lavinium.
Rōmānus, -a, -um	Roman	The adjective used to describe the people of Rome and places near Rome.
Lāvīnium, -ī, n.	Lavinium	The city that Aeneas founded in Italy after he defeated the Rutulians later in the epic.
Lāvīnia, -ae, f.	Lavinia	The daughter of Latinus whom Aeneas later married and after whom he named the town of Lavinium.
Lāvīn(i)us, -a, -um	Lavinian	The adjective used to describe the people of Lavinium and places near Lavinium.

LANGUAGE FACT

SUBSTANTIVES (ADJECTIVES USED AS NOUNS)

An adjective used as a noun is sometimes called a "substantive" or its use is termed the "substantival" use of the adjective. Substantives are very common in Latin.

When an adjective is a substantive, a noun is to be understood in Latin. The most common nouns to be understood are "man," "woman," and "thing" and their respective plurals. In order to know what noun must be supplied, the case, number, and gender of the adjective must be determined. Consider this example from line 5 of the passage you have just read.

> *multa quoque et bellō passus*
> "having endured also many things in war"

The phrase *multa . . . passus* contains the substantive *multa*. In order to understand *multa*, you need to recognize that it is neuter plural accusative. Its plural number and neuter gender signify that the word to be understood is "things." Substantives can occur in all cases, numbers, and genders. Here are a few examples of substantives in the nominative case.

bonus	a good man	bona	a good woman	bonum	a good thing
bonī	good men	bonae	good women	bona	good things

▶ EXERCISE 2

Practice translating these substantives into English. Watch out for singular vs. plural and masculine vs. feminine vs. neuter. Remember that some endings can be more than one case or gender.

1. bonō
2. bonae
3. bonōrum
4. bonōs
5. bonās
6. altās
7. alta
8. altae
9. caelestia
10. multōrum

11. saevī
12. saevae
13. saeva
14. memorēs
15. memoris
16. prīmī
17. prīma
18. prīmōs
19. superīs
20. superī

A Roman mosaic depicts the Greek hero Odysseus on his journey home after ten years at war against the Trojans. Vergil models his epic tale of the Trojan hero Aeneas's mission to found his destined new Troy in unknown western lands on the Homeric epics. Aeneas is delayed by an attractive woman just as Odysseus overcame the charms of several women on the course of his journey home. This scene shows him listening to the alluring Sirens and their song while bound to the mast lest he yield to their charms. He had stuffed his comrades' ears with wax so that they would not be able to hear and then be tempted.

READING 1 REDUX

You are now ready to read these lines exactly as Vergil wrote them. For this reason, the words in parentheses and the special fonts are no longer used. You have already seen notes in the first version of these lines, and you may refer to those notes if you need to. Additional notes are given below the text.

1   Arma virumque canō, Trōiae quī prīmus ab ōrīs

     Italiam fātō profugus Lāvīnaque vēnit

     lītora—multum ille et terrīs iactātus et altō

     vī superum, saevae memorem Iūnōnis ob īram,

5   multa quoque et bellō passus, dum conderet urbem

     īnferretque deōs Latiō—genus unde Latīnum

     Albānīque patrēs atque altae moenia Rōmae.

     Mūsa, mihī causās memorā, quō nūmine laesō

     quidve dolēns rēgīna deum tot volvere cāsūs

10   īnsignem pietāte virum, tot adīre labōrēs

     impulerit. Tantaene animīs caelestibus īrae?

BY THE WAY

The first three words in the *Aeneid, arma virumque canō,* are Vergil's way of showing that his epic is in the tradition of Homer's epics. The noun *arma,* "weapons," refers to war, the central theme of the *Iliad* as well as of the *Aeneid,* and *virum,* "man," refers to Aeneas, the central character of the *Aeneid,* just as the word "man" in the first line of the *Odyssey* refers to its central character, namely Odysseus. The use of the word *canō* refers to the tradition of reciting ancient epics aloud, which was common practice even in Vergil's time.

NOTES AND VOCABULARY

Line 2:   **Italiam:** Prepositions must be frequently understood in the *Aeneid,* especially with places. Since *Italiam* is accusative, *ad* or *in* is the word to be understood.

          Lāvīnaque: *Lāvīna* is the alternate spelling of *Lāvīnia* and is an adjective, not the name of Latinus's daughter.

Line 3:   **terrīs . . . altō:** the preposition *in* is understood with both of these words.

          iactātus: this perfect passive participle modifies *ille.*

Line 4:   **superum:** the contracted form of *superōrum*

BY THE WAY

In the phrase *saevae . . . īram* in line 4, note how *saevae* modifies *Iūnōnis* while *memorem* modifies *īram* to create the following pattern:

saevae	*memorem*	*Iūnōnis*	*īram*
A	B	A	B

This placement of words in an A B A B pattern is a figure of speech called SYNCHESIS or INTERLOCKED WORD ORDER, the purpose of which is to connect closely the four words in the pattern, Juno's anger, cruelty, and memory.

REMINDER

The adjective *memorem* is a TRANSFERRED EPITHET, a figure of speech first learned on p. 120 in the Catullus chapter of this book; although the adjective modifies *īram*, it should be translated as if it modifies Juno.

Line 5: **bellō:** supply the preposition "in."

Lines 6–7: **genus . . . Rōmae:** a word such as *sunt* (or *orta sunt*) should be supplied.

Line 7: **altae moenia Rōmae:** Logically Rome's walls are high, but grammatically *altae* modifies *Rōmae*. This is another example of a TRANSFERRED EPITHET.

Line 8: **Mūsa, mihī:** note the ALLITERATION. In Latin poetry, the final *-i* of *mihi* can be either long or short. While the final *-i* is long here, in Book 2.710, for example, the final *-i* is short.

Lines 9–10: **tot volvere . . . tot adīre:** the conjunction *et* is to be understood between these two infinitive phrases. Note the repetition of *tot*.

Line 11: **īrae:** Translate this plural noun as singular and supply *sunt*. Note the RHETORICAL QUESTION.

ESSAY

In lines 1–11 Vergil sets forth some of the themes that he will explore in the rest of the poem. Identify and discuss these themes in a short, well-organized essay.

Support your assertions with references drawn from throughout the passage. All Latin words must be copied or their line numbers provided, AND they must be translated or paraphrased closely enough so that it is clear you understand the Latin. Direct your answer to the question; do not merely summarize the passage. Please write your essay on a separate piece of paper.

SCANSION

Name the meter and scan the following lines.

vī superum, saevae memorem Iūnōnis ob īram

multa quoque et bellō passus, dum conderet urbem

īnferretque deōs Latiō—genus unde Latīnum

READING 2

The rest of the Vergilian passages in this book will no longer feature the words in parentheses and the use of special fonts. Use the notes below the poem to help you.

After informing Aeneas and Achates that they are on the shore of Africa and that their missing ships are safe, Venus hides them in a cloud so that they can travel into the city of Carthage safely. From a hilltop, the Trojans look down at the growing city. Vergil compares the Carthaginians building their city to a hive of bees. Aeneas admires the rising walls and expresses his envy of the Carthaginians, who have already mastered the difficulties of finding the land and resources to found a new city.

THE CONSTRUCTION OF CARTHAGE

VERGIL *AENEID* 1.421–440

Meter: Dactylic Hexameter

> Mīrātur mōlem Aenēās, māgālia quondam,
>
> mīrātur portās strepitumque et strāta viārum.
>
> Īnstant ardentēs Tyriī: pars dūcere mūrōs
>
> mōlīrīque arcem et manibus subvolvere saxa,
>
> 425 pars optāre locum tēctō et conclūdere sulcō;
>
> iūra magistrātūsque legunt sānctumque senātum.
>
> Hīc portūs aliī effodiunt; hīc alta theātrīs
>
> fundāmenta locant aliī, immānīsque columnās
>
> rūpibus excīdunt, scaenīs decora alta futūrīs.

NOTES AND VOCABULARY

Line 421: **mīror** (1) to wonder (at), admire

mōlēs, mōlis, f. mass, burden, structure, construction

māgālia, māgālium, n. pl. huts, hovels

quondam, *adv.* once, at some time

Lines 421–422: **mīrātur . . . mīrātur:** note the ANAPHORA here—as often—combined with ASYNDETON.

Line 422: **porta, -ae,** f. gate, door, opening

strepitus, strepitūs, m. noise, uproar

strātum, -ī, n. pavement, bed; in the phrase *strāta viārum*, *viārum* is a partitive genitive; translate "paved roads."

Line 423: **īnstō, īnstāre, īnstitī** to urge on, press on (+ *dat.*)

ardeō, ardēre, arsī, arsum to burn, be eager

dūcere: to extend; this and the following infinitives either depend on *īnstant* or are to be construed as historical infinitives.

mūrus, -ī, m. (city) wall, rampart

Lines 423–425: **pars:** This repeated *pars* in line 423 and in line 425 is in apposition to the *Tyriī* (line 423).

Line 424: **mōlior, mōlīrī, mōlītus sum** to work, effect, make, construct

subvolvō, subvolvere, subvolvī, subvolūtum to roll up

Line 425: **optō** (1) to choose, desire, hope (for)

tēctō: translate "for a house." *Tēctō* is a dative of purpose. Note the SYNECDOCHE.

conclūdō, conclūdere, conclūsī, conclūsum to (en)close

sulcus, -ī, m. furrow, trench, ditch

Line 426: **iūs, iūris,** n. law, justice, decree

magistrātus, magistrātūs, m. magistrate, officer; *magistrātūs* is accusative plural.

legō, legere, lēgī, lēctum to choose, gather

sānctus, -a, -um sacred, holy, revered; note the ALLITERATION.

senātus, senātūs, m. Senate, council of elders

Line 427: **portus, portūs,** m. port, harbor

effodiō, effodere, effōdī, effossum to dig out, excavate

theātrum, -ī, n. theatre; poetic plural

STUDY TIP

Be careful to distinguish among these words that look so similar.

porta, portae, f. gate	FIRST DECLENSION
portus, portūs, m. port, harbor	FOURTH DECLENSION
portō (1) to carry	FIRST CONJUGATION VERB

Lines 427–428: **aliī . . . aliī:** some . . . others

Line 428: **fundāmentum, -ī,** n. foundation

locō (1) to place, locate, establish

immānis, immāne, huge

columna, -ae, f. column, pillar

Line 429: **rūpēs, rūpis,** f. rock, cliff, crag; *(ex) rūpibus:* the typical open-air theatre of classical Greece (less frequently, Rome) was commonly excavated from a hillside.

excīdō, excīdere, excīdī, excīsum to cut out, destroy

scaena, -ae, f. stage, background; dative case; note the CHIASMUS.

decus, decoris, n. ornament, beauty, dignity; *decora* is in apposition with *columnās*.

VERGIL *AENEID* 1.421–440, CONTINUED

430   Quālis apēs aestāte novā per flōrea rūra

      exercet sub sōle labor, cum gentis adultōs

      ēdūcunt fētūs, aut cum līquentia mella

      stīpant et dulcī distendunt nectare cellās,

      aut onera accipiunt venientum, aut agmine factō

435   ignāvum fūcōs pecus ā praesēpibus arcent;

      fervet opus redolentque thymō fragrantia mella.

      "Ō fortūnātī, quōrum iam moenia surgunt!"

      Aenēās ait et fastīgia suspicit urbis.

      Īnfert sē saeptus nebulā—Mīrābile dictū!—

440   per mediōs, miscetque virīs neque cernitur ūllī.

NOTES AND VOCABULARY

Line 430:   **quālis, quāle** just as, such (as), of what sort, as

               apis, apis, f. bee

               aestās, aestātis, f. summer; *aestāte novā* is an ablative of time.

               flōreus, -a, -um flowery

               rūs, rūris, n. the country

Lines 430–431: **(tālis est labor illīs) quālis (labor) exercet apēs:** this SIMILE is famous and is considered an
               EXTENDED SIMILE. The HYPERBATON is striking, with *quālis . . . labor* acting as a frame for
               the main clause. Vergil emphasizes the noun *labor* by postponing it until the end.

BY THE WAY

A SIMILE is considered an EXTENDED SIMILE when after making a comparison, the author then elaborates on the idea for several lines.

Line 431:   **exerceō, exercēre, exercuī, exercitum** to busy, train

               sōl, sōlis, m. sun; day

               adultus, -a, -um grown, adult

Line 432:   **ēdūcō, ēdūcere, ēdūxī, ēductum** to lead forth

               fētus, fētūs, m. offspring, brood, swarm

               līquēns, līquentis liquid, flowing

               mel, mellis, n. honey

Line 433:   **stīpō** (1) to stuff, crowd, stow

               dulcis, dulce sweet, dear, fresh

               distendō, distendere, distendī, distentum to distend, stretch

               nectar, nectaris, n. nectar

               cella, -ae, f. cell, storeroom

Line 434: **onus, oneris,** n. burden, load

agmen, agminis, n. line, line of battle

STUDY TIP

Be careful to distinguish between *onus, oneris,* n. "burden, load" (line 434) and *opus, operis,* n. "work, deed, toil" (line 436).

Line 435: **ignāvus, -a, -um** lazy, idle

fūcus, -ī, n. drone; *fūcōs* is in apposition to *ignāvum pecus.*

pecus, pecoris, n. flock, herd, swarm

praesēpe, praesēpis, n. stall, hive

arceō, arcēre, arcuī to keep off, defend

Line 436: **ferveō, fervēre, ferbuī** to glow, boil, heat up

opus, operis, n. work, deed, toil

redoleō, redolēre, redoluī to be fragrant, smell (of)

thymum, -ī, n. thyme, a flowering plant

fragrāns, fragrantis fragrant, sweet-smelling

Line 437: **fortūnātus, -a, -um** fortunate, blessed; *Ō fortūnātī* is to be taken substantively; translate "O fortunate ones!" In this instance of APOSTROPHE, Aeneas addresses the Carthaginians who cannot see him because he is cloaked in a cloud.

iam moenia surgunt: Aeneas was impatiently looking forward to the time when the walls of his own city would rise.

Line 438: **ait:** the third singular of *aiō,* "say"

fastīgium, -ī, n. summit, top, height

suspiciō, suspicere, suspexī, suspectum to look up (at)

Line 439: **īnferō, īnferre, intulī, illātum** to bear (in, into)

saepiō, saepīre, saepsī, saeptum to hedge in, enclose

nebula, -ae, f. cloud, mist, fog

mīrābilis, mīrābile wonderful, marvelous; *dictū* is an ablative supine of respect with *mīrābile* (see Language Fact later in this chapter on p. 251).

Line 440: **per mediōs (virōs):** translate "through the midst (of) the men."

misceō, miscēre, miscuī, mixtum to mix, mingle; *(sē) miscet virīs: virīs* is dative with *miscet.*

cernō, cernere, crēvī, crētum to discern

BY THE WAY

In line 440, *ūllī* is a dative of agent. In prose a dative of agent, which is translated in the same way as an ablative of agent, is found with passive periphrastics and perfect passive participles. In poetry, the dative of agent can be used with any passive verb. The ablative of agent features the preposition *ā, ab* plus the ablative case. The dative of agent is in the dative case without a preposition. Translate *ūllī* "by anyone."

COMPREHENSION QUESTIONS

1. At what three aspects of the new city does Aeneas marvel? Cite the Latin.

2. List at least four activities in which the eager Tyrians are engaged, according to lines 423–425.

3. To what are the bees in line 430 being compared?

4. List at least four things that the bees are seen doing in lines 431–435. Cite the Latin.

5. Why is Aeneas not seen when he enters Carthage?

▶ EXERCISE 1

1. What is the case and use of *māgālia* in line 421?

2. What is the case and use of *strāta* in line 422?

3. What is the case, tense, voice, and form of *ardentēs* in line 423?

4. In line 424, what is the case and use of *manibus*?

5. What is the case and use of *iūra* in line 426?

6. What is the case and use of *portūs* in line 427?

7. What is the case and use of *theātrīs* in line 427?

8. What Latin word does *immānis* in line 428 modify?

9. In line 429, what is the tense, voice, and mood of *excīdunt*?

10. What Latin word does *novā* in line 430 modify?

11. In line 432, what is the case and use of *mella*?

12. In line 433, what is the case and use of *nectare*?

13. In line 434, what is the tense, voice, and form of *venientum*?

14. In line 434, what is the case and use of *agmine*?

15. In line 435, what is the case and use of *praesēpibus*?

16. In line 437, what is the case and use of the substantive *fortūnātī*?

17. In line 437, what is the case and use of *moenia*?

18. In line 439, what is the tense, voice, and form of *saeptus*?

LANGUAGE FACT

SUPINES

The Latin supine is a fourth declension noun formed from the perfect passive participle, which is the fourth principal part of a Latin verb. Only the accusative and ablative singular of the supine are used. The supine is translated as an infinitive in English.

Examples:

parātum or *parātū*	"to prepare"	*ductum* or *ductū*	"to lead"
habitum or *habitū*	"to have, to hold"	*dictum* or *dictū*	"to say"
		audītum or *audītū*	"to hear"

- **The Accusative Supine**

  The supine is used in the accusative to express purpose with verbs of motion.

  > *Venīmus vīsum.* "We are coming to see."
  > "We are coming (in order) to see."

- **The Ablative Supine**

  The supine is also used in the ablative to express respect with some adjectives and with certain phrases.

  > *Mīrābile dictū!* (Vergil *Aeneid* 1.439)
  > "A wonderful thing to say!"

STUDY TIP

The supine that ends in *–ū* functions as an ablative of respect but is limited to being used with adjectives denoting ease, difficulty, or the effect on one's feelings and senses or with the phrases *opus est, fās est,* and *nefās est.* Nouns in an ablative of respect show in respect to what something is being done or exists. Remember that a supine of respect translates "to . . . ," but a noun ablative of respect translates "in (respect to) . . . ."

▶ EXERCISE 2

Translate each of the following phrases and indicate whether the supine is expressing purpose or respect or whether a noun is showing respect.

1. fortūnātum vīsū

2. differentēs linguā

3. dulce dictū

4. veniunt audītum

5. nefārium factū

6. fortūnātī moenibus surgentibus

7. īnstant ductum mūrōs

8. sānctum dictū

ESSAY

What emotions does Aeneas reveal in this passage, and what literary features does Vergil use to draw our attention to this throughout the text?

Support your assertions with references drawn from throughout the passage. All Latin words must be copied or their line numbers provided, AND they must be translated or paraphrased closely enough so that it is clear you understand the Latin. Direct your answer to the question; do not merely summarize the passage. Please write your essay on a separate piece of paper.

SCANSION

Name the meter and scan the following lines.

aut onera accipiunt venientum, aut agmine factō

ignāvum fūcōs pecus ā praesēpibus arcent;

fervet opus redolentque thymō fragrantia mella.

The ruins of Carthage perched on the Byrsa Hill and overlooking the sea evoke Dido and Aeneas as well as the Punic Empire. Carthage became the seat of the powerful empire, with which Rome waged three wars. While tradition contends that the Romans destroyed the city and sowed the soil with salt, the archaeology indicates that the destruction was not as great as the legend would lead us to believe.

THE TRAVELS OF AENEAS

EURŌPA

CORSICA

ITALIA

Rōma* Alba Longa
         Lāvīnium
              Caiēta
              Cūmae
Sibylla

SARDINIA

Mare
Tyrrhēnum

Tempestās ab
lūnōne excitāta

Sepulcrum
Anchīsae

Carthāgō

SICILIA

Scylla et
Charybdis

Cȳclops

MELITA

Mare Hādriāticum

GRAECIA

Būthrōtum

Actium

ITHACA

Harpȳiārum
Īnsula

Mare
Īonium

Mare Internum

THRĀCIA
              Aenos

              Trōia

         Pergamum

Mare
Aegaeum

DĒLOS

CRĒTA

Pontus
Euxīnus

AFRICA

* Rome not yet founded

© 2008 Bolchazy–Carducci Publishers, Inc.

READING 3

Aeneas has been invited to a banquet at Dido's palace in Carthage. Near the end of the banquet Dido asks Aeneas to tell her and her court about the fall of Troy. Aeneas explains how a huge wooden horse filled with Greek soldiers was left on the plain in front of the gates of Troy, while the rest of the Greeks sailed away to the nearby island of Tenedos, where they hid in order to convince the Trojans that they had returned to Greece. Most of the Trojans wanted to bring the wooden horse inside the city walls, but the priest Laocoon tried to convince them that this would not be a good idea. To make his point that the wooden horse might be a trick on the part of the Greeks, Laocoon hurled a spear at the side of the wooden horse. A hollow sound was made on impact. This should have convinced the Trojans that it was not safe to bring the horse inside the city. But Sinon, a Greek left behind on the plain at Troy, persuaded the Trojans that the wooden horse was an offering to the goddess Minerva, a portent that would bring good luck to the Trojans. At this point a terrifying omen appeared: two snakes made their way from the sea to the shore. The snakes from Tenedos, attacking first the sons of Laocoon and then their father, strangled the bodies in their spiraling coils. The monsters then sought shelter at the shrine of Minerva. Sinon said that they were a punishment for Laocoon's having struck the wooden horse with his spear.

The ancient Romans placed great importance on omens/portents as indicators of good or bad luck. Priests, such as Laocoon, were often entrusted with interpreting these omens. In this passage the Trojans are faced with two different interpretations of the wooden horse—one from Laocoon and one from Sinon. Laocoon realizes that the horse is a bad omen for the Trojans. Sinon and the gods, it seems, see the horse as a good omen for the Greeks. Vergil assumes that his readers understand that it was fated for Troy to fall and that these snakes were sent by the gods to persuade the Trojans to take the horse into the city. It is important to keep in mind that Aeneas, an eyewitness to these events, is telling the story from a Trojan point of view.

DEATH OF LAOCOON AND HIS SONS

VERGIL *AENEID* 2.201–222
Meter: Dactylic Hexameter

> Lāocoōn, ductus Neptūnō sorte sacerdōs,
>
> sollemnīs taurum ingentem mactābat ad ārās.
>
> Ecce autem geminī ā Tenedō tranquilla per alta
>
> —horrēscō referēns—immēnsīs orbibus anguēs
>
> 205 incumbunt pelagō pariterque ad lītora tendunt;

NOTES AND VOCABULARY

Line 201:   **Lāocoōn, Lāocoōntis,** m. Trojan priest of Neptune

Neptūnus, -ī, m. Neptune, god of the sea; *Neptūnō*: dative of reference

sors, sortis, f. lot, fate, destiny, oracle; translate *ductus sorte* "drawn (chosen) by lot."

sacerdōs, sacerdōtis, m. (f.) priest(ess)

BY THE WAY

Diaresis is a term that refers to the coincidence of the end of a metrical foot and the end of a word. A diaeresis appears between feet. In line 201, a diaresis occurs between the fourth and fifth foot (*Nep*)*tunō* and *sorte*. Caesura is a term that refers to the lack of coincidence between the end of a metrical foot and the end of a word. A caesura occurs within a metrical foot. In line 201 a caesura occurs in the third foot, between (*duc*)*tus* and *Nep*(*tunō*). Both caesura and diaeresis result in a pause in the line.

Line 202:   **sollemnis, sollemne** annual, customary, solemn

taurus, taurī, m. bull, bullock, ox

mactō (1) to sacrifice, slaughter; honor

ad: translate "at, beside."

Line 203:   **ecce,** *interjection* see! look! behold! *Ecce* is intended to make the narrative more vivid and to draw the reader into the scene by calling attention, in this instance, to something surprising that is about to happen.

autem, *adv.* moreover, but, however

Tenedos, -ī, f. Tenedos, small island near Troy‡

tranquillus, -a, -um tranquil, calm

altum, -ī, *n.* the deep (sea)

Lines 203–204: **ecce autem . . . anguēs:** the snakes from Tenedos foreshadow and symbolize the later coming of the Greek ships from Tenedos, bringing destruction with them. Note the HYPERBATON.

Line 204:   **horrēscō, horrēscere, horruī** to shudder, tremble; understand *haec* ("these things") as a direct object of *horrēscēns.*

referō, referre, rettulī, relātum to tell, bring back, withdraw; *horrēscō referēns*: Aeneas was indeed an eyewitness, and his use of the present tense through much of this passage makes the recollection vivid for his listeners.

immēnsus, -a, -um immense, immeasurable

orbis, orbis, m. circle, fold, coil; earth; *immēnsīs orbibus* is an ablative of quality or manner; translate "with huge coils."

anguis, anguis, m. (f.) snake, serpent; understand *venientēs* with *geminī anguēs.*

Line 205:   **incumbō, incumbere, incubuī, incubitum** to lean upon, hang over, lower (over) (+ *dat.*)

pelagus, -ī, n. sea; *pelagō* is a dative with compound *incumbent.*

pariter, *adv.* equally, side by side

tendō, tendere, tetendī, tentum or **tēnsum** to go, advance, strive, stretch

VERGIL *AENEID* 2.201–222, CONTINUED

> pectora quōrum inter flūctūs arrēcta iubaeque
>
> sanguineae superant undās; pars cētera pontum
>
> pōne legit sinuatque immēnsa volūmine terga.
>
> Fit sonitus spūmante salō; iamque arva tenēbant
>
> 210 ardentīsque oculōs suffectī sanguine et ignī
>
> sībila lambēbant linguīs vibrantibus ōra.
>
> Diffugimus vīsū exsanguēs. Illī agmine certō

NOTES AND VOCABULARY

Line 206: **pectus, pectoris,** n. breast, chest; with *arrēcta*: the snakes seem almost to stand on the water.

quōrum: connecting relative

flūctus, flūctūs, m. wave, tide

arrigō, arrigere, arrēxī, arrēctum to raise, rear; translate *arrēcta* with *sunt* understood as "were raised."

iuba, -ae, f. mane, crest

Line 207: **sanguineus, -a, -um** bloody, blood-red

superō (1) to surmount, overcome, survive

cēterus, -a, -um rest, remaining, other; *pars cētera*, the remaining part, refers to the rear part of the snakes' bodies.

pontus, -ī, m. sea, waves

STUDY TIP

Be careful to distinguish the adverb *pōne* ("behind, after") that derives from *post* + *ne* from the verb *pōnō, pōnere, posuī, positum* that means "to put, place."

Line 208: **pōne,** *adv.* behind, after

legō, legere, lēgī, lēctum to choose; skim

sinuō (1) to fold, curve, twist, wind

immēnsus, -a, -um immense, immeasurable

volūmen, volūminis, n. fold, coil, roll; *volūmine* is an ablative of manner or respect; translate "in a coil."

tergum, -ī, n. back, body, rear

Line 209: **fīō, fierī, factus sum** to become, arise

sonitus, sonitūs, m. sound, roar, noise, crash

spūmō (1) to foam, froth, spray

salum, -ī, n. sea, swell (of the sea); *spūmante salō* is an ablative absolute.

arvum, -ī, n. field; literally the clause *arva tenēbant* means "they held the fields." Translate "they arrived upon the fields."

BY THE WAY

Note the SIBILANCE and ONOMATOPOEIA in line 209. The ALLITERATION of "s" in *sonitus spūmante salō* is intended to suggest the sound made by the hissing of the waves. The SIBILANCE carries over into the next lines as well with *suffectī sanguine . . . sībila*.

Line 210:   **ardeō, ardēre, arsī, arsum** to burn; *ardentīs* is the poetic accusative plural form of the present active participle.

oculus, -ī, m. eye; *oculōs*: direct object of the participle *suffectī*, treated here as a middle/reflexive participle capable of having a direct object ("having suffused their eyes"); alternatively, *oculōs* is an accusative of respect translated "suffused with respect to their eyes." (See Language Fact later in this chapter on p. 262.)

sufficiō, sufficere, suffēcī, suffectum to supply, suffuse; the participle *suffectī* modifies the third plural subject ("they") of *tenēbant*.

sanguine *and* **ignī:** both words are ablatives of means. *Ignī* (instead of *igne*) often occurs as the ablative singular.

BY THE WAY

The repeated sound of "l"—*sībi-la lambēbant linguīs*—is suggestive of the snakes licking their mouths. The English word SIBILANCE, the use of words that repeat the "s" sound, derives from the Latin base *sībil–*.

Line 211:   **sībilus, -a, -um** hissing, whirring

lambō, lambere, lambī to lick, lap

lingua, -ae, f. tongue, language

vibrō (1) to quiver, vibrate, dart

ōs, ōris, n. face, mouth; *ōra* is neuter accusative plural; note the CHIASMUS.

Line 212:   **diffugiō, diffugere, diffūgī** to flee apart, scatter; Aeneas inserts himself and his companions again into the scene.

vīsus, vīsūs, m. sight, view, vision, aspect; *vīsū* is either ablative of cause with *exsanguēs* or ablative of separation with *diffugimus*.

exsanguis, exsangue bloodless, lifeless, pale; modifies the first plural subject ("we") of *diffugimus*.

certus, -a, -um sure, fixed, certain, reliable; *agmine certō* is an ablative of means; translate "in a sure line."

BY THE WAY

Interestingly, Vergil uses the adjective *exsanguis* (*ex* + *sanguis*), "bloodless," hence "pale," to describe those witnessing the assault of the snakes, which are associated with "blood" a few lines earlier (*sanguineae* in line 207 and *sanguine* in line 210).

VERGIL *AENEID* 2.201–222, CONTINUED

Lāocoönta petunt; et prīmum parva duōrum

corpora nātōrum serpēns amplexus uterque

215   implicat et miserōs morsū dēpascitur artūs;

post ipsum auxiliō subeuntem ac tēla ferentem

corripiunt spīrīsque ligant ingentibus; et iam

bis medium amplexī, bis collō squāmea circum

terga datī superant capite et cervīcibus altīs.

220   Ille simul manibus tendit dīvellere nōdōs

perfūsus saniē vittās ātrōque venēnō,

clāmōrēs simul horrendōs ad sīdera tollit.

NOTES AND VOCABULARY

STUDY TIP

When Greek names of persons and places occur in Latin, the authors used either the appropriate Latin ending on the noun or the original Greek endings. In the accusative singular, most Greek nouns in Latin end in *–an*, *–on*, *–en*, or *–a*. Be careful not to confuse a Greek accusative *–a* (e.g., *Lāocoönta* in line 213) with a Latin feminine singular nominative ending (e.g., *iuba*) or a Latin accusative plural ending (e.g., *corpora* in line 214).

Line 213:   **prīmum:** an accusative adjective, as in Greek, can function as an adverb. Translate "first."

           duo, duae, duo two

Lines 213–14: Note the SYNCHESIS.

Line 214:   **nātus, nātī,** m. son

           serpēns, serpentis, m. (f.) serpent, snake

           amplector, amplectī, amplexus sum to embrace, enfold; *amplexus* as a perfect passive participle of a deponent verb translates actively. Thus *amplexus* means "having enfolded."

           uterque, utraque, utrumque each, both

Line 215:   **implicō, implicāre, implicāvī (uī), implicātum (itum)** to entwine

           morsus, morsūs, m. bite, biting, jaws, fangs

           dēpascor, dēpascī, dēpāstus sum to feed on, devour

           artus, artūs, m. joint, limb, body

Line 216:   **post,** *adv.* afterward; *prep. + acc.* after, behind

           ipse, ipsa, ipsum –self; *ipsum* modifies *Lāocoönta*, which is understood.

           auxilium, -ī, n. help, aid, assistance; *auxiliō* is a dative of purpose.

           subeō, subīre, subiī, subitum to approach; *subeuntem* is the present participle of *subeō.*

Line 217:   **corripiō, corripere, corripuī, correptum** to seize, snatch up

spīra, -ae, f. fold, coil, spire

ligō (1) to bind, tic, fasten

BY THE WAY

The series of two monosyllabes (*et iam*) that end line 217 combined with the monosyllabic *bis* that begins 218 is quite striking and calls attention to the horror of this scene.

Line 218:   **bis** twice

collum, -ī, n. neck; *collō* is dative with the compound *circumdatī*.

squāmeus, -a, -um scaly

Lines 218–219: Take *circum* with *datī* (i.e., *circumdatī*) and translate "placed around."

BY THE WAY

The separation of the parts of a compound word into two distinct words is called TMESIS (from the Greek word for "cutting"). Note that through the use of TMESIS here, the verb *circumdatī* surrounds and thereby emphasizes *terga,* the (scaly) backs of the two snakes.

Line 219:   **tergum, -ī,** n. back, body, rear; *terga* is the direct object of the participle *circumdatī* ("having placed"), treated here as a middle/reflexive participle capable of having a direct object. (See the Language Fact later in this chapter on p. 262.)

caput, capitis, n. head; *capite* for *capitibus*, which could not be used in dactylic verse because of its three successive short syllables; *capite* is an ablative of means.

cervīx, cervīcis, f. neck

Line 220:   **ille:** refers to Laocoon.

manus, manūs, f. hand; *manibus* is an ablative of means.

dīvellō, dīvellere, dīvellī (or **dīvulsī**), **dīvulsum** to tear apart

nōdus, -ī , m. knot; fold, coil

Lines 220–222: **simul . . . simul** not only . . . but at the same time

Line 221:   **perfundō, perfundere, perfūdī, perfūsum** to soak, drench

saniēs, saniēī, f. blood, gore; *saniē, ātrōque, venēnō* are ablatives of means.

vitta, -ae, f. fillet, garland, band; *vittās* is an accusative object of the participle *perfūsus*, treated here as a middle/reflexive participle capable of having a direct object ("having soaked his headbands"). (See the Language Fact later in this chapter on pp. 262–263.)

venēnum, -ī, n. poison, venom, drug

Line 222:   **horrendus, -a, -um** horrible, horrifying

sīdus, sīderis, n. star

tollō, tollere, sustulī, sublātum to raise

TAKE NOTE

Many islands ending in *–us/-os* are feminine gender in Latin. Examples include Tenedos (line 203), Cypros (Cyprus), Chios, and others.

This copy of the famous Laocoon statue group sits near the Legion of Honor and its art collection in San Francisco, CA. Ever since the Roman copy was uncovered in 1506 near the Baths of Trajan on the Esquiline hill, the statue group has enjoyed celebrity status. Pope Julius II purchased it that March and it has been part of the Vatican collections ever since. The Laocoon group influenced such Renaissance artists as Michelangelo, who was summoned to the site when the work was first found. Francis I of France negotiated with the pope for permission to cast a copy that was placed in the court at Fontainebleau. The Roman copy in marble, probably commissioned by the emperor Titus, was based on a bronze original of the second century BCE. Pliny the Elder in his *Natural History* notes that it was sculpted by the Rhodians Hagesander, Athanadoros, and Polydoros.

COMPREHENSION QUESTIONS

1. What was Laocoon doing as the snakes appeared? Cite the Latin.

2. Where were the snakes coming from?

3. What parts of the snakes were raised above the waves?

4. With what did the snakes' eyes burn? Cite the Latin.

5. Who fled the sight of the snakes?

6. Whom did the snakes attack first?

7. How many times did the snakes coil around Laocoon's body?

8. What does Laocoon raise to the sky?

VOCABULARY BUILDER

There are five groups of synonyms in the list below. List each word according to the group to which it belongs. Give the English meaning for each group of synonyms. These words can be found in the passage above.

anguis, anguis, m. (f.)

serpēns, serpentis, m. (f.)

unda, -ae, f.

volūmen, volūminis, n.

salum, -ī, n.

collum, -ī, n.

fluctus, -ūs, m.

spīra, -ae, f.

pelagus, -ī, n.

nodus, -ī, m.

altum, -ī, n.

cervīx, cervīcis, f.

pontus, -ī, m.

orbis, orbis, m.

▶ EXERCISE 1

1. In line 201, what is the case and use of *sorte*?

2. What is the case and use of *Tenedō* in line 203?

3. In line 204, what is the tense, voice, and form of *referēns*?

4. In line 205, what is the tense, voice, and mood of *incumbunt*?

5. What is the case and use of *lītora* in line 205?

6. In line 206, what is the case and use of *iubae*?

7. In line 209, what is the tense and mood of *fit*?

8. What is the case and use of *salō* in line 209?

9. In line 211, what is the case and use of *ōra*?

10. In line 213, what is the case and use of *Lāocoönta*?

11. In line 214, what is tense, mood, and form of *amplexus*?

12. In line 217, what is the case and use of *spīrīs*?

13. What is the case and use of *cervīcibus* in line 219?

14. What is the case and use of *clāmōrēs* in line 222?

15. What is the tense, mood, and voice of *tollit* in line 222?

LANGUAGE FACT

REFLEXIVE/MIDDLE VOICE

The voice of a verb indicates whether the subject is acting (active voice) or being acted upon (passive voice). Greek has a third voice (middle) used to indicate that the subject is acting upon itself. English and Latin usually express the middle voice by the use of reflexive pronouns.

ACTIVE	PASSIVE	MIDDLE/REFLEXIVE
"They soak."	"They are soaked."	"They soak themselves."
Perfundunt.	*Perfunduntur.*	*Perfundunt sē.*

Latin authors, however, sometimes use a passive verb form as a middle/reflexive verb form. Passive verbs do not normally take a direct object. A Latin verb in the passive voice with a direct object is usually being used as a reflexive/middle voice verb. Look at these examples from the passage you have just read.

> *... oculōs suffectī sanguine et ignī ...* (Vergil *Aeneid* 2.210)
> "Having suffused his eyes with blood and fire"

> *... perfūsus saniē vittās ....* (Vergil *Aeneid* 2.221)
> "Having soaked his garlands with blood"

Now compare the passive and middle voices in these Latin sentences.

> *vittae suae saniē perfūsae sunt.* **PASSIVE**
> "His garlands were soaked with blood."

> *ille vittās saniē perfūsus est.* **MIDDLE**
> "He soaked his garlands with blood."

> *oculī suī sanguine et ignī suffectī sunt.* **PASSIVE**
> "Their eyes were suffused with blood and fire."

> *eī oculōs sanguine et ignī suffectī sunt.* **MIDDLE**
> "They suffused their eyes with blood and fire."

BY THE WAY

Some prefer to treat the middle voice participle, actually a Greek usage found in Latin, as a true passive voice with an accusative of respect. An accusative of respect is translated "as to" or "with respect to" and is used with references to body parts or articles of apparel. Be careful not to confuse the accusative of respect, which is a Greek usage transferred into Latin, with the ablative of respect, the Latin usage (See p. 20 and p. 209 for the ablative of respect).

> *ille vittās saniē perfūsus est.*
> "He was soaked as to his garlands with blood."

> *oculōs suffectī sunt sanguine et ignī.*
> "They were suffused with respect to their eyes with blood and fire."

This close-up of Laocoon reveals the agony and contorted emotion of Laocoon as he attempts to uncoil the snakes. The Hellenistic era reveled in portraying intense drama and emotion. Indeed, the Laocoon group is often referenced as the most influential portrayal of suffering and violent motion from the ancient world.

▶ EXERCISE 2

Translate these sentences based on this passage. Identify whether the verb in bold is active, passive, or middle voice.

1. Anguēs inter flūctūs pectora **arrēctī sunt**.

2. Serpentēs ad arva iērunt, ardentēs oculōs **suffectī** sanguine.

3. Lāocoön **ligātus est** ingentibus spīrīs.

4. Ille **perfūsus** saniē caput tēla fert.

5. Bis squāmeīs tergīs illum **superant**.

6. Serpentēs collō Lāocoöntis **circum** terga **datī sunt**.

7. Nodōs anguium manibus **dīvellit.**

8. Magnī clāmōrēs ad sīdera **tolluntur**.

9. Lāocoönta serpentēs medium corporis amplectentēs immēnsibus orbibus **līgant**.

10. Anguēs parva nātōrum corpora **amplexī** miserōs artūs dēpascuntur.

ESSAY

The description of the snakes and their actions (lines 201–222) is extraordinarily vivid. How does Vergil achieve this effect? What senses does his description include? Present your response in a well-organized essay.

Support your assertions with references drawn from throughout the passage indicated by each essay. All Latin words must be copied or their line numbers provided, AND they must be translated or paraphrased closely enough so that it is clear you understand the Latin. Direct your answer to the question; do not merely summarize the passage. Please write your essay on a separate piece of paper.

SCANSION

Name the meter and scan the following lines.

Ecce autem geminī ā Tenedō tranquilla per alta

horrēscō referēns immēnsīs orbibus anguēs

incumbunt pelagō pariterque ad lītora tendunt

The story of the Trojan Horse has seized the imagination through the millennia. From fifth-century Greek vase paintings to modern renditions like the one depicted, artists and craftsmen have sought to celebrate the great trick of the Greeks. After the snakes attacked Laocoon seemingly for having advised the Trojans not to bring the wooden horse inside the city walls, the tricky Sinon convinces the war-weary Trojans that the horse was left behind as an offering. So, the Trojans, in their eagerness to believe the Greeks had returned home, bring the horse into the city, spend the night in revelry only to be awakened by a maurading Greek army that had sprung from the belly of the wooden horse.

READING 4

In the passage that immediately precedes this one, Priam is forced to witness the death of his son, Polites, at the hand of Pyrrhus, Achilles's son. In anger, Priam upbraids Pyrrhus, observing that Achilles (who is now dead) treated him with respect as a suppliant. Pyrrhus responds to this rebuke sarcastically before he murders Priam and his wife Hecuba, who have taken refuge on the household altar, where suppliants are supposed to be safe. As Aeneas witnesses from a distance the brutal death and senseless mutilation of Priam, his thoughts turn for the first time to the fate of his own family.

PYRRHUS AND THE DEATH OF PRIAM

VERGIL *AENEID* 2.547–566

Meter: Dactylic Hexameter

> Cui Pyrrhus: "Referēs ergō haec et nuntius ībis
>
> Pēlīdae genitōrī. Illī mea tristia facta
>
> dēgeneremque Neoptolemum nārrāre mementō.
>
> 550 Nunc morere." Hoc dīcēns altāria ad ipsa trementem
>
> trāxit et in multō lāpsantem sanguine nātī,
>
> implicuitque comam laevā, dextrāque coruscum
>
> extulit ac laterī capulō tenus abdidit ēnsem.

NOTES AND VOCABULARY

Line 547: **cui:** the referent is Priam; translate "to him."

Pyrrhus, -ī, m. Neoptolemus, son of Achilles; note the ELLIPSIS of *dīxit*, the verb that goes with Pyrrhus.

referō, referre, rettulī, relātum to bring back, tell; the future tense verbs *referēs et ībis* are used with the force of imperatives; translate "go and tell."

ergō, *adv.* therefore, then, consequently

nuntius, -(i)ī, m. messenger, message; translate "(as) a messenger."

BY THE WAY

In line 547, *referēs et ībis* are an example of HYSTERON PROTERON, a figure of speech in which there is a reversal of the natural order of events. The reversal gives importance to the first item mentioned, in this instance, "the telling."

Line 548: **Pēlīdēs, -ae,** m. descendant of Peleus, Achilles

genitor, genitōris, m. father; understand *meō* with *genitōrī = Achillī.*

ille, illa, illud that, he, she, it; *illī* is dative singular and refers to Achilles, Neoptolemus's father.

tristis, triste sad; the *tristia facta* refer to Pyrrhus's killing of Polites.

factum, -ī, n. deed, exploit, undertaking; *mea tristia facta dēgeneremque Neoptolemum* are ironical and mocking: Neoptolemus's deeds have caused sadness, not for himself but for Priam and his family.

Line 549: **dēgener, dēgeneris** degenerate, ignoble, base

Neoptolemus, -ī, m. Pyrrhus, son of Achilles

meminī, meminisse to remember, recall; *mementō* is a future imperative. In classical Latin the form of the future imperative seldom appears and with only a few verbs.

Line 550: **morior, morī, mortuus sum** to die, perish; *morere* is the imperative of a deponent verb.

altāria, altārium, n. pl. altar; Vergil mentions this detail (*altāria ad ipsa*) to emphasize the impiety of Neoptolemus's deed.

tremō, tremere, tremuī to tremble, shake, quiver. Understand *eum,* "him," referring to Priam, with *trementem.* Priam is trembling probably less from fear than from old age and anger.

Line 551: **lāpsō, lāpsāre** to slip, stumble, totter, fall; the added detail of his slipping in the blood of his son (*lāpsantem sanguine nātī*) increases the vividness of the terrible scene, as it evokes our pathos for Priam. The frequentative verb *lāpsō* (from *lābor, lābī, lāpsus* sum) appears to have been coined by Vergil.

nātī: refers to Polites, one of Priam's sons. In lines 526–531 Pyrrhus kills Polites while Priam and Hecuba look on.

BY THE WAY

Note how the one slipping (*lāpsantem*), namely Priam, is in the middle of the copious blood (*multō . . . sanguine*). The arrangement of the words forms a picture of what the reader is to see in his or her mind. Vergil draws another picture for his reader with *laevā, dextrāque* in line 552 in which *laevā,* which means "left," is on the left while *dextrā,* which means "right," is on the right. Thus the reader is encouraged to see in his or her mind how Pyrrhus grabs Priam's hair with his left hand and unsheathes his sword with his right hand.

Line 552: **implicō, implicāre, implicāvī (-uī), implicātum (-itum)** to entwine

coma, -ae, f. hair, locks, tresses

laeva, -ae, f. left hand

dextra, -ae, f. right hand; the noun *dextra* (or *dextera*) derives from the adjective *dexter, dextra, dextrum,* meaning "to the right" or "right" (the forms *dextera, dexterum,* etc. are less common).

coruscus, -a, -um flashing, bright, waving; modifies *ēnsem* in line 553.

Line 553: **efferō, efferre, extulī, ēlātum** to raise, lift

latus, lateris, n. side, flank; *laterī = in latus:* dative of direction or motion

capulus, -ī, m. hilt, handle

tenus, *prep. + abl.* to, up to, as far as; this preposition normally follows the ablative (*capulō* here) it governs.

abdō, abdere, abdidī, abditum to hide, bury

ēnsis, ēnsis, m. sword

VERGIL *AENEID* 2.547–566, CONTINUED

Haec fīnis Priamī fātōrum, hic exitus illum

555   sorte tulit Troiam incēnsam et prōlāpsa videntem

Pergama, tot quondam populīs terrīsque superbum

rēgnātōrem Asiae. Iacet ingēns lītore truncus,

āvulsumque umerīs caput et sine nōmine corpus.

    At mē tum prīmum saevus circumstetit horror.

560   Obstipuī; subiit cārī genitōris imāgō,

ut rēgem aequaevum crūdēlī vulnere vīdī

vītam exhālantem, subiit dēserta Creūsa

et dīrepta domus et parvī cāsus Iūlī.

NOTES AND VOCABULARY

Line 554:   **fīnis, fīnis,** m. (f.) end; *haec* is attracted to the gender of the predicate noun, *fīnis*, which is here feminine, though ordinarily masculine. Supply *fuit.*

         exitus, exitūs, m. exit, issue, end. In the phrase *hic exitus*, the word *vītae* is to be understood. The quantity of the adjective *hic* is lengthened here, perhaps as a reminiscence of the word's earlier spelling, *hicc(e).*

Line 555:   **sors, sortis,** f. lot, fate, destiny; oracle

         incendō, incendere, incendī, incēnsum to burn, inflame

         prōlābor, prōlābī, prōlāpsus sum to slide, fall, perish. *Prōlāpsa*, which modifies Troy, echoes *lāpsantem* in line 551, which modified Priam. Vergil's purpose is to link the fate of Troy with that of its ruler.

Line 556:   **Pergama, Pergamōrum,** n. pl. (citadel of) Troy; Vergil often uses *Pergama* as a synonym for Troy.

         tot so many

         populus, -ī, m. people, nation; *populīs terrīsque* are ablatives of cause with *superbum.*

         superbus, -a, -um proud, haughty

Line 557:   **rēgnātor, rēgnātōris,** m. ruler, sovereign, lord

         Asia, -ae, f. Asia (Minor); *Asiae* is an objective genitive with *rēgnātōrem.*

         iaceō, iacēre, iacuī, iacitum to lie (low, outspread)

         ingēns, ingentis huge, immense

         lītus, lītoris, n. shore; understand *in* with *lītore*. Priam's headless corpse is thrown out on the beach for the dogs and birds to devour.‡

         truncus, -ī, m. trunk, body, torso

Line 558:   **āvellō, āvellere, āvellī** or **āvulsī, āvulsum** to tear from

STUDY TIP

Be careful to distinguish between the second conjugation verb *iaceo*, "to lic," and the third conjugation verb *iaciō*, "to throw."

| iaceō, iacēre, iacuī | lie | SECOND CONJUGATION |
| iaciō, iacere, iēcī, iactum | throw | THIRD *IO* CONJUGATION |

Line 559:   **circumstō, circumstāre, circumstetī** to surround, stand around

horror, horrōris, m. shudder(ing), horror, alarm

Line 560:   **obstipēscō, obstipēscere, obstipuī** to be dazed, stand agape

subeō, subīre, subiī, subitum to approach; understand *meam mentem* with *subiit* as an implied direct object, or take intransitively, "arose."

cārus, -a, -um dear, beloved, fond

imāgō, imāginis, f. image, picture, likeness

Line 561:   **aequaevus, -a, -um** of equal age; Anchises was about the same age as Priam.

crūdēlis, crūdēle cruel, bloody, bitter

vulnus, vulneris, n. wound, deadly blow

STUDY TIP

The synonyms *crūdēlis* and *saevus*, both of which mean "cruel," appear in lines 559 and 561. While Vergil often uses the same word in a similar context to provide a verbal echo, he also likes to use synonyms.

Line 562:   **exhālō** (1) to breathe out, exhale

dēserō, dēserere, dēseruī, dēsertum to desert, forsake

Creūsa, -ae, f. wife of Aeneas, lost during the sack of Troy

Line 563:   **dīripiō, dīripere, dīripuī, dīreptum** to plunder, ravage; *dīrepta*: i.e., in Aeneas's imagination

domus, domūs, f. home, house; *domus* is nominative singular with the final syllable to be marked long (instead of short) for the sake of the meter. Aeneas's home may at this point have been ravaged; the unusual metrical effect emphasizes Aeneas's sense of loss.

cāsus, cāsūs, m. fortune, misfortune, chance

Iūlus, -ī, m. Ascanius, son of Aeneas; it should be noted that Iulus has three syllables: *I - ū- lus*.

VERGIL *AENEID* 2.547–566, CONTINUED

Respiciō et quae sit mē circum cōpia lūstrō.

565 Dēseruēre omnēs dēfessī, et corpora saltū

ad terram mīsēre aut ignibus aegra dedēre.

NOTES AND VOCABULARY

Line 564: **respiciō, respicere, respexī, respectum** to look back; Aeneas on the roof of the palace had been so transfixed in looking down on the murder of Priam that he had forgotten everything else. He now looks around for his followers and finds them gone.

mē circum = *circum mē*

cōpia, -ae, f. abundance, plenty, forces, troops; *quae sit . . . cōpia (virōrum)* is an indirect question.

lūstrō (1) to survey; traverse; purify

BY THE WAY

The phrase *mē circum* in line 564 is an example of ANASTROPHE, a figure of speech in which there is an inversion of the usual order of words. By postponing *circum*, Vergil slows down the line by creating a string of single words with long or lengthened syllables (*quae, sit, mē*; *et* is elided with *respiciō*), a retardation that reflects the context of Aeneas's taking time to scan the area, looking for fellow Trojans. The ANASTROPHE also allows Vergil to create ALLITERATION through the repeated sound of hard "c" (*cir-cum cōpia*).

Line 565: **dēfessus, -a, -um** tired, weary, worn

saltus, saltūs, m. leap, bound, dancing; *saltū* is an ablative of means or manner.

Lines 565–566: **dēseruēre, mīsēre, dedēre:** the contracted forms of *dēseruērunt, mīsērunt, dedērunt*

Line 566: **aeger, aegra, aegrum** sick, weary, wretched, wounded; the HYPERBATON, which separates *aegra* from *corpora* in line 565, emphasizes the weary and wounded state of the bodies.

TAKE NOTE

In his fourth century CE commentary on the *Aeneid*, Servius suggests that in line 557 Vergil has in mind the fate of Pompey, who was one of the world's most powerful men. Pompey was defeated in the battle of Pharsalus in 48 BCE. After fleeing to Egypt, he was killed and beheaded by agents of King Ptolemy XIII on the Egyptian shore, where his body was cast out and allowed to lie on the beach.

COMPREHENSION QUESTIONS

1. What does Pyrrhus tell Priam to relate to his dead father Achilles? Cite the Latin.

2. Where did Pyrrhus drag Priam in order to kill him?

3. In what was Priam slipping?

4. What weapon did Pyrrhus use to kill Priam?

5. Who was described as once the proud ruler of Asia?

6. What three relatives came to Aeneas's mind as he saw the dead body of Priam? Cite the Latin.

7. What happened to many of Aeneas's comrades who had been with him until this time?

▶ EXERCISE 1

1. What is the tense, mood, and voice of *referēs* in line 547?

2. In line 548, what is the case and use of the phrase *mea tristia facta*?

3. In line 550, what is the tense, voice, and form of *dīcēns*?

4. In line 552, what is the case and use of *laevā*?

5. In line 553, what is the tense, voice, and mood of *abdidit*?

6. In line 554, what is the case and use of *exitus*?

7. What word does *ingēns* in line 557 modify?

8. What is the tense, voice, and form of *āvulsum* in line 558?

9. What Latin word does *saevus* in line 559 modify?

10. In line 561, what is the English meaning of *ut*?

11. In line 564, what is the tense, mood, and use of *sit*?

12. What is the case and use of *ignibus* in line 566?

LANGUAGE FACT

PATRONYMICS AND OTHER NAMES

Vergil often refers to characters by more than one name. Sometimes a character has another name or a nickname. For example, Pyrrhus's nickname is Neoptolemus, a name that means "new to the war." Aeneas's son Ascanius also goes by Iulus. Vergil may use a patronymic to refer to a character, a way of calling a son by the name of his father. Thus, Achilles's patronymic Pelides means "son of Peleus." Patronymics can be recognized in Latin by the characteristic "-des" at the end of the father's name. Vergil also uses adjectival forms of names. So *Aenēius* means "of Aeneas" or "related to Aeneas." Here are some examples of patronymics and other names from the *Aeneid*.

Name	Another Name	Adjective	Patronym	Son
Anchīsēs			Anchīsiadēs	Aenēās
Aenēās		Aenēius	Aeneadēs	Ascānius
Ascānius	Iūlus			
Achillēs		Achillēus	Achillīdēs	Pyrrhus
Pyrrhus	Neoptolemus			
Atreus			Atrīdēs	Agamemnōn/Menelāus
Hector		Hectoreus		
Pēleus			Pēlīdēs	Achillēs
Priamus		Priamēius	Priamidēs	Hector/Helenus/Polītēs

▶ EXERCISE 2

Match the names that refer to the same person.

1. Ascānius   Anchīsiadēs

2. Achillēs   Achillīdēs

3. Hector   Atrīdēs

4. Agamemnōn   Pēlīdēs

5. Aenēās   Aeneadēs

6. Pyrrhus   Priamidēs

Likewise, countries and cities often are referred to by multiple names. Citizens are called by these different names (usually an adjective in form), sometimes derived from the name of the country or city, and sometimes derived from other sources, like a founding ancestor or an early king. Here are a few examples.

City/Country	Latin Names	Citizen
Troy	Trōia	Trōiānus
	Īlium	Iliacus
	Pergama	Pergameus
		Dardanius
		Teucrius
		Phrygius
Greece	Argos	Argivus
		Argolicus
	Graecia	Grāius
		Achaicus
		Danaus
		Doricus
		Achivus
Carthage	Karthāgō	
	Tyrus	Tyrius
Italy	Italia	Italus
	Latium	Latīnus
	Hesperia	Hesperius
	Ausonia	Ausonius
	Lāvīnium	Lāvīnus

▶ EXERCISE 3

Match the citizen to his country or city.

1. Italus   Pergama

2. Tyrius   Argos

3. Teucrī   Karthāgō

4. Achivus   Ausonia

BY THE WAY

Before the fall of Troy, the young son of Aeneas, Ascanius, was called Ilus which meant "little boy of Troy," from the other name for Troy, which was Ilium. Later by an addition of the letter "u," Ilus became known as Iulus. After the fall of Troy, Aeneas and Iulus settled in Italy. Much later the Julian (Iulian) family in Rome took great pride in tracing their lineage back to Iulus. The most famous member of the Julian family was Julius Caesar.

ESSAY

Lines 547–566 focus on the family. Discuss how Vergil uses theme and language to associate Achilles and Anchises, Polites and Iulus, and Iulus and Priam and how the emphasis on the family is significant for the interpretation of the passage.

Support your assertions with references drawn from throughout the passage. All Latin words must be copied or their line numbers provided, AND they must be translated or paraphrased closely enough so that it is clear you understand the Latin. Direct your answer to the question; do not merely summarize the passage. Please write your essay on a separate piece of paper.

SCANSION

Name the meter and scan the following lines.

> ut rēgem aequaevum crūdēlī vulnere vīdī
>
> vītam exhālantem; subiit dēserta Creūsa
>
> et dīrepta domus et parvī cāsus Iūlī.

Benjamin Robert Haydon (1786–1846) drew from the *Homeric Hymn to Aphrodite* as the inspiration for his painting of Venus and Anchises. Here, Anchises having taken a break from herding cattle on Mt. Ida is visited by the goddess of beauty. Sir John Leycester, who had commissioned the painting, begged Haydon to send it to the Royal Academy for exhibit. Haydon, who acquiesced to his patron's request, was pleased to remark later that the painting was well received.

READING 5

As Anchises finishes begging Aeneas to save his family from the Greek invaders, the roar of fire is heard and its heat comes closer. Aeneas returns home and plans for an escape from the city are made. Aeneas tells his father to get on his back so that he can carry him out of the city. His little son Iulus and his wife Creusa will come with them. He instructs the household servants to meet him at an old temple of Ceres just outside the city. Aeneas also tells his father to carry the Penates, since it would be a sacrilege for Aeneas himself to touch them with his bloody hands. Aeneas then covers his shoulders with a lion skin and puts his father on his back. Iulus holds his father's right hand and Creusa follows behind as they flee through the darkness.

FLIGHT FROM TROY

VERGIL *AENEID* 2.705–729

Meter: Dactylic Hexameter

705 Dīxerat ille, et iam per moenia clārior ignis

audītur, propriusque aestūs incendia volvunt.

"Ergō, age, cāre pater, cervīcī impōnere nostrae;

ipse subībō umerīs nec mē labor iste gravābit;

quō rēs cumque cadent, ūnum et commūne perīclum,

710 ūna salūs ambōbus erit. Mihi parvus Iūlus

sit comes, et longē servet vestīgia coniūnx.

NOTES AND VOCABULARY

Line 705: **ille:** refers to Anchises.

clārus, -a, -um clear, bright; translate the comparative adjective *clārior* as a comparative adverb "more clearly."

Line 706: **prope,** *adv.* near; (*comp.*) **proprius** nearer

aestus, aestūs, m. flood, tide, surge; heat; translate the poetic plural as a singular in English. Translate *aestūs incendia volvunt* "the fires roll the heat." In English we would say, "the fires increase the heat."

incendium, -ī, n. fire, flame, conflagration

Line 707: **ergō,** *adv.* therefore, then, consequently

agō, agere, ēgī, āctum to do. Here the word *age* is being used informally in conversation; translate *age* as "come on."

cārus, -a, -um dear, beloved

cervīx, cervīcis, f. neck; *cervīcī . . . nostrae* is dative after the compound verb *impōnere*; translate "on my neck."

impōnō, impōnere, imposuī, impositum (+ *dat.*) to place (on); although *impōnere* looks like a present active infinitive, it is being used as a middle/reflexive imperative; translate "place yourself."

Line 708:　**subeō, subīre, subiī, subitum** to go under, support, follow, approach; Vergil expects his reader to supply *tē*, "you," as the direct object of *subībō*.

umerus, -ī, m. shoulder; *umerīs* is an ablative of means.

iste, ista, istud that (of yours)

gravō (1) to burden, load

STUDY TIP

Be careful to distinguish between *iste, ista, istud* that (of yours) and *ipse, ipsa, ipsum* –self.

Line 709:　**quō . . . cumque (quōcumque),** *conj.* wherever, wheresoever, to whatever place; note the TMESIS. Translate *quōcumque* "in whatever place."

cadō, cadere, cecidī, cāsum to fall, happen

commūnis, commūne common, mutual, general; in the phrase *ūnum et commūne*, do not translate "and."

perīc(u)lum, -ī, n. danger, peril, risk; understand *erit*, "will be," with *perīclum*. *Perīclum* is the contracted form of *perīculum*.

Line 710:　**salūs, salūtis,** f. safety, health

ambō, -ae, -ō (pl.) both

parvus: an EPITHET for Iulus

Iūlus, -ī, m. Ascanius, son of Aeneas

Line 711:　**comes, comitis,** m. companion; *comes (cum + eō)* means literally "to go with [someone]," hence "companion."

longē, *adv.* far (away), (from) afar

vestīgium, -ī, n. step, track, trace; translate *servet vestīgia* as "follow." Both *sit* and *servet* are volitive subjunctives.

VERGIL *AENEID* 2.705–729, CONTINUED

Vōs, famulī, quae dīcam animīs advertite vestrīs.

Est urbe ēgressīs tumulus templumque vetustum

dēsertae Cereris, iuxtāque antīqua cupressus

715 religiōne patrum multōs servāta per annōs.

Hanc ex dīversō sēdem veniēmus in ūnam.

Tū, genitor, cape sacra manū patriōsque penātīs;

Mē bellō ē tantō dīgressum et caede recentī

attrectāre nefās, dōnec mē flūmine vivō

720 abluerō."

NOTES AND VOCABULARY

Line 712: **famulus, -ī,** m. servant, attendant

quae dīcam: the understood antecedent of *quae* is *ea* or *haec*. Translate "these things that I will say."

animus, -ī, m. mind; *animīs . . . vestrīs* is a dative with a compound verb. Translate "direct your minds to."

advertō, advertere, advertī, adversum to turn or direct . . . to

vester, vestra, vestrum your(s), your own

Line 713: **ēgredior, ēgredī, ēgressus sum** to depart, go out; perfect passive participles of deponent verbs translate actively. The participle *ēgressīs* is a dative of reference. Translate *(vōbīs) ēgressīs urbe*" "to (you) having departed from the city."

tumulus, -ī, m. mound, hill

templum, -ī, n. temple, shrine, sanctuary

vetustus, -a, -um old, ancient, former

Line 714: **dēserō, dēsere, dēseruī, dēsertum** to desert; the participle *dēsertae* that modifies *Cereris* grammatically refers to *templum* in context and is an example of a TRANSFERRED EPITHET. Translate with *vetustum* "an old, deserted temple."

Cerēs, Cereris, f. Ceres, the goddess of grain

iuxtā, *adv.* near (by), close

cupressus, -ī, f. cypress (tree); names of trees in Latin are feminine. Thus *antīqua* modifies *cupressus.*

Line 715: **religiō, religiōnis,** f. religion, sanctity; some texts read the poetic and less common form *relligiōne.*‡

annus, -ī, m. year, season

Line 716: **dīversus, -a, -um** different, various; the singular phrase *ex dīversō (locō)* instead of the plural *ex dīversīs (locīs)* is used, which means literally "from a different place." Translate "from different directions."

Line 717: **sacer, sacra, sacrum** holy, sacred; *sacra* is a neuter plural substantive; translate "sacred objects."

patrius, -a, -um fatherly, ancestral

penātēs, penātium, m. (pl.) the gods of Troy; the poetic accusative form *-īs* for *-ēs* is used.

Line 718: **mē:** this pronoun is accusative after the impersonal verb *nefās (est)*. Translate "for me."

dīgredior, dīgredī, dīgressus sum to (de)part, go away; the perfect participle *dīgressum,* which should be translated actively, modifies *mē.*

caedēs, caedis, f. slaughter, blood(shed), murder

recēns, recentis recent, fresh, new, late

Line 719: **attrectō** (1) to handle, touch

nefās, n. *indeclin.* guilt, impiety, wrong‡

dōnec, *conj.* until, as long as, while

flūmen, flūminis, n. river, stream, flood

vīvus, -a, -um living, alive; running; translate *vīvō* as "running."

Line 720: **abluō, abluere, abluī, ablūtum** to wash, purify; a short line like this one is usually thought to be a sign of the unfinished nature of the *Aeneid*. If Vergil had lived longer, he might have eliminated such short lines by reworking the passage.

VERGIL *AENEID* 2.705–729, CONTINUED

> Haec fātus lātōs umerōs subiectaque colla
> veste super fulvīque īnsternor pelle leōnis,
> succēdōque onerī; dextrae sē parvus Iūlus
> implicuit sequiturque patrem nōn passibus aequīs;
> 725 pōne subit coniūnx. Ferimur per opāca locōrum,
> et mē, quem dūdum nōn ūlla iniecta movēbant
> tēla neque adversō glomerātī ex agmine Grāiī,
> nunc omnēs terrent aurae, sonus excitat omnis
> suspēnsum et pariter comitīque onerīque timentem.

NOTES AND VOCABULARY

Line 721:   **for, fārī, fātus sum** to speak; *fātus* is the perfect passive participle of the deponent verb *for, fārī*. Translate actively as "having spoken [these words]."‡

lātus, -a, -um broad, wide, spacious

subiciō, subicere, subiēcī, subiectum to bend, stoop

collum, -ī, n. neck

STUDY TIP

Don't confuse *lātus, -a, -um* "broad, wide" with *latus, lateris* n. "side" or with *lateō, latēre* "to lie hidden."

REMINDER

As you read on p. 33 in the Caesar chapter of this book, HENDIADYS (as in *veste . . . fulvīque . . . pelle* in line 722) is a rhetorical figure of speech in which two nouns linked by a conjunction express one idea.

Line 722:   **vestis, vestis,** f. cloth(ing), garment, robe; can be translated as "with a garment of yellow skin" or "hide." Note the HENDIADYS.

super is an adverb and should be translated "over."

fulvus, -a, -um yellow, tawny, blond

īnsternō, īnsternere, īnstrāvī, īnstrātum to lay on, cover, spread; the verb *īnsternor* is being used as a middle/reflexive present tense verb. Translate "I cover my."

pellis, pellis, f. hide, skin, pelt

leō, leōnis, m. lion

Line 723:   **succēdō, succēdere, successī, successum** (+ *dat.*) to go under, advance, succeed

onus, oneris, n. burden, load, weight; *onerī* is dative after the compound verb *succēdō*; translate "I take on the burden."

dextrae: The Latin adjectives for "right" and "left" can be used in the feminine with *manus* ("hand") understood to refer to the right (*dextra*) or left hand (*sinistra*). *Dextrae* is dative with a compound verb.

Line 724: **implicō, implicāre, implicāvī** or **implicuī, implicātum** or **implicitum** (*+ dat.*) to enfold, wind, twine, cling; *implicuit* literally means "he entwined himself in my right hand" but translate "he held my right hand."

passus, passūs, m. step, pace, gait, stride; *nōn passibus aequīs* is an ablative of means.

aequus, -a, -um equal, even, just

Line 725: **pōne,** *adv.* behind, from behind

ferimur, from *ferō, ferre, tulī, lātum*

opācus, -a, -um dark, obscure, gloomy; *opāca* is a neuter plural substantive; this is literally "through the dark things of the places" but translate "through dark places."

Line 726: **mē:** this word is the object of *terrent* (728).

dūdum, *adv.* lately, previously

iniciō, inicere, iniēcī, iniectum to cast on

moveō, movēre, mōvī, mōtum: in this context the meaning of this word is more emotional than physical, as in the English expression "I was moved by his tears." Translate here as "bothered" or "disturbed."

Line 727: **adversus, -a, -um** opposing, facing

glomerō (1) to roll together, assemble

agmen, agminis, n. line of battle

Grāius, -a, -um Greek

Line 728: **terreō, terrēre, terruī, territum** to terrify, frighten

aura, -ae, f. breeze

sonus, -ī, m. sound, noise, roar; in the phrase *omnēs terrent aurae, sonus excitat omnis* note the ASYNDETON and the CHIASMUS.

excitō (1) to arouse, startle, stir (up)

STUDY TIP

Be careful to distinguish among these three nouns that look similar to one another but are from different declensions and have different meanings.

aura, -ae, f. breeze	FIRST DECLENSION
aurum, -ī, n. gold	SECOND DECLENSION NEUTER
auris, auris, f. ear	THIRD DECLENSION

Line 729: **suspēnsus, -a, -um** doubtful, anxious

pariter equally, side by side

comes, comitis, m. comrade; both *comitī* and *onerī* are datives of reference. Since *-que* is with each noun, translate "for both my companion and my burden."

onus, oneris, n. burden, load, weight

timeō, timēre, timuī to fear, dread, be anxious

TAKE NOTE

1. *Religiō* derives from *ligō*, "to bind" and *re–* "back" or "strongly." Etymologically, religion bound people by rituals and practices.

2. *Nefās (ne + for, fārī, fātus sum)* refers to something contrary to divine law. It thus signifies an offense or event so wicked that one should not talk about it.

3. *Fātum, -ī,* n. derives from *for, fārī, fātus* to speak. Literally, *fātum* means "a [divine] statement." In addition to "fate," other English words that derive from this Latin family of words include affable, preface, infant, infantry, fable, fame, defame, infamous, nefarious, and fairy.

COMPREHENSION QUESTIONS

1. How does Aeneas intend to get his aged father out of the burning city?

2. How does Aeneas intend for his son and wife to escape from the city?

3. Where does Aeneas say that all his people should meet? Cite the Latin.

4. What does Aeneas tell his father to carry? Why?

▶ EXERCISE 1

1. In line 705, what is the tense, mood, and voice of *dīxerat*?

2. In line 708, what is the case and use of *mē*?

3. What is the tense, mood, and voice of *cadent* in line 709?

4. What is the case and use of *ambōbus* in line 710?

5. What is the tense and mood of *sit* in line 711?

6. In line 711, what is the case and use of *vestīgia*?

7. In line 712, what is the case and use of *famulī*?

8. What is the tense and mood of *dīcam* in line 712?

9. What word does *antīqua* in line 714 modify?

10. What is the case and use of *religiōne* in line 715?

11. What word does *ūnam* in line 716 modify?

12. In line 717, what word does *patriōs* modify?

13. What word does *fulvī* in line 722 modify?

14. What is the tense, voice, and form of *glomerātī* in line 727?

15. What is the tense, voice, and form of *timentem* in line 729?

The iconic image of filial devotion is captured in this terracotta statue of Aeneas supporting his father Anchises on his shoulder and holding the hand of his son. The three generations represent the tradition of Troy and hearken to its future. Note that Anchises holds a small shrine for the images of the state gods of Troy that Aeneas must bring on his journey so that he can establish them in the new land that is promised him. The figure is dated to the first century CE and was found in Pompeii.

VOCABULARY BUILDER

Vergil has a repertoire of synonyms. In this passage he uses two different words for "father," *pater* and *genitor*. In creating synonyms, Vergil often uses a part for the whole, *tēctum* ("roof") for *domus* ("house"), for example, a figure of speech called SYNECDOCHE. Being familiar with these synonyms will make it easier to read the *Aeneid*. Here are a few examples of synonyms, some of which you have already seen, some of which are new. As you read more of the poem, try building on this list.

Identify the Latin words that qualify as synonyms by SYNECDOCHE only.

father	house	speak	sea
pater	domus	dīcō	mare
parēns	tēctum ("roof")	for, fārī	altum ("deep")
genitor	līmen ("threshold")	ait	fretum ("strait")
	ātrium	inquit	aequor ("level")
	sēdēs	exclāmō	pelagus
		fert	salum
			pontus
			unda
			fluctus

god	city	ship	death
deus	urbs	nāvis	mors
nūmen ("divine power")	arx ("citadel")	puppis ("stern")	lētum
caelestēs ("heavenly")	rēgnum	carīna ("keel")	exitus
dīvus	moenia		obitus

LANGUAGE FACT

ASSIMILATION AND DATIVE WITH COMPOUND VERBS

- **Compound Verbs and Assimilation**

Some Latin words are formed by adding a prefix like *ad–*, *ante–*, *con–*, *in–*, or *ob–* to the base. These are called compound words.

Sometimes the two parts are simply combined:

īnstō	from in + stō	to urge on
obstō	from ob + stō	to hinder, oppose
īnferō	from in + ferō	to bring against
subeō	from sub + eō	to go under, support, follow, approach

Sometimes the combination of consonants results in a blending of sounds called assimilation:

accēdō	from ad + cedō	to approach, reach
conclūdō	from cum + claudō	to (en)close
succedō	from sub + cedō	to go under, advance, succeed
impōnō	from in + pōnō	to place on
implicō	from in + plicō	to fold in, entwine

These are the Latin prefixes that may undergo assimilation: *ad–*, *con–*, *dis–*, *ex–*, *in–*, *ob–*, and *sub–*.

Some of these Latin compound verbs take a dative object while others govern an accusative and a dative.

- **Dative with Compound Verbs**

The dative used with compound verbs is expressed with a preposition in English or as an English direct object in the sentence.

> *Illīs senibus adulēscentēs successērunt.*
> "The young men succeeded those old men."
> (Here the dative *illīs senibus* functions as a simple direct object in English.)

> *Cervīcī impōnere.* (Vergil *Aeneid* 2.707)
> "Place yourself on my neck."
> (Here "neck" is the object of the preposition "on," which in Latin is seen in the prefix *im-* in *impōnere*.)

- **Accusative and Dative with Compound Verbs**

In Latin compound verbs governing an accusative and a dative, the accusative expresses the direct object of the verb, and the dative expresses the thing or person concerned.

> *Dextrae sē parvus Iūlus implicuit.* (Vergil *Aeneid* 2.723–724)
> "Small Iulus enfolded himself in [my] right hand."
> (Here *sē* is the direct object and *dextrae* is the dative of the thing concerned.)

▶ EXERCISE 2

Give the unassimilated forms of the prefix in the following words.

1. impōnō
2. dīversus
3. attrectō
4. suspēnsus
5. ēgredior

▶ EXERCISE 3

Identify the compound verb and the dative or the accusative with the dative in each sentence. Then translate the sentence.

1. Templō vetustō dēsertae Cereris subeāmus.
2. Nihil obstat Aenēae et comitibus ex urbe ēgredientibus.
3. Sonus aurae mē terret sed nōn tēla iniecta mihi.
4. Aenēās patrem suō cervīcī imposuit.
5. Incendia moenibus succēdunt.

ESSAY

In what ways does Aeneas show more attention to his father and his son than his wife in this passage?

Support your assertions with references drawn from throughout the passage. All Latin words must be copied or their line numbers provided, AND they must be translated or paraphrased closely enough so that it is clear you understand the Latin. Direct your answer to the question; do not merely summarize the passage. Please write your essay on a separate piece of paper.

SCANSION

Name the meter and scan the following lines.

quō rēs cumque cadent, ūnum et commūne perīclum,

ūna salūs ambōbus erit. Mihi parvus Iūlus

sit comes, et longē servet vestīgia coniūnx.

Forced to preside over the beauty contest among the goddesses Athena, Juno, and Venus, Paris, depicted with golden apple in hand, chose Venus the winner because she promised him the most beautiful mortal woman in the world. Paris abducted his prize Helen from her Greek husband Menelaus and brought her back to Troy. The Greeks rallied around their insulted countryman and soon were besieging the city of Troy to defend Menelaus's honor and the honor of all Greece against the "barbarians" who had taken Helen. The other half of the panel shows Jupiter directing the three goddesses towards the half with Paris. Painted in the fifteenth century in Tuscany, Italy, the panel is stylistically related to the work of the painter of panels illustrating the story of the Argonauts.

READING 6

Aeneas, Dido, and their followers go on a hunt together. A torrential storm causes the group to scatter. Dido and Aeneas find shelter in the same cave. Rumor swiftly spreads the news of their romantic relationship throughout the cities of Libya.

AENEAS AND DIDO IN THE CAVE

VERGIL *AENEID* 4.160–192

Meter: Dactylic Hexameter

160 Intereā magnō miscērī murmure caelum

  incipit, īnsequitur commixtā grandine nimbus,

  et Tyriī comitēs passim et Trōiāna iuventūs

  Dardaniusque nepōs Veneris dīversa per agrōs

  tēcta metū petiēre; ruunt dē montibus amnēs.

165 Spēluncam Dīdō dux et Trōiānus eandem

  dēveniunt. Prīma et Tellūs et prōnuba Iūnō

  dant signum; fulsēre ignēs et cōnscius aether

  cōnūbiīs summōque ululārunt vertice Nymphae.

  Ille diēs prīmus lētī prīmusque malōrum

170 causa fuit; neque enim speciē fāmāve movētur

  nec iam fūrtīvum Dīdō meditātur amōrem:

  coniugium vocat, hōc praetexit nōmine culpam.

NOTES AND VOCABULARY

Line 160: **intereā,** *adv.* meanwhile, (in the) meantime

  misceō, miscēre, miscuī, mixtum to mix, mingle, confuse

  murmur, murmuris, n. murmur, roar, rumble; note the ALLITERATION and ONOMATOPOEIA.

Line 161: **incipiō, incipere, incēpī, inceptum** to begin, undertake

  īnsequor, īnsequī, īnsecūtus sum to follow

  commisceō, commiscēre, commiscuī, commixtum to mix, mingle

  grandō, grandinis, f. hail (storm, stones)

  nimbus, -ī, m. rainstorm, (storm) cloud

Line 162: **Tyrius, -a, -um** Tyrian, Carthaginian

  passim, *adv.* everywhere, all about

  iuventūs, iuventūtis, f. youth, young men

Line 163: **Dardanius, -a, -um** Dardanian, Trojan

  nepōs, nepōtis, m. grandson; descendant; *nepōs Veneris* = Ascanius

  dīversus, -a, -um separated, different

Line 164: **tēctum, -ī,** n. roof, shelter; by METONYMY this word comes to mean "house."

metus, metūs, m. fear, fright, anxiety

petō, petere, petīvī, petītum to seek; *petiēre = petīvērunt*

amnis, amnis, m. river, stream

Line 165: **spēlunca, -ae,** f. cave, cavern, grotto

dux, ducis, m. (f.) leader, guide, chief

Trōiānus, -a, -um Trojan, of Troy

BY THE WAY

The word *dux* in line 165 can describe either Dido or the Trojan, i.e., Aeneas. Hence the translation can read "Dido the leader and the Trojan . . ." or "Dido and the Trojan leader." Note the CHIASMUS.

Line 166: **dēveniō, dēvenīre, dēvēnī, dēventum** to come (down), arrive (at)

tellūs, tellūris, f. land

prōnuba, -ae, f. matron of honor, bride's attendant; the *prōnuba* was the matron whose function it was to join the hand of the bride to that of the groom at the wedding.

Lines 166–168: Vergil here recalls the various features in a Roman wedding and represents Nature herself as performing these ceremonies. Earth and Heaven, parents of the universe, take the part of human parents in bringing the couple together; lightning (*ignēs*) represents the wedding torches (*taedae*); Juno performs the duty of the matron of honor (*prōnuba*), and the cries of the mountain nymphs take the place of the wedding song and festal cries. *Prīma Tellūs*: Earth was called *prīma* as the oldest of the gods; as Mother Earth, the producer and nurse of life, she presided over marriage.

Line 167: **signum, -ī,** n. sign, signal, token, mark; *dant signum:* i.e., for the wedding

fulg(e)ō, fulgēre (or ere), fulsī to shine, flash, gleam

ignis, ignis, m. fire, lightning; lightning is present instead of marriage torches.

cōnscius, -a, -um privy to; as a substantive, accomplice; here "witness" (to the marriage)

aether, aetheris, m. upper air, heaven, ether

Line 168: **cōnūbium, -ī,** n. marriage; translate "to the marriage"; poetic plural; the first -i- is pronounced as a consonant (i.e., as "y"), for the sake of the meter.

ululō (1) to howl, wail, shout, shriek; *ululārunt* is contracted from *ululā(vē)runt*. Note the ONOMATOPOEIA.

vertex, verticis, m. peak, summit, head, top

nympha, -ae, f. nymph, minor female divinity of the forests, waters, etc.

Line 169: **lētum, -ī,** n. death, destruction, ruin

malum, -ī, n. evil, misfortune, trouble

Line 170: **speciēs, speciēī,** f. appearance, sight, aspect; **speciē fāmāve:** ablative of cause; translate "by (regard for) appearances or (for) her reputation."

Line 171: **fūrtīvus, -a, -um** secret, stolen

meditor, meditārī, meditātus sum to meditate, design

Line 172: **coniugium, -ī,** n. wedlock, marriage

praetexō, praetexere, praetexuī, praetextum to fringe, cloak

nōmen, nōminis, n. name; *hōc nōmine* is an ablative of means.

culpa, -ae, f. fault, offense, guilt, blame

VERGIL *AENEID* 4.160–192, CONTINUED

Extemplō Libyae magnās it Fāma per urbēs,

Fāma, malum quā nōn aliud vēlōcius ūllum:

175   mōbilitāte viget vīrēsque adquīrit eundō,

parva metū prīmō, mox sēsē attollit in aurās

ingrediturque solō et caput inter nūbila condit.

Illam Terra parēns īrā inrītāta deōrum

extrēmam, ut perhibent, Coeō Enceladōque sorōrem

180   prōgenuit pedibus celerem et pernīcibus ālīs,

mōnstrum horrendum, ingēns, cui quot sunt corpore plūmae,

tot vigilēs oculī subter (mīrābile dictū),

tot linguae, totidem ōra sonant, tot subrigit aurēs.

NOTES AND VOCABULARY

Line 173:   **extemplō,** *adv.* immediately, at once, suddenly

   Libya, -ae, f. Libya, country of North Africa

   Fāma, -ae, f. Rumor

Line 174:   **quā:** ablative with comparative *vēlōcius*; understand *est* with *nōn.*

   vēlōx, vēlōcis swift, quick, rapid, fleet

BY THE WAY

In lines 173–174 (*Fāma … Fāma*), EPANALEPSIS occurs, a figure of speech in which the same word is repeated in the same sentence after other words have intervened. Vergil repeats the word *Fāma* to emphasize it.

Line 175:   **mōbilitās, mōbilitātis,** f. activity, motion, speed

   vigeō, vigēre, viguī to flourish, be strong, thrive

   adquīrō, adquīrere, adquīsīvī, adquīsītum to acquire, gain

   eundō: ablative of means, from the gerund of *eō, īre, iī, itum,* "to go"

Line 176:   **metus, metūs,** m. fear, fright, anxiety; *metū* is an ablative of cause.

   prīmō, *adv.* at first, in the beginning

   mox, *adv.* soon, presently

   attollō, attollēre to lift, rear, raise

Line 177:   **ingredior, ingredī, ingressus sum** to enter, proceed

   solum, -ī, n. ground, soil, earth; *(in) solō = (in) terrā*

   nūbila, nūbilōrum, n. pl. clouds, cloudiness

   condō, condere, condidī, conditum to establish, hide

STUDY TIP

Be careful to distinguish among these words with similar spellings.

sōlus, -a, -um	alone, only	ADJECTIVE
solum, -ī, n.	ground, soil	NOUN, SECOND DECLENSION
sōlum, *adv.*	only	ADVERB
sōl, sōlis, m.	sun	NOUN, THIRD DECLENSION
soleō, solēre, solitus sum	to be accustomed	VERB, SECOND CONJUGATION
solea, -ae, f.	sandal, shoe	NOUN, FIRST DECLENSION
solvō, solvere, soluī	to loosen, set sail	VERB, THIRD CONJUGATION

Line 178:   **inrītō** (1) to vex, enrage, provoke

      deōrum: is objective genitive with *īrā.*

Line 179:   **extrēmus, -a, -um** final, last, furthest

      perhibeō, perhibēre, perhibuī, perhibitum to present, say; Vergil often uses phrases like *ut perhibent* to signal that he is alluding to an earlier work. Here, he is recalling the cosmic myths of Hesiod's *Theogony,* where the battle of the Olympians and Titans is described.

      Coeus, -ī, m. one of the Titans

      Enceladus, -ī, m. one of the Giants

Line 180:   **prōgignō, prōgignere, prōgenuī, prōgenitum** to bring forth, bear

      celer, celeris, celere swift, speedy, quick

      pernīx, pernīcis active, nimble, swift

      āla, -ae, f. wing

Line 181:   **mōnstrum, -ī, n.** prodigy, portent, monster

      horrendus, -a, -um awful, terrible, dire

      cui: a dative of possession

      quot as many as

      corpore: ablative of respect or specification

      plūma, -ae, f. feather, plume

Line 182:   **tot** so many, as many

      vigil, vigilis wakeful, watchful, sleepless

      subter, *adv.; prep + acc.* beneath, below; understand *sunt.*

      mīrābilis, mīrābile wonderful, marvelous

      dictū: ablative of respect with *mīrābile*

Line 183:   **totidem** the same number, so many

      sonō, sonāre, sonuī, sonitum (re)sound, roar

      subrigō, subrigere, surrēxī, surrēctum raise, rise; translate *(Fāma) subrigit tot aurēs* "Rumor raises as many listening ears."

      auris, auris, f. ear

VERGIL *AENEID* 4.160–192, CONTINUED

    Nocte volat caelī mediō terraeque per umbram

185 strīdēns, nec dulcī dēclīnat lūmina somnō;

    lūce sedet custōs aut summī culmine tēctī

    turribus aut altīs, et magnās territat urbēs,

    tam fictī prāvīque tenāx quam nuntia vērī.

    Haec tum multiplicī populōs sermōne replēbat

190 gaudēns, et pariter facta atque īnfecta canēbat:

    vēnisse Aenēān Trōiānō sanguine crētum,

    cui sē pulchra virō dignētur iungere Dīdō.

NOTES AND VOCABULARY

BY THE WAY

Do not confuse *volō* (1), "to fly," and *volō, velle, voluī*, "to wish, want"

Line 184:	**volō** (1) to fly, flit, move with speed
	medium, -ī, n. middle, center; translate *caelī mediō terraeque* "between heaven and earth." Note how the Latin word order imitates the meaning of the phrase.
Line 185:	**strīd(e)ō, strīdēre (or -ere), strīdī** to hiss, whir, rustle; *strīdēns*: with her wings as she flies, referring to the buzz of gossip.
	dulcis, dulce sweet, dear, fond
	dēclīnō (1) to turn aside, bend down, close (of eyes)
	lūmina (sua) = *oculōs*, as often
Line 186:	**lūx, lūcis,** f. light; translate *lūce* "by day," ablative of time.
	sedeō, sedēre, sēdī, sessum to sit (down), settle
	custōs, custōdis, m. (f.) guard(ian), sentinel
	culmen, culminis, n. roof, summit, top, peak
Line 187:	**turris, turris,** f. tower, turret
	territō (1) to frighten, terrify, alarm
Line 188:	**tam,** *adv.* so, as, such
	fictum, -ī, n. falsehood, fiction; *fictī prāvīque . . . vērī*: genitive with *tenāx*
	prāvum, -ī, n. wrong, perverse act
	tenāx, tenācis tenacious, holding (to)
	tam . . . quam so . . . as
	nuntia, -ae, f. messenger
	vērum, -ī, n. truth, right, reality
Line 189:	**haec** = *Fāma*.
	multiplex, multiplicis manifold, multiple

populus, -ī, m. people, nation

sermō, sermōnis, m. conversation, gossip

repleō, replēre, replēvī, replētum to fill, stuff

Line 190:   **gaudeō, gaudēre, gāvīsus sum** to rejoice, exult

pariter, *adv.* equally, alike

factum, -ī, n. deed, act, exploit; translate *facta atque īnfecta* "fact and fiction," *lit.*, "things done and not done." Note the elisions that join *facta atque īnfecta*; the effect is to intermingle and blur fact and fiction, which rumor often does.

īnfectus, -a, -um not done, false

canō, canere, cecinī, cantum to sing (of), chant, tell, proclaim, prophesy; followed by indirect statement

Line 191:   **Trōiānus, -a, -um** Trojan, of Troy; *Trōiānō sanguine* is an ablative of origin with *crētum*.

crētus, -a, -um grown, sprung

Line 192:   **pulcher, pulchra, pulchrum** beautiful, handsome, splendid, illustrious, noble

virō = *coniugī*

dignor, dignārī, dignātus sum to deem worthy

iungō, iungere, iūnxī, iūnctum to join, yoke; *iungere* is a complementary infinitive.

COMPREHENSION QUESTIONS

1. When the storm begins, where do the Tyrian and Trojan youth flee and where do Aeneas and Dido find shelter? Cite the Latin.

2. How does Vergil employ natural phenomena to recreate a typical wedding ceremony? Cite the Latin.

3. What do lines 169–172 foreshadow?

4. In the PERSONIFICATION of Fama (lines 173–190), Vergil gives one of the most vivid descriptions of a monster in ancient literature. Though Fama has a frightening appearance, its greatest destructiveness appears in lines 188–190. What is it that makes Fama so harmful?

▶ EXERCISE 1

1. In line 160, what Latin word does *magnō* modify?

2. What is the tense, voice, and form of *miscērī* in line 160?

3. In line 161, what is the voice, tense, and mood of *incipit*?

4. In line 162, what Latin word does *Trōiāna* modify?

5. In line 164, what is the alternate form of *petiēre*?

6. In line 166, what Latin word does *prīma* modify?

7. In line 168, what is the uncontracted form of *ululārunt*?

8. In line 171, what is the tense and mood of *meditātur*?

9. What is the case and use of *urbēs* in line 173?

10. What is the nominative singular form of *vīrēs* (line 175)?

11. What is the case and use of *aurās* in line 176?

12. What is the case and use of *caput* in line 177?

13. What is the case and use *of pedibus* in line 180?

14. What is the case and use of *plūmae* in line 181?

15. What is the tense, mood, and voice of *subrigit* in line 183?

16. What is the case and use of *nocte* in line 184?

17. What word does *dulcī* in line 185 modify?

18. What is the case and use of *culmine* in line 186?

19. In line 189, what word does *multiplicī* modify?

20. What is the tense, voice, and form of *vēnisse* in line 191?

LANGUAGE FACT

FIGURES OF SPEECH AND MEANING

In prose and poetry, Latin authors use figures of speech for a variety of reasons.

- A figure of speech may be used to emphasize or call attention to something. Note how in this example the ANAPHORA of *mirātur* underscores Aeneas's amazement and wonder at the construction of the city as the repeated word also links the construction with specific parts already built, the gates and paved streets.

> *Mīrātur mōlem Aenēās, māgālia quondam,*
> *mīrātur portās strepitumque et strāta viārum.* (Vergil *Aeneid* 1.421–422)

> "Aeneas admires the construction [of the city], formerly huts,
> he admires the gates and the noise and the paved streets."

- Sometimes a figure of speech may highlight the coming together of sound and meaning. In the example below, the ALLITERATION of the letter "m" accentuates and creates the sound of the rumbling of the storm.

> *Intereā magnō miscērī murmure caelum / incipit* (Vergil *Aeneid* 4.160–161)
> "Meanwhile the sky begins to be mixed with a great murmur."

- Still other times a figure of speech may complement the meaning of line. In this example of CHIASMUS observe how Dido and the Trojan (i.e., Aeneas) are located between the words *spēluncam* and *eandem* just as they are together inside the cave.

> *Spēluncam Dīdō dux et Troiānus eandem / dēveniunt*
> (Vergil *Aeneid* 4.165–166)
> "The leader Dido and the Trojan (or Dido and the Trojan
> leader) come down to the same cave."

- And in other instances figures of speech such as POLYSYNDETON can decelerate the action while ASYNDETON can accelerate it. The POLYSYNDETON in the following passage serves to complement Vergil's lengthy description of the brutality of Priam's death.

> Hoc dīcēns altāria ad ipsa trementem
> trāxit et in multō lāpsantem sanguine nātī,
> implicuitque comam laevā, dextrāque coruscum
> extulit ac laterī capulō tenus abdidit ēnsem. (Vergil *Aeneid* 2.550–553)

> "Saying this, he [Pyrrhus] drew the man, trembling and slipping in the abundant blood of [Priam's] son, to the altars themselves, and he entwined [Priam's] hair in his left hand, and with his right he took out his flashing sword and buried it up to the hilt in [Priam's] side."

▶ EXERCISE 2

Identify the figure of speech (there may be more than one) in each sentence and explain how it affects what the author is saying.

1. et Tyriī comitēs passim et Troiāna iuventūs / Dardaniusque nepōs Veneris dīversa per agrōs / tēcta metū petiēre (*Aeneid* 4.162–164).

2. mōbilitāte viget vīrēsque adquīrit eundō (*Aeneid* 4.175).

3. tot vigilēs oculī subter (mīrābile dictū), / tot linguae, totidem ōra sonant, tot subrigit aurēs. (*Aeneid* 4.182–183).

4. strīdēns nec dulcī dēclīnat lūmina somnō (*Aeneid* 4.185).

5. cui sē pulchra virō dignētur iungere Dīdō (*Aeneid* 4.192).

ESSAY

How does Vergil create a sense of foreboding in lines 160–172? Present your response in a well-organized essay.

Support your assertions with references drawn from throughout lines 160–172. All Latin words must be copied or their line numbers provided, AND they must be translated or paraphrased closely enough so that it is clear you understand the Latin. Direct your answer to the question; do not merely summarize the passage. Please write your essay on a separate piece of paper.

SCANSION

Name the meter and scan the following lines.

> Ille diēs prīmus lētī prīmusque malōrum
>
> causa fuit; neque enim speciē fāmāve movētur
>
> nec iam fūrtīvum Dīdō meditātur amōrem

READING 7

Aeneas has been told by the gods that he must leave Carthage to fulfill his destiny. Dido is heart-broken and angry when she learns of his plans since Aeneas attempts to depart without telling her. Because she has made Aeneas the central focus of her life, she now feels totally abandoned and consequently decides to commit suicide. This passage describes how Dido climbs a pyre piled high with all the mementos of her relationship with Aeneas and ends her life.

DIDO'S SUICIDE

VERGIL *AENEID* 4.642–666

Meter: Dactylic Hexameter

> At trepida et coeptīs immānibus effera Dīdō
> sanguineam volvēns aciem, maculīsque trementēs
> interfūsa genās et pallida morte futūrā,
> 645 interiōra domūs inrumpit līmina et altōs
> cōnscendit furibunda rogōs ēnsemque reclūdit
> Dardanium, nōn hōs quaesītum mūnus in ūsūs.
> Hīc, postquam Īliacās vestēs nōtumque cubīle
> cōnspexit, paulum lacrimīs et mente morāta
> 650 incubuitque torō dīxitque novissima verba:

NOTES AND VOCABULARY

Line 642: **trepidus, -a, -um** trembling, excited

coeptum, -ī, n. undertaking, beginning; *coeptīs* is an ablative of cause with *effera* and refers to Dido's preparations for her death. Translate "wild because of the undertakings."

immānis, immāne huge, large

efferus, -a, -um wild, savage, mad

Dīdō: the subject of *inrumpit* (645), *cōnscendit* (646), and *reclūdit* (646)

Line 643: **sanguineus, -a, -um** bloody, bloodshot

aciēs, aciēī, f. edge, line, eye(sight); translate here as "eyes."

macula, -ae, f. spot, splotch, stain

tremō, tremere, tremuī, to tremble, quiver, shake; the TRANSFERRED EPITHET *trementēs* grammatically modifies *genās* but refers in sense to *Dīdō* (642).

Line 644: **interfundō, interfundere, interfūdī, interfūsum** to pour among, suffuse; *genās* is an accusative of respect with *interfūsa*; translate "suffused with respect to her cheeks." Alternatively, *genās* is the accusative direct object of the middle/reflexive participle *interfūsa.*

gena, -ae, f. cheek

pallidus, -a, -um pale, wan, pallid; *morte* is an ablative of cause with *pallida*; translate "pale because of death."

Line 645: **interior, interius** inner, interior

domus, domūs, f. house; *domūs* is genitive singular.

inrumpō, inrumpere, inrūpī, inruptum to burst into, rush in

līmen, līminis, n. threshold; this threshold leads into a courtyard in the middle of Dido's palace. Translate "courtyard."

STUDY TIP

Be careful to distinguish between *līmen, līminis,* n. "threshold" and *lūmen, lūminis,* n. "light."

Line 646: **cōnscendō, cōnscendere, cōnscendī, cōnscensum** to mount, climb

furibundus, -a, -um wild, frenzied; translate this adjective as an adverb, "wildly."

rogus, -ī, m. funeral pyre

reclūdō, reclūdere, reclūsī, reclūsum to open, unsheathe

Line 647: **Dardan(i)us, -a, -um** Trojan, Dardanian; modifies *ēnsem.* The sword is Trojan because it used to belong to Aeneas.

mūnus, mūneris, n. gift; the phrase *Dardanium mūnus* is accusative neuter singular in apposition to *ēnsem* (line 646). Vergil uses the adjective Dardanian to emphasize the IRONY of Dido's committing suicide with a sword that Aeneas had given her.

ūsus, ūsūs, m. use, service, employment; *hōs* agrees with the accusative masculine plural *ūsūs;* translate *in hōs ūsūs* "for these purposes."

Line 648: **hīc:** translate "hereupon" or "then."

postquam, *conj.* after, when

Īliacus, -a, -um Trojan, Ilian; *Īliacās* modifies *vestīs,* another gift of Aeneas.

vestis, vestis, f. cloth(ing), garment, robe

nōtus, -a, -um (well) known, familiar; translate *nōtum* as "familiar."

cubīle, cubīlis, n. couch, bed

Line 649: **cōnspiciō, cōnspicere, cōnspexī, cōnspectum** to catch sight of, see, notice

paulum, *adv.* (a) little, slightly, somewhat

lacrima, -ae, f. tear; the phrase *lacrimīs et mente* is an ablative of manner. *Lit.,* "with (her) tears and with (her) mind." Translate either "with a tearful mind" or "in tearful recollection." Note the HENDIADYS.

moror (1) to delay, hesitate, hinder; *morāta* refers to Dido. Translate "having delayed."

Line 650: **incumbō, incumbere, incubuī, incubitum** (+ *dat.*) to recline on

torus, -ī, m. (banqueting) couch, bed; *torō* is dative with the compound verb *incubuit.*

verbum, -ī, n. word, speech, talk; *novissima verba* literally means "(her) most recent words." In English we would say "her last words."

VERGIL *AENEID* 4.642–666, CONTINUED

"Dulcēs exuviae, dum fāta deusque sinēbat,

accipite hanc animam mēque hīs exsolvite cūrīs.

Vīxī et quem dederat cursum fortūna perēgī,

et nunc magna meī sub terrās ībit imāgō.

655   Urbem praeclāram statuī, mea moenia vīdī,

ulta virum poenās inimīcō ā frātre recēpī,

fēlīx, heu nimium fēlīx, sī lītora tantum

numquam Dardaniae tetigissent nostra carīnae."

NOTES AND VOCABULARY

Line 651:   **dulcis, dulce** sweet, dear, fond; the adjective *dulcēs* should be taken closely with *dum*.

        exuviae, -ārum, f. (pl.) spoils, relics, mementos; *exuviae* is vocative plural. Dido is speaking to all the mementos of her time with Aeneas. Note the PERSONIFICATION.

        sinō, sinere, sīvī, situm to permit, allow

Line 652:   **exsolvō, exsolvere, exsoluī, exsolūtum** to loose(n), free; *mē* is the object of *exsolvite*.

        cūrīs: ablative of separation with *exsolvite*; "free me from these cares." *Cūra* is referring to the "cares" that are closely associated with love, or, in other words, the "pain of love."

Line 653:   **vīvō, vīvere, vīxī, vīctum** to live, be alive; Dido uses the perfect tense *vīxī* to emphasize that her life is over: "I have lived."

        cursus, cursūs, m. course (of life); The relative pronoun *quem* refers to *cursum*. Translate "the course which."

        peragō, peragere, perēgī, perāctum to accomplish, finish

Line 654:   **meī:** genitive singular personal pronoun with *imāgō*.

        sub terrās: *sub* takes the accusative here to show "direction to." Dido is going "down under the earth."

        imāgō, imāginis, f. likeness, image, ghost, soul, form; translate *imāgō* "ghost" or "soul." The adjective *magna* modifies *imāgō*.

BY THE WAY

In line 654, *sub terrās ībit* is a EUPHEMISM, a figure of speech in which something less offensive or disagreeable is substituted for something more offensive or disagreeable. A similar expression *īre sub umbrās* occurs in line 660. EUPHEMISMS often are used in reference to death (cf. "pass away" for "die").

Line 655:   **praeclārus, -a, -um** very renowned

        statuō, statuere, statuī, statūtum to set (up), found

Line 656: **ulcīscor, ulcīscī, ultus sum** to avenge, punish; *ulta* is the perfect participle of the deponent verb *ulcīscor*. Translate "having avenged."

virum: this man is Sychaeus, Dido's first husband, who was killed by her brother Pygmalion. Translate "my husband."

inimīcus, -a, -um hostile, enemy, unfriendly

recipiō, recipere, recēpī, receptum to receive, take; translate *poenās . . . recēpī* "I took revenge."

Line 657: **fēlīx, fēlīcis** happy, fortunate, blessed; *fēlīx, heu nimium fēlīx:* with these words understand the pluperfect subjunctive *fuissem* in the conclusion of a contrary to fact condition. Translate "I would have been happy."

nimium, *adv.* too (much), excessively

tantum, *adv.* so much, only, merely; translate this word with *sī,* "if only."

Line 658: **tangō, tangere, tetigī, tāctum** to touch, reach

nostra: modifies *lītora* (657).

carīna, -ae, f. keel; ship, boat; note the SYNECDOCHE.

Joseph Staellert (1825–1903) in his *La mort de Didon* presents a fanciful rendition of Dido's suicide. In the distance, where Dido gestures with her right hand, Aeneas and his ships sail away. Presumably the woman with the light-colored hair attending Dido is her beloved sister Anna.

VERGIL *AENEID* 4.642–666, CONTINUED

Dīxit, et ōs impressa torō "Moriēmur inultae,

660   sed moriāmur" ait. "Sīc, sīc iuvat īre sub umbrās.

Hauriat hunc oculīs ignem crūdēlis ab altō

Dardanus, et nostrae sēcum ferat ōmina mortis."

Dīxerat, atque illam media inter tālia ferrō

conlāpsam aspiciunt comitēs, ēnsemque cruōre

665   spūmantem sparsāsque manūs. It clāmor ad alta

ātria: concussam bacchātur Fāma per urbem.

NOTES AND VOCABULARY

Line 659:   **imprimō, imprimere, impressī, impressum** to press (upon), imprint; *impressa* is a middle participle. Translate with *ōs* as "having pressed (her) mouth." In other words, Dido kisses the couch.

        torō: dative with the compound verb *impressa*; translate "on the couch."

        morior, morī, mortuus sum to die, perish; *moriēmur* is future indicative of a deponent verb.

        inultus, -a, -um unavenged, unpunished; *inultae* agrees with an understood *nōs*.

BY THE WAY

Note the regal plural in "we will die." The use of a first person plural pronoun instead of a first person singular pronoun is referred to as the ROYAL OR EDITORIAL "WE." This rhetorical device often lends a certain authority to those passages in which this plural is used. Here it may be intended to remind us of Dido's royal status.

Line 660:   **moriāmur:** present subjunctive of a deponent verb; volitive. Note the CHIASMUS in lines 559–560.

        iuvō, iuvāre, iūvī, iūtum to help, please; *iūvat* is used impersonally here, i.e., its subject is the infinitive *īre*. Translate "it is pleasing."

        sub umbrās: *sub* takes the accusative case here to indicate direction toward. A similar EUPHEMISM occurred in line 654.

Line 661:   **hauriō, haurīre, hausī, haustum** to drain, drink (in); *hauriat* is a volitive subjunctive. Translate "let him drink." Note the METAPHOR.

        oculīs: ablative of means; translate "with his eyes."

        ignem: the fire of her funeral pyre

        crūdēlis, crūdēle cruel, heartless; *crūdēlis* modifies *Dardanus* (662).

        altum, -ī, n. the deep (sea); Dido is imagining Aeneas on his ship at sea.

Line 662:   **Dardanus:** the subject of *hauriat* (661), refers to Aeneas

        ōmen, ōminis, n. portent, omen, sign; *ōmina,* the signs Dido is referring to include Aeneas's sorrow at leaving her and the misfortunes his unfaithfulness will bring him. Dido thus sees her death as an omen of Aeneas's future suffering.

REMINDER

As you learned in the Cicero chapter, p. 199, be careful to distinguish *ōmen, ōminis*, n. "omen" from *omnis, omne* "all."

Line 663:
dīxerat: Note that the action of the pluperfect *dīxerat* ("she had spoken") takes place before the action of the present tense *aspiciunt* (664).

illam: direct object of *aspiciunt* (664)

media inter tālia: *tālia* is a neuter plural substantive modified by the adjective *media*. Translate "among the middle of such things." Dido speaks, kisses the couch, takes hold of Aeneas's sword, and in the middle of such things (i.e., these three actions) the servants watch her collapse.

ferrō = *in ferrum*; Dido collapses on the sword.

Line 664:
conlābor, conlābī, conlāpsus sum to fall in a heap, collapse, faint; *conlāpsam* modifies *illam* (663); translate "having collapsed."

a(d)spiciō, a(d)spicere, a(d)spexī, a(d)spectum to see, behold; this verb has three direct objects: *illam* (663), *ēnsem* (664), and *manūs* (665). The subject of *aspiciunt* is *comitēs*.

cruor, cruōris, m. blood, gore; the ablative of means *cruōre* should be understood with both *spūmantem* and *sparsās* (665).

Line 665:
spūmō (1) to foam, froth, spray; *spūmantem* modifies *ēnsem* (664). Note the CHIASMUS. Note also the SIBILANCE and ONOMATOPOEIA. The repeated "sp-" sound in *spūmantem* and *sparsāsque* contributes to the graphic picture here of "spurting" blood.

spargō, spargere, sparsī, sparsum to scatter, sprinkle

Line 666:
ātrium, -ī, n. hall, court, atrium

concutiō, concutere, concussī, concussum to shake, shatter; *concussam* modifies *urbem*.

bacchor (1) to rave, rush wildly

Fāma: translate "Rumor."

COMPREHENSION QUESTIONS

1. Describe Dido's appearance at the beginning of this passage by citing and translating the Latin.

2. What did Dido look at before she spoke her last words?

3. What does Dido wish upon Aeneas just before she commits suicide?

4. Who spreads the news that Dido has died?

▶ EXERCISE 1

1.   What is the tense, voice, and form of *volvēns* in line 643?

2.   What Latin word does *futūrā* in line 644 modify?

3.   What is the case and use of *līmina* in line 645?

4.   What Latin word does *altōs* in line 645 modify?

5.   What case and use is *gradūs* in line 646?

6.   In line 648, what Latin word does *nōtum* modify?

7.   What is the tense, mood, and voice of *cōnspexit* in line 649?

8.   What is the case and use of *exuviae* in line 651?

9.   What is the case, use, and gender of *quem* in line 653?

10. What is the tense, mood, and voice of *statuī* in line 655?

11. What Latin word does *inimīcō* in line 656 modify?

12. What is the case and use of *lītora* in line 657?

13. What is the case and use of *ōs* in line 659?

14. What Latin word does *crūdēlis* in line 661 modify?

15. What Latin word does *nostrae* in line 662 modify?

VOCABULARY BUILDER

In this passage you saw the Latin word *līmen, līminis*, n. "threshold," which looks very much like *lūmen, lūminis*, n. "light." Give the English meanings of these look-alike words that were seen in earlier passages of Vergil.

solum, -ī., n.   aura, -ae, f.
sōlus, -a, -um   auris, auris, m.
soleō, solēre   aurum, -ī, n.

iaceō, iacēre, iacuī   pōne
iaciō, iacere, iēcī, iactum   pōnō, pōnere, posuī, positum

latus, lateris, n.   iste, ista, istud
lātus, -a, -um   ipse, ipsa, ipsum

opus, operis, n.   portus, portūs, m.
onus, oneris, n.   porta, -ae, f.
                           portō, portāre, portāvī, portātum

LANGUAGE FACT

ALTERNATE ENDINGS AND SYNCOPATED WORDS

Latin words sometimes have alternate or syncopated (i.e., contracted) endings, especially in poetry. The most important of these endings, some of which you have seen before, are:

- In third declension nouns, adjectives, and participles in the accusative plural, *–īs* can be used instead of *–ēs.*

> . . . *Īliacās vestīs nōtumque cubīle / cōnspexit . . .* (Vergil *Aeneid* 4.648–649)
> *Vestīs* is found as an alternate for *vestēs* in some texts.
> "She looked at the Trojan garments and the familiar bed."

- In third declension *i*-stems,

> *–im* for *–em* in the accusative singular with words like *Tiberim, puppim* ("stern") and *turrim* ("tower.") (But Vergil also uses the *–em* ending for other *i*-stem words like *nāvem.*)

> *pontus / in puppim ferit*   *puppim = puppem*
> (Vergil *Aeneid* 1.114–115)
> "The sea strikes against the stern."

> *–ī* for *–e* in ablative singular often occurs with words like *ignī* ("fire"), *turrī* ("tower"), and *amnī* ("river.")

> . . . *ardentīsque oculōs suffectī sanguine et ignī . . .*   *ignī = igne*
> (Vergil *Aeneid* 2.210)
> "having suffused their burning eyes with
>   blood and fire"

> *–um* instead of *–ium* in the genitive plural of third declension *i*-stem nouns such as *volucrum* and *vātum,* and present active participles such as *venientum.*

> *Apēs . . . onera accipiunt venientum.*   *venientum = venientium*
> (Vergil *Aeneid* 1.430–434)
> "The bees receive the loads of those
>   coming."

- In first and second declension nouns, *–um* is sometimes used instead of the genitive plural *–ārum* or *–ōrum.*

> . . . *vī superum saevae memorem Iūnōnis ob īram . . .*   *superum = superōrum*
> (Vergil *Aeneid* 1.4)
> ". . . by the force of the gods above because of
>   the mindful anger of cruel Juno . . ."

- In verbs, as you have already seen on pp. 99, 157, and 167,

  - in the perfect active indicative, third person plural: *–ēre* can be used instead of *–ērunt* in the perfect active indicative, third person plural. For example, *tenuēre* for *tenuērunt*.

    > *Dēseruēre omnēs dēfessī . . .*   *dēseruēre = dēseruērunt*
    >   (Vergil *Aeneid* 2.565)
    > "Being tired, they all deserted."

  - in all verbs formed from the third principle part: the syllables *–vi–* and *–ve–* in the perfect tenses can be omitted. For example, *audīerat* for *audīverat* and *amāsse* for *amāvisse*.

    > *. . . Tyriī comitēs . . . tēcta metū petiēre . . .*   *petiēre = petīvērunt*
    >   (Vergil *Aeneid* 4.162–164)
    > "The Tyrian comrades sought roofs/
    >   houses from fear."

  - in all second singular passive verb forms that end in *–ris*. The passive ending *–ris* is syncopated by using the ending *–re* instead. For example, *amābāre* for *amābāris* "you were loved."

    > *. . . cervīcī impōnere nostrae . . .*   *impōnere = impōneris*
    >   (Vergil *Aeneid* 2.707)
    > "Place yourself on my neck."

STUDY TIP

Some syncopated and alternate forms are easily confused with other forms. Be careful to distinguish among

- an accusative plural third declension noun ending in *–īs* with a first or second declension dative or ablative plural noun.

vestis, vestis, f.	THIRD DECLENSION	vestīs, accusative plural
lacrima, -ae, f.	FIRST DECLENSION	lacrimīs, dative or ablative plural
torus, -ī, m.	SECOND DECLENSION	torīs, dative or ablative plural

- a masculine or feminine ablative singular ending in *–ī* in third declension *i*-stems with the dative singular that also ends in *–ī*. All neuter *i*-stems have an *–ī* in the ablative singular as well as in the dative singular.

- syncopated perfect endings with the endings of present infinitives in the second conjugation, e.g., *tenuēre* ("they held") and *tenēre* ("to hold"). Recalling the perfect stem of a verb often helps to distinguish a syncopated form from a present infinitive, e.g., *dīcere* and *dīxēre*.

- a verb form with a syncopated *–re* for *–ris* ending with an infinitive, e.g., *dūcēre* ("you will be led") for *dūcere* ("to lead"). Only the macron marks the difference between the two. The present passive second person singular *dūcere* ("you are led") can only be distinguished from *dūcere* ("to lead") by context.

▶ EXERCISE 2

Translate each of the following nouns and participles and give the regular spelling of the word in the case and number indicated.

1. ardentīs (acc. pl. of ardēns)
2. accipientum (gen. pl. of accipiēns)
3. febrim (acc. sg. of febris)
4. venientīs (acc. pl. of veniēns)
5. nāvim (acc. sg. of nāvis)
6. sequentum (gen. pl. of sequēns)
7. deum (gen. pl. of deus)
8. virum (gen. pl. of vir)

▶ EXERCISE 3

For each of the following syncopated forms, give the unsyncopated form and translate the word into English.

Example:

Syncopated Form	Unsyncopated Form	Translation
tenuēre	tenuērunt	they have held

1. petīvēre
2. quaesīerās
3. iactāsse
4. conspiciēre
5. ululārant
6. servāsset
7. dēclīnarit

ESSAY

How is the description of Dido's physical appearance and her activities as she prepares to die intended to make her a less sympathetic figure?

Support your assertions with references drawn from throughout this passage (lines 160–172 only). All Latin words must be copied or their line numbers provided, AND they must be translated or paraphrased closely enough so that it is clear you understand the Latin. Direct your answer to the question; do not merely summarize the passage. Please write your essay on a separate piece of paper.

SCANSION

Name the meter and scan the following lines.

Dulcēs exuviae, dum fāta deusque sinēbat,

accipite hanc animam mēque hīs exsolvite cūrīs.

Vīxī et quem dederat cursum fortūna perēgī

A plaque of painted enamel on silvered copper presents an interesting version of Dido's death. It is one of a series whose designs were based on woodcut illustrations of a 1502 edition of Vergil. The scene is faithful to several elements of Vergil's story—a flight of four stairs, a funeral pyre, Aeneas's sword, the familiar bed. His garments, which Dido claimed she was going to burn in a ritual of cleansing him from her system, are depicted as the prostrate body of Aeneas with his Turkish turban and very un-Roman trousers. Dido stabs herself with Aeneas's sword as she stands atop a flight of four stairs near a funeral pyre on which are already burning "the Trojan garb and the familiar bed." The funeral fire roars but Dido has not yet plunged the sword into her chest. Her Carthaginian subjects crowd the pyre with Anna at the front. At the same time, Iris looking very much like an angel has arrived on the scene ready to release Dido's soul.

CHAPTER 5

QUINTUS HORATIUS FLACCUS

Deponent Verbs that Govern the Ablative Case; Infinitive of Purpose, Review of Purpose Constructions, and Review of Infinitive Uses

Enjambment

Luca Signorelli (1445–1523) spent four years painting a series of frescoes in the Capella Nuova in the Duomo of Orvieto. A set of decorative panels includes this imaginative portrait of Horace. Four panels of scenes from the poet's works surround the portrait. Signorelli's Horace joins portraits of Dante, Virgil, Ovid, Horace, Lucan, Homer, and Empedocles.

MEMORĀBILE DICTŪ

Nōn omnis moriar

"I will not die completely." (Horace *Odes* 3.30)

Horace ends the three books of the *Odes* with a poem that elaborates upon this phrase. For like many writers of great literature, artists, musicians, architects, and originators of other types of creative productions, Horace believes that his works will live on after him.

INTRODUCTION TO HORACE

HORACE'S IMPORTANCE AS A POET

Horace is one of Augustan Rome's greatest poets. His two books of *Satires,* or "Conversations," served as a model and inspiration for the later Roman satirists Persius and Juvenal, and also for the English satirists Pope, Dryden, and Swift. His lyric poems were so extraordinary that few Latin poets after Horace attempted to write lyric. Horace's lyric poems were quite popular in the sixteenth and seventeenth centuries and were translated and widely imitated by English, French, Spanish, and Italian poets of that era. His *Ars poētica,* a work on poetic composition, was profoundly influential for western writers from the seventeenth century and beyond. Further, Horace's verve at creating memorable maxims has had a lasting impact on our own language. Here are just a few examples that are cited regularly both in English and in Latin: "seize the day" (*carpe diem*), which is sometimes freely translated as "seize the opportunity"; "foot and a half long," or very long, words (*sesquipedālia verba*); "it is sweet and noble to die for one's country" (*dulce et decōrum est prō patriā morī*); and the "golden mean" (*aurea mediocritās*).

Horace wrote at a time that included great political upheaval and great literary achievement. In the works of Horace and of his contemporary and friend, Vergil, who is best known for the *Aeneid,* an underlying dilemma can be detected regarding how to write in times that are turbulent as well as how to write when absolute rule emerges as the solution to the problems of the Roman Republic. How the works of both authors "comment" on Augustan rule has been the subject of ongoing literary debate.

HORACE'S LIFE

The main sources about Horace's life are his own writings and a short biography transmitted along with some of the manuscripts of his work. This biography very likely derives from the *Dē poētīs* of Suetonius (born c. 69 CE), which formed a section of a larger collection of biographies entitled *Dē virīs illūstribus.* Quintus Horatius Flaccus was born on December 8th, 65 BCE, in the town of Venusia (modern Venosa), located on the border between Apulia and Lucania in southern Italy. He was the son of a freedman, or an ex-slave, who worked as an auction agent or *coāctor argentārius.* Nothing is known of Horace's mother.

Despite his social status Horace's father must have had sufficient resources to provide his son with the kind of education typical for those from families of the equestrian or senatorial class. His father took him to Rome for his early education and later sent him to Athens in 44 BCE to pursue studies in philosophy. There Horace made the acquaintance of Cicero's son Marcus. Later that year Brutus, one of the assassins of Julius Caesar, recruited both Horace and Marcus to join the cause of reestablishing the Roman Republic. Horace fought on the losing side at the battle of Philippi in 42 BCE, which secured the defeat of the republican cause and the victory of Antony and Octavian, the heirs to Caesar's power.

After Octavian declared an amnesty for all who had fought against him, Horace returned to Italy. He found himself without his paternal home and estate, which were probably confiscated for Octavian's victorious soldiers. Horace was able to secure for himself the job of *scrība quaestōrius,* clerk to the quaestors, an important position, held for life, with duties involving public finances and the public records. The job only intermittently required a great deal of work, yet always brought in a salary, thus providing an excellent situation that enabled the poet to pursue his writing.

By the early thirties, around 39–38 BCE, Horace must have begun to circulate his writing. He became friends with Varius (a leading epic and tragic poet) and Vergil, both of whom introduced him to Maecenas (Gaius Cilnius Maecenas). Nine months after the introduction, Maecenas invited Horace to become part of his circle of friends, which already included Vergil, Varius, and several other authors. Maecenas, a quite wealthy equestrian, served as an important advisor to Octavian until the late twenties BCE. Horace became connected with the absolute leader of the Roman state through his friendship with Maecenas. Horace's addressing the first poem of his initial lyric collection to Maecenas (*Odes*, Books 1–3) as well as the beginning poems of the *Epodes*, *Satires* Book 1, and *Epistles* Book 1 illustrates how important Maecenas's relationship was to him.

Little is known of Horace's later life. While he accepted Augustus's commission to write the *Carmen saeculāre,* a poem written to be performed by a chorus of young men and women at the Secular Games in 17 BCE, he graciously turned down a request by Augustus to serve as his personal secretary. Horace died on November 27th, 8 BCE, shortly after the death of Maecenas. Interestingly, in *Odes* 2.17, a poem in which he expresses deep friendship for Maecenas, Horace predicts that they will die at the same time, "companions prepared to take that final journey together" (11–12), a prediction that turned out to be true.

HORACE'S WRITINGS

Horace wrote poetry over a period of about thirty years. His first publication in 35 BCE, at the age of thirty, was Book 1 of the *Satires* or *Sermōnēs* ("Conversations"), followed five years later by Book 2. Latin satire is verse in a conversational style on a variety of topics written from an individual point of view. Horace's satires, composed in dactylic hexameter, touch on a variety of literary, social, and ethical topics and include humorous or playful attacks on various human faults. By contrast, satire today refers to a literary work that uses derision, wit, strong irony, or exaggeration to expose or criticize human vices or stupidity.

Like the *Satires,* the *Epodes*, or *Iambī* as they are sometimes called, were written early in Horace's career. These poems follow in the tradition of the early Greek poet Archilochus of Paros, who wrote poems of attack and blame. According to Horace, his meters and spirit come from Archilochus, but the subject matter and words do not. The *Epodes* include several poems with political themes as well as several on erotic topics.

In 23 BCE Horace published Books 1–3 of his collection of lyric poetry, the *Odes* or *Carmina.* (These terms come from the Greek for "song" and the Latin for "song" or "poem.") He returned to lyric ten years later and published Book 4 of the *Odes*, which includes much that is in praise of Augustus. Horace wrote 103 lyric poems in all, with 88 appearing in Books 1–3 and 15 in Book 4.

Lyric poetry originally signified poetry written to the accompaniment of the lyre. While Horace makes allusion to the musical quality of his lyrics, scholars generally agree that his lyric poems were spoken and not sung. To the Romans, lyric poetry meant poetry written in the meters used by the Greek lyric poets. Sappho and Alcaeus were the Greek lyric poets to whom Horace especially looked for inspiration. They lived and wrote at the close of the seventh century BCE on the island of Lesbos, in Aeolia, part of the Greek area of Asia Minor. While Catullus, writing a generation earlier than Horace, wrote some poems in the lyric meters used by the Greek lyric poets (for example, Poem 51 is his translation and adaptation of a poem by Sappho), Horace took great pride in being the first to do so on a large scale. When expressing both his hopes for his lyric collection in *Odes* 1.1 and his pride in his lyric achievement in *Odes* 3.30 (a poem included in this text), Horace alludes to Sappho and Alcaeus through the phrases *Lesbōum . . . barbiton* ("Lesbian lyre") and *Aeolium carmen* ("Aeolic song"). Like his predecessor Catullus, Horace was influenced by the Alexandrian aesthetics of the Hellenistic Greek poet Callimachus (third century BCE), and thus wrote small, learned, carefully crafted poems.

A late fifth-century BCE Greek vase painting shows the poet Alcaeus paying homage to the poetess Sappho. The two poets each hold a lyre, the instrument the poet plucked as he recited his verse. This red figure Attic kalathos is a fine example of the classical period with its emphasis on depicting the human body naturally and in proportion.

The odes range widely in subject matter and include the themes of politics, love, literature, death's inevitability, life's brevity, friendship, and more. The personal is often mixed with the public. While Horace was self-consciously writing in a long literary tradition that included much Greek influence, his poems are very contemporary. In addition to the Roman political world that pervades the *Odes*, the social environment Horace inhabited is evident. The *Odes* in this volume include 1.5 (to Pyrrha), 1.11 (to Leuconoe), 1.23 (to Chloe), 2.10 (on the golden mean), and 3.30 (the epilogue).

Horace's lyrics stand out in that his exploitation of the possibilities of the Latin language is really quite extraordinary. Word order, which in Latin is already flexible, is with Horace even more so. Words that agree with each other may be separated widely, creating a kind of framing or phrasing effect (for instance, *mē . . . inermem* frames the third stanza of *Odes* 1.22). Also, Horace regularly separates adjectives from the nouns they modify. Lines 13–14 of *Odes* 1.5 (*tabulā sacer / vōtīvā pariēs*) well illustrate this technique of an interlocked word order, with *sacer* in line 13 modifying *pariēs* in line 14 and with *vōtīvā* in line 14 modifying *tabulā* in line 13. In addition, words placed right next to each may not agree grammatically but may affect each other in terms of sense. For example, in lines 11–12 of *Odes* 1.23, *dēsine mātrem / tempestīva sequī virō*, the verb *dēsine* at first seems to have *mātrem* as its direct object ("stop the mother"), while *sequī*

virō suggests "following a man," even though *virō* is not its grammatical object. Read in this way, these lines appear to reinforce the message of the poem that Chloe has reached an age appropriate for love. The best readers of Horace will be open to these types of aural and visual effects of his language. Most odes have an addressee, which makes the poems appear immediate and personal. Finally, each poem is carefully constructed, often with the close of the poem verbally or thematically recalling the beginning. For example, nautical metaphors begin and end *Odes* 2.10.

HORATIAN METERS

Horace used a wide variety of meters in his poetry. This text includes poems in the following meters: Sapphic, First or Lesser Asclepiadean, Fourth Asclepiadean, and Fifth or Greater Asclepiadean. (The basics of Latin metrical scansion are to be found in Appendix B. There, too, metrical schemes of the meters for the poems are provided.)

READING 1

In Latin prose and poetry, the reader often needs to "understand" or supply words that are not in the Latin text. Words to be understood are in parentheses in the text below. Different fonts point out words that belong together.

Odes 1.5 is the first love poem in the three-book collection of Horace's *Odes*. The subject of this poem is the inconstancy of love. Horace exploits the METAPHOR of the "seas of love" in describing the young man's present (and possibly Horace's own past) romantic relationship with Pyrrha. While the more specific involvement of the speaker revealed in the final stanza is something of a surprise, his presence is felt from the beginning of the poem where he interrogates the present relationship between Pyrrha and her young man.

THE CHANGEABILITY OF LOVE

HORACE *ODES* 1.5

Meter: Fourth Asclepiadean

1   **Quis** multā **gracilis** tē **puer** in rosā

    perfūsus liquidīs urget odōribus

        grātō, Pyrrha, sub antrō?

           cui flāvam religās comam

NOTES AND VOCABULARY

Line 1:   **quis:** interrogative adjective modifying *puer*. Translate "what."

          gracilis, gracile slender, thin

          rosa, -ae, f. rose

          multā . . . in rosā: translate "amid many a rose" or "among many roses."

BY THE WAY

Roses are associated with Venus, the goddess of love.

Line 2:   **perfundō, perfundere, perfūdī, perfūsum** to pour over, fill with; *perfūsus* translates *lit.,* "having been poured/filled," more naturally, "drenched." Men, as well as women, wore perfume in Horace's Rome. In modern terms, the boy is wearing too much cologne.

          liquidus, -a, -um flowing, clear, liquid; *liquidīs . . . odōribus* is an ablative of means.

          urgeō, urgēre, ursī to press

          odor, odōris, m. smell, odor, perfume

Line 3:   **Pyrrha, -ae,** f. Pyrrha, woman's name

             sub: translate "under the shelter of."

             antrum, -ī, n. cave, hollow space, grotto

Line 4:   **flāvus, -a, -um** yellow, golden, blond, auburn

             religō (1) to tie back, fasten behind

The Romans were very fond of roses. Archaeologists have found evidence of their presence in Roman gardens from Pompeii to the Fishbourne Palace near Chichester, England. Roses were used like confetti at celebrations, for medicinal purposes, and to make perfume. Noble families planted large rose gardens in the south of ancient Rome.

5   (tū) simplex munditiīs? Heu quotiēns *fidem (mūtātam)*

mūtātōsque deōs flēbit et aspera

    nigrīs aequora ventīs

        ēmīrābitur īnsolēns,

quī nunc **tē** fruitur crēdulus **aureā,**

10   quī *(tē)* semper *vacuam, (tē)* semper *amābilem (futūram esse/fore)*

    spērat, nescius aurae

        fallācis. Miserī (sunt illī), quibus

intemptāta nitēs. Mē tabulā *sacer*

vōtīvā *pariēs* indicat *ūvida*

15   suspendisse *potentī*

    vestīmenta maris *deō.*

NOTES AND VOCABULARY

Line 5:   **simplex, simplicis** simple, artless, plain

        munditia, -ae, f. neatness, elegance; *munditiīs* is an ablative of respect. Translate "in (your) neatness, elegance, etc."

        heu, *interj.* expressing grief or pain, oh, alas

        quotiēns, *adv.* how often

        fidem: understand the sense of *mūtātōs* with *fidem* as well as with *deōs.* "Changed faith" equals "faithlessness."

Line 6:   **mūtō** (1) to change

        fleō, flēre, flēvī, flētum to weep for, lament

        asper, -a, -um fierce, rough

Lines 6–7:   **aspera nigrīs aequora ventīs:** note the SYNCHESIS.

Line 8:   **ēmīror** (1) to wonder at exceedingly, be astonished at‡

        īnsolēns, īnsolentis unaccustomed, excessive; *īnsolēns* modifies the subject of *ēmīrābitur.*

Line 9:   **fruor, fruī, fructus sum** (+ *abl.*) to enjoy

        crēdulus, -a, -um credulous, naïve, trustful

        aureus, -a, -um golden, splendid‡

REMINDER

In Book 2 of Vergil, on p. 281, you were introduced to these words that begin with *aur-*. Now add *aureus, -a, -um* to this list of commonly confused words.

aura, -ae, f. breeze	FIRST DECLENSION NOUN
aurum, -ī, n. gold	SECOND DECLENSION NEUTER NOUN
auris, auris, f. ear	THIRD DECLENSION NOUN
aureus, -a, -um golden	FIRST AND SECOND DECLENSION ADJECTIVE

Line 10:   **vacuus, -a, -um** empty, free, available

                amābilis, amābile lovable, loving, delightful

Lines 10–11:   Translate *quī . . . spērat* "who hopes (that) you will be."

Line 11:   **spērō** (1) to hope, hope for, expect

                nescius, -a, -um ignorant, unaware; *nescius* takes the genitive. Translate "ignorant of."

Line 12:   **fallāx, fallācis** deceitful, deceptive

                miserī: translate "unhappy (are those)."

Lines 13–16:   Note the two examples of SYNCHESIS in these lines.

Line 13:   **intemptātus, -a, -um** untried, unattempted

                niteō, nitēre, nituī to shine, be radiant with beauty

                tabula, -ae, f. board, plank, writing tablet, (votive) tablet

Lines 13–14:   **tabulā . . . vōtīvā:** ablative of means

Line 14:   **vōtīvus, -a, -um** votive, relating to a vow

                pariēs, parietis, m. wall; *sacer pariēs* = temple wall

                indicō, (1) to point out, show, declare; *indicat* sets up the indirect statement *mē . . . suspendisse.*

                ūvidus, -a, -um wet

Line 15:   **suspendō, suspendere, suspendī, suspēnsum,** to hang up

Line 16:   **vestīmentum, -ī,** n. clothes, garments

BY THE WAY

The noun *deō* can refer to Venus as well as to Neptune, for the masculine form of the noun *deus* can be used of a female deity. It is likely that Horace ingeniously intended the word to refer to both deities, with Neptune (god of the sea) the natural recipient on a literal level and with Venus (goddess of the seas of love) the natural recipient on a metaphorical level.

TAKE NOTE

1. Horace appears to have coined the verb *ēmīror* (line 8), which appears only here in Latin literature. The prefix *"ex-, ē-"* intensifies the meaning of the simple form of the verb *mīror*.

2. The adjective *aureus* (line 9) comes to mean "of great excellence" or "of great beauty." Consequently, *aureus* can mean "stunningly beautiful." In Latin, words having to do with "shining" or "being bright" can take on the meaning of "beautiful." *Candidus*, for example, means "white, fair," and comes to mean "beautiful" (cf. Catullus 13.4, *nōn sine candidā puellā*). Similarly, *niteō* (line 13) means "to shine, to be bright" and, by extension, "to be radiant with beauty."

COMPREHENSION QUESTIONS

1. According to lines 1–3, where are Pyrrha and the boy? Cite the Latin.

2. Describe the storm mentioned in lines 6–7. Cite the Latin.

3. For what two things does the boy hope?

4. To whom were the wet garments dedicated?

▶ EXERCISE 1

1. In line 1, what is the case and use of *tē*?

2. What is the tense, voice, and form of *perfūsus* in line 2?

3. In line 4, what is the case and use of *cui*?

4. What is the case and use of *fidem* in line 5?

5. In line 7, what is the case and use of *ventīs*?

6. In line 8, what is the subject and translation of *ēmīrābitur*?

7. What noun does *fallācis* in line 12 modify?

8. In line 13, what is the case and use of *mē*?

9. What is the subject of *indicat* in line 14?

10. What is the tense, voice, and form of *suspendisse* in line 15?

LANGUAGE FACT

DEPONENT VERBS THAT GOVERN THE ABLATIVE CASE

You read this line in Horace, *Odes* 1.5.

> *quī nunc tē fruitur crēdulus aureā* (Horace *Odes* 1.5.9)
> "who now, being naïve, enjoys you beautiful"

Notice how the object of *fruitur* is the ablative phrase, *tē . . . aureā*.

Of course you are familiar with the "ablative of means." One particular variety of this ablative is the use of the ablative with five deponent verbs and their compounds:

ūtor, ūtī, ūsus sum	use, enjoy
fruor, fruī, frūctus sum	enjoy, derive pleasure from
fungor, fungī, functus sum	perform, experience
potior, potīrī, potītus sum	get possession of, obtain, possess
vescor, vescī, —	enjoy, feed on, eat

REMINDER

As you read in a note in the Caesar chapter of this book on p. 45, in the writings of some authors, *potior* is also found with a genitive object.

BY THE WAY

A mnemonic to help you remember the verbs above is to think of them as the PUFFV (pronounce "puffy") verbs.

P	potior
U	ūtor
F	fruor
F	fungor
V	vēscor

If you look at the following translations, you can see how the use of the ablative with these verbs is a kind of ablative of means:

Vītā fruor.   "I enjoy life." (natural English translation)
"I enjoy myself (by means of) life." (literal English translation showing the ablative of means)

▶ EXERCISE 2

Choose the correct form of the ablative to complete the following Latin sentences. Consider the tense of each verb. Then translate the sentence into English two ways, "naturally" and "more literally."

1. Puer _____ fruitur.   (tū, tuī, tē)

2. Puer _____ fruētur.   (multīs, multās, multōs)

3. Puer _____ fruēbātur   (Pyrrha, Pyrrham, Pyrrhā)

4. Pyrrha _____ fruitur.   (puer, puerum, puerō)

5. Pyrrha _____ frūcta est.   (aurīs, aura, auram)

READING 1 REDUX

You are now ready to read the poem exactly as Horace wrote it. For this reason the words in parentheses and the special fonts are no longer used. You have already seen notes in the first version of this poem, and you may refer to those notes if you need to. Additional notes for this poem are given below the text.

1   Quis multā gracilis tē puer in rosā

     perfūsus liquidīs urget odōribus

        grātō, Pyrrha, sub antrō?

           cui flāvam religās comam

5   simplex munditiīs? heu quotiēns fidem

     mūtātōsque deōs flēbit et aspera

        nigrīs aequora ventīs

           ēmīrābitur īnsolēns,

     quī nunc tē fruitur crēdulus aureā,

10   quī semper vacuam, semper amābilem

        spērat, nescius aurae

           fallācis. miserī, quibus

     intemptāta nitēs. mē tabulā sacer

     vōtīvā pariēs indicat ūvida

15   suspendisse potentī

        vestīmenta maris deō.

NOTES AND VOCABULARY

Line 1:   **multā . . . in rosā:** this is a primarily poetic usage of *multus, -a, -um* where the singular is used with a singular noun, standing for a plural noun. This phrase refers either to the couple lying on rose petals or to roses garlanding the grotto.

BY THE WAY

Note the CHIASMUS in line 1: *Quis multā **gracilis** tē **puer** in rosā. Multā* (A) modifies *rosā* (A), while *gracilis* (B) modifies *puer* (B). The pronoun *tē* is in the middle of these pairs, thereby emphasizing Pyrrha, the subject of the poem.

Line 3:   The Greek base for fire (*pyr–*), contained in the name Pyrrha, may suggest flame-colored hair or a fiery nature. Latin has the image of the "fire" of love, as we do in English. Her name thus may be underscoring the context of love already established in the poem; because of the destructive nature of fire, Horace may subtly be suggesting the emotional havoc that will result from the *puer*'s relationship with her. The name Pyrrha also sets up a contrast with the water imagery in this poem.

Line 15:   **suspendisse:** those who escaped from danger as a thanks-offering to the gods often attached to a temple wall a tablet with a picture depicting the escape; sailors who eluded death sometimes dedicated the garments that they wore at the time. Horace combines the two ideas here and cleverly transfers this practice to his being rescued as a shipwrecked sailor from the seas of love. *Odes* 1.5 may be considered the *tabula* that Horace, the experienced sailor on the seas of love, dedicates in thanksgiving.

ESSAY

In *Odes* 1.5 Horace skillfully portrays Pyrrha and the *puer* who is in love with her. Discuss how Horace characterizes each individual.

Support your assertions with references drawn from throughout the poem. All Latin words must be copied or their line numbers provided, AND they must be translated or paraphrased closely enough so that it is clear you understand the Latin. Direct your answer to the question; do not merely summarize the passage. Please write your essay on a separate piece of paper.

SCANSION

Name the meter and scan the following lines.

> Quis multā gracilis tē puer in rosā
>
> perfūsus liquidīs urget odōribus
>
> grātō, Pyrrha, sub antrō?
>
> cui flāvam religās comam

READING 2

The rest of the Horace poems in this book will no longer feature the words in parentheses and the use of special fonts. Use the notes below the poem to help you.

In this ode the speaker exhorts Leuconoe not to worry about what tomorrow will bring; instead, she should enjoy the present. This is one of several odes that deal with the theme of life's brevity. In this poem Horace introduces the quite novel METAPHOR from viticulture of "plucking" the day. This phrase, which signifies "seizing an opportunity" or "embracing the present," is still commonly used today.

SEIZE THE DAY

HORACE *ODES* 1.11

Meter: Fifth or Greater Asclepiadean

1   Tū nē quaesīeris (scīre nefās), quem mihi, quem tibi

     fīnem dī dederint, Leuconoē, nec Babylōniōs

     temptāris numerōs. ut melius, quidquid erit, patī!

     seu plūrīs hiemēs, seu tribuit Iuppiter ultimam,

NOTES AND VOCABULARY

Line 1:   **tū** at the start of the poem is very emphatic. Latin poets may emphasize first or last words, or both, in a poem. For example, the word "nose" provides an unexpected and quite striking ending for Poem 13 of Catullus.

        nē quaesīeris: *nē* + the perfect subjunctive is used to express a prohibition or negative command. *Quaesīeris* is the syncopated form of *quaesīveris*.

        nefās, n. *indeclin.,* crime, offense against divine law, sacrilege; understand *est* with *scīre nefās.* This phrase is parenthetical, "interrupting" the sentence.

Lines 1–2:   **quem:** understand *fīnem* with each *quem.*

STUDY TIP

Be careful not to confuse *deus* (*dī,* line 2), the Latin word for "god," with *diēs* (line 8), which means "day," or with *dīvus, -a, -um* "divine." Compare and contrast *diēs* (nominative singular and accusative plural of "day"), *dī* (nominative plural of *deus*), *dīs* (dative and ablative plural of *deus*), and *dīvī* (nominative plural of *dīvus*).

Line 2:   **dī:** alternate form of *deī,* nominative plural of *deus.*‡

        dederint: perfect subjunctive in indirect question dependent on *quem fīnem. Quem* is an interrogative adjective here.

        Leuconoē, Leuconoēs, f. Leuconoe, woman's name

BY THE WAY

The name of the woman to whom the poem is addressed, Leuconoe, comes from the Greek *leukos* ("clear, bright, white") and *nous* ("mind") and may suggest equally "clear-minded" or "empty-minded" ("empty-headed"). The notion of "white" in her name ties in with the season of winter in line 4.

Lines 2–3: **Babylōnius, -a, -um** Babylonian; Babylonian numbers or astrological tables predicting the future.

Line 3: **temptō** (1) to try, attempt; *temptāris = temptā(ve)ris* This is the syncopated, or shortened, form of the verb.

ut: translate "how."

melius: comparative adjective, nominative singular neuter. Translate as "better." Understand *est*.

quidquid erit: direct object of *patī*.

patior, patī, passus sum to suffer, endure; the infinitive *patī* functions as the predicate nominative of the understood *est*. Translate "to suffer" or "to endure."

Line 4: **seu . . . seu:** translate "whether . . . or." The first clause has subject and verb understood (to be supplied from looking at the second clause): *plūrīs hiemēs [Iuppiter tribuit]*; the second clause has the direct object understood (to be supplied from the first clause): *Iuppiter tribuit ultimam [hiemem]*.

plūrīs = *plūrēs*; third declension adjective alternate ending, masculine/feminine accusative plural

hiems, hiemis, f. winter, storm; this is METONYMY for "year." The sense of "winter" as a way of reckoning years, however, is significant for the theme of death that pervades the poem.

tribuō, tribuere, tribuī, tribūtum to allot, assign; *tribuit* can be present or perfect tense (same form).

ultimam: understand *hiemem*.

HORACE *ODES* 1.11, CONTINUED

5   quae nunc oppositīs dēbilitat pūmicibus mare

    Tyrrhēnum: sapiās, vīna liquēs et spatiō brevī

    spem longam resecēs. dum loquimur, fūgerit invida

    aetās: carpe diem, quam minimum crēdula posterō.

NOTES AND VOCABULARY

Line 5:   **quae:** a relative pronoun

        oppōnō, oppōnere, opposuī, oppositum to place against, place in front, proffer; *oppositīs . . . pūmicibus* is ablative of means. Translate "with its hostile pumice-stones." Note that the stones are what make the sea become weakened, not the reverse.

        dēbilitō (1) to weaken

        pūmex, pūmicis, m. pumice-stone

Lines 5–6:   **mare Tyrrhēnum:** direct object of *dēbilitat*

Line 6:   **Tyrrhēnus, -a, -um** Tyrrhenian, Etruscan

        sapiās . . . liquēs: volitive subjunctives

        vīna: plural for singular

        liquō, liquāre to melt, strain; before drinking their wine, the Romans strained it to remove the sediment.

        spatiō brevī: best taken as a causal ablative. Translate "because of the brief time." Understand after this phrase "of our lives."

        spatium, spatiī, n. space, period of time, span of life

Line 7:   **resecō, resecāre, resecuī, resectum,** to cut back, prune, restrain; *resecēs* is a volitive subjunctive.

        loquor, loquī, locūtus sum to speak

        fūgerit: future perfect. Translate "will have fled."

        invidus, -a, -um envious, jealous

BY THE WAY

Time, *aetās,* is personified in the poem when it is described as "jealous," *invida.*

Line 8:   **aetās, aetātis,** f. time, age

        carpō, carpere, carpsī, carptum to pluck, seize

        quam minimum: *quam* with the superlative (as . . . as possible). Translate "to the least extent possible" or "as little as possible."

        crēdulus, -a, -um credulous, trustful; *crēdula* takes dative *posterō.*

        posterus, -a, -um next, following, future, later; understand the noun *diēī* with *posterō.*

STUDY TIP

You read the word *aetās, aetātis,* f. "age" in line 8 above. Don't confuse *aetās* with *aestās, aestātis,* f. "summer," or with *aestus, aestūs,* m. "flood," a word you saw in Vergil 2.706.

Horace's famous phrase "seize the day" has been popularized in America beginning with the Robin Williams movie *Dead Poets Society*. Subsequently it has been placed on coffee mugs, t-shirts, sweatshirts, and the like.

BY THE WAY

The *carpe diem* theme, which comes from this poem, encompasses time, the seasons, and even death.

TAKE NOTE

The nouns *deus, diēs,* and *dīvus* ("god") all belong to the same word family, which has the basic idea of "brightness."

COMPREHENSION QUESTIONS

1. What is Leuconoe told not to do? Cite the Latin.

2. It is said to be better to endure what? Cite the Latin.

3. What three things is Leuconoe encouraged to do?

4. According to this poem, what should not be trusted?

▶ EXERCISE 1

1. In line 1, what part of speech is *quem*?

2. What is the case and use of *mihi* and *tibi* in line 1?

3. In line 2, what is the case and use of *Leuconoē*?

4. What is the case and use of *quidquid* in line 3?

5. What is the tense and form of *patī* in line 3?

6. What is the case and use of *hiemēs* in line 4?

7. What is the antecedent, case, and use of *quae* in line 5?

8. What is the case and use of *vīna* in line 6?

9. What is the case and use of *posterō* in line 8?

VOCABULARY BUILDER

The theme of time is a significant one in Horace's *Odes*. Here are some important "time" words from the *Odes* that would be good to learn.

NOUNS

hōra, -ae, f. hour, time, season

diēs, diēī, m. (f.) day

aetās, aetātis, f. time, age

aestās, aestātis, f. summer

vēr, vēris, n. spring

hiems, hiemis, f. winter, storm

spatium, spatiī, n. space, period of time

ADJECTIVES

ultimus, -a, -um last

posterus, -a, -um next, following, future

brevis, breve short

longus, -a, -um long

▶ EXERCISE 2

Translate the following phrases into English using the "time" words above. Identify the case of the time phrase. If there are two possibilities, list them both.

Example:

Latin	English translation	case(s)
vēr breve	short spring	nom., acc.

1. longa aetās

2. hiems postera

3. vēr longum

4. aestātis brevis

5. hōra ultima
   (translate *hōra* using three different meanings)

6. longum diem

7. spatiō longō

8. aetās postera

9. brevium diērum

ESSAY

This ode makes a contrast between aspects over which an individual has no control and those aspects that an individual can control. In a short essay discuss how the speaker develops this contrast to help him set forth advice about how to live.

Support your assertions with references drawn from throughout lines 1–8. All Latin words must be copied or their line numbers provided, AND they must be translated or paraphrased closely enough so that it is clear you understand the Latin. Direct your answer to the question; do not merely summarize the passage. Please write your essay on a separate piece of paper.

SCANSION

Name the meter and scan the following lines.

quae nunc oppositīs dēbilitat pūmicibus mare

Tyrrhēnum: sapiās, vīna liquēs et spatiō brevī

spem longam resecēs. dum loquimur, fūgerit invida

aetās: carpe diem, quam minimum crēdula posterō.

READING 3

Odes 1.23 has as its subject a girl's coming of age. The speaker attempts to convince Chloe, the poem's addressee, not to avoid his advances. In his opinion she is sufficiently mature to be involved in a romantic relationship. The strong imagery in the poem may suggest a sense of danger that runs counter to the speaker's reassurances.

CHLOE'S MATURITY

HORACE *ODES* 1.23

Meter: Fourth Asclepiadean

1   Vītās inuleō mē similis, Chloē,

      quaerentī pavidam montibus āviīs

          mātrem nōn sine vānō

             aurārum et siluae metū.

5   nam seu mōbilibus vēris inhorruit

      adventus foliīs, seu viridēs rubum

          dīmovēre lacertae,

             et corde et genibus tremit.

    atquī nōn ego tē tigris ut aspera

10   Gaetulusve leō frangere persequor:

      tandem dēsine mātrem

          tempestīva sequī virō.

NOTES AND VOCABULARY

REMINDER

As noted at the beginning of Cicero's *First Catilinarian Oration* on p. 165 of this book, do not confuse *vītō* (1) "to avoid" with *vīta, -ae,* f. "life" or with *vīvō, vīvere, vīxī, vīctum* "to live."

Line 1:   **vītō** (1) to avoid, shun

          in(n)uleus, -ī, m. fawn; *inuleō* is dative with *similis.*

          Chloē, Chloēs, f. Chloe, woman's name; the *oe* is not a diphthong in the name; rather, this is a two-syllable or bisyllabic word.‡

Line 2:   **pavidus, -a, -um** frightened, terrified, trembling, fearful

          montibus: ablative of place where; *in* is frequently to be understood in poetry.

          āvius, -a, -um pathless, remote

Line 3:	**nōn sine:** note the LITOTES.
	vānus, -a, -um empty, groundless, imaginary
Line 4:	**aura, -ae,** f. breeze
	siluae: three syllables here; the letter "v/u" is being treated as a vowel, not a consonant.
	metus, metūs, m. fear
Line 5:	**mōbilis, mōbile** movable, changeable, inconstant, pliant
	vēr, vēris, n. spring
	inhorrēscō, inhorrēscere, inhorruī to begin to tremble, bristle, become stiffly erect

STUDY TIP

Don't confuse *vēr, vēris,* n. "spring" with *vērus, -a, -um* "true." The genitive singular of *vēr, vēris* and the dative/ablative plural of *vērus, -a, -um* are both spelled *v·e·r·i·s.* The dative/ablative *vērīs* has a macron on the ending *–īs* but the genitive singular *vēris* does not.

Line 6:	**adventus, adventūs,** m. arrival, approach
	folium, foliī, n. leaf
	viridis, viride green, fresh, young
	rubus, -ī, m. bramble, prickly bush
Line 7:	**dīmoveō, dīmovēre, dīmōvī, dīmōtum** to move apart, separate; *dīmōvēre* is the alternate form of *dīmōvērunt.*
	lacerta, -ae, f. lizard
Line 8:	**cor, cordis,** n. heart
	genu, genūs, n. knee
	tremō, tremere, tremuī to tremble, quiver

STUDY TIP

Be careful to distinguish *atquī,* "but," from *atque,* "and."

Line 9:	**atquī,** *conj.* but, nevertheless
	tigris, tigris/tigridis, f. (also, m.) tiger
	asper, aspera, asperum fierce, rough
Lines 9–10:	**atquī . . . persequor:** note how the literal sense of these two lines ("I am not chasing you, etc.") is countered by the fierceness of the imagery (lion and tiger) and observe the postponement of the word *persequor* until the very end, with its negative (*nōn*) long forgotten.
Line 10:	**Gaetulus, -a, -um** Gaetulian, of Gaetulia, region of northwest Africa known for its lions
	frangō, frangere, frēgī, frāctum to break, crush; *frangere:* infinitive expressing purpose
	persequor, persequī, persecūtus sum to pursue, chase
Line 11:	**dēsinō, dēsinere, dēsiī, dēsitum** to stop, cease; *dēsine* takes the infinitive *sequī;* translate "stop following."
Line 12:	**tempestīvus, -a, -um** timely, seasonable, ripe
	virō: dative, with *tempestīva*

TAKE NOTE

Chloe in Greek means "green bud" or "shoot." The name appears as an EPITHET of the Greek goddess of agriculture, Demeter; there is inscriptional evidence of a festival of Demeter Chloe and Kore (which refers to her daughter, Persephone) at Eleusis in Greece. Thus through its association with Demeter, the name Chloe suggests simultaneously both female youth (Persephone) and female maturity (Demeter). Horace's use of this name in the poem evokes both the image of spring and the life cycle of women.

COMPREHENSION QUESTIONS

1. According to stanza one, what is the fawn doing?

2. According to stanza two, what two things does the fawn fear? Cite the Latin.

3. According to stanza three, how is the poet not following Chloe? Cite the Latin.

4. According to the end of this poem, what should Chloe do?

▶ EXERCISE 1

1. In line 1, what is the case and use of *mē*?

2. What figure of speech is in line 1?

3. What word does *quaerentī* (line 2) modify?

4. What word does *pavidam* (line 2) modify?

5. What is the case and use of *montibus āviīs* in line 2?

6. For what word does *mātrem* (line 3) serve as object?

7. What word does *vānō* (line 3) modify?

8. What figure of speech is in lines 2–3?

9. In line 4, what is the case and use of *aurārum et siluae*?

10. In line 5, what is the case and use of *vēris*?

11. In line 6, what is the case and use of *adventus*?

12. What does *viridēs* (line 6) modify?

13. What is the case and use of *rubum* in line 6?

14. In line 7, the verb *dīmovēre* is an alternative of what verb?

15. In line 8, what is the case and use of *corde*?

16. What two figures of speech are in line 9?

17. What is the case and use of *tigris* in line 9?

18. In line 10, what is the case and use of *leō*?

19. What figure of speech is in lines 9–10?

20. In line 11, what is the case and use of *mātrem*?

21. What word does *tempestīva* (line 12) modify?

22. What is the tense and form of *sequī* in line 12?

23. What is the case and use of *virō* in line 12?

Modern Venosa that rose near the ancient Venusia is proud of its favorite son, the poet Horace. A museum filled with Roman reproductions of items one would find in a poet's home are housed in this venerable building by tradition called the Casa di Orazio Flacco.

LANGUAGE FACT

INFINITIVE OF PURPOSE, REVIEW OF PURPOSE CONSTRUCTIONS, AND REVIEW OF INFINITIVE USES

- **Infinitive of Purpose**

  The infinitive of purpose is the least common way to show purpose in Latin and generally occurs only in poetry.

  > *Nōn ego tē . . . frangere persequor* (Horace *Odes* 1.23.9–10)
  > "I do not pursue you to break you."

- **Other Purpose Constructions**

   Remember these other more frequently used ways of showing purpose.

Mātrem sequere nē ā mē frangāris. "Follow your mother so that you are not broken by me."	**PURPOSE** **CONSTRUCTION** **WITH *UT/NĒ***
Chloē mātrem quaerit ad mē vītandum. "Chloe seeks her mother for the purpose of avoiding me."	***AD* + GERUND/** **GERUNDIVE IN A** **PURPOSE CLAUSE**

- **Infinitive Uses**

   The infinitive of purpose is one use of the infinitive. Consider the other infinitive uses in these examples.

Dēsine . . . sequī. (Horace *Odes* 1.23.11–12) "Stop following."	**COMPLEMENTARY** **INFINITIVE**
Inuleus mātrem quaerere potest. "The fawn is able to seek her mother."	**COMPLEMENTARY** **INFINITIVE**
Placet inuleō matrem quaerere. "It is pleasing to the fawn to seek her mother."	**INFINITIVE WITH** **IMPERSONAL VERB**
Dīcō inuleum tremere. "I say that the fawn is trembling."	**INFINITIVE IN** **INDIRECT STATEMENT**
Sciō Gaetulum leōnem tē frāctūrum esse. "I know that the Gaetulian lion will break you."	**INFINITIVE IN** **INDIRECT STATEMENT**

▶ EXERCISE 2

Translate the following Latin sentences and state which one of the four uses of the infinitive each Latin sentence contains.

Example:

Latin Sentence	English Translation	Type of Infinitive
Dēsine tremere.	Stop trembling.	Complementary

1. Dēsine sequī!

2. Tē tremere dīcō.

3. Frangere eōs persecūta sum.

4. Putāsne (Do you think) leōnēs tremere?

5. Dēsine mē quaerere!

6. Libet lacertīs dīmovēre folia.

7. Nōn tē frangere persequor.

8. Tē sequī nōn possum.

9. Leōnem esse bonum dīcō.

ESSAY

In *Odes* 1.23 Horace encourages Chloe to recognize that she has reached an age appropriate for love. In a short essay discuss how Chloe's name suits her characterization in the poem and how it connects closely with the seasons and nature.

Support your assertions with references drawn from throughout the poem. All Latin words must be copied or their line numbers provided, AND they must be translated or paraphrased closely enough so that it is clear you understand the Latin. Direct your answer to the question; do not merely summarize the passage. Please write your essay on a separate piece of paper.

SCANSION

Name the meter and scan the following lines.

> nam seu mōbilibus vēris inhorruit
>
> adventus foliīs, seu viridēs rubum
>
> > dīmovēre lacertae,
>
> > > et corde et genibus tremit.

READING 4

The speaker advises Licinius that moderation is the best course in living one's life. Good and bad circumstances should be accepted with composure. Warning against extremes of excessiveness, the poem focuses on the notion that people who are in positions of power or prominence are particularly susceptible to a change in circumstance.

THE GOLDEN MEAN

HORACE *ODES* 2.10
Meter: Sapphic

1 Rēctius vīvēs, Licinī, neque altum

  semper urgendō, neque—dum procellās

  cautus horrēscis—nimium premendō

   lītus inīquum.

5 auream quisquis mediocritātem

  dīligit, tūtus caret obsolētī

  sordibus tēctī, caret invidendā

   sōbrius aulā.

  saepius ventīs agitātur ingēns

10 pīnus et celsae graviōre cāsū

  dēcidunt turrēs feriuntque summōs

   fulgura montīs.

NOTES AND VOCABULARY

Line 1: **rēctus, -a, -um** straight, right, correct, proper

   Licinīus, -ī, m. Licinius‡

   altum: this nautical language introduces the METAPHOR of the "sea" of life or of politics.

Line 2: **urgeō, urgēre, ursī** to push, press upon, make for

   procella, -ae, f. violent wind, storm, trouble

Line 3: **cautus, -a, -um** on one's guard, wary, cautious, prudent

   horrēscō, horrēscere, horruī to shudder at, tremble at

   nimium, *adv.* too, too much, very

   premō, premere, pressī, pressum to press, follow closely, hug

Line 4: **lītus, lītoris,** n. shore, coast, beach

   inīquus, -a, -um uneven, unfavorable, treacherous, discontented

Line 5: **aureus, -a, -um** golden, splendid

   mediocritās, mediocritātis, f. mean, moderation, keeping of a middle course

BY THE WAY

Horace coined the phrase "the golden mean." The inspiration for the coinage comes from Aristotle's *Nicomachean Ethics,* which suggests excellence lies in between two extremes.

Line 6: **dīligō, dīligere, dīlēxī, dīlēctum** to love, esteem, hold dear, have special regard for

tūtus, -a, -um safe, secure; translate *tūtus* and *sōbrius* in line 8 adverbially.

careō, carēre, caruī, caritum (+ *abl.*) to lack, be without, avoid

obsolētus, -a, -um worn out, shabby, ordinary

STUDY TIP

Be careful to distinguish between *tūtus, -a, -um* "safe, secure" and *tōtus, -a, -um* "whole, entire."

Lines 6–8: Note the repetition of *caret*, which highlights the extremes, as well as the ASYNDETON, which makes the alternatives more obvious.

Line 7: **sordēs, sordis,** f. dirt, squalor, baseness; often used in plural.

tēctum, -ī, n. roof; house, dwelling

invideō, invidēre, invīdī, invīsum to envy, begrudge, refuse; translate *invidendā* "to be envied." See p. 75 for information on this use of the gerundive.

Line 8: **sōbrius, -a, -um** sober, moderate, sensible

aula, -ae, f. noble residence, palace, hall

Line 9: **agitō** (1) to drive, agitate, excite

ingēns, ingentis huge

Line 10: **pīnus, pīnūs,** f. pine‡

celsus, -a, -um high, lofty, proud

cāsus, cāsūs, m. fall, event, misfortune, chance

REMINDER

As noted in the Cicero chapter of this book on p. 184, don't confuse *cāsus, cāsūs,* m. "fall, event" with *casa, casae,* f. "hut, house" and *causa, causae,* f. "reason."

Line 11: **dēcidō, dēcidere, dēcidī** to fall down, collapse, die

turris, turris, f. tower

feriō, ferīre to strike, hit

Line 12: **fulgur, fulguris,** n. lightning, a flash of lightning, flash of light

montīs = *montēs*

STUDY TIP

Be careful to distinguish between *feriō, ferīre* "to strike, hit" and *ferō, ferre* "to bring, carry, bear."

HORACE *ODES* 2.10, CONTINUED

> spērat īnfestīs, metuit secundīs
> alteram sortem bene praeparātum

15 pectus; īnfōrmīs hiemēs redūcit
> Iuppiter, īdem

> submovet. nōn, sī male nunc, et ōlim
> sīc erit: quondam citharā tacentem
> suscitat Mūsam, neque semper arcum

20 tendit Apollō.

> rēbus angustīs animōsus atque
> fortis appārē: sapienter īdem
> contrahēs ventō nimium secundō
> turgida vēla.

NOTES AND VOCABULARY

Line 13: **spērō** (1) to hope, hope for

īnfestus, -a, -um dangerous, hostile, insecure, adverse

secundus, -a, -um following, second, favorable

īnfestīs ... secundīs: understand a word like *rēbus* ("circumstances"); *īnfestīs* and *secundīs* may be either datives of reference or ablative absolutes with *rēbus* understood. Translate the datives using the preposition "for"; translate as ablative absolutes using the conjunction "when."

spērat ... secundīs: note the SYNCHESIS.

Line 14: **sors, sortis,** f. lot, share, fortune

praeparō (1) to prepare

STUDY TIP

There is only a one-letter difference between *pectus, pectoris*, n. "heart, chest, mind" and *pecus, pecoris*, n. "flock, herd." Don't confuse them!

Line 15: **pectus:** subject of *spērat* and *metuit* (line 13)

īnfōrmis, īnfōrme shapeless, deformed, ugly; *īnfōrmīs* = *īnfōrmēs*

hiems, hiemis, f. winter, storm

Line 16: **īdem:** (*lit.,* "same [person]") translate "likewise" or "also."

BY THE WAY

Lines 15–17 illustrate the technique of clausal ENJAMBMENT, whereby the sentence in lines 15–16 continues beyond the end of the stanza into line 17. The clausal ENJAMBMENT here is striking because all the other stanzas form self-contained units. Horace's purpose appears to be to link the two divine exemplars of the golden mean in this poem, Jupiter and Apollo.

Line 17:   **submoveō, submovēre, submōvī, submōtum** to move away, remove, ward off, banish
sī male nunc: supply *sit*. Translate "if things go badly now" (*lit.,* "if it is badly now").
et: an adverb here; translate "also."
ōlim, *adv.* formerly, once, on an occasion, at some future date

STUDY TIP

The adverbs *ōlim* in line 17 and *quondam* in line 18 are synonyms.

Line 18:   **quondam,** *adv.* once, formerly, sometimes, in the future
cithara, -ae, f. lyre
taceō, tacēre, tacuī, tacitum to be silent
Line 19:   **suscitō, suscitāre, suscitāvī, suscitātum** to rouse, awaken
arcus, arcūs, m. bow
Line 20:   **tendō, tendere, tetendī, tentum/tēnsum** to stretch out, extend, proceed
Apollō, Apollinis, m. Apollo, son of Jupiter and Latona/Leto, brother of Diana, god of archery, music, poetry, etc.
Line 21:   **rēbus angustīs:** ablative absolute; translate "when circumstances are difficult."
angustus, -a, -um narrow, limited, difficult (of circumstances)
animōsus, -a, -um spirited, bold; of winds, violent
Line 22:   **appāreō, appārēre, appāruī, appāritum** to appear, show yourself
sapienter, *adv.* wisely
īdem: see line 16
Line 23:   **contrahō, contrahere, contrāxī, contrāctum** to draw together, narrow
nimium, *adv.* too, too much, very
secundō: see line 13.
Line 24:   **turgidus, -a, -um** swollen, turgid
vēlum, -ī, n. sail

BY THE WAY

The poem closes as it opened with a METAPHOR from sailing.

TAKE NOTE

1. Some believe that the Licinius of this poem is Lucius Licinius Murena, a prominent politician and brother-in-law of Maecenas, who was executed when trying to escape after his alleged participation in a conspiracy against Augustus. If this identification is correct, extra point would be added to Horace's advice for moderation and his comments on the dangers of being in a position of power. This Licinius also was a follower of Aristotle's school of philosophy that promoted the notion of moderation (*mediocritās*).

2. Trees, like islands as noted earlier on p. 259, are generally feminine in Latin.

COMPREHENSION QUESTIONS

1. What advice does the poet offer Licinius in the first stanza?

2. What two things will the person who esteems the golden mean avoid, according to the second stanza? Cite the Latin.

3. What three things represent great height, according to the third stanza? Cite the Latin.

4. Give two examples of extremes described in the second half of the poem.

▶ EXERCISE 1

1. In line 1, what tense is *vīvēs*?

2. In line 2, what is the case and use of *urgendō,* and what is its object?

3. In line 7, what is the case and use of *sordibus*?

4. In line 7, what is the case and use of *tēctī*?

5. What is the case and use of *invidendā* in line 7?

6. In line 9, what is the case and use of *ventīs*?

7. What is the case and use of *cāsū* in line 10?

8. What two figures of speech are in line 13?

9. In line 15, what does *īnfōrmīs* modify?

10. What figure of speech is in lines 13–15?

11. What is the object of *submovet* (line 17)?

12. In line 18, what is the case and use of *citharā*?

13. What is the subject of *suscitat* in line 19?

14. What is the tense, voice, and form of *appārē* in line 22?

15. In line 23, what is the object of *contrahēs*?

VOCABULARY BUILDER

In *Odes* 2.10, Horace uses adjectives frequently, and some of these are synonyms of adjectives seen earlier in this book and in beginning textbooks. Other parts of speech that are synonyms are also given. It will increase your vocabulary to know these.

Adjectives used in 2.10	Synonymous adjectives
animōsus, -a, -um bold	audāx, audācis bold
ingēns, ingentis huge	magnus, -a, -um large
īnfestus, -a, -um dangerous, hostile	perīculōsus, -a, -um dangerous
cautus, -a, -um wary, cautious, prudent	prūdēns, prūdentis prudent
celsus, -a, -um high, lofty, proud	altus, -a, -um tall, high

Other parts of speech in 2.10	Synonymous words
dīligō, dīligere, dīlēgī, dīlēctum to love	amō (1) to love
dēcidō, dēcidere, dēcidī to fall down, die (NB: note that *dēcidō* is a compound of *dē* + *cadō*)	cadō, cadere, cecidī, cāsum to fall, die
pectus, pectoris, n. heart, mind, soul	animus, animī, m. soul, mind, heart
metuō, metuere, metuī to fear	timeō, timēre, timuī to fear
praeparō (1) to prepare	parō (1) to prepare
suscitō (1) to rouse, awaken	excitō (1) to awaken, arouse
altum, -ī, n. the deep (sea)	māre, māris, n. sea
procella, -ae, f. storm, trouble	tempestās, tempestātis, f. storm
tēctum, tēctī, n. roof, house	domus, domūs, f. house
quondam once	ōlim once
sors, sortis, f. decision by lot, fate, fortune	fortūna, fortūnae, f. fortune
taceō, tacēre, tacuī, tacitum to be silent	sileō, silēre, siluī to be silent

Proud of its Roman heritage, Romania salutes Horace with
a commemorative stamp. Modern Romanian is one of the
Romance languages that evolved from the Latin language.

▶ EXERCISE 2

Substitute the synonym for the word indicated in bold. Then translate the sentence.

1. Et **cautum** pectus et bene **praeparātum** auream mediocritātem **dīligit**.

2. **Ōlim** in **mārī** erat **ingēns tempestās**.

3. Rēbus angustīs **animōsus** atque fortis appārēt.

4. Alteram **sortem** in secundīs rēbus **metuunt**.

5. Quondam citharā **tacentem** Mūsam **suscitat** Apollō.

ESSAY

Odes 2.10 contains many references to weather. Discuss how Horace uses the imagery of weather to link key stanzas and thus to provide a coherent structure for the poem.

Support your assertions with references drawn from throughout the poem. All Latin words must be copied or their line numbers provided, AND they must be translated or paraphrased closely enough so that it is clear you understand the Latin. Direct your answer to the question; do not merely summarize the passage. Please write your essay on a separate piece of paper.

SCANSION

Name the meter and scan the following lines.

saepius ventīs agitātur ingēns

pīnus et celsae graviōre cāsū

dēcidunt turrēs feriuntque summōs

    fulgura montīs.

The great patron of the arts, Augustus's virtual minister for cultural affairs, Maecenas is honored by the Irish who erected this portrait bust in Coole Park, County Galway. Coole Park was the home of Lady Augusta Gregory, the dramatist, who with W. B. Yeats and Edward Martyn founded the famous Abbey Theatre of Dublin. The ancestral home of Lady Gregory was a gathering place for members of the Irish Literary Revival that took place in the first decades of the twentieth century. Similarly, Maecenas welcomed Horace, Vergil, the historian Livy, and other leading intellectuals of the day to his home in Rome.

READING 5

With this ode Horace closes the three-book lyric collection of eighty-eight odes he published in 23 BCE. In this poem he takes on a tone of supreme confidence and lays claim to an enduring literary achievement: the adaptation to the Latin language of the genre of Greek lyric poetry. Horace's claim that he will live on through his lyric poetry reflects his great pride in his poetic achievement. This seemingly excessive pride is balanced by the reference to humble beginnings and the prayer-like address to the Muse, whom he indirectly asks to approve of his work. It is difficult to read this ode without incorporating our knowledge that, in fact, Horace's work has endured long past the time of Roman rule.

THE IMMORTALITY OF THE POET

HORACE *ODES* 3.30

Meter: First or Lesser Asclepiadean

1   Exēgī monumentum aere perennius

     rēgālīque sitū pȳramidum altius,

     quod nōn imber edāx, nōn Aquilō inpotēns

     possit dīruere aut innumerābilis

5   annōrum seriēs et fuga temporum.

     nōn omnis moriar, multaque pars meī

     vītābit Libitīnam: ūsque ego posterā

     crēscam laude recēns, dum Capitōlium

NOTES AND VOCABULARY

Line 1:   **exigō, exigere, exēgī, exāctum** to drive out, complete, execute

        monumentum, -ī, n. monument, memorial

        aes, aeris, n. copper, bronze, money; statues and public records frequently were made of bronze.

        perennis, -e lasting throughout the year, lasting for many years, enduring

BY THE WAY

A *monumentum* is anything that "reminds or recalls" (the root in the word is the verb *moneō*); the word often refers to inscriptions in bronze or stone.

Line 2:   **rēgālis, rēgāle** royal, regal; the adjective may be construed as a TRANSFERRED EPITHET modifying *pȳramidum*.

    situs, sitūs, m. site, structure

    situs, sitūs, m. deterioration, neglect

    pȳramis, pȳramidis, f. pyramid

    rēgālī ... pȳramidum: the pyramids of Egypt

STUDY TIP

In line 2, *sitū* can be from either *situs*; since both words make sense, it is best to keep the ambiguity.

Line 3:   **nōn ... nōn:** ANAPHORA with ASYNDETON

    imber, imbris, m. rain, rain shower, water

    edāx, edācis greedy, devouring, destructive

    Aquilō, Aquilōnis, m. the north wind

    inpotēns, inpotentis powerless, weak, wild, violent

Line 4:   **possit:** subjunctive in a relative clause of characteristic.

    dīruō, dīruere, dīruī, dīrūtum to cause to fall in ruin, demolish

    innumerābilis, innumerābile countless, numberless

Line 5:   **seriēs, seriēī,** f. series, sequence, succession

    fuga, -ae, f. flight, rout

Line 6:   **omnis:** all; translate "completely." English would use an adverb here where Latin uses an adjective; *omnis* contrasts with *pars*.

    morior, morī, mortuus sum to die

    meī: partitive genitive

Line 7:   **vītō** (1) to avoid, shun

    Libitīna, -ae, f. Libitīna, the goddess of funerals; *Libitīnam* means death, by METONYMY.

    usque, *adv.* continuously, continually, all the way

    posterus, -a, -um next, following, future, later

Line 8:   **crēscō, crēscere, crēvī, crētum** to arise, multiply, expand, increase

    recēns, recentis fresh, recent, modern

    Capitōlium, Capitōliī, n. Capitolium, the Capitoline hill in Rome on which the Capitoline gods, Jupiter, Juno, and Minerva, were worshipped

HORACE *ODES* 3.30, CONTINUED

scandet cum tacitā virgine pontifex.

10 dīcar, quā violēns obstrepit Aufidus

et quā pauper aquae Daunus agrestium

rēgnāvit populōrum, ex humilī potēns

prīnceps Aeolium carmen ad Ītalōs

dēdūxisse modōs. sūme superbiam

15 quaesītam meritīs et mihi Delphica

laurō cinge volēns, Melpomenē, comam.

NOTES AND VOCABULARY

BY THE WAY

In lines 8–9, *dum . . . pontifex*, the Pontifex Maximus, or chief priest, and the Vestal Virgins represent Rome's state religion. Their continued walk up the Capitolium symbolizes the continuity of Roman culture and institutions.

Line 9: **scandō, scandere** to climb, ascend, mount

tacitus, -a, -um silent

pontifex, pontificis, m. high priest, pontiff

BY THE WAY

Note the contrast between the Vestal Virgin's silence (*tacitā*, line 9) and the roaring Aufidus of the next line as well as Horace's voice as poet and the voice of posterity, which will increase his fame.

Line 10: **quā,** *adv.* where

violēns, violentis violent, vehement

obstrepō, obstrepere, obstrepuī, obstrepitum to make a loud noise, roar, drown by louder noise

Aufidus, -ī, m. Aufidus, river in Apulia

Lines 10–12: He is powerful, although from humble origins (a reference both to his status as a freedman's son and his small town beginnings), and his fame will exist in the Apulian area of his childhood.

Line 11: **pauper, pauperis** poor (with genitive of reference)

Daunus, -ī, m. Daunus, legendary king of Apulia; here the noun refers both to the king as well as to his kingdom, which was "poor in water."

agrestis, agreste of the country, rustic, rural

Lines 11–12:	**agrestium . . . populōrum:** genitive with *rēgnāvit* (a Greek construction for verbs of ruling)
Line 12:	**humilis, humile** humble, low; neuter as noun, low position; masculine as a noun, humble person
	potēns, potentis able, powerful, potent
Line 13:	**prīnceps, prīncipis** first in time, leading, first
	Aeolius, -a, -um Aeolian, Aeolic; referring to Aeolia, the Greek area of Asia Minor, including the island of Lesbos where the Greek poets Sappho and Alcaeus lived, as well as to the dialect of Greek in which they wrote.
	carmen, carminis, n. solemn or ritual utterance, song, poem, lyric poetry
	Ītalus, -a, -um Italian; the initial "i" is long here.

BY THE WAY

The word *prīnceps* suggests temporal priority as well as leadership. Originality was an important concept for poets writing at this time as it was for the neoteric poets. (*Prīnceps* is also the title Augustus officially used of himself, so the term has Roman political resonance as well.)

Lines 13–14:	**prīnceps . . . modōs:** this is Horace's claim that he was the first to adapt Aeolic poetry, that is, the Greek lyric poetry of Sappho and Alcaeus, to the Latin language. Of course, Catullus wrote two poems in the Sapphic meter (11 and 51), but Horace's accomplishment in this area was on a far greater scale.
Line 14:	**dēdūcō, dēdūcere, dēdūxī, dēductum** to compose, lead away, escort; here translate "adapt."
	modus, -ī, m. limit, way, rhythmic pattern; *in plural,* poetry
	sūmō, sūmere, sūmpsī, sūmptum to take, take on
	superbia, -ae, f. pride, arrogance; the Muse, Melpomene, deserves to be proud because of Horace's poetic achievement.
Line 15:	**meritum, -ī,** n. that which one deserves, due reward, service, meritorious action (the arts, among other things)
	Delphicus, -a, -um Delphic, pertaining to the Delphic oracle of Apollo (god of poetry) at Delphi, Greece

BY THE WAY

By not using a possessive adjective with the word *meritīs*, Horace leaves open whose "meritorious actions" have earned Melpomene her pride. Are they Horace's actions as evidenced in his lyric achievement, or are they the "services" of inspiration provided by the muse?

Line 16:	**laurus, -ī/-ūs,** f. laurel tree; the laurel tree was sacred to Apollo.
	cingō, cingere, cīnxī, cīnctum to surround, encircle, crown
	volēns, volentis willing; here, as in line 6, the Latin uses an adjective where English would use an adverb.
	Melpomenē, Melpomenēs, f. Melpomene, one of the Muses

BY THE WAY

Horace ends his final poem by referring to his "hair" (*comam*). He does this so that the final word of the final poem complements the closing word of the first poem of the collection, which ends by referring to his "head" (*verticem*). *Odes* 1.1 and 3.30, the only poems in the collection written in the First or Lesser Asclepiadean, have in common the theme of the poet's immortality.

TAKE NOTE

The Greek lyric poet Pindar also speaks in Pythian 6 of poems that cannot be destroyed by wind and rain.

COMPREHENSION QUESTIONS

1. To what monument is the poet referring in line 1?

2. According to lines 3–5, list three things that will not destroy the poet's monument. Cite the Latin.

3. What does the poet claim is his highest achievement?

The Great Pyramids of Giza continue to amaze viewers both with their massive size and with their having survived the millennia.

► EXERCISE 1

1. In line 1, what is the case and use of *aere*?

2. What does *perennius* (line 1) modify?

3. In line 2, what is the case and use of *situ*?

4. What is the antecedent of *quod* (line 3)?

5. What two figures of speech are in line 5?

6. What is the case and use of *temporum* (line 5)?

7. In line 8, what is the case and use of *laude*?

8. In line 9, what is the case and use of *virgine*?

9. In line 13, what is the case and use of *carmen*?

10. On what verb does *dēdūxisse* (line 14) depend?

11. In lines 13–14, what three figures of speech are in these lines?

12. In line 15, what is the case and use of *mihi*?

13. What is the case and use of *laurō* in line 16?

14. What is the case and use of *comam* in line 16?

ESSAY

In this ode, Horace reflects on his finished three books of *Odes*. In a brief, well-organized essay, show how Horace uses references to time to talk about his poetic accomplishments. You may discuss, but are not limited to, verb tenses, imagery, or mythological and historical references.

Support your assertions with references drawn from throughout the poem. All Latin words must be copied or their line numbers provided, AND they must be translated or paraphrased closely enough so that it is clear you understand the Latin. Direct your answer to the question; do not merely summarize the passage. Please write your essay on a separate piece of paper.

SCANSION

Name the meter and scan the following lines.

> Exēgī monumentum aere perennius
>
> rēgālīque situ pȳramidum altius,
>
> quod nōn imber edāx, nōn Aquilō inpotēns
>
> possit dīruere aut innumerābilis

CHAPTER 6

PUBLIUS OVIDIUS NASO

Genitive of Quality and Ablative of Quality; Review of Possession and Dative of Possession; Indirect Questions; Fear Clauses

Antithesis, Golden Line, Zeugma, Paradox, Assonance, Polyptoton

This image of Pyramus and Thisbe is taken from a manuscript commissioned in 1490 by the courtier Raphael de Marcatelis. As is common for medieval depictions of classical subject matter, the architecture and dress reflect the contemporary world. The woman looking from the bushes is identified as Alcithoe, one of the daughters of Minyas, who in the *Metamorphōsēs* tells the tale of Pyramus and Thisbe.

MEMORĀBILE DICTŪ

Ars adeō latet arte suā.

"Art is so concealed by its own art." (Ovid *Metamorphōsēs* 10.252)

Ovid's words, quoted often both in Latin and in translation, refer to the effect of art. The best art appears to be effortless, spontaneous, or natural and thus conceals the careful craftsmanship of the artist. In this case Pygmalion's art is so lifelike that it deludes even its creator.

AN INTRODUCTION TO OVID

OVID'S LIFE AND WORKS

By the time he was in his twenties, Ovid (Publius Ovidius Naso) had established himself as a successful poet in Rome. By the time he reached his fifties, he was at the pinnacle of his career and was the toast of the city. In 8 CE, however, disaster struck; the *prīnceps* Augustus exiled Ovid to Tomis, a bleak outpost on the Black Sea and as far from Rome as a truly urban Roman could get. Of such drama are fictional lives made, but these are true events in the life of a poet whose existence spanned exciting days in Rome's history and whose poetry continues to excite the interest of readers and scholars alike long after his death.

We know much of Ovid's life from his own poem, *Tristia* 4.10, written while he was in exile. There he tells us that he was born into a wealthy equestrian family of Sulmo (modern Sulmona), located in the central part of Italy to the east of Rome; his date of birth is March 20th, 43 BCE. His family wanted him to pursue the civil/military career expected of every upper-class Italian or Roman after a traditional education and some entry-level political posts. Instead, Ovid turned to the writing of poetry and published his first poetic work, the five original books of the *Amōrēs,* by 17 BCE. This collection of poems was later revised and published in three books. Between these two editions Ovid published the *Herōidēs,* a series of letters from various heroic women to their husbands or lovers. He then turned to mock-didactic poems, works that purport to educate an audience, and published the *Medicāmina facēī fēmineae,* a work on women's cosmetics; the *Ars amātōria,* a treatise on how to meet women in Rome; and the *Remēdia amōris,* a sequel to the *Ars amātōria* that deals with how to end a relationship.

All of these works contributed enormously to Ovid's popularity as a virtuoso poet and a writer who had his finger on the pulse of elite Rome. But it was his longer poems, the *Metamorphōsēs* and the *Fastī* (of which only six books survive), that have ensured his immortality. The *Metamorphōsēs* has become one of the most important literary sources for Greek and Roman mythology. It is a highly complex epic poem in fifteen books whose design and purpose continue to challenge scholars. In the poem Ovid brings together his erudition, his enormous wit, an intricate plan that incorporates, among other structures, the Hellenistic design of tales within tales, and his inventive and easy to read poetic style. The work begins with the creation of the world and ends with the power and might of Rome; within this framework a variety of tales appears that combines the charming and the violent, the wistful and the hilarious. No one who reads the *Metamorphōsēs* in English or in Latin can forget the twenty lines of poetry devoted to listing dogs' names in "the Story of Actaeon"—with none of these dogs actually featured in the destruction of the man-turned-stag. Or the gently comic scene of the aged Baucis and Philemon attempting to capture the wily goose so that they can produce a modest feast for their disguised divine guests. The *Metamorphōsēs* has been called a "modern epic," and truly it is a feast for ancient and modern readers alike. The *Fastī* combines a detailed calendar of Rome's festivals with the recounting of relevant myths, and as such it provides invaluable information on Roman life and religion.

Ovid was occupied with the writing and publication of these epics until 8 CE, when his life took an unexpected and tragic turn, and he was exiled by Augustus. Ovid supplies two reasons for his banishment, "a poem and a mistake" (*carmen et error*). The *carmen* probably refers to the *Ars amātōria*, a poem published at least a decade before his exile, while the *error* remains unknown, although clearly it was the principal reason he was expelled from Italy.

Ovid continued to write in exile: his two works, the *Tristia* and the *Epistulae ex Pontō*, combine descriptions of his journey and new life with entreaties for forgiveness and an end to his banishment. The death of Augustus in 14 CE raised his hopes that he might win over Augustus's successor Tiberius to allow his return to Rome. Ovid did not prevail, however, and he himself died three years later in 17 CE.

OVID'S INFLUENCE

> ergo etiam cum mē suprēmus adederit ignis,
> vīvam, parsque meī multa superstes erit.
>
> (Amōrēs 1.15.41–42)

> "Therefore, even when the final fire consumes me,
> I shall live, and a large part of me will remain alive."

When Ovid wrote the words that concluded the first book of the *Amōrēs*, he may have been reiterating the expectation of immortality that many Greek and Roman poets assumed for themselves. We like to think, then, that he would be enormously pleased not only that the bulk of his writings remains extant, but also that his poetry, studied in schools from the Renaissance on, has had and continues to have great influence on literature and art of all periods. Within thirty years of the printing of the Gutenberg Bible, the first text with movable type, the first English translation of the *Metamorphōsēs* was published—in all likelihood by William Caxton. Before 1483, the works of Ovid appeared in the Romance languages and inspired numerous medieval and Renaissance authors who either made reference to Ovid in their works or used his poetry as a departure for their own. In his *Midsummer's Night Dream* Shakespeare envisions a performance, a play within a play, to entertain his human audience. What better choice of subject than the tragic tale of Pyramus and Thisbe, the doomed lovers forced to communicate through a chink in a wall until their desire compels them to meet, and, through a series of tragic misunderstandings, to die? Shakespeare inserts the story pretty much as told by Ovid into this play, but it is also likely that this tiny piece of the *Metamorphōsēs* inspired the sources for his *Romeo and Juliet*, which in turn inspired the 1960s musical *West Side Story*.

To enumerate all of the later authors who fell under Ovid's spell is impossible. We find traces of Ovid in the entire tradition of courtly love that fed the cycle of Arthurian legend in the Middle Ages, in Spenser, in Milton, and in many Victorian poets. The poetry of Oscar Wilde, whose own life reveals distinct parallels to Ovid's, contains countless references to the myths of the *Metamorphōsēs* and *Fastī*. Specific myths from these works have enjoyed a long tradition in art and literature. The Apollo and Daphne story, especially the scene of Daphne's transformation into a tree, has inspired artists for centuries. Bernini's statue is but one example of the grace with which this scene has been rendered. The fall of Icarus is also a favorite. The magic of a boy who flies and whose enthusiasm leads to his destruction is irresistibly attractive. Ovid's story of Pygmalion became a play of the same name in the twentieth century. Written by George Bernard Shaw, the play concerned the transformation of a cockney street vendor into a true lady under the tutelage of Professor Higgins. Still later, the play became the great musical *My Fair Lady*, and the theme of creating the perfect mate continues to intrigue writers and cinematographers today.

The universality of Ovid's themes and the appeal of the stories themselves have ensured his immortality. While we may live in a practical and prosaic world driven by technology, we never let go of our imaginative lives. The popularity of current fantasy—Harry Potter and the *Chronicles of Narnia,* for example—proves our need to experience a world apart from our everyday life. So, in Ovid, we have boys who fly, humans who transform into vegetation or animals or the opposite gender, and statues that become human. At the same time these stories are about unrequited love, love obtained, the fulfillment of wishes and fantasies, heroic journeys, and painful and sometimes bitter break-ups of romantic relationships, all of which are part of our own experience. The expression of reality in a format that is so obviously yet charmingly unreal explains Ovid's enormous appeal to audiences of all ages. He continues to enchant audiences literally and metaphorically. He graces our world just as he graced the streets of Rome twenty centuries ago.

MYTH AND THE *METAMORPHŌSĒS*

While the *Metamorphōsēs* meets the criteria for the genre of epic poetry in terms of length, scope, meter, and other elements such as extended similes, storms, and battles, it is as unlike the works of Homer and Apollonius and Vergil's *Aeneid* as any poem can be. It does not have a coherent plot per se; any attempt to provide a summary reduces the epic to a list of the myths that occur in each book. The work forms a coherent whole through its overriding theme of transformation, although scholars have noted that sometimes the transformations are peripheral or incidental to a particular story, and in some cases nonexistent.

Mythological stories informed nearly all the literature of all ages of Greece. The one exception was comedy, which, after Aristophanes, tended more to stories set firmly in the human realm. The lyric poets of the Archaic Age incorporated myth into their poems, and Pindar and Bacchylides in particular are valuable sources for extended stories. The tragic poets of the fifth century BCE focused, for the most part, on the great myths of Agamemnon, Oedipus, Medea, and others; and the Hellenistic poets wrote either myth-based works, such as, the *Argonautica* of Apollonius of Rhodes and the *Hymns* of Callimachus, or they departed from the mythological world altogether and focused on "real life" in their mimes. Early Roman authors focused on historical epic or translations of Greek epics and tragedies, or they stayed strictly practical with treatises on agriculture and the like. In the first century BCE when the poet Catullus began to experiment with literary composition similar to that of the Greek lyric and Hellenistic poets, he began to integrate myth into some of his poetry, and later Roman poets did the same. The Roman poet Vergil deftly combined myth and history (although the Romans would not have made this distinction) in his *Aeneid* by establishing Troy as the homeland of Rome's forefather Aeneas; he incorporated myth into his *Georgics* and *Eclogues* as well.

We can draw several conclusions from this too brief and too general survey. First, what we call myth was as much a part of the lives of Greeks and Romans as the stories of the founding and settlement of our country are to us. Second, what survives of the ancient sources for mythology is a sadly small percentage of what existed. Finally, Ovid as an educated Roman would have had access to all of these sources; as a creative Roman poet, he would have chosen which versions of the myth to incorporate into his work, and he, like every other literary author, would have shaped the myth into his own conception. We know this because when we have sources for Ovid's myths, we can see the choices he made, and sometimes we can speculate as to why he made these choices. His story of Medea in the *Metamorphōsēs*, for instance, covers all of the events of Medea's relationship with Jason, but focuses on the gruesome murder of Jason's uncle rather than on Medea's murder of her own children. He makes this choice possibly because Pelias's death is so deliciously nasty—after all Medea manipulates Pelias's own daughters into killing the feeble old man—or possibly because he did not want to compete with Euripides's brilliant tragedy that dealt in great detail with Medea's murder of her children. In the same way, when he comes to explain Teiresias's double sex change, Ovid uses the story of the snakes in the woods: Teiresias saw snakes mating, struck them apart (why, we don't know), and lo, became a woman! Seven years later he saw them again, struck them again and changed back to a man. Callimachus used a different approach: Teiresias saw Athena in her bath and she struck him blind. The *Metamorphōsēs* is more than a mere retelling of myth. It combines an erudition common to all educated Romans with a poetic genius that enables Ovid to make traditional stories his own.

Since the 1960s Ovid has emerged from the shadow of his predecessors and contemporaries to assume a key role in the study of Latin literature. Before that time, Ovid was seen as a pale imitator of both elegiac and epic poets. His love poetry, the *Amōrēs,* was considered "insincere" and "artificial" when compared to the poetry of Catullus, Propertius, and Tibullus; and his epic, the *Metamorphōsēs,* although charming in places, was seen as a lesser epic when compared to Vergil's great national epic, the *Aeneid.* Fortunately our understanding of Ovid has evolved as we have begun to study the poet on his own terms. This has resulted in a greater appreciation of Ovid as a highly talented and innovative poet. In the *Metamorphōsēs,* and indeed in everything he wrote, Ovid situates his writing within a tradition, which provides a point of departure for his innovations and his unique perspective.

READING 1

In Latin prose and poetry, the reader often needs to "understand" or supply words that are not in the Latin text. Words to be understood are in parentheses in the text below. Different fonts point out words that belong together.

The exotic city of Babylon, home to the legendary queen Semiramis, is the setting for this tale of two star-crossed lovers, Pyramus (male) and Thisbe (female). They are neighbors, and their proximity to each other causes them to fall in love. They want marriage, but their parents are opposed to the match, and the lovers are left to devise ways to communicate and, eventually, to meet.

Ovid describes how the young lovers first discover a means by which they can communicate: there is a small fissure in a wall common to their two homes. Through this small hole they can whisper to each other even though they cannot touch or even kiss.

The lovers devise a plan to meet outside the city after dark. Unforeseen events result in disastrous consequences. In the end, the lovers who were separated in life are joined together in death.

THE CHINK IN THE WALL

OVID *METAMORPHŌSĒS* 4.65–77

Meter: Dactylic Hexameter

65   Fissus erat **tenuī rīmā,** quam dūxerat ōlim,

       cum fieret, pariēs **domuī** commūnis **utrīque.**

       id vitium nūllī per saecula longa **notātum** (est)—

       quid nōn sentit amor?—prīmī vīdistis amantēs

       et vōcis fēcistis iter, **tūtae**que per illud (vitium)

70   (cum) **murmure blanditiae minimō** trānsīre solēbant.

NOTES AND VOCABULARY

Line 65:   **findō, findere, fidī, fissum** to split, separate, divide

             tenuis, tenue thin, slender

             rīma, -ae, *f.* crack, fissure; *tenuī rīmā* is an ablative of means.

             quam: relative pronoun whose antecedent is *rīmā.*

             dūxerat: translate "had formed."

             ōlim, *adv.* once

REMINDER

Pariēs is the Latin word that Ovid uses to refer to the wall between Pyramus's and Thisbe's house. *Mūrus, -ī*, m. and *moenia, moenium*, n. pl. refer to the walls of a city, as you have seen in Cicero and Vergil.

Lines 65–66:   **fissus erat . . . pariēs:** *pariēs* is the subject of *fissus erat.*

Line 66:   **fiō, fierī, factus sum** to be made, be done, happen, become; "it," referring to *pariēs,* is the subject of both *fieret* and *dūxerat.*

       commūnis, commūne common; the dative *domuī* depends on *commūnis.*

       uterque, utraque, utrumque each

REMINDER

In the Cicero chapter of this book on p. 165, you learned not to confuse *vītō* with *vīta.* Now add *vitium* to this list of look-alike words.

vītō (1) to avoid	FIRST CONJUGATION VERB
vīta, -ae, f. life	FIRST DECLENSION NOUN
vitium, -ī, n. defect	SECOND DECLENSION NOUN

Line 67:   **vitium, -ī,** n. defect

       nūllī: dative of agent with the passive verb *notātum est.* Remember that *nūllus* belongs to the "naughty nine," a group of pronouns that have *–īus* in the genitive singular and *–ī* in the dative singular. Translate "this defect (*id vitium*) was noticed by no one."‡

       saeculum, -ī, n. age, generation

Line 68:   **quid:** interrogative pronoun and the object of *sentit.*

       prīmī . . . amantēs: in apposition to the understood subject "you" of the verb; *amantēs* is the present participle being used as a noun, i.e., substantively. Translate "you lovers first saw."

Line 70:   **blanditia, -ae,** f. flirtation, flattery

       trānseō, trānsīre, trānsiī, trānsitum to go across, pass over; *transīre* is a complementary infinitive with *solēbant.*

OVID *METAMORPHŌSĒS* 4.65–77, CONTINUED

saepe, ubi cōnstiterant hinc Thisbē, Pȳramus illinc,

inque vicēs fuerat captātus anhēlitus ōris,

"invide" dīcēbant **"pariēs,** quid amantibus obstās?

quantum erat, ut sinerēs **tōtō** nōs **corpore** iungī,

75   aut, hoc sī nimium est, vel ad ōscula danda patērēs?

nec sumus ingrātī: tibi nōs dēbēre fatēmur,

quod datus est verbīs ad **amīcās** trānsitus **aurīs."**

NOTES AND VOCABULARY

Line 71:   **cōnsistō, cōnsistere, cōnstitī** to stand, take one's place, stop, pause; the subjects, Pyramus and Thisbe, occur after the verb.

    hinc, *adv.* on one side

    Thisbē, Thisbēs, f. Thisbe (a Greek name)

    Pȳramus, -ī, m. Pyramus

    illinc, *adv.* on the other side

Line 72:   **vicis** (gen. only), **vicem,** pl. **vicēs, vicibus** turn, alternation

    captō (1) to catch; *fuerat captātus* is unusual and we would expect *captātus erat* instead. Translate "the breath had been caught."

    anhēlitus, anhēlitūs, m. breath, exhalation

REMINDER

In the Vergil chapter of this book on p. 237, you learned not to confuse *ōra, -ae,* f. "shore" with *ōra,* the nominative and accusative plural of *ōs, ōris,* n. "mouth, face."

Line 73:   **invidus, -a, -um** envious, envying; *invide* is vocative masculine singular, modifying *pariēs.*

    quid: here the interrogative means "why."

    amantibus: dative with *obstō*

Line 74:   **quantus, -a, -um** how great, how much (pl. many); translate *quantum erat* "how much [trouble] would it be . . . ."

STUDY TIP

sinō, sinere, sīvī, situm and *patior, patī, passus sum* are synonyms. Both verbs mean "allow." Remember that Cicero wrote *nōn feram, nōn sinam, nōn patiar* in *In Catilīnam* I 1.10.27 (see p. 176).

REMINDER

As noted on p. 176 of the Cicero chapter of this book and p. 65 of the Caesar chapter, be careful to distinguish among these verbs: *patior, patī, passus sum* "to allow"; *pateō, patēre, patuī* "to be/lie open"; *partior, partīrī, partītus sum* "to divide"; and *potior, potīrī, potītus sum* "to gain possession of."

Lines 74–75:   **sinerēs ... patērēs:** both imperfect subjunctives are in result clauses. Translate "(that) you allow ... that you allow ... "; *sinō* introduces an accusative (*nōs*) and infinitive (*iungī*) construction.

Line 75:   **vel,** *adv.* if you will, even, at least

   ōsculum, -ī, n. kiss; *ad ōscula danda* is a gerundive in a purpose construction. Translate "for giving kisses."‡

REMINDER

As noted on p. 186 of the Cicero chapter, the verb *dēbeō, dēbēre, dēbuī, dēbitum* has two distinct meanings: "to owe" and "ought." If *dēbeō* takes a complementary infinitive, it means "ought"; otherwise, *dēbeō* means "owe."

Line 76:   **ingrātus, -a, -um** ungrateful

   fateor, fatērī, fassus sum to confess, admit; *nōs dēbēre* is an indirect statement after *fatēmur.*

STUDY TIP

The Latin word *amīcus* can be either a noun or an adjective. If *amīcus* is modifying a noun, it is the adjective *amīcus, -a, -um* "friendly"; otherwise, it is the noun *amīcus, -ī,* m. "friend." Similarly, the adjective *inimīcus, -a, -um* means "unfriendly, hostile" while the noun *inimīcus, -ī.* m., means "enemy."

Line 77:   **amīcus, -a, -um** friendly

   trānsitus, trānsitūs, m. a passage; subject of *quod datus est.* Translate "that a passage has been given ... ."

   auris, auris, f. the ear; *aurīs = aurēs*

REMINDER

As noted in the Vergil chapter of this book on p. 281 and in Horace on p. 315, do not confuse *auris, auris,* f. "ear" with *aurum, -ī,* n. "gold" or with *aureus, -a, -um,* "golden" or *aura, -ae,* f. "breeze."

TAKE NOTE

1. The meaning of *nūllus* as an adjective is "no, not any"; as a pronoun the word means "no one, nobody," or "nothing." The form *nūllus* is a combination of *nē* ("not") and *ūllus* ("any").

2. Latin has three words for "kiss": *bāsium, ōsculum,* and *suāvium.* As was indicated on page 94, Catullus introduced the word *bāsium* to the Latin language, and it is this word for "kiss" that he uses most often in his very conversational poems, the polymetra (poems 1–60). Other Latin authors of the late Republic and Augustan period, however, prefer to use the less colloquial *ōsculum* ("little mouth") or *suāvium* ("sweetness" or "delight").

COMPREHENSION QUESTIONS

1. Where was the fissure located? Cite the Latin.

2. For what purpose did Pyramus and Thisbe use the fissure? Cite the Latin.

3. What would Pyramus and Thisbe have preferred to be able to do? Cite the Latin.

A Hungarian stamp from the 1980s recreates the fabulous gardens and palace of Semiramis, the famous queen of Babylon whose romance with Ninus was legendary.

▶ EXERCISE 1

1. What word is the subject of *fissus erat* (line 65)?

2. In line 65, what is the tense and voice of *dūxerat*?

3. In line 66, what is the mood and use for *fieret*?

4. What word modifies *domuī* (line 66)?

5. What is the case and use of *vōcis* in line 69?

6. In line 74, what is the mood and use for *sinerēs*?

7. What is the tense, voice, and form of *iungī* in line 74?

8. What is the case and number of *ingrātī* in line 76?

9. What is the case and use of *nōs* in line 76?

10. In line 77, what word does *amīcās* modify?

VOCABULARY BUILDER

Each of the following English words comes from a Latin word in this passage. Cite the Latin word from the lines above that supplies the English derivative and give its vocabulary entry.

Example:

	Latin Word in Text	Vocabulary Entry
domicile	domuī	domus, domūs, f. house

1. communal

2. null

3. primal

4. vocal

5. murmur

6. blandishments

7. minimal

8. corporeal

9. ungrateful

10. transition

READING 1 REDUX

You are now ready to read these lines exactly as Ovid wrote them. For this reason the words in parentheses and the special fonts are no longer used. You have already seen notes in the first version of this poem, and you may refer to those notes if you need to. Additional notes for this poem are given below the text.

65   Fissus erat tenuī rīmā, quam dūxerat ōlim,

       cum fieret, pariēs domuī commūnis utrīque.

       id vitium nūllī per saecula longa notātum—

       quid nōn sentit amor?—prīmī vīdistis amantēs

       et vōcis fēcistis iter, tūtaeque per illud

70   murmure blanditiae minimō trānsīre solēbant.

       saepe, ubi cōnstiterant hinc Thisbē, Pȳramus illinc,

       inque vicēs fuerat captātus anhēlitus ōris,

       "invide"dīcēbant "pariēs, quid amantibus obstās?

       quantum erat, ut sinerēs tōtō nōs corpore iungī,

75   aut, hoc sī nimium est, vel ad ōscula danda patērēs?

       nec sumus ingrātī: tibi nōs dēbēre fatēmur,

       quod datus est verbīs ad amīcās trānsitus aurīs."

NOTES AND VOCABULARY

Lines 65–66:   The word order here is complex. An ablative phrase and two subordinate clauses occur between the verb, *fissus erat,* and its subject, *pariēs.* Note how Ovid emphasizes both the wall and the crack in it. He stresses the crack by placing *fissus erat* at the beginning of the sentence; he stresses the wall by postponing *paries* as the subject until the middle of the next line. He also suggests the commonality of the wall to each home through the INTERLOCKED WORD ORDER (SYNCHESIS) that concludes line 66 (*pariēs domuī commūnis utrīque*).

Line 67:   Supply *est* to complete the meaning of the verb *notātum.*

Line 68:   Note the RHETORICAL QUESTION.

       prīmī vīdistis amantēs: Ovid breaks the third person narrative here with a dramatic address to Pyramus and Thisbe. This is an example of APOSTROPHE.

Line 69:   **illud:** i.e., *vitium*

Line 71:   Note how the CHIASMUS, *hinc Thisbē, Pȳramus illinc,* contradicts what Ovid is saying. Pyramus and Thisbe are in opposite places (*hinc . . . illinc*) but Ovid puts them together.

Line 73:   Note the PERSONIFICATION and the APOSTROPHE.

Line 74:   **quantum erat:** introduces two result (*ut*) clauses. Forms of the verb "to be" can be used in the indicative to express the subjunctive.

Line 77:   **quod datus est:** substantive noun clause introduced by *quod*

ESSAY

The wall functions as both a barrier and a conduit between the lovers. Discuss its dual role; include in your discussion the effect of the personification of the wall in lines 73–77.

Support your assertions with references from lines 73–77. All Latin words must be copied or their line numbers provided, AND they must be translated or paraphrased closely enough so that it is clear you understand the Latin. Direct your answer to the question; do not merely summarize the passage. Please write your essay on a separate piece of paper.

BY THE WAY
Remember that for the purposes of scansion, "h" does not count as a consonant.

SCANSION

Name the meter and scan the following lines.

> saepe, ubi cōnstiterant hinc Thisbē, Pȳramus illinc,
>
> inque vicēs fuerat captātus anhēlitus ōris,
>
> invide dīcēbant pariēs, quid amantibus obstās?

READING 2

The rest of the Ovid passages in this book will no longer feature the words in parentheses and the use of special fonts. Use the notes below the poem to help you.

In the manner of teenagers everywhere, Pyramus and Thisbe agree to meet at night without their parents' knowledge. They choose a place outside the city gates at the tomb of Ninus, a former king of Babylon. The location may seem unusual, but it contains a beautiful tree and a pleasant stream. Thisbe arrives first and sits under the tree to await her lover.

THISBE'S ARRIVAL FOR A NIGHTTIME RENDEZVOUS

OVID *METAMORPHŌSĒS* 4.78–96

Meter: Dactylic Hexameter

> tālia dīversā nēquīquam sēde locūtī
>
> sub noctem dīxēre "valē" partīque dedēre
>
> 80 ōscula quisque suae nōn pervenientia contrā.
>
> postera nocturnōs Aurōra remōverat ignēs,
>
> sōlque pruīnōsās radiīs siccāverat herbās:
>
> ad solitum coiēre locum. tum murmure parvō
>
> multa prius questī statuunt, ut nocte silentī
>
> 85 fallere custōdēs foribusque excēdere temptent,
>
> cumque domō exīerint, urbis quoque tēcta relinquant,
>
> nēve sit errandum lātō spatiantibus arvō,

NOTES AND VOCABULARY

Line 78: **dīversus, -a, -um** separate

nēquīquam, *adv.* in vain, to no purpose

sēdēs, sēdis, f. house, dwelling

loquor, loquī, locūtus sum to speak, talk

BY THE WAY

Line 78 is a nicely balanced line with the adjective/noun pair (*dīversā . . . sēde*), which describes the house, separated by the adverb *nēquīquam* just as the wall separates the two houses.

Line 79: **sub:** with a word indicating time *sub* means "shortly before, about up to."

dīxēre: third person plural perfect active alternate form, as are *dedēre* and *coiēre* (line 83).

Line 80: **quisque, quaeque, quidque** each; here nominative singular, in apposition to the third person plural subject of *dīxēre* and *dedēre*.

contrā, *adv.* on the other side

Line 81: **posterus, -a, -um** following, next

Aurōra, -ae, f. Aurora, goddess of the dawn; by METONYMY, Aurora means "dawn."

Line 82: **pruīnōsus, -a, -um** frosty

radius, -ī, m. ray of light

siccō (1) to dry, dry up

herba, -ae, f. grass

Line 83: **soleō, solēre, solitus sum** to be accustomed

coeō, coīre, coiī, coitum to go/come together, meet; *coiēre* is the alternate form of *coiērunt.*

Line 84: **prius,** *adv.* first

queror, querī, questus sum to complain, complain of

statuō, statuere, statuī, statūtum to decide; *statuō* is followed by a series of indirect commands containing the subjunctives *temptent, relinquant, conveniant,* and *lateant.*

nocte silentī: ablative of time when

Line 85: **fallō, fallere, fefellī, falsum** to deceive

custōdēs: *custōdēs* are traditional obstacles to the fulfillment of love; translate "doorkeepers."

foris, foris, f. door, double door

temptō (1) to test, try

Line 86: **relinquō, relinquere, relīquī, relictum** to leave behind

BY THE WAY

As the lovers, driven by the power of their passions, leave behind the protection of their parents, their doorkeepers, and the city, they expose themselves to the wilderness that will destroy them in the end.

Line 87: **nēve,** *adv.* and not; *nēve* introduces a negative purpose clause with *nē* + *-ve*, hence the continued use of the subjunctive.

errō (1) to miss the right way, lose oneself, go astray; *sit errandum* is the passive periphrastic with an impersonal "it" as the grammatical subject. Translate literally "so that it must not be gone astray by them walking about in the broad countryside." *Eīs* is the understood dative of agent modified by *spatiantibus* and refers to the lovers. For a more natural translation, use *eīs spatiantibus* as the subject of *sit errandum* and translate "so that they, walking about in the broad countryside, would not go astray" (i.e., miss each other).

spatior (1) to walk about; here, a present participle referring to the two lovers.

latus, -a, -um wide, broad

arvum, -ī, n. field, plain, countryside

OVID *METAMORPHŌSĒS* 4.78–96, CONTINUED

    conveniant ad busta Ninī lateantque sub umbrā

    arboris: arbor ibī niveīs ūberrima pōmīs,

90   ardua mōrus, erat, gelidō contermina fontī.

    pacta placent; et lūx, tardē discēdere vīsa,

    praecipitātur aquīs, et aquīs nox exit ab īsdem.

    callida per tenebrās versātō cardine Thisbē

    ēgreditur fallitque suōs adopertaque vultum

95   pervenit ad tumulum dīctāque sub arbore sēdit.

    audācem faciēbat amor.

NOTES AND VOCABULARY

REMINDER

As noted in the Vergil chapter on p. 280, do not confuse *lātus, -a, -um* "wide, broad," with *latus, lateris,* n. "side." Also, be careful to distinguish these two words from the verb *lateō, latēre, latuī* "to hide."

Line 88:   **bustum, -ī,** n. a tomb; a poetic plural for a singular

        Ninus, -ī, m. king of Assyria and second husband to Semiramis; the romance between Ninus and Semiramis was legendary.

        lateō, latēre, latuī to hide

Line 89:   **niveus, -a, -um** snow-white, snowy

        ūber, ūberis abounding in, plentiful, abundant

        pōmum, -ī, n. fruit

Line 90:   **arduus, -a, -um** tall, lofty; the emphatic wording in this elaborate description of the mulberry tree reminds us that it provides the essential *aition* (origin) for the tale.

        mōrus, -ī, f. the mulberry tree

        gelidus, -a, -um icy, cold; dative after the adjective *contermina*

        conterminus, -a, -um nearby, adjacent

BY THE WAY

Aition, from the Greek word for "cause" or "reason," explains the origin of something; in this case Ovid is providing an explanation for why the color of the mulberry is dark red.

    Myths that give an explanation for something are said to be aetiological (also spelled etiological).

Line 91:   **pactum, -ī,** n. agreement, plan; again, poetic plural where English would use a singular.

        Supply *eīs* (= the lovers) after the verb *placent.*

BY THE WAY

Three of the six feet in line 91 are spondees. Together with the two monosyllabic words, *et* and *lūx*, the spondees slow down the rhythm of the line to mimic the day, which is slow to depart.

Line 92:   **praecipitō** (1) to fall, sink; in contrast to line 91, this line is filled with dactyls, which quicken the pace of the line, which in turn suggests the notion that after the day sets, the night comes quickly.

īsdem: an alternate ablative plural form of *īdem*. This does not mean the same spot in which the sun set but rather the same region, i.e., the sea.

Line 93:   **callidus, -a, -um** clever, resourceful

versō (1) to turn

cardō, cardinis, m. hinge

Line 94:   **suōs:** supply *custōdēs* of line 85, which the same verb, *fallō*, governs there as here.

adoperiō, adoperīre, adoperuī, adopertum: to cover up, cover over

vultus, vultūs, m. face; an accusative of respect with *adoperta* or, alternatively, an accusative direct object of the middle/reflexive participle *adoperta*

Line 95:   **tumulum, -ī,** n. grave, tomb

dictā: modifies *arbore*; translate, "under the appointed tree."

Line 96:   **audāx, audācis** bold; understand *eam*, "her."

faciēbat: the shift to the imperfect tense after a series of perfect verbs stresses the continuous effect love is having on her. Love is transforming her into something she had not been before.

COMPREHENSION QUESTIONS

1. According to lines 78–80, what are Pyramus and Thisbe doing?

2. What plan did the couple make the next day? Cite the Latin.

3. Describe the tree located near the tomb of Ninus. Cite the Latin.

▶ EXERCISE 1

1. What is the tense, voice, and form of *pervenientia* in line 80?

2. In line 82, what is the case and use of *radiīs*?

3. In line 84, what is the case and use of the substantive *multa*?

4. In line 86, what is the case and use of *domō*?

5. What is the tense, voice, and mood of *exīerint* in line 86?

6. What is the tense, voice, and mood of *conveniant* in line 88?

7. What is the case and degree of *ūberrima* in line 89?

8. In line 90, what is the case, number, and gender of *mōrus*?

9. What form is *tardē* in line 91?

10. In line 93, what is the case and use of *versātō cardine*?

11. What is the case and use of *vultum* in line 94?

ESSAY

The place where Pyramus and Thisbe plan to meet seems idyllic. In a short essay describe the pleasant features of the place that suggest it is an ideal spot for a rendezvous. Include also in your discussion non-idyllic elements in this scene that foreshadow that all will not turn out well.

Support your assertions with references drawn from throughout the passage. All Latin words must be copied or their line numbers provided, AND they must be translated or paraphrased closely enough so that it is clear you understand the Latin. Direct your answer to the question; do not merely summarize the passage. Please write your essay on a separate piece of paper.

SCANSION

Name the meter and scan the following lines.

fallere custōdēs foribusque excēdere temptent,

cumque domō exīerint, urbis quoque tēcta relinquant,

nēve sit errandum lātō spatiantibus arvō

OVIDIUS

SULMO TOMIS

R. P. ROMÎNĂ POSTA LEI 1.75

The Roman province of Dacia is today's Romania, whose native tongue, Romanian, is a Latin-derived language. Exiled by Augustus in 8 CE, Ovid spent the last nine years of his life in the provincial Roman town of Tomis on the Black Sea. These years were bleak for Ovid, a bon vivant who thrived on the cosmopolitan bustle of Rome. This circa 1957 Romanian stamp commemorates the great Roman poet. The stamp notes his birthplace Sulmo, Italy and where he died, Tomis, Romania. The image of Ovid is a drawing of a statue that stands in Constanta, the modern city built over the Roman Tomis.

READING 3

While Thisbe awaits Pyramus, a lioness appears with jaws smeared with blood from a recent kill. Thisbe flees in fear into a dark cave, accidentally dropping her veil as she goes. The lioness comes upon the veil and shreds it, leaving it bloodied. Pyramus then arrives. He sees the tracks of a lion and discovers Thisbe's garment stained with blood.

PYRAMUS'S FATAL MISTAKE

OVID *METAMORPHŌSĒS* 4.96–127
Meter: Dactylic Hexameter

>   venit ecce recentī
> caede leaena boum spūmantīs oblita rīctūs
> dēpositūra sitim vīcīnī fontis in undā;
> quam procul ad lūnae radiōs Babylōnia Thisbē
> 100   vīdit et obscūrum timidō pede fūgit in antrum,
> dumque fugit, tergō vēlāmina lapsa relīquit.
> ut lea saeva sitim multā conpēscuit undā,
> dum redit in silvās, inventōs forte sine ipsā
> ōre cruentātō tenuēs laniāvit amictūs.

NOTES AND VOCABULARY

Line 96:   **venit:** the historical present tense enlivens the story and shifts the reader's perspective back to Thisbe's immediate situation.

          ecce, *adv.* lo and behold, see, look; this adverbial demonstrative makes the reader an eyewitness.

STUDY TIP

Consider the word *veniō, venīre, vēnī, ventum* "to come." In form, the third person singular and the first person plural are spelled the same in both the present and perfect tenses. Only the macron on the "e" in the third principal part distinguishes the forms in the perfect tense (*vēnit, vēnimus*) from those in the present (*venit, venimus*). Other verbs that work the same way include *fugiō, fugere, fūgī, fūgitum* and *legō, legere, lēgī, lēctum.*

Line 97:   **caedēs, caedis,** f. blood, gore; murder

          bōs, bovis, m./f. cattle; *boum* is genitive plural depending on *recentī caede. Boum* occurs regularly instead of the uncontracted form *bovum.*

          spūmō (1) to foam, froth; here, the final syllable is long, making this the accusative plural of the present participle with *i*-stem endings. The participle modifies *rīctūs.*

          oblinō, oblinere, oblēvī, oblitum: to besmear, make dirty; *oblita* modifies *leaena.*

          rīctus, rīctūs, m. jaws, the opening of the jaws; accusative of respect with *oblita* or, alternatively, an accusative direct object of the middle/reflexive participle *oblita.*

Line 98: **dēpōnō, dēpōnere, dēposuī, dēpositum** to quench; *dēpositūra* is a future active participle that agrees with *leaena* (line 97) and expresses purpose.

sitis, sitis, f. thirst

Line 99: **quam:** connecting relative referring to the *leaena*; translate "this one" or "her."

ad: by the light of

Babylōnia Thisbē: a reference to the city of her birth; translate "Babylonian Thisbe."

Line 100: **obscūrus, -a, -um** dim, dark

timidus, -a, -um trembling, fearful; her recent boldness disappears quickly with the threat from the lioness.

antrum, -ī, n. cave

Line 101: **vēlāmen, vēlāminis,** n. veil, cloak, garment. The meaning is singular.

labor, labī, lapsus sum to slip

STUDY TIP

Be careful to distinguish among these look-alike words.

labor, labī, lāpsus sum to slip	THIRD CONJUGATION DEPONENT VERB
labor, labōris, m. toil, work	THIRD DECLENSION NOUN
labōrō (1) to work	FIRST CONJUGATION VERB

Line 102: **conpēscō, conpēscere, conpēscuī** to quench, check

Line 103: **fors, fortis,** f. chance; translate *forte* "by chance," which may be taken with either *inventōs* or *sine ipsā*, or both. It reminds us of the purely accidental cause of this tragedy.

ipsā: refers to Thisbe.

STUDY TIP

Don't confuse these look-alike words:

fors, fortis, f. chance	THIRD DECLENSION NOUN
fortis, forte brave, strong	THIRD DECLENSION ADJECTIVE

Line 104: **cruentō** (1) to stain with blood

tenuis, tenue thin, slender

laniō (1) to shred, tear, mangle

amictus, amictūs, m. garment, covering, cloak; modified by *inventōs* (103). Note the CHIASMUS.‡

OVID *METAMORPHŌSĒS* 4.96–127, CONTINUED

105   sērius ēgressus vestīgia vīdit in altō

     pulvere certa ferae tōtōque expalluit ōre

     Pȳramus; ut vērō vestem quoque sanguine tīnctam

     repperit, "ūna duōs" inquit "nox perdet amantēs,

     ē quibus illa fuit longā dignissima vītā;

110   nostra nocēns anima est. ego tē, miseranda, perēmī,

     in loca plēna metūs quī iussī nocte venīrēs

     nec prior hūc vēnī. nostrum dīvellite corpus

     et scelerāta ferō cōnsūmite vīscera morsū,

NOTES AND VOCABULARY

Line 105:   **sērus, -a, -um** late, after the expected time; *sērius* is the comparative adverb.

     ēgredior, ēgredī, ēgressus sum to depart, leave, step out

     vestīgium, -ī, n. footprint

Line 106:   **pulvis, pulveris,** m. dust, sand

     certus, -a, -um unmistakeable, plain; note the HYPERBATON *vestīgia . . . certa ferae* in lines 105–106; the point is to emphasize that the footprints were plainly those of a wild animal.

     fera, -ae, f. wild animal

     expallēscō, expallēscere, expalluī to turn pale

STUDY TIP

Differentiating among Latin words that begin with *fer–* can be difficult. Here is a list of these words to help you.

ferō, ferre, tulī, lātum to bring, carry	IRREGULAR VERB
fera, -ae, f. wild beast	FIRST DECLENSION NOUN
ferus, -a, -um untamed, wild	FIRST/SECOND DECLENSION ADJECTIVE
ferōx, ferōcis courageous, arrogant	THIRD DECLENSION ADJECTIVE
ferōcia, -ae, f. courage, ferocity	FIRST DECLENSION NOUN
feriō, ferīre to strike	FOURTH CONJUGATION VERB
ferē, *adv.* almost	ADVERB

It is also necessary to distinguish *ferō, ferre* (cf. above) from *ferrum, -ī,* n. iron, sword.

Line 107:   **ut vērō:** translate "but when."

     tingō, tingere, tīnxī, tīnctum to wet, soak

BY THE WAY

In line 108, *ūna duōs* is an example of ANTITHESIS, a figure of speech in which two words that are opposites are juxtaposed. Here the ANTITHESIS adds emphasis.

Line 108:	**reperiō, reperīre, repperī, repertum** to find, discover
	ūna duōs: note the word order of *ūna duōs . . . nox . . . amantēs.*
	perdō, perdere, perdidī, perditum to destroy, ruin
Line 109:	**dignus, -a, -um** (+ *abl.*) worthy of; the ablative *longā . . . vītā* depends on *digna.*

STUDY TIP

Instead of the genitive of the whole (for this grammatical construction, see p. 86), the prepositions *dē* or *ex* with the ablative usually are used with *quidam* and the cardinal numbers (except for *mīlia*) to express a partitive idea (cf. *ē plūribus ūnum*). Ovid uses *ē quibus* in line 109 (instead of *quōrum*), therefore, because of the cardinal number *duōs* in line 108.

Line 110:	**nostra:** the meaning is singular, as it also is in line 112; translate "my."
	nocēns, nocentis guilty, harmful
	ego . . . perēmī: these words, referring to Pyramus, embrace the words, *tē, miseranda,* referring to Thisbe. For the second time in this lament, for dramatic effect, Ovid's narrator draws attention to Pyramus's words by APOSTROPHE.
	miseror (1) to pity; translate "to be pitied."
	perimō, perimere, perēmī, perēmptum to kill
Line 111:	**plēnus, -a, -um** (+ *gen.*) full of
	metus, metūs, m. fear; *metūs* is genitive with *plēna.*
	iubeō, iubēre, iussī, iussum to order; *iussī* is used here with the imperfect subjunctive *venīrēs* without the expected *ut* to introduce an indirect command.
Line 112:	**prior, prius,** *comp. adv.* prior, earlier
	hūc, *adv.* here
	dīvellō, dīvellere, dīvulsī, dīvulsum to tear apart, tear open, tear in two
Line 113:	**scelerātus, -a, -um** wicked, accursed, impious
	ferus, -a, -um savage, fierce
	vīscera, vīscerum (pl. only), n. pl. internal organs, bowels
	morsus, morsūs, m. a bite

BY THE WAY

In line 113, *et . . . morsū* is a GOLDEN LINE. A GOLDEN LINE is a line of dactylic hexameter consisting of a pair of adjacent adjectives and a pair of adjacent nouns, with a verb separating the two pairs.

Here the first adjective (*scelerāta*) modifies the first noun (*vīscera*) and the second adjective (*ferō*) modifies the second noun (*morsū*). The verb *cōnsūmite* occupies the middle of the pattern.

Schematically a GOLDEN LINE looks like this: A B Verb A B.

OVID *METAMORPHŌSĒS* 4.96–127, CONTINUED

  ō quīcumque sub hāc habitātis rūpe leōnēs!

115 sed timidī est optāre necem." vēlāmina Thisbēs

  tollit et ad pactae sēcum fert arboris umbram,

  utque dedit nōtae lacrimās, dedit ōscula vestī,

  "accipe nunc" inquit "nostrī quoque sanguinis haustūs!"

  quōque erat accīnctus, dēmīsit in īlia ferrum,

120 nec mora, ferventī moriēns ē vulnere trāxit.

  ut iacuit resupīnus humō, cruor ēmicat altē,

  nōn aliter quam cum vitiātō fistula plumbō

  scinditur et tenuī strīdente forāmine longās

  ēiaculātur aquās atque ictibus āera rumpit.

125 arboreī fētūs adspergine caedis in ātram

  vertuntur faciem, madefactaque sanguine rādīx

  purpureō tinguit pendentia mōra colōre.

NOTES AND VOCABULARY

Line 114: **quīcumque, quaecumque, quodcumque** whoever, whatever; *quīcumque* modifies *leōnēs*.

    rūpēs, rūpis, f. rocky cliff

    leōnēs: vocative case

Line 115: **timidī:** a genitive of quality/characteristic with *hominis* understood; translate "of a timid man."

    optō (1) to wish for

    nex, necis, f. death

    Thisbēs: a Greek genitive ending

Line 116: **tollō, tollere, sustulī, sublātum** to lift, pick up

    pacīscor, pacīscī, pactus sum to agree upon

Line 117: **ut:** translate "when."

    nōtus, -a, -um known, familiar; note the ELLIPSIS with *dedit nōtae* (*vestī*) *lacrimās* and *dedit ōscula* (*nōtae*) *vestī*.

Line 118: **haustus, haustūs,** m. a drawn quantity of liquid, a drink

Line 119: **quōque** = *et quō*; the antecedent of *quō* is *ferrum*.

    accingō, accingere, accīnxī, accīnctum to gird, equip; translate *accīnctus erat* "was girt."

    dēmittō, dēmittere, dēmīsī, dēmissum to let sink, plunge into

    īlia, īlium, n. pl. gut, groin

Line 120: **mora, -ae,** f. delay; translate *nec mora* "immediately" or "with no delay."

    fervēns, ferventis hot, fresh

    trahō, trahere, trāxī, trāctum to draw, drag

Line 121: **iaceō, iacēre, iacuī** to lie

resupīnus, -a, -um lying on one's back, supine

humus, -ī, f. ground, earth; *humō* is ablative and is equivalent to the locative *humī*.

cruor, cruōris, m. blood, gore

ēmicō (1) to spurt, shoot forth

Line 122: **nōn aliter quam:** translate "not otherwise than"; an example of LITOTES, which introduces a SIMILE.

vitiō (1) to impair, cause defects in

fistula, -ae, f. pipe, tube

plumbum, -ī, n. lead

REMINDER

In the Horace and Ovid chapters on pp. 326 and 353 respectively, the difference between *vītō*, *vīta*, and *vitium* was noted. The noun *vitium*, which means "defect," is related to the verb *vitiō* with the meaning "to cause defects in." Translate *vitiātus*, the perfect passive participle from *vitiō*, as "defective."

Line 123: **scindō, scindere, scidī, scissum** to split, tear open

strīdō, strīdere, strīdī to make a high-pitched sound; to whistle, shriek, hiss

forāmen, forāminis, n. a hole, aperture

Line 124: **ēiaculor** (1) to shoot forth

ictus, ictūs, m. a blow, stroke, thrust

āēr, āeris, m. the air; this is a three-syllable word with a Greek accusative ending. Remember that Greek nouns in the accusative singular may end in *–an*, *–on*, *–en*, or *–a*.

rumpō, rumpere, rūpī, ruptum to break, split

STUDY TIP

Don't confuse *āēr, āeris,* m. "air" with *aes, aeris,* n. "copper coin."

Line 125: **arboreus, -a, -um** of a tree

fētus, fētūs, m. fruit or product of a plant

adspergō, adsperginis, f. a sprinkling, scattering, splashing

caedēs, caedis, f. blood, gore; murder

āter, ātra, ātrum black, dark-colored, stained

Line 126: **vertō, vertere, vertī, versum** to turn, change

faciēs, faciēī, f. appearance, looks

madefaciō, madefacere, madefēcī, madefactum to soak, drench

rādīx, rādīcis, f. root, foot, base

Line 127: **purpureus, -a, -um** purple, crimson

tinguō, tinguere, tīnxī, tīnctum to dye, tinge

pendeō, pendēre, pependī to hang

mōrum, -ī, n. the fruit of the mulberry tree

REMINDER

You read in the Caesar chapter of this book on p. 50 about not confusing *mora, morior,* and *moror.* Here are two more look-alike words that you should be careful to tell apart.

mora, -ae, f. delay (line 120)	FIRST DECLENSION NOUN
morior, morī, mortuus sum to die	THIRD *–IO* CONJUGATION DEPONENT VERB
moror, morārī, morātus sum to delay	FIRST CONJUGATION DEPONENT VERB
mōrum, -ī, n. mulberry (line 127)	SECOND DECLENSION NOUN, NEUTER
mōrus, -ī, f. the mulberry tree	SECOND DECLENSION NOUN, FEMININE

TAKE NOTE

Ovid uses the words *amictus, vēlāmen,* and *vestis* interchangeably as synonyms meaning "veil" or "garment" in this passage even though there are slight differences in their meanings. Elsewhere *vēlāmen* has the meaning "veil" or "garment" while *amictus* often refers to an outer cloak, and *vestis* is the general word for an item of clothing.

COMPREHENSION QUESTIONS

1. What had the lioness recently killed? Cite the Latin.
2. How did the lioness get Thisbe's veil?
3. What did Pyramus see in the dust and how did he react?
4. Why did Pyramus feel he was responsible for Thisbe's death?
5. How did Pyramus kill himself? Cite the Latin.
6. What metamorphosis did the fruit of the mulberry tree undergo?

The Romanesque tympanum from the twelfth-century church of Saint-Gery-au-Mont-des-Boeufs, Cambrai, France celebrates the love of Pyramus and Thisbe and shows them joined in death. Medieval culture regularly recalled stories from the classical world and Christianized them. For example, in the popular *Ovid Moralisé*, Pyramus represents Christ, Thisbe, the Christian soul, and the lion, the Devil. The wall symbolizes the original sin of Adam and Eve, which has created a barrier between humankind and God. Perhaps that is what the upper register of the relief sculpture illustrates.

▶ EXERCISE 1

1. In line 97, what is the case of *oblita*?
2. What is the case and use of *rīctūs* in line 97?
3. In line 101, what is the case and number of *lapsa*?
4. In line 102, what is the case and use of *sitim*?
5. What Latin word does *inventōs* (line 103) modify?
6. In line 105, what is the case and use of *vestīgia*?
7. In line 106, what is the case and use of *pulvere*?
8. In line 107, what is the tense, voice, and form of *tīnctam*?
9. What is the tense of *perdet* in line 108?
10. What is the case of *miseranda* in line 110?
11. In line 111, what is the case and use of *loca*?
12. What is the tense and mood of *venīrēs* in line 111?
13. What is the tense, voice, and form of *dīvellite* in line 112?

14. What is the case and use of *corpus* in line 112?

15. What is the case and use of *leōnēs* in line 114?

16. In line 116, what is the tense, voice, and form of *pactae*?

17. Translate *ut* in line 117.

18. In line 117, what Latin word does *nōtae* modify?

19. What is the tense, voice, and form of *accipe* in line 118?

20. What is the tense, voice, and mood of *erat accīnctus* in line 119?

21. What is the case and use of *ictibus* in line 124?

22. What Latin word does *ātram* (line 125) modify?

23. In line 127, what is the tense, voice, and form of *pendentia*?

24. What is the case and use of *mōra* in line 127?

LANGUAGE FACT

GENITIVE OF QUALITY AND ABLATIVE OF QUALITY

A noun in the genitive, modified by an adjective, may denote the quality or describe the noun. The ablative of quality works the same way but more often physical qualities are in the ablative.

The genitive and ablative of quality are sometimes called the genitive and ablative of characteristic.

sed timidī est optāre necem
  (Ovid *Metamorphōsēs* 4.115)
"But to wish for death is [a characteristic/quality] of a timid [man]."

GENITIVE OF QUALITY/ CHARACTERISTIC

Mōra sunt purpureō colōre.
"The mulberries are of a purple color."

ABLATIVE OF QUALITY/ CHARACTERISTIC

The bright berries of the mulberry tree contrast with the green of its leaves. The Latin name for this tree is *Mōrus alba*. Its leaves are fed to silkworms.

▶ EXERCISE 2

Translate and identify the Latin words that are the genitive or ablative of quality.

1. Amantēs, adulēscentēs bonārum familiārum, nocte domō ēgrediuntur.

2. Leōnēs sunt magnā fortitūdine (strength).

3. Vēlāmen Thisbēs erat pulchrō colōre.

4. Rūpēs erat magnā altitūdine (height).

5. Animus bonī hominis est magnae dignitātis (worth).

ESSAY

In this passage Ovid pairs the following key words and themes:

Lines 101 and 115	the veil (*vēlāmen*)
Lines 102–104 and 112–114	lions shredding/tearing
Lines 105 and 112	Pyramus's late departure
Lines 108 and 110	verbs of destruction (*perdō/perimō*)

Briefly discuss the relationship between these pairs and be sure to include in your discussion Ovid's purpose in making lines 108–111 the centerpiece of the passage.

Support your assertions with references drawn from throughout lines 101–115. All Latin words must be copied or their line numbers provided, AND they must be translated or paraphrased closely enough so that it is clear you understand the Latin. Direct your answer to the question; do not merely summarize the passage. Please write your essay on a separate piece of paper.

SCANSION

Name the meter and scan the following lines.

sed timidī est optāre necem. vēlāmina Thisbēs

tollit et ad pactae sēcum fert arboris umbram,

utque dedit nōtae lacrimās, dedit ōscula vestī

READING 4

Meanwhile Thisbe, who has been hiding in the cave, gathers up her courage and returns to the grove, where she finds Pyramus on the point of death.

LOVERS UNITED IN DEATH

OVID *METAMORPHŌSĒS* 4.128–166

Meter: Dactylic Hexameter

<blockquote>

ecce metū nōndum positō, nē fallat amantem,

illa redit iuvenemque oculīs animōque requīrit,

130 quantaque vītārit nārrāre perīcula gestit;

utque locum et vīsā cognōscit in arbore fōrmam,

sīc facit incertam pōmī color: haeret, an haec sit.

dum dubitat, tremebunda videt pulsāre cruentum

membra solum, retrōque pedem tulit, ōraque buxō

135 pallidiōra gerēns exhorruit aequoris īnstar,

quod tremit, exiguā cum summum stringitur aurā.

</blockquote>

NOTES AND VOCABULARY

Line 128: **ecce:** signals a shift in scene and character. Thisbe returns to the scene.

pōnō, pōnere, posuī, positum to put down, lay aside

fallō, fallere, fefellī, falsum to deceive, disappoint

STUDY TIP

Don't confuse *redeō*, "to return" with *reddō*, "to give back." What these two words have in common is the prefix *red–* (a variation of *re–*) that means "back." The root verb of *redeō* is *eō, īre* and thus *redeō* means "to go back" or "to return," while the root verb of *reddō* is *dō, dare* and thus the definition of *reddō* is "to give back."

Line 129: **redeō, redīre, rediī, reditum** to return

iuvenis, iuvenis, m./f. youth, young person

requīrō, requīrere, requīsīvī, requīsītum to look for, search

Line 130: **vītō** (1) to avoid; here the syncopated form of the perfect subjunctive is used in an indirect question.

gestiō, gestīre, gestīvī to desire eagerly, want, be anxious to

Line 131: **utque:** when *ut* is paired with *sīc* (line 132) in a contrasting sense, the meaning is "while . . . at the same time."

Line 132:   **haereō, haerēre, haesī, haesum** to be brought to a standstill, be perplexed, hesitate

    sit: present subjunctive in an indirect question. The pause (diaeresis) at the end of the fourth foot with the word *color* and the three monosyllabic words that end the line (*an haec sit*) reflect Thisbe's reluctance to proceed toward the tree.

Line 133:   **dubitō** (1) to hesitate, doubt

    tremebundus, -a, -um trembling, quivering

    pulsō (1) to beat repeatedly

    cruentus, -a, -um bloody

Line 134:   **membrum, -ī, n.** limb

    solum, -ī, n. earth, soil. Note that *solum* and *membra* follow their adjectives (*tremebunda . . . cruentum*) and appear in a separate line. The slowed resolution of the adjective with its noun may mimic Thisbe's own gradual realization of what has happened.

    retrō, *adv.* backward

    buxus, -ī, f. boxwood; the wood of the boxwood tree is well known for its light color.

REMINDER

As noted in the Vergil chapter of this book on p. 291, do not confuse the adverb *sōlum*, "only," *sōlus, -a, -um,* "one, alone," or *sōl, sōlis,* m. "sun" with *solum, -ī,* n., "soil," which has a short "o" in its first syllable, in contrast with the other words, which have a long "o."

Line 135:   **pallidus, -a, -um** pale, wan

    exhorrēscō, exhorrēscere, exhorruī to shudder

    aequor, aequoris, n. sea, waves

    īnstar, n. *indecl.* like, just like, with genitive object; *īnstar* sets up a SIMILE.

Line 136:   **tremō, -ere, tremuī** to tremble, quiver, shudder; *tremit* connects Thisbe to Pyramus's *tremebunda membra.*

    exiguus, -a, -um small, slight

    summus, -a, -um highest, top; here a noun meaning "surface"

    stringō, stringere, strīnxī, strictum to graze

OVID *METAMORPHŌSĒS* 4.28–166, CONTINUED

> sed postquam remorāta suōs cognōvit amōrēs,
>
> percutit indignōs clārō plangōre lacertōs
>
> et laniāta comās amplexaque corpus amātum
>
> 140   vulnera supplēvit lacrimīs flētumque cruōrī
>
> miscuit et gelidīs in vultibus ōscula fīgēns
>
> "Pȳrame," clāmāvit, "quis tē mihi cāsus adēmit?
>
> Pȳrame, respondē! tua tē cārissima Thisbē
>
> nōminat; exaudī vultūsque attolle iacentēs!"

NOTES AND VOCABULARY

Line 137:   **remoror** (1) to linger, delay

       amōrēs: translate "beloved."

Line 138:   **percutiō, percutere, percussī, percussum** to beat, strike

       clārus, -a, -um loud, shrill

       plangor, plangōris, m. beating, lamentation; Thisbe's actions here and in line 139 are the typical ritual gestures of the woman as mourner in the ancient world.

       lacertus, -ī, m. upper arm

Line 139:   **laniō** (1) to tear, mangle

       coma, -ae, f. hair; an accusative of respect with *laniāta* or alternatively an accusative direct object of the middle/reflexive participle *laniāta*.

       amplector, amplectī, amplexus sum to embrace

Line 140:   **suppleō, supplēre, supplēvī, supplētum** to fill up; *vulnera supplēvit lacrimīs* is an example of HYPERBOLE.

       flētus, flētūs, m. crying, weeping

       cruor, cruōris, m. bloodshed, gore; *cruōrī* and *lacrimīs* are in the dative case because *misceō* can take *cum*, the dative, or the ablative to express the sense of "with."

STUDY TIP

Cruor refers to blood that flows from a wound, while *sanguis, -is*, m. refers to blood circulating in the body as well as to blood shed from a wound.

Line 141:   **misceō, miscēre, miscuī, mixtum** to mix with, blend

       gelidus, -a, -um cold

       vultus, vultūs, m. face; *vultibus* is a poetic plural; translate in the singular.

       fīgō, fīgere, fīxī, fīxum to fasten, fix

Line 142:   **mihi:** a dative of separation; translate "from me."

       adimō, adimere, adēmī, adēmptum to take away, remove

REMINDER

Diaeresis is a term that refers to the coincidence of the end of a metrical foot and the end of a word. The vocative *Pȳrame* at the beginning of lines 142 and 143 fills out the first metrical foot of each line and offers a good example of diaeresis.

Line 143:   **Pȳrame:** the repetition adds pathos to Thisbe's lament.

respondē: the first of three imperatives setting up a TRICOLON.

tua tē: the ALLITERATION links the two lovers.

Line 144:   **nōminō** (1) to call by name

exaudiō, exaudīre, exaudīvī, exaudītum to listen to, heed

attollō, attollere to lift up, raise

iaceō, iacēre, iacuī, iacitum to lie prostrate, to lie on the ground

OVID *METAMORPHŌSĒS* 4.28–166, CONTINUED

145   ad nōmen Thisbēs oculōs iam morte gravātōs

Pȳramus ērēxit vīsāque recondidit illā.

quae postquam vestemque suam cognōvit et ēnse

vīdit ebur vacuum, "tua tē manus" inquit "amorque

perdidit, īnfēlīx! est et mihi fortis in ūnum

150   hoc manus, est et amor: dabit hīc in vulnera vīrēs.

persequar extīnctum lētīque miserrima dīcar

causa comesque tuī: quīque ā mē morte revellī

heu sōlā poterās, poteris nec morte revellī.

NOTES AND VOCABULARY

Line 145:   **Thisbēs:** it is the mention of her name, not his, that stirs Pyramus.

        gravō (1) to make heavy, weigh down. The many spondees weigh down the line just as Pyramus's eyes are weighed down by death.

Line 146:   **ērigō, ērigere, ērēxī, ērēctum** to raise

        recondō, recondere, recondidī, reconditum to close again

Line 147:   **quae:** feminine nominative singular referring to Thisbe; translate "she." The connecting relative, along with *-que*, links this sentence to the previous one.

        ēnsis, ēnsis, m. a sword

STUDY TIP

Ēnsis, gladius, and *ferrum* (by METONYMY) all mean "sword" and thus are synonyms.

Line 148:   **ebur, eboris,** n. ivory; through SYNECDOCHE *ebur* means "scabbard." Translate "ivory scabbard."

        vacuus, -a, -um empty (+ *abl.*); *ēnse* is the ablative here.

        tua tē: *tua* modifies *manus* and *tē* refers to Pyramus; *tua tē* echoes the same phrase at line 143.

BY THE WAY

In line 149 *perdidit* is an example of ZEUGMA, a figure of speech in which one word modifies or governs two or more words that are joined grammatically, but is appropriate for only one of them. Here, literally speaking, Pyramus's hand destroyed him by plunging the sword into his loins; the destructive quality of love is metaphorical. ZEUGMA comes from a Greek word that means "yoke" or "join."

Line 149:   **īnfēlīx, īnfēlīcis** unlucky

et: translate this *et* and the one in line 150 adverbially as "also."

mihi: dative of possession with *est*; translate "I have."

ūnum: translate *in ūnum hoc* "for this one thing."

Line 150:   **amor:** here *amor* will give her strength; in line 96 *amor* made her bold. *Est . . . amor* with *mihi* understood from line 149 is another dative of possession; translate "I (also) have love."

hīc: antecedent is *amor*, giving precedence to the power of her love. The "i" in *hic* is lengthened for the sake of the meter.

REMINDER

As you read in the Caesar chapter of this book on p. 64, remember that *vīrēs, vīrium* is the plural of *vīs*, "strength," while *virī, virōrum* is the plural of *vir*, "man."

Line 151:   **persequor, persequī, persecūtus sum** to follow all the way, accompany

extinguō, extinguere, extīnxī, extīnctum to kill, destroy; understand *tē* with *extīnctum.*

lētum, -ī, n. death

Lines 150–151: **lētīque . . . tuī:** note the HYPERBATON.

Line 152:   **quīque** = *et quī*; the antecedent of *quī* is the "you" of *poterās.*

revellō, revellere, revellī, revulsum to remove, tear away. The two occurrences of this verb, here and in 153, form a PARADOX: death, which has taken him away from her, will, in fact, not take him away from her because of her own suicide.

Line 153:   **nec** not even

BY THE WAY

PARADOX is a figure of speech in which a statement appears self-contradictory but yet may be true or may prove to be true. The paradoxical statement here draws attention to the complex idea Thisbe is expressing. This figure is often confused with OXYMORON, which properly only involves two apparently self-contradictory words.

OVID *METAMORPHŌSĒS* 4.28–166, CONTINUED

hoc tamen ambōrum verbīs estōte rogātī,

155 ō multum miserī meus illīusque parentēs,

ut, quōs certus amor, quōs hōra novissima iūnxit,

conpōnī tumulō nōn invideātis eōdem;

at tū quae rāmīs arbor miserābile corpus

nunc tegis ūnīus, mox es tēctūra duōrum,

160 signa tenē caedis pullōsque et lūctibus aptōs

semper habē fētūs, geminī monimenta cruōris."

dīxit et aptātō pectus mucrōne sub īmum

incubuit ferrō, quod adhūc ā caede tepēbat.

vōta tamen tetigēre deōs, tetigēre parentēs;

165 nam color in pōmō est, ubi permātūruit, āter,

quodque rogīs superest, ūnā requiēscit in urnā.

NOTES AND VOCABULARY

Line 154:   **hoc ... rogātī:** a heavily spondaic line. The slow, plodding meter lends weight and importance to the request she is about to make. The passive *rogātī* takes the accusative *hoc*.

estōte: this is the future plural imperative of *sum* emphatically expressing a command to be carried out in the future. Thisbe directly addresses the absent parents in an APOSTROPHE. Translate *hoc ... estōte rogātī* "be asked this."

Line 155:   **ō:** sets up a direct address.

multum: adverbial modifying the adjective *miserī;* translate "very."

miserī: vocative case modifying *parentēs* at the line's end. Thisbe earlier used this adjective to describe herself in line 151.

meus: the use of the singular adjective refers to Thisbe's parents as the genitive *illīus* refers to Pyramus's.

Line 156:   **ut:** introduces an indirect command after *rogātī* (154).

quōs ... quōs: these relative pronouns, together an example of ANAPHORA, are each direct objects in their own clauses. The implied antecedent of each *quōs* is *eōs*, "those."

novissimus, -a, -um last, final

iungō, iungere, iūnxī, iūnctum to join

Line 157:   **conpōnō, conpōnere, conposuī, conpositum** to join, place together; *conpōnī:* a present passive infinitive used in an indirect statement with *invideātis*.

tumulō ... eōdem: translate "in the same tomb."

invideō, invidēre, invīdī, invīsum to refuse, be unwilling

Line 158:   **tū ... arbor:** note the APOSTROPHE.

Line 159: **tegō, tegere, tēxī, tēctum** to cover; *es tēctūra* is an active periphrastic expressing what is about to be; translate "you are about to cover."

Line 160: **tenē:** imperative singular, continuation of the direct address to the tree (as is *habē* in line 161); translate "preserve." The metamorphosis and *aition* are established.

 pullus, -a, -um dingy, somber, drab-colored

 luctus, luctūs, m. grief, mourning

 aptus, -a, -um (+ *dat.*) appropriate, fitting, suited

Line 161: **fētus, fētūs,** m. offspring, fruit; once again a noun is held until the end of its clause to create suspense and to bring an emphatic end to the declaration.

 geminus, -a, -um double

 monimentum, -ī, n. memorial

Line 162: **aptō** (1) to adjust, make ready

 pectus, pectoris, n. chest, heart

 mucrō, mucrōnis, m. tip, point of a sword

 īmus, -a, -um lowest

Line 163: **incubō, incubāre, incubuī, incubitum** to throw oneself upon

 tepeō, tepēre to be warm, tepid; the line begins and ends with gruesome verbs marking Thisbe's suicide.

Line 164: **vōtum, -ī,** n. prayer, vow

 tangō, tangere, tetigī, tāctum to touch; *tetigēre* is the alternate form of *tetigērunt*.

Line 165: **permātūrēscō, permātūrēscere, permātūruī** to become fully ripe

Line 166: **rogus, -ī,** m. funeral pyre. In the plural because there were two funeral pyres. *Rogīs* is dative with *supersum*, a compound and intransitive verb.

 supersum, superesse, superfuī, superfutūrus to remain, be left over

 ūnā . . . urnā: Ovid ends this tale of star-crossed lovers with a strong image symbolizing their union—a single urn for their combined ashes.

COMPREHENSION QUESTIONS

1. After she leaves the cave, what does Thisbe plan to do when she meets up with Pyramus? Cite the Latin.

2. How does Thisbe feel when she returns and sees the mulberry tree again? Cite the Latin.

3. What makes Thisbe turn pale?

4. How does Thisbe react after she recognizes Pyramus? Cite the Latin.

5. What made Pyramus briefly open his eyes?

6. What does Thisbe decide to do after seeing her veil?

7. What last request does Thisbe make of his and her parents?

Lions and tigers were familiar to people in the ancient world. This Roman mosaic, an example of the *opus sectile* "cut stone" technique, is housed at the Capitoline Museum in Rome. Its artist catches the tigress at a dramatic moment.

▶ EXERCISE 1

1. In line 128, what is the tense, voice, and mood of *fallat*?

2. What is the case and use of *oculīs* in line 129?

3. In line 131, what is the tense, voice, and form of *vīsā*?

4. What is the case and use of *membra* in line 134?

5. In line 134, what is the case and use of *buxō*?

6. What is the case and use of *plangōre* in line 138?

7. What is the tense, voice, and form of *laniātā* in line 139?

8. In line 141, what Latin word does *gelidīs* modify?

9. In line 142, what is the case and use of *Pȳrame*?

10. In line 145, what is the case and use of *morte*?

11. In line 148, what Latin word does *vacuum* modify?

12. What is the tense, voice, and mood of *dīcar* in line 151?

13. In line 152, what is the tense, voice, and form of *revellī*?

14. What is the case and use of *illīus* in line 155?

15. In line 157, what is the tense, voice, and mood of *invideātis*?

16. What Latin word does *geminī* in line 161 modify?

17. In line 162, what case is *pectus* and what Latin word modifies *pectus*?

VOCABULARY BUILDER

Give the English meaning for each group of synonyms.

Group A	Group B	Group C
vultus, vultūs, m.	caedes, caedis, f.	cruor, cruōris, m.
ōs, ōris, n.	mors, mortis, f.	sanguis, sanguinis, m.
faciēs, faciēī, f.	lētum, -ī, n.	
	nex, necis, f.	

Group D	Group E
ferrum, -ī, n.	membrum, -ī, n.
ēnsis, ēnsis, m.	artus, artūs, m.
gladius, -ī, m.	

LANGUAGE FACT

REVIEW OF POSSESSION AND DATIVE OF POSSESSION

In this passage you read two examples of a dative of possession. Latin shows possession in several ways; here is a short review of these.

- **Possessive Adjectives**

  The Latin adjectives *meus, -a, -um* (my, mine), *tuus, -a,-um* (your, sing.), *suus, -a, -um* (his, her, its), *noster, nostra, nostrum* (our), *vester, vestra, vestrum* (your, pl.), and *suus, -a, -um* (their) are the usual way of expression possession. (See p. 530.)

... **tua** *tē cārissima Thisbē* ... (Ovid, *Metamorphōsēs* 4.143) "**your** most dear Thisbe ... you"	**POSSESSIVE ADJECTIVE**
... *postquam remorāta* **suōs** *cognōvit amōrēs* ... (Ovid, *Metamorphōsēs* 4.137) "having delayed, after she recognized **her** love"	**POSSESSIVE ADJECTIVE OF A REFLEXIVE**

- **The Genitive Case of Nouns and Pronouns**

  The genitive case of Latin nouns can show possession. The genitive of only a few pronouns [*illīus/eius/huius* (of him/his, of her/her, of it/its), *illōrum/eōrum/hōrum* (of them/their)] can be used to show possession. The genitive of other Latin pronouns [*meī* (of me), *tuī* (of you), *suī/*), *nostrī/nostrum* (of us), *vestrī/vestrum* of you, *suī* (of him/his, of her/her, of it/its, of them/their)] is **not** used to show possession but is used as an objective or partitive genitive.

sīc facit incertam **pōmī** *color* (Ovid *Metamorphōsēs* 4.132) "the color **of the fruit** makes her uncertain"	**POSSESSIVE GENITIVE OF A NOUN**
ad nōmen **Thisbēs** *oculōs* ... *Pȳramus ērēxit* (Ovid *Metamorphōsēs* 4.145–146) "at the name **of Thisbe** Pyramus raised [his] eyes"	**POSSESSIVE GENITIVE OF A GREEK NOUN**
ō ... *miserī* ... **illīus**que *parentēs* (Ovid *Metamorphōsēs* 4.155) "o the miserable parents **of that one**"	**POSSESSIVE GENITIVE OF A PRONOUN**

- **Dative of Possession**

The dative case of nouns and pronouns, when used with a form of *sum,* can also show possession. The possessor is in the dative case and the thing being possessed stands in the nominative case. There are several ways to translate sentences in which there is a dative of possession.

> **Tibi** *nōmen est Pȳramus.*   **DATIVE OF POSSESSION**
> "**To you** is the name Pyramus"
>   OR "**You** have the name Pyramus,"
>   OR "**Your** name is Pyramus."

> *est et **mihi** fortis in ūnum hoc manus*   **DATIVE OF POSSESSION**
>   (Ovid *Metamorphōsēs* 4.149–150)
> "**To me** is a brave hand for this one thing."
>   OR "**I** have a brave hand for this one thing."
>   OR "**My** hand is brave for this one thing."

▶ EXERCISE 2

Translate; identify the possessive word and the type of possession it represents. There may be more than one possessive word in a sentence.

1. Ō, meī miserī parentēs!

2. Pȳramō erat ēnsis.

3. Thisbae erant et fortis manus et fortis amor.

4. Pȳramī manus in īlia ferrum dēmīsit.

5. Pȳramō Thisbaeque semper erit amor īnfēlīx.

6. Extemplō Libyae magnās it Fāma per urbēs.

7. Haec ego omnia vixdum etiam coetū vestrō dīmissō comperī.

8. Satis facere reī pūblicae vidēmur, sī istīus furōrem ac tēla vītāmus.

9. Nam tuī Catullī plēnus sacculus est arāneārum.

10. Vīvāmus, mea Lesbia, atque amēmus, rumōrēsque senum sevēriōrum omnēs ūnius aestimēmus assis!

ESSAY

The story of the star-crossed lovers Pyramus and Thisbe is poignant and tragic. Ovid suggests several reasons for the tragic outcome. In a short essay, discuss what you believe are the major causes of the tragedy.

Support your assertions with references drawn from throughout lines 65–166. All Latin words must be copied or their line numbers provided, AND they must be translated or paraphrased closely enough so that it is clear you understand the Latin. Direct your answer to the question; do not merely summarize the passage. Please write your essay on a separate piece of paper.

SCANSION

Name the meter and scan the following lines.

> signa tenē caedis pullōsque et lūctibus aptōs
>
> semper habē fētūs, geminī monimenta cruōris.
>
> dīxit et aptātō pectus mucrōne sub īmum

An ancient mosaic presents the master musician and poet Orpheus "soothing the surrounding savage beasts," mesmerized by his voice and the beautiful music of his lyre. Orpheus narrated the Pygmalion story as a means of processing the grief and guilt he felt at the loss of his wife. Orpheus's wife Eurydice had died suddenly. Orpheus, trusting in the power of his music, descended to the Underworld in the hopes of cajoling Hades into allowing him to bring his wife back to the world. Charmed by Orpheus's music, Hades granted Eurydice a reprieve on the condition that Orpheus take the lead on the ascent back to the world and that he not look back at his wife who would follow. Unfortunately, Orpheus felt compelled to look back and instantly lost his wife again to the Underworld.

READING 5

Ovid's Pygmalion is one of the stories told by the singer/poet Orpheus in an effort to assuage his grief over the loss of his bride Eurydice. The tale of Pygmalion follows a brief account of the Propoetides, who had denied the divinity of Venus. The goddess punished this group of women by forcing them into prostitution and later turning them into stone. Pygmalion, an artist, is so disgusted by the foul activities of the daughters of Propoetus that he avoids all real women. Instead, he creates for himself the ideal woman out of ivory, a statue of such exquisite beauty that he falls in love with its perfection. As a misogynist, he abhors real, flesh-and-blood women, and can love only a lifeless image. At a festival honoring Venus, whom he genuinely reveres, he wishes silently that his statue come to life. When he returns home and caresses the ivory, it softens and turns to flesh beneath his hands. Venus sanctifies Pygmalion's union with his ideal wife, a union that produces a child named Paphos.

The tale of Pygmalion has through the ages inspired plays, poems, ballets, operas, and paintings. Shakespeare in *The Winter's Tale* was fascinated by the idea of changing a woman's identity. George Bernard Shaw, in his play called *Pygmalion*, which is set in nineteenth-century London, and Lerner and Lowe, creators of *My Fair Lady*, a musical based on Shaw's play, turn their modern Pygmalion, Professor Henry Higgins, into an arrogant male, who transforms a humble seller of flowers into an upper-class lady as a kind of scientific experiment. The tale of Pygmalion and the literary works it inspires are appealing because we are fascinated by the idea of the transformative power of art in the hands of a great creative artist.

PYGMALION'S LOVE FOR HIS IVORY GIRL

OVID *METAMORPHŌSĒS* 10.243–269

Meter: Dactylic Hexameter

> quās quia Pygmaliōn aevum per crīmen agentīs
>
> vīderat, offēnsus vitiīs, quae plūrima mentī
>
> 245   fēmineae nātūra dedit, sine coniuge caelebs
>
> vīvēbat thalamīque diū consorte carēbat.
>
> intereā niveum mīrā fēlīciter arte
>
> sculpsit ebur fōrmamque dedit, quā fēmina nāscī
>
> nūlla potest, operisque suī concēpit amōrem.

NOTES AND VOCABULARY

Line 243:   **quās:** translate this connecting relative as "these women." *Quās* is the direct object of *vīderat* and refers to a group of women called the Propoetides, whose foul activities Ovid relates in the story preceding this one; his contempt for their activities results in Pygmalion's total rejection of women in general.

                quia, *conj.* because

Pygmaliōn, Pygmaliōnis, m. Pygmalion; a legendary king of Cyprus although Ovid never refers to him as a king.

aevum, -ī, n. lifetime, age

per, *prep.* + *acc.* through, for the sake of

crīmen, crīminis, n. guilt, crime

agō, agere, ēgī, āctum to spend, lead; note the poetic accusative ending *–īs* on *agentīs* (see p. 303). The present participle *agentīs* modifies *quās.*

Line 244: **offēnsus, -a, -um** offended, displeased

vitium, -ī, n. vice, moral failing

quae: neuter accusative plural relative pronoun whose antecedent is *vitiīs.*

plūrimus, -a, -um very much; *plūrima* modifies *quae* whose antecedent is *vitia*; translate *quae plurima* "very many of which."

Line 245: **fēmineus, -a, -um** feminine

caelebs, caelibis unmarried (male), bachelor; the juxtaposition of this adjective with *coniuge* clearly sets forth the dilemma of this story. Pygmalion, a hater of women, wants and needs a woman.

Line 246: **thalamus, -ī,** m. bedroom, marriage chamber

cōnsors, cōnsortis, m./f. partner; *cōnsorte* is an ablative of separation with *carēbat.*

careō, carēre, caruī (+ *abl.*) to lack, be without

Line 247: **intereā,** *adv.* meanwhile, nevertheless

niveus, -a, -um white, snowy-white; this adjective connotes a cold white, emblematic of the lifeless beauty Pygmalion has created. Note the HYPERBATON.

mīrus, -a, -um wonderful

fēlīciter, *adv.* successfully

Line 248: **sculpō, sculpere, sculpsī, sculptum** to carve

ebur, eboris, n. ivory

fōrma, -ae, f. form, shape, beauty

quā: translate "with which."

nāscor, nāscī, nātus sum to be born, be produced

Line 249: **opus, operis,** n. work; objective genitive with *amōrem*

concipiō, concipere, concēpī, conceptum: to conceive, to fall (in love)

REMINDER

Remember that nouns indicating action, agency, or feeling such as *amōrem* in line 249 govern an objective genitive—a noun that would be the direct object if the noun of action, agency, or feeling were a verb.

250 virginis est vērae faciēs, quam vīvere crēdās,

et, sī nōn obstet reverentia, velle movērī:

ars adeō latet arte suā. mīrātur et haurit

pectore Pygmaliōn simulātī corporis īgnēs.

saepe manūs operī temptantēs admovet, an sit

255 corpus an illud ebur, nec adhūc ebur esse fatētur.

ōscula dat reddīque putat loquiturque tenetque

et crēdit tāctīs digitōs īnsīdere membrīs

et metuit, pressōs veniat nē līvor in artūs,

et modo blanditiās adhibet, modo grāta puellīs

NOTES AND VOCABULARY

Line 250:   **faciēs, faciēī,** f. face, appearance

crēdās: translate this subjunctive verb "you would believe." The poet's address to the reader in *crēdās* makes the story more vivid.

BY THE WAY

Crēdās is a potential subjunctive of the second person singular present. A potential subjunctive describes something that could potentially happen. The negative is *nōn*. The potential subjunctive functions as the main verb in the main clause of the sentence.

Line 251:   **obstō, obstāre, obstitī, obstātum** to stand in the way, block the path; *sī nōn obstet* is one half of a future less vivid condition, with *velle* being construed as equivalent to *velit* ("[and] if modesty should not stand in the way, would wish . . . ").

reverentia, -ae, f. awe, shyness, modesty; refers to the feelings of the statue, as if it were alive.

velle movērī: the *et* joins *vīvere* and *velle*, both of which depend on *crēdās; movērī* can be construed as a present middle/reflexive infinitive; nakedness is viewed as less licentious if the woman does not move.

BY THE WAY

ars adeō latet arte suā in line 252 offers a good example of ASSONANCE, a figure of speech in which the same or similar vowel(s) are repeated in a series of two or more words. The repeated "a" is suggestive of the wonder Pygmalion experiences gazing at the lifelike work he has created. This same line also illustrates another figure of speech, POLYPTOTON, in which words from the same base/root, but in a different form, appear in close proximity. The repetition of *ars/arte* serves to emphasize artistic creation.

Line 252:   **adeō,** *adv.* so, truly, indeed

lateō, latēre, latuī to lie hidden, be concealed, escape notice

ars adeō latet arte suā: "To such an extent art is concealed by its own art." This line refers to the effect of art. The most successful art is that which appears effortless or natural and does not appear to have been produced by the artist. Here Pygmalion's art is so lifelike that it deludes even its creator.

mīror (1) to be amazed at, admire

hauriō, haurīre, hausī, haustum to consume, drink

REMINDER

As noted in the Horace chapter of this book on p. 334, be careful to distinguish between *pectus, pectoris,* n. "chest, heart" and *pecus, pecoris,* n. "flock, herd."

Line 253:   **pectus, pectoris,** n. chest, heart

        simulō (1) to imitate, copy, represent; *simulātī corporis* is an objective genitive.

        īgnēs: in poetry this word often refers to the fire of love.

Line 254:   **temptō** (1) to try, test; *temptantēs* modifies *manūs* and introduces the indirect question *an sit.*

        admoveō, admovēre, admōvī, admōtum to move, bring or apply something (in the accusative), *manūs,* to something (in the dative), *operī*

Lines 254–255: **an . . . an** whether . . . or

Line 255:   **adhūc,** *adv.* yet, still

        fateor, fatērī, fassus sum to admit, acknowledge

Line 256:   **reddō, reddere, reddidī, redditum** to return, give back; *reddī* is an infinitive in indirect statement with its accusative subject, *ōscula,* understood.

Line 257:   **tangō, tangere, tetigī, tāctum** to touch

        digitus, -ī, m. finger

        īnsīdō, īnsīdere, īnsēdī, īnsessum to sink in, become embedded

STUDY TIP

There are three verbs in Latin that mean "to fear." It will increase your Latin vocabulary to know these.

timeō, timēre, timuī	SECOND CONJUGATION
vereor, verērī, veritus sum	SECOND CONJUGATION DEPONENT
metuō, metuere, metuī, metūtum	THIRD CONJUGATION

Line 258:   **metuō, metuere, metuī, metūtum** to fear, be afraid; note the present tense.

        premō, premere, pressī, pressum to press, squeeze

        veniat nē (= *nē veniat*): a fear clause

        līvor, līvōris, m. bluish coloring, bruise

        artus, artūs, m. arm, leg, limb

Line 259:   **modo . . . modo:** now . . . now, at one time . . . at another

        blanditia, -ae, f. flattery, compliment, word of endearment

        adhibeō, adhibēre, adhibuī, adhibitum to apply, offer

        grātus, -a, -um pleasing, agreeable

OVID *METAMORPHŌSĒS* 10.243–269, CONTINUED

260 mūnera fert illī conchās teretēsque lapillōs

et parvās volucrēs et flōrēs mille colōrum

līliaquē pictāsque pilās et ab arbore lāpsās

Hēliadum lacrimās; ōrnat quoque vestibus artūs,

dat digitīs gemmās, dat longa monīlia collō,

265 aure levēs bācae, redimīcula pectore pendent:

cūncta decent; nec nūda minus fōrmōsa vidētur.

conlocat hanc strātīs conchā Sīdōnide tīnctīs

adpellatque torī sociam adclīnātaque colla

mollibus in plūmīs, tamquam sēnsūra, repōnit.

NOTES AND VOCABULARY

Line 260: **mūnus, mūneris,** n. gift

concha, -ae, f. shell; this noun stands in apposition to *mūnera* as do the next six accusative nouns: *lapillōs* (260), *volucrēs* (261), *flōrēs* (261), *līliaque* (262), *pilās* (262), and *lacrimās* (263). The long list of items that Pygmalion gives to the sculpted statue is intended to be humorous.

teres, teretis smooth, round; note the POLYSYNDETON here and throughout this description.

lapillus, -ī, m. small stone

Line 261: **volucris, volucris,** f. bird

Line 262: **līlium, -ī,** n. lily; note that the *-que* of *līliaque,* the first syllable of the second foot, must be long here for the sake of the meter.

pingō, pingere, pīnxī, pictum to paint, color

pila, -ae, f. ball, sphere

lābor, lābī, lāpsus sum to slip, fall

Line 263: **Hēliadēs, Hēliadum,** f. pl. the Heliades, daughters of the sun god Helios

ōrnō (1) to adorn, decorate

REMINDER

You have read previously on p. 237 to be careful to distinguish between *ōs, ōris,* n. "mouth" and *ōra, ōrae,* f. "shore." Now look at this more complete list of look-alike words.

ōs, ōris, n. "mouth"	THIRD DECLENSION NOUN
ōra, ōrae, f. "shore"	FIRST DECLENSION NOUN
os, ossis, n. "bone"	THIRD DECLENSION NOUN
orō (1) "to beg, pray"	FIRST CONJUGATION VERB
ōrnō (1) "to decorate"	FIRST CONJUGATION VERB

Line 264: **gemma, -ae,** f. jewel, gem

monīle, monīlis, n. necklace

collum, -ī, n. neck

Line 265: **auris, auris,** f. ear

levis, leve light, slight

bāca, -ae, f. pearl

redimīculum, -ī, n. band, wreath, garland

pendeō, pendēre, pependī to hang down

Line 266: **cūnctus, -a, -um** all, every

decet, decēre, decuit it is fitting

nec . . . minus: note the LITOTES.

nūdus, -a, -um bare, naked

fōrmōsus, -a, -um beautiful

Line 267: **conlocō** (1) to arrange

hanc: this demonstrative refers to the statue.

strātum, -ī, n. coverlet, bedcover

conchā Sīdōnide: refers to a shellfish indigenous to the waters off Sidon, a Phoenician city,
    from which came a rare purple dye. Sidon was synonymous with the production of dye;
    hence the *concha Sīdōnis* came to stand for the color purple—rare and regal. Note the
    CHIASMUS.

tingō, tingere, tīnxī, tīnctum to dye, stain

Line 268: **appellō (adpellō)** (1) to call

torus, -ī, m. bed; *torī* is objective genitive with *sociam.*

socia, sociae, f. partner

adclīnō (1) to lean, rest on

colla: Ovid frequently uses the plural for singular parts of the body.

Line 269: **mollis, molle** soft

plūma, -ae, f. feather

tamquam, *adv.* as if, as though

sentiō, sentīre, sēnsī, sēnsum to feel, sense

repōnō, repōnere, reposuī, repositum to lay to rest

 ## TAKE NOTE

Helios and Clymene were the parents of Phaethon. Phaethon's sisters were changed into
poplar trees, and their tears of mourning for the loss of their brother became amber. The
aetiological myth explains the origin of amber.

COMPREHENSION QUESTIONS

1. Why did Pygmalion live alone without a spouse?

2. After Pygmalion presses his fingers on the statue, what does he fear?

3. List five gifts and another five adornments that Pygmalion brings to the statue. Cite the Latin
   and the English.

▶ EXERCISE 1

1. In line 243, what is the case and use of *agentīs*?

2. What is the case and use of *vitiīs* in line 244?

3. What is the case and use of *arte* in line 247?

4. In line 248, what is the tense and form of *nāscī*?

5. In line 250, what Latin word does *vērae* modify?

6. In lines 250–251, what is the tense, voice, and mood of *crēdās* and *obstet*?

7. In line 251, what is the tense and form of *velle*?

8. In line 253, what is the tense, voice, and form of *simulātī*?

9. In line 254, what is the case and use of *operī*?

10. What is the case and use of *ōscula* in line 256?

11. In line 257, what is the case and use of *digitōs*?

12. In line 260, what is the case and use of *illī*?

13. What is the case and use of *artūs* in line 263?

14. In line 264, what is the case and use of *collō*?

15. In line 267, what is the case and use of *conchā*?

16. What is the tense, voice, and form of *sēnsūra* in line 269?

LANGUAGE FACT

INDIRECT QUESTIONS

An indirect question is a subordinate clause, introduced by a main verb of asking, doubting, or knowing, and so forth, and an interrogative pronoun or adverb. The verb of the indirect question is in the subjunctive and follows the sequence of tenses.

In the first example *temptō* governs the indirect question introduced by *an*.

> *Saepe manūs operī temptantēs admovet, an sit / corpus an illud ebur . . .*
> (Ovid *Metamorphōsēs* 10.254–255)
> "Often he moves his hands to the work, testing whether it is a body
> or that ivory . . ."

In the second example, the verb *nesciō* governs the indirect question introduced by *cūr*.

> *Pygmaliōn nescīvit cūr fēminae crīmen per aevum agerent.*
> "Pygmalion did not know why women were committing crime[s]
> over a period of time."

STUDY TIP

Be careful to distinguish an indirect question from an indirect statement or indirect command.

Indirect Question

| verb of asking, uncertainty | + interrogative word | + nominative subject | + subjunctive verb |

Indirect Command

| verb of asking, urging | + ut/nē | + nominative subject | + subjunctive verb |

Indirect Statement

| verb of saying, thinking | | + accusative subject | + infinitive |

| *Pygmaliōn sē rogāvit cūr ōscula nōn redderentur.* "Pygmalion asked himself why the kisses were not being returned." | INDIRECT QUESTION |

| *Venus imperat ut ebur fiat vīvum.* "Venus orders that the ivory become alive." | INDIRECT COMMAND |

| *. . . nec adhūc ebur esse fatētur.* (Ovid *Metamorphōsēs* 10.255) ". . . and he does not confess that it is still ivory." | INDIRECT STATEMENT |

▶ EXERCISE 2

Identify whether each sentence below contains an indirect statement, indirect command, or indirect question. Then translate the sentences.

1. Rogāvērunt cūr sine coniuge caelebs vīveret Pȳgmaliōn.

2. Dīcō tē priōre nocte vēnisse inter falcāriōs.

3. Nescīvit quās fēminās Pȳgmaliōn amāret.

4. Pȳgmaliōn scīvit sē vitiīs fēminārum offēnsum esse.

5. Cīvitātī persuāsit ut dē fīnibus suīs cum omnibus cōpiīs exīrent.

6. Rogāmus quid Pȳgmaliōn sculpat.

7. Quaerunt quis ōrnet quoque vestibus artūs et det digitīs gemmās.

8. Pȳgmaliōn putat tāctīs digitōs īnsīdere membrīs.

9. Statuistī quō quemque proficīscī placēret.

10. Pȳgmaliōn sē hortātus est ut sine coniuge caelebs vīveret.

LANGUAGE FACT

FEAR CLAUSES

After a verb of fearing (*metuere, timēre, verērī*) the values of *ut* and *nē* are reversed. This is the only subjunctive construction introduced by *ut/nē* with reversed values.

> *et metuit, pressōs veniat nē līvor in artūs, . . .* (Ovid *Metamorphōsēs* 10.258)
> "and he fears that a bruise may come onto the pressed limbs, . . ."

BY THE WAY

This usage may have grown out of a negative wishing statement that eventually was used with a verb of fearing.

> *Nē veniat!* = "May he not come!" After a verb of fearing, you might translate in the following way: *Metuō nē veniat!* = "I fear lest he come!" or "I fear that he is coming!"

Thus, since *nē* had fallen into use in an affirmative clause of fearing, by default, *ut* was used in a negative clause of fearing. *Metuō ut veniat* = "I fear that he is not coming." Sometimes *nē nōn* is found instead of *ut*.

▶ EXERCISE 3

Translate the following fear clauses.

1. Vereor ut Pygmaliōn fēminās amet.

2. Saepe manūs operī admovet, timēns ut corpus sit.

3. Pygmaliōn verētur nē omnēs fēminae malae sint.

4. Pygmaliōn metuit ut puellae mūnera essent grāta.

5. Omnēs timuērunt nē Pygmaliōn statuam amāret.

ESSAY

The story of Pygmalion, who rejects women but falls in love with a statue of a woman he created, lends itself to humor. In a short essay, identify and discuss some of the humorous elements in this passage that enhance the mythological tale.

Support your assertions with references drawn from throughout lines 243–269. All Latin words must be copied or their line numbers provided, AND they must be translated or paraphrased closely enough so that it is clear you understand the Latin. Direct your answer to the question; do not merely summarize the passage. Please write your essay on a separate piece of paper.

SCANSION

Name the meter and scan the following lines.

conlocat hanc strātīs conchā Sīdōnide tīnctīs

adpellatque torī sociam adclīnātaque colla

mollibus in plūmīs, tamquam sēnsūra, repōnit.

READING 6

The time comes for the festival in honor of Venus, the patron goddess of Cyprus. Sacrifice is made, and as Pygmalion brings a gift to her altar, he humbly requests that he find a wife as perfect as his statue.

THE GRANTING OF PYGMALION'S SECRET DESIRE

OVID *METAMORPHŌSĒS* 10.270–297
Meter: Dactylic Hexameter

270   fēsta diēs Veneris tōtā celeberrima Cyprō

        vēnerat, et pandīs inductae cornibus aurum

        conciderant ictae niveā cervīce iuvencae,

        tūraque fūmābant, cum mūnere fūnctus ad ārās

        cōnstitit et timidē "sī, dī, dare cūncta potestis,

275   sit coniūnx, optō," nōn ausus "eburnea virgō"

        dīcere, Pygmaliōn "similis mea" dīxit "eburnae."

        sēnsit, ut ipsa suīs aderat Venus aurea fēstīs,

        vōta quid illa velint et, amīcī nūminis ōmen,

        flamma ter accēnsa est apicemque per āera dūxit.

NOTES AND VOCABULARY

Line 270:   **fēstus, -a, -um** festive, (with *diēs*) holiday, festival

             diēs: usually masculine but feminine when it refers to a specific or appointed day as here.

             celeber, celebris, celebre popular, well-known, festive

             Cyprus, -ī, f. Cyprus, an island in the eastern Mediterranean Sea known for its worship of Venus.

Line 271:   **pandus, -a, -um** curved, bent, bowed

             indūcō, indūcere, indūxī, inductum to cover, spread on, spread over

             aurum: an accusative of respect with *inductae* to describe the material used for the gilding or, alternatively, an accusative direct object of the middle/reflexive participle.

Line 272:   **concidō, concidere, concidī** to fall, collapse

             īciō, icere, īcī, ictum to strike, beat

             niveus, -a, -um white, snowy-white; another use of the color of cold snow associated with purity as in line 247.

             cervix, cervīcis, f. the neck, back of the neck

             iuvenca, -ae, f. a young cow, heifer

Line 273: **tūs, tūris,** n. incense

fūmō (1) to smoke

mūnus, mūneris, n. ritual duty, gift

fungor, fungī, fūnctus sum (+ *abl.*) to perform

Line 274: **cōnstō, cōnstāre, cōnstitī** to take up a position; to stand with

cūnctus, -a, -um all; *cūncta* is neuter plural being used as a noun. Translate "all things."

Line 275: **sit:** a subjunctive verb because *optō* is taking a substantive clause as a direct object, here without *ut*.

optō (1) to wish

audeō, audēre, ausus sum to dare; perfect participles of semi-deponent verbs translate "having + perfect participle."

eburneus, -a, -um of ivory. Another form of this word, *eburnus, -a, -um*, has the same meaning "of ivory" and is seen in line 276.

REMINDER

As noted on p. 171 of the Cicero chapter of this book, be careful to distinguish between *audeō, audēre, ausus sum* "to dare" and *audiō, audīre, audīvī, audītum* "to hear."

Line 276: **similis mea:** the word order here is jumbled and reflects Pygmalion's state of mind as he hesitates in speaking his wish. Note the HYPERBATON with *coniūnx . . . mea.*

Line 277: **sentiō, sentīre, sēnsī, sēnsum** to know, understand; the subject of *sēnsit* is Venus, who also is the subject of the next clause.

Line 278: **vōtum, -ī,** n. prayer, vow, oath

volō, velle, voluī to mean, signify, wish, want

quid illa velint: indirect question.

nūmen, nūminis, n. divinity, divine power

STUDY TIP

Don't confuse these two words that are only one letter apart from being spelled the same: *nūmen, nūminis,* n. "divinity" and *nōmen, nōminis,* n. "name."

BY THE WAY

The number three is always significant and often implies divine intervention. Here, since Venus is present at her own festival, it signifies her direct response.

Line 279: **ter,** *adv.* three times

accendō, accendere, accendī, accēnsum to brighten, stir up

apex, apicis, m. a tip of a flame. Here *apicemque . . . dūxit* is best translated "and the flame leapt up."

āēr, āeris, m. the air

OVID *METAMORPHŌSĒS* 10.270–297, CONTINUED

280 ut rediit, simulācra suae petit ille puellae

incumbēnsque torō dedit ōscula: vīsa tepēre est;

admovet ōs iterum, manibus quoque pectora temptat:

temptātum mollēscit ebur positōque rigōre

subsīdit digitīs cēditque, ut Hymettia sōle

285 cēra remollēscit tractātaque pollice multās

flectitur in faciēs ipsōque fit ūtilis ūsū.

dum stupet et dubiē gaudet fallīque verētur,

rūrsus amāns rūrsusque manū sua vōta retractat.

corpus erat! saliunt temptātae pollice vēnae.

NOTES AND VOCABULARY

BY THE WAY

The reference to the statue as well as the girl in *simulācra suae . . . puellae* anticipates the transformation, while the abrupt shift to the present tense in *simulācra suae . . . puellae* makes the following description of the miracle more vivid.

Line 280:	**simulācrum, -ī,** n. an image, statue; poetic plural
Line 281:	**incumbō, incumbere, incubuī** to lie or lean on
	torus, -ī, m. couch, bed
	tepeō, tepēre, tepuī to be warm, tepid; often used of the passion of love
Line 282:	**iterum,** *adv.* again
	quoque, *adv.* also
	temptō (1) to try, attempt; here *temptat* means "he tries out" in the sense of "he touches."
Line 283:	**mollēscō, mollēscere** to become soft
	rigor, rigōris, m. stiffness, rigidity
Line 284:	**subsīdō, subsīdere, subsēdī** to give way
	cēdō, cēdere, cessī, cessum to yield
	ut: translate "as." Note the SIMILE.
	Hymettius, -a, -um: of Hymettus; the adjectival form of Hymettus, a mountain near Athens that was known for its honey; modifies *cēra* in line 285.
Line 285:	**cēra, -ae,** f. wax
	tractō (1) to handle, manage
	pollex, pollicis, m. thumb

Line 286: **flectō, flectere, flexī, flexum** to bend, twist, direct

faciēs, faciēī, f. shape

fīō, fīerī, factus sum to become, happen, be made, be done

ūtilis, ūtile useful

ūsus, ūsūs, m. use

Line 287: **stupeō, stupēre, stupuī** to be amazed

dubiē, *adv.* doubtfully

gaudeō, gaudēre, gāvīsus sum to rejoice

fallō, fallere, fefellī, falsum to deceive

vereor, verērī, veritus sum to fear, be afraid

Line 288: **rūrsus,** *adv.* again

amāns, amantis, m. lover

sua vōta: refers to those things he had wished for and prayed for, i.e., that his statue become a wife.

retractō (1) to handle, feel for a second time

Line 289: **saliō, salīre, saluī, saltum** to leap, i.e., to pulse

temptātae pollice: nearly the same phrase as used in the SIMILE in 284–285.

vēna, -ae, f. blood vessel, vein

OVID *METAMORPHŌSĒS* 10.270–297, CONTINUED

290 tum vērō Paphius plēnissima concipit hērōs

verba, quibus Venerī grātēs agat, ōraque tandem

ōre suō nōn falsa premit, dataque ōscula virgō

sēnsit et ērubuit timidumque ad lūmina lūmen

attollēns pariter cum caelō vīdit amantem.

295 coniugiō, quod fēcit, adest dea, iamque coāctīs

cornibus in plēnum noviēns lūnāribus orbem

illa Paphon genuit, dē quā tenet īnsula nōmen.

NOTES AND VOCABULARY

Line 290: **Paphius, -a, -um** of or pertaining to the city of Paphos on the island of Cyprus

concipiō, concipere, concēpī, conceptum to form, produce, conceive

hērōs, hērōis, m. a hero

Line 291: **grātēs, grātium,** f. pl. thanks‡

Line 292: **nōn falsa:** genuine, real; LITOTES for emphasis

Line 293: **ērubēscō, ērubēscere, ērubuī** to blush with shame or modesty. This reference to modesty at the end of the story is reminiscent of the statue's *reverentia* in line 251.

lūmen: here meaning "eye"; by juxtaposing *lūmina lūmen* Ovid is playing on the double meaning of *lūmen*, which signifies "light" and "eye."

STUDY TIP

Be careful to distinguish between *lūmen, lūminis,* n. "light, eye" and *līmen, līminis,* n. "threshold."

Line 294: **attollō, attollere** to lift up, raise

pariter, *adv.* at the same time, equally

Line 295: **coniugium, -ī,** n. marriage; dative with the verb *adsum,* "to be present at"

cōgō, cōgere, coēgī, coāctum to gather, assemble

Line 296: **cornū, cornūs,** n. horn; with *coāctīs* describes the crescent phases of the moon

noviēns, *adv.* nine times

lūnāris, lūnāre lunar, of or pertaining to the moon

Line 297: **illa:** refers to the ivory statue that is now a woman; translate "she."

Paphos, -ī, m./f. the child of Pygmalion. By tradition a son who became the founder of the Cyprian city of Paphos, which was sacred to Venus. Ovid ends his tale with an *aition* (origin) of how the city received its name.

gignō, gignere, genuī, genitum to give birth to

quā: the gender of this relative pronoun is problematic, as it should refer to the masculine Paphos. Some texts prefer *quō.*

TAKE NOTE

Grātēs occurs in the nominative and accusative plural and is used of thanks given to the gods. The more common *grātiās agere* is the usual way of expressing thanks to humans. Both *grātēs* and *grātia* are related to the Latin word *grātus, -a, -um* that means "pleasing" or "grateful."

COMPREHENSION QUESTIONS

1. What does Pygmalion ask from the gods, according to lines 274–275?

2. How did Venus show her response to Pygmalion's request?

3. What happened after Pygmalion returned home and kissed the statue?

4. What deity was present at Pygmalion's marriage? Cite the Latin.

5. Who is Paphos? Cite the Latin.

The association of Aphrodite with the city of Paphos lives on in the Rock of Aphrodite in Ramiou, Cyprus.

VOCABULARY BUILDER

Here are some of the Latin words for body parts that you saw in the first reading about Pygmalion in lines 243–269. Copy this list of words and include the English meaning for each. Identify which words are synonyms.

> pectus, pectoris, n. (line 253)
>
> manus, manūs, f. (line 254)
>
> digitus, -ī, m. (line 257)
>
> membrum, -ī, n. (line 257)
>
> artus, -ūs, m. (line 258)
>
> collum, -ī, n. (line 264)
>
> auris, auris, f. (line 265)

▶ EXERCISE 1

Find all the Latin words for body parts used in lines 270–297. Include these words in the list you made for the Vocabulary Builder above along with the Latin dictionary entry, the English meaning of each, and the line number. The same word may be used in more than one line; list the word each time it is used.

▶ EXERCISE 2

1. In line 271, what Latin word does *pandīs* modify?
2. In line 272, what Latin word does *niveā* modify?
3. In line 273, what is the case and use of *mūnere*?
4. In line 274, what is the case and use of *dī*?
5. Translate *ut* in line 277.
6. In line 278, what is the tense, voice, and mood of *velint*?
7. In line 281, what is the tense, voice, and form of *incumbēns*?
8. In line 283, what is the tense, voice, form, and use of *positō*?
9. What is the case and use of *ūsū* in line 286?
10. In line 287, what is the tense, voice, and form of *fallī*?
11. In line 291, what is the case, use, and antecedent of *quibus*?
12. In line 297, what is the case and use of *nōmen*?

ESSAY

In a short essay, identify from lines 270–297 one example of each of the following rhetorical figures: alliteration, assonance, litotes, simile, chiasmus, and hyperbaton, and discuss how these rhetorical figures enhance the meaning of the passage.

Support your assertions with references drawn from throughout lines 270–297. All Latin words must be copied or their line numbers provided, AND they must be translated or paraphrased closely enough so that it is clear you understand the Latin. Direct your answer to the question; do not merely summarize the passage. Please write your essay on a separate piece of paper.

SCANSION

Name the meter and scan the following lines.

ut rediit, simulācra suae petit ille puellae

incumbēnsque torō dedit ōscula: vīsa tepēre est;

admovet ōs iterum, manibus quoque pectora temptat

PART 3

Authors from the Post-antique Era

- **DESIDERIUS ERASMUS ET ALIĪ**
- **FRANCISCUS PETRARCHUS**
- **JOHN PARKE**

WHY POST-ANTIQUE LATIN

To say that Latin literature did not end with the Romans would be an understatement. In fact the Roman contribution to Latin, however fundamental, is a mere beginning. The amount of surviving Latin literature written in Europe since the collapse of the Western Roman Empire in the late fifth century CE is almost inconceivably larger than the surviving corpus of literature left by the Romans themselves.

This heritage of post-Roman Latin literature was anything but a sterile idiom reserved for a few reclusive monks. The very pulse of western European civilization, as it developed through the Middle Ages and the Renaissance, moved primarily to the rhythms of Latin prose and poetry.

The language of Caesar and Cicero performed new functions and came to be used in ways unimagined by the ancient Romans. Latin became the vehicle for sciences as refined as ballistics and hydrodynamics. Latin exclusively provided the academic and philosophical vocabulary for the expression of Europe's most sophisticated thoughts. Latin was the language in which fundamental concepts, such as gravity and the heliocentric solar system, received their first coherent expression. Latin, along with some revived terms from ancient Greek, supplied the language of botany and zoology. Latin was the international language of cartography, geography, history, and ethnography, the sciences through which the discoveries of Renaissance explorers gradually became part of the consciousness of European civilization. Latin, and not any of the nascent national tongues, was the primary linguistic vehicle for all of this before about 1750 CE.

But medieval and Renaissance Latin was not merely the language of scholars, scientists, and philosophers; it also produced poetry, letters, satire, fiction, and many other genres—including works widely recognized as monuments and masterpieces of world literature, ranging from the stories of the Venerable Bede and the *Carmina Burāna* to Thomas More's *Ūtopia* and Erasmus's *Praise of Folly*. Even as the language of creative literature, Latin still rivaled the vernacular tongues in the Renaissance.

This international and multicultural role of Latin was in some ways already anticipated in the literature of the Roman Empire, when the peoples of the Roman provinces, especially in the West, began using Latin and not their native tongues as their means of literary expression. Thus Quintilian and Seneca, who were from Spain, wrote in Latin just as the African Apuleius also produced his literary work in Latin. This multicultural role for Latin was even more pronounced in the Middle Ages and Renaissance, when Latin served as an international language and a vehicle for a literary tradition that eventually extended even to the New World. Moreover, in the Middle Ages and Renaissance, Latin was no longer anyone's native tongue, and this long-lasting phenomenon of the Latin language, based on stable written sources rather than

fluid popular usage, supporting such a vast, varied, and dynamic literature from about 450 CE to about 1750 CE, is arguably more distinctive and significant than any literature produced by people who wrote in their native tongue.

The existence of Latin curricula in the secondary schools is often defended because Latin offers access to the origins of Western civilization. The literary heritage of the Romans is certainly fundamental. But the Latin literature produced after the time of the ancient Romans is no less central to our culture, language, and institutions than the literature of the ancient Romans. If "cultural literacy" is one of the goals of our education, teachers of Latin should think seriously about broadening their perspective and consistently exploiting post-antique as well as Roman Latin.

Latin helps students build vocabulary and verbal skills in English and modern languages. Students who have taken Latin in secondary school typically earn higher verbal scores in college entrance exams than their peers who never studied Latin. However, Latin could offer even more linguistic resources and verbal power if more attention were paid to post-antique Latin in secondary school curricula. Medieval Latin lies at the basis of nearly the whole spectrum of the vocabulary for modern universities, degrees, and academic institutions (and this includes basic English words, such as "faculty," "dean," "chancellor," "graduate," etc.). Medieval and Renaissance Latin is the source for our terminology for telling time (the Romans had no mechanical clocks). The list of our word debts to post-Roman Latin would embrace physics, astronomy, botany, and many other sciences, not to mention such disciplines as philosophy and law.

Yet Latin is typically taught, and Latin teachers are typically prepared, in a way that assumes that Latin is only about the ancient Romans—and not even the entire Roman tradition (since most of Roman literature produced after about 120 CE has little place in canonical curricula). What other literary and linguistic discipline focuses so exclusively on its origins alone? It is time for a change. Both teachers and students of Latin should make the most of what the Latin tradition actually has to offer. In the long run, the place of Latin in our educational system will be more secure if such a broadening of perspective can be achieved. Some idea of the immense contributions to our culture made by Latin after the time of the Romans and selected readings of some of the astoundingly rich post-Roman Latin literature should be a basic part of the teaching of Latin today at all levels. As in *Latin for the New Millennium,* Level 2, this text endeavors to provide teachers, and students who are still learning the fundamentals of the Latin language, with the readings and cultural information that will help to add this wider and richer perspective to the Latin classroom.

Latin learning in the new millennium should take full account of the fact that Latin literature is a phenomenon spanning the millennia.

TERENCE TUNBERG
University of Kentucky

CHAPTER 7

DESIDERIUS ERASMUS AND OTHER POST-ANTIQUE LATIN WRITERS

Cum Circumstantial Clauses; Substantive Clauses of Result

At the University of Paris, Erasmus served as a private tutor. He was especially esteemed as a tutor for Latin composition. Edouard Hamman (1819–1888) recreates a scene from 1511 with Erasmus lecturing the young Archduke Charles, the future Charles V King of Spain and later the Holy Roman emperor. In the dedication to his Gospel of Matthew, Erasmus praises Charles, "Caesar is not a doctor of the gospels but their champion."

MEMORĀBILE DICTŪ

Bis puerī senēs.

"Old men are twice children (boys)." (Erasmus *Adagia* 1.5.36)

Erasmus demonstrated a wry sense of humor and perspective on the human condition. In his collection of proverbs *Adagia*, both the pithy statements like this one and longer ones reveal his playful nature.

INTRODUCTION TO POST-ANTIQUE WRITERS

As Professor Tunberg details in his overview essay for this section, the corpus of post-antique Latin is a vast and very rich one that spans academic disciplines, continents, and ages. This section seeks to provide a glimpse into this bounty of Latin by presenting readings from Petrarch, one of the animators of the Italian Renaissance; from Erasmus, the leading humanist of the Northern Renaissance; and from John Parke, a Revolutionary War soldier who wrote Latin poetry. The passages from Petrarch and Parke reveal the enduring influence of Horace and Vergil, whose poetry you studied earlier in this text. The readings from Erasmus and his circle of fellow intellectuals provide insight into the personality of this genius and the interconnectedness of the scholars of the period. Additionally, these letters demonstrate that Latin was the international language of the Renaissance. Erasmus and friends from Italy, England, France, Germany, Flanders, and the Netherlands not only wrote to one another in Latin but also spoke in Latin when face to face. Students familiar with *Latin for the New Millennium*, Level 2, encountered both Petrarch and Erasmus in that text. Here, they will read unadapted Latin from these two intellectual giants. Since the chapter highlights Erasmus, this essay concentrates on his life and accomplishments.

ERASMUS'S EARLY YEARS

Erasmus was born in Rotterdam (hence his frequent identification as Erasmus Roterodamus) in the Netherlands on October 27th, probably in 1466 but the exact year is not certain. His name has been the subject of discussion as some believe he was christened Erasmus after St. Erasmus, an early Christian martyr and bishop of Formiae, Italy, while others assert that his real name was Gerard Gerardson. However, he became known as Erasmus Desiderius—*Erasmus*, bad Greek for "beloved," and *Desiderius*, bad Latin for "beloved." Erasmus's godson, the son of his Basle printer Johann Froben, was baptized Erasmius, the proper Greek spelling. Erasmus dedicates his *Colloquia* to this godson in 1524 and notes, "You might say it (the *Colloquia*) too was an ἐράσμιον, the delight of the Muses, who foster sacred things." The *Colloquia* (see pp. 234–35, *Latin for the New Millennium*, Level 2) was Erasmus's second most popular work after the *Adagia*. A series of dialogues about topics of contemporary interest, the book was intended to acclimate students as quickly as possible to reading Latin. His friends, later noting Erasmus's many travels, made a pun on his name and called him "*mūs errāns*," a "wandering mouse."

At age nine Erasmus began his Latin studies at the humanist Hegius's school in Deventer in the Netherlands. When he was orphaned at age fifteen, his guardians first sent him to a monastery school for two years and then, it is believed because the inheritance ran out, forced the teenager to enter the monastery of Emmaus near Gouda in the Netherlands. While Erasmus did not feel a vocation to the priesthood (see his letter to Arnoldus Bostius, p. 420), he did enjoy and seize the opportunity to immerse himself in studies and in the Latin texts of classical masters like Cicero and Jerome.

A LIFE OF TRAVELS, STUDIES, AND MAKING FRIENDS

Erasmus's excellent command of Latin earned him an escape from the monastery when the Bishop of Cambrai took him on as his secretary and companion for a journey to Italy. That pilgrimage did not take place, but Erasmus convinced the bishop to sponsor him as a student at the University of Paris. Here, he befriended the Italian scholar and poet Faustus Andrelinus. Erasmus did not like the living conditions or the food at the university and so moved off campus. There he supplemented his stipend from the bishop by tutoring students like William Blount, who later invited Erasmus to come to England. One of his teaching strategies while tutoring was the daily exchange, with his tutees, of letters written in Latin. The visit to England proved providential as it introduced Erasmus to future lifelong friends John Colet and Thomas More as well as to a wider circle of England's great thinkers of the time including the future Henry VIII as well as proponents of the study of Greek like William Grocyn, Thomas Linacre, and John Latimer. As a result of these new friendships, Erasmus determined to return to Paris and take up the study of Greek. At this time, he also stayed in Orleans and Louvain whenever some epidemic arose in Paris. In his letters in this chapter, it is evident how frequently Erasmus experienced health problems. It was on a stay in Louvain in 1504 that he discovered Lorenzo Valla's unpublished manuscript *Annotātiōnēs in Novum Testāmentum*. Erasmus acted boldly and decided to have Valla's treatise, which is critical of the Vulgate, the Latin translation of the Bible in use at the time, published. He added his own introduction to it and was inspired to use his recently acquired mastery of ancient Greek to work on and to produce his own translation of the New Testament.

The following year found Erasmus again in England where he earned a Bachelor of Divinity degree at Cambridge and joined the scholars who taught at the University of London. He stayed with Thomas More at his new home in Chelsea and regularly traveled along the Thames to visit Lambeth Palace where William Warham, the Archbishop of Canterbury, gathered the leading intellectuals of the day. While in England, he was asked to accompany Henry VII's royal physician on a trip to Italy as tutor to the doctor's sons. Erasmus made the most of the opportunity, earning a doctorate in divinity at the University of Turin, meeting with scholars at the venerable universities of Bologna and Padua, befriending the famous Venetian printer Aldus Manutius, and printing the second edition of his *Adagia*. While in Bologna, he received permission from Pope Julius II to lay aside his monastic garb, a significant concession for that era, and dress as the people did. In Rome, the leading scholars welcomed Erasmus as one of their own.

Upon learning of the death of Henry VII in England, Erasmus hurried north with hopes of some significant role in the court of the humanist Henry VIII. En route to England, Erasmus composed notes that became *Moriae Encomium* or *Laus Stultitiae* ("Praise of Folly"), which he completed while staying with Thomas More. Some claim the work's title is a pun on More's name. Unfortunately, Erasmus's hopes of a great posting never bore fruit as Henry VIII put aside his interests in the New Learning and instead waged war. While in England, John Fisher, Bishop of Rochester, found his friend a teaching post at Cambridge, where Erasmus lectured on Greek and was appointed the Lady Margaret Reader in Divinity. He also advised John Colet on the founding of his new school for boys and wrote some texts for the use of the young scholars. During this stay in England, Erasmus also wrote commentaries on the early Christian Fathers and began work on his New Testament.

Erasmus left Cambridge in 1514 and settled in Basle, Switzerland, where he spent the rest of his life. Here he befriended Johann Froben and became part of his extended family. Froben and Erasmus were also business associates as the scholar entrusted his many works to the printer. In the wake of religious strife brought on by the Reformation, Erasmus sought refuge in Freiburg from 1529 to 1535. Erasmus spent the last year of his life in Basle and was buried in the former Catholic cathedral, which had become a Reformed church.

THE INFLUENCE OF ERASMUS

Erasmus was heralded as the outstanding figure of the northern humanists, if not of all humanists. Rulers and scholars alike sought his advice and insights and were honored to be included in his extensive circle of friends and correspondents. The letters in this chapter illustrate the connections between Erasmus and his fellow scholars. Erasmus had friends throughout Europe—had there been LinkedIn or Facebook in Erasmus's day, the number of his contacts and friends would have been most impressive. He is often likened to Cicero, whom he much admired and in whose *hūmanitās* tradition of education he believed strongly, as they were both great correspondents and writers on a breadth of topics. Erasmus's voluminous correspondence, however, more than rivals Cicero's output and fills some eight volumes.

Erasmus produced an impressive output of books that included treatises, commentaries, collections of proverbs, and a definitive edition of the New Testament as well as manuals for parents, students, and teachers. The book for which he is most celebrated is *Praise of Folly*, in which he gently and humorously reproaches the state of society and especially the church. The personified Folly, perhaps inspired by the Neoplatonism of the Italian Renaissance scholars Ficino and Pico, delivers sermons that critique every group in society from the clergy to scholars. The work resonated with the educated, who appreciated its exposure of clerical hypocrisy and monkish superstition. Those seeking reform in the church saw Erasmus as an ally but faulted him for showing too much restraint in his criticism while Roman Catholics felt betrayed. Like his English humanist friends, More and Colet, Erasmus sought to reform the church from within. That desire was the impetus for his commentaries on the early church fathers and his publication of the New Testament. Erasmus even promoted the idea of publishing the scriptures in the vernacular languages. However, the forces for change were far more radical and once Martin Luther nailed his Ninety-five Theses on the doors of Mainz Cathedral in 1517, volcanic change burst forth—surprising even Luther.

Erasmus and Luther had been friendly colleagues regularly corresponding and sharing ideas. Luther, like Reuchlin (see the reading on pp. 454–456), had hoped Erasmus would join their reform movement. However, the issue of free will drove a wedge between the two scholars. In 1524 Erasmus asserted in *Diatriba dē līberō arbitriō* ("A Treatise Concerning Free Will"), that the human will was free and cited the biblical command that sinners repent as evidence. Luther retorted with *Dē servō arbitriō* ("Concerning Slave Will"), a strongly worded tract that rejected free will, claiming that the human will was irrevocably flawed and that salvation was only possible through God's grace. The two scholars never communicated again.

ERASMUS'S STYLE

Erasmus learned the Latin of the Renaissance, the Latin of Cicero that Petrarch had set as the standard for the academic and literary worlds. However, Erasmus was also inspired by Lorenzo Valla whose *Ēlegantiārum linguae Latīnae librī sex* ("Six Books Concerning Proper Uses of the Latin Language"), proposed looking to other polished Roman writers as a source for Latin composition. (See *Latin for the New Millennium*, Level 2, pp. 159–164.) A copious vocabulary and an extraordinary command of the best classical Latin are the hallmarks of Erasmus's Latin. Aside from some peculiar medieval spellings and an occasional lapse in syntax, probably due to writing in haste, the ancients would surely have approved of Erasmus's style as well as that of his correspondents. Texts like his *Colloquia* and his manuals for parents, teachers, and students promoted classical learning.

In old Prague's Lesser Town, a house on Mostecká street boasts a striking bronze door entitled "Dialogues." Sculptor Petr Cisarovsky (b. 1957) celebrates the relationships between the Dutch and Czech peoples by portraying two great thinkers, the Czech Jan Amos Comenius on the left and the Dutchman Erasmus, of Rotterdam sharing a common desk. Though they lived in different eras, both were heralded as Christian humanists who significantly impacted the world of learning.

THE WORLD OF ERASMUS TIMELINE

World Events and Key Figures in Erasmus's Life		Events in Erasmus's Life
Petrarch	1304–74	
Lorenzo Valla	1407–57	
Renaissance	**ca. 1400–ca. 1600**	
Constantinople taken by Ottomans; last battle of Hundred Years War fought	1453	
Gutenberg prints his Bible	1455	
Thomas Linacre	1460–1520	
	1466	birth of Erasmus
Copernicus	1473–1543	
Thomas More	1478–1535	
	1481	Erasmus orphaned, enters monastery
Dias sails around the Cape of Good Hope	1488	
	1491	Bishop of Cambrai appoints Erasmus as his secretary
Ferdinand and Isabella sponsor Columbus's transatlantic journey, expel the Jews from Spain, and defeat the last Moorish ruler in Spain	1492	
Maximilian I shores up Holy Roman Empire	1495	Erasmus studies at University of Paris
Faustus Andrelinus named poet laureate of France by Charles VIII	1496	
	1497	Thomas Linacre teaches Erasmus Greek
Vasco da Gama sails around Africa to India	1497–98	
	1499	Erasmus travels to England at Lord Mountjoy's invitation; befriends John Colet and Thomas More
	1500	*Adagia* published
Pope Julius II, patron of Michelangelo, begins his papacy	1503	
	1504	Erasmus discovers Valla's *Adnotātiōnēs in Novum Testāmentum*
	1505	Erasmus earns Bachelor of Divinity at Cambridge, also studies at London
	1506–09	Erasmus travels to Italy
Michelangelo paints the Sistine Chapel ceiling	1508–12	
	1509–14	Henry VII dies and Erasmus returns to England
	1509	*Praise of Folly* published
	1510–11	John Colet founds St. Paul's School, London; Erasmus serves as advisor

	1514–29	Erasmus settles in Basle and works with the printer Johann Froben
Francis I becomes King of France	1515	
	1516	Thomas More's *Utopia* published; Erasmus's New Testament published
Luther presents his Ninety-Five Theses beginning Protestant Reformation	1517	Erasmus experiences perilous landing at Bolougne-sur-Mer
Royal College of Physicians founded in London	1518	Erasmus in Basle
Charles V, King of Spain, becomes Holy Roman emperor	1519	
Cortés takes Aztec capital	1521	
	1524	Erasmus publishes the *Colloquia*
	1529–35	Erasmus leaves Basle due to religious strife and stays in Freiburg
Pizarro takes Inca Empire	1533	
Henry VIII establishes Church of England	1534	
Bishop John Fisher and Thomas More executed	1535	Erasmus returns to Basle
	1536	Erasmus dies in Basle and is buried in the cathedral
Ignatius of Loyola founds Jesuit Order, key group in Catholic Counter-Reformation	1540	
John Calvin starts Reformed Church	1541	
Council of Trent formulates Roman Catholic Counter-Reformation	1545–1563	

READING 1

Fonts, underlined words, and words in parentheses will no longer be used.

This is one of two letters that Erasmus sent to his fellow humanist Arnold Bostius, a Carmelite friar who lived in Ghent. At this time Ghent in East Flanders was controlled by Spain. Today it is in modern Belgium. Bostius served as prior of his monastery and is the author of some theological treatises and of historical works about the Carmelites.

He was friends with many of the scholars of his day and served a pivotal role in the exchanges among humanists of Italy, Paris, and northern Europe. Bostius sought copies of scholars' works and shared them with his many contacts.

The letter finds Erasmus once again suffering from some ailments that threaten to keep him from traveling to Italy, a deep desire that he had nourished from his youth. His desire was to earn a degree in theology from the venerable University of Bologna and to visit Rome in the Jubilee Year. Another recurring theme in Erasmus's letters concerns his lack of funds—here, he complains that his patron, the Bishop of Cambrai, is a bit stingy! While he was not able to visit Rome for the Jubilee, Erasmus did journey there in 1506. On that trip with King Henry VII's physician and his two young sons, Erasmus earned his doctor of divinity in Turin. He was received with great acclaim by the scholars of the universities of Bologna and Padua. On his visit to Venice, he met the famous printer Aldus Manutius, to whom he entrusted the second printing of the *Adagia*, and began another lifelong friendship. In Rome, he enjoyed the company of such celebrities as Cardinal Giovanni de' Medici (the subsequent Pope Leo X) and others who encouraged him to take up residence in Rome.

A DREAM DEFERRED AND A FIT OF DEPRESSION

ERASMUS TO ARNOLD BOSTIUS

1   Salvē, mī Arnolde. Iam sēsquimēnsem graviter labōrō febrī nocturnā, lentā quidem illā

       sed quotīdiānā, quae mē penitus exstīnxit. Nōndum sum morbō līber, sed tamen

       aliquantō recreātior; nōndum vīvō, sed affulget aliqua vītae spēs. Petis ut tibi animī meī

       cōnsilium commūnicem; hoc ūnum habē, mundum mihi iamdūdum obolēre; damnō

5   spēs meās. Nihil aliud cupiō quam mihi darī ōtium, in quō possim tōtus ūnī Deō vīvere,

       dēflēre peccāta aetātis incōnsultae, versārī in scriptūrīs sacrīs, aliquid aut legere aut

       scrībere. Id in sēcessū aut collēgiō nōn possum. Nihil enim mē tenerius; nec vigiliās, nec

       iēiūnia, nec ūlla incommoda fert haec valētūdō, etiam cum est prosperrima.

NOTES AND VOCABULARY

Line 1:   **sēsquimēnsis, -is,** m. one and a half months (about six weeks)

             labōrō (1) to suffer

             febris, febris, f. fever

nocturnus, -a, -um nightly

lentus, -a, -um lasting, persistent

Line 2:   **quotīdiānus, -a, -um** daily; often seen with the spelling *cottīdiānus*

penitus, *adv.* utterly, thoroughly

exstinguō, exstinguere, exstīnxī, exstīnctum to destroy

nōndum, *adv.* not yet

morbus, -ī, m. disease

Line 3:   **aliquantō,** *adv.* somewhat

recreātus, -a, -um restored to health; note the adjective is comparative in form from *recreō* (1) "to revive."

affulgeō, affulgēre, affulsī to shine forth, appear

tibi: translate "with you."

Line 4:   **commūnicō** (1) to share (with), impart

habē = "know"

iamdūdum, *adv.* for a long time

oboleō, obolēre, oboluī *lit.,* to smell of; translate here "grows stale."

damnō (1) to condemn

Line 5:   **tōtus:** translate adverbially for better sense in English, "completely, entirely."

ūnī Deō: dative of reference; translate "for God alone."

Line 6:   **dēfleō, dēflēre, dēflēvī, dēflētum** to lament bitterly

peccātum, -ī, n. sin

aetās, aetātis, f. life

incōnsultus, -a, -um ill-advised, thoughtless, indiscreet

versor (1) to be engaged (in), be busy (with)

scrīptūra, scrīptūrae, f. scripture

Line 7:   **sēcessus, sēcessūs,** m. solitude

collēgium, -ī, n. college‡

id . . . possum: supply "to do."

REMINDER

In line 7 *tenerius* is a comparative adjective modifying *nihil* with *est* to be understood. Watch for a comparative adverb as well as a superlative adjective later in this passage. To review comparative and superlative forms in Latin, see pp. 113–115.

nihil: translate "no one." Erasmus may well mean nothing as well as no one.

tener, tenera, tenerum delicate, weak

vigiliae, -ārum, f. pl. keeping awake, periods of keeping awake

Line 8:   **iēiūnium, -ī,** n. fast

incommodum, -ī, n. inconvenience

valētūdō, valētūdinis, f. state of health

prosper, -a, -um favorable

ERASMUS TO ARNOLD BOSTIUS, CONTINUED

Hīc ubi tantīs
in dēliciīs vīvō, subinde in morbum incidō; quid facerem inter labōrēs collēgiālēs?
10 Dēcrēveram in Ītaliam hōc annō concēdere et Bonōniae aliquot mēnsēs theologiae
operam dare, atque illīc doctōris insigne accipere, deinde in annō iubileō Rōmam
vīsere; quibus cōnfectīs ad meōs redīre atque istīc vītam compōnere. Sed vereor nē
haec ut volumus cōnficere nōn possīmus. Metuō imprīmīs nē tantum iter et regiōnis
aestum valētūdō haec nōn ferat. Dēnique reputō nec in Italiam venīrī nec illīc vīvī sine
15 summō sumptū. Ad titulum quoque parandum grandī summā est opus. Et Episcopus
Cameracēnsis dat perparcē. Omnīnō benignius amat quam largitur, et prōlixius omnia
pollicētur quam praestat. Ipse propemodum in causā sum quī nōn īnstem; et sunt tam
multī quī vel extorqueant. Faciam tamen prō tempore quod factū vidēbitur optimum.
Bene valē.

NOTES AND VOCABULARY

Line 9:   **dēliciae, -ārum,** f. pl. delights, pleasures
            subinde, *adv.* immediately after‡
            facerem: deliberative subjunctive
            collēgiālis, -e connected with a college
Line 10:   **dēcernō, dēcernere, dēcrēvī, dēcrētum** to decide
            concēdō, concēdere, concessī, concessum to depart
            Bonōnia, -ae, f. modern Bologna
            aliquot some; indeclinable adjective modifying *mēnsēs*
            theologia, -ae, f. theology; *theologiae* is dative case with *operam dare.*
Line 11:   **operam dare:** translate "to pay attention to (to the study of)."
            illīc, *adv.* there
            doctōris īnsigne: the badge of doctor, i.e., indicating the doctoral degree. Consider the academic
                gowns worn by faculty at a college commencement and sometimes at a high school graduation.
            iubileus, -a, -um: used substantively as "Jubilee"‡
Line 12:   **vīsō, vīsere, vīsī, vīsum** to look at, go to see, visit
            quibus: a connecting *qui*; the infinitives *redīre* and *compōnere* depend on *dēcrēveram.*
            cōnficiō, cōnficere, cōnfēcī, cōnfectum to complete
            ad meōs: understand *domōs.*
            istīc, *adv.* translate "there where you are," i.e., in Flanders; Bostius lived in Ghent.
            compōnō, compōnere, composuī, compositum to settle, arrange, put together
            vereor, verērī, veritus sum to fear; negative clauses of fearing may be introduced by either *ut*
                or *nē . . . nōn.*
Line 13:   **ut volumus:** a clause embedded in the fear clause; translate "as we wish."
            possīmus: subjunctive after verbs of fearing; see also *ferat* in line 14.

metuō, metuere, metuī to fear

imprīmīs = *in prīmīs* especially (*lit.*, "among the first things")

REMINDER

As you read in the Ovid chapter of this book on p. 393, the verbs *metuō, vereor,* and *timeō* are synonyms.

Line 14:   **aestus, aestūs,** m. heat

reputō (1) to consider; the complementary infinitives *venīrī* and *vīvī* are used in the sense of the Greek middle voice.

REMINDER

The Greek middle voice, expressed in Latin with the passive voice, indicates that the subject is acting upon itself. See pp. 262–263.

Line 15:   **sūmptus, sūmptūs,** m. expense, cost

titulus, -ī, m. title, degree

parō (1) to procure, get, buy

grandī summā: ablative with *est opus.* Translate "there is need of a large sum."

Episcopus, -ī, m. bishop

Line 16:   **Cameracēnsis, -is** of Cambrai

perparcē, *adv.* very stingily

omnīnō, *adv.* in general

benignus, -a, -um lavish

largior, largīrī, largītus sum to give, bestow, confer

prōlixus, -a, -um willing, copious

Line 17:   **praestō, praestāre, praestetī, prōstātum** *or* **prōstitum** to show, provide, excel

propemodum, *adv.* almost

in causā: translate "at fault."

īnstō, īnstāre, īnstitī to pursue, press, insist

Line 18:   **quī:** introduces a causal clause.

vel, *adv.* even, actually

extorqueō, extorquēre, extorsī, extortum to extort, obtain by force

quī . . . extorqueant: relative clause of characteristic

prō tempore: *lit.*, "according to the time"; translate "according to circumstances."

factū: supine

REMINDER

The supine is derived from the fourth principal part and is translated into English as an infinitive. See p. 251 for more information on the two types of supines.

TAKE NOTE

1. The medieval and Renaissance university comprised a set of colleges as the university still does today. Erasmus studied at the Collège de Montaigu, a college within the University of Paris. John Calvin, one of the leaders of the Reformation, studied philosophy at the Collège de Montaigu until his father decided to send him elsewhere to study law. Scholars believe Calvin's father saw law as a more lucrative profession. Yet Calvin went on to become a great religious leader of his day. In America, the Dutch Reformed Church and the Presbyterian Church are part of Calvin's legacy. Ignatius of Loyola, one of the leaders of the Catholic Counter-Reformation, also studied at the Collège de Montaigu.

2. With reference to *vigiliās* (line 7) and *iēiūnia* (line 8), Erasmus recalls the rigors of his early years living in the monastery before he entered the service of the Bishop of Cambrai. Monks regularly fasted and were awakened during the night to meet in chapel for prayer. In many letters he declares that his physical inability to endure the rigors of a monastic life was one of the main reasons for his abandoning it. He also found the living conditions in the College in Paris too much for his delicate constitution. In spite of his ill health, however, he lived to the age of 70.

3. The term "Jubilee Year" is applied to a holy year—special privileges are granted by the Roman Catholic Church for a pilgrimage to Rome and a special indulgence is proclaimed. The tradition of making the pilgrimage to Rome, center of Christendom where St. Peter, the apostle and first bishop of Rome, is buried, is ages old. The first holy year was celebrated in 1300. Holy years occurred at fifty-year intervals, but in 1473 this period was reduced to twenty-five years. Occasionally, a special Jubilee Year is proclaimed, e.g., to celebrate the conclusion of the Second Vatican Council in 1966. In the Jubilee Year of 1975, the first American-born saint, Elizabeth Ann Seton, was canonized.

COMPREHENSION QUESTIONS

1. From what has Erasmus been suffering? Cite the Latin.

2. What does Erasmus contend would be his prime desire? Cite the Latin.

3. What does Erasmus hope to accomplish in Bologna?

4. What are Erasmus's fears with respect to that hope?

5. Explain how this letter corroborates the statement that Erasmus regularly found himself in financial need.

► EXERCISE 1

1. What is the case and use of *Arnolde* in line 1?

2. What is the case and use of *sēsquimēnsem* in line 1?

3. What is the case and use of *febrī nocturnā* in line 1?

4. Identify the case and use of *morbō* in line 2.

5. Identify the use of *commūnicem* in line 4.

6. What is the case and use of *mundum* in line 4?

7. What is the case and use of *mē* in line 7?

8. What is the case and use of *Bonōniae* in line 10?

9. What is the case and use of *annō iubileō* in line 11?

10. What is the case and use of *Rōmam* in line 11?

11. Identify the construction of *quibus cōnfectīs* (line 12).

12. What figure of speech is illustrated in lines 11–12 (*operam . . . vīsere*)?

13. To what does *illīc* in line 14 refer?

14. Identify the use of *ad . . . parandum* (line 15).

15. To what does *titulum* in line 15 refer?

ESSAY

Erasmus's letter to Arnold Bostius provides some insights into Erasmus's character. Discuss what the letter reveals about Erasmus.

Support your assertions with references drawn from throughout the passage. All Latin words must be copied or their line numbers provided, AND they must be translated or paraphrased closely enough so that it is clear that you understand the Latin. Direct your answer to the question; do not merely summarize the passage. Please write your essay on a separate piece of paper.

READING 2

In Paris, Erasmus earned additional income serving as a tutor to students at the university. His most important student was the young Englishman William Blount, who later succeeded his father as Lord Mountjoy. An adaptation of a letter from Erasmus to Mountjoy can be found in *Latin for the New Millennium*, Level 2, pp. 188–189. In the summer of 1499, Mountjoy brought his teacher over to England. While staying near Greenwich, Thomas More, whom Erasmus had met in London, paid him a visit. In the course of a walk in the country, More led them to Eltham Palace where the royal children lived at the time.

The following account of that visit with King Henry VII's children, and the circumstances under which it came about, comes from his work *A Catalogue* that contains Erasmus's reflections on his various publications. In this essay, Erasmus describes how he ended up composing a poem in praise of King Henry VII and England. Note how Erasmus was embarrassed when More presented Prince Henry, the later King Henry VIII, with a prepared composition, and Erasmus had to promise that he would write something after the visit. The essay gives a glimpse of the life of the princes and princesses as well as an insight into the relationship between Erasmus and Thomas More, with whom he maintained a lifelong friendship.

A ROYAL EMBARRASSMENT

ERASMUS ON HIS POEM TO HENRY VII

1   Ēdidimus ōlim carmen dē laudibus rēgis Henricī septimī et illīus līberōrum, nec nōn

ipsīus Britanniae. Is erat labor trīduī, et tamen labor, quod iam annōs aliquot nec legeram

nec scrīpseram ūllum carmen. Id partim pudor ā nōbīs extorsit, partim dolor. Pertrāxerat

mē Thomas Morus, quī tum mē in praediō Montiōiī agentem invīserat, ut animī causā in

5   proximum vīcum exspatiārēmur. Nam illīc ēducābantur omnēs līberī rēgiī, ūnō Arturō

exceptō, quī tum erat nātū maximus. Ubi ventum erat in aulam, convēnit tōta pompa,

nōn sōlum domūs illīus vērum etiam Montioiicae. Stābat in mediō Henricus annōs nātus

novem, iam tum indolem quandam rēgiam prae sē ferēns, hoc est animī celsitūdinem cum

singulārī quādam hūmānitāte coniūnctam.

NOTES AND VOCABULARY

Line 1:   **ēdō, ēdere, ēdidī, ēditum** to produce, publish

ōlim, *adv.* once

carmen, carminis, n. song, poem

nec nōn: translate "also"; note the LITOTES.

BY THE WAY

Henry VII was king of England at the time of the visit. He reigned from 1487 to 1509 and was succeeded by his son Henry (*Henricus*, line 7), who became Henry VIII and ruled until 1546. Henry VIII was a man of the Renaissance; he was interested in scholarly matters, wrote poetry, played musical instruments, and composed music among other pursuits. Henry VIII is also well known for his attempts to acquire a male heir and for establishing the Church of England.

Line 2: **trīduum, -ī,** n. period of three days

et tamen labor: translate "and labor indeed it was" (*lit.*, "and nevertheless labor").

aliquot several

Line 3: **partim,** *adv.* partly

pudor, pudōris, n. sense of shame

extorqueō, extorquēre, extorsī, extortum to twist out, extort

dolor, dolōris, m. resentment, annoyance, grief, pain

pertrahō, pertrahere, pertrāxī, pertractum to drag, entice, take by force

Line 4: **praedium, -ī,** n. estate

Montiōius = William Blount (Lord Mountjoy)

agentem: translate "living"; cf. *vītam agere*.

invīsō, invīsere, invīsī, invīsum to visit

animī causā: *lit.*, "for the sake of the mind, spirit"; translate "for amusement, recreation."

Line 5: **vīcus, -ī,** m. village

exspatior (1) to go for a walk

līberī, -ōrum, m. children

rēgius, -a, -um royal, regal

Line 6: **nātū maximus:** idiom for "oldest by birth"; in common English, "oldest"

ventum erat: impersonal passive; translate "we had come, we had arrived."

aula, -ae, f. palace, royal court

pompa, -ae, f. retinue

Line 7: **Montioiicae:** an adjective modifying an understood *domus* in the genitive singular

Henricus, -ī, m. Henry; the young Henry VIII

Lines 7–8: **annōs nātus novem:** *lit.*, "born for nine years"; translate "nine years old."

Line 8: **indolēs, indolis,** f. nature, character

prae sē: translate "openly."

hoc est = "that is"

celsitūdō, celsitūdinis, f. loftiness

Line 9: **singulāris, singulāre** remarkable

hūmānitās, hūmānitātis, f. kindness, culture

ERASMUS ON HIS POEM TO HENRY VII, CONTINUED

Ā dextrīs erat Margarēta, ūndecim fermē
10 annōs nāta, quae post nūpsit Jacōbō Scotōrum rēgī. Ā sinistrīs Marīa lūsitāns annōs nāta
quattuor. Nam Edmondus adhūc īnfāns in ulnīs gestābātur. Morus cum Arnoldō sodālī
salūtātō puerō Henricō, quō rēge nunc flōret Britannia, nesciōquid scrīptōrum obtulit.
Ego, quoniam nihil huiusmodī exspectābam, nihil habēns quod exhibērem, pollicitus sum
aliquō pactō meum ergā ipsum studium aliquandō dēclārātūrum. Interim subīrāscēbar
15 Morō quod nōn praemonuisset, et eō magis quod puer, epistoliō inter prandendum ad mē
missō, meum calamum prōvocāret. Abiī domum, ac vel invītīs Mūsīs, cum quibus iam
longum fuerat dīvortium, carmen intrā trīduum absolvī.

NOTES AND VOCABULARY

Line 9: **ā dextrīs** = "on the right"; cf. *ā sinistrīs,* line 10.
ferē, fermē, *adv.* almost, about

BY THE WAY

The verb *nūbō* is used in Latin to refer to a bride getting married, while *in mātrimōnium dō* is the idiom used when a man is marrying a woman.

Line 10: **nūbō, nūbere, nūpsī, nūptum** (+ *dat.*) to marry
Jacōbus = James IV, King of Scotland‡
ā sinistrīs: understand *esse.*
lūsitō (1) to play, frequentative of *lūdō*; translate *ā sinistrīs . . . quattuor*: "On the left was Maria, almost four years old, playing about . . . . "

Line 11: **nam:** the sentence begins with this word to give the reason why Edmund was not "playing about" like Mary, or possibly why he was not present at all.
adhūc, *adv.* still
ulna, -ae, f. arm; Edmund was still a babe in arms at this time and may not have been present at all.
gestō (1) to carry
sodālis, sodālis, m. friend

Lines 11–12: **Arnoldō sodālī salūtātō puerō Henricō:** translate "after saluting the boy Henry along with his friend Arnold."

Line 12: **quō rēge:** translate "under whom as king."
flōreō, flōrēre, flōruī to flourish
nesciōquis, nesciōquid someone or other; something or other; this word is frequently seen as two words, *nesciō quis* and *nesciō quid.*
scrīptum, -ī, n. composition
offerō, offerre, obtulī, oblātum to present, offer

Line 13:   **quoniam** since, because

huiusmodī = *hic* + *modus*; translate "of this sort."

exhibeō, exhibēre, exhibuī, exhibitum to produce; relative clause of purpose

Line 14:   **aliquō pactō** = *aliquot modō*, somehow, in some way

ergā, *prep.* + *acc.,* to

ipsum = Henry

studium: translate "literary work."

aliquandō, *adv.* (at) some time

dēclārō (1) to show; understand *mē* as the subject of *dēclārātūrum.*

subīrāscor, subīrāscī, subīrātus sum to be rather angry

BY THE WAY

Note how Erasmus carefully words his reaction to this embarrassing moment before the prince—e.g., the repetition in *nihil huiusmodī . . . nihil habēns* and then the use of the double indefinites, *aliquō . . . aliquandō.* The word after each *nihil* starts with "h"— almost as if he were gasping. Note the ANAPHORA.

Line 15:   **Morō:** dative with intransitive verbs

praemoneō, praemonēre, praemonuī, praemonitum to forewarn; understand *mē* as the direct object. *Praemonuisset* is subjunctive because the clause gives the reason in Erasmus's mind. English might require the awkward "as I thought to myself" to bring this thought across completely.

eō magis: translate "all the more."

epistolium, -ī, n. a note (*lit.,* "a little letter")

inter prandendum: gerund; *lit.,* "in the midst of lunching"; translate "while lunching, during lunch."

Line 16:   **calamus, -ī,** m. pen

prōvocō (1) to provoke, call out, challenge; subjunctive probably by attraction since there is no grammatical need for it here.

Line 17:   **dīvortium, -ī,** n. separation

absolvō, absolvere, absolvī, absolūtum to bring to completion, complete

TAKE NOTE

In 1502 King Henry VII of England arranged the marriage of his daughter Margaret Tudor (1489–1541) to James IV, King of Scotland (1473–1518), as a means of maintaining peace between the two countries. The wedding took place at Holyrood Castle, Edinburgh, Scotland, in August 1503. The peace between England and Scotland only lasted a decade as James marched on England and lost his life in the Battle of Flodden on September 9th, 1513. They were the grandparents of Mary, Queen of Scots, the most famous member of that family.

COMPREHENSION QUESTIONS

1. Why did Erasmus write this piece?

2. With whom did Thomas More and Erasmus visit?

3. How does Erasmus describe young Henry's demeanor? Cite the Latin.

4. How did Thomas More embarrass Erasmus?

5. How did Erasmus make amends to the prince? Cite the Latin.

6. Why does Erasmus mention the Muses in the last sentence?

▶ EXERCISE 1

1. What is the case and use of *annōs* in line 2?

2. Identify the case and use of *Arturō* in line 5.

3. Identify the case and use of *scrīptōrum* in line 12.

4. What verb sets up the indirect statement with *dēclārātūrum* in line 14?

5. Identify the case and use of *missō* in line 16.

6. Identify the case and use of *domum* in line 16.

7. Identify the case and use of *invītīs Mūsīs* in line 16.

ESSAY

Explain how Erasmus's encounter with young Prince Henry was not as auspicious as he would have liked. Discuss how Erasmus handled it.

Support your assertions with references drawn from throughout the passage. All Latin words must be copied or their line numbers provided, AND they must be translated or paraphrased closely enough so that it is clear that you understand the Latin. Direct your answer to the question; do not merely summarize the passage. Please write your essay on a separate piece of paper.

The statue of Sir Thomas More sculpted by L. Cubitt Bevis sits alongside Chelsea Old Church. More built a home in Chelsea beside the banks of the Thames River, along which he would travel to visit Henry VIII at Hampton Court or to attend to Lord Chancellor business at Westminster. More hosted his friend Erasmus at this home. While most of the church was destroyed by bombs in World War II, the chapel, which More renovated, survived the air raids.

READING 3

Faustus Andrelinus was an Italian poet who spent much of his life in France. He was a brilliant and popular lecturer at the University of Paris who was appointed Poet Laureate of France by Charles VIII in 1496. Andrelinus and Erasmus began a lasting friendship when Erasmus first arrived at the university. Andrelinus wrote this letter of praise for Erasmus's *Adagia* in June of 1500 as the work was being printed. Erasmus had the letter included in the book along with a dedication to Lord Mountjoy. Consider how Catullus's relationship with Cornelius Nepos (see Catullus Poem 1) is similar to the friendship Andrelinus and Erasmus share. Written while he was convalescing, Erasmus intended the *Adagia*, a collection of quotations from the Latin and Greek classics, to serve as a model for scholars wanting to compose elegant Latin.

MUTUAL ADMIRATION AND A LETTER OF PRAISE

THE POET ANDRELINUS TO ERASMUS

Faustus Andrelinus Poēta Regius Herasmō Suō S.

1   Lēgī ego nōn sine maximā voluptāte quae ad mē mīsistī Adagia, dulcissime Herasme.

Ea sunt meā quidem sententiā quae vel inimīcō iūdice probārī possint; adeō ūtile dulcī

commiscent, ut omnia certē suffrāgantium pūncta prōmereantur. Tam iucundās tamque

frūgiferās lūcubrātiōnēs ut in pūblicum prōferās nōn hortor modo, vērum etiam familiārī

5   quōdam iūre praecipiō, nē scīlicet videāris omnīnō vel sūdōrem tuum vel exspectātam

iamdiū ēditiōnem aspernārī. Neque timendī sunt hī quī aliēna scrīpta subsānnāre soleant.

Nōn dēbent nāsūtum quempiam rhīnocerōta formīdāre, cum nōn parvam sint et

oblectātiōnem et ūtilitātem allātūra.

Parīsiī, MCCCCC, xv Iūniī.

NOTES AND VOCABULARY

        suō: the use of the personal possessive adjective emphasizes the esteem with which the writer holds the recipient of his letter

        s. = *salutat* from *salutō* (1) to greet

Line 1:   **voluptās, voluptātis,** f. pleasure

        quae: refers to *Adagia* (neuter plural) in line 1.

Line 2:   **sententia, -ae,** f. opinion

        vel, *adv.* even

        iūdex, iūdicis, m. judge

        probō (1) to approve

        adeō, *adv.* in fact, to such an extent

        ūtile: the object of *commisceō*

        dulcī: ablative with *commisceō*

Line 3: **commisceō, commiscēre, commiscuī, commixtum** to mix (something in the accusative) with, mingle

suffrāgor (1) to vote for, support

pūnctum, -ī, n. vote

prōmereor, prōmerērī, prōmeritus sum to deserve, earn

Line 4: **frūgifer, -a, -um** fruitful, profitable

lūcubrātiō, lūcubrātiōnis, f. work by lamplight, nocturnal study; translate "literary compositions." The word with this meaning is a favorite with Erasmus and his correspondents.

in pūblicum prōferās: translate "you bring out into the public (i.e., you publish)."

nōn . . . modo, vērum etiam not only . . . but also; correlatives

Lines 4–5: **familiārī quōdam iūre:** *lit.*, "by a certain friendly right"; translate "on the basis of our friendship."

Line 5: **praecipiō, praecipere, praecēpī, praeceptum** to order, admonish

scīlicet, *adv.* of course

omnīnō, *adv.* altogether, at all, generally

sūdor, sūdōris, m. sweat; METAPHOR for "labor"

Line 6: **iamdiū:** translate "already for a long time"

aspernor (1) to disdain, despise, reject

aliēnus, -a, -um someone else's

subsānnō (1) to mock, deride, insult by derisive gestures

Line 7: **dēbent:** subject is *Adagia*

nāsūtus, -a, -um big-nosed

quispiam, quaepiam, quippiam some

formīdō (1) to fear; the poet Martial has preserved the proverbial saying "*nāsum rhīnocerōtis habēre,*" meaning "to turn up one's nose at everything."

Line 8: **oblectātiō, oblectātiōnis,** f. delight

afferō, afferre, attulī, allātum to contribute, bring about

BY THE WAY

Though Erasmus uses the Roman numeral for the day of the month in *xv Iūniī*, "15th of June," he renders it with the modern system of dating. Note also how the date is at the bottom of the letter instead of at the top where we are accustomed to seeing the date in modern correspondence.

COMPREHENSION QUESTIONS

1. What prompted Faustus to write this letter to Erasmus?

2. To what extent does Faustus praise the *Adagia*? Cite the Latin.

3. Faustus gives three variations in his advice to Erasmus on how to handle the critics. What is that advice? Cite the Latin.

4. What previous statement that he made does Faustus's final statement in this letter echo? Cite the Latin.

▶ EXERCISE 1

1. Identify the case and use of *Herasme* in line 1.

2. What is the antecedent of *ea* in line 2?

3. What type of clause is introduced by *ut* in line 3?

4. Identify the case and number of *suffrāgantium* in line 3.

5. What is the case and use of *iūre* in line 5?

6. Identify the construction of *timendī sunt* in line 6.

7. Identify the tense and mood of *soleant* in line 6.

8. What figure of speech is illustrated by *nōn parvam* in line 7?

9. Identify the form of *allātūra* in line 8.

10. Find three sets of correlatives in this passage. Cite the Latin and line numbers.

ESSAY

Catullus's Poem 1 to Cornelius Nepos and Andrelinus's letter to Erasmus exhibit many similarities in their content. In a well-organized essay compare and contrast the content of these two literary works.

Support your assertions with references drawn from throughout the two passages. All Latin words must be copied or their line numbers provided, AND they must be translated or paraphrased closely enough so that it is clear that you understand the Latin. Direct your answer to the question; do not merely summarize the passage. Please write your essay on a separate piece of paper.

The Collège de Sorbonne was founded in 1257 by Robert Sorbonne, chaplain to King Louis IX of France, as a constituent of the already famous University of Paris. The college matriculated twenty students and acquired a reputation for excellence. As the university quarter was quite compact, Erasmus would have been familiar with the Sorbonne. Though suppressed by the French Revolution, a theology school survived until 1882. At that time the college was secularized and the courtyard in the photograph was constructed in 1889. Since that time, the name Sorbonne has come to mean the University of Paris.

READING 4

This reading is excerpted from a letter Erasmus wrote in 1521 to his German friend Jodocus Jonas. A professor at the University of Erfurt, Jonas had asked Erasmus to tell him about John Colet, the founder of St. Paul's School, London. In a letter the month prior, Erasmus had tried to dissuade Jonas from aligning himself with Martin Luther. Erasmus's advice did not prevail, and the following year Jonas joined Luther and took on a position at the University of Wittenberg.

John Colet and Thomas More were Erasmus's two best friends in England. With Colet, Erasmus had traveled about England and made the customary pilgrimage to the shrine of Thomas à Becket at Canterbury Cathedral. Colet sought his friend's advice about the new school he was establishing in London when Erasmus made this third visit to England in 1510–1511. Tradition holds that Colet asked Erasmus to be the new school's founding High Master. The school Erasmus describes is a far cry from his own. In all likelihood, Erasmus learned his Latin in a class with as many as two hundred other boys. Books were quite rare in those days; the Gutenberg printing press dates from 1450, so Erasmus and his classmates would copy down the teacher's lecture. St. Paul's School now in a suburban setting continues to flourish and is considered one of the top ten secondary schools in the United Kingdom.

THE FOUNDING OF A SPECIAL SCHOOL

ERASMUS TO JODOCUS JONAS

1   Quicquid ē sacerdōtiīs redībat, id in ūsūs domesticōs oeconomō suō dispensandum
    relīquit; quod erat patrimōniī (erat autem amplissimum) ipse in piōs usūs distribuēbat.
    Nam patre dēfūnctō, cum ingentem pecūniae vim accēpisset ex hērēditāte, nē servāta
    gigneret in eō aliquid morbī, novam scholam exstrūxit in coemeteriō Sanctī Paulī, puerō
5   Iēsū sacram, opere magnificō. Adiēcit aedēs magnificās, in quibus agerent duo lūdī
    magistrī, quibus amplum salārium dēsignāvit, quō grātuītō docērent, sed sīc ūtī schola
    nōn capiat nisi certum numerum. Eam distīnxit in partēs quattuor. Prīmus ingressus habet
    ceu catechūmenōs. Nūllus autem admittitur nisi quī iam nōrit et legere et scrībere.

NOTES AND VOCABULARY

Line 1:   **sacerdōtium, -ī,** n. priestly office, living, income

redeō, redīre, rediī, redditum to return, come in (understand money or income as the
        subject); translate "whatever income came from the duties of his priestly offices" or simply
        "his priestly work."

oeconomus, -ī, m. steward, one who manages a household and its expenses‡

dispensō (1) to manage, distribute; understand *esse* with *dispensandum*; together they form a
        passive periphrastic.

Line 2:   **patrimōnium, -ī,** n. inheritance; translate *quod erat patrōmoniī* "his private means" (*lit.,* "that which belonged to his inheritance").

    distribuēbat: translate "in the habit of distributing" since the imperfect tense communicates continuous action.

Line 3:   **dēfungor, dēfungī, dēfūnctus sum** to die

    vīs, vim, vī, f. rare meaning here of "amount"

    hērēditās, hērēditātis, f. inheritance

    servāta: translate this nominative singular feminine participle with a conditional force: "if the money were hoarded."

Line 4:   **gignō, gignere, genuī, genitum** to produce

    morbus, -ī, m. disease, sickness (of the mind); a vice or fault

    exstruō, exstruere, exstrūxī, exstrūctum to build

    coemeterium, -ī, n. cemetery

Line 5:   **Iēsū:** dative

    adiciō, adicere, adiēcī, adiectum to add

    aedēs, aedium, f. pl. house

    agerent: translate "were to live."

Line 6:   **salārium, -ī,** n. salary‡

    dēsignō (1) to arrange

    grātuītō, *adv.* without pay

    quō . . . docērent: relative clause of purpose; *quō* for *ut* is generally reserved for purpose clauses containing a comparative adjective or adverb; in this type of purpose clause, *quō* would be an ablative of comparison.

    sīc ūtī: *lit.,* "thus that"; translate "with the limitation that." The school was to be limited to an enrollment of 153 boys.

BY THE WAY

John Colet equated the number of boys to be taught at his school to the total of 153 fish in the second miraculous catch (John 21:1–14). This event took place the morning after the Resurrection. The precision of this number has given rise to countless interpretations and discussions, but two theories now seem to prevail: Either John has some symbolism in mind but has hidden the significance well, or there is no significance.

Line 7:   **capiō, capere, cēpī, captum** to hold, contain

    distinguō, distinguere, distīnxī, distīnctum to separate, divide

    prīmus ingressus: *lit.,* "the first entrance"; translate "the first part, as you enter."

Line 8:   **ceu,** *adv.* as if

    catechūmenus, -ī, m. candidate under instruction for Confirmation; translate *ceu catechūmenōs* "what I might call catechumens." Erasmus speaks figuratively.‡

    nūllus = *nēmō*

    nōscō, nōscere, nōvī, nōtum to get to know; in the perfect tense, know. *Nōrit* is the syncopated form of *nōverit.*

ERASMUS TO JODOCUS JONAS, CONTINUED

Secunda pars habet eōs quōs hypodidascalus īnstituit. Tertia quōs superior ērudit.

10 Alteram ab alterā dīrimit vēlum quoddam, quod addūcitur ac dīdūcitur cum libet. Suprā cathedram praeceptōris sedet puer Iēsūs singulārī opere, docentis gestū, quem tōtus grex adiēns scholam ac relinquēns hymnō salūtat. Et imminet Patris faciēs dīcentis "Ipsum audīte": nam haec verba mē auctōre ascrīpsit. In postrēmō sacellum est, in quō licet rem dīvīnam facere. Tōta schola nūllōs habet angulōs aut sēcessūs, adeō ut nec cēnāculum sit

15 ūllum aut cubiculum. Puerīs singulīs suus est locus in gradibus paulātim ascendentibus, distīnctīs spatiīs. Quaeque classis habet sēdecim, et quī in suā classe praecellit, sellulam habet cēterīs paulō ēminentiōrem. Nec quōsvīs admittunt temerē, sed dēlectus fit indolis et ingeniōrum.

NOTES AND VOCABULARY

Line 9:   **hypodidascalus, -ī,** m. (Greek) Under Master. This title is still in use at St. Paul's.

īnstituō, īnstituere, īnstituī, īnstitūtum to instruct, teach

superior: *didascalus* is understood, *ergo,* High Master. This is still the proper title of the Head Master of St. Paul's.

ērudiō, ērudīre, ērudiī, ēruditum to teach

Line 10:   **alteram . . . alterā:** the one . . . the other

dīrimō, dīrimere, dīrēmī, dīremptum to separate

vēlum, -ī, n. curtain

addūcō, addūcere, addūxī, adductum to draw together

dīdūcō, dīdūcere, dīdūxī, dīductum to draw apart

libet, *impers.* it is pleasing, pleases

suprā, *prep. + acc.* above, beyond

STUDY TIP

The two compounds of *dūcō* in line 10 are antonyms and illustrate the power of learning prefixes for vocabulary building in both Latin and English. The prefix *ad–* means "to, toward" or, in terms of a curtain, "together." The prefix *dī–* is a variation on *dis–,* which means "apart."

Line 11:   **cathedra, -ae,** f. chair, bishop's throne‡

praeceptor, praeceptōris, m. teacher

singulārī opere: "a remarkable work"; Erasmus refers to a painting.

gestus, gestūs, m. attitude, manner; translate *docentis gestū,* "in the posture of one teaching."

grex, gregis, m. flock, company, throng; Erasmus uses *grex* as "flock" in referring to the students but also plays on the METAPHOR from the Christian scriptures of Christ as the good shepherd and humankind as his flock. In the framework of a religious school like St. Paul's, the teachers are the shepherds and the students, the flock. The whole undertaking is dedicated to God.

Line 12: **adeō, adīre, adiī, aditum** to go toward, approach

hymnus, -ī, m. hymn, religious song; *hymnō* is ablative of means.

immineō, imminēre to be above

Lines 12–13: **Ipsum audīte:** translate "(This is my Beloved Son,) hear him."

Line 13: **mē:** Note that Erasmus references himself. He had served as an advisor to Colet in the founding of the school and suggested the inscription, if not the whole painting of Christ as teacher.

auctor, auctōris, m. advisor

ascrībō, ascrībere, ascrīpsī, ascriptum to add (in writing)

postrēmus, -a, -um last

sacellum, -ī, n. shrine in classical Latin; chapel in later Latin

BY THE WAY

This command from God *Ipsum audīte* is found in the gospels of Matthew (18:2–5), Luke (9:35), and Mark (9:7). All three sources agree that a voice from a cloud spoke these words during the transfiguration of Christ, which took place while he was conversing with Moses and Elijah on the mountain, with Peter, James, and John as witnesses.

Lines 13–14: **rem dīvīnam facere:** translate "to hold divine services."

Line 14: **angulus, -ī,** m. corner

sēcessus, sēcessūs, m. alcove, room

adeō, *adv.* in fact, indeed, so

cēnāculum, -ī, n. dining room

Line 15: **cubiculum, -ī,** n. bedroom

singulī, -ae, -a one each, one at a time

puerīs singulīs: dative of possession

gradus, gradūs, m. step

paulātim, *adv.* gradually, little by little

Line 16: **distīnctīs spatiīs:** translate "separated by spaces."

classis, classis, f. class, fleet

praecellō, praecellere to excel

sellula, -ae, f. diminutive of *sella*, little bench, seat

Line 17: **ēminēns, ēminentis** lofty, raised

quīvīs, quaevīs, quodvīs anyone you like

temerē, *adv.* rashly, hastily; translate "without due consideration."

dēlectus, dēlectūs, m. choice, selection

indolēs, indolis, f. character

Lines 17–18: **indolis et ingeniōrum:** genitive of description; translate "based on character and talents."

Line 18: **ingenium, -ī,** n. intellect, talents

TAKE NOTE

1. English derives "economics" and "economy" from two Greek words, *oikos* (house) and *nomos* (law); *oikonomia* meant, literally, "the law of the house" and referred to household management emphasizing thrift and frugal expenditure. Using the words to refer to the wealth and resources of a country dates from the 1650s, and the idea of economics as a science began in 1835. The spelling of the words was affected by their passage through Latin (*oeconomicus*) and the French *economicque*.

2. The English word "salary" is derived from the Latin word for salt (*sāl, salis*, m.). The related word *salārium* originally referred to a soldier's allowance for the purchase of salt. By the mid-fourteenth century it had come to mean "compensation or payment for regular service" (through the Old French and Anglo-French *salarie*). Note that Erasmus's Latin reflects that fourteenth-century meaning.

3. The term *catechūmenus* is referenced in Galatians 6:6. Those seeking to become members of the Christian faith undertook a program of instruction in the doctrine of the church. As they studied this "catechism" with their teacher, known as a "catechist," they were known as catechumens. In the early church, catechumens, not yet initiated into the sacred mysteries of the Christian faith, gathered in the narthex of the church, the back of the nave at the entrance of the church, and were obliged to leave the service at the beginning of those rites. In current practice, catachumens usually are received into the Roman Catholic Church on Holy Saturday, the day prior to Easter. At this ceremony, the catachumens receive the sacraments of baptism, holy communion, and confirmation.

4. The term "cathedral" refers specifically to the church where the bishop's chair, *cathedra,* or throne, is located. Thus, a city would only have one Roman Catholic, Anglican, or Episcopalian cathedral. The cathedral in Rome is St. John Lateran, the church of the bishop of Rome, i.e., the Pope. St. Peter's Basilica, on the other hand, where the Pope often presides, is not the cathedral but is a very significant church nonetheless. St. Paul's School originally stood near London's famous St. Paul's Cathedral.

COMPREHENSION QUESTIONS

1. How did John Colet pay for the construction of St. Paul's? Cite the Latin.

2. Why did he decide to spend that money in this way? Cite the Latin.

3. Describe the physical layout of the school.

4. How would one recognize that this was a religious school?

5. If you were to have visited St. Paul's, how would you recognize those students who excelled?

6. What criteria were used in evaluating potential students for St. Paul's?

7. Is this a day school or a boarding school? Cite the Latin.

Václav Hollar, a native of Bohemia, spent much of his adult life in England where he served in the court of the Earl of Arundel. Hollar was a prolific illustrator whose corpus includes over 2,700 etchings that provide insight into life in the sixteenth century and reveal the breadth of Hollar's interests and contacts. He is noted for the set of illustrations he made for Homer's and Vergil's poems. In this etching, Hollar provides his day's equivalent of a photograph of John Colet's tomb. Note the piety implicit in the presence of the skulls and the skeleton—reminders of humankind's mortality.

▶ EXERCISE 1

1. What is the case and use of *oeconomō suō* in line 1?

2. What is the case and use of *patrimōniī* (line 2)?

3. Identify the construction of *nē . . . gigneret* in lines 3–4.

4. Identify the construction of *quō . . . docērent* in line 6.

5. Identify the case and use of *hymnō* in line 12.

6. Identify the construction of *mē auctōre* in line 13.

7. To whom does *mē auctōre* in line 13 refer?

8. Identify the construction of *ut . . . sit* in line 14.

9. Identify the construction of *distīnctīs spatiīs* in line 16.

10. What is the case and use of *cēterīs* (line 17)?

VOCABULARY BUILDER

One of the key ways to build your Latin vocabulary is to track synonyms. The Erasmus passages yield the following for you to master. What does each group of synonyms mean in English? Explain any differences between the synonyms in each pair.

> Group A
> cōgnōscō, cōgnōscere, cōgnōvī, cōgnitum
> nōscō, nōscere, nōvī, nōtum
>
> Group B
> īnstituō, īnstituere, īnstituī, īnstitūtum
> ērudiō, ērudīre, ērudīvī, ērudītum
>
> Group C
> dīrimō, dīrimere, dīrēmī, dīrēmptum
> distinguō, distinguere, distīnxī, distīnctum
>
> Group D
> dēliciae, -ārum, f. pl.
> oblectātiō, -ōnis, f.
>
> Group E
> cathedra, -ae, f.
> sellula, -ae, f.

ESSAY

John Colet's plans for St. Paul's School included some very specific features. Describe those features and explain, where possible, the reasoning behind them.

Support your assertions with references drawn from throughout the passage. All Latin words must be copied or their line numbers provided, AND they must be translated or paraphrased closely enough so that it is clear that you understand the Latin. Direct your answer to the question; do not merely summarize the passage. Please write your essay on a separate piece of paper.

John Colet brought Erasmus to Canterbury Cathedral, the center of Christianity in England where the missionary Augustine established the first Christian church in England in 597 CE. The shrine to Archbishop Thomas à Becket, who was murdered in the cathedral in 1170, has attracted pilgrims like Erasmus and Colet through the centuries. Such pilgrimages inspired Geoffrey Chaucer to compose *The Canterbury Tales*. The Archbishop of Canterbury oversees the Church of England, founded by Henry VIII.

READING 5

Thomas Linacre (1460–1520) was a pioneer in the study of Greek. As an assistant to Henry VII's ambassador to the Papal States, Linacre studied Greek and medicine. When he returned to Oxford, he was one of Erasmus's teachers of Greek. From about 1500 he lived in London and devoted himself to medicine, becoming one of the founders of the Royal College of Physicians in 1518.

Once again, Erasmus is plagued by ill-health and seeks Linacre's assistance in procuring some medicine for him. The letter, nonetheless, offers significant insight into Erasmus's thinking as we find him taking pleasure in the favorable reception of his translation of the New Testament from the original Greek into Latin. Since he had learned Greek from Linacre, the student took great pleasure in sharing this success with his teacher.

SELF-PRAISE AND NEED OF A PRESCRIPTION

ERASMUS TO THOMAS LINACRE, MD

Erasmus Roterodamus Thomae Linacrō Medicō Rēgiō S.D.

1　Tametsī novum nōn erat, tamen grātissimum fuit quod ex Morī līterīs cognōvī tē tam amīcē nōbīs favēre, licet immerentibus. Novum Testāmentum adeō placet ubīque doctīs, etiam ex ōrdine theologōrum, ut indoctī pudōre obticēscant. Febrīcula subitō oborta fuit in causā quōminus mē nāvigātiōnī commīserim, praesertim dissuādente medicō

5　Ghisbertō. Maiōrem in modum tē rogō ut pharmacum, quod, cum essem proximē Londīnī, sumpsī tē auctōre, dēnuō dēscrīptum mihi trānsmittās; nam puer schedulam apud pharmacopōlam relīquit. Erit id mihi grātissimum. Cētera ex Morō cognōscēs.

Bene valē.

Ex dīvō Audumarō. Nōnīs Jūliīs.

NOTES AND VOCABULARY

　　　　medicus, -ī, m. doctor
　　　　s.d. = *salūtem dīcit*
Line 1:　**tametsī,** *conj.* although
　　　　Morī = Sir Thomas More
　　　　līterīs: an alternate spelling for *litterīs*

REMINDER

The poetic plural is often called the EDITORIAL OR ROYAL "WE." For more information, consult p. 300 in the Vergil chapter.

STUDY TIP

Note how the conjunction *licet* in line 2 is a synonym of *tametsī* in line 1. *Cum* in a concessive clause also means "although." The conjunction *licet* is from the impersonal verb *licet, licuit, licitum est* "it is allowed."

Lines 1–2:	**quod . . . immerentibus** serves as the subject of *erat* and *fuit*.
Line 2:	**amīcē,** *adv.* translate "in so friendly a fashion."
	nōbīs = *mihi*
	faveō, favēre, fāvī, fautum (+ *dat.*) to be well disposed to
	licet, *conj.* although
	immerēns, immerentis undeserving; modifies *nōbīs* (line 2)
	Novum Testāmentum: Erasmus edited it in the original Greek and also translated it into a Latin more accurate than the Vulgate version.‡
	adeō, *adv.* indeed, to such an extent
	ubīque, *adv.* everywhere
	doctus, -a, -um learned, educated
Line 3:	**pudor, pudōris,** m. shame
	obticēscō, obticēscere, obticuī to grow silent
	febrīcula, -ae, f. slight fever; note the diminutive ending.
	oborior, oborīrī, obortus sum to spring up, occur
Lines 3–4:	**fuit in causā quōminus:** translate "was the reason why I did not . . . ."
Line 4:	**nāvigātiō, nāvigātiōnis,** f. sea voyage
	committō, committere, commīsī, commissum to entrust; subjunctive with verbs of hindering ("a fever kept me from . . .")
	praesertim, *adv.* especially
Line 5:	**Ghisbertō:** Ghisbert was a doctor at St. Omer and closely connected with the Abbey of St. Bertin, where Erasmus frequently stayed.
	maiōrem in modum: translate "please" (*lit.*, "in a rather grand manner").
	pharmacum, -ī, n. medicine; here translate "a prescription for the medicine."
	proximē, *adv.* most recently, lastly
Lines 5–6:	**ut . . . trānsmisttās:** *pharmacum . . . dēnuō dēscrīptum mihi trānsmittās* make up the *ut* clause that forms the object of the verb *rogō*.
Line 6:	**dēnuō,** *adv.* again
	dēscrībō, dēscrībere, dēscrīpsī, dēscrīptum to write again
	puer: servant of Erasmus
	schedula, -ae, f. prescription
Line 7:	**pharmacopōla, -ae,** f. pharmacy, drugstore
Line 9:	**dīvus** = *sanctus*
	Audumarus (Sanctus) = St. Omer
	nōnīs Iūliīs: translate "on the Nones of July"; an ablative of time when.

REMINDER

In the classical Latin calendar, the Kalends of the month are the first day, the Nones are the fifth or seventh day, and the Ides are the thirteenth or fifteenth. For more information on dates in Latin, see p. 69.

TAKE NOTE

The Renaissance evoked an interest not only in the ancient works of the Greeks and Romans but also in the early texts of Christianity including both the New Testament and the writings of the Church Fathers. Erasmus, one of the great scholars of humanism, the expression of Renaissance thinking in northern Europe, committed considerable energy to this endeavor of rediscovering and learning from the early Christian fathers and their writings. In 1505, he published Lorenzo Valla's *Annotātiōnēs* to the New Testament, the manuscript of which he had found in a monastery at Brussels. In the introduction to this work, Erasmus expressed the necessity of a new translation, a return to the original text, and respect for the literal sense. Among Erasmus's editions of the Church Fathers are nine volumes on Jerome and an edition of Hilary of Poitiers, Irenaeus of Lyons, Ambrose, Augustine, and Chrysostom. He did not live to finish his edition of Origen.

Latin for the New Millennium, Level 2, presented Lorenzo Valla's work on the Latin language, *Ēlegantiārum linguae Latīnae librī sex* ("Six Books Concerning Proper Uses of the Latin Language"). Erasmus read Valla's text and took his advice to heart. This led Erasmus to publish his *Adagia* and not to model his own Latin solely on Cicero's. His discovery of Valla's treatise on the New Testament stimulated Erasmus's interest in the original Greek of the gospels. Erasmus's translation of the New Testament served as one of the models for the King James Bible translation of 1611.

COMPREHENSION QUESTIONS

1. What is the relationship among More, Linacre, and Erasmus? Cite the Latin.

2. How has Erasmus's edition of the New Testament been received? Cite the Latin.

3. Why did Erasmus not sail to England at this time?

4. What happened to the medicine Linacre had prescribed for Erasmus?

▶ EXERCISE 1

1. What is the case and use of *tē* in line 1?

2. In line 3 what is the case and use of *pudōre*?

3. Identify the form, case, and use of *dissuādente* in line 4.

4. What type of clause does *cum* in line 5 introduce?

The medieval cathedral of St. Omer with its Gothic spires remains a important landmark of the town, recalling the bishop for whom the town is named. St. Omer was born to a distinguished family around 600 CE at Guldendal, Switzerland. He studied at the monastery of Luxeil near Besançon, France, where he acquired remarkable proficiency in the study of the scriptures. When King Dagobert requested the appointment of a bishop for the important city of Terouenne, the capital of the ancient territory of the Morini in Belgic Gaul, he was appointed and consecrated in 637. There, he strengthened the people's Christian faith and established two monasteries including St. Bertin, which Erasmus frequented. Today, the French town bears St. Omer's name.

5. What is the case and use of *Londīnī* in line 6?

6. What is the case and construction of *tē auctōre* (line 6)?

7. What is the mood and use of *trānsmittās* in line 6?

ESSAY

In his letter to Thomas Linacre, we hear Erasmus raise concerns presented in the previous letters in this chapter. Discuss those similarities and how they contribute to our understanding of Erasmus. Make sure your citations specifically note from which letter you are quoting (e.g., Reading 2, lines 3–4.)

Support your assertions with references drawn from throughout the readings. All Latin words must be copied or their line numbers provided, AND they must be translated or paraphrased closely enough so that it is clear that you understand the Latin. Direct your answer to the question; do not merely summarize the passage. Please write your essay on a separate piece of paper.

READING 6

Erasmus writes this letter to his good friend Thomas More from Antwerp in 1517. More, with Erasmus's letter of introduction, had befriended Peter Aegidius, also known as Peter Gilles, when he visited Antwerp on some diplomatic business. Aegidius served as city clerk and was both a humanist and a printer. The three humanists became fast friends.

Some attribute the font of More's *Utopia* to Aegidius. Erasmus oversaw the printing of the book's first edition at Louvain. More's preface is addressed to Aegidius and the book may well have been a New Year's present. Erasmus and Aegidius decided to have Antwerp's leading painter, Quentin Matsys, create a double portrait for them to give to their mutual friend Thomas More. The Renaissance nurtured the rise of the portrait as both a sign of one's status and, in this case, a memento of friendship.

A PORTRAIT OF LIFELONG FRIENDSHIP

ERASMUS TO THOMAS MORE

1 Kalendīs Māiī ventīs invalēscentibus iamque etiam adversīs mediō noctis scaphulā
   nauticā nōn sine perīculō in rupēs quāsdam ēiectī sumus, in Galliam haud procul ā
   Bolōniā. Mox ventī asperrimī, quōs reliquō itinere lītus vīcīnum nōbīs exasperāvit. Iī
   multōs apud nōs cynanchē et pleuritide occīdērunt et occīdunt.

5 Petrus Aegidius et ego pingimur in eādem tabulā: eam tibi dōnō brevī mittēmus. Vērum
   incidit incommodē quod reversus Petrum offenderim nesciōquō morbō graviter
   labōrantem, nec citrā perīculum; unde nec adhūc satis revaluit.

NOTES AND VOCABULARY

STUDY TIP

Verbs ending in *–scō* like *invalēscō* in line 1 indicate a sense of beginning. These verbs, called inceptives or inchoatives, are formed from other verbs by adding *–sco* to the present stem. All inceptive or inchoative verbs belong to the third conjugation. In addition to *invalēscō*, you have met *obticēscō* in the previous selection.

Line 1:   **Kalendīs Māiī:** in classical Latin "May" would have been an adjective, not a noun, i.e., *Kalendīs Māiīs*; ablative of time when.

invalēscō, invalēscere, invaluī to grow stronger

adversus, -a, -um (of winds) blowing against, contrary

mediō noctis: in classical Latin, "middle" would be an adjective, not a noun, i.e., *mediā nocte*.

scaphula, -ae, f. little boat; ablative of place from which

STUDY TIP

Be careful to distinguish between the noun *ventus, -ī,* m. wind and the fourth principal part of the verb *veniō, ventum.*

Line 2: **nauticus, -a, -um** nautical; translate *scaphulā nauticā* "a ship's boat."
ēiciō, ēicere, ēiēcī, ēiectum to put on shore
haud procul: translate "not far."

Line 3: **Bolōnia, -ae,** f. the modern Boulogne-sur-Mer, France
asper, -a, -um harsh, severe
ventī asperrimī: supply an understood *fiēbant.*
reliquō itinere: ablative of time; the ablative sometimes conveys duration of time within which.
lītus, lītoris, n. shore
vīcīnus, -a, -um neighboring
exasperō (1) to roughen, make harsh
iī: alternate plural of masculine nominative of *is, ea, id*

Line 4: **cynanchē, cynanchēs,** f. sore throat
pleurītis, pleurītidis, f. pleurisy
occīdō, occīdere, occīdī, occīsum to kill

BY THE WAY

Quinsy is an inflammation of the tonsils accompanied by the formation of pus while pleurisy is an inflammation of the double membrane (*pleura*) that lines the inside of the chest cavity and surrounds each of the lungs. These are Greek medical terms already Latinized in classical times; Roman medicine relied entirely on the Greeks.

Line 5: **pingō, pingere, pīnxī, pictum** to paint, color
tabula, -ae, f. portrait, painting
dōnō: dative of purpose; *lit.,* "for a gift"
brevī: supply an understood *tempore.*
vērum but

Line 6: **incidit . . . quod** = *accidit ut;* translate "it happened that." Although a subjunctive would normally follow *accidit ut* (substantive clause of result), Erasmus did not need to use one in this construction since the statement is a fact.
incommodē, *adv.* unfortunately
revertor, revertī, reversus sum to return
offendō, offendere, offendī, offensum to find

Line 7: **citrā,** *prep.* + *acc.,* short of; translate the phrase *nec citrā perīculum* "dangerously ill."
unde: translate "from it" (that is, the disease).
adhūc, *adv.* still
revalēscō, revalēscere, revaluī to recover

ERASMUS TO THOMAS MORE, CONTINUED

Nōs bellē valēbāmus
sed nesciōquō modō medicō vēnit in mentem ut purgandae bīlī iubēret mē pilulās aliquot
sūmere, et quod ille stultē suāsit, ego stultius fēcī. Iam pingī coeperam; vērum ā pharmacō
10   sūmptō cum ad pictōrem redīrem, negāvit eundem esse vultum. Dīlāta est igitur pictūra
in diēs aliquot, dōnec fiam paulō alacrior.... Scrībam fūsius intrā mēnsem, cum mittam
tabellam. Dē equō nihil adhūc audiō, atquī nunc fuisset ūsuī. Bene valē cum suāvissimā
coniuge līberīsque dulcissimīs. Petrus Aegidius ūnā cum Cornēliolā suā tē tuamque
plūrimum salvēre iubet.

NOTES AND VOCABULARY

Line 7:   **bellē,** *adv.* fairly

Lines 8–9:   The Latin here is difficult. In the main clause, *nesciōquō modō medicō vēnit in mentem, vēnit* is
an impersonal verb. Literally, *vēnit in mentem* means "it came into mind." *Medicō* is in the
dative case showing possession with *mentem.* This phrase, in turn, is taking a noun result
clause as its object (*ut . . . sūmere*). Translate "somehow it came into the doctor's mind to
order me to take some pills for purging bile."

            bīlis, -is, f. bile, poison

            purgandae bīlī: dative of purpose with a gerundive

            pilula, -ae, f. little ball, pill

REMINDER

Note how the diminutive of *pila,* "ball" becomes a "little ball," which then becomes a
"pill." For more on diminutives, consult p. 89.

Line 9:   **quod:** relative pronoun; understand *id* as its antecedent.

            stultē, *adv.* foolishly

            suādeō = *persuādeō*

Lines 9–10:   **ā pharmacō sūmptō:** translate "from having taken the medicine." This is an odd use of the
preposition.

Line 10:   **pictor, pictōris,** m. painter

            vultus, vultūs, m. complexion

            differō, differe, distulī, dīlātum to postpone

Line 11:   **in diēs aliquot:** translate "for some days."

            fiam: subjunctive in a temporal clause implying expectancy

            alacer, alacris, alacre healthy

            fūsē, *adv.* fully, copiously; in text as comparative.

            intrā, *prep. + acc.* within

Line 12: **tabella, -ae,** f. painting

equō: Erasmus references a very bad experience with this horse on a previous journey.

atquī and yet

fuisset: apodosis ("then" half) of a contrary to fact condition

ūsuī: dative of purpose; translate "of use."

bene valē: be well, be in good health

suāvis, suāve pleasant

REMINDER

The pluperfect subjunctive is used in the past contrary to fact condition. To review conditional statements, see p. 109.

Line 13: **ūnā,** *adv.* along

Cornēliolā: wife of Peter Gilles; note the diminutive.

tuam: supply *familiam.*

Line 14: **plūrimum,** *adv.* most of all; in today's English, this superlative seems strange with *salvēre.*

COMPREHENSION QUESTIONS

1. Summarize the problems Erasmus encountered on his landing in France.

2. Who will be depicted on the portrait?

3. To whom will the portrait be given as a gift?

4. Why has Erasmus not yet presented the portrait gift? Cite the Latin.

5. What is Erasmus's intent in the use of the superlatives in the last two sentences? Cite the Latin.

▶ EXERCISE 1

1. Identify the construction of *ventīs . . . adversīs* in line 1.

2. What is the case and use of *mediō* in line 1?

3. What is the case and use of *noctis* in line 1?

4. What is the case and use of *scaphulā* in line 1?

5. What is the case and use of *brevī* in line 5?

6. What is the form of *stultius* in line 9?

7. What is the tense, voice, and form of *pingī* in line 9?

8. Identify the construction of *pharmacō sūmptō* in lines 9–10.

9. In line 10, what is the mood, tense, and voice of *redīrem*?

10. What is the case and use of *paulō* in line 11?

LANGUAGE FACT

CUM CIRCUMSTANTIAL CLAUSES

There are four types of *cum* clauses, three of which you have already met in the Catullus chapter. Let's review those.

- ### *Cum* Temporal Clauses

  > *Scrībam ... cum mittam tabellam.*
  > "I will write [at that time] when I (will) send the painting."
  >> (Erasmus Letter to Thomas More, lines 11–12)

  The verb in *cum* temporal clauses is in the indicative and *cum* is translated as "when." *Cum* temporal clauses indicate the point of time at which the main action takes place.

- ### *Cum* Causal Clauses

  > *Cum Erasmus invalidus esset, Rōmam nōn iter fēcit.*
  > "Since Erasmus was ill, he did not travel to Rome."

  The verb in *cum* causal clauses is subjunctive and *cum* is translated as "since."

- ### *Cum* Concessive Clauses

  > *Cum Vergilius in pāgō quī Andes dīcitur nātus esset, Mantua tamen*
  >> *eum adrogāvit.*
  > "Although Vergil was born in a village called Andes, Mantua
  >> nevertheless claimed him as her own."

  In *cum* concessive clauses, the verb is in the subjunctive and *cum* translates with "although." In the main clause of sentence that contains a *cum* concessive clause, the word *tamen* is usually present or implied.

- ### *Cum* Circumstantial Clauses

  > *Cum ad pictōrem redīrem, negāvit eundem esse vultum.*
  >> (Erasmus Letter to Thomas More, line 10)
  > "When I returned to the painter, he denied that it was the
  >> same face."

  The fourth type of *cum* clause, mentioned briefly in the Catullus chapter, is called a circumstantial clause because it gives the circumstances under which the action of the main verb occurs. The clause affects that action. The *cum* in these clauses is translated "when." Circumstantial *cum* clauses contain a subjunctive mood verb. Note in the example how Erasmus's illness implied in the *cum* clause is the circumstance that affected the painter's response.

Caveat: Sometimes it is difficult to distinguish between a circumstantial clause and a causal one. Carefully consider the broader context of the clause to determine which use of the cum the author intended.

> *Animal, cum vulnerātum esset, in silvam fūgit.*
> "When the animal was wounded, it fled into the forest."

>> or

> "Because the animal was wounded, it fled into the forest."

▶ EXERCISE 3

Identify the type of *cum* clause and translate the complete sentence.

1. Nec ūlla incommoda fert haec valētūdo, etiam cum est prosperrima.

2. Cum essem proximē Londīnī, pharmacum tē auctōre sūmpsī.

3. Illī castīgātōrēs formīdāre nōn dēbent, cum nōn parvam sint ūtilitātem scrīpta allātūra.

4. Cum ingentem pecūniae vim accēpisset ex hērēditāte, novam scholam exstruxit.

5. Cum Novum Testāmentum meum indoctīs non placēret, doctīs tamen placuit.

6. Cum nūlla spēs victōriae esset, Gallī pācem petere coāctī sunt.

ESSAY

From this letter to Thomas More, we again see the themes of friendship and healthfulness. Construct a short essay that addresses these two themes.

Support your assertions with references drawn from throughout the passage. All Latin words must be copied or their line numbers provided, AND they must be translated or paraphrased closely enough so that it is clear that you understand the Latin. Direct your answer to the question; do not merely summarize the passage. Please write your essay on a separate piece of paper.

READING 7

John Fisher, the Bishop of Rochester, was another of Erasmus's English friends. Erasmus had tutored Fisher in Greek, and Fisher had found Erasmus a teaching position at Queens' College in Cambridge. Fisher, himself a scholar, had previously served as chancellor of the university. The tower at Queens' where Erasmus lived is still called Erasmus's tower.

John Fisher, like Thomas More, remained faithful to the Catholic faith and his conscience and thus refused to swear to Henry VIII's Acts of Succession and Supremacy. Their failure to do so was considered treasonous and saw them both executed in 1535.

Fisher's letter is another testament to the interconnectedness of the scholars of the day. He complains that More has not yet passed the German scholar Reuchlin's book on to him. Fisher praises Erasmus's translation of the New Testament but complains that, given some errors in the text, the printer must not have known Greek.

IN PRAISE OF YOUR TRANSLATION DESPITE PRINTER'S ERRORS

BISHOP JOHN FISHER TO ERASMUS

Episcopus Roffensis Dominō Erasmō S.D.

1 Quantum erat molestum audīre tuae nāvigātiōnis discrīmen, tantum sānē laetor quod salvus incolumisque ēvāserās. Iūstum quidem erat ut poenam dēpenderēs tantae properātiōnis tuae ā mē, apud quem tūtus ab omnī iactātiōne pelagī quiēscere potuistī. Liber ille quō mē scrībis ā Reuchlinō dōnātum, nōndum ad mē pervēnit. Morus tuus

5 epistolam ad mē mīsit, at librum adhūc suō mōre dētinet. Plūrimum tibi dēvincior, Erasme, quum ob alia tuae in mē hūmānitātis studia, tum quod tantopere annīteris ut Reuchlinus tam dīligenter meminerit meī.

NOTES AND VOCABULARY

REMINDER

Certain words (called "correlatives") when used as a pair such as *quantum* and *tantum* in line 1 possess a different meaning than when they are used singly. See p. 216 for more information about correlatives.

Line 1: **quantum . . . tantum:** translate "however much . . . so much."

molestus, -a, -um distressing

discrīmen, discrīminis, n. danger

sānē, *adv.* of course

laetor (1) to rejoice

Line 2: **salvus, -a, -um** safe, sound

incolumis, incolume safe, unharmed; translate the phrase *salvus incolumisque* "safe and sound."

ēvādō, ēvādere, ēvāsī, ēvāsum to escape

quidem, *adv.* indeed

dēpendō, dēpendere, dēpendī, dēpensum to pay

Line 3: **properātiō, properātiōnis,** f. hasty departure

apud, *prep.* + *acc.* at the house of . . .

iactātiō, iactātiōnis, f. tossing

pelagus, -ī, n. sea

quiēscō, quiēscere, quiēvī, quiētum to be quiet, rest

Line 4: **quō . . . scrībis:** translate "with which you . . . ."

Reuchlinus, -ī, m. Reuchlin‡

Morus: Sir Thomas More

BY THE WAY

Epistola, transliterated from the Greek, is an alternate spelling of *epistula*. Note that the letters of Paul in the New Testament are also called "epistles."

Line 5: **adhūc,** *adv.* up to now (this point), still

suō mōre: translate "according to his habit, in keeping with his habit, as is his custom."

dētineō, dētinēre, dētinuī, dētentum to keep back

plūrimum: used adverbially

dēvinciō, dēvincīre, dēvīnxī, dēvīnctum to lay under an obligation, bind

Line 6: **quum** = *cum*; *quum* forms part of a correlative with *tum* later in line 6; translate "not only . . . but also."

ob, *prep.* + *acc.* on account of

in: translate "for, toward."

hūmānitās, hūmānitātis, f. kindness, culture

studia: translate "proofs." The plural of abstract words like *studium* often implies "instances" of the quality or feeling contained in the word; e.g., *īrae* means "outbursts of anger."

tantopere, *adv.* so greatly

annītor, annītī, annīsus sum to strive, make an effort

Lines 6–7: **ut . . . meminerit:** result clause

Line 7: **meminī, meminisse** (+ *gen.*) to remember

BISHOP JOHN FISHER TO ERASMUS, CONTINUED

Eum animō tōtō complector; cui inter ea dōnec
perlēctō librō ad eum scrībam, significēs precor mē grātiās illī quantās animō cogitāre
possum, habēre maximās.

10 In Testāmentō Novō per tē ad commūnem omnium ūtilitātem trāductō nēmō quī
sapit offendī potest, quandō nōn sōlum innumera in eō loca tuā ēruditiōne plūrimum
illustrāstī, vērum etiam ūniversō operī integerrimam adhibuistī commentātiōne ut nunc
multō quam ante grātius multōque iūcundius ab ūnōquōque et lēgī et intelligī possit. At
vereor sānē nē crēbrius dormitārit impressor. Nam ipse mē exercitāns in lēctiōne Paulī
15 iuxtā praeceptiōnēs tuās, repperī saepenumerō dictiōnēs Graecās illum omīsisse, ac
nōnnunquam sententiās integrās. Tibi et istud dēbeō, Erasme, quod conicere aliquōusque
possum, ubi nōn omnīnō Latīnīs Graeca respondeant. Utinam aliquot mēnsēs licuisset
habēre tē praeceptōrem.

Fēlīx valē ex Roffā.

20 Discipulus tuus Io. Roffēnsis.

NOTES AND VOCABULARY

complector, complectī, complexus sum to care for

dōnec, *conj.* until

Lines 7–9: This sentence is complex. *Cui*, a connecting relative, is serving as the indirect object of
significēs; precor ("I beg") is taking an indirect command, with an understood *ut* (*[ut]*
significēs precor mē grātiās illī habēre maximās); the dative *illī* should be taken with *grātiās*
habēre maximās; grātiās is the antecedent of the clause *quantās animō cogitāre possum.*

Line 8: **perlegō, perlegere, perlēgī, perlēctum** to read through

significō (1) to make known, signify, mean; *significēs* introduces an indirect statement.

precor (1) to beg, pray, entreat

cogitō (1) to conceive

Line 10: **per tē:** translate "through your efforts."

ūtilitās, ūtilitātis, f. usefulness

trādūcō, trādūcere, trādūxī, trāductum to translate

Line 11: **sapiō, sapere, sapīvī** to be wise

offendō, offendere, offendī, offēnsum to meet with, be offensive to, upset

quandō, *conj.* when, since

ēruditiō, ēruditiōnis, f. learning, erudition

Line 12: **illustrō** (1) to shed light upon, illuminate

integer, integra, integrum honest, entire, whole; translate "very complete."

adhibeō, adhibēre, adhibuī, adhibitum to employ, show

commentātiō, commentātiōnis, f. commentary

Line 13: **grātius:** the adverb is one of a series of comparatives.

iūcundus, -a, -um pleasant

ūnusquisque, ūnaquaeque, ūnumquidque each one, everyone

Line 14: **vereor, verērī, veritus sum** to fear

crēber, crēbra, crēbrum frequent, numerous

dormitō (1) to sleep, doze; *dormitārit* is a perfect subjunctive after a verb of fearing.

impressor, impressōris, m. printer

exercitō (1) to practice, exercise

mē: reflexive use of the personal pronoun with the verb *exercitō*

lēctiō, lēctiōnis, f. reading

Line 15: **iuxtā,** *prep. + acc.* near, close to, in accordance with

praeceptiō, preceptiōnis, f. instruction

reperiō, reperīre, repperī, repertum to find

saepenumerō, *adv.* often

dictiō, dictiōnis, f. word

illum = *impressor*; accusative subject

omittō, omittere, omīsī, omissum to omit, let go, disregard, pass over

Line 16: **nōnnunquam,** *adv.* sometimes; note the LITOTES.

et: translate "also."

quod: refers to *istud* (line 16).

coniciō, conicere, coniēcī, coniectum to conjecture, guess, infer

aliquōūsque, *adv.* to some extent

Line 17: **omnīnō,** *adv.* at all

Latīnīs: supply *verbīs.*

Graeca: supply *verba.*

ubi . . . respondeant: temporal clause used as the protasis (the "if" half) of a present simple condition

respondeō, respondēre, respondī, respōnsum to agree with

utinam . . . licuisset: optative subjunctive; translate "if only it had been permitted . . ."

mēnsis, mēnsis, m. month

Line 18: **praeceptor, praeceptōris,** m. teacher

Line 19: **Roffā:** in ecclesiastical Latin, Rochester was called *Roffa.*

Line 20: **Io.** = Iohannes, Latin for John

Roffēnsis, Roffēnse of Roffa

TAKE NOTE

Johann Reuchlin was a distinguished scholar and humanist who was among the first to introduce the study of Hebrew and Greek into Germany. When he was handed over to the Inquisition as a heretic, Erasmus wrote letters in his defense. With the rise of the Reformation, Reuchlin's case was forgotten, and he was released from prison. Reuchlin sided with Martin Luther and the Reformation. He had tried unsuccessfully to persuade Erasmus to join him.

COMPREHENSION QUESTIONS

1. Explain how Fisher's home proved a refuge for Erasmus.
2. To what does Fisher attribute the dangers of Erasmus's journey? Cite the Latin.
3. What had Reuchlin given to Fisher?
4. How has Fisher characterized Thomas More? Cite the Latin.
5. Why does Fisher feel an obligation to Erasmus?
6. What does Fisher think of Reuchlin's book? Cite the Latin.
7. What does Fisher think of Erasmus's New Testament?
8. Of what does Fisher accuse the printer of the New Testament?
9. From what language and into what language did Erasmus translate the New Testament?
10. What does *discipulus tuus* in line 20 indicate?
11. With what in the text of the letter is that phrase connected?

▶ EXERCISE 1

1. What is the form and use of *audīre* in line 1?
2. What is the tense of *ēvāserās* in line 2?
3. Identify the form and use of *quiēscere* in line 3.
4. Identify the construction of *mē . . . dōnātum* in line 4.
5. In line 6, what is the case and use of *Erasme*?
6. What construction does *ut* in line 6 introduce?
7. Identify the case and use of *animō tōtō* in line 7.
8. Identify the construction of *perlēctō librō* in line 8.
9. What is the case and use of *illī* in line 8?
10. Identify the case and use of *tuā ēruditiōne* in line 11.
11. What is the case and use of *multō* in line 13?
12. In line 13, what is the case and use of *ūnōquōque*?
13. What is the case and use of *illum* in line 15?
14. In line 17, what is the case and use of *mēnsēs*?
15. What word is understood with *fēlīx* in line 19?

His hometown of Pforzheim, Germany, named its municipal museum for their celebrity theologian, Johannes Reuchlin, who joined Martin Luther as one of the leaders of the Reformation in Germany.

LANGUAGE FACT
SUBSTANTIVE CLAUSES OF RESULT

A substantive clause is one used as a noun usually in the nominative or accusative case. (Remember that the word "substantive" means "to stand in place of.") The clause and the main verb reinforce each other.

Substantive clauses of result denote the accomplishment of an effort. They are introduced by *ut* or *ut nōn* and follow the rules for the sequence of tenses.

> *Faciam ut praemium recipiās.*
> "I shall see to it that you receive a reward."

When substantive clauses are used as subjects, the main verb is impersonal and translated with the word "it." Such introductory verbs are *accidit* and *efficit*.

> *Accidit ut imperātor victus esset.*
> "It happened that the general had been defeated."

> *Accidit ut imperātor vulnerātus sit.*
> "It happens that the general was wounded."

Because *accidit* looks the same in the present and perfect tenses, check the tense of the subjunctive verb and apply the rules for the sequence of tenses to determine the tense in each example.

Neuter adjectives can also be followed by a substantive clause of result. These include *necesse*, *reliquum*, and *iustum*.

> *Necesse est ut nōn bellum in Gallōs gerātis.*
> "It is necessary that you do not wage war against the Gauls."

▶ EXERCISE 3

Translate each of the sentences.

1. Reliquum erat ut Cicero ōrātiōnem habēret.

2. Effēcit ut exercitus Galliam relinqueret.

3. Iūstum erat ut poenam dēpenderēs.

4. Incidit ut Petrum gravī morbō laborantem offenderim.

5. Faciam ut praemium recipiās.

ESSAY

Bishop Fisher's letter to Erasmus mentions several friends they share. Discuss what those relationships tell us about the nature of the academic community of that period.

Support your assertions with references drawn from throughout the passage. All Latin words must be copied or their line numbers provided, AND they must be translated or paraphrased closely enough so that it is clear that you understand the Latin. Direct your answer to the question; do not merely summarize the passage. Please write your essay on a separate piece of paper.

Hans Holbein the Younger (ca. 1497–1543) was one of the master portrait painters of his day. His clients included those on the continent as well as a roster of famous individuals of Tudor England whom he painted through his work as court painter for Henry VIII. Holbein's "Portrait of Erasmus of Rotterdam Writing" done in 1523 is now at the Louvre while a similar portrait is in Basle.

Rochester Castle recalls the bustle of castle and fortress building conducted by the Norman rulers of England. Its Norman tower-keep was built about 1127 by William of Corbeil, Archbishop of Canterbury, with the encouragement of Henry I. In 1215 King John besieged rebel nobles who holed up in the castle for two months until they were starved out. The castle stands at a strategic point by the Medway River and the London Road.

READING 8

The celebrated Italian humanist Petrarch (1304–1374) was devoted to maintaining the Latin literary tradition. His two heroes of Latin literature were Cicero and Vergil. An adaptation of his letter to Cicero is presented in *Latin for the Millennium,* Level 2, pp. 144–146. In his own writing, Petrarch consciously modeled his Latin on that of Cicero and he inspired a generational change that saw Ciceronian, that is classical, Latin replace the medieval Latin of the previous centuries. In his letter of praise to Vergil, Petrarch writes in dactylic hexameters, the meter of Vergil's *Aeneid.* Note that he refers to Cicero obliquely in the first line of the letter—*Latiae spēs altera linguae,* where he describes Vergil as "the other hope of the Latin language."

ODE TO VERGIL

PETRARCH
Meter: Dactylic Hexameter

1   Ēloquiī splendor, Latiae spēs altera linguae,

     clāre Marō, tantā quem fēlīx Mantua prōle

     Rōmānum genuisse decus per saecula gaudet,

     quis tē terrārum tractus, quotus arcet Avernī

5   circulus, an raucam cytharam tibi fuscus Apollō

     percutit, et nigrae contexunt verba sorōrēs?

NOTES AND VOCABULARY

Line 1:   **ēloquium, -ī,** n. diction, eloquence; objective genitive

          splendor, splendōris, m. brilliance, splendor; vocative

          Latius, -a, -um of Latium, Latin

          spēs, speī, f. hope, expectation

          altera: Petrarch here refers to Cicero.

Line 2:   **clārus, -a, -um** famous

          Marō = Publius Vergilius Marō

          quem: refers to *Marō.*

          fēlīx, fēlīcis happy, fortunate

          Mantua: Vergil was born in Andes, near Mantua in northern Italy.

          prōlēs, prōlis, f. offspring

Line 3:   **gignō, gignere, genuī, genitum** to bear, produce, give birth

          decus, decoris, n. glory, honor; an appositive to *quem*

          saeculum, -ī, n. age, generation

Line 4:   **quis:** commonly used as an interrogative adjective

terrārum = of the Earth

tractus, tractūs, m. region

quotus, -a, -um what number, how many

arceō, arcēre, arcuī, arcitum to enclose

Avernus, -ī, m. a lake near Cumae in Campania, south of Rome, said to be an entrance to the Underworld. Used here as METONYMY for the Underworld or in Petrarch's Christian idiom, Hell.

BY THE WAY

Quotus circulus probably refers to the nine circles of Hell described by Dante in his epic poem *The Inferno*. Vergil serves as Dante's guide to the Underworld.

Line 5:   **circulus, -ī,** m. circle; *quotus . . . circulus*: translate "which of the many circles of Hell." By using *quotus* Petrarch evokes the multiple circles of hell though the adjective modifies the singular *circulus*.

an or, perhaps

raucus, -a, -um hoarse, harsh

cythara, -ae, f. cithara; stringed instrument associated with Apollo

fuscus, -a, -um dark, swarthy

BY THE WAY

Petrarch's description of Apollo as *fuscus* is unusual since the god is associated with the sun and the color of gold. However, the adjective also can be used to describe a voice as "muffled," which would give the idea that he is far away and associated with the *nigrae . . . sorōrēs* in line 6.

Line 6:   **percutiō, percutere, percussī, percussum** to strike, strike through

niger, nigra, nigrum black, dark; *nigrae . . . sorōrēs* = the Fates

contexō, contexere, contexuī, contextum to interweave, devise, construct

PETRARCH ODE TO VERGIL, CONTINUED

> An pius Ēlysiam permulcēs carmine sylvam,
>
> Tartareumque Helicōna colis, pulcherrime vātum,
>
> et simul ūnanimus tēcum spatiātur Homērus?
>
> 10 Sōlivagīque canunt Phoebum per prāta poētae,
>
> Orpheus ac reliquī, nisi quōs violentia relēgat
>
> Mors propriā cōnscīta manū, saevīque ministrī
>
> obsequiō, quālis Lūcānum in fāta volentem
>
> impulit: arteriās medicō dedit ille cruentō
>
> 15 suppliciī graviōre metū mortisque pudendae:
>
> sīc sua Lūcrētium mors abstulit ac ferus ardor
>
> longē aliīs, ut fāma, locīs habitāre coēgit.

NOTES AND VOCABULARY

Line 7:   **pius, -a, -um** loyal, devoted; modifies the subject of *permulcēs*

Ēlysius, -a, -um Elysian, of or pertaining to Elysium, that region of the Underworld where the blessed souls reside.

permulceō, permulcēre, permulsī, permulsum to charm

sylva, -ae, f. forest, a variation of the more familiar *silva, -ae*

BY THE WAY

Petrarch employs a series of three adjectives—*fuscus Apollō* (line 5), *nigrae . . . sorōrēs* (line 6), and *Tartareumque Helicōna* (line 8)—that present an image of the gloomy Underworld. Note, also, how all three adjectives precede their nouns, thereby constituting both TRICOLON and parallel structure.

Line 8:   **Tartareus, -a, -um** infernal; having to do with Tartarus, a region of the Underworld

Helicōn, Helicōnis, m. Helicon, a mountain in Greece sacred to Apollo and the Muses; note the Greek accusative. See p. 258 in the Vergil chapter. Remember that an initial "h" is disregarded for the purpose of scansion.

colō, colere, coluī, cultum to inhabit, cultivate

pulcherrime: translate "most glorious."

vātīs, vātis, m. bard, poet

Line 9:   **simul,** *adv.* together

ūnanimus, -a, -um of one mind, in accord

spatior (1) to walk

Homērus, -ī, m. Homer, the celebrated Greek epic poet

Line 10:   **sōlivagus, -a, -um** wandering alone, not gregarious, solitary; modifies *Orpheus ac reliquī.*

canō, canere, cecinī, cantum to sing, sing about, celebrate

Phoebus, -ī, m. another name for Apollo, god of music and poetry. See also lines 5–6 above.

prātum, -ī, n. meadow

Line 11: **Orpheus, -ī,** m. Orpheus, Thracian singer who went to the Underworld to rescue his wife Eurydice

nisi quōs: translate "except those whom."

violentia: for the purpose of scansion, construe *–tia* as *–tya*.

relēgō (1) to send away, banish

Line 12: **proprius, -a, -um** one's own

consciscō, consciscere, conscīvī, conscītum to inflict; *conscīta* modifies *mors*. Translate "death inflicted (by their own hand)." Note the SYNCHESIS.

minister, ministrī, m. servant, agent, tool

Line 13: **obsequium, -ī,** n. obedience; refers to poets like Nero who were cruel in the exercise of their authority.

quālis, quāle like, of such a sort

Lūcānus, -ī, m. Lucan, Roman poet‡

volentem: present participle from *volō, velle, voluī*

REMINDER

As you learned in the Vergil chapter of this text, p. 292, do not confuse *volō* (1), "to fly," and *volō, velle, voluī*, "to wish, want."

Line 14: **impellō, impellere, impulī, impulsum** to strike

arteria, -ae, f. artery

cruentus, -a, -um bloody, cruel

Line 15: **supplicium, -ī,** n. punishment, execution

pudendus, -a, -um shameful

supliciī . . . pudendae: translate "because of a deeper fear of a shameful execution and death."

Line 16: **sua:** implies suicide

Lūcrētius, -ī, m. Roman poet and philosopher. For the purpose of scansion, construe *–ium* as *–yum*.‡

auferō, auferre, abstulī, ablatus to take away, steal

BY THE WAY

In the chapter on Vergil, p. 284, you learned about assimilation. In *auferō, auferre, abstulī, ablatus*, we see an example of vocalization. The "b" in the prefix *ab–* has been vocalized, i.e., changed to a vowel, the "u." That way, the compound *auferō* is distinguished from *afferō*, the compound of *ad– + ferō*.

ferus, -a, -um wild, savage

ardor, ardōris, m. passion

Line 17: **alius, -a, -um** different

ut fāma: translate "as rumor has it."

cōgō, cōgere, coēgī, coāctum to force, compel

TAKE NOTE

1. Lucan (39–65 CE) wrote an epic poem *Pharsālia* about the Civil Wars, and was forced to commit suicide by Nero, who was jealous of his poetic talents. Lucan was the nephew of Seneca the Younger, who also committed suicide in 65 when sentenced to death by Nero.

   Both Lucan and Seneca took their lives by opening their veins. The writer Petronius, upon falling out of favor, also committed suicide.

2. Lucretius (ca. 95–ca. 55 BCE) wrote *Dē rērum nātūrā* ("On the Nature of Things" or "On the Nature of the Universe"). The philosophical poet defends the beliefs of Epicureanism in six books of hexameter. The only extant biographical reference is found in Jerome (*Chronicle Olympiad* 171.3), whose few and savage words against the poet suggest that Lucretius was driven mad by a love potion, wrote his poetry between fits of insanity, and committed suicide. Note that Jerome's description might be negatively influenced by the early Christian rejection of Epicurean thought.

COMPREHENSION QUESTIONS

1. How does Petrarch communicate that Vergil is dead? Cite the Latin.

2. Why does Petrarch make reference to Apollo?

3. Cite a phrase that demonstrates Petrarch's praise for Vergil. Provide the Latin and its English translation.

4. Did Vergil suffer the same death as Lucan or Lucretius? Explain.

▶ EXERCISE 1

1. What does *altera* (line 1) modify?

2. What is the case of *clāre* in line 2?

3. What does *tantā* (line 2) modify?

4. What is the case and use of *decus* in line 3?

5. What is the subject of *permulcēs* (line 7)?

6. In line 8 what is the degree and case of *pulcherrime*?

7. What is the case and use of *vātum* in line 8?

8. In line 9 to whom does the *tē* in *tēcum* refer?

9. In line 12 what is the case and use of *manū*?

10. In line 14 to whom does *ille* refer?

11. What is the case and use of *mortis* (line 15)?

12. What is the tense of *abstulit* (line 16)?

ESSAY

Vergil is Petrarch's most beloved Roman poet. Discuss the ways Petrarch praises Vergil in his "Ode to Vergil."

Support your assertions with references drawn from throughout the passage. All Latin words must be copied or their line numbers provided, AND they must be translated or paraphrased closely enough so that it is clear that you understand the Latin. Direct your answer to the question; do not merely summarize the passage. Please write your essay on a separate piece of paper.

SCANSION

Scan the following lines.

> An pius Ēlysiam permulcēs carmine sylvam,
>
> Tartareumque Helicōna colis, pulcherrime vātum,
>
> et simul ūnanimus tēcum spatiātur Homērus?

When the Renaissance architect Vasari designed the colonnaded portico of the Uffizi Gallery, he left a series of empty niches intended to highlight the pure beauty of the architectural forms. In the nineteenth century, a humble Florentine printer, Vincenzo Batelli, rallied his fellow citizens encouraging them to fill the niches with statues of famous Florentines. Batelli created a list of political, artistic, and other geniuses, and a group of sculptors carved images of twenty-eight such individuals. The great Italian humanist and animator of the Italian Renaissance, Petrarch, crowned with the laurel looks heavenward in his no longer empty niche.

READING 9

John Parke (1754–1789) was born in Dover, Delaware. He received a BA degree from the College of Philadelphia and studied law for four years earning an MA also from the College of Philadelphia in the spring of 1775. He thereupon joined the Continental Army and, in the course of active military campaigns, he continued his project of translating classical Greek and Latin poetry. He continued this project after he resigned his colonel's commission. Parke is known today for the first American translation of the *Odes* and *Epodes* of Horace. He dedicated the volume to General George Washington.

Parke also composed some original Latin poems. This poem, a tribute to Horace, demonstrates Parke's knowledge of Horace's poetry and his own command of Latin.

AN ODE IN PRAISE OF HORACE

JOHN PARKE

Meter: Alcaic

1   Ferrī secundō mēns avet impetū,

     quā cygniformēs per liquidum aethera,

         tē, dīva, vim praebente, vātēs

            explicuit Venusīnus ālās,

5   sōlers modōrum seu puerum trucem

     cum mātre flāvā, seu caneret rosās

         et vīna, Cyrrhaeīs Hetruscum

            rīte beāns equitem sub antrīs.

NOTES AND VOCABULARY

Line 1:   **ferrī:** present passive infinitive of *ferō*.

         secundus, -a, -um favorable, fortunate, propitious

         aveō, avēre to desire, long for

         impetus, impetūs, m. rapid motion, rush, impulse, passion

BY THE WAY

The formal greeting *avē* as in *Avē, Caesar* "Hail, Caesar!" with which you are probably familiar is the imperative of *aveō*. Note that the verb has only two principal parts because it exists only in the present tense in Latin. Some sources trace its origin to the Punic language.

Line 2:   **quā,** *adv.* where

         cygniformis, cygniforme swan-shaped; modifies *ālās* in line 4.

         liquidus, -a, -um flowing, clear, pure

         aether, aetheris, m. air, sky, heaven

BY THE WAY

Parke is referring to Horace, *Odes* 2.20, where the poet transforms into a swan in front of his readers' eyes. The theme of *Odes* 2.20 is Horace's transcendence of death through his poetry. The swan is the bird of epic; the transformation is in preparation for the epic-like themes of the Roman Odes that directly follow on this poem. The phrase *per liquidum aethera* comes directly from *Odes* 2.20, line 2.

Line 3:   **vīs, vim, vī,** f. power, force

praebeō, praebēre, praebuī, praebitum to give, supply

vātēs: Horace likes to use the word *vātēs* for poet; originally, the word meant "prophet." In *Odes* 2.20 Horace refers to himself as a *biformis . . . vātēs* (lines 2–3).

Line 4:   **explicō** (1) to spread out, open

Venusīnus, -a, -um Venusian; modifies *vātēs*. Horace was born in Venusia in southern Italy.

Line 5:   **sōlers** = *sōllers, sōllertis* skilled, expert

modus, -ī, m. measure, meter, music; objective genitive with *solers*. Horace introduced many Greek meters to the Latin language.

trux, trucis savage, grim, wild; the "wild boy" is Cupid.

Lines 5–6:   **seu . . . seu** whether . . . or

BY THE WAY

The language in lines 5–6 may echo that in lines 5–7 of *Odes* 1.30; this poem is addressed to Venus, who is told to hasten to the shrine of Glycera, accompanied by her *fervidus . . . puer* (her "passionate son") = Cupid.

Line 6:   **flāvus, -a, -um** golden; the "golden mother" is Venus. *Flāvus* may refer to Venus's hair as many goddesses are described as "blond."

canō, canere, cecinī, cantus sing; *caneret* is a potential subjunctive.

Line 7:   **Cyrrhaesis, Cyrrhaese:** refers to Cyrrha, a city in Syria‡

Hetruscus, -a, -um Etruscan; modifies *equitem* in line 8. The *equitem Hetruscum* probably refers to Maecenas.

Lines 7–8:   **Cyrrhaeīs . . . sub antrīs:** possibly intended to recall *grātō . . . sub antrō* from *Odes* 1.5

BY THE WAY

Maecenas was a member of the equestrian class and, as you have read, was one of Augustus's closest advisors and the patron of several writers, including Horace. Maecenas's family was of Etruscan origin. To this day, we use "Maecenas" to refer to a wealthy and significant patron of the arts.

Line 8:   **rīte,** *adv.* rightly, properly

beō (1) to bless, gladden

eques, equitis, m. knight

antrum, -ī, n. cave

TAKE NOTE

The Syrians and others in the area worshipped a goddess, equivalent to the Greek Aphrodite and the Roman Venus, named Atargatis. The Syrians did not eat fish or doves because of how the goddess was born. According to their tradition, a huge egg fell into the Euphrates River. Fish rolled it to shore and doves hatched it. Out stepped Aphrodite (cf. Hyginus's *Fabulae*). The Cyrrhaesian caves, therefore, belong to Venus.

A swan spreads its wings for stunning effect.

COMPREHENSION QUESTIONS

1. With what reference does the poet let the reader know he is talking about Horace?

2. What does the poet use to connect Horace to the Muse? Cite the Latin.

3. In mentioning both Venus and Cupid, to what kind of poetry is the poet alluding? Explain.

▶ EXERCISE 1

1. What is the case and use of *impetū* in line 1?

2. What is the case and use of *tē* in line 3?

3. What is the case and use of *dīva* in line 3?

4. What is *beāns* (line 8) modifying?

ESSAY

Parke praises Horace implicitly by using diction (words, allusions, poetic features) that echoes the diction of Horace. In a short, well-organized essay, explain how Parke honors Horace without mentioning him by name in the poem itself.

Support your assertions with references drawn from throughout the passage. All Latin words must be copied or their line numbers provided, AND they must be translated or paraphrased closely enough so that it is clear that you understand the Latin. Direct your answer to the question; do not merely summarize the passage. Please write your essay on a separate piece of paper.

SCANSION

Name the meter and scan the following lines.

> sōlers modōrum seu puerum trucem
>
> cum mātre flāvā, seu caneret rosās
>
> > et vīna, Cyrrhaeīs Hetruscum
>
> > > rīte beāns equitem sub antrīs.

APPENDIX A

HISTORICAL TIMELINE

TIMELINE FOR THE LATE REPUBLIC AND AUGUSTAN PRINCIPATE IN ROME

Historical/ Political Events	Dates	Caesar	Catullus	Cicero	Vergil	Horace	Ovid
birth of Marius	157 BCE						
Third Punic War; destruction of Carthage	149–146 BCE						
birth of Sulla	138 BCE						
Tribunate of Tiberius Gracchus	133 BCE						
Tribunate of Gaius Gracchus	123–122 BCE						
	119 BCE			birth of Archias			
Marius serves consecutive terms as consul	107–101 BCE						
	106 BCE			birth of Cicero			
	102 BCE			Archias arrives in Rome			
birth of Cornelius Nepos	ca. 100 BCE	birth of Caesar					
	89 BCE			Archias granted Roman citizenship			

Historical/ Political Events	Dates	Caesar	Catullus	Cicero	Vergil	Horace	Ovid
Conflict between Marius and Sulla: First Civil War/ Social War	89–88 BCE						
Sulla elected to consulship	88 BCE						
death of Marius	86 BCE						
	84 BCE		birth of Catullus				
Golden Age of Roman Literature	83 BCE– 17 CE						
Sulla's dictatorship	82–80 BCE						
	80 BCE			*Prō Sextō Rosciō*			
death of Sulla	79 BCE						
	76 BCE			Cicero serves quaestor- ship in Sicily			
Spartacus and slave revolt	73–71 BCE						
Pompey and Crassus elected to consulship/ birth of Maecenas	70 BCE			*In Verrem*	birth of Vergil		
Pompey given *imperium* in war against Mithridates	69 BCE			Cicero's aedileship			
Pompey rids Mediterranean of pirates	67 BCE						
	67–66 BCE			Catiline's quaestor- ship in Africa			

Historical/ Political Events	Dates	Caesar	Catullus	Cicero	Vergil	Horace	Ovid
	66 BCE			Cicero's praetorship			
	65 BCE	Caesar's aedileship				birth of Horace	
Catilinarian conspiracy	63 BCE	Caesar elected *Pontifex Maximus*		Cicero's consulship; Catilinarian conspiracy			
Clodius Pulcher violates *Bona Dea* festival	62 BCE			Cicero defends Archias			
	61 BCE	Caesar's quaestorship in Hispania					
First Triumvirate formed: Caesar, Crassus, Pompey	60 BCE*	Caesar's consulship					
	58 BCE			Cicero exiled			
	57 BCE			Cicero recalled from exile, returns to Rome			
	57–56 BCE		Catullus serves quaestorship in Bithynia				
Caesar's conquest of Gaul	58–51 BCE	Caesar's conquest of Gaul					
	56 BCE			*Prō Caeliō*			
	54 BCE	death of Julia, Caesar's daughter	Year traditionally assigned for death of Catullus				

* Some date the First Triumvirate's formation in 59 BCE.

Historical/ Political Events	Dates	Caesar	Catullus	Cicero	Vergil	Horace	Ovid
Crassus dies in Parthia	53 BCE						
Pompey given sole consulship	52 BCE	Caesar defeats Gauls at Alesia					
Caesar crosses the Rubicon: Second Civil War	49 BCE	Caesar crosses the Rubicon: Second Civil War					
Battle of Pharsalus	48 BCE	Battle of Pharsalus					
	46 BCE	Caesar gains sole control of Rome					
	45 BCE			death of his daughter Tullia results in Cicero's turning to philosophy			
	44 BCE (March 15)	Caesar's Assassination		Cicero publishes *Philippics*		Horace studies in Athens	
Second Triumvirate formed: Antony, Lepidus, Octavian	43 BCE			Cicero assassinated			birth of Ovid
Defeat of Brutus and Cassius at Philippi: Third Civil War	42 BCE					Horace fought for losing side at Philippi	
	39–38 BCE				Vergil befriends Horace	Horace befriends Vergil, meets Maecenas	

Historical/ Political Events	Dates	Caesar	Catullus	Cicero	Vergil	Horace	Ovid
Asinius Pollio begins to build a library on slopes of Capitoline	39 BCE						
	37 BCE				*Eclogues* published		
	35 BCE					*Sermonēs* 1 published	
Octavian declares war on Antony	32 BCE						
Defeat of Antony and Cleopatra at the Battle of Actium	31 BCE						
	30 BCE				*Georgics* published	*Sermonēs* 2 published	
Augustus's Principate	27 BCE– 14 CE						
Octavian assumes the name Augustus/ Augustus proclaims that he has restored the Republic; Agrippa builds Pantheon	27 BCE						
Nepos dies	ca. 25 BCE						
Augustus given *tribūnicia potestās*/his nephew and heir Marcellus dies	23 BCE					*Odes* 1–3 published	
	19 BCE				death of Vergil in Brundisium		

Historical/ Political Events	Dates	Caesar	Catullus	Cicero	Vergil	Horace	Ovid
	17 BCE					*Carmen Saeculāre* published	*Amorēs* published
Augustus establishes permanent, professional army	13 BCE						
	1 BCE						*Ars amātōria* published
death of Maecenas	8 CE					death of Horace (and Maecenas)	Ovid exiled to Tomis/ *Metamorphōsēs* published
Roman defeat at Teutoberg Forest	9 CE						Ovid begins writing exilic poems
death of Augustus	14 CE						
Tiberius	14 CE–37 CE						
	17 CE						death of Ovid

APPENDIX B

LATIN METERS

The meters of Latin poetry derive from those of Greek poetry and are constructed on patterns of long and short syllables. The process of marking the quantity of syllables as long or short and of dividing lines of poetry into feet is called "scansion."

In Latin, every syllable contains a vowel or a diphthong; a diphthong combines two vowels that make a single sound, such as the "au" in *laudō* or the "ae" in *puellae*. A Latin word contains as many syllables as it has vowels or diphthongs. So, *me-a* has two syllables; *ā-ri-dō* has three. A syllable whose quantity is long (i.e., a long mark [macron] appears over the vowel) takes longer to read than a syllable whose quantity is short (i.e., the vowel lacks a macron). For this reason meters in classical poetry are referred to as "quantitative verse." It should be noted that when "u" is combined with "q" or "g," the "u" in "qu" and "gu" is not counted as a separate syllable. So, *e-quus* and *a-qua* have two syllables; *san-gui-ne-us* has four.

DETERMINATION OF A VOWEL'S LENGTH

- All diphthongs (ae, au, ei, eu, oe, and ui) are long **by nature**.

- All vowels marked by a macron are long **by nature**. For example, the "a" in the first syllable of *māter* is long by nature because a long mark (macron) appears over the vowel, while the "e" in the second syllable is short by nature because the vowel lacks a macron.

- Short vowels may become long **by position**. If a syllable containing a short vowel is followed by two of more consonants or a double consonant "x" (pronounced cs) or "z" (pronounced ds), the syllable is considered long by position. In a line of poetry, the short initial "i" of *in-gredior* becomes long by position because the vowel is followed by two consonants. This rule also applies to a short vowel followed by a single consonant in the final syllable of a word, where the short vowel is considered long if the next word begins with a consonant. For example, in the phrase *miser Catulle*, the "e" in *miser* becomes long by position because "r" is followed by a consonant ("C"), and the entire phrase should be marked ◡ – ◡ – ◡. The vowel syllable lengthened by position is still pronounced short.

TWO DOUBLE CONSONANT EXCEPTIONS

- If a short syllable is followed by a consonant cluster that involves a mute (b, c, d, g, p, t) and a liquid (l or r), the syllable may be long or short. The quantity of the syllable will depend on what the metrical scheme requires.

- For the purposes of scansion, the letter "h" should not be regarded as a consonant, and so will **not** lengthen the quality of a vowel if the word or syllable that precedes it ends in a single consonant. For example, in the phrase *quidquid hoc libellī*, the second syllable of *quidquid* is short because the "h" of *hoc* is disregarded. Similarly, in the word *anhēlitus*, the first syllable, "an" is marked or scanned as short because the "*an-*" is followed by an "h."

TWO RULES ABOUT WORDS ENDING IN A VOWEL OR *–M*

- **Elision**, derived from the Latin verb *elidō*, which means "to knock out" or "to eliminate," takes place when a vowel, diphthong, or a vowel plus "-m" ends one word and is followed by a word beginning with an "h," a vowel, or a diphthong. In the following examples, note how the final vowel or vowel plus "m" is "knocked out" and how the word is combined with the next word in which the initial "h" also may be eliminated. The opening words of line 8 of Catullus Poem 1, *quārē habē* illustrate the elimination of both a vowel ("e") and an "h": through elision *quārē habē* becomes *quārē habē* (*quārabe*). In line 554 of Vergil's *Aeneid* Book 2, the "*–um*" of *fātōrum* and *hic* come together to create *fātōrum hic* (*fātōric*). In line 268 of Book 10 of Ovid's *Metamorphōsēs,* the "-am" of *sociam* and the "ac-" of *adclīnātaque* produce the following elision: *sociam adclīnātatque* (*sociadclīnātaque*). The most common type of elision, however, involves eliminating the final vowel of one word before combining that word with the next word that begins with a vowel as in this example from *Aeneid* 1.424: *mōlīrī arcem* (*mōlīrarcem*).

- **Prodelision** is a special form of elision that applies to only two Latin words, *es* and *est*. When these verbs follow a word ending in a vowel, diphthong, or a vowel combined with "–m," the "e" of *es* or *est* is eliminated instead of the final vowel, diphthong, or the vowel combined with "–m" of the preceding word. For example, in line 281 of Ovid *Metamorphōsēs* Book 10, the "e" in *est* is eliminated in eliding *tepēre* and *est*: *tepēre est* (*teperest*). In line 13 of Catullus 51, the "e" in *est* is eliminated in eliding *molestum* and *est*: *molestumst*. Prodelision, then, is the opposite of elision in that it eliminates the vowel in *es* and *est* and retains the final vowel, diphthong, or vowel combined with "–m" of the preceding word.

METERS

In Latin poetry, a foot is a metrical unit of at least two syllables. Look at the following examples of feet, each of which has its own name.

dactyl	– ‿ ‿	— ‿ ‿ cētera
spondee	– –	— — rēgēs
trochee	– ‿	— ‿ mēnsa
iamb	‿ –	‿ — amō
choriamb	– ‿ ‿ –	— ‿ ‿ — sanguineae

- **Alcaic Stanza:** This meter is used in Horace's *Odes* more often than any other meter. It is named after Alcaeus, a Greek lyric poet from the island of Lesbos. The first two lines have the same meter. There is typically a diaeresis (‖), or pause and break between words, after the fifth syllable in the first two lines. John Parke uses this meter in his tribute to Horace.

  This is the metrical pattern of the Alcaic stanza:

  $$\times - \cup - - \, \| - \cup \cup - \cup \times$$
  $$\times - \cup - - \, \| - \cup \cup - \cup \times$$
  $$\times - \cup - - - \cup - \times$$
  $$- \cup \cup - \cup \cup - \cup - \times$$

  Example from Horace's *Ode* 1.9.21–24.

  $$\bar{} \quad \bar{} \cup \bar{} \bar{} \quad \bar{} \cup \cup - \cup \times$$
  nunc et latentis ‖ proditor intumō

  $$\bar{} \bar{} \quad \cup \bar{}\bar{} \quad \bar{} \cup \cup - \cup \times$$
  gratus puellae ‖ risus ab angulō

  $$\bar{} \quad \bar{} \quad \cup \bar{}\bar{} \quad \bar{} \cup \bar{} \times$$
  pignusque derēptum lacertīs

  $$\bar{} \quad \cup \cup \bar{} \quad \cup \cup \quad \bar{} \cup \bar{} \times$$
  aut digitō male pertinacī

- **Dactylic Hexameter.** The meter of ancient epic, the dactylic hexameter begins with Homer. Vergil used this meter in composing the *Aeneid*, and Ovid used the same meter for his epic, the *Metamorphōsēs*. The dactylic hexameter consists of six feet. A line of dactylic hexameter could be considered as consisting of a pattern of five consecutive feet made up of dactyls ($- \cup \cup$), with the sixth foot consisting of a long syllable and an anceps ($\times$). The *syllaba anceps* indicates that the final syllable can be either long or short. The first four feet allow a substitution of a spondee ($- -$); the fifth foot is nearly always a dactyl. The metrical pattern for a dactylic hexameter line, then, looks like this:

  $$\bar{} \cup \cup \mid \bar{} \cup \cup \mid \bar{} \cup \cup \mid \bar{} \cup \cup \mid \bar{} \cup \cup \mid \bar{} \times$$
  $$\quad 1 \qquad 2 \qquad 3 \qquad 4 \qquad 5 \qquad 6$$

  Several examples of the hexameter line follow; two lines are taken from Vergil and two from Ovid.

  $$\bar{} \quad \cup \cup \quad \bar{} \cup \cup \quad \bar{} \quad \bar{} \quad \bar{} \cup\cup \quad \bar{} \times$$
  sanguine|ae supe|rant un|dās; pars| cētera| pontum

  (Vergil *Aeneid* 2.207)

  $$\bar{} \cup \cup \quad \bar{} \cup \cup \quad \bar{} \quad \bar{} \cup \cup \quad \bar{} \cup \cup \quad \bar{} \times$$
  pōne le|git sinu|atque im|mēnsa vo| lūmine| terga

  (Vergil *Aeneid* 2.208)

$$\bar{} \quad \bar{} \quad \bar{} \quad \smile \smile \quad \bar{} \quad \smile \smile \quad \bar{} \quad \smile \smile \quad \bar{} \quad \times$$

aut, hōc| sī nimi|um (e)st, vel ad| ōscula| danda pa|tērēs?

(Ovid *Metamorphōsēs* 4.75)

$$\bar{} \quad \smile \quad \smile \quad \times \quad \bar{} \quad \bar{} \quad \bar{} \quad \bar{} \quad \smile \smile \quad \bar{} \quad \times$$

nec sumus| ingrā|tī: tibi| nōs dē|bēre fa|tēmur,

(Ovid *Metamorphōsēs* 4.76)

- **The Hendecasyllable.** This is the most common meter found in Poems 1–60 of Catullus. Consisting of eleven syllables that are organized in five feet, this meter largely is made up of trochees ($-\smile$), with the exception of the second foot, which is a dactyl ($-\smile\smile$). Substitutions are allowed in the final syllable of the line, which may be long or short, and in the first two syllables of the line, where either the first or second syllable of the foot may be long or short. The pattern of the line follows.

$$-\times \text{ or } \times - \mid - \smile \smile \mid - \smile \mid - \smile \mid - \times$$
$$1 \qquad\qquad 2 \qquad 3 \qquad 4 \qquad 5$$

The examples of the hendecasyllable provided below illustrate the three possible variations in the quantities in the first foot of the hendecasyllable (a spondee, a trochee, and an iamb).

$$\bar{} \quad \bar{} \quad \bar{} \quad \smile \smile \quad \bar{} \quad \smile \quad \bar{} \quad \smile \quad \bar{} \quad \times$$

vīvā|mus, mea| Lesbi| a, atque a|mēmus   (Poem 5.1)

$$\bar{}\smile \quad \bar{} \quad \smile \smile \quad \bar{} \quad \smile \quad \bar{} \quad \smile \quad \bar{} \quad \times$$

āri|dā modo| pūmi|ce expo| lītum   (Poem 1.2)

$$\smile \quad \bar{} \quad \bar{} \quad \smile \smile \quad \bar{} \quad \smile \quad \bar{} \smile \quad \bar{} \quad \times$$

meās| es se ali| quid pu|tāre| nūgās   (Poem 1.4)

In order to determine that you have not missed any elided syllables, count the syllables to make sure they total eleven, for that is what hendecasyllable means, "eleven syllables" (*hendeca* = eleven).

- **Limping Iambics.** Catullus composed roughly one-sixth of Poems 1–60 in limping iambics ($\smile -$). Perhaps the most well-known of the poems written in this meter is Poem 8, where Catullus warns Lesbia that she will be sorry when they are no longer a couple. This meter allows a spondee ($- -$) in place of an iamb ($\smile -$) in the first and third feet (but not the fifth). The last syllable of the line is an anceps. This is the pattern:

$$\times - \mid - - \mid \times - \mid - - \mid \smile - \mid - \times$$
$$1 \qquad 2 \qquad 3 \qquad 4 \qquad 5 \qquad 6$$

Two examples follow. Note that line 1 of Poem 8 is made up entirely of iambs except for the sixth foot, while line 3 admits spondees in both the first and third feet.

$$\breve{}\; - \;|\; \breve{}\; - \;|\; \breve{}\; - \;|\; \breve{}\; - \;|\; \breve{}\; - \;|\; - \times$$
miser| Catull|e dē|sinās| inep| tīre   (Poem 8.1)

$$- \;-\; \breve{}\;|\; -\; |\; -\;|\; -\; |\; \breve{}\; - \;|\; \breve{}\; - \;|\; - \times$$
fulsē|re quon|dam can|didī| tibi| sōlēs   (Poem 8.3)

- **Sapphic Stanza.** Sappho of Lesbos, a celebrated Greek poetess of the sixth century BCE, gives her name to the Sapphic meter, which she apparently invented. Catullus composed only two poems in this meter, which happen to be two of his most famous Lesbia poems, Poems 11 and 51. Horace, on the other hand, composed many of his lyric poems in the Sapphic meter. This meter forms a stanza or strophe of four lines each. The first three lines repeat the same pattern, in which the choriamb ($- \; \smile \; \smile \; -$) forms the centerpiece. Catullus allows either a short or a long in the fourth syllable of the line (marked below as an anceps), while in Horace's Sapphic stanzas that syllable is always long. The pattern for the first three lines is this:

$$- \; \smile \; - \; \times \;|\; - \; \smile \; \smile \; - \;|\; \smile \; - \; \times \;|$$

The fourth line of the stanza consists of five syllables that make up two feet, the first of which is a dactyl and the second of which may be either a spondee or a trochee. Since the last syllable may be long or short, this syllable is marked as an anceps: $- \; \smile \; \smile \;|\; - \; \times$. The first example that follows is taken from Catullus, Poem 51, the second from *Odes* 2.10.

$$- \smile - \quad \breve{} \quad - \smile \smile - \quad \smile \; - \quad \times$$
ōtium Ca| tulle tibi| molestum (e)st

$$- \smile - \quad - \quad - \quad \smile \; \smile - \quad \smile \; - \; \times$$
ōtiŏ exsul|tās nimium|que gestis

$$- \smile \quad - \quad - \; - \quad \smile \smile \; - \quad \smile - \times$$
ōti(um) et rē|gēs prius et| beātās

$$- \; \smile \; \breve{} \quad - \; \times$$
perdidit| urbēs   (Catullus 51.13–16)

$$- \smile - \quad - \quad - \quad \smile \; \smile - \quad \smile - \times$$
auream quis|quis medio|critatem

$$- \smile - \; - \quad \smile \; \smile \; - \quad \smile - \times$$
dīligit tū|tus caret ob|solētī

$$- \; \smile \; - \quad - \quad - \; \smile \; \smile \quad - \quad \smile \; - \quad \times$$
sordibus tēc| tī caret in| videndā

$$- \quad \smile \smile \quad - \; \times$$
sōbrius| aulā   (Horace *Odes* 2.10.5–8)

- **The First, the Fourth, and the Fifth Ascleapiadean.** The other four Horatian odes in this book are written in Ascelepiadeans, the First (*Odes* 3.30), the Fourth (*Odes* 1.5 and 1.23), and the Fifth (*Odes* 1.11). The First Asclepiadean does not consist of stanzas; every line follows this metrical scheme:

$$- - \mid - \cup \cup - \| - \cup \cup - \mid \cup \times$$

Note that the center is made up of a pair of choriambs ($- \cup \cup -$), with a strong pause, called a diaeresis and marked below with the double vertical lines, in the middle of the line. Horace reserved the First Asclepiadean for the first and last poems of his three books of *Odes* to indicate the structural integrity of this large collection of poems. Two examples of this meter taken from *Odes* 3.30 follow.

$$\overline{-} \quad \overline{-} \quad \overline{-} \quad \overset{\smile}{-}\overset{\smile}{-} \quad \overline{-} \quad \overline{-} \quad \overset{\smile}{-}\overset{\smile}{} \quad \overline{-} \quad \overset{\smile}{}\times$$
quaesi| tam meritīs || et mihi Del| phica

$$\overline{-} \quad \overline{-} \quad \overline{-} \quad \cup \cup - \quad \overline{-} \quad - \cup \cup \quad \overline{-} \quad \cup \times$$
laurō| cinge volēns || Melpomenē| comam.   (Horace *Odes* 3.30.15–16)

The first two lines of the Fourth Asclepiadean repeat the metrical scheme of the First Asclepiadean:

$$- - \mid - \cup \cup - \| - \cup \cup - \mid \cup \times$$

Lines three and four of the Fourth Asclepiadean are shortened versions of this pattern, in which the choriamb still occupies the center.

Line 3: $- - - \cup \cup - \times$

Line 4: $- - - \cup \cup - \cup \times$

The example that follows is taken from the final stanza of Horace's *Odes* 1.5.

$$\overline{-} \quad \overline{-} \quad \overline{-} \cup \cup - \quad \overline{-} \cup \cup - \cup \times$$
Intemp| tāta nitēs || mē tabulā sacer

$$\overline{-}\overline{-} \quad \overline{-} \quad \cup \cup - \quad \overline{-} \cup \cup - \cup \times$$
vōtī| vā pariēs || indicat ū vida

$$\overline{-} \quad \overline{-} \quad \overline{-} \cup \quad \cup - \times$$
suspendisse potentī

$$\overline{-}\overline{-} \quad \overline{-} \cup \quad \cup - \quad \cup \times$$
vestīmenta maris deō.   (Horace *Odes* 1.5.13–16)

As with the First Asclepiadean, every line of the Fifth Asclepiadean follows a single metrical scheme. The Fifth Asclepiadean differs from the First in that there are three choriambs instead of two. It is because of the number of choriambs that the Fifth Asclepiadean is sometimes referred to as the Greater Asclepiadean and the First is sometimes referred to as the Lesser Asclepiadean.

$$- - \mid - \cup \cup - \parallel - \cup \cup - \parallel - \cup \cup - \mid \cup \times$$

Odes 1.11 is one of three odes (along with 1.18 and 4.10) written in this meter.

Tū nē quaesieris ||(scīre nefās),|| quem mihi, quem tibi

fīnem dī dederint,|| Leuconoē,|| nec Babylōniōs
    (*Odes* 1.11.1–2)

APPENDIX C

FIGURES OF SPEECH/LITERARY TERMS

ALLITERATION

Consonants (usually initial) are repeated in a series of two or more words.

> **Example:** *receptōs ad sē sociōs sibi ascīscunt.* (Caesar *Dē bellō Gallicō* 1.5.17)

ANAPHORA

The same word or words are repeated for emphasis at the beginning of a series of phrases or clauses.

> **Example:** *dein mīlle altera, dein secunda centum, / deinde ūsque altera mīlle, deinde centum / dein, cum mīlia multa fēcerīmus.*
> (Catullus 5.8–10)

ANASTROPHE

An inversion of the usual order of words.

> **Example:** *mē circum.* (Vergil *Aeneid* 2.564)

ANTITHESIS

Two words that are opposites are juxtaposed.

> **Example:** *"ūna duōs" inquit "nox perdet amantēs . . . ."* (Ovid *Metamorphōsēs* 4.108)

APOSTROPHE

A sudden shift in addressee to some person or personified object, absent or present.

> **Example:** *sed obstinātā mente perfer, obdūrā. / vāle, puella. iam Catullus obdūrat.*
> (Catullus 8.11–12)

ASSONANCE

The same or similar vowel(s) are repeated in a series of two or more words.

> **Example:** *ars adeō latet arte suā.* (Ovid *Metamorphōsēs* 10.252)

ASYNDETON

The omission of a connective such as *et* or *–que*.

> **Example:** *Hī omnēs linguā, īnstitūtīs, lēgibus inter sē differunt.*
> (Caesar *Dē bellō Gallicō* 1.1.2–3)

CHIASMUS

An A-B-B-A arrangement of pairs of words.

Example: *Vīvāmus, mea Lesbia, atque amēmus.* (Catullus 5.1)

CLIMAX

High point of an argument following a CRESCENDO.

Example: *Polliceor hōc vōbīs, patrēs cōnscrīptī, tantam in nōbīs cōnsulibus fore dīligentiam, tantam in vōbīs auctōritātem, tantam in equitibus Rōmānīs virtūtem, tantam in omnibus bonīs cōnsēnsiōnem* **ut Catilīnae profectiōne omnia patefacta, illūstrāta, oppressa, vindicāta esse videātis.**
(Cicero *In Catilīnam* I 13.13–16)

CRESCENDO

Words or phrases are gradually built in order of importance or intensity.

Example: *Polliceor hōc vōbīs, patrēs cōnscrīptī, tantam in nōbīs cōnsulibus fore dīligentiam, tantam in vōbīs auctōritātem, tantam in equitibus Rōmānīs virtūtem, tantam in omnibus bonīs cōnsēnsiōnem ut Catilīnae profectiōne omnia patefacta, illūstrāta, oppressa, vindicāta esse videātis.*
(Cicero *In Catilīnam* I 13.13–16)

EDITORIAL "WE" (ROYAL "WE")

The use of a first person plural pronoun instead of a first person singular pronoun; often used to lend a certain authority to a passage.

Example: *Moriēmur inultae.* (Vergil *Aeneid* 4.659)

ELLIPSIS

The omission of one or more words needed to complete the thought in one or more clauses.

Example: *Gallia est omnis dīvīsa in partēs trēs, quārum ūnam incolunt Belgae.*
(Caesar *Dē bellō Gallicō* 1.1.1)

ENJAMBMENT (ALSO SPELLED ENJAMBEMENT)

In poetry, the running on of a phrase, clause, or sentence from one line to the next line or between two stanzas.

Example: *īnfōrmīs hiemēs redūcit / Iuppiter, īdem / submovet.* (Horace *Odes* 2.10.15–17)

EPANALEPSIS

The same word is repeated in the same sentence after other words have intervened. Sometimes the repeated word occurs at the beginning and end of the sentence.

Example: *Fāma . . . Fāma.* (Vergil *Aeneid* 4.173–174)

EPITHET

A descriptive word or phrase about a character, hero, or location with which the author emphasizes a characteristic of the person or place.

Example: *īnsignem pietāte virum.* (Vergil *Aeneid* 1.10)

EUPHEMISM

An expression in which something less offensive or disagreeable is substituted for something more offensive or disagreeable; often used in reference to death.

Example: *sub terrās ībit.* (Vergil *Aeneid* 4.654)

EXTENDED SIMILE

A comparison using a word for "like" or "as" that the author elaborates on for several lines.

Example: *Quālis apēs aestāte novā per flōrea rūra / exercet sub sōle labor, cum gentis adultōs / ēdūcunt fētūs, aut cum līquentia mella . . . .* (Vergil *Aeneid* 1.430–432)

GOLDEN LINE

A line of dactylic hexameter consisting of a pair of adjacent adjectives and a pair of adjacent nouns, with a verb separating the two pairs in an A B Verb A B arrangement of words.

Example: *et scelerāta ferō cōnsūmite vīscera morsū.* (Ovid *Metamorphōsēs* 4.113)

HENDIADYS

Two nouns linked by a conjunction, used instead of a noun and adjective, to express one idea.

Example: *bellī atque fortitūdinis.* (Caesar *Dē bellō Gallicō* 1.2.10–11)

HYPERBATON

The separation of words, often adjectives and nouns, that belong together.

Example: *paucīs, sī tibi dī favent, diēbus.* (Catullus 13.2)

HYPERBOLE

Great exaggeration for effect.

Example: *huius urbis atque adeō dē orbis terrārum exitiō cōgitent.* (Cicero *In Catilīnam* I 4.10)

HYSTERON PROTERON

A reversal of the natural order of events.

Example: *Referēs ergō haec et nuntius ībis.* (Vergil *Aeneid* 2.547)

IRONY

One thing is said but the opposite is meant.

Example: *Nōs autem, fortēs virī, satis facere reī pūblicae vidēmur, sī istīus (virī) furōrem ac tēla vītāmus.*
(Cicero *In Catilīnam* I 2.11–12)

LITOTES

Understatement; frequently found with a double negative.

Example: *neque abest suspiciō.* (Caesar *Dē bellō Gallicō* 1.4.7)

METAPHOR

A comparison made without using the words for "like" or "as."

Example: *quot ego tuās petitiōnēs ita coniectās ut vītārī posse nōn vidērentur parvā quādam dēclīnātiōne et, ut aiunt, corpore effūgī!*
(Cicero *In Catilīnam* I 6.3–4)

METONYMY

One word is used for another with which it is closely associated.

Example: *quōs ferrō trucīdārī oportēbat.* (Cicero *In Catilīnam* I 4.11)

ONOMATOPOEIA

The sound of the word(s) suggests the actual sound.

Example: *magnō miscērī murmure* (Vergil *Aeneid* 4.160)

OXYMORON

An expression using contradictory terms.

Example: *quōdam modō tacita loquitur.* (Cicero *In Catilīnam* I 7.20)

PARADOX

A statement appears self-contradictory but yet may be true or prove to be true.

Example: *quīque ā mē morte revellī / heu sōlā poterās, poteris nec morte revellī.*
(Ovid *Metamorphōsēs* 4.152–153)

PERSONIFICATION

Human qualities are attributed to inanimate objects.

Example: *Nunc tē patria, quae commūnis est parēns omnium nostrum, ōdit ac metuit et iam diū nihil tē iūdicat nisi dē parricīdiō suō cōgitāre: huius tū neque auctōritātem verēbere nec iūdicium sequere nec vim pertimēscēs?*
(Cicero *In Catilīnam* I 7.17–19)

POLYPTOTON

Words from the same base/root, but in a different form, appear in close proximity.

Example: *ars adeō latet artē suā.* (Ovid *Metamorphōsēs* 10.252)

POLYSYNDETON

Many connectives in close succession, where one or more could be omitted.

Example: *Rauracīs et Tulingīs et Latōbrigīs.* (Caesar *Dē bellō Gallicō* 1.5.14–15)

PRETERITION (PRAETERITIO)

To include precisely what a speaker indicates he will not discuss.

Example: *iam illa omittō neque enim sunt aut obscūra, aut nōn multa commissa.*
(Cicero *In Catilīnam* I 6.1)

RHETORICAL QUESTION

A question is asked but an answer is not expected.

Example: *quae tibi manet vīta? / quis nunc tē adibit? cui vidēbēris bella? / quem nunc
amābis? cūius esse dīcēris? / quem bāsiābis? cui labella mordēbis?*
(Catullus 8.15–18)

SIBILANCE

The repetition of the "s" sound; this is a form of ALLITERATION.

Example: *rūmōrēsque senum sevēriōrum / omnēs ūnius aestimēmus assis!*
(Catullus 5.2–3)

SIMILE

An analogy or comparison is made using a word for "like" or "as."

Example: *Ut saepe hominēs aegrī morbō gravī, cum aestū febrīque iactantur, sī
aquam gelidam bibērunt, prīmō relevātī videntur, deinde multō gravius
vehementiusque afflictantur, sīc hīc morbus quī est in rē pūblicā relevātus
istīus poenā vehementius reliquīs vīvīs ingravēscet.*
(Cicero *In Catilīnam* I 13.5–8)

SYNCHESIS (INTERLOCKED WORD ORDER)

An A-B-A-B arrangement of words.

Example: *saevae memorem Iūnōnis ob īram.* (Vergil *Aeneid* 1.4)

SYNECDOCHE

Part of something is used to represent the whole, or the whole is used to represent a part.

Example: *ā tēctīs urbis ac moenibus.* (Cicero *In Catilīnam* I 13.24)

TMESIS

The separation of the parts of a compound word into two distinct words.

Example: *bis medium amplexī, bis collō squāmea circum / terga datī superant*
capite et cervīcibus altīs.
　　(Vergil *Aeneid* 2.218–219)

TRANSFERRED EPITHET

A word describing an essential quality of one word that grammatically modifies a different word.

Example: *geminā teguntur / lūmina nocte.* (Catullus 51.11–12)

TRICOLON

Three words, phrases, or clauses arranged in a particular order; ANAPHORA often is used to mark off a set of three.

Example: *nōn feram, nōn patiar, nōn sinam.* (Cicero *In Catilīnam* I 5.28)

ZEUGMA

One word modifies or governs two or more words that are joined grammatically, but strictly is appropriate for only one of them.

Example: *"tua tē manus"* inquit *"amorque / perdidit, īnfēlīx!"*
　　(Ovid *Metamorphōsēs* 4.148–149)

GRAMMATICAL FORMS, PARADIGMS, AND SYNTAX

Forms taught in *Latin for the New Millennium*, Levels 1, 2, and 3, are listed in this appendix. In parentheses are poetic, syncopated (contracted), or alternate endings.

NOUNS

DECLENSIONS OF NOUNS

First Declension: *puella*

	Singular	Plural
Nominative	puella	puellae
Genitive	puellae	puellārum (-um)
Dative	puellae	puellīs*
Accusative	puellam	puellās
Ablative	puellā	puellīs*
Vocative	puella	puellae

*The nouns *dea* and *filia* have irregular dative and ablative plurals: *deābus* and *filiābus*.

Second Declension: *amīcus*

	Singular	Plural
Nominative	amīcus	amīcī
Genitive	amīcī	amīcōrum (-um)
Dative	amīcō	amīcīs
Accusative	amīcum	amīcōs
Ablative	amīcō	amīcīs
Vocative	amīce	amīcī

Second Declension: *puer*

	Singular	Plural
Nominative	puer	puerī
Genitive	puerī	puerōrum (-um)
Dative	puerō	puerīs
Accusative	puerum	puerōs
Ablative	puerō	puerīs
Vocative	puer	puerī

Second Declension: *ager*

	Singular	Plural
Nominative	ager	agrī
Genitive	agrī	agrōrum (-um)
Dative	agrō	agrīs
Accusative	agrum	agrōs
Ablative	agrō	agrīs
Vocative	ager	agrī

Second Declension: *vir*

	Singular	Plural
Nominative	vir	virī
Genitive	virī	virōrum (-um)
Dative	virō	virīs
Accusative	virum	virōs
Ablative	virō	virīs
Vocative	vir	virī

Second Declension Irregular Noun: *deus*

	Singular	Plural
Nominative	deus	deī (dī)
Genitive	deī	deōrum (-um)
Dative	deō	deīs (dis)
Accusative	deum	deōs
Ablative	deō	deīs (dis)
Vocative	—	deī, dī

Second Declension: *bellum*

	Singular	Plural
Nominative	bellum	bella
Genitive	bellī	bellōrum (-um)
Dative	bellō	bellīs
Accusative	bellum	bella
Ablative	bellō	bellīs
Vocative	bellum	bella

Third Declension
Masculine and Feminine Nouns: *sol*

	Singular	Plural
Nominative	sol	solēs
Genitive	solis	solum
Dative	solī	solibus
Accusative	solem	solēs
Ablative	sole	solibus
Vocative	sol	solēs

Third Declension Neuter Nouns: *tempus*

	Singular	Plural
Nominative	tempus	tempora
Genitive	temporis	temporum
Dative	temporī	temporibus
Accusative	tempus	tempora
Ablative	tempore	temporibus
Vocative	tempus	tempora

Third Declension Pure *I*-stem Nouns†: *īgnis*
Same Number of Syllables (Masculine and Feminine)

	Singular	Plural
Nominative	īgnis	īgnēs
Genitive	īgnis	īgnium
Dative	īgnī	īgnibus
Accusative	īgnem	īgnīs (-ēs)
Ablative	īgnī (-e)	īgnibus
Vocative	īgnis	īgnēs

† Pure *i*-stem nouns (those with the same number of syllables in the nominative and genitive singular except those with –*es* in the nominative singular and –*is* in the genitive singular) may have the ending –*im* in the accusative singular, in addition to the alternate endings shown in parentheses. Not all nouns allow for the same variations.

Third Declension Mixed *I*-stem Nouns‡: *urbs*
Different Number of Syllables (Masculine and Feminine)

	Singular	Plural
Nominative	urbs	urbēs
Genitive	urbis	urbium
Dative	urbī	urbibus
Accusative	urbem	urbēs (-īs)
Ablative	urbe	urbibus
Vocative	urbs	urbēs

‡In mixed *i*-stems (*i*-stems that are not pure *i*-stems), the singular has the same endings as a regular third-declension noun while the plural has the same endings as a pure *i*-stem noun.

Third Declension *I*-stem Nouns: *mare*
Neuters in -*al*, -*ar*, -*e* in the Nominative Singular

	Singular	Plural
Nominative	mare	maria
Genitive	maris	marium
Dative	marī	maribus
Accusative	mare	maria
Ablative	marī	maribus
Vocative	mare	maria

Third Declension
Irregular Mixed *I*-stem Noun: *vīs*

	Singular	Plural
Nominative	vīs	vīrēs
Genitive	—	vīrium
Dative	—	vīribus
Accusative	vim	vīrīs (-ēs)
Ablative	vī	vīribus
Vocative	vīs	vīrēs

Fourth Declension
Masculine and Feminine Nouns: *tumultus*

	Singular	Plural
Nominative	tumultus	tumultūs
Genitive	tumultūs	tumultuum
Dative	tumultuī	tumultibus
Accusative	tumultum	tumultūs
Ablative	tumultū	tumultibus
Vocative	tumultus	tumultūs

Fourth Declension Neuter Nouns: *cornū*

	Singular	Plural
Nominative	cornū	cornua
Genitive	cornūs	cornuum
Dative	cornū	cornibus
Accusative	cornū	cornua
Ablative	cornū	cornibus
Vocative	cornū	cornua

Fourth Declension Irregular Noun: *domus*

	Singular	Plural
Nominative	domus	domūs
Genitive	domūs	domuum (domōrum)
Dative	domuī (domō)	domibus
Accusative	domum	domōs (domūs)
Ablative	domō (domū)	domibus
Vocative	domus	domūs

Fifth Declension: *rēs*

	Singular	Plural
Nominative	rēs	rēs
Genitive	reī	rērum
Dative	reī	rēbus
Accusative	rem	rēs
Ablative	rē	rēbus
Vocative	rēs	rēs

Fifth Declension: *diēs*

	Singular	Plural
Nominative	diēs	diēs
Genitive	diēī	diērum
Dative	diēī	diēbus
Accusative	diem	diēs
Ablative	diē	diēbus
Vocative	diēs	diēs

ADJECTIVES

DECLENSIONS OF POSITIVE ADJECTIVES

Adjectives of the First and Second Declension: *durus*

	Singular			Plural		
	Masculine	**Feminine**	**Neuter**	**Masculine**	**Feminine**	**Neuter**
Nominative	dūrus	dūra	dūrum	dūrī	dūrae	dūra
Genitive	dūrī	dūrae	dūrī	dūrōrum	dūrārum	dūrōrum
Dative	dūrō	dūrae	dūrō	dūrīs	dūrīs	dūrīs
Accusative	dūrum	dūram	dūrum	dūrōs	dūrās	dūra
Ablative	dūrō	dūrā	dūrō	dūrīs	dūrīs	dūrīs
Vocative	dūre	dūra	dūrum	dūrī	dūrae	dūra

Adjectives of the First and Second Declension: *pulcher*

	Singular			Plural		
	Masculine	**Feminine**	**Neuter**	**Masculine**	**Feminine**	**Neuter**
Nominative	pulcher	pulchra	pulchrum	pulchrī	pulchrae	pulchra
Genitive	pulchrī	pulchrae	pulchrī	pulchrōrum	pulchrārum	pulchrōrum
Dative	pulchrō	pulchrae	pulchrō	pulchrīs	pulchrīs	pulchrīs
Accusative	pulchrum	pulchram	pulchrum	pulchrōs	pulchrās	pulchra
Ablative	pulchrō	pulchrā	pulchrō	pulchrīs	pulchrīs	pulchrīs
Vocative	pulcher	pulchra	pulchrum	pulchrī	pulchrae	pulchra

Adjectives of the First and Second Declension: *miser*

	Singular			Plural		
	Masculine	**Feminine**	**Neuter**	**Masculine**	**Feminine**	**Neuter**
Nominative	miser	misera	miserum	miserī	miserae	misera
Genitive	miserī	miserae	miserī	miserōrum	miserārum	miserōrum
Dative	miserō	miserae	miserō	miserīs	miserīs	miserīs
Accusative	miserum	miseram	miserum	miserōs	miserās	misera
Ablative	miserō	miserā	miserō	miserīs	miserīs	miserīs
Vocative	miser	misera	miserum	miserī	miserae	misera

Adjectives of the Third Declension with Three Nominative Endings**: *celeber*

	Singular			Plural		
	Masculine	**Feminine**	**Neuter**	**Masculine**	**Feminine**	**Neuter**
Nominative	celeber	celebris	celebre	celebrēs	celebrēs	celebria
Genitive	celebris	celebris	celebris	celebrium	celebrium	celebrium
Dative	celebrī	celebrī	celebrī	celebribus	celebribus	celebribus
Accusative	celebrem	celebrem	celebre	celebrīs (-ēs)	celebrīs (-ēs)	celebria
Ablative	celebrī	celebrī	celebrī	celebribus	celebribus	celebribus
Vocative	celeber	celebris	celebre	celebrēs	celebrēs	celebria

** Third-declension adjectives that have two or three forms are considered pure *i*-stem. Like pure *i*-stem nouns, they admit variations such as substituting –*ēs* instead of –*īs* for the masculine and feminine accusative plural.

Adjectives of the Third Declension with Two Nominative Endings: *fortis*

	Singular		Plural	
	Masculine/Feminine	**Neuter**	**Masculine/Feminine**	**Neuter**
Nominative	fortis	forte	fortēs	fortia
Genitive	fortis	fortis	fortium	fortium
Dative	fortī	fortī	fortibus	fortibus
Accusative	fortem	forte	fortīs (-ēs)	fortia
Ablative	fortī	fortī	fortibus	fortibus
Vocative	fortis	forte	fortēs	fortia

Adjectives of the Third Declension with One Nominative Ending: *fēlīx*

	Singular			Plural		
	Masculine	**Feminine**	**Neuter**	**Masculine**	**Feminine**	**Neuter**
Nominitive	fēlīx	fēlīx	fēlīx	fēlīcēs	fēlīcēs	fēlīcia
Genitive	fēlīcis	fēlīcis	fēlīcis	fēlīcium	fēlīcium	fēlīcium
Dative	fēlīcī	fēlīcī	fēlīcī	fēlīcibus	fēlīcibus	fēlīcibus
Accusative	fēlīcem	fēlīcem	fēlīx	fēlīcīs (-ēs)	fēlīcīs (-ēs)	fēlīcia
Ablative	fēlīcī	fēlīcī	fēlīcī	fēlīcibus	fēlīcibus	fēlīcibus
Vocative	fēlīx	fēlīx	fēlīx	fēlīcēs	fēlīcēs	fēlīcia

DECLENSIONS OF COMPARATIVE ADJECTIVES

Declension of Comparative Adjectives: *fortior*

	Singular		Plural	
	Masculine/Feminine	**Neuter**	**Masculine/Feminine**	**Neuter**
Nominative	fortior	fortius	fortiōrēs	fortiōra
Genitive	fortiōris	fortiōris	fortiōrum	fortiōrum
Dative	fortiōrī	fortiōrī	fortiōribus	fortiōribus
Accusative	fortiōrem	fortius	fortiōrēs (-īs)	fortiōra
Ablative	fortiōre (-ī)	fortiōre (-ī)	fortiōribus	fortiōribus
Vocative	fortior	fortius	fortiōrēs	fortiōra

Declension of Comparative Adjectives Ending in –*er*: *pulcher*

	Singular		Plural	
	Masculine/Feminine	**Neuter**	**Masculine/Feminine**	**Neuter**
Nominative	pulchrior	pulchrius	pulchriōrēs	pulchriōra
Genitive	pulchriōris	pulchriōris	pulchriōrum	pulchriōrum
Dative	pulchriōrī	pulchriōrī	pulchriōribus	pulchriōribus
Accusative	pulchriōrem	pulchrius	pulchriōrēs (-īs)	pulchriōra
Ablative	pulchriōre (-ī)	pulchriōre (-ī)	pulchriōribus	pulchriōribus
Vocative	pulchrior	pulchrior	pulchriōrēs	pulchriōra

Declension of Comparative Adjectives Ending in –er: *miser*

	Singular		Plural	
	Masculine/Feminine	**Neuter**	**Masculine/Feminine**	**Neuter**
Nominative	miserior	miserius	miseriōrēs	miseriōra
Genitive	miseriōris	miseriōris	miseriōrum	miseriōrum
Dative	miseriōrī	miseriōrī	miseriōribus	miseriōribus
Accusative	miseriōrem	miserius	miseriōrēs (-īs)	miseriōra
Ablative	miseriōre (-ī)	miseriōre	miseriōribus	miseriōribus
Vocative	miserior	miserior	miseriōrēs	miseriōra

DECLENSIONS OF SUPERLATIVE ADJECTIVES

Declension of Superlative Adjectives: *fortissimus*

Singular			
	Masculine	**Feminine**	**Neuter**
Nominative	fortissimus	fortissima	fortissimum
Genitive	fortissimī	fortissimae	fortissimī
Dative	fortissimō	fortissimae	fortissimō
Accusative	fortissimum	fortissimam	fortissimum
Ablative	fortissimō	fortissimā	fortissimō
Vocative	fortissime	fortissima	fortissimum

Plural			
	Masculine	**Feminine**	**Neuter**
Nominative	fortissimī	fortissimae	fortissima
Genitive	fortissimōrum	fortissimārum	fortissimōrum
Dative	fortissimīs	fortissimīs	fortissimīs
Accusative	fortissimōs	fortissimās	fortissima
Ablative	fortissimīs	fortissimīs	fortissimīs
Vocative	fortissimī	fortissimae	fortissima

Declension of Superlative Adjectives ending in –er: *pulcherrimus*

Singular

	Masculine	Feminine	Neuter
Nominative	pulcherrimus	pulcherrima	pulcherrimum
Genitive	pulcherrimī	pulcherrimae	pulcherrimī
Dative	pulcherrimō	pulcherrimae	pulcherrimō
Accusative	pulcherrimum	pulcherrimam	pulcherrimum
Ablative	pulcherrimō	pulcherrimā	pulcherrimō
Vocative	pulcherrime	pulcherrima	pulcherrimum

Plural

	Masculine	Feminine	Neuter
Nominative	pulcherrimī	pulcherrimae	pulcherrima
Genitive	pulcherrimōrum	pulcherrimārum	pulcherrimōrum
Dative	pulcherrimīs	pulcherrimīs	pulcherrimīs
Accusative	pulcherrimōs	pulcherrimās	pulcherrima
Ablative	pulcherrimīs	pulcherrimīs	pulcherrimīs
Vocative	pulcherrimī	pulcherrimae	pulcherrima

Declension of Superlative Adjectives ending in –lis††: *facillimus*

Singular

	Masculine	Feminine	Neuter
Nominative	facillimus	facillima	facillimum
Genitive	facillimī	facillimae	facillimī
Dative	facillimō	facillimae	facillimō
Accusative	facillimum	facillimam	facillimum
Ablative	facillimō	facillimā	facillimō
Vocative	facillime	facillima	facillimum

Plural

	Masculine	Feminine	Neuter
Nominative	facillimī	facillimae	facillima
Genitive	facillimōrum	facillimārum	facillimōrum
Dative	facillimīs	facillimīs	facillimīs
Accusative	facillimōs	facillimās	facillima
Ablative	facillimīs	facillimīs	facillimīs
Vocative	facillimī	facillimae	facillima

††Only the Latin adjectives *facilis, difficilis, similis, dissimilis, gracilis,*
and *humilis* are formed in this way in the superlative.

IRREGULAR COMPARATIVE AND SUPERLATIVE DEGREES OF ADJECTIVES

Common Irregular Comparatives and Superlatives

Positive degree	Comparative degree	Superlative degree
bonus, a, um – good	melior, melius – better	optimus, a, um – best
malus, a, um – bad	peior, peius – worse	pessimus, a, um – worst
magnus, a, um – great	maior, maius – greater	maximus, a, um – greatest
multus, a, um – much	plūs (neuter noun) – more	plūrimus, a, um – most
multī, ae, a – many	plūrēs, plūra – more	plūrimī, ae, a – most
parvus, a, um – small	minor, minus – smaller	minimus, a, um – smallest
superus, a, um – upper, higher	superior, superius – upper, higher	supremus, a, um – uppermost, highest

Declension of *plūs, plūris*‡‡

	Singular	Plural	
	Neuter	Masculine/Feminine	Neuter
Nominative	plūs	plūrēs	plūra
Genitive	plūris	plūrium	plūrium
Dative	—	plūribus	plūribus
Accusative	plūs	plūrēs (-īs)	plūra
Ablative	plūre	plūribus	plūribus
Vocative	—	plūrēs	plūra

‡‡The singular of *plūs, plūris* is a neuter noun while in the plural it is an adjective.

Adjectives with a Genitive in –*īus* and Dative in –*ī*

1. alius, alia, aliud – another, other
2. alter, altera, alterum – the other (of two)
3. neuter, neutra, neutrum – neither, none (of two)
4. nūllus, nūlla, nūllum – none
5. sōlus, sōla, sōlum – alone, only
6. tōtus, tōta, tōtum – whole, entire
7. ūllus, ūlla, ūllum – any
8. ūnus, ūna, ūnum – one
9. uter, utra, utrum – who, which (of two)

Declension of *sōlus****

	Singular			Plural		
	Masculine	**Feminine**	**Neuter**	**Masculine**	**Feminine**	**Neuter**
Nominative	sōlus	sōla	sōlum	sōlī	sōlae	sōla
Genitive	sōlīus	sōlīus	sōlīus	sōlōrum	sōlārum	sōlōrum
Dative	sōlī	sōlī	sōlī	sōlīs	sōlīs	sōlīs
Accusative	sōlum	sōlam	sōlum	sōlōs	sōlās	sōla
Ablative	sōlō	sōlā	sōlō	sōlīs	sōlīs	sōlīs
Vocative	sōle	sōla	sōlum	sōlī	sōlae	sōla

(masculine vocative rarely seen)

****Alius, ūnus, tōtus, nūllus,* and *ūllus* decline like *sōlus,* and *uter* declines like *neuter.*

Declension of *alter*

	Singular			Plural		
	Masculine	**Feminine**	**Neuter**	**Masculine**	**Feminine**	**Neuter**
Nominative	alter	altera	alterum	alterī	alterae	altera
Genitive	alterīus	alterīus	alterīus	alterōrum	alterārum	alterōrum
Dative	alterī	alterī	alterī	alterīs	alterīs	alterīs
Accusative	alterum	alteram	alterum	alterōs	alterās	altera
Ablative	alterō	alterā	alterō	alterīs	alterīs	alterīs
Vocative	alter	altera	alterum	alterī	alterae	altera

Declension of *neuter****

	Singular			Plural		
	Masculine	**Feminine**	**Neuter**	**Masculine**	**Feminine**	**Neuter**
Nominative	neuter	neutra	neutrum	neutrī	neutrae	neutra
Genitive	neutrīus	neutrīus	neutrīus	neutrōrum	neutrārum	neutrōrum
Dative	neutrī	neutrī	neutrī	neutrīs	neutrīs	neutrīs
Accusative	neutrum	neutram	neutrum	neutrōs	neutrās	neutra
Ablative	neutrō	neutrā	neutrō	neutrīs	neutrīs	neutrīs
Vocative	neuter	neutra	neutrum	neutrī	neutrae	neutra

****Alius, ūnus, tōtus, nūllus,* and *ūllus* decline like *sōlus,* and *uter* declines like *neuter.*

DECLENSIONS OF PARTICIPLES AND THE GERUNDIVE

Declension of the Present Active Participle

	Singular			Plural		
	Masculine	Feminine	Neuter	Masculine	Feminine	Neuter
Nominative	parāns	parāns	parāns	parantēs	parantēs	parantia
Genitive	parantis	parantis	parantis	parantium	parantium	parantium
Dative	parantī	parantī	parantī	parantibus	parantibus	parantibus
Accusative	parantem	parantem	parāns	parantīs (-ēs)	parantīs (-ēs)	parantia
Ablative	parantī (-e)	parantī (-e)	parantī (-e)	parantibus	parantibus	parantibus
Vocative	parāns	parāns	parāns	parantēs	parantēs	parantia

Declension of the Perfect Passive Participle

	Singular			Plural		
	Masculine	Feminine	Neuter	Masculine	Feminine	Neuter
Nominative	parātus	parāta	parātum	parātī	parātae	parāta
Genitive	parātī	parātae	parātī	parātōrum	parātārum	parātōrum
Dative	parātō	parātae	parātō	parātīs	parātīs	parātīs
Accusative	parātum	parātam	parātum	parātōs	parātās	parāta
Ablative	parātō	parātā	parātō	parātīs	parātīs	parātīs
Vocative	parāte	parāta	parātum	parātī	parātae	parāta

Declension of the Future Active Participle

	Singular			Plural		
	Masculine	Feminine	Neuter	Masculine	Feminine	Neuter
Nominative	parātūrus	parātūra	parātūrum	parātūrī	parātūrae	parātūra
Genitive	parātūrī	parātūrae	parātūrī	parātūrōrum	parātūrārum	parātūrōrum
Dative	parātūrō	parātūrae	parātūrō	parātūrīs	parātūrīs	parātūrīs
Accusative	parātūrum	parātūram	parātūrum	parātūrōs	parātūrās	parātūra
Ablative	parātūrō	parātūrā	parātūrō	parātūrīs	parātūrīs	parātūrīs
Vocative	parātūre	parātūra	parātūrum	parātūrī	parātūrae	parātūra

Declension of the Gerundive

	Singular			Plural		
	Masculine	**Feminine**	**Neuter**	**Masculine**	**Feminine**	**Neuter**
Nominative	parandus	paranda	parandum	parandī	parandae	paranda
Genitive	parandī	parandae	parandī	parandōrum	parandārum	parandōrum
Dative	parandō	parandae	parandō	parandīs	parandīs	parandīs
Accusative	parandum	parandam	parandum	parandōs	parandās	paranda
Ablative	parandō	parandā	parandō	parandīs	parandīs	parandīs
Vocative	parande	paranda	parandum	parandī	parandae	paranda

NUMBERS

Declension of Numbers†††

	Ūnus			Duo			Trēs	
Nominative	ūnus	ūna	ūnum	duo	duae	duo	trēs	tria
Genitive	ūnīus	ūnīus	ūnīus	duōrum	duārum	duōrum	trium	trium
Dative	ūnī	ūnī	ūnī	duōbus	duābus	duōbus	tribus	tribus
Accusative	ūnum	ūnam	ūnum	duōs	duās	duo	trēs	tria
Ablative	ūnō	ūnā	ūnō	duōbus	duābus	duōbus	tribus	tribus

	Mīlle†††	Mīlia†††
Nominative	mīlle	mīlia
Genitive	mīlle	mīlium
Dative	mīlle	mīlibus
Accusative	mīlle	mīlia
Ablative	mīlle	mīlibus

†††Other numbers are listed in Appendix E on p. 562 and the use of *mille/milia*
can be found in the syntax section of this appendix on p. 538.

ADVERBS

Comparison of Adverbs

Positive			Comparative	Superlative	
dūrē	harshly	dūrius	more/too/rather harshly	dūrissimē	most/very harshly
pulchrē	beautifully	pulchrius	more/too/rather beautifully	pulcherrimē	most/very beautifully
fortiter	bravely	fortius	more/too/rather bravely	fortissimē	most/very bravely

Irregular Positive Degree of Adverbs

Adjective	Adverb
bonus, a, um	bene
magnus, a, um	magnopere
multus, a, um	multō/multum
malus, a, um	male
parvus, a, um	parum
facilis, facile	facile
tristis, triste	triste
tūtus, a, um	tūtō (tūtē is a rare form)

PRONOUNS

DECLENSIONS OF PERSONAL AND REFLEXIVE PRONOUNS

Personal Pronouns: First and Second Person

	First singular	Second singular	First plural	Second plural
Nominative	ego	tū	nōs	vōs
Genitive	meī	tuī	nostrī/nostrum	vestrī/vestrum
Dative	mihi	tibi	nōbīs	vōbīs
Accusative	mē	tē	nōs	vōs
Ablative	mē	tē	nōbīs	vōbīs

Personal Pronoun: Third Person; Demonstrative Pronoun and Adjective: *is, ea, id*

	Singular			Plural		
	Masculine	**Feminine**	**Neuter**	**Masculine**	**Feminine**	**Neuter**
Nominative	is	ea	id	eī (iī)	eae	ea
Genitive	eius	eius	eius	eōrum	eārum	eōrum
Dative	eī	eī	eī	eīs (iīs)	eīs (iīs)	eīs (iīs)
Accusative	eum	eam	id	eōs	eās	ea
Ablative	eō	eā	eō	eīs (iīs)	eīs (iīs)	eīs (iīs)

Third Person Singular and Plural Reflexive Pronoun

Nominative	—
Genitive	suī
Dative	sibi
Accusative	sē
Ablative	sē

Possessive Adjectives

First Person Singular	meus, mea, meum
Second Person Singular	tuus, tua, tuum
Third Person Singular	suus, sua, suum/eius
First Person Plural	noster, nostra, nostrum
Second Person Plural	vester, vestra, vestrum
Third Person Plural	suus, sua, suum/eōrum, eārum, eōrum

DECLENSIONS OF DEMONSTRATIVE PRONOUNS/ADJECTIVES

Demonstrative Pronoun/Adjective: *hic, haec, hoc*

	Singular			Plural		
	Masculine	**Feminine**	**Neuter**	**Masculine**	**Feminine**	**Neuter**
Nominative	hic	haec	hoc	hī	hae	haec
Genitive	huius	huius	huius	hōrum	hārum	hōrum
Dative	huic	huic	huic	hīs	hīs	hīs
Accusative	hunc	hanc	hoc	hōs	hās	haec
Ablative	hōc	hāc	hōc	hīs	hīs	hīs

Demonstrative Pronoun/Adjective: *ille, illa, illud*

	Singular			Plural		
	Masculine	**Feminine**	**Neuter**	**Masculine**	**Feminine**	**Neuter**
Nominative	ille	illa	illud	illī	illae	illa
Genitive	illīus	illīus	illīus	illōrum	illārum	illōrum
Dative	illī	illī	illī	illīs	illīs	illīs
Accusative	illum	illam	illud	illōs	illās	illa
Ablative	illō	illā	illō	illīs	illīs	illīs

Demonstrative Pronoun/Adjective: *iste, ista, istud*

	Singular			Plural		
	Masculine	**Feminine**	**Neuter**	**Masculine**	**Feminine**	**Neuter**
Nominative	iste	ista	istud	istī	istae	ista
Genitive	istīus	istīus	istīus	istōrum	istārum	istōrum
Dative	istī	istī	istī	istīs	istīs	istīs
Accusative	istum	istam	istud	istōs	istās	ista
Ablative	istō	istā	istō	istīs	istīs	istīs

Demonstrative Pronoun/Adjective: *īdem, eadem, idem*

	Singular			Plural		
	Masculine	**Feminine**	**Neuter**	**Masculine**	**Feminine**	**Neuter**
Nominative	īdem	eadem	idem	eīdem	eaedem	eadem
Genitive	eiusdem	eiusdem	eiusdem	eōrundem	eārundem	eōrundem
Dative	eīdem	eīdem	eīdem	eīsdem	eīsdem	eīsdem
Accusative	eundem	eandem	idem	eōsdem	eāsdem	eadem
Ablative	eōdem	eādem	eōdem	eīsdem	eīsdem	eīsdem

DECLENSION OF THE INTENSIVE PRONOUN/ADJECTIVE

Intensive Pronoun/Adjective: *ipse, ipsa, ipsum*

	Singular			Plural		
	Masculine	**Feminine**	**Neuter**	**Masculine**	**Feminine**	**Neuter**
Nominative	ipse	ipsa	ipsum	ipsī	ipsae	ipsa
Genitive	ipsīus	ipsīus	ipsīus	ipsōrum	ipsārum	ipsōrum
Dative	ipsī	ipsī	ipsī	ipsīs	ipsīs	ipsīs
Accusative	ipsum	ipsam	ipsum	ipsōs	ipsās	ipsa
Ablative	ipsō	ipsā	ipsō	ipsīs	ipsīs	ipsīs

DECLENSION OF THE RELATIVE PRONOUN

Relative Pronoun: *quī, quae, quod*

	Singular			Plural		
	Masculine	**Feminine**	**Neuter**	**Masculine**	**Feminine**	**Neuter**
Nominative	quī	quae	quod	quī	quae	quae
Genitive	cūius	cūius	cūius	quōrum	quārum	quōrum
Dative	cui	cui	cui	quibus	quibus	quibus
Accusative	quem	quam	quod	quōs	quās	quae
Ablative	quō	quā	quō	quibus	quibus	quibus

DECLENSIONS OF INTERROGATIVE PRONOUNS AND ADJECTIVES

Interrogative Pronoun: *quis, quid?*

	Singular		Plural		
	Masculine/Feminine	**Neuter**	**Masculine**	**Feminine**	**Neuter**
Nominative	quis	quid	quī	quae	quae
Genitive	cūius	cūius	quōrum	quārum	quōrum
Dative	cui	cui	quibus	quibus	quibus
Accusative	quem	quid	quōs	quās	quae
Ablative	quō/quā	quō	quibus	quibus	quibus

Interrogative Adjective: *quī, quae, quod?*

	Singular			Plural		
	Masculine	**Feminine**	**Neuter**	**Masculine**	**Feminine**	**Neuter**
Nominative	quī	quae	quod	quī	quae	quae
Genitive	cūius	cūius	cūius	quōrum	quārum	quōrum
Dative	cui	cui	cui	quibus	quibus	quibus
Accusative	quem	quam	quod	quōs	quās	quae
Ablative	quō	quā	quō	quibus	quibus	quibus

VERBS

CONJUGATIONS OF REGULAR VERBS

Present Active Indicative

	First conjugation	Second conjugation	Third conjugation	Fourth conjugation	Third conjugation –*iō*
First person singular	parō	teneō	petō	audiō	capiō
Second person singular	parās	tenēs	petis	audīs	capis
Third person singular	parat	tenet	petit	audit	capit
First person plural	parāmus	tenēmus	petimus	audīmus	capimus
Second person plural	parātis	tenētis	petitis	audītis	capitis
Third person plural	parant	tenent	petunt	audiunt	capiunt

Present Passive Indicative

	First conjugation	Second conjugation	Third conjugation	Fourth conjugation	Third conjugation –iō
First person singular	paror	teneor	petor	audior	capior
Second person singular	parāris (-re)	tenēris (-re)	peteris (-re)	audīris (-re)	caperis (-re)
Third person singular	parātur	tenētur	petitur	audītur	capitur
First person plural	parāmur	tenēmur	petimur	audīmur	capimur
Second person plural	parāminī	tenēminī	petiminī	audīminī	capiminī
Third person plural	parantur	tenentur	petuntur	audiuntur	capiuntur

Imperfect Active Indicative

	First conjugation	Second conjugation	Third conjugation	Fourth conjugation	Third conjugation –iō
First person singular	parābam	tenēbam	petēbam	audiēbam	capiēbam
Second person singular	parābās	tenēbās	petēbās	audiēbās	capiēbās
Third person singular	parābat	tenēbat	petēbat	audiēbat	capiēbat
First person plural	parābāmus	tenēbāmus	petēbāmus	audiēbāmus	capiēbāmus
Second person plural	parābātis	tenēbātis	petēbātis	audiēbātis	capiēbātis
Third person plural	parābant	tenēbant	petēbant	audiēbant	capiēbant

Imperfect Passive Indicative

	First conjugation	Second conjugation	Third conjugation	Fourth conjugation	Third conjugation –iō
First person singular	parābar	tenēbar	petēbar	audiēbar	capiēbar
Second person singular	parābāris (-re)	tenēbāris (-re)	petēbāris (-re)	audiēbāris (-re)	capiēbāris (-re)
Third person singular	parābātur	tenēbātur	petēbātur	audiēbātur	capiēbātur
First person plural	parābāmur	tenēbāmur	petēbāmur	audiēbāmur	capiēbāmur
Second person plural	parābāminī	tenēbāminī	petēbāminī	audiēbāminī	capiēbāminī
Third person plural	parābantur	tenēbantur	petēbantur	audiēbantur	capiēbantur

Future Active Indicative

	First conjugation	Second conjugation	Third conjugation	Fourth conjugation	Third conjugation –iō
First person singular	parābō	tenēbō	petam	audiam	capiam
Second person singular	parābis	tenēbis	petēs	audiēs	capiēs
Third person singular	parābit	tenēbit	petet	audiet	capiet
First person plural	parābimus	tenēbimus	petēmus	audiēmus	capiēmus
Second person plural	parābitis	tenēbitis	petētis	audiētis	capiētis
Third person plural	parābunt	tenēbunt	petent	audient	capient

Future Passive Indicative

	First conjugation	Second conjugation	Third conjugation	Fourth conjugation	Third conjugation –*iō*
First person singular	parābor	tenēbor	petar	audiar	capiar
Second person singular	parāberis (-re)	tenēberis (-re)	petēris (-re)	audiēris (-re)	capiēris (-re)
Third person singular	parābitur	tenēbitur	petētur	audiētur	capiētur
First person plural	parābimur	tenēbimur	petēmur	audiēmur	capiēmur
Second person plural	parābiminī	tenēbiminī	petēminī	audiēminī	capiēminī
Third person plural	parābuntur	tenēbuntur	petentur	audientur	capientur

	Perfect Active Indicative	Perfect Passive Indicative
First person singular	parāvī	parātus, parāta, (parātum) sum
Second person singular	parāvistī	parātus, parāta, (parātum) es
Third person singular	parāvit	parātus, parāta, parātum est
First person plural	parāvimus	parātī, parātae, (parāta) sumus
Second person plural	parāvistis	parātī, parātae, (parāta) estis
Third person plural	parāvērunt (-ēre)	parātī, parātae, parāta sunt

	Pluperfect Active Indicative	Pluperfect Passive Indicative
First person singular	parāveram	parātus, parāta, (parātum) eram
Second person singular	parāverās	parātus, parāta, (parātum) erās
Third person singular	parāverat	parātus, parāta, parātum erat
First person plural	parāverāmus	parātī, parātae, (parāta) erāmus
Second person plural	parāverātis	parātī, parātae, (parāta) erātis
Third person plural	parāverant	parātī, parātae, parāta erant

	Future Perfect Active Indicative	Future Perfect Passive Indicative
First person singular	parāverō	parātus, parāta, (parātum) erō
Second person singular	parāveris	parātus, parāta, (parātum) eris
Third person singular	parāverit	parātus, parāta, parātum erit
First person plural	parāverimus	parātī, parātae, (parāta) erimus
Second person plural	parāveritis	parātī, parātae, (parāta) eritis
Third person plural	parāverint	parātī, parātae, parāta erunt

Present Active Subjunctive

	First conjugation	Second conjugation	Third conjugation	Fourth conjugation	Third conjugation –iō
First person singular	parem	teneam	petam	audiam	capiam
Second person singular	parēs	teneās	petās	audiās	capiās
Third person singular	paret	teneat	petat	audiat	capiat
First person plural	parēmus	teneāmus	petāmus	audiāmus	capiāmus
Second person plural	parētis	teneātis	petātis	audiātis	capiātis
Third person plural	parent	teneant	petant	audiant	capiant

Present Passive Subjunctive

	First conjugation	Second conjugation	Third conjugation	Fourth conjugation	Third conjugation –iō
First person singular	parer	tenear	petar	audiār	capiar
Second person singular	parēris (-re)	teneāris (-re)	petāris (-re)	audiāris (-re)	capiāris (-re)
Third person singular	parētur	teneātur	petātur	audiātur	capiātur
First person plural	parēmur	teneāmur	petāmur	audiāmur	capiāmur
Second person plural	parēminī	teneāminī	petāminī	audiāminī	capiāminī
Third person plural	parentur	teneantur	petantur	audiantur	capiantur

Imperfect Active Subjunctive

	First conjugation	Second conjugation	Third conjugation	Fourth conjugation	Third conjugation –iō
First person singular	parārem	tenērem	peterem	audīrem	caperem
Second person singular	parārēs	tenērēs	peterēs	audīrēs	caperēs
Third person singular	parāret	tenēret	peteret	audīret	caperet
First person plural	parārēmus	tenērēmus	peterēmus	audīrēmus	caperēmus
Second person plural	parārētis	tenērētis	peterētis	audīrētis	caperētis
Third person plural	parārent	tenērent	peterent	audīrent	caperent

Imperfect Passive Subjunctive

	First conjugation	Second conjugation	Third conjugation	Fourth conjugation	Third conjugation –iō
First person singular	parārer	tenērer	peterer	audīrer	caperer
Second person singular	parārēris (-re)	tenērēris (-re)	peterēris (-re)	audīrēris (-re)	caperēris (-re)
Third person singular	parārētur	tenērētur	peterētur	audīrētur	caperētur
First person plural	parārēmur	tenērēmur	peterēmur	audīrēmur	caperēmur
Second person plural	parārēminī	tenērēminī	peterēminī	audīrēminī	caperēminī
Third person plural	parārentur	tenērentur	peterentur	audīrentur	caperentur

	Perfect Active Subjunctive	**Perfect Passive Subjunctive**
First person singular	parāverim	parātus, parāta, (parātum) sim
Second person singular	parāveris	parātus, parāta, (parātum) sīs
Third person singular	parāverit	parātus, parāta, parātum sit
First person plural	parāverimus	parātī, parātae, (parāta) sīmus
Second person plural	parāveritis	parātī, parātae, (parāta) sītis
Third person plural	parāverint	parātī, parātae, parāta sint

	Pluperfect Active Subjunctive	**Pluperfect Passive Subjunctive**
First person singular	parāvissem	parātus, parāta, (parātum) essem
Second person singular	parāvissēs	parātus, parāta, (parātum) essēs
Third person singular	parāvisset	parātus, parāta, parātum esset
First person plural	parāvissēmus	parātī, parātae, (parāta) essēmus
Second person plural	parāvissētis	parātī, parātae, (parāta) essētis
Third person plural	parāvissent	parātī, parātae, parāta essent

Note that the neuter participle for the first and second person is in parentheses
because the first and second person usually refer to a person and not a thing.

Present Active Imperatives and Prohibitions

	First conjugation	Second conjugation	Third conjugation	Fourth conjugation	Third conjugation –iō
Second person singular positive	parā	tenē	pete	audī	cape‡‡‡
Second person plural positive	parāte	tenēte	petite	audīte	capite
Second person singular negative	nōlī parāre‡‡‡	nōlī tenēre	nōlī petere	nōlī audīre	nōlī capere
Second person plural negative	nōlīte parāre	nōlīte tenēre	nōlīte petere	nōlīte audīre	nōlīte capere

‡‡‡The second person singular positive imperatives of a few verbs are irregular in the singular: *dīc, dūc, fac, fer.* Negative imperatives (also called prohibitions) may also be formed by using *cavē* + present subjunctive, *nē* + perfect subjunctive, and in poetry *nē* + present active imperative.

Present Passive Imperatives

	First conjugation	Second conjugation	Third conjugation	Fourth conjugation	Third conjugation –iō
Second person singular positive	parāre	tenēre	petere	audīre	capere
Second person plural positive	parāminī	tenēminī	petiminī	audīminī	capiminī

Participles

	Active	Passive
Present	parāns, parantis	—
Perfect	—	parātus, parāta, parātum
Future	parātūrus, parātūra, parātūrum	—

Infinitives

	Active	Passive
Present	parāre	parārī
Perfect	parāvisse	parātus, parāta, parātum esse
Future	parātūrus, parātūra, parātūrum esse	—

CONJUGATIONS OF DEPONENT VERBS

Present Passive Indicative

	First conjugation	Second conjugation	Third conjugation	Fourth conjugation	Third conjugation –iō
First person singular	hortor	vereor	sequor	partior	patior
Second person singular	hortāris (-re)	verēris (-re)	sequeris (-re)	partīris (-re)	pateris (-re)
Third person singular	hortātur	verētur	sequitur	partītur	patitur
First person plural	hortāmur	verēmur	sequimur	partīmur	patimur
Second person plural	hortāminī	verēminī	sequiminī	partīminī	patiminī
Third person plural	hortantur	verentur	sequuntur	partiuntur	patiuntur

Imperfect Passive Indicative

	First conjugation	Second conjugation	Third conjugation	Fourth conjugation	Third conjugation –iō
First person singular	hortābar	verēbar	sequēbar	partiēbar	patiēbar
Second person singular	hortābāris (-re)	verēbāris (-re)	sequēbāris (-re)	partiēbāris (-re)	patiēbāris (-re)
Third person singular	hortābātur	verēbātur	sequēbātur	partiēbātur	patiēbātur
First person plural	hortābāmur	verēbāmur	sequēbāmur	partiēbāmur	patiēbāmur
Second person plural	hortābāminī	verēbāminī	sequēbāminī	partiēbāminī	patiēbāminī
Third person plural	hortābantur	verēbantur	sequēbantur	partiēbantur	patiēbantur

Future Passive Indicative

	First conjugation	Second conjugation	Third conjugation	Fourth conjugation	Third conjugation –iō
First person singular	hortābor	verēbor	sequar	partiar	patiar
Second person singular	hortāberis (-re)	verēberis (-re)	sequēris (-re)	partiēris (-re)	patiēris (-re)
Third person singular	hortābitur	verēbitur	sequētur	partiētur	patiētur
First person plural	hortābimur	verēbimur	sequēmur	partiēmur	patiēmur
Second person plural	hortābiminī	verēbiminī	sequēminī	partiēminī	patiēminī
Third person plural	hortābuntur	verēbuntur	sequentur	partientur	patientur

Perfect Passive Indicative

	First conjugation	Second conjugation	Third conjugation	Fourth conjugation	Third conjugation –iō
First person singular	hortātus, a, um sum	veritus, a, um sum	secūtus, a, um sum	partītus, a, um sum	passus, a, um sum
Second person singular	hortātus, a, um es	veritus, a, um es	secūtus, a, um es	partītus, a, um es	passus, a, um es
Third person singular	hortātus, a, um est	veritus, a, um est	secūtus, a, um est	partītus, a, um est	passus, a, um est
First person plural	hortātī, ae, a sumus	veritī, ae, a sumus	secūtī, ae, a sumus	partītī, ae, a sumus	passī, ae, a sumus
Second person plural	hortātī, ae, a estis	veritī, ae, a estis	secūtī, ae, a estis	partītī, ae, a estis	passī, ae, a estis
Third person plural	hortātī, ae, a sunt	veritī, ae, a sunt	secūtī, ae, a sunt	partītī, ae, a sunt	passī, ae, a sunt

Pluperfect Passive Indicative

	First conjugation	Second conjugation	Third conjugation	Fourth conjugation	Third conjugation –iō
First person singular	hortātus, a, um eram	veritus, a, um eram	secūtus, a, um eram	partītus, a, um eram	passus, a, um eram
Second person singular	hortātus, a, um erās	veritus, a, um erās	secūtus, a, um erās	partītus, a, um erās	passus, a, um erās
Third person singular	hortātus, a, um erat	veritus, a, um erat	secūtus, a, um erat	partītus, a, um erat	passus, a, um erat
First person plural	hortātī, ae, a erāmus	veritī, ae, a erāmus	secūtī, ae, a erāmus	partītī, ae, a erāmus	passī, ae, a erāmus
Second person plural	hortātī, ae, a erātis	veritī, ae, a erātis	secūtī, ae, a erātis	partītī, ae, a erātis	passī, ae, a erātis
Third person plural	hortātī, ae, a erant	veritī, ae, a erant	secūtī, ae, a erant	partītī, ae, a erant	passī, ae, a erant

Future Perfect Passive Indicative

	First conjugation	Second conjugation	Third conjugation	Fourth conjugation	Third conjugation –iō
First person singular	hortātus, a, um erō	veritus, a, um erō	secūtus, a, um erō	partītus, a, um erō	passus, a, um erō
Second person singular	hortātus, a, um eris	veritus, a, um eris	secūtus, a, um eris	partītus, a, um eris	passus, a, um eris
Third person singular	hortātus, a, um erit	veritus, a, um erit	secūtus, a, um erit	partītus, a, um erit	passus, a, um erit
First person plural	hortātī, ae, a erimus	veritī, ae, a erimus	secūtī, ae, a erimus	partītī, ae, a erimus	passī, ae, a erimus
Second person plural	hortātī, ae, a eritis	veritī, ae, a eritis	secūtī, ae, a eritis	partītī, ae, a eritis	passī, ae, a eritis
Third person plural	hortātī, ae, a erunt	veritī, ae, a erunt	secūtī, ae, a erunt	partītī, ae, a erunt	passī, ae, a erunt

Present Passive Subjunctive

	First conjugation	Second conjugation	Third conjugation	Fourth conjugation	Third conjugation –iō
First person singular	horter	verear	sequar	partiar	patiar
Second person singular	hortēris (-re)	vereāris (-re)	sequāris (-re)	partiāris (-re)	patiāris (-re)
Third person singular	hortētur	vereātur	sequātur	partiātur	patiātur
First person plural	hortēmur	vereāmur	sequāmur	partiāmur	patiāmur
Second person plural	hortēminī	vereāminī	sequāminī	partiāminī	patiāminī
Third person plural	hortentur	vereantur	sequantur	partiantur	patiantur

Imperfect Passive Subjunctive

	First conjugation	Second conjugation	Third conjugation	Fourth conjugation	Third conjugation –iō
First person singular	hortārer	verērer	sequerer	partīrer	paterer
Second person singular	hortārēris (-re)	verērēris (-re)	sequerēris (-re)	partīrēris (-re)	paterēris (-re)
Third person singular	hortārētur	verērētur	sequerētur	partīrētur	paterētur
First person plural	hortārēmur	verērēmur	sequerēmur	partīrēmur	paterēmur
Second person plural	hortārēminī	verērēminī	sequerēminī	partīrēminī	paterēminī
Third person plural	hortārentur	vererentur	sequerentur	partīrentur	paterentur

Perfect Passive Subjunctive

	First conjugation	Second conjugation	Third conjugation	Fourth conjugation	Third conjugation –*iō*
First person singular	hortātus, a, um sim	veritus, a, um sim	secūtus, a, um sim	partītus, a, um sim	passus, a, um sim
Second person singular	hortātus, a, um sīs	veritus, a, um sīs	secūtus, a, um sīs	partītus, a, um sīs	passus, a, um sīs
Third person singular	hortātus, a, um sit	veritus, a, um sit	secūtus, a, um sit	partītus, a, um sit	passus, a, um sit
First person plural	hortātī, ae, a sīmus	veritī, ae, a sīmus	secūtī, ae, a sīmus	partītī, ae, a sīmus	passī, ae, a sīmus
Second person plural	hortātī, ae, a sītis	veritī, ae, a sītis	secūtī, ae, a sītis	partītī, ae, a sītis	passī, ae, a sītis
Third person plural	hortātī, ae, a sint	veritī, ae, a sint	secūtī, ae, a sint	partītī, ae, a sint	passī, ae, a sint

Pluperfect Passive Subjunctive

	First conjugation	Second conjugation	Third conjugation	Fourth conjugation	Third conjugation –*iō*
First person singular	hortātus, a, um essem	veritus, a, um essem	secūtus, a, um essem	partītus, a, um essem	passus, a, um essem
Second person singular	hortātus, a, um essēs	veritus, a, um essēs	secūtus, a, um essēs	partītus, a, um essēs	passus, a, um essēs
Third person singular	hortātus, a, um esset	veritus, a, um esset	secūtus, a, um esset	partītus, a, um esset	passus, a, um esset
First person plural	hortātī, ae, a essēmus	veritī, ae, a essēmus	secūtī, ae, a essēmus	partītī, ae, a essēmus	passī, ae, a essēmus
Second person plural	hortātī, ae, a essētis	veritī, ae, a essētis	secūtī, ae, a essētis	partītī, ae, a essētis	passī, ae, a essētis
Third person plural	hortātī, ae, a essent	veritī, ae, a essent	secūtī, ae, a essent	partītī, ae, a essent	passī, ae, a essent

Participles

	Active	Passive
Present	hortāns, hortantis	—
Perfect	—	hortātus, a, um
Future	hortātūrus, a, um	—

Infinitives

	Active	Passive
Present	—	hortārī
Perfect	—	hortātus, a, um esse
Future	hortātūrus, a, um esse	—

CONJUGATIONS OF IRREGULAR VERBS

SUM, ESSE, FUĪ, FUTŪRUM

Indicative

	Present	Imperfect	Future	Perfect	Pluperfect	Future perfect
First person singular	sum	eram	erō	fuī	fueram	fuerō
Second person singular	es	erās	eris	fuistī	fuerās	fueris
Third person singular	est	erat	erit	fuit	fuerat	fuerit
First person plural	sumus	erāmus	erimus	fuimus	fuerāmus	fuerimus
Second person plural	estis	erātis	eritis	fuistis	fuerātis	fueritis
Third person plural	sunt	erant	erunt	fuērunt (-ēre)	fuerant	fuerint

Subjunctive

	Present	Imperfect	Future	Perfect	Pluperfect	Future perfect
First person singular	sim	essem	—	fuerim	fuissem	—
Second person singular	sīs	essēs	—	fueris	fuissēs	—
Third person singular	sit	esset	—	fuerit	fuisset	—
First person plural	sīmus	essēmus	—	fuerimus	fuissēmus	—
Second person plural	sītis	essētis	—	fueritis	fuissētis	—
Third person plural	sint	essent	—	fuerint	fuissent	—

Present Imperatives

Second person singular positive	es
Second person plural positive	este

Infinitives

	Active	Passive
Present	esse	—
Perfect	fuisse	—
Future	futūrus, a, um esse	—

POSSUM, POSSE, POTUĪ, —

Indicative

	Present	Imperfect	Future	Perfect	Pluperfect	Future perfect
First person singular	possum	poteram	poterō	potuī	potueram	potuerō
Second person singular	potes	poterās	poteris	potuistī	potuerās	potueris
Third person singular	potest	poterat	poterit	potuit	potuerat	potuerit
First person plural	possumus	poterāmus	poterimus	potuimus	potuerāmus	potuerimus
Second person plural	potestis	poterātis	poteritis	potuistis	potuerātis	potueritis
Third person plural	possunt	poterant	poterunt	potuērunt (-ēre)	potuerant	potuerint

Subjunctive

	Present	Imperfect	Future	Perfect	Pluperfect	Future perfect
First person singular	possim	possem	—	potuerim	potuissem	—
Second person singular	possīs	possēs	—	potueris	potuissēs	—
Third person singular	possit	posset	—	potuerit	potuisset	—
First person plural	possīmus	possēmus	—	potuerimus	potuissēmus	—
Second person plural	possītis	possētis	—	potueritis	potuissētis	—
Third person plural	possint	possent	—	potuerint	potuissent	—

Participles

Active

Present	potēns, potentis

Infinitives

Active

Present	posse
Perfect	potuisse

EŌ, ĪRE, ĪVĪ, ITUM

Indicative

	Present	Imperfect	Future	Perfect	Pluperfect	Future perfect
First person singular	eō	ībam	ībō	īvī	īveram	īverō
Second person singular	īs	ībās	ībis	īvistī	īverās	īveris
Third person singular	it	ībat	ībit	īvit	īverat	īverit
First person plural	īmus	ībāmus	ībimus	īvimus	īverāmus	īverimus
Second person plural	ītis	ībātis	ībitis	īvistis	īverātis	īveritis
Third person plural	eunt	ībant	ībunt	īvērunt (-ēre)	īverant	īverint

Subjunctive

	Present	Imperfect	Future	Perfect	Pluperfect	Future perfect
First person singular	eam	īrem	—	īverim	īvissem	—
Second person singular	eās	īrēs	—	īveris	īvissēs	—
Third person singular	eat	īret	—	īverit	īvisset	—
First person plural	eāmus	īrēmus	—	īverimus	īvissēmus	—
Second person plural	eātis	īrētis	—	īveritis	īvissētis	—
Third person plural	eant	īrent	—	īverint	īvissent	—

Present Imperatives

Second person singular positive	ī
Second person plural positive	īte
Second person singular negative	nōlī īre
Second person plural negative	nōlīte īre

Participles

	Active	Passive
Present	iēns, euntis	—
Perfect	—	—
Future	itūrus, itūra, itūrum	—

Infinitives

	Active
Present	īre
Perfect	īvisse
Future	itūrus, a, um esse

VOLŌ, VELLE, VOLUĪ

Indicative

	Present	Imperfect	Future	Perfect	Pluperfect	Future perfect
First person singular	volō	volēbam	volam	voluī	volueram	voluerō
Second person singular	vīs	volēbās	volēs	voluistī	voluerās	volueris
Third person singular	vult	volēbat	volet	voluit	voluerat	voluerit
First person plural	volumus	volēbāmus	volēmus	voluimus	voluerāmus	voluerimus
Second person plural	vultis	volēbātis	volētis	voluistis	voluerātis	volueritis
Third person plural	volunt	volēbant	volent	voluērunt (-ēre)	voluerant	voluerint

Subjunctive

	Present	Imperfect	Future	Perfect	Pluperfect	Future perfect
First person singular	velim	vellem	—	voluerim	voluissem	—
Second person singular	velīs	vellēs	—	volueris	voluissēs	—
Third person singular	velit	vellet	—	voluerit	voluisset	—
First person plural	velīmus	vellēmus	—	voluerimus	voluissēmus	—
Second person plural	velītis	vellētis	—	volueritis	voluissētis	—
Third person plural	velint	vellent	—	voluerint	voluissent	—

Participles

Active

Present	volēns, volentis

Infinitives

Active

Present	velle
Perfect	voluisse

NŌLŌ, NŌLLE, NŌLUĪ

Indicative

	Present	Imperfect	Future	Perfect	Pluperfect	Future perfect
First person singular	nōlō	nōlēbam	nōlam	nōluī	nōlueram	nōluerō
Second person singular	nōn vīs	nōlēbās	nōlēs	nōluistī	nōluerās	nōlueris
Third person singular	nōn vult	nōlēbat	nōlet	nōluit	nōluerat	nōluerit
First person plural	nōlumus	nōlēbāmus	nōlēmus	nōluimus	nōluerāmus	nōluerimus
Second person plural	nōn vultis	nōlēbātis	nōlētis	nōluistis	nōluerātis	nōlueritis
Third person plural	nōlunt	nōlēbant	nōlent	nōluērunt (-ēre)	nōluerant	nōluerint

Subjunctive

	Present	Imperfect	Future	Perfect	Pluperfect	Future perfect
First person singular	nōlim	nōllem	—	nōluerim	nōluissem	—
Second person singular	nōlīs	nōllēs	—	nōlueris	nōluissēs	—
Third person singular	nōlit	nōllet	—	nōluerit	nōluisset	—
First person plural	nōlīmus	nōllēmus	—	nōluerimus	nōluissēmus	—
Second person plural	nōlītis	nōllētis	—	nōlueritis	nōluissētis	—
Third person plural	nōlint	nōllent	—	nōluerint	nōluissent	—

Present Imperatives

Second person singular positive	nōlī
Second person plural positive	nōlīte

Participles

Active

Present	nōlēns, nōlentis

Infinitives

Active

Present	nōlle
Perfect	nōluisse

MĀLŌ, MĀLLE, MĀLUĪ

Indicative

	Present	Imperfect	Future	Perfect	Pluperfect	Future perfect
First person singular	mālō	mālēbam	mālam	māluī	mālueram	māluerō
Second person singular	māvīs	mālēbās	mālēs	māluistī	māluerās	mālueris
Third person singular	māvult	mālēbat	mālet	māluit	māluerat	māluerit
First person plural	mālumus	mālēbāmus	mālēmus	māluimus	māluerāmus	māluerimus
Second person plural	māvultis	mālēbātis	mālētis	māluistis	māluerātis	mālueritis
Third person plural	mālunt	mālēbant	mālent	māluērunt (-ēre)	māluerant	māluerint

Subjunctive

	Present	Imperfect	Future	Perfect	Pluperfect	Future perfect
First person singular	mālim	māllem	—	māluerim	māluissem	—
Second person singular	mālīs	māllēs	—	mālueris	māluissēs	—
Third person singular	mālit	māllet	—	māluerit	māluisset	—
First person plural	mālīmus	māllēmus	—	māluerimus	māluissēmus	—
Second person plural	mālītis	māllētis	—	mālueritis	māluissētis	—
Third person plural	mālint	māllent	—	māluerint	māluissent	—

Infinitives

Active

Present	mālle
Perfect	māluisse

FERŌ, FERRE, TULĪ, LĀTUM

Indicative Active

	Present	Imperfect	Future	Perfect	Pluperfect	Future perfect
First person singular	ferō	ferēbam	feram	tulī	tuleram	tulerō
Second person singular	fers	ferēbās	ferēs	tulistī	tulerās	tuleris
Third person singular	fert	ferēbat	feret	tulit	tulerat	tulerit
First person plural	ferimus	ferēbāmus	ferēmus	tulimus	tulerāmus	tulerimus
Second person plural	fertis	ferēbātis	ferētis	tulistis	tulerātis	tuleritis
Third person plural	ferunt	ferēbant	ferent	tulērunt (-ēre)	tulerant	tulerint

Indicative Passive

	Present	Imperfect	Future	Perfect	Pluperfect	Future perfect
First person singular	feror	ferēbar	ferar	lātus, a, um sum	lātus, a, um eram	lātus, a, um erō
Second person singular	ferris (-re)	ferēbāris (-re)	ferēris (-re)	lātus, a, um es	lātus, a, um erās	lātus, a, um eris
Third person singular	fertur	ferēbātur	ferētur	lātus, a, um est	lātus, a, um erat	lātus, a, um erit
First person plural	ferimur	ferēbāmur	ferēmur	lātī, ae, a sumus	lātī, ae, a erāmus	lātī, ae, a erimus
Second person plural	feriminī	ferēbāminī	ferēminī	lātī, ae, a estis	lātī, ae, a erātis	lātī, ae, a eritis
Third person plural	feruntur	ferēbantur	ferentur	lātī, ae, a sunt	lātī, ae, a erant	lātī, ae, a erunt

Subjunctive Active

	Present	Imperfect	Future	Perfect	Pluperfect	Future perfect
First person singular	feram	ferrem	—	tulerim	tulissem	—
Second person singular	ferās	ferrēs	—	tuleris	tulissēs	—
Third person singular	ferat	ferret	—	tulerit	tulisset	—
First person plural	ferāmus	ferrēmus	—	tulerimus	tulissēmus	
Second person plural	ferātis	ferrētis	—	tuleritis	tulissētis	
Third person plural	ferant	ferrent	—	tulerint	tulissent	

Subjunctive Passive

	Present	Imperfect	Future	Perfect	Pluperfect	Future perfect
First person singular	ferar	ferrer	—	lātus, a, um sim	lātus, a, um essem	—
Second person singular	ferāris	ferrēris (-re)	—	lātus, a, um sīs	lātus, a, um essēs	—
Third person singular	ferātur	ferrētur	—	lātus, a, um sit	lātus, a, um esset	—
First person plural	ferāmur	ferrēmur	—	lātī, ae, a sīmus	lātī, ae, a essēmus	—
Second person plural	ferāminī	ferrēminī	—	lātī, ae, a sītis	lātī, ae, a essētis	—
Third person plural	ferantur	ferrentur	—	lātī, ae, a sint	lātī, ae, a essent	—

Present Imperatives

Second person singular positive	fer
Second person plural positive	ferte
Second person singular negative	nōlī ferre
Second person plural negative	nōlīte ferre

Participles

	Active	Passive
Present	ferēns, ferentis	—
Perfect	—	lātus, lāta, lātum
Future	lātūrus, lātūra, lātūrum	—

Infinitives

	Active	Passive
Present	ferre	ferrī
Perfect	tulisse	lātus, lāta, lātum esse
Future	lātūrus, a, um esse	—

FĪŌ, FIERĪ, FACTUS SUM

Indicative

	Present	Imperfect	Future	Perfect	Pluperfect	Future perfect
First person singular	fīō	fīēbam	fīam	factus, a, um sum	factus, a, um eram	factus, a, um ero
Second person singular	fīs	fīēbās	fīēs	factus, a, um es	factus, a, um erās	factus, a, um eris
Third person singular	fit	fīēbat	fīet	factus, a, um est	factus, a, um erat	factus, a, um erit
First person plural	fīmus	fīēbāmus	fīēmus	factī, ae, a sumus	factī, ae, a erāmus	factī, ae, a erimus
Second person plural	fītis	fīēbātis	fīētis	factī, ae, a estis	factī, ae, a erātis	factī, ae, a eritis
Third person plural	fīunt	fīēbant	fīent	factī, ae, a sunt	factī, ae, a erant	factī, ae, a erunt

Subjunctive

	Present	Imperfect	Future	Perfect	Pluperfect	Future perfect
First person singular	fīam	fierem	—	factus, a, um sim	factus, a, um essem	—
Second person singular	fīās	fierēs (-re)	—	factus, a, um sīs	factus, a, um essēs	—
Third person singular	fiat	fieret	—	factus, a, um sit	factus, a, um esset	—
First person plural	fīāmus	fierēmus	—	factī, ae, a sīmus	factī, ae, a essēmus	—
Second person plural	fīātis	fierētis	—	factī, ae, a sītis	factī, ae, a essētis	—
Third person plural	fīant	fierent	—	factī, ae, a sint	factī, ae, a essent	—

Participles

	Active	Passive
Present	—	—
Perfect	—	factus, facta, factum

Infinitives

	Active	Passive
Present	fierī	—
Perfect	—	factus, facta, factum esse

GERUNDS AND GERUNDIVES

Formation of the Gerund

Conjugation		Gerund in the Genitive Singular
First	parō, parāre	parandī
Second	teneō, tenēre	tenendī
Third	colō, colere	colendī
Fourth	audiō, audīre	audiendī
Third –*io*	capiō, capere	capiendī

Gerunds of Irregular Verbs

eō, īre	eundī
ferō, ferre	ferendī

Declension of the Gerund

Genitive	parandī
Dative	parandō
Accusative	(ad) parandum
Ablative	parandō

Formation of Gerundives

Conjugation		Gerundives in the Nominative Singular
First	parō, parāre	parandus, paranda, parandum
Second	teneō, tenēre	tenendus, tenenda, tenendum
Third	colō, colere	colendus, colenda, colendum
Fourth	audiō, audīre	audiendus, audienda, audiendum
Third –*io*	capiō, capere	capiendus, capienda, capiendum

Declension of the Gerundive

	Singular			Plural		
	Masculine	**Feminine**	**Neuter**	**Masculine**	**Feminine**	**Neuter**
Nominative	parandus	paranda	parandum	parandī	parandae	paranda
Genitive	parandī	parandae	parandī	parandōrum	parandārum	parandōrum
Dative	parandō	parandae	parandō	parandīs	parandīs	parandīs
Accusative	parandum	parandam	parandum	parandōs	parandās	paranda
Ablative	parandō	parandā	parandō	parandīs	parandīs	parandīs

LATIN SYNTAX

Only syntax taught in *Latin for the New Millennium*, Levels 1, 2, and 3 is listed in this appendix. For additional syntax not taught in this book, see Appendix E.

NOUNS

BASIC USE OF CASES***

Case	Function
Nominative	Subject. Predicate Nominative (noun or adjective).
Genitive	Modifier (often possession). Partitive. Objective. Quality/characteristic. Charge/penalty. Indefinite Value.
Dative	Indirect object. Possession. Purpose. Agent (with passive periphrastic and passive verbs in poetry). With compound verbs. Direction. With adjectives "near, dear, kind, friendly," etc.
Accusative	Direct object. Place to which. Greek Accusative of Respect. Duration of Time and Extent of Space. Exclamation.
Ablative	Agent (with passive voice). Manner. Instrument (means). Separation. Place from which. Place where. Accompaniment. Partitive using *ex, dē* with cardinal numerals and *quīdam*. Comparison. With certain deponent verbs. Quality/characteristic. Respect. Degree of Difference. Cause. Time When (or Within Which).
Vocative	Address.
Locative	Place where.

***For additional case uses, see Appendix E.

PRONOUNS

EXPRESSION OF POSSESSION WITH PERSONAL PRONOUNS, DEMONSTRATIVES, AND POSSESSIVE ADJECTIVES

The genitive forms of the personal pronouns, *ego, tū, nōs, vōs*, and of the reflexive pronoun of the third person, *suī, sibi, sē, sē*, are not used to indicate possession. If you need to express possession with these words, use the possessive adjectives, *meus, tuus, noster, vester, suus*.

Examples:

Librum meum habeō.	"I have my book."
Librum tuum habeō.	"I have your book."
Librum vestrum habeō.	"I have your (pl.) book."
Librum nostrum habētis.	"You (pl.) have our book."
Librum suum habent.	"They have their (own) book."
Librum suum habet.	"S/he has her/his (own) book."

However, the genitive of the third person non-reflexive pronouns is used to indicate possession.

Examples:

Librum eius habet.	"S/he has her/his (someone else's) book."
Librum eōrum habent.	"They have their (other people's) book."

In general, the genitive often shows possession.

Example:

liber puellae	"the book of the girl"

Possession can also be expressed by the dative of possession.

Example:

Mihi sunt multī librī.	"I have many books."

USE OF THE RELATIVE PRONOUN

The relative pronoun always refers to a preceding word, which is usually expressed, but sometimes implied. The preceding word is called an antecedent. The relative pronoun has the gender and number of the antecedent, but its case is determined by its function in its own clause. When a relative clause explains something and is factual, the verb is in the indicative. Other types of relative clauses that take subjunctive verbs are on pp. 542–543 of this appendix.

Example:

Hī sunt librī quōs habēmus.	"These are the books that we have."

When a form of the relative pronoun is found at the beginning of a Latin sentence, it is sometimes being used to link the sentence to a noun or idea in the previous sentence. This use is called the "connecting *quī*" or "connecting relative," and is translated by the corresponding form in English of *is, hic,* or *ille.*

Examples:

Quī in Galliā bellum gerunt.	"They wage war in Gaul."
Quā dē causā Helvētiī frumentum comburunt.	"For this reason the Helvetians burn their grain."

INTENSIVE AND REFLEXIVE PRONOUNS

The intensive pronoun/adjective *ipse, ipsa, ipsum* means "self" and should be carefully distinguished from the reflexive pronoun *suī, sibi, sē, sē,* which we also translate "self." The intensive pronoun/adjective is used for emphasis; it agrees with what it refers to and has a nominative form, whereas the reflexive pronoun refers to the subject of its own clause or sentence and does not have a nominative form.

Examples:

Nauta ipse haec dīxit.	"The sailor himself said these things."
Nauta haec sibi dīxit.	"The sailor said these things to himself."

DEMONSTRATIVE PRONOUNS/ADJECTIVES

The demonstratives *is, ea, id; hic, haec, hoc;* and *ille, illa, illud* may be used as pronouns or adjectives. As pronouns, all three demonstratives are the third person pronouns "he, she, it, they." As with other pronouns, the case of the demonstrative pronoun is determined by its use in the sentence.

As adjectives, the demonstratives agree with the noun they modify in case, number, and gender. The demonstrative *is, ea, id* means "this/these" or "that/those" while *hic, haec, hoc* means "this/these," and *ille, illa, illud* means "that/those."

Examples:

Hic mox respondēbit.	"He (this <man>) will reply soon."
Hic vir mox respondēbit.	"This man will reply soon."

The demonstrative *īdem, eadem, idem* means "same."

Example:

Īdem vir mox respondēbit.	"The same man will reply soon."

The demonstrative *iste, ista, istud* means "that [of yours]." The notion "of yours" may be literally true, or it may simply refer figuratively to a connection between the thing indicated by the demonstrative and something else. In some cases—but certainly not always—the use of this pronoun may have a derogatory or dismissive connotation.

Example:

> *Cōnsilium istud nōn probō.*   "I do not approve of that plan of yours."

INDEFINITE PRONOUNS, ADJECTIVES, AND RELATIVES

INDEFINITE PRONOUNS/ADJECTIVES

Latin is rich in these words, and many of them have subtle distinctions in meaning.

The indefinite *aliquis, aliquid*:

This pronoun means "someone" in an affirmative statement. Its adjective form is *aliquī, aliqua, aliquod.*

Example:

> *Aliquis hoc dīxit.*   "Somebody said this (though we don't know who)."

The pronoun *quis, quid* ("anyone, anything") and its adjective *quī, qua/quae, quod* are used instead of *aliquis/aliquī* after *sī, nisi, num,* and *nē.*

Example:

> *Sī quis illam pecūniam mihi dederit, eum amābō!*
> "If anyone gives me that money, I will like him!"

The indefinite *quisquam, quidquam/quicquam*:

This pronoun means "anyone, anything at all," and its adjective *ūllus, a, um* is used after negative words such as *nec* or *vix* and after verbs of prohibiting, preventing, and denying. They are used in questions and *sī* clauses where a negative force is implied. Unlike *aliquis*, we find *quisquam* in negative or virtually negative statements.

Examples:

> *Ad urbem noctū vēnī, nec quisquam mē cōnspexit.*
> "I arrived at the city by night, and no one saw/caught sight of me."

> *Estne quisquam, quī hoc dīxerit?*
> "Is there anyone who has said this?" (It is implied that there is no one.)

The indefinites *quispiam, quippiam* and *nesciō quis, nesciō quid*:

This pronoun means "someone or other" and is not negative but is vaguer than *aliquis*.

>   **Example:**
>
>   *Dīxerit tunc quispiam . . . .*   "Then someone or other would say . . . ."

This pronoun means "someone or other." Its adjective *nesciō quī, nesciō quae, nesciō quod* is similar to *quispiam* except that the sense of *nesciō quis* is typically contemptuous. The "verbal" part, *nesciō,* never changes its form, regardless of the construction of *quis/quid*.

>   **Example:**
>
>   *Nesciō quis hoc dīxit.*   "Someone (of little account, i.e., I don't know who) said this."

The indefinite *quīdam, quaedam, quoddam*:

This pronoun/adjective means "a certain one/thing," and it is sometimes used in much the same way as "one" is used in English. Please note that the Latin *ūnus* is very rarely (in the more polished authors, at least) used as an indefinite.

>   **Examples:**
>
>   *Erat in Atticī mōribus grātia, sed etiam quaedam gravitās.*
>   "There was agreeableness in Atticus' personality, but also a
>   certain seriousness/weightiness."
>
>   *Tertiō autem diē quīdam ē nautīs lūmen cōnspexit.*
>   "But on the third day one of the sailors observed a light."

The indefinite *quīvīs, quaevīs, quodvīs* (for adjectives) and *quidvīs* (for pronouns) and *quīlibet, quaelibet, quodlibet* (for adjectives) and *quidlibet* (for pronouns):

These mean "any one/thing you like" or "any one/thing which you please."

>   **Example:**
>
>   *Mūcius Scaevola quodlibet perīculum prō patriā patī parātus erat.*
>   "Mucius Scaevola was prepared to endure any danger whatsoever
>   for the sake of [his] fatherland."

THE INDEFINITE RELATIVE

The indefinite relative *quīcumque, quaecumque, quodcumque* and *quisquis, quicquid/quidquid*:

These indefinite relative pronouns mean "whoever, whatever." In later authors they are sometimes used as nonrelative indefinite pronouns, but in classical Latin they are almost always relatives (like *quī, quae, quod*).

>   **Example:**
>
>   *Quīcumque Rōmam vēnerit lūcrum faciet.*
>   "Whoever comes to Rome will make a profit."

ADJECTIVES

NOUN-ADJECTIVE AGREEMENT

The adjective agrees with the noun in number, gender, and case.

Examples:

Ōrātiōnem longam audīvī.	"I heard a long speech."
Librum celebrem legō.	"I am reading a renowned book."

SUBSTANTIVE ADJECTIVES, ESPECIALLY NEUTER PLURAL

Sometimes adjectives, used in the appropriate gender, and when the context makes the frame of reference clear, may be used without an expressed noun to indicate persons or things.

Examples:

Fortēs fugere nōn solent.	"Brave people are not accustomed to flee."
Bonī mala nōn laudant.	"Good people do not praise bad things."

WAYS OF EXPRESSING A COMPARISON

When two or more things are compared with a comparative adjective or adverb, the word for "than" is expressed by the adverb *quam,* or the second member of the comparison is put in the ablative case.

This is called the ablative of comparison and is not used unless the first of the two things being compared is in the nominative or accusative, and it is usually avoided when the second member of the comparison has a modifier.

Examples:

Nēmō est miserior quam ego.	"No one is more wretched than I."
Nēmō est miserior mē.	"No one is more wretched than I."

Sometimes comparatives, but especially superlatives, express a part of a whole. The whole then is expressed by a genitive. Sometimes this "part of the whole" or "partitive" relationship with superlatives is expressed with the prepositions *ex, dē,* or *inter* instead of the genitive especially after forms of *quīdam, quaedam, quoddam,* and numerals.

Examples:

Fīliam rēgī omnium praeclārissimō dedit.
"He gave [his] daughter to the most distinguished king of all."

Fīliam rēgī ex omnibus praeclārissimō dedit.
"He gave [his] daughter to the most distinguished king of all."

THE USES OF *QUAM*

When *quam* is linked to a superlative adjective or adverb, it means "as . . . as possible." A form of *possum* may be a part of this superlative expression.

Examples:

quam fortissimus	"as brave as possible"
quam vehementissimē	"as strongly as possible"
quam plūrimī	"as many as possible"
quam maximō potest itinere	"by as great a journey as possible"

When *quam* is used with a comparative adjective or adverb, it means "than."

Example:

Haec ars est ūtilior quam illa.   "This skill is more useful than that one."

The accusative singular feminine of the relative pronoun is *quam* and it means "whom," "which," or "that."

Example:

Haec est rēgīna quam laudāvī.   "This is the queen whom I praised."

The accusative singular feminine of the interrogative adjective is also *quam* and it means "which, what."

Example:

Quam puellam Catullus bāsiāvit?   "Which girl did Catullus kiss?"

When *quam* is used in an exclamation, it means "how."

Example:

Quam celeriter mīlitēs proficīscuntur!   "How fast the soldiers set off!"

PREPOSITIONS AND PHRASES

Preposition	Case	Meaning	Grammatical Name
ā, ab	ablative	by, from	Agent, Separation
ad	accusative	toward, to, into	Place to Which
ante	accusative	in front of	Miscellaneous
apud	accusative	at the house of	Miscellaneous
circum	accusative	around	Miscellaneous
contrā	accusative	against	Miscellaneous
cum	ablative	with	Accompaniment, Manner
dē	ablative	about, concerning, down from, of	Miscellaneous, Place from Which, Partitive after *quidam* and numbers
ē, ex	ablative	from, out of	Place from Which, Partitive
in	ablative	in, on	Place Where
in	accusative	into, to, toward, against	Place to Which
inter	accusative	between, among	Miscellaneous; Partitive
ob	accusative	on account of	Miscellaneous
per	accusative	through	Miscellaneous
post	accusative	after	Miscellaneous
prō	ablative	for, on behalf of	Miscellaneous
prope	accusative	near	Miscellaneous
propter	accusative	because of	Miscellaneous
sine	ablative	without	Miscellaneous
subter	accusative	beneath, below	Miscellaneous
tenus	ablative	to, up to, as far as	Miscellaneous
trans	accusative	across	Miscellaneous
ultrā	accusative	beyond	Miscellaneous

PLACE WHERE, PLACE TO WHICH, AND PLACE FROM WHICH WITH NAMES OF TOWNS

Place Where:

To express "place where" Latin uses *in* with the ablative.

Example:

> *Vīvō in pulchrā terrā.*   "I live in a nice land."

However, "place where" with the names of cities, towns, and small islands is expressed with a locative for singular nouns of the first and second declension and with the ablative for plural nouns of the first and second declension. The ablative also expresses "place where" for nouns of the third declension in both the singular and the plural. The ending of the locative singular for the first declension is -*ae* and for the second declension is –*ī*.

Examples:

Vīvō Rōmae.	"I live in Rome."
Carolus vīvit Aquīsgrānī.	"Charles lives in Aachen."
Vīvō Athēnīs.	"I live in Athens."
Hannibal vīvēbat Carthāgine.	"Hannibal lived in Carthage."

Place to Which:

To express "place to which" Latin uses *in* or *ad* with the accusative.

Example:

Mīlitēs ad Italiam dūcō.	"I lead soldiers to Italy."

However, "place to which" with the names of cities, towns, and small islands is expressed with a simple accusative.

Example:

Mīlitēs Rōmam, Aquīsgrānum,	"I lead soldiers to Rome, Aachen,
Athēnās, Carthāginem dūcō.	Athens, Carthage."

Place from Which:

To express "place from which" Latin uses *ā, ab, dē,* or *ē, ex* with the ablative.

Example:

Ab Germāniā veniō.	"I am coming from Germany."

However, "place from which" with the names of cities, towns, and small islands is expressed with a simple ablative.

Examples:

Rōmā, Aquīsgrānō,	"I am coming from Rome, Aachen,
Athēnīs, Carthāgine veniō.	Athens, Carthage."

THE USE OF MĪLLE AND MĪLIA

In the singular *mīlle* is an indeclinable adjective. In the plural *mīlia* is a third declension noun and is used with a partitive genitive.

Examples:

> *Cum mīlle mīlitibus vēnit.*
> "S/he came with a thousand soldiers."

> *Cum decem mīlibus mīlitum vēnit.*
> "S/he came with ten thousand soldiers."

VERBS

SUBJECT-VERB AGREEMENT

The subject agrees with the verb in number.

Example:

> *Puer currit.*   "The boy is running."

The predicate nominative agrees with the verb in number. If the predicate nominative is a noun, it agrees with the subject in number and case; if it is an adjective, it agrees with the subject in number, gender, and case.

Examples:

> *Vīta est gaudium.*   "Life is joy."
>
> *Praemium est magnum.*   "The prize is great."

TRANSITIVE AND INTRANSITIVE VERBS

Transitive verbs express the subject acting on something else and usually take the accusative.

Example:

> *Librum teneō.*   "I hold a book."

Intransitive verbs express the state or condition of the subject and cannot take an accusative.

Examples:

> *Liber est meus.*   "The book is mine."
>
> *In casā meā maneō.*   "I am staying in my house."

HISTORICAL PRESENT

In a narration (especially in histories) of a series of actions that took place in the past, the present tense is sometimes employed to make the action seem more vivid and present. This use of the present may occur in the context of other verbs that retain their past tense.

Example:

> Caesar Gallōs nōn esse parātōs cōnspexerat: itaque mīlitēs suōs
>   impetum facere iubet.
> "Caesar had noticed the Gauls were unprepared: so he orders
>   (i.e., ordered) his soldiers to launch an attack."

Similar to this "historical present" is the use of the "literary present." In this use of the present tense an author, who may be long since dead, is conventionally said to speak in the present time.

Example:

> Nepos dīcit Atticum ab omnibus Athēniēnsibus amātum esse.
> "Nepos says (as if he were speaking now) that Atticus was loved
>   by all the Athenians."

REFLEXIVE/MIDDLE VOICE OF VERBS

The voice of a verb indicates whether the subject is acting (active voice) or being acted upon (passive voice). Greek has a third voice (middle) used to indicate that the subject is acting upon itself. English and Latin usually express the middle voice by the use of reflexive pronouns.

In Latin poetry, however, passive verbs (often perfect passive participles) sometimes take a direct object and are used as though they were Greek verbs in the middle voice. Some prefer to treat the middle voice in Latin as a true passive voice that takes an accusative of respect. An accusative of respect, which regularly is a part of the body or to an item of apparel, is translated "as to" or "with respect to"; some call this the "Greek accusative of respect" to distinguish it from the Latin ablative of respect.

Examples:

	Middle Translation	Passive Translation with Accusative of Respect.
Ōs torō impressa est.	"She pressed [her] mouth on the couch."	"She was pressed as to [her] mouth on the couch."
Nec vultum movetur.	"Nor does he move [his] facial expression."	"Nor is he moved as to [his] facial expression."
Fallit custodēs suōs adoperta vultum.	"Having covered [her] face, she deceives the guards."	"Having been covered as to [her] face, she deceives the guards."

FUNCTIONS OF THE SUBJUNCTIVE IN THE MAIN CLAUSE

The subjunctive in a main clause usually shows the action as desirable or possible.

1. The volitive subjunctive is a somewhat milder command than the imperative OR it indicates an exhortation or strong advice, usually in the first or third person. Its negative is accompanied by *nē*.

    Examples:

Rēs parēs!	"Prepare the things!"
	"You should/must prepare the things!"
Ad īnsulam nāvigēmus!	"Let us sail to the island!"
Nē meum respectet, ut ante, amōrem.	"Let her not look back at my love as before."

2. The optative subjunctive indicates a wish and is often, but not always, accompanied by the word *utinam*. Its negative is expressed by *nē*. The present subjunctive is used for a wish about the future, that could still come true. The imperfect subjunctive is used for a wish about the present that has not become true. The pluperfect subjunctive is used for a wish about the past that has not become true.

    Examples:

(Utinam) illam vōcem audiam!	"If only I may hear that voice!"
(Utinam) illam vōcem audīrem!	"If only I were hearing that voice!"
(Utinam) illam vōcem audīvissem!	"If only I had heard that voice!"

3. The deliberative subjunctive is used in questions or exclamations to express doubt, indignation, or the impossibility of something's being done. The present subjunctive is used for present time and the imperfect subjunctive for past time. These questions often are rhetorical and do not expect an answer. The negative is *nōn*.

    Examples:

Quid agam?	"What am I to do?"
Quid agerem?	"What was I to do?"

4. The potential subjunctive appears in the principal clause of a sentence with a meaning that is often described as potential (or one of conditioned futurity). In this usage the speaker/writer makes a statement about something that could potentially happen but that is far from certain. The present, and very often the perfect subjunctive, is used for a present potential statement pertaining to some vague future time.

    Examples:

    Mōrēs tālium hominum probem . . . .
    "I would approve of the character of such people . . . ."
    (should I perchance meet people of such a kind)

Vix crēdiderim tālia esse vēra . . . .

"I should scarcely believe such things are true . . . ."

(should such things perchance happen).

The potential of the past, with its effect often being valid up to the present, is expressed by the imperfect subjunctive (the pluperfect subjunctive is rarely employed for the past potential).

Example:

Crēderēs eōs esse victōs . . . .

"You would think (and would still think) those people were conquered . . . ."

(if you had seen them).

FUNCTIONS OF THE SUBJUNCTIVE IN A DEPENDENT CLAUSE

Purpose Clauses:

Purpose clauses are introduced by *ut*, "in order to," "so that," or *nē*, "in order not to," "lest" for a negative purpose. They are constructed with the present subjunctive depending on a primary tense (present, future, future perfect), or with the imperfect subjunctive depending on a secondary tense (imperfect, perfect, pluperfect). (See p. 553 in this appendix for a fuller discussion of purpose constructions.)

Examples:

Epistulam mittō ut sciās mē bene valēre.

"I am sending a letter so that you may know that I am well."

Epistulam mīsī ut scīrēs mē bene valēre.

"I sent a letter so that you might know that I was well."

Indirect Questions:

Indirect questions are introduced by verbs of asking, doubting, or knowing. They begin with an interrogative word, such as the interrogative pronoun or adjective, and have a subjunctive verb according to the sequence of tenses.

Examples:

Interrogō tē quid agās.	"I am asking you what you are doing."
Interrogō tē quid ēgeris.	"I am asking you what you were doing."
Interrogāvī tē quid agerēs.	"I asked you what you were doing."
Interrogāvī tē quid ēgissēs.	"I asked you what you had done."

Indirect Commands:

An indirect command is used after verbs of requesting, commanding, persuading, and wishing like *ōrō*, "to ask, entreat" or *imperō*, "to order" or *rogō*, "to request, ask." It is introduced with the conjunction *ut*, or with the conjunction *nē*, if the command is negative. The indirect command has the present subjunctive, if the tense in the main clause is primary, and the imperfect subjunctive if the tense in the main clause is secondary.

Examples:

Ōrō ut ad mē veniās.	"I ask you to come to me."
Ōrāvī ut ad mē venīrēs.	"I asked you to come to me."

Result Clauses:

Result clauses show what would happen as a result of the action in the main clause and are introduced by *ut*, or by *ut nōn* if the result is negative. When trying to recognize a result clause in Latin, look for a clue word in the main clause such as *tam*, "so," *ita*, "in such a way," *tantus*, "so great," *tālis*, "such," *tot* "so many," etc.

Examples:

Terra est tam ingēns ut ā nōbīs tōta cōnspicī nōn possit.
"The earth is so huge that [as a] whole it cannot be observed by us."

Antīquōrum ars nōn erat ita magna ut illī omnia dē terrā intellegerent.
"The science of the ancients was not so great that they understood everything about the earth."

Substantive Clauses of Result

Substantive clauses of result denote accomplishment of an effort. They are introduced by *ut* or *ut nōn* and follow the rules for the sequence of tenses. When substantive clauses are used as subjects, the main verb is impersonal. Such introductory verbs include *accidit, effēcit, contingit, ēvēnit, fit, fierī potest,* and *mōs est.*

Example:

Fit ut āthlētae optimī praemia accipiant.
"It happens that the best athletes get prizes."

Relative Clauses:

A relative clause introduced by *quī, quae, quod* and containing a subjunctive verb may express purpose.

Example:

Missī sunt duo equitēs Rōmānī quī tē interficerent.
"Two Roman knights were sent to kill you."

A relative clause with a subjunctive verb also may suggest a characteristic; the antecedent of the relative pronoun is often an indefinite or negative word.

Example:

> *Hīc in senatū sunt eī quī mē interficere velint.*
> "Here in the Senate are those who wish to kill me."

Cum Clauses:

The conjunction *cum* is used with the indicative when it indicates a general unspecified circumstance that could occur any time. This *cum* with the indicative occurs most often when the tense of the main verb is present and it means "when."

Example:

> *Cum nimis dolēmus, lacrimās fundimus.*
> "When we feel too much pain, we shed tears."

The conjunction *cum* with a pluperfect indicative verb means "whenever" and functions somewhat like the protasis of a conditional sentence.

Example:

> *Cum rēgīna moenia surgentia urbis spectāverat, erat laeta.*
> "Whenever the queen saw the walls of the city rising, she was happy."

The conjunction *cum* with the imperfect subjunctive refers to a concrete or specific circumstance in the past during which the action in the main clause occurred. It is translated with "when."

Example:

> *Cum nimis diū legerem, oculī dolēbant.*
> "When I was reading for too long a time, my eyes were hurting."

The conjunction *cum* with the pluperfect subjunctive refers to a concrete or specific circumstance in the past, which occurred before the action in the main clause. In this case *cum* means "after."

Example:

> *Cum haec omnia audīvisset, nautās quidem timēre coepit Colōnus.*
> "After he had heard all these things, Columbus indeed began to fear
>   the sailors."

When a causal meaning of the conjunction *cum* fits the context better than a temporal meaning, translate *cum* "since." Causal *cum* clauses feature a verb in the subjunctive mood.

Example:

> *Cum tam diū nāvigārent, nautae cupere coepērunt domum petere.*
> "Since they were sailing for such a long time, the sailors began to
>   desire to go home."

When a *cum* clause has a concessive meaning, translate *cum* "although." Concessive *cum* clauses contain a subjunctive mood verb.

Temporal Clauses:

In addition to *cum* temporal clauses, several other temporal clauses feature indicative verbs.

Temporal Conjunctions			
Conjunction	**Mood/Tense**	**Meaning**	**Example**
Cum	indicative	when	Cum legimus, discimus. "When we read, we learn."
Cum	imperfect subjunctive	when	Cum nimis diū legerem, oculī dolēre coepērunt. "When I was reading for too long a time, my eyes began to hurt."
Cum	pluperfect subjunctive	after	Cum librum lēgissem, alium petīvī. "After I had read the book, I looked for another one."
Cum	pluperfect indicative	whenever	Cum librum legeram, laetus eram. "Whenever I read the book, I was happy."
Dum	indicative	while	Dum est spēs, spērāre dēbēmus. "While there is hope, we must hope."
Postquam	indicative	after	Postquam mē vocāvistī, ad tē vēnī. "After you called me, I came to you."
Quotiēs	indicative	as often as	Quotiēs tē videō, gaudium mē capit. "As often as I see you, joy seizes me."
Simul ac	indicative	as soon as	Simul ac verba illa audīvī, timēre coepī. "As soon as I heard those words, I began to fear."

Causal Clauses:

The two most used causal conjunctions in Latin are *quia* and *quod*.

If a causal clause presents the cause as a statement, its verb is in the indicative.

Example:

> *Discimus quia plūra scīre necesse est.*
> "We learn because it is necessary to know more."

If a causal clause presents the cause as the thought of a person in the narrative, but not necessarily that of the author, its verb is often in the subjunctive.

Example:

> *Ille nōn vēnit quod tempus nōn habēret.*
> "He did not come because [according to what he said/thought]
>   he did not have (the) time."

The conjunction *cum* with the subjunctive may also be employed to introduce a causal clause. The causal meaning (rather than temporal or concessive) is typically clear from the context.

Example:

> *Cum mare esset vacuum, nautae spērāre nōlēbant.*
> "Since the sea was empty, the sailors were unwilling to hope."

Concessive Clauses:

A subordinate clause beginning with *quamquam* is concessive. It states a fact despite which the action in the main clause happens or is true. The two most used concessive conjunctions in Latin are *quamquam*, which is used with the indicative and presents the concession as a fact, and *quamvīs*, which is used with the subjunctive and presents the concession as the thought of a person in the narrative, but not necessarily that of the author.

Examples:

> *Quamquam iter est longum, īre dēbēbimus.*
> "Although the trip is long, we will need to go."

> *Quamvīs mēcum venīre nōlīs, hoc tamen facere dēbēs.*
> "Although you do not want to come with me, nevertheless
>   you have to do this."

The conjunction *cum* may also be used with a concessive meaning. When *cum* has this meaning, the verb in the subordinate clause is subjunctive, and in the main clause the adverb *tamen* is usually present or implied, so that it is obvious that the meaning of *cum* is not temporal or causal.

Example:

> *Cum mēcum venīre nōlīs, hoc tamen facere dēbēs.*
> "Although you do not want to come with me, nevertheless
>   you have to do this."

Note that in this sentence *cum* has the same meaning as *quamvīs*.

Statements Dependent on Verbs of Fearing:

The subordinate constructions that depend on verbs expressing fear are quite distinctive.

What we fear might happen in the future is expressed by a clause, introduced by *nē*, whose verb is subjunctive. In such cases, *nē* has a meaning similar to the English "lest."

Example:

> *Caesar timēbat nē ab hostibus facile cōnspicerētur.*
> "Caesar was afraid that/lest he would easily be observed
>   by the enemy."

What we fear might not happen is expressed by a clause, introduced by *ut* or *nē nōn*, whose verb is subjunctive.

Examples:

> *Caesar timēbat ut ā mīlitibus suīs cōnspicerētur.*
> "Caesar was afraid that he would not be observed by his [own] soldiers."

> *Caesar timēbat nē mīlitēs tālibus verbīs nōn firmārentur.*
> "Caesar was afraid that [his] soldiers would not be strengthened by
>   such words."

CONDITIONAL SENTENCES

Type of Conditional Sentence	Subordinate Clause	Main Clause
Future More Vivid	Future Perfect Indicative (or Future Indicative)	Future Indicative
	Sī pecūniam habuerō, "If I have money,	*dōnum pulcherrimum tibi parābō.* I will prepare for you a very beautiful gift."
Future Less Vivid	Perfect subjunctive (or present subjunctive)	Present Subjunctive
	Sī pecūniam habuerim, "If I should have money,	*dōnum pulcherrimum tibi parem.* I would prepare for you a very beautiful gift."
Present Contrary to Fact	Imperfect Subjunctive	Imperfect Subjunctive
	Sī pecūniam habērem, "If I were to possess money,	*dōnum pulcherrimum tibi parārem.* I would prepare for you a very beautiful gift." (but I don't have money and I am not preparing you any gift)
Past Contrary to Fact	Pluperfect Subjunctive	Pluperfect Subjunctive
	Sī pecūniam habuissem, "If I had possessed money,	*dōnum pulcherrimum tibi parāvissem.* I would have prepared for you a very beautiful gift." (but I did not have money and I did not prepare you any gift)
Simple Present (Present General)	Present Indicative	Present Indicative
	Sī pecūniam habeō, "If I [ever] have money,	*dōnum pulcherrimum tibi parō.* I [always] prepare for you a very beautiful gift." (i.e., if the condition of my having money exists)
Simple Past (Past General)	Past Indicative	Past Indicative
	Sī pecūniam habēbam, "If I [ever] had money,	*dōnum pulcherrimum tibi parābam.* I [always] used to prepare for you a very beautiful gift." (i.e., if the condition of my having money was present)

SEQUENCE OF TENSES

The sequence of tenses describes the relationship of the tense of a subordinate subjunctive to that of the main verb.

1. If the main verb is in a present or future tense, the present subjunctive is used in the subordinate clause if the verb in the subjunctive refers to the same time as that of the main verb (or just after). The perfect subjunctive is used in the subordinate clause if the verb in the subjunctive refers to a time before that of the main verb.

   Examples:

   > *Etiam victōrēs sentīre possunt quam terribilis sit haec clādēs.*
   > "Even the victors can feel how terrible this disaster is."

> *Etiam victōrēs sentīre possunt quam terribilis fuerit haec clādēs.*
> "Even the victors can feel how terrible this disaster was."

2. If the main verb is in any past tense, the imperfect subjunctive is used in the subordinate clause if the verb in the subjunctive refers to the same time as that of the main verb (or just after). The pluperfect subjunctive is used in the subordinate clause if the verb in the subjunctive refers to a time before that of the main verb.

   Examples:

   > *Tunc hostēs intellēxērunt quanta esset clādēs.*
   > "Then the enemy realized how great the disaster was."

   > *Prīmō nec nostrī nec hostēs sciēbant quid hominēs in aliā urbis parte fēcissent.*
   > "At first, neither our men nor the enemy were aware of what people had done in the other part of the city."

Complete Sequence of Tenses		
Independent Clause (Main Verb)	Subordinate Clause Same Time, Time Just After	Subordinate Clause Time Before
Primary Tense Verb/ Primary Sequence: Present, Future, Future Perfect Indicative	Present Subjunctive	Perfect Subjunctive
Secondary Tense Verb/ Secondary Sequence: Imperfect, Perfect Indicative	Imperfect Subjunctive	Pluperfect Subjunctive

USE OF THE SUPINES

The perfect passive participle is formed from the fourth principal part of verbs (e.g., *parātum, tentum, cultum, audītum, captum*). This part of the verb itself, with the *–um* ending, is called the supine ending in *–um* or the first supine. The first supine is used after verbs of movement to indicate purpose.

Examples:

Eō dormītum.	"I go to sleep."
Veniō petītum pācem.	"I come to ask for peace."

The second supine, the supine in –ū, is also formed from the perfect passive participle. The supine ending in –ū is similar to an ablative of respect. It is used with the noun phrases *opus* ("there is need of"), *fās* ("it is right"), *nefās* ("it is wrong"), and with adjectives denoting "ease," "difficulty," or the effect on one's feelings and senses. A relatively limited number of supines occur in classical Latin; these supines include *audītū, dictū, factū, inventū, memorātū (memorō, -āre,* to mention), *nātū,* and *vīsū.* Supines appear more frequently in later Latin.

Examples:

Sī hoc est fās dictū.	"If this is legitimate to say."
Quaerunt quid optimum factū sit.	"They ask what is the best thing to do."

NB: In each chapter of the three levels of *LNM,* you have seen the supine in –ū in the phrase *memorābile dictū* found on the first page of each chapter.

USES OF THE GERUND

The gerund has a specific use in each of its four cases. The gerund usually does not have a direct object but sometimes it does take an object in the appropriate case.

Genitive:

The gerund is used with nouns or adjectives that take the genitive, or it may precede *causā* or *gratiā* to show purpose. (For a fuller discussion of purpose, see p. 553 in this appendix.)

Examples:

Eram discendī studiōsus.	"I was fond of/eager for learning."
Est in meō animō spēs fugiendī.	"Hope of fleeing is in my mind."
Excedendī causā, multa parāvērunt.	"For the sake of leaving, they prepared many things."
Proficīscendī gratiā, multa parāvērunt.	"For the sake of setting out, they prepared many things."

Dative:

The dative is sometimes used to indicate the purpose of the action.

Example:

Quaerō locum habitandō.	"I am looking for a place for living (i.e., to live)."

Accusative:

The accusative, usually accompanied by the preposition *ad,* indicates the purpose of the action. (For a fuller discussion of purpose, see p. 553 in this appendix.)

Example:

> *Parātus sum ad pugnandum.*   "I am ready to fight/I am ready for fighting."

Ablative:

The ablative indicates means or instrument.

Example:

> *Discimus legendō.*   "We learn through/by reading."

USES OF THE GERUNDIVE

The gerundive has two functions and therefore two translations.

1. The gerundive usually replaces a gerund that would have a direct object. (Gerunds sometimes take direct objects when the gerund is not in the accusative case.) The gerundive agrees with its object in gender and number, while it takes the case that the gerund would have taken. In this situation, the gerundive translates into English with –ing.

   Example:

   > *Caesar hostis vincendī cupidus erat.*
   > "Caesar was desirous of defeating (eager to defeat) the enemy."

2. The gerundive is used as a verbal adjective with a passive sense that expresses necessity or appropriateness. As a verbal adjective it should be translated "to be . . . ."

   Example:

   > *Virum nōbilem admirandumque . . . .*
   > "a man noble and to be admired."

   When the gerundive as a verbal adjective is used in conjunction with a form of *sum*, this is called the passive periphrastic. (For a fuller discussion of the passive periphrastic see p. 550 in this appendix.)

   Example:

   > *Iter per prōvinciam nōn faciendum est.*
   > "A journey must not be made through the province."

The following examples illustrate the differences between the use of the gerund and the gerundive in the various cases.

Examples:

	Gerund	**Gerundive**
Genitive:	*Eram studiōsus videndī.*	*Eram studiōsus videndae spēluncae.*
	"I was fond of seeing."	"I was fond of seeing the cave."
	Celeriter adveniendī gratiā (causā), sēcum multa nōn tulērunt.	*Pacis faciendae causā (gratiā), amīcitiam celeriter confirmant.*
	"For the sake of arriving quickly, they did not bring many things with them."	"For the sake of making peace, they establish friendship quickly."
Dative:	*Quaerō locum aedificandō.*	*Quaerō locum aedificandae domuī.*
	"I am looking for a place to build."	"I am looking for a place for building a house."
Accusative:	*Habēbam tēlum ad repellendum.*	*Habēbam tēlum ad repellenda animālia.*
	"I had a spear for repelling."	"I had a spear for repelling animals (to repel animals)."
Ablative:	*Discimus legendō.*	*Discimus legendīs librīs.*
	"We learn through/by reading."	"We learn through/by reading books." (literally "by books to be read")

THE PASSIVE PERIPHRASTIC

The gerundive may be used with a form of "to be" to express obligation or necessity. As a passive periphrastic it should be translated "must be, had to be, will have to be" depending on the tense of the verb *sum*.

Examples:

Librī sunt legendī.   present passive periphrastic
"Books must be/have to be read."

Librī erunt legendī.   future passive periphrastic
"Books will have to be read."

Librī erant legendī.   past passive periphrastic
"Books had to be read."

In order to indicate who is the agent of the action, the dative of agent is used (not the ablative of agent, which is usually used with the passive voice).

Example:

> *Librī mihi sunt legendī.*
> "Books have to be read by me" or, its active equivalent,
> > "I have to read books."

INFINITIVES

FUNCTIONS OF THE INFINITIVE

1. **Complementary with *dēbeō, possum, soleō, coepī, dubitō, desinō*:**

   The infinitive completes the meanings of these verbs, each of which has an incomplete meaning by itself.

   Example:

   > In the sentence *legere dēbeō*, which means "I ought to read," the infinitive completes the meaning of "I ought."

2. **Infinitives with Impersonal Verbs:**

   Many impersonal verbs govern an infinitive. The person doing the action in these phrases is sometimes in the dative case and other times in the accusative.

   Examples:

   > *Nōn placet mihi scrībere magnum librum.*
   > "It does not please me to write a large book."
   >
   > *Necesse est mē scrībere doctum libellum.*
   > "It is necessary for me to write a learned little book."

3. **Indirect statement after verbs of saying and thinking:**

   In English a subordinate statement after a verb of saying or thinking begins with the conjunction "that." In classical Latin no such conjunction is used: instead, the subordinate statement is expressed in the accusative and infinitive as a kind of object of the verb of saying or thinking. Consider the English sentence "I think that the book is good." In Latin the same sentence is *Putō librum esse bonum.*

4. **Nominative and infinitive:**

   In Latin, when a verb of saying or thinking is in the passive, the accusative and infinitive is typically not used. The subject of the indirect statement is the same as the subject of the verb of saying or thinking, and so it is in the nominative. The verb in the indirect statement is still an infinitive. In this case, Latin is much closer to English. Consider the English sentence "The book is thought to be good." In Latin the same sentence is *Liber bonus esse putātur.*

5. **Accusative and infinitive with *volō, nōlō* and *mālō*:**

The verbs *volō, nōlō,* and *mālō* are used with the accusative and infinitive. But it should be noted that if the subject of the main verb and the infinitive are the same, then the subject of the infinitive is not expressed.

Examples:

Accusative and Infinitive	No Change in Subject
Volō tē ad mē venīre.	*Volō ad tē venīre.*
"I want you to come to me."	"I want to come to you."
Nōn vīs mē ad tē venīre.	*Nōn vīs ad mē venīre.*
"You do not want me to come to you."	"You do not want to come to me."
Mālumus vōs ad nōs venīre.	*Mālumus ad vōs venīre.*
"We prefer that you come to us."	"We prefer to come to you."

6. **The Infinitive of Purpose:**

The infinitive of purpose is the least common way to show purpose in Latin and generally is seen only in poetry.

Example:

> *Nōn tē . . . frangere persequor.*   "I do not pursue you to break you."

7. **Historical Infinitive:**

In a narration (especially in histories) that involves a rapid sequence of events, the present infinitive instead of the indicative is sometimes employed. In such cases there are usually several infinitives in succession, and their subjects, if expressed, are nominative (not accusative).

Example:

> *Tunc Catilīna cum mīlitibus prīmīs versārī, laesīs auxilium dare,*
>   *omnia cūrāre, ferōciter ipse pugnāre . . . .*

> "Then Catiline was occupied with the front rank of soldiers:
>   he was helping the wounded, he was taking charge of everything,
>   and he himself was fighting fiercely . . . ."

TENSES OF THE INFINITIVE IN INDIRECT STATEMENT

In Latin, when the accusative and infinitive construction of indirect statement is used, the tense of the infinitive is always relative to the main verb of saying or thinking.

Indirect Statements		
Infinitive	**Time in relation to main clause**	**Example**
Present Infinitive	SAME	*Putō multōs hominēs librum legere.* "I think that many people are reading the book." *Putābam multōs hominēs librum legere.* "I used to think that many people were reading the book."
Perfect Infinitive	BEFORE	*Putō multōs hominēs librum lēgisse.* "I think that many people have read the book." *Putābam multōs hominēs librum lēgisse.* "I used to think that many people had read the book."
Future Infinitive	AFTER	*Putō multōs hominēs librum lēctūrōs esse.* "I think that many people will read/are going to read/are going to be reading the book." *Putābam multōs hominēs librum lēctūrōs esse.* "I used to think that many people would read/were going to read/were going to be reading the book."

PURPOSE CONSTRUCTIONS

There are several ways to express purpose in Latin. The following examples illustrate these various constructions.

Examples	Purpose Construction	Translation
Hunc mihi timōrem ēripe ut tandem timēre dēsinam.	Purpose Clause with *ut/nē* + subjunctive verb	"Take this fear from me so that finally I may cease being afraid."
Repertī sunt duo Rōmānī quī tē interficerent.	Relative Clause of Purpose + subjunctive verb	"Two Romans were found who were to kill you." (i.e., in order to kill you)
Vēnērunt ad vescendum nōbīscum.	Accusative Gerund in a Purpose Construction with *ad*	"They came to eat with us."
Ad cōnficiendās rēs, Orgetorīx dēligitur.	Accusative Gerundive in a Purpose Construction with *ad*	"Orgetorix is chosen to complete the matters."
Loquendī pūblicē causā, Orgetorīx ōrātiōnem parāvit.	Genitive Gerund in a Purpose Construction with *causā/gratiā*	"For the sake of speaking publicly, Orgetorix prepared a speech."
In solitum locum convēnērunt fallendōrum custōdum causā.	Genitive Gerundive in a Purpose Construction with *causā/gratiā*	"They came together into the customary place for the sake of deceiving [their] guards."
Eōs mē salūtātum mīsistī.	Supine of Purpose	"You sent them to greet me."
Vīnum fert bibere amicō.	Infinitive of Purpose	"He brings [his] friend wine to drink."

PARTICIPLES

USE OF PARTICIPLES

A participle is both an adjective and a verb. Like verbs, participles express an action and can be modified by adverbial constructions. Like adjectives, participles agree with a noun, expressed or implied, in case, number, and gender.

Participles have literal meanings but also temporal and occasionally causal meanings.

The present active participle indicates an action that happens *at the same time* as the action of the main verb. It is translated literally with *-ing* in English or, less literally, with a clause beginning with a relative pronoun (e.g., "who, which, that") or a temporal conjunction such as "while."

Example:

> *Arbitrāntēs angustōs sē fīnēs habēre, Helvētiī excēdere constituērunt.*
> "Thinking that they had narrow territory, the Helvetians decided to leave."

The perfect passive participle indicates an action that happened *before* the action of the main verb. It can often be translated literally into English by "having been," or it can be translated by a clause beginning with a temporal conjunction such as "when" or "after."

Examples:

> *Rēgnī cupiditāte inductus coniūrātiōnem nōbilitātis fēcit.*
> "(Having been) influenced by the desire for a kingdom,
>   he made a conspiracy of the nobility."

> *Lāvīnaque vēnit lītora, multum ille et terrīs iactātus et altō.*
> "He came to the Lavinian shores, after he had been tossed
>   much on both the lands and the sea."

The future active participle indicates an action that is intended to happen *after* the action of the main verb. It can be translated literally into English by "about to," "going to," or "intending to" or, less literally, by a clause beginning with a relative pronoun or temporal conjunction.

Examples:

> *Venit ecce leaena dēpositūra sitim vīcīnī fontis in undā.*
> "Look a lioness comes about to/intending to quench
>   [her] thirst in the water of a nearby spring."

> *Fortūna semper discessūra nihil dat.*
> "Fortune, which is always about to go away, gives nothing."

When the future active participle combines with a form of *sum*, this construction is called the active periphrastic. The future active participle and the form of *sum* retain their meanings. In an active periphrastic, the future active participle agrees with the subject of the sentence and thus is most often in the nominative case but may be in the accusative when the subject is the subject of an indirect statement.

Example:

> *Frūmentum sēcum portātūrī erant.*
> "They were about (or intended) to carry the grain with them."

Sometimes participles have nuances that go beyond the temporal meaning and may express cause, as in the following example:

Example:

> *Aliī putantēs monīlia esse vincula et lēgātōs esse servōs,*
>   *illa vincula reprehendēbant.*
>
> "Other [people], because they were thinking that the
>   necklaces were chains and the ambassadors were slaves,
>   criticized those chains."

Deponent verbs have a present participle, a future participle with an active meaning (*ūtēns*, "using," *ūsūrus*, "going to use"), and a perfect participle with an active meaning also (*ūsus*, "having used").

THE ABLATIVE ABSOLUTE

The ablative absolute is a dependent clause that expresses circumstances logically linked to what is happening in the main clause of a sentence but that is not tied grammatically to the main clause. The ablative absolute is made up of a noun or pronoun in the ablative agreeing with a participle, along with other words depending on them or modifying them. Sometimes an adjective or another noun can take the place of the participle, such as *Caesare duce* ("with Caesar as general"). Note that there are no subordinating conjunctions like *cum*, *postquam*, or *quamquam* in an ablative absolute. The subject of the ablative absolute is, with only very rare exceptions, different from the subject of the main clause.

The perfect participle in an ablative absolute refers to a time *before* the time of the verb in the main clause while a present participle refers to the *same* time as that of the verb in the main clause. When a present participle is in an ablative absolute, it usually ends in *–e*, not in *–ī*. When the perfect participle is used in the ablative absolute, the action indicated in the ablative absolute has to be said passively, even if the same action could be expressed actively using a different type of construction such as a *cum* clause. Since only deponent verbs in Latin can have a perfect participle with an active meaning, this is an exception to perfect participles being phrased in the passive in ablative absolutes. The use of a deponent perfect participle in an ablative absolute, however, is not common and is limited (in classical Latin) to deponent verbs without an object.

Example:

> *Caesare mortuō, multī cīvēs bellum timēre coepērunt.*
> "After Caesar had died, many citizens began to fear war."

The ablative absolute can fulfill the same functions as temporal, causal, conditional, and concessive clauses. The temporal, causal, conditional, or concessive meaning is inferred from the context. Sometimes the presence of the word *tamen* in the main clause is an indication that the meaning is concessive.

Examples:

Temporal Meaning

Caesare duce dictō, mīlitēs sē ad iter parāre coepērunt.
"When Caesar had been named leader, the soldiers prepared
   themselves for the journey."

Causal Meaning

Hostibus appropinquantibus, cōnsul exercitum parāvit.
"Because the enemy was approaching, the consul prepared
   an/the army."

Concessive Meaning

Hostibus appropinquantibus, cōnsul tamen exercitum nōn parāvit.
"Although the enemy was approaching, nevertheless the consul
   did not prepare an/the army."

CONJUNCTIONS

Latin	English
atque, ac	and
atquī	but, nevertheless
aut	or
autem††††	however
cum	when, after
dum	while
enim††††	for, in fact
et	and
itaque	and so
nam	for, in fact
nec, neque	and not, nor
nōn sōlum . . . sed etiam	not only . . . but also
postquam	after
-que	and
sed	but
sī	if
sive, seu	whether, or if
tamen	however

†††† The conjunctions *autem* and *enim* are postpositive.

INTERROGATIVE WORDS

Latin	English
cūr?	why?
-ne?	interrogative particle
nōnne?	interrogative expecting a positive answer
num?	interrogative expecting a negative answer
qualis?	of what sort, what kind of?
quam?	to what extent, how?
quandō?	when?
quantus?	of what size, how great?
quī? quae? quod?	which? what?
quis? quid?	who? what?
quōmodo?	how?
quot?	how many?
quotiēns, quotiēs?	how often?
ubi?	where?

CORRELATIVES

Correlatives are conjunctions and adverbs used in pairs to make parallel or balanced clauses. Most correlatives can be used alone with one meaning but when used with a paired word mean something else.

Used Alone		Used as Correlatives	
et	and	et ... et	both ... and
aut	or	aut ... aut	either ... or
neque (nec)	nor, and ... not	neque (nec) ... neque (nec)	neither ... nor
sive	whether	sīve ... sīve	whether ... or
tantus	so great	tantus ... quantus	as much ... as
quantus	how great		
tam	so	tam ... quam	so ... as
quam	how		
tālis	such	tālis ... quālis	such ... as
quālis	of what sort		
tot	so many	tot ... quot	so many ... as
quot	how many		
totiēns	so often	totiēns ... quotiēns	so often ... as
quotiēns	how often		
cum	when	tum ... cum	not only ... but also
tum	then		

APPENDIX E

SUPPLEMENTARY GRAMMAR, MORPHOLOGY, AND SYNTAX

This appendix contains additional information on grammar and syntax that is NOT covered in Levels 1, 2, or 3 of *Latin for the New Millennium* and is intended for students continuing with another Latin course.

CASE USES

GENITIVE

Subjective Genitive:

The genitive indicates the subject.

> **Example:**
>> *Patriae beneficia.*
>> "The benefits of the fatherland." (i.e., the benefits given by the fatherland)

Genitive with Verbs of Memory:

Verbs of reminding, remembering, and forgetting take the genitive (some of these verbs also take the accusative).

> **Example:**
>> *Hārum rērum semper meminī.*
>> "I always am mindful of these things."

DATIVE

Dative of Purpose:

A noun in the dative may indicate the purpose or tendency of an act or situation. These dative nouns are not modified by any adjectives other than those of magnitude or extent. This dative is often joined with another dative that indicates the person affected. The verb is usually *esse*, although a few other verbs such as *habēre*, *dūcere*, and *dare* are also used in this construction.

> **Examples:**
>> *Cōnsilia tua mihi magnō auxiliō fuērunt.*
>> "Your suggestions were a source of great help to me."
>>
>> *Verba huius poētae mihi sunt gaudiō.*
>> "The words of this poet are a source of joy to me."

Ethical Dative:

This dative indicates a person interested in the action; its grammatical and logical link with the rest of the sentence is quite loose.

Example:

> *Tālia mihi dicta dēfendis?*
> "Do you defend such sayings (in my sight)?"

ACCUSATIVE

Adverbial Accusative:

A neuter adjective or pronoun expresses the type or extent of an action.

Examples:

> *Plūs valeō quam tū.*
> "I have more strength than you."
>
> *In carminibus legendīs plūrimum potest.*
> "In reading poetry s/he is the most effective."

Double Accusative:

A group of verbs may take two objects, one expressing the thing done, and the other expressing the personal object of the action. This construction occurs with some very common verbs, including *docēre* ("to teach"), *rogāre* ("to ask"), *pōscere* ("to demand"), and *cēlāre* ("to hide").

Examples:

> *Rogō tē tuam sententiam.*   "I ask you your opinion."
>
> *Doceō tē hanc artem.*   "I teach you this skill."

Note that many of these verbs, including those in the examples above, may also take alternate constructions, such as the accusative of the person affected with the preposition *dē* and the ablative indicating the thing involved; for example: *Tē dē hīs rēbus docēbō* ("I will teach you about these things").

ABLATIVE

Ablative of Price:

Specific price is expressed by the ablative with verbs of buying and selling.

Example:

> *Agrum eōrum vigintī talentīs ēmī.*
> "I bought their field for twenty talents."

NUMBERS
Numbers may be divided into four categories.

Cardinal numbers:

These answer the question *quot?* ("how many?").

Example:

> *Quīnque sunt nautae.*   "There are five sailors."

Ordinal numbers:

These answer the question *quotus?* ("which in order?").

Example:

> *Hic est nauta quīntus.*   "This is the fifth sailor."

Distributive numbers:

These answer the question *quotēnī?* ("how many each?"), and they are regularly used in Latin when one indicates how many items are to be associated with each person or each set of persons/things. The distributives are also used with nouns that have plural forms with singular meanings, such as *castra* ("a camp") and *litterae* ("a letter").

Examples:

> *Quīnquāgēnī nautae in singulīs nāvibus erant.*
> "In each ship there were fifty sailors."
>
> *Mīlitēs Caesaris in bīnīs castrīs exspectābant.*
> "Caesar's soldiers were waiting in two camps."

Numerical adverbs:

These answer the question *quotiēs?* ("how often?"), and they indicate how many times something happened.

Example:

> *Quīnquiēns rogāvērunt Colōnum ut in Hispāniam redīrent.*
> "Five times they asked Columbus that they turn back to Spain."

The declension of the cardinal number adjectives *ūnus, a, um* ("one"); *duo, duae, duo* ("two"); and *trēs, tria* ("three") are found in Appendix D on p. 506.

The other cardinal numbers from *quattuor* to *centum* are indeclinable. The rest of the cardinals up to *mīlle* are adjectives of the first and second declension, as are all the ordinals and distributives.

	CARDINAL	ORDINAL	DISTRIBUTIVE	ADVERBS
I.	ūnus, a, um	prīmus, a, um	singulī, ae, a	semel
II.	duo, duae, duo	secundus, alter	bīnī	bis
III.	trēs, trēs, tria	tertius	ternī/trīnī	ter
IV.	quattuor	quārtus	quaternī	quater
V.	quīnque	quīntus	quīnī	quīnquiēns
VI.	sex	sextus	sēnī	sexiēns
VII.	septem	septimus	septēnī	septiēns
VIII.	octō	octāvus	octōnī	octiēns
IX.	novem	nōnus	novēnī	noviēns
X.	decem	decimus	dēnī	deciēns
XI.	ūndecim	ūndecimus	ūndēnī	ūndeciēns
XII.	duodecim	duodecimus	duodēnī	duodeciēns
XIII.	trēdecim	tertius decimus	ternī dēnī	terdeciēns
XIV.	quattuordecim	quārtus decimus	quaternī dēnī	quaterdeciēns
XV.	quīndecim	quīntus decimus	quīnī dēnī	quīndeciēns
XVI.	sēdecim	sextus decimus	sēnī dēnī	sēdeciēns
XVII.	septendecim	septimus decimus	septēnī dēnī	septiēns deciēns
XVIII.	duodēvīgintī	duodēvīcēsimus	duodēvīcēnī	duodēvīciēns
XIX.	ūndēvīgintī	ūndēvīcēsimus	ūndēvīcēnī	ūndēvīciēns
XX.	vīgintī	vīcēsimus	vīcēnī	vīciēns
XXI.	ūnus et vīgintī	ūnus et vīcēsimus	vīcēnī singulī	semel et vīciēns
XXX.	trīgintā	trīcēsimus	trīcēnī	trīciēns
XL.	quadrāgintā	quadrāgēsimus	quadrāgēnī	quadrāgiēns
L.	quīnquāgintā	quīnquāgēsimus	quīnquāgēnī	quīnquāgiēns
LX.	sexāgintā	sexāgēsimus	sexāgēnī	sexāgiēns
LXX.	septuāgintā	septuāgēsimus	septuāgēnī	septuāgiēns
LXXX.	octōgintā	octōgēsimus	octōgēnī	octōgiēns
XC.	nōnāgintā	nōnāgēsimus	nōnāgēnī	nōnāgiēns
C.	centum	centēsimus	centēnī	centiēns
CC.	ducentī	ducentēsimus	ducēnī	ducentiēns
CCC.	trecentī	trecentēsimus	trecēnī	trecentiēns
CCCC.	quadringentī	quadringentēsimus	quadringēnī	quadringentiēns
D.	quīngentī	quīngentēsimus	quīngēnī	quīngentiēns
DC.	sescentī	sescentēsimus	sescēnī	sescentiēns
DCC.	septingentī	septingentēsimus	septingēnī	septingentiēns
DCCC.	octingentī	octingentēsimus	octingēnī	octingentiēns
DCCCC.	nōngentī	nōngentēsimus	nōngēnī	nōngentiēns
M.	mīlle	mīllēsimus	mīllēnī	mīlliēns
MM.	duo mīlia	bis mīllēsimus	bīna mīlia	bis mīlliēns

SUPPLEMENTAL INFORMATION ON VERB FORMS

FUTURE PASSIVE INFINITIVE IN INDIRECT SPEECH

The equivalent of a future passive infinitive in indirect speech may be formed in two ways: by using (1) the supine ending in *–um* with *īrī* (the passive infinitive of *īre*) or (2) *fore* (the future active infinitive of *esse* in shortened form) with *ut* and a result clause. The supine form in *–um*, of course, never changes its ending, regardless of its implied "subject."

> **Examples:**
>
> *Caesar multōs cīvēs servātum īrī pollicitus est.*
> "Caesar promised that many citizens would be saved."
>
> *Caesar fore ut multī cīvēs servārentur pollicitus est.*
> "Caesar promised that many citizens would be saved."

FUTURE IMPERATIVE

There is also a future active and passive imperative of most verbs that indicates a more formal sort of request. Note that in the passive only singular forms occur.

	First conjugation	Second conjugation	Third conjugation	Fourth conjugation	Third conjugation *–iō*
Active					
Second person singular positive	amātō (you shall love)	monētō (you shall warn)	petitō (you shall seek)	audītō (you shall hear)	capitō (you shall capture)
Second person plural positive	amātōte (you shall love)	monētōte (you shall warn)	petitōte (you shall seek)	audītōte (you shall hear)	capitōte (you shall capture)
Passive					
Second person singular positive	amātor (you shall be loved)	monētor (you shall be warned)	petitor (you shall be sought)	audītor (you shall be heard)	capitor (you shall be captured)

IMPERSONAL VERBS

Some impersonal verbs, such as *paenitet* ("it repents/is a cause of regret"), *pudet* ("it causes shame"), *taedet* ("it bores"), and *piget* ("it causes regret"), may be constructed with genitive and infinitive.

> **Example:**
>
> *Īrae meae mē paenitet.*
> "I regret/am sorry for my anger."

Sometimes intransitive verbs can be used impersonally in the third person singular passive to indicate a general action. If the tense is perfect, the participial part of the verb must be in the neuter nominative singular.

Examples:

> *Ad forum itur.*
> "There is a going to the forum/One goes to the forum."

> *Ad urbem ventum est.*
> "There was an arrival at the city/[They] came to the city."

Verbs that take a dative instead of an accusative direct object, such as *parcō* ("to spare"), *persuādeō* ("to persuade"), *noceō* ("to harm"), and *īgnōscō* ("to pardon"), are only used impersonally in the passive.

Examples:

Tibi nōn nocētur.	"You are not being harmed."
Nōbīs ā Cicerōne persuādētur.	"We are persuaded by Cicero."
Nēminī parcēbātur.	"No one was being spared."

PASSIVE PERIPHRASTIC

Sometimes, the passive periphrastic is used impersonally, that is, no person is specified in association with the necessary action. In this situation, the gerundive is neuter—since the subject is impersonal.

Example:

> *Legendum est.*
> "There must be reading./People have to read./One has to read./
>   One must read."

EXCLAMATORY QUESTIONS

Exclamatory questions may be expressed with the subjunctive, with or without *ut*.

Example:

> *Egone tibi pauper, hominī tam dīvitī, pecūniam dare dēbeam?*
> "I, a poor man, ought to give money to you, so wealthy a man?"

MORE ON THE SUBJUNCTIVE IN DEPENDENT CLAUSES

Futurity in Indirect Questions

If the verb in an indirect question is active and refers to a time after that of the main verb, this future time may be indicated by the use of the future active participle with the subjunctive of *esse*. The tense of the subjunctive of *esse* normally conforms to the rules for sequence of tenses.

Examples:

> Mīles rogat *quid dīxerimus.*
> "The soldier is asking what we said."

> Mīles rogat *quid dictūrī sīmus.*
> "The soldier is asking what we are going to say."

> Mīles rogāvit *quid dicerēmus.*
> "The soldier asked what we were saying."

> Mīles rogāvit *quid dictūrī essēmus.*
> "The soldier asked what we were going to say."

Clauses after Verbs of Hindering and Preventing: *nē, quōminus, quīn*

If a verb of hindering or preventing is positive, the clause depending on it is in the subjunctive mood introduced by *nē* or *quōminus.*

Example:

> *Impedior nē/quōminus dē hīs rēbus loquar.*
> "I am prevented from speaking about these things."

If the verb of hindering or preventing is negative or implies a negative, or is joined with the adverbs *vix* or *aegrē,* the clause depending on it is in the subjunctive mood introduced by *quīn* or (more rarely) *quōminus.*

Example:

> *Mīlitēs impedīrī nōn poterant quīn arma caperent.*
> "The soldiers could not be prevented from seizing arms."

More Clauses with *quīn*

The word *quīn* has several distinctive and widely differing functions and meanings.

A clause introduced by *quīn* with its verb in the subjunctive depends on negative (and never affirmative) phrases of doubting.

Examples:

> *Nōn erat dubium quīn mīlitēs arma capere vellent.*
> "There was no doubt that the soldiers wanted to seize arms."

> *Nōn dubitō quīn Vergilius poēta fuerit optimus.*
> "I do not doubt that Vergil was the best poet."

Very often *quīn* is the equivalent of *ut nōn* in result clauses if the main verb is negative, or an interrogative implying a negative, or is joined with the adverbs *vix* or *aegrē* (which mean "hardly," or "scarcely"). In such sentences *quīn* is the equivalent of a relative with a negative (i.e., *quī, quae, quod + nōn*). It is generally used instead of a relative in the nominative case (and occasionally in place of a relative in the accusative).

Example:

> *Nūllus homō est tam doctus quīn aliquid aliud discere possit.*
> "No person is so learned that he cannot learn something else."

Quīn introducing an interrogative sentence sometimes means "why not(?)."

Example:

> *Quīn pācem petimus?*   "Why do we not seek peace?"

Explicative Clauses

An entire clause, that has an explicative or "completing the circumstances" meaning and is introduced by *quod* with its verb in the indicative is used as the object of certain set phrases, the most common of which are: *addō* ("I add"), *praetereō* ("I pass over"), and *mittō* ("I disregard"). *Quod* in such sentences means "the fact that."

Example:

> *Praetereō quod cīvēs nostrī cibō indigent.*
> "I pass over the fact that our citizens need food."

An entire clause that has an explicative or "completing the circumstances" meaning, and is introduced by *quod* with its verb in the indicative, is used as the subject of certain set phrases, such as *bonum/malum/(etc.) est* ("it is good or bad that"), *accēdit* ("[the fact] is added that"), *bene/male/(etc.) accidit, ēvenit, fit* ("it turns out well/badly [etc.] that").

Example:

> *Accēdit quod nē ūnum quidem amīcum inter iūdicēs cōnspiciō.*
> "Added is the fact that I do not observe even one friend among the jurors."

Comparative Clauses

In a comparative sentence that expresses likeness or difference as a fact, the indicative is used in both clauses. Common correlative words expressing likeness are *sīc/ita . . . ut* ("just/so . . . as"), or *perinde/iuxtā . . . atque* ("just/so . . . as"), and *pariter aequē . . . atque* ("equally . . . as").

Example:

> *Perinde fēcī, atque dēbuī.*
> "As I ought [to have acted], so I acted."

Common correlative words expressing difference or unlikeness in a comparison of fact are *aliter/secus . . . atque* ("differently . . . from," "otherwise . . . than"), *contrā . . . atque/quam* ("contrarily . . . to").

Examples:

> *Contrā quam putāvī, nēmō vēnit.*
> "Contrary to my supposition, no one came."

> *Aliter dīxit atque fēcit.*
> "His words were different from his action."

In comparative sentences that are hypothetical, conditional, or contrary to fact, the verb of the subordinate clause is subjunctive. The most common comparative conjunctions in such sentences are *quam sī* ("than/as . . . if"), *quasi, ut sī, tamquam sī, velut sī* ("as . . . if"). Occasionally we find simply *tamquam* or *velut* with a subjunctive verb.

Examples:

> *"Mātris tuae negōtia,"* inquit Atticus, *"cūrāvī, velut sī essent mea."*
> "I managed your mother's business affairs," said Atticus, "as though they were mine."

> *Omnēs, quī (quidem) hīc maneant, Atticum laudāre volunt.*
> "Everyone, at least [of] those who are staying here, wants to praise Atticus."

MORE ON CONDITIONAL SENTENCES

Hypothetical conditions may pertain to the future, in which case they are often called "future-less-vivid conditions." Generally, in such conditions the verbs in both the main and subordinate clause are in the present subjunctive although the verb in the subordinate clause may be in the perfect subjunctive if the action clearly happened before that of the main clause.

Examples:

> *Sī Rōmae habitētis, sītis fēlīcēs.*
> "Should you (pl.) live in Rome, you would be happy."

> *Sī aedēs in urbe positās ēmerim, Rōmae saepius maneam.*
> "If I should buy a house located in the city, I would stay in Rome more often."

Hypothetical conditions of the past usually have verbs in the imperfect subjunctive in both the "if-clause" and the main clause. In appearance they resemble unfulfilled or contrary to fact conditions of the present. In fact, they are to be distinguished from such conditional sentences because of subtle differences in meaning. These conditions are not actually contrary-to-fact or unfulfilled, but rather present a hypothetical or potential statement about a past time.

Example:

> *Sī Caesar mīlitēs in eōrum terram ad eōs iuvandōs mittere vidērētur,*
> *nōn tam bellum gerere quam hostēs repellere putārētur.*

> "Were Caesar to seem to send soldiers into their territory in order
> to help them, he would be thought not so much to wage war as
> to repel enemies."

MORE ON INDIRECT STATEMENT/DISCOURSE

Subordinate clauses that are really part of indirect speech have their verb(s) in the subjunctive, even if this/these verb(s) would have been in the indicative in the direct statement.

Example:

> *Caesar sē quoque ā mīlitibus, quōs ipse vidēre posset, facile cōnspicī*
> *posse intellēxit.*
> "Caesar realized that he too could be easily observed by the soldiers
> whom he himself could see." (The phrase *quōs ipse vidēre posset* is a
> part of what Caesar realized.)

Subordinate clauses in a passage of indirect discourse that are not part of the thought of the subject of the indirect discourse (such as explanatory remarks of the author) have verb(s) in the indicative.

Example:

> *Thēseus sē in Crētam, quae est īnsula, cum adulēscentibus Athēniēnsibus*
> *nāvigātūrum esse prōmīsit.*
> "Theseus promised that he would sail with the Athenian youths to Crete,
> which is an island." (The phrase *quae est īnsula* is an explanation given
> by the author rather than a part of what Theseus promised.)

Pronouns, as well as adverbs of place and time, fit the point of view of indirect speech introduced by a third person verb. Therefore, *hic* in direct speech becomes *ille* in the indirect speech, *hīc* becomes *ibi*, *nunc* becomes *tunc* (if the main verb introducing the indirect speech is in a past tense), and so forth.

Examples:

(Direct) *Haec praemia sunt optima.*
(These are the words of the athletes.) "These prizes are the best."

(Indirect) *Āthlētae illa praemia esse optima crēdēbant.*
(Someone else is reporting the words/thoughts of the athletes.)
   "The athletes believed that those prizes were the best."

(Direct) *Hīc templum aedificābō.*
(These are the words of the queen.) "Here I shall build a temple."

(Indirect) *Rēgīna sē templum ibi aedificātūram esse dīxit.*
(Someone else is reporting the words of the queen.) "The queen
   said that she would build a temple there."

(Direct) *Multās nāvēs vidēre nunc possum!*
(These are the words of the sailor.) "Now I can see many ships."

(Indirect) *Nauta multās sē nāvēs vidēre tunc posse clāmāvit.*
(Someone else is reporting the words of the sailor.) "The sailor
   shouted that he was then able to see many ships."

Questions and commands, which would have indicative and imperative moods in direct speech, are expressed in indirect discourse with subjunctive verbs.

Examples:

(Direct) *Hostēs ferōcissimī ā vōbīs sunt victī. Propter virtūtem vestram*
   Carthāginiēnsēs ab omnibus gentibus timentur. Cūr igitur nunc Alpēs,
   montēs nōn hominēs, montēs nōn hostēs, timētis? Timōrem exstinguite!
   Sarcinās parāte! Nōlīte in castrīs manēre!
"The most ferocious enemies have been defeated by you. Because of your
   courage the Carthaginians are feared by all peoples. Why do you now fear
   the Alps, mountains not people, mountains not enemies? Destroy fear!
   Prepare the baggage! Do not stay in the camp!"

(Indirect) *Hannibal īrātus dīxit hostēs ferōcissimōs ab illīs esse victōs. Propter*
   eōrum virtūtem Carthāginiēnsēs ab omnibus gentibus timērī. Cūr igitur tunc
   Alpēs, montēs nōn hominēs, montēs nōn hostēs, timērent? Timōrem
   exstinguerent! Sarcinās parārent! Nē in castrīs manērent!
"Angered, Hannibal said that the most ferocious enemies had been defeated
   by them (i.e., the soldiers). Because of their courage the Carthaginians
   were feared by all peoples. Why then were they afraid of the Alps,
   mountains not people, mountains not enemies? They should destroy fear!
   They should prepare <their> baggage! They must not stay in the camp!"

Sometimes, however, RHETORICAL QUESTIONS, which are not real questions but are asked just for effect and expect no answer, are expressed with the accusative and infinitive rather than the subjunctive in indirect speech.

Example:

> (Direct) *Hostēs ferōcissimī ā vōbīs sunt victī. Propter virtūtem vestram Carthāginiēnsēs ab omnibus gentibus timentur. Cūr igitur nunc Alpēs, montēs nōn hominēs, montēs nōn hostēs, timētis? Quis umquam rem tam turpem vīdit?! Timōrem exstinguite! Sarcinās parāte! Nōlīte in castrīs manēre!*
>
> "The most ferocious enemies have been defeated by you. Because of your courage the Carthaginians are feared by all peoples. Why do you now fear the Alps, mountains not people, mountains not enemies? Who ever saw a thing so shameful?! Destroy fear! Prepare the baggage! Do not stay in the camp!"

> (Indirect) *Hannibal īrātus dīxit hostēs ferōcissimōs ab illīs esse victōs. Propter eōrum virtūtem Carthāginiēnsēs ab omnibus gentibus timērī. Cūr igitur tunc Alpēs, montēs nōn hominēs, montēs nōn hostēs, timērent? Quem umquam rem tam turpem vīdisse?! Timōrem exstinguerent! Sarcinās parārent! Nē in castrīs manērent!*
>
> "Angered, Hannibal said that the most ferocious enemies had been defeated by them (i.e., the soldiers). Because of their courage the Carthaginians were feared by all peoples. Why were they then afraid of the Alps, mountains not people, mountains not enemies? Who had ever seen a thing so shameful?! They should destroy fear! They should prepare <their> baggage! They must not stay in the camp!"

MORE ON INTERROGATIVE WORDS: *NUM, NŌNNE, NECNE, ANNŌN*

Num introducing a direct question expects a negative answer.

Example:

> *Num mōrēs hōrum hominum malōs probās?*
> "Surely you do not approve of the bad character of these people, [do you]?" (Expected answer: "Of course not.")

Num introducing an indirect question does not have this force. In indirect questions, *num* is a neutral interrogative particle that indicates no expectation about the type of answer.

Example:

> *Amīcum meum rogābō num carmina Vergilī lēgerit.*
> "I shall ask my friend whether he has read the poems of Vergil."
> (I have no expectation about what his answer might be.)

Nōnne introducing a direct question expects an affirmative answer.

Example:

> *Nōnne hoc aedificium esse pulchrum putās?*
> "Don't you think this building is beautiful?"
> (Expected answer: "Yes indeed, I do.")

Annōn means "or not" and is typically used in direct questions.

Example:

> *Suntne hī hominēs cīvēs, annōn?*
> "Are these people citizens, or not?"

Necne means "or not" and is typically used in indirect questions.

Example:

> *Rogāvimus pecūnia mīlitibus esset data necne.*
> "We asked whether the money had been given to the soldiers or not."

LATIN TO ENGLISH GLOSSARY

This glossary contains the vocabulary needed to facilitate reading the Latin passages and completing the Language Fact exercises in *Latin for the New Millennium*, Level 3.

*All words from the **Vocabulary to Learn** of Levels 1 and 2 are asterisked. Those from Level 2 are additionally coded: e.g., C12 means the word first appeared as **Vocabulary to Learn** in Chapter 12 while A3 means the word first appeared in the third Atticus selection (those following Chapters 1–15) at the back of the text. Additional meanings presented for these words in the course of Level 3 have been added to the meanings from the prior levels.

Words marked with an asterisk and no chapter or Atticus selection reference are from the **Vocabulary to Learn** of Level 1.

LIST OF ABBREVIATIONS:

(1) = first conjugation	indeclin. = indeclinable
abl. = ablative	inf. = infinitive
acc. = accusative	interj. = interjection
adj. = adjective	m. = masculine
adv. = adverb	n. = neuter
conj. = conjunction	pl. = plural
dat. = dative	prep. = preposition
f. = feminine	sg. = singular
gen. = genitive	

NOTE:

The genitive of second declension words ending in *–ius* or *–ium* is indicated with a single *–ī*, which is the genitive ending itself. Note that in the full form of the genitive there is normally a double *–i*: *fīlius, -ī* (= *fīliī*); *gaudium, -ī* (= *gaudiī*).

A

ā *or* **ab,** *prep. + abl.,* by, from, away from*

abdō, -ere, abdidī, abditum, to hide, bury

abeō, -īre, -īvī/iī, -itum, to go away, depart

abhorreō, -ēre, abhorruī, —, + *abl.,* to be averse to, be different from, be inconsistent with

abluō, -ere, abluī, ablūtum, to wash, purify

absēns, absentis, *adj.,* away, absent* C13

absolvō, -ere, absolvī, absolūtum, to bring to completion, complete

absum, abesse, āfuī, —, to be away, be absent, missing, be absent from*

abutor, abutī, abusus sum, + *abl.,* to abuse

ac, *conj.,* and, and moreover

ac, shortened form of **atque**

accendō, -ere, accendī, accēnsum, to brighten, stir up

accidō, -ere, accidī, —, to fall upon, happen, occur, happen to (+ *dat. of person affected*)* A7

accingō, -ere, accīnxī, accīnctum, to gird on, arm, equip

accipiō, -ere, -cēpī, -ceptum, to accept, receive*

aciēs, -ēī, *f.,* line of battle, sharp edge, edge, line, eye(sight)

ācrius, *comparative adv.,* more keenly

ad, *prep. + acc.,* toward, to, into, near*

adclīnō (1), to lean, rest on

addūcō, -ere, addūxī, adductum, to draw together, lead toward, bring in, influence, sway

adeō, *adv.,* to such an extent, even, in fact, so, thus, truly, indeed* A8

adeō, adīre, adiī/adīvī, aditum, to approach, go toward

adferō, adferre, attulī, allātum, to bring, carry to a place

adficiō, -ere, adfēcī, adfectum, to influence, afflict, impair, affect

adfluō, -ere, adflūxī, adflūxum, to abound, overflow with

adhibeō, -ēre, adhibuī, adhibitum, *+ dat.,* to apply, offer, invite, call in, employ, show* A10

adhūc, *adv.,* still, up to this time, yet, up to now (this point)* C8

adiciō, -ere, adiēcī, adiectum, to add

adimō, -ere, adēmī, ademptum, to take away, remove

admīrātiō, -ōnis, *f.,* admiration

admittō, -mittere, admīsī, admissum, to let in, admit

admoveō, -ēre, admōvī, admotum, to move, bring or apply something (*acc.*) to something (*dat.*)

adoperiō, -īre, adoperuī, adopertum, to cover up, cover over

adpellō (1), to call upon, address

adquīrō, -ere, adquīsīvī, adquisītum, to acquire, gain

adspectus see **aspectus**

adspergō, -ginis, *f.,* sprinkling, scattering, splashing

adspiciō see **aspiciō**

adsum, adesse, adfuī, —, to be present

adulēscēns, -entis, *m./f.,* young man, young lady, young woman, youth*

adulēscentulus, -ī, *m.,* young man, youth

adultus, -a, -um, *adj.,* grown, adult

adveniō, -īre, advēnī, adventum, to arrive

adventus, -ūs, *m.,* arrival, approach* A2

adversus, -a, -um, *adj.,* opposite, facing, adverse, opposing; (*of winds*) blowing against, contrary

advertō, -ere, advertī, adversum, to pay attention

aedēs, -is, *f.,* (*in the singular*) a temple; (*in the plural*) a dwelling or house* C10

aedificium, -ī, *n.,* building* A5

Aeduus, -a, -um, *adj.,* Aeduan, of the Aedui

aeger, -gra, -grum, *adj.,* sick, weary, wretched, wounded

Aenēās, Aenēae, *m.,* Aeneas

Aeolius, -a, -um, *adj.,* Aeolian, Aeolic, referring to Aeolia

aequaevus, -a, -um, *adj.,* of equal age

aequor, aequoris, *n.,* delta, sea, waves

aequus, -a, -um, *adj.,* even, fair, equal, just; **aequō animō,** indifferently*

āēr, -ris, *m.,* air

aes, aeris, *n.,* bronze, copper, money; **aes aliēnum,** debt

aestās, -ātis, *f.,* summer; **aestāte,** in the summer

aestimō (1), to regard, esteem, assess*

aestus, -ūs, *m.,* heat, glow, flood, tide, surge

aetās, -ātis, *f.,* age, time of life, life* C7

aeternus, -a, -um, *adj.,* eternal

aethēr, -ēris, *m.,* upper air, heaven, ether, sky, air

aevum, -ī, *n.,* age, history, time, lifetime

afferō, afferre, attulī, allātum, to bring, contribute, bring about

afflictō (1), to distress, torment

affulgeō, -ēre, affulsī, to shine forth, appear

ager, agrī, *m.,* field, territory, land*

agitō (1), to drive, agitate, excite, aspire, persecute

agmen, -minis, *n.,* marching column, line of battle* C4

agnōscō, -ere, agnōvī, agnitum, to recognize, acknowledge

agō, -ere, ēgī, āctum, to drive, lead, do, behave, treat, spend*

agrestis, -e, *adj.,* of the country, rustic, rural

aiō, ais, ait, aiunt, *defective verb,* to say

āla, -ae, *f.,* wing

alacer, -cris, -cre, *adj.,* healthy

Albānus, -a, -um, *adj.,* Alban

aliēnus, -a, -um, *adj. + prep. ā/ ab + abl.,* foreign to, inconsistent with, that which belongs to another, someone else's; **aes aliēnum, aeris aliēnī,** *n.,* debt*

aliquandō, *adv.,* (at) some time, at last

aliquantō, *adv.,* somewhat

aliquis, aliqua, aliquid, *indefinite pronoun;* **aliquī, aliqua, aliquod,** *indefinite adj.,* some, any; someone, something, anyone, anything* A6

aliquis, aliquis, aliquid, *indefinite pronoun,* anyone, anything

aliquō, *adv.,* to somewhere, somewhere

aliquot, *indeclin. indefinite pronoun and adj.,* some, several, a few, some

aliquōūsque, *adv.,* to some extent

aliter, *adv.,* otherwise

alius, alia, aliud, *adj.,* another, other, different*

Allobrogēs, -um, *m. pl.,* Allobroges

Ālpēs, -ium, *f.,* Alps

altāria, -ium, *n. pl.,* altar

alter, altera, alterum, *adj.,* the other (of two), another*

altum, -ī, *n.,* the deep (sea); heaven, high place or position

altus, -a, -um, *adj.,* tall, high, deep* C2

amābilis, -e, *adj.,* lovable, loving, delightful

amāns, -antis, *m.,* lover

ambō, -ae, -ō, *adj. pl.,* both

amentia, -ae, *f.,* madness, folly

amīcitia, -ae, *f.,* friendship

amictus, -ūs, *m.,* garment, covering, cloak

amīcus, -a, -um, *adj.,* friendly* A1

amīcus, -ī, *m.,* friend*

amnis, -is, *m.,* river, stream

amō (1), to love*

amor, -ōris, *m.,* love, love affair*

amplector, -ī, amplexus sum, to embrace, enfold

amplus, -a, -um, *adj.,* large, eminent, distinguished, powerful, strong, prominent

an, *conj.,* or (*in a disjunctive question*), perhaps

anguis, -is, *m./f.,* snake, serpent

angulus, -ī, *m.,* corner

angustus, -a, -um, *adj.,* narrow, limited, difficult (of circumstances), close

anhēlitus, -ūs, *m.,* breath, exhalation

anima, -ae, *f.,* soul, spirit

animōsus, -a, -um, *adj.,* spirited, bold

animus, -ī, *m.,* spirit, soul, mind, will, judgment, courage*

annītor, annītī, annīsus sum, to strive, make an effort

annus, -ī, *m.,* year, season* C2

ante, *adv.,* before, in front, previously

ante, *prep. + acc.,* in front of*

antecellō, -ere, —, to surpass, distinguish oneself before

Antiochīa, -ae, *f.,* Antioch, the most important city for the Romans in the province of Syria; Antioch is located in modern-day Turkey

antīquus, -a, -um, *adj.,* ancient, old, ancestral* C8

antrum, -ī, *n.,* cave, hollow space, grotto

apex, apicis, *m.,* tip of a flame

apis, -is, *f.,* bee

Apollō, -linis, *m.,* Apollo, son of Jupiter and Latona/Leto, brother of Diana, god of archery, music, poetry, etc.

appāreō, -ēre, appāruī, to appear, be found, show oneself* A7

appellō (1), to call upon, name, address, call, call (by name)

aptō (1), to adjust, make ready

aptus, -a, -um, *adj.,* fitted, appropriate, fitting, suited* A7

apud, *prep. + acc.,* at the house of, among*

aqua, -ae, *f.,* water, water supply, aqueduct*

Aquilō, -ōnis, *m.,* the north wind

Aquītānī, -ōrum, *m. pl.,* Aquitanians

Aquītānia, -ae, *f.,* Aquitane, a region of Gaul

Aquītānius, -a, -um, *adj.,* Aquitanian

āra, -ae, *f.,* altar

arānea, -ae, *f.,* spider's web

arbitror, arbitrārī, arbitrātus sum, to judge, consider, be of the opinion, suppose, think, decide, judge* A6

arbor, -oris, *f.,* tree*

arboreus, -a, -um, *adj.,* of a tree

arceō, -ēre, arcuī, to keep *someone in the acc.* away from *something ab + abl.,* keep off, defend, enclose

arcus, -ūs, *m.,* bow

ārdeō, -ēre, ārsī, —, to burn, be on fire, be eager*

ardor, -ōris, *m.,* passion

arduus, -a, -um, *adj.,* tall, lofty

āridus, -a, -um, *adj.,* dry

arma, -ōrum, *n. pl.,* weapons, arms, tools of war*

arrigō, -ere, arrēxī, arrēctus, to raise, rear

ars, artis, *f.,* science, art, skill, (*pl.*) liberal arts, humanities* C8

arteria, -ae, *f.,* artery

artus, -ūs, *m.,* joint, limb, body, arm, leg

arvum, -ī, *n.,* field, plain, countryside

arx, arcis, *f.,* citadel

as, assis, *m.,* coin, penny

ascendō, -dere, ascendī, ascensum, climb, mount, rise

ascīscō, -ere, ascīvī, ascītum, to receive, adopt, summon from elsewhere, take as an ally

ascrībō, -ere, ascrīpsī, ascrīptum, to impute, ascribe, attribute, add (in writing)

Āsia, -ae, *f.,* Asia Minor

aspectus, -ūs, *m.,* seeing, sight, view, vision, aspect

asper, -a, -um, *adj.,* fierce, rough, harsh, severe

aspernor (1), to disdain, despise, reject

aspiciō, -ere, aspexī, aspectum, to look at, catch a glimpse of* C1, observe, see, look at, behold

assequor, assequī, assecūtus sum, to accomplish, gain

assidō, -ere, assedī, to sit down

at, *conj.,* but, yet* C3

ater, -tra, -trum, *adj.,* black, dark-colored, stained

atque, *conj.,* and, and also*

atquī, *conj.,* but, nevertheless, and yet

ātrium, -ī, *n.,* hall, court, atrium

attingō, -ere, attigī, attāctum, to touch, engage in, reach, border (on)

attollō, -ere, to lift, rear, raise, lift up

attrectō (1), to handle, touch

auctor, -tōris, *m./f.,* originator, supporter, advisor

auctoritās, -tātis, *f.,* authority, power, influence

audācia, -ae, *f.,* boldness, recklessness

audāx, -ācis, *adj.,* bold

audeō, -ēre, ausus sum (*semideponent*), to dare, be bold

audiō, -īre, audīvī, audītum, to hear, listen*

auferō, auferre, abstulī, ablātum, to take away, steal

Aufidus, -ī, *m.,* Aufidus, river in Apulia

aula, -ae, *f.,* noble residence, palace, hall, royal court

aura, -ae, *f.,* breeze

aureus, -a, -um, *adj.,* golden, splendid, beautiful

auris, -is, *f.,* ear* C9

Aurōra, -ae, *f.,* Aurora, goddess of the dawn

aurum, -ī, *n.,* gold, thing(s) made of gold, gold ornaments* C2

Ausonius, -a, -um, *adj.,* Italian

auspicium, -ī, *n.,* sign, omen

aut, *conj.,* or; **aut . . . aut . . . ,** either . . . or . . .* A2

autem, *conj.,* moreover, however, on the other hand, but, however

auxilium, -ī, *n.,* help, aid, assistance*

āvellō, -ere, āvellī/āvulsī, āvulsum, to tear from

aveō, -ēre, —, to desire, long for

Avernus, -ī, *m.,* a lake near Cumae, Italy

avius, -a, -um, *adj.,* pathless, remote

B

Babylōnius, -a, -um, *adj.,* Babylonian

bāca, -ae, *f.,* pearl

bacchor (1), to rave, rush wildly

bāsiō (1), to kiss

bāsium, -ī, *n.,* kiss

beātus, -a, -um, *adj.,* blessed

Belgae, -ārum, *m. pl.,* Belgians

bellē, *adv.,* fairly

bellō (1), to wage war, fight

bellum, -ī, *n.,* war*

bellus, -a, -um, *adj.,* pretty

belua, -ae, *f.,* beast, animal

bene, *adv.,* well*

benevolentia, -ae, *f.,* goodwill, kindness, affection* C13

benignus, -a, -um, *adj.,* lavish

beō (1), to bless, gladden

bibō, -ere, bibī, —, to drink* C5

biennium, -ī, *n.,* two-year period, two years

bīlis, -is, *f.,* bile, poison

bis, *adv.,* twice

blanditia, -ae, *f.,* word(s) of endearment, flattery, compliment, *pl.,* flatteries

Boiī, -ōrum, *m. pl.,* Boii

Bolōnia, -ae, *f.,* Boulogne-sur-Mer, France

Bonōnia, -ae, *f.,* modern Bologna, Italy

bonus, -a, -um, *adj.,* good*

bōs, bovis, *m./f.,* cattle

brevis, -e, *adj.,* short, brief* C2

bustum, -ī, *n.,* a tomb

buxus, -ī, *f.,* boxwood

C

cachinnus, -ī, *m.,* loud laughter

cadō, -ere, cecidī, cāsum, to fall, happen*

caducus, -a, -um, *adj.,* frail, transitory, perishable

caedēs, -is, *f.,* slaughter, murder, blood(shed), blood, gore

caelebs, -bis, *m.,* unmarried (male), bachelor

caeles, -itis, *m.,* heaven-dweller, god

caelestis, -e, *adj.,* celestial, divine, heavenly

caelum, -ī, *n.,* sky, heaven, weather*

Caesar, -aris, *m.,* emperor (initially the cognomen of Julius Caesar), Caesar* A4

calamus, -ī, *m.,* pen

callidus, -a, -um, *adj.,* clever, cunning, resourceful

Cameracēnsis, -e, *adj.,* of Cambrai

candidus, -a, -um, *adj.,* bright, radiant, beautiful

canō, -ere, cecinī, cantum, to sing of, sing about, chant, tell, proclaim, prophesy, celebrate, recite* A7

capiō, -ere, cēpī, captum, to take, adopt, capture, seize, hold, contain; **cōnsilia capere,** to make plans*

Capitōlium, -ī, *n.,* Capitolium, the Capitoline hill in Rome

captō (1), to catch, try to catch

capulus, -ī, *m.,* handle, hilt

caput, -itis, *n.,* head, chief, ringleader*

cardō, -dinis, *m.,* hinge

careō, -ēre, caruī, + *abl.,* to be without, go without, lack, avoid

carīna, -ae, *f.,* keel; ship, boat

cāritās, -tātis, *f.,* regard; love, affection

carmen, -inis, *n.,* poem, song, lyric poetry, solemn or ritual utterance* C5

carpō, -ere, carpsī, carptum, to pluck, seize

carrus, -ī, *m.,* cart, wagon

carta, -ae, *f.,* a sheet of papyrus

cārus, -a, -um, *adj.,* dear, beloved, fond* C12

Casticus, -ī, *m.,* Casticus, son of Catamantaloedes

castīgātor, -ōris, *m.,* castigator

castra, -ōrum, *n. pl.,* camp*

cāsus, -ūs, *m.,* accident, chance occurrence, chance, mishap, misfortune, fortune, fall, event

catechūmenus, -ī, *m.,* candidate under instruction for confirmation

cathedra, -ae, *f.,* chair, bishop's throne

causa, -ae, *f.,* cause, reason, case, occasion; **causā,** + *preceding gen.,* for the sake of, because of; **causam dīcō, -ere, dīxī, dictum,** to plead a case*

cautus, -a, -um, *adj.,* on one's guard, wary, cautious, prudent

caveō, -ēre, cāvī, cautum, to take care, beware

cēdō, -ere, cessī, cessum, to go away (from), withdraw, move, yield, depart

celeber, -bris, -bre, *adj.,* renowned, well-known, crowded, busy, populous, popular, festive*

celebritās, -ātis, *f.,* reputation, crowded conditions

celebrō (1), to attend in large numbers, frequent

celer, -is, -e, *adj.,* swift, speedy, quick

celeriter, *adv.,* swiftly, quickly*

cella, -ae, *f.,* cell, storeroom

celsitūdō, -dinis, *f.,* loftiness

celsus, -a, -um, *adj.,* high, lofty, proud

Celtae, -ārum, *m. pl.,* Celts

cēna, -ae, *f.,* dinner

cēnāculum, -ī, *n.,* dining room

cēnō (1), to dine* A6

centum, *numeral and indeclin. adj.,* one hundred

cēra, -ae, *f.,* wax

Cerēs, Cereris, *f.,* goddess of grain and agriculture (in Greek, Demeter)

cernō, -ere, crēvī, crētum, to see, distinguish by the eyes* C15

certus, -a, -um, *adj.,* certain, sure, specific, fixed, reliable, unmistakable, plain; **certiōrem faciō, -ere, fēcī, factum,** to inform

cervīx, cervīcis, *f.,* neck, back of the neck

cēterus, -a, -um, *adj.,* other, remaining, rest; *in pl.,* the rest* A5

ceu, *adv.,* as if

Chloē, -oēs, *f.,* Chloe, woman's name

cibāria, -ōrum, *n. pl.,* food, allowance of food

cibus, -ī, *m.,* food* C5

cingō, -ere, cīnxī, cīnctum, to surround, encircle, crown

circulus, -ī, *m.,* circle

circum, *prep. + acc.,* around*

circumstō, -āre, circumstetī, circumstatum, to surround, stand around

cithara, -ae, *f.,* lyre

citrā, *prep + acc.,* short of

cīvis, -is, *m./f.,* citizen*

cīvitās, cīvitātis, *f.,* city, community of citizens, state, political entity, citizenship, body of citizens, community, clan

clāmō (1), to shout, call by name; scream* C15

clamor, -ōris, *m.,* shout, outcry, clamor

clārus, -a, -um, *adj.,* bright, clear, famous, distinguished, loud, shrill* C2

classis, -is, *f.,* fleet, class*

claudō, -ere, clausī, clausum, to close, imprison

cliēns, -entis, *m.,* client, dependent (of a patron)

clīvus, -ī, *m.,* slope, incline

coemeterium, -ī, *n.,* cemetery

coemō, -ere, coēmī, coēmptum, to buy up, purchase

coeō, coīre, coīvī, coitum, to go, come together, meet

coepī, coepisse, coeptum, + *inf.,* to begin to, have begun* C4

coeptum, -ī, *n.,* undertaking, beginning, design

coetus, -ūs, *m.,* meeting, gathering

Coeus, -ī, *m.,* one of the Titans, a giant, son of Earth

cōgitō (1), to think, conceive*

cognitiō, cognitiōnis, *f.,* acquaintance

cōgnōscō, -ere, cōgnōvī, cōgnitum, to come to know, find to be, know, learn* A1

cōgō, -ere, coēgī, coāctum, to compel, force (together), gather, assemble, bring together, collect* A5

collēgiālis, -e, *adj.,* connected with a college

collēgium, -ī, *n.,* college

collum, -ī, *n.,* neck

colō, -ere, coluī, cultum, to worship, cultivate, revere, honor, esteem, inhabit*

color, -ōris, *m.,* color

columna, -ae, *f.,* column, pillar

coma, -ae, *f.,* hair, locks, tresses, foliage

combūrō, -ere, combussī, combustum, to burn up, ruin

comes, comitis, *m.,* count; companion, associate, comrade, partner

commentātiō, -iōnis, *f.,* commentary

commeō (1), to come and go

commisceō, -ēre, commiscuī, commixtum, to mix, mingle

committō, -ere, commīsī, commissum, to entrust, commit

commūnicō (1), to share (with), impart

communis, -e, *adj.,* common, joint, mutual, general

comparō (1), to collect, prepare, plan

comperiō, -īre, comperī, compertum, to find out, discover

complector, complectī, complexus sum, to embrace, hug, seize, care for

complūrēs, complūrium, *adj.,* not a few, several, many

compōnō, -ere, composuī, compositum, to settle, arrange, put together

conātum, -ī, *n.,* attempt

concēdō, -ere, concessī, concessum, to allow, pardon, retreat, grant, give up, depart

concha, -ae, *f.,* shell

concidō, -ere, concidī, to fall, collapse

conciliō (1), to bring together, form, unite, bring about, win over

concipiō, -ere, concēpī, conceptum, to conceive, fall (in love), form, produce, conceive

conclūdō, -ere, conclusī, conclusum, to (en)close

concursus, -ūs, *m.,* gathering

concutiō, -ere, concussī, concussum, to shake, shatter, agitate

condō, -ere, -didī, -ditum, to found, establish, hide, put away, store

condūcō, -ere, condūxī, conductum, to assemble

cōnferō, cōnferre, contulī, collātum, to compare, bring together, collect, contribute, (reflexive with **sē**) to apply oneself

cōnficiō, -ere, cōnfēcī, cōnfectum, to make, compose, accomplish, make ready, complete

cōnfirmō (1), to confirm, strengthen, encourage, establish, affirm

congregō (1), to assemble

coniciō, -ere, coniēcī, coniectum, to throw together, hurl, conjecture, guess, infer

coniugium, -ī, *n.,* wedlock, marriage

coniūnctus, -a, -um, *adj.,* connected, friendly

coniungō, -ere, -iūnxī, -iūnctum, to connect, join together* A4

coniūnx, -iūgis, *m./f.,* spouse* C3

coniūrātiō, -ōnis, *f.,* conspiracy, plot

conlābor, conlābī, conlāpsus sum, to fall in a heap, collapse, faint

conlocō (1), to arrange

cōnor, cōnārī, cōnātus sum, to try, attempt* C9

conpescō, -ere, conpescuī, to quench, check

conpōnō, -ere, conposuī, conpositum, to join, place together

conquiēscō, -ere, conquiēvī, rest, relax

cōnscendō, -ere, cōnscendī, cōnscēnsum, to mount, climb

conscientia, -ae, *f.,* common knowledge

cōnsciscō, -ere, cōnscīvī, cōnscītum, to decide on, inflict

cōnscius, -a, -um, *adj.,* privy to

cōnscriptus, -a, -um, *adj.,* enrolled

cōnsēnsiō, cōnsēnsiōnis, *f.,* agreement, unanimity, harmony

cōnsilium, -ī, *n.,* plan, advice, debate, council, deliberation, decision, planning* C1

cōnsistō, -ere, cōnstitī, to stand, take one's place, stop, pause

cōnsors, -ortis, *m./f.,* partner

cōnspiciō, -ere, -spexī, -spectum, to look at, observe, catch sight of, see, notice*

cōnstituō, -ere, cōnstituī, cōnstitūtum, to establish, set up, institute, decide, designate, worship, organize, determine, arrange, appoint, judge* A4

cōnstō, -āre, cōnstitī, —, + *abl.,* to consist in, take up a position, stand with* A5

constringō, -ere, constrīnxī, constrictum, to bind, restrain

consuētūdō, -ūdinis, *f.,* custom, habit, companionship* A6

cōnsul, -ulis, *m.,* consul, the highest political office in Rome*

cōnsulāris, -e, *adj.,* of consular rank, consular

cōnsulātus, -ūs, *m.,* consulship

cōnsūmō, -ere, -sūmpsī, -sūmptum, to consume*

contendō, -ere, contendī, contentum, to struggle, fight, aim for, march, hasten, compete

conterminus, -a, -um, *adj.,* nearby, adjacent

contexō, -ere, contexuī, contextum, to join by weaving, compose, weave together, entwine, interweave, devise, construct

continenter, *adv.,* constantly, continuously

contineō, -ēre, continuī, contentum, to hold, keep together, contain, embrace, sustain, preserve, keep, hem in, bound by* C14

contingō, -ere, contigī, contactum, + *dat.,* to happen to

contrā, *adv.,* in return, on the other side

contrā, *prep.* + *acc.,* against*

contrahō, -ere, contrāxī, contrāctum, to restrict, draw together, unite, narrow

contumēlia, -ae, *f.,* reproach, insult

conturbō (1), to mix up, jumble

cōnubium, -ī, *n.,* marriage

conveniō, -īre, convēnī, conventum, to meet; + *dat.,* to be becoming to, be appropriate for*

convincō, -ere, convicī, convictum, to prove wrong

convocō (1), to call together

cōpia, -ae, *f.,* abundance, plenty, supply, resource(s), wealth, *pl.,* troops, forces; possessions

cōpiōsus, -a, -um, *adj.,* abundant, well supplied

cor, cordis, *n.,* heart*

Cornēliola, -ae, *f.,* wife of Peter Gilles

cornū, -ūs, *n.,* horn*

corpus, -oris, *n.,* body*

corripiō, -ere, -ripuī, -reptum, to seize, snatch up, snatch away*

coruscus, -a, -um, *adj.,* flashing, bright, waving

cottīdiānus, -a, -um, *adj.,* daily, of every day* C14

crēber, -bra, -brum, *adj.,* frequent, numerous

crēdō, -ere, crēdidī, crēditum, + *dat.,* to believe somebody, lend money, trust, suppose*

crēdulus, -a, -um, *adj.,* credulous, naïve, trustful

cremō (1), to burn, burn alive

crescō, -ere, crēvī, crētum, to arise, multiply, expand, increase, grow

crētus, -a, -um, *adj.,* grown, sprung

Creūsa, -ae, *f.,* wife of Aeneas, lost during the sack of Troy

crīmen, crīminis, *n.,* crime, illegal action, accusation, charge, indictment, guilt

crūdēlis, -e, *adj.,* cruel, bloody, heartless, bitter*

cruentō (1), to stain with blood

cruentus, -a, -um, *adj.,* bloody, cruel

cruor, -ōris, *m.,* blood, gore, bloodshed

cubiculum, -ī, *n.,* bedroom

cubīle, -is, *n.,* couch, bed

culmen, -minis, *n.,* roof, summit, top, peak

culpa, -ae, *f.,* fault, offense, guilt, blame

cultus, -ūs, *m.,* care, management, maintenance, way of living, culture, civilization* A6

cum, *conj.,* + *indicative,* when; + *imperfect subjunctive,* although, since; + *pluperfect subjunctive,* after* C12

cum, *prep.* + *abl.,* with*

cūnctus, -a, -um, *adj.,* all, all together, every

cupiditās, -ātis, *f.,* greed, immoderate desire, desire, eagerness, ambition

cupīdō, -inis, *m.,* desire, eagerness

Cupīdō, -inis, *m.,* god of love

cupidus, -a, -um, *adj.,* + *gen.,* longing, desirous, longing for, fond of

cupiō, -ere, -īvī, -ītum, to wish, be eager for, desire*

cupresus, -ī, *f.,* cypress (tree)

cūr, *adv.,* why?*

cūra, -ae, *f.,* care, pain, sorrow, concern, worry* A6

curia, -ae, *f.,* the Senate house

cursus, -ūs, *m.,* course (of life), direction, way, going

custōs, -ōdis, *m./f.,* guard, guardian, sentinel, doorkeeper* C2

cygniformis, -e, *adj.,* swan-shaped

cynanchē, -ēs, *f.,* sore throat

Cyprus, -ī, *f.,* Cyprus, an island in the eastern Mediterranean Sea

Cyrrhaesis, -e, *adj.,* from or of Cyrrha

cythara, -ae, *f.,* cithara; stringed instrument associated with Apollo

D

damnō (1), to condemn

Dardanius, -a, -um (variant without the -i-), *adj.,* Dardanian, Trojan

Daunus, -ī, *m.,* Daunus, legendary king of Apulia

dē, *prep.* + *abl.,* about, concerning; down from, from*

dea, -ae, *f.,* goddess*

dēbeō, -ēre, dēbuī, dēbitum, + *inf.,* ought, must, should; to owe*

dēbilitō (1), to weaken

decem, *indecl. adj.,* ten

dēcernō, -ere, -crēvī, -crētum, + *inf.,* to decide, determine, settle*

decet, decēre, decuit (*impersonal verb*), it is becoming, befitting

dēcidō, -ere, dēcidī, to fall down, collapse, die

dēclārō (1), to demonstrate, indicate, show* C13

dēclīnātiō, -ōnis, *f.,* a bending, sidestep

dēclīnō (1), to turn aside, bend down, droop

decor, -ōris, *m.,* beauty

decus, decoris, *n.,* ornament, beauty, dignity, glory, honor

dēdūcō, -ere, dēdūxī, dēductum, to lead away, compose, escort, bring home

dēfessus, -a, -um, *adj.,* tired, weary, worn

dēfīgō, -ere, dēfīxī, dēfīxum, to plunge

dēfleō, -ēre, dēflēvī, dēflētum, to lament bitterly

dēfungor, dēfungī, dēfūnctus sum, to die

dēgener, -neris, *adj.,* degenerate, ignoble, base

deinde (also, **dein**), *adv.,* then*

dēlectō (1), to delight, please*

dēlectus, -ūs, *m.,* choice, selection

dēlīberō (1), to think over, consider carefully, deliberate

dēliciae, -ārum, *f. pl.,* delight, pet, delights, pleasures*

dēligō, -ere, dēlēgī, dēlēctum, to choose, pick

Dēlos, -ī, *f.,* a small island in the Aegean, birthplace of Apollo and Diana

Delphicus, -a, -um, *adj.,* Delphic, pertaining to Delphi, site of the Pythian oracle and sanctuary sacred to Apollo

dēmanō (1), to flow down

dēmittō, -ere, -mīsī, -missum, to send down, let fall, drop, lower, let sink, plunge into; **animum dēmittō,** to let my spirit sink, become dejected* C9

dēnique, *adv.,* finally, in short

dēnuō, *adv.,* again

dēpascor, -ī, dēpāstus sum, to feed on, devour

dēpendō, -ere, dēpendī, dēpēnsum, to pay

depōnō, -ere, deposuī, depositum, to quench

dēscendō, -ere, -scendī, -scēnsum, to descend, fall, stoop, resort to, lower oneself*

describō, -ere, descrīpsī, descrīptum, to describe, mark out, map, write again

dēserō, -ere, dēseruī, dēsertum, to desert, forsake, abandon

dēsīderō (1), to long for, miss, desire, need, require* A7

dēsignātus, -a, -um, *adj.,* elect; with *cōnsul* consul-elect

dēsignō (1), to indicate, assign, arrange

dēsinō, -ere, dēsiī, dēsitum, to cease, stop*

desistō, -ere, destitī, destitum, to stop, cease

dēstinātus, -a, -um, *adj.,* determined

dētineō, -ēre, dētinuī, dētentum, to keep back

deus, -ī, *m.,* god*

dēveniō, -īre, dēvēnī, dēventum, to come (down), arrive (at)

dēvinciō, -īre, dēvīnxī, dēvīnctum, to tie up, oblige, attach, lay under an obligation, bind

dēvoveō, -ēre, dēvōvī, devōtum, to devote, consecrate, curse

dextra, -ae, *f.,* right hand*

dīcō, -ere, dīxī, dictum, to say, explain, describe, speak, tell; **causam dīcō,** to plead a case*

dictiō, -ōnis, *f.,* speaking, word

dīdūcō, -ere, dīdūxī, dīductum, to draw apart

diēs, -ēī, *m./f.,* day*

differō, differre, distulī, dīlātum, to differ, postpone

difficilis, -e, *adj.,* difficult*

diffugiō, -ere, diffūgī, to flee apart, scatter

digitus, -ī, *m.,* finger*

dignitās, dignitātis, *f.,* dignity, status, social position, worth, reputation, authority

dignor (1), + *abl.,* to deem worthy, deign

dignus, -a, -um, *adj.* + *abl.,* worthy, deserving, worthy of

dīgredior, -ī, dīgressus sum, to (de)part, go away

diligenter, *adv.,* diligently, carefully* A8

dīligentia, -ae, *f.,* carefulness, attentiveness, diligence, attention, energy* A1

dīligō, -ere, dīlēxī, dīlēctum, to esteem highly, love, hold dear, have special regard for* C6

dīmittō, -ere, dīmīsī, dīmissum, to send away, adjourn, dismiss, let go

dīmoveō, -ēre, dīmōvī, dīmōtum, to move apart, separate

dīreptiō, -onis, *f.,* plundering, pillaging

dīrimō, -ere, dīrēmī, dīrēmptum, to pull apart, separate, break up

dīripiō, -ere, dīripuī, dīreptum, to plunder, ravage

dīruō, -ere, dīruī, dīrutum, to cause to fall in ruin, demolish

discēdō, -ere, -cessī, -cessum, to depart, leave*

disciplīna, -ae, *f.,* learning, instruction, science, education, knowledge, system, discipline, doctrine

discipulus, -ī, *m.,* male student [**discipula, -ae,** *f.,* female student* C3]

discrībō, -ere, discrīpsī, discriptum, to distribute, assign

discrīmen, -minis, *n.,* danger, distinction, difference

disertus, -a, -um, *adj.,* articulate, eloquent

dispēnsō (1), to manage, distribute

dissuādeō, -ēre, dissuāsī, dissuāsum, to advise against, to dissuade

distendō, -ere, distendī, distentum, to distend, stretch

distinguō, -ere, distīnxī, distinctum, to separate, divide

distribuō, -ere, distribuī, distributum, to divide, assign

dītissimus, -a, -um, *adj.,* richest, wealthiest

diū, *adv.,* for a long time*

diūtius, *adv.,* longer

dīvellō, -ere, dīvellī (*or* dīvulsī), **dīvulsum,** to tear apart, tear open, tear in two

dīversus, -a, -um, *adj.,* different, various, separated, separate

Diviciacus, -ī, *m.,* Diviciacus

dīvidō, -ere, dīvīsī, dīvīsum, to divide

dīvīnus, -a, -um, *adj.,* divine, holy*

dīvitiae, -ārum, *f. pl.,* wealth, riches*

dīvortium, -ī, *n.,* separation

dīvus, -a, -um, *adj.,* divine, pertaining to a god

dīvus, -ī, *m.,* god, deified emperor

dō, dăre, dedī, dătum, to give; **in mātrimōnium dō,** to give in matrimony, to marry*

doceō, -ēre, docuī, doctum, to teach*

doctor, -ōris, *m.,* teacher; **doctōris īnsigne,** the badge of doctor, i.e., indicating the doctoral degree from a university

doctus, -a, -um, *adj.,* learned, knowledgeable, educated*

doctus, -ī, *m.,* wise man, learned man

doleō, dolēre, doluī, dolitum, to grieve (over), be sorry, be angry (at), to feel pain, hurt*

dolor, -ōris, *m.,* grief, pain, passion, anger, resentment, annoyance*

domesticus, -a, -um, *adj.,* domestic

domus, -ūs, *f.,* house, home*

dōnec, *conj.,* until, as long as, while

dōnō (1), to give, reward, gift with + *abl.,* bestow; + *acc.* + *abl.,* to present someone with something

dormiō, -īre, -īvī, -ītum, to sleep*

dormītō (1), to sleep, doze

dubiē, *adv.,* doubtfully

dubitō (1), to hesitate, doubt

dubius, -a, -um, *adj.,* doubtful

dūcō, -ere, dūxī, ductum, to lead, take, extend, consider*

dūdum, *adv.,* lately, previously

dulce, *adv.,* sweetly

dulcis, -e, *adj.,* sweet, dear, fond, fresh* C5

dum, *conj.,* while; + *subjunctive,* until*

Dumnorīx, -rīgis, *m.,* Dumnorix, chieftain of the Aeduans

duo, duae, duo, *numeral,* two* C6

duodecim, *indecl. adj.,* twelve

dux, ducis, *m.,* leader, guide, chief, general (in medieval Latin often means "duke")*

E

ē *or* **ex,** *prep.* + *abl.,* from, out of*

ebur, eboris, *n.,* ivory

eburneus, -a, -um, *adj.,* (of) ivory

eburnus, -a, -um, *adj.,* (of) ivory

ecce, *interj.,* look here!, see!, look!, behold!, lo and behold*

edāx, edācis, *adj.,* greedy, devouring, destructive

ēditiō, -ōnis, *f.* statement, publication, edition (of a book)

ēdō, -ere, ēdidī, ēditum, to produce, give forth, publish* C4

ēdūcō, -ere, ēdūxī, ēductum, to lead, draw out, lead forth

effēminō (1), to weaken, make effeminate

efferō, efferre, extulī, ēlātum, to carry out, set, raise, lift, bring out, express, publish, spread

efferus, -a, -um, *adj.,* wild, savage, mad

efficiō, -ere, -fēcī, -fectum, *often* + *ut,* to cause to happen, bring about, effect, bring to effect, to accomplish* A4

effodiō, -ere, effōdī, effossus, to dig out, excavate

effrenātus, -a, -um, *adj.,* unbridled, unrestrained

effugiō, -ere, effūgī, —, to escape, avoid

egeō, -ēre, eguī, —, + *abl.,* to lack something, need, want*

ego, *personal pronoun,* I*

ēgredior, ēgredī, ēgressus sum, to go out, leave, depart, step out

ēiaculor (1), to shoot forth

ēiciō, -ere, ēiēcī, ēiectum, to put on shore

ēlābor, ēlābī, ēlāpsum, to slip away, escape

ēlegāns, -antis, *adj.,* careful in choosing, tasteful* A5, elegant

ēloquium, -ī, *n.,* diction, eloquence

ēlūdō, -ere, ēlūsī, ēlūsum, to mock

Ēlysius, -a, -um, *adj.,* Elysian, of or pertaining to Elysium

ēmicō (1), to spurt, shoot forth

ēminēns, -entis, *adj.,* lofty, raised

ēmīror, ēmīrārī, to wonder at exceedingly, be astonished at

Enceladus, -ī, *m.,* one of the Giants

enim, *conj.,* for, indeed, in fact, truly*

ēnsis, -is, *m.,* sword

ēnuntiō (1), to reveal, express, say

eō, *adv.,* for that reason

eō, īre, īvī/iī, itum, to go* C10

eōdem, *adv.,* to the same place, in the same place

episcopus, -ī, *m.,* bishop

epistolium, -ī, *n.,* note, a little letter

eques, -itis, *m.,* horseman, knight, member of the equestrian order, cavalryman, rider* C2 A4

Erasmus (-ī) Roterodamus, -ī, *m.,* Erasmus of Rotterdam

ergā, *prep.* + *acc.,* to

ergō, *conj.,* therefore, then, consequently* C14

ērigō, -ere, ērēxī, ērēctum, to raise, set up

ēripiō, -ere, -ripuī, -reptum, to snatch away*, take away; **sē ēripiō,** to escape

errō (1), to wander, make a mistake*

ērubēscō, -ere, ērubuī, to blush with shame or modesty

ērudiō, -īre, ērudīvī, ērudītum, to educate, instruct, teach

ēruditiō, -tiōnis, *f.,* learning, erudition

ērudītus, -a, -um, *adj.,* learned, scholarly

ērumpō, -ere, ērūpī, ēruptum, to break out, rush out

et, *adv.,* also

et, *conj.,* and; **et . . . et . . . ,** both . . . and . . . * C1

etenim, *adv.,* and indeed, and really

etiam, *adv.,* even, also, still*

ēvādō, -ere, ēvāsī, ēvāsum, to escape

ēvertō, -ere, ēvertī, ēversum, to overthrow

exasperō (1), to roughen, make harsh

exaudiō, -īre, exaudīvī, exaudītum, to listen to, heed

excēdō, excēdere, excessī, excessum, to go away, depart

excidō, -ere, excidī, to fall out, fall

excīdō, -ere, excīdī, excīsum, to cut out, destroy

excipiō, -ere, excēpī, exceptum, to take out, remove, accept, receive

excitō (1), to awaken, wake up, rouse, stir up, call up, raise, arouse, startle, inspire*

exclūdō, -ere, exclūsī, exclūsum, to shut out

exeō, -īre, -iī, -itum, to go out, leave, march out, escape

exerceō, -ēre, exercuī, exercitum, to be busy, train

exercitō (1), to practice, exercise

exercitus, -ūs, *m.,* army* C6

exhālō (1), to breathe out, exhale

exhibeō, -ēre, exhibuī, exhibitum, to produce

exhorrescō, -ere, exhorruī, to shudder

exigō, -ere, exēgī, exāctum, to drive out, complete, execute

exiguus, -a, -um, *adj.,* small, slight

exīstimō (1), to value, esteem, think, deem, suppose, consider, judge* A1

exitium, -ī, *n.,* ruin, destruction

exitus, -ūs, *m.,* exit, issue, end, outlet, egress

expallescō, -escere, -uī, to turn pale

expedītus, -a, -um, *adj.,* unobstructed, convenient

expetō, -ere, expetīvī, expetītum, to desire

explicō (1), to explain, spread out, open

expoliō, -īre, -īvī, -ītum, to polish

exsanguis, -e, *adj.,* bloodless, lifeless, pale

exsequor, exsequī, exsecūtus sum, to carry out, perform, enforce

exsistō, -ere, exstitī, to appear, arise, come forth

exsolvō, -ere, exsoluī, exsolūtum, to loose(n)

exspatior (1), to go for a walk

exspectātiō, -ōnis, *f.,* expectation, anticipation

exspectō (1), to wait for, await, expect*

exstinguō, -ere, exstīnxī, exstīnctum, to quench, destroy, extinguish*

exstruō, -ere, exstrūxī, exstrūctum, to build

exsultō (1), to revel in

extemplō, *adv.,* immediately, at once, suddenly

exstinguō, -ere, exstīnxī, exstīnctum, to kill, destroy

extorqueō, -ēre, extorsī, extortum, to wrest away, take by force, extort, obtain by force, twist out

extrēmus, -a, -um, *adj.,* situated or occurring at the end, last, furthest, final, utmost, farthest, outermost* A7

exūrō, -ere, exussī, exustum, to burn down, destroy

exuviae, -ārum, *f. pl.,* spoils, relics, mementos

F

Fabullus, -ī, *m.,* Fabullus, friend of Catullus

faciēs, -ēī, *f.,* face, appearance, looks, shape*

facile, *adv.,* easily*

facilis, -e, *adj.,* easy, favorable, ready*

facinus, facinoris, *n.,* deed, crime, outrage

faciō, -ere, fēcī, factum, to do, make; **certiōrem faciō,** to inform*

facultās, facultātis, *f.,* ability, opportunity, capacity; *f. pl.,* resources, riches

falcariī, -ōrum, *m. pl.,* Scythe Makers' Street; **inter falcariōs,** to the Scythe Makers' Street

fallāx, fallācis, *adj.,* deceitful, deceptive

fallō, -ere, fefellī, falsum, to deceive, disappoint

falsus, -a, -um, *adj.,* false, deceitful, mock

fāma, -ae, *f.,* fame, name, reputation* C3

Fāma, -ae, *f.,* Rumor

familia, -ae, *f.,* family, household; slaves in household*

familiāris, familiāre, *adj.,* belonging to the same family, intimate person or thing, familiar, intimate

famulus, -ī, *m.,* servant, attendant

fās, *n. indeclin.,* right according to the divine law, right, divine law

fastīgium, -ī, *n.,* highest part, roof, top, summit, height

fateor, -ērī, fassus sum, to confess, admit, acknowledge

fātum, -ī, *n.,* fate, destiny*

faveō, -ēre, fāvī, fautum, + *dat.,* to favor

fax, facis, *f.,* torch, firebrand

febrīcula, -ae, *f.,* slight fever

febris, -is, *f.,* fever* A10

fēlīciter, *adv.,* successfully

fēlīx, -īcis, *adj.,* fortunate, happy, blessed*

fēmina, -ae, *f.,* woman, wife*

fēmineus, -a, -um, *adj.,* feminine

fera, -ae, *f.,* wild animal

ferē, *adv.,* for the most part, almost, usually, nearly, generally, about

feriō, -īre, to hit, strike, blow, kill

fermē, *adv.,* almost, about

ferō, ferre, tulī, lātum, to carry, bear, endure, tolerate* C9

ferrum, -ī, *n.,* iron

ferus, -a, -um, *adj.,* savage, fierce, wild

fervēns, -entis, *adj.,* hot, fresh

ferveō, -ēre, ferbuī, to glow, boil, heat up

fēstus, -a, -um, *adj.,* festive, holiday, festival

fētus, -ūs, *m.,* offspring, brood, swarm, fruit, product of a plant

fictum, -ī, *n.,* falsehood, fiction

fidēs, -eī, *f.,* faith, honor, pledge, promise, trust* C7

fīgō, -ere, fīxī, fīxum, to fasten, fix, pierce

fīlia, -ae, *f.,* daughter*

fīlius, -ī, *m.,* son*

findō, -ere, fidī, fissum, to split, separate, divide

fīnis, -is, *m.,* end, limit; *pl.,* boundaries, territory* C2

fīnitimus, -a, -um, *adj.,* neighboring

fīnitimus, -ī, *m.,* neighbor

fīō, fierī, factus sum, to be made, become, arise, be done; (*impersonally*) to happen* C9

firmō (1), to strengthen*

firmus, -a, -um, *adj.,* strong

fistula, -ae, *f.,* pipe, tube, panpipe

Flaccus, -ī, *m.,* Quintus Horatius Flaccus, the poet Horace

flāgitium, -ī, *n.,* deed of shame, outrage, disgrace

flamma, -ae, *f.,* flame*

flāvus, -a, -um, *adj.,* yellow, golden, blond, auburn

flectō, -ere, flexī, flexum, to bend, twist, direct

fleō, -ēre, flēvī, flētum, to cry, weep for, lament*

flētus, -ūs, *m.,* crying, weeping

flōreō, -ēre, flōruī, —, to blossom, flourish* A3

flōreus, -a, -um, *adj.,* flowery

flōs, -ōris, *m.,* flower

fluctus, -ūs, *m.,* wave, breaker, tide

flūmen, -minis, *n.,* river, stream, flood* C5

fluō, -ere, flūxī, fluxum, to flow*

foedus, -deris, *n.,* pact, treaty, alliance, contract, agreement, bond

folium, -ī, *n.,* leaf

fons, fontis, *m.,* spring, fountain, source

for, fārī, fātus sum, speak

forāmen, -minis, *n.,* hole, aperture

foris, -is, *f.,* door, double-door

fōrma, -ae, *f.,* form, appearance, beauty, shape*

formīdō (1), to fear

fōrmōsus, -a, -um, *adj.,* beautiful

fors, fortis, *f.,* chance

fortasse, *adv.,* perhaps*

fortis, -e, *adj.,* brave, strong*

fortitūdō, -inis, *f.,* courage, bravery*

fortūna, -ae, *f.,* fortune, the goddess Fortune; *f. pl.,* financial resources

fortūnātus, -a, -um, *adj.,* fortunate, blessed

fragrāns, -antis, *adj.,* fragrant, sweet-smelling

Franciscus (-ī) Petrarca, -ae, *m.,* Francis Petrarch (His name in Italian is Francesco Petrarca.)

frangō, -ere, frēgī, frāctum, to break, crush

frāter, -ātris, *m.,* brother* C3

frequentia, -ae, *f.,* crowd

frīgidus, -a, -um, *adj.,* cold

frons, frontis, *f.,* forehead, front, brow

frūctus, -ūs, *m.,* fruit, gain, profit, revenue

frūgifer, -era, -erum, *adj.,* fruitful, profitable

frūmentum, -ī, *n.,* grain

fruor, fruī, fruitus/frūctus sum, + *abl.,* to enjoy, enjoy the society of* C10 A9

fūcus, -ī, *m.,* drone

fuga, -ae, *f.,* flight, rout

fugiō, -ere, fūgī, fugitum, to flee, run away*

fulgeō, -ēre, fulsī, —, to shine, flash, gleam, glitter

fulgō see **fulgeō**

fulgur, -uris, *n.,* lightning, a flash of lightning, flash of light

fulvus, -a, -um, *adj.,* yellow, tawny, blond

fūmō (1), to smoke

fundāmentum, -ī, *n.,* basis, foundation

fungor, fungī, fūnctus sum, + *abl.,* to use, perform, enjoy

furibundus, -a, -um, *adj.,* wild, frenzied

furor, -ōris, *m.,* madness, fury, insanity, frenzy

fūrtīvus, -a, -um, *adj.,* secret, stolen

fuscus, -a, -um, *adj.,* dark, swarthy

fūsē, *adv.,* fully, copiously

G

Gaetulus, -a, -um, *adj.,* Gaetulian, of Gaetulia, region of northwest Africa known for its lions

Gallī, -ōrum, *m. pl.,* the Gauls, the inhabitants of France

Gallia, -ae, *f.,* Gaul, a region of modern France and northern Italy

Gallicus, -a, -um, *adj.,* of Gaul

Gallus, -a, -um, *adj.,* Gallic, of Gaul

Garumna, -ae, *m.,* Garrone river

gaudeō, -ēre, gāvīsus sum, + *abl.,* to rejoice, be glad, exult, rejoice in

gelidus, -a, -um, *adj.,* very cold, icy, cold

geminus, -a, -um, *adj.,* twin, both, double

gemma, -ae, *f.,* gem, precious stone, jewel* C11

gena, -ae, *f.,* cheek

Genāva, -ae, *f.,* Geneva

genitor, -oris, *m.,* father

gēns, gentis, *f.,* tribe, population, people, nation* C1

genu, genūs, *n.,* knee

genus, -eris, *n.,* type, kind, origin, family, class, race* C9

Germānī, -ōrum, *m. pl.,* Germans

Germānus, -a, -um, *adj.,* German

gerō, -ere, gessī, gestum, to carry, wear; to administer in civil politics, wage; **sē gerit,** s/he behaves; **bellum gerō,** to wage war* C2

gestiō, gestīre, gestīvī, gestītum, to desire eagerly, want, be anxious to

gestō (1), to carry

gestus, -ūs, *m.,* attitude, manner

Ghisbertus, -ī, *m.,* Ghisbert, a doctor at St. Omer

gignō, -ere, genuī, genitum, to produce, give birth, give birth to, bear* C1

gladius, -ī, *m.,* sword*

glomerō (1), to roll together, assemble

glōria, -ae, *f.,* glory, fame, honor, distinction* C7

gracilis, -e, *adj.,* slender, thin*

gradus, -ūs, *m.,* step, gait, pace, stride

Graecia, -ae, *f.,* Greece

Graecus, -a, -um, *adj.,* Greek, of Greece

Grāius, -a, -um, *adj.,* Greek

grandis, -e, *adj.,* large, great

grandō, grandinis, *f.,* hail(storm, stones)

grātēs, -ium, *f. pl.,* thanks

grātia, -ae, *f.,* agreeableness, favor, grace; winning character, influence, charm; **grātiās agere,** to give thanks* A4

grātuītō, *adv.,* without pay

grātus, -a, -um, *adj.,* thankful, appreciative, gratifying, agreeable* A1

gravis, -e, *adj.,* heavy, serious, weighty, grave, severe* C2

graviter, *adv.,* heavily, severely, harshly

gravō (1), to burden, load, make heavy, weigh down

grex, gregis, *m.,* flock, herd; group, crowd

H

habeō, -ēre, habuī, habitum, to have*

habitō (1), to live, dwell*

haereō, -ēre, haesī, haesum, to be brought to a standstill, be perplexed, hesitate

haud, *adv.,* not

hauriō, -īre, hausī, haustum, to drain, drink (in), consume

haustus, -ūs, *m.,* a drawn quantity of liquid, a drink

Hēliadēs, -um, *f. pl.,* the Heliades, daughters of the sun god Helios

Helicōn, -ōnis, *m.,* mountain in Greece sacred to Apollo and the Muses

Helvētiī, -ōrum, *m. pl.,* Helvetians

Helvētius, -a, -um, *adj.,* Helvetian

Henricus, -ī, *m.,* Henry

herba, -ae, *f.,* plant, vegetation, grass*

hērēditās, -ātis, *f.,* inheritance* A5

hērōs, -ōis, *m.,* hero, mighty warrior

Hetruscus, -a, -um, *adj.,* Etruscan

heu, *interj.,* alas!, expressing grief or pain, oh

hīc, *adv.,* here

hic, haec, hoc, *demonstrative pronoun and adj.,* this*

hiems, hiemis, *f.,* winter, storm* A2

hinc, *adv.,* on one side

Hispānia, -ae, *f.,* Hispania, modern-day Spain

Hispānus, -a, -um, *adj.,* Spanish

Homērus, -ī, *m.,* Homer, Greek epic poet

homō, -inis, *m.,* man (*i.e., human being*); *pl.,* people*

honor *or* **honōs, -ōris,** *m.,* mark of honor, office; honor, esteem, public office or distinction*

hōra, -ae, *f.,* hour, time

horrendus, -a, -um, *adj.,* horrible, horrifying, awful, terrible, dire

horrēscō, -ere, horruī, to shudder (at), tremble (at)

horribilis, -e, *adj.,* rough

horror, -ōris, *m.,* shudder(ing), horror, alarm

hortor (1), to exhort, urge, encourage* C8

hospitium, -ī, *n.,* hospitality

hostis, -is, *m.,* enemy*

hūc, *adv.,* to this place, hither, here

hūmānitās, -ātis, *f.,* human character, kindness; culture, humanity, refinement befitting a human, human feeling, civilization* A7

hūmānus, -a, -um, *adj.,* human*

humilis, -e, *adj.,* low, humble*

humus, -ī, *f.,* ground, earth

Hymettius, -a, -um, *adj.,* of Hymettus

hymnus, -ī, *m.,* religious song

hypodidascalus, -ī, *m.,* Under Master

I

iaceō, -ēre, iacuī, — , to lie down (low, outspread), be inert, to lie prostrate, to lie on the ground*

iactātiō, -ōnis, *f.,* tossing

iactō (1), to show (himself/herself/itself) off, throw, hurl, toss

iam, *adv.,* already; anymore, now; *w/ future tense,* soon*

iamdiū, *adv.,* already for a long time

iamdūdum, *adv.,* for a long time

ibi, *adv.,* there, then*

īciō, -ere, īcī, ictum, to strike, beat

ictus, -ūs, *m.,* blow, strike, thrust

īdem, eadem, idem, *demonstrative pronoun and adj.,* the same, the same one/thing* C13

identidem, *adj.,* again and again

iēiūnium, -ī, *n.,* fast

Iēsūs, -ū, (declined: Iēsūs, Iēsū, Iēsū, Iēsūm, Iēsū), *m.,* Jesus

igitur, *adv.,* therefore*

ignāvus, -a, -um, *adj.,* lazy, idle

ignis, -is, *m.,* fire, lightning, heat of the sun*

ignōrō (1), to have no knowledge, be ignorant of, be unaware of, fail to recognize

īlia, -ium, *n. pl.,* groin, gut

Īliacus, -a, -um, *adj.,* Trojan, Ilian

ille, illa, illud, *demonstrative pronoun and adj.,* that, he, she, it*

illīc, *adv.,* there

illinc, *adv.,* on the other side

illustrō (1), to make clear, shed light upon, illuminate

imāgō, -inis, *f.,* image, picture, likeness, ghost, soul, form* A8

imber, -bris, *m.,* rain, rain shower, water

immānis, -e, *adj.,* huge, enormous

immēnsus, -a, -um, *adj.,* immeasurable, immense, endless* C14

immerēns, -entis, *adj.,* undeserving

immineō, -ēre, to be above

immō, *conj.,* on the contrary, nay rather; no, rather

immortālis, -e, *adj.,* undying, immortal* A3

impediō, -īre, -īvī, -ītum, to impede, prevent, hinder*

impellō, -ere, -pulī, -pulsum, to drive, force, strike

impendeō, -ēre, to overhang, loom over

imperātor, -ōris, *m.,* emperor, leader, general, commanding officer* A2

imperium, -ī, *n.,* rule, power, empire, dominion, command, supreme authority, absolute authority* C6

imperō (1), to requisition from, demand from, order, command

impetus, -ūs, *m.,* impetus, force, attack, rapid motion, rush, impulse, passion*

impius, -a, -um, *adj.,* irreverent, wicked, shameless, impious

implicō, -āre, implicāvī/ implicuī, implicitum/ implicātum, + *dat.,* to involve into, implicate, entwine, enfold, wind, twine, cling

impōnō, -ere, imposuī, impositum, + *dat.,* to place (on), impose, establish

importō (1), to bring or carry in

impressor, -ōris, *m.,* printer

imprimō, -ere, impressī, impressum, to press (upon), imprint

improbus, -a, -um, *adj.,* bad, wicked, base, shameless* C3

impunitus, -a, -um, *adj.,* unpunished, unchecked

īmus, -a, -um, *adj.,* lowest, bottom of

in prīmīs (imprīmīs), especially, above all, first of all, among the first

in, *prep.* + *abl.,* in, on*

in, *prep.* + *acc.,* in, into, toward (*when referring to feelings or attitude to someone*)*

inānis, -e, *adj.,* empty

incendium, -ī, *n.,* conflagration, eruption, flame, fire; *pl.,* arson*

incendō, -ere, incendī, incēnsum, to set on fire, irritate, burn, inflame

incertus, -a, -um, *adj.,* uncertain, unsure

incidō, -ere, incidī, incāsum, to fall into, fall in, happen, occur

incipiō, -ere, incēpī, inceptum, to begin, undertake

incitō (1), to stimulate, instigate, incite, stir up

inclūdō, -ere, inclūsī, inclūsum, to shut in, enclose

incolō, -ere, incoluī, to inhabit, dwell, live, live in

incolumis, -e, *adj.,* safe, unharmed

incommodē, *adv.,* unfortunately

incommodum, -ī, *n.,* disadvantage, harm, misfortune, inconvenience* A4

incōnsultus, -a, -um, *adj.,* ill-advised, thoughtless, indiscreet

increpō (1), to rattle, sound, make a noise

incubō, -āre, incubuī, incubitum, to throw oneself upon, to lie on

incumbō, -ere, incubuī, incubitum, + *dat.,* to lean upon, hang over, lower (over), recline on, lie on, lean on

indicium, -ī, *n.,* indication, proof, evidence (*given against someone*), disclosure

indicō (1), to show, indicate, point out, declare

indignus, -a, -um, *adj.,* + *abl.,* unworthy of

indoctus, -a, -um, *adj.,* untaught, unlearned, untrained; uninformed, ignorant

indolēs, -is, *f.,* nature, character

indūcō, -ere, indūxī, inductum, to cover, spread on, spread over, induce

ineō, -īre, inīvī/iniī, initum, to go into, enter into, attempt; **cōnsilium inīre,** to form a plan

ineptiō, ineptīre, to make a fool of oneself

īnfāns, -antis, *m./f.,* baby, infant

īnfectus, -a, -um, *adj.,* not done, false

īnfēlīx, -īcis, *adj.,* unhappy, unlucky

īnferior, -ius, *adj.,* lower

īnferō, -ferre, -tulī, illātum, to bring (into), bear (in, into), bring forward, produce; **bellum īnferre,** to make or wage war

īnfestus, -a, -um, *adj.,* hostile, dangerous, insecure, adverse

īnfīnītus, -a, -um, *adj.,* boundless, unlimited, infinite, immense* C14

īnflammō (1), to set on fire

īnfōrmis, -e, *adj.,* shapeless, deformed, ugly

īnfōrmō (1), to shame, conform

ingenium, -ī, *n.,* ability, talent, genius, natural talent, intellect

ingēns, ingentis, *adj.,* huge, immense* C4

ingrātus, -a, -um, *adj.,* unwelcome, unpleasant, ungrateful

ingravēscō, -ere, *defective verb,* to worsen, become aggravated

ingredior, ingredī, ingressus sum, to enter, proceed, step, stride

ingressus, -ūs, *m.,* entrance, entry; gait

inhorrēscō, -ere, inhorruī, to begin to tremble, bristle, become stiffly erect

iniciō, -ere, iniēcī, iniectum, to cast on

inimīcus, -a, -um, *adj.,* unfriendly, hostile, enemy

inimīcus, -ī, *m.,* enemy, opponent* A2

inīquus, -a, -um, *adj.,* unjust, harsh, uneven, unfavorable, treacherous, discontented

initiō (1), to initiate, consecrate

initium, -ī, *n.,* beginning*

iniūria, -ae, *f.,* unjust treatment, injury, injustice, harm, wrongdoing, oppression* A3

innumerābilis, -e, *adj.,* countless, numberless

innumerus, -a, -um, *adj.,* countless

inpotens, inpotentis, *adj.,* powerless, weak, wild, violent

inquam, I say/I said (*only introducing direct speech*)*

inrītō (1), to vex, enrage, provoke

inrumpō, -ere, inrūpī, inruptum, to burst into, rush in

īnscrībō, -ere, īnscrīpsī, īnscrīptum, to write upon

īnsequor, īnsequī, īnsecūtus sum, to pursue (in a hostile manner), follow

insidiae, -ārum, *f. pl.,* ambush; trap, plot

insidior (1), + *dat.,* to lie in wait for, plot against

īnsīdō, -ere, īnsēdī, īnsessum, to sink in, become embedded

īnsignis, -e, *adj.,* distinguished, marked, noteworthy

īnsolēns, -entis, *adj.,* unaccustomed, excessive

īnstar, *n. indeclin.,* (often + *gen.*) likeness, presence, weight, dignity, like, just like

īnsternō, -ere, īnstrāvī, īnstrātum, to lay on, cover, spread

īnstituō, -ere, īnstituī, īnstitūtum, + *acc.* + *abl.,* to train or educate someone in some skill, set up, establish, put in place, build, instruct, teach

īnstitūtum, -ī, *n.,* way, manner, custom, habit

īnstō, īnstāre, īnstitī, + *dat.,* to urge on, press on, pursue, press, insist

insula, -ae, *f.,* island* C12

integer, -gra, -grum, *adj.,* whole, untouched, upright, entire, honest

intellegō, -ere, intellēxī, intellēctum, to understand, perceive*

intempestīvus, -a, -um, *adj.,* out of season

intemptātus, -a, -um, *adj.,* untried, unattempted

inter, *prep.* + *acc.,* between, among*

intercēdō, -ere, intercessī, intercessum, to go between, intervene, pass

interdīcō, -ere, interdixī, interdictum, to banish (someone) from

intereā, *adv.,* meanwhile, (in the) meantime, nevertheless

interficiō, -ere, interfēcī, interfectum, to kill

interfundō, -ere, interfūdī, interfūsum, to pour among, suffuse

interior, -ius, *adj.,* inner, interior

interitus, -ūs, *m.,* ruin, destruction

interpretor (1), to explain, interpret, understand, call

intersum, interesse, interfuī, + *dat.,* to get involved in, participate in, take part in, attend to

intrā, *prep.* + *acc.,* within

in(n)uleus, -ī, *m.,* fawn

inultus, -a, -um, *adj.,* unavenged, unpunished

invalēscō, -ere, invaluī, to grow stronger

invalidus, -a, -um, *adj.,* ill, weak, feeble

inveniō, -īre, invēnī, inventum, to come upon, find* C1

invideō, -ēre, invīdī, invīsum, + *dat.,* to envy someone, to cast an evil eye upon, begrudge, refuse*

invidus, -a, -um, *adj.,* envious, jealous, envying

invīsō, -ere, invīsī, invīsum, to visit

invītus, -a, -um, *adj.,* unwilling, reluctant

iocōsus, -a, -um, *adj.,* joking, playful

Iohannes, -is, *m.,* John

ipse, ipsa, ipsum, *demonstrative pronoun and adj.,* –self* C13

īra, -ae, *f.,* anger, wrath*

is, ea, id, *personal and demonstrative pronoun and adj.,* s/he, it, this*

iste, ista, istud, *demonstrative pronoun and adj.,* that (of yours), this* C13

istīc, *adv.,* there (by you)

ita, *adv.,* so, in such a way; yes*

Italia, -ae, *f.,* Italy* A2

Italus, -a, -um, *adj.,* Italian

itaque, *conj.,* and so*

item, *adv.,* likewise

iter, itineris, *n.,* road, trip, journey* C9

iterum, *adv.,* again* C15

iuba, -ae, *f.,* mane, crest

iubeō, -ēre, iussī, iussum, + *acc.* + *inf.,* to order somebody to do something*

iubileus, -a, -um, *adj.,* used substantively as "Jubilee."

iūcundus, -a, -um, *adj.,* pleasant, agreeable, delightful* C10

iūdex, -icis, *m.,* judge*

iūdicium, -ī, *n.,* court, court case, judgment, sentence, trial, decision; **iūdicium . . . habēre,** to be involved in a court case

iūdicō (1), to decide, judge*

iugum, -ī, *n.,* yoke

Iūlius, -ī, *m.,* July

Iūlus, -ī, *m.,* Ascanius, son of Aeneas

iūmentum, -ī, *n.,* beast of burden, mule, pack animal

iungō, -ere, iūnxī, iūnctum, to join, yoke* C3

Iūnius, -ī, *m.,* June

Iūra, -ae, *m.,* a chain of mountains north of the Alps

iūs, iūris, *n.,* law, justice, decree, right, prerogative; **in iūs īre,** to go to court, take legal action

iūs iūrandum, iūris iūrandī, *n.,* oath

iūstus, -a, -um, *adj.,* legitimate, just, right*

iuvenca, -ae, *f.,* young cow, heifer

iuvenis, -is, *m./f.,* youth, young (man, woman), young person

iuventūs, -ūtis, *f.,* youth, young men, young people* C5

iūvō, -āre, iūvī, iūtum, to help, please

iuxtā, *adv.,* near (by), next, close, close to, in accordance with; *prep.* + *acc.*

J

Jacōbus, -ī, *m.,* James

K

Kalendae, -ārum, *f. pl.,* Kalends, the first day of the month on the Roman calendar

L

labellum, -ī, *n.,* little lip

lābor, lābī, lāpsus sum, to slide, slip, glide down, fall* C9

labor, -ōris, *m.,* labor, toil* C10

labōriōsus, -a, -um, *adj.,* full of (involving) work

laborō (1), to work, suffer, toil

lacerta, -ae, *f.,* lizard

lacertus, -ī, *m.,* upper arm, arm

lacrima, -ae, *f.,* tear*

lacus, -ūs, *m.,* lake

laedō, -ere, laesī, laesum, to harm, hurt, offend* C10

laetor (1), to rejoice

laetus, -a, -um, *adj.,* happy, joyful

laeva, -ae, *f.,* left hand

lambō, lambere, lambī, to lick, lap, wash

laniō (1), to shred, tear, mangle

Lāocoōn, Lāocoöntis, *m.,* Trojan priest of Neptune

lapillus, -ī, *m.,* small stone

lapsō (1), to slip, stumble, totter, fall

largior, largīrī, largītus sum, to give, bestow, confer

lātē, *adv.,* far and wide, widely

lateō, -ēre, latuī, to hide, lie hidden, be concealed, escape notice, escape the notice of, be unknown to

Latīnus, -a, -um, *adj.,* Latin, pertaining to Latin, of Latium* C8

lātitūdō, -dinis, *f.,* width, breadth

Latium, -ī, *n.,* Latium, the region around Rome

Latius, -a, -um, *adj.,* of Latium, Latin

latrō, -ōnis, *m.,* thief, robber

latrōcinium, -ī, *n.,* robbery, banditry, band of robbers

lātus, -a, -um, *adj.,* broad, wide, spacious

latus, lateris, *n.,* side, flank, extreme part or region, lungs, body

laudō (1), to praise* C6

laurus, -ī/-ūs, *f.,* laurel tree

laus, laudis, *f.,* praise

lea, -ae, *f.,* lioness

leaena, -ae, *f.,* lioness

lēctiō, -ōnis, *f.,* reading

lectus, -ī, *m.,* bed, couch

lēgātiō, -ōnis, *f.,* embassy, mission

legātus, -ī, *m.,* ambassador, deputy, envoy* C11

legiō, -ōnis, *f.,* legion

legō, -ere, lēgī, lēctum, to read, choose, gather, skim*

Lemannus, -ī, *m.,* Lake Geneva

lentus, -a, -um, *adj.,* lasting, persistent

leō, -ōnis, *m.,* lion

lepidus, -a, -um, *adj.,* charming, delightful

lētum, -ī, *n.,* death, destruction, ruin

Leuconoē, Leuconoēs, *f.,* Leuconoe, woman's name

levis, -e, *adj.,* light, easy, trivial, slight* C5

lēx, lēgis, *f.,* law*

libellus, -ī, *m.,* little book

līber, lībera, līberum, *adj.,* free* C10

līberālis, -e, *adj.,* befitting a free man, generous, of the liberal arts; **artēs līberālēs,** the liberal arts (*typically grammar, rhetoric, and dialectic*)

līberī, -ōrum, *m. pl.,* children

līberō (1), + *acc.* + *abl.,* to free someone from something*

libet, libuit, it is pleasing, it pleases

Libitīna, -ae, *f.,* Libitina, the goddess of funerals; funeral couch

Libya, -ae, *f.,* country of North Africa

licet, *conj.,* although

licet, + *dat.* + *inf.,* it is allowed, it is permitted for someone to do something*

Licinius, -ī, *m.,* Licinius

ligō (1), to tie, bind, fasten

līlium, -ī, *n.,* lily

līmen, -minis, *n.,* doorway, threshold

lingua, -ae, *f.,* language, tongue (*as physical part of the mouth*)* C8

līquēns, līquentis, *adj.,* liquid, flowing

liquidus, -a, -um, *adj.,* flowing, clear, melodious, liquid, pure

liquō (1), to melt, strain

lītera, see **littera**

littera, -ae, *f.,* letter of the alphabet; **litterae, -ārum,** *f. pl.,* literature, letter (epistle), writing*

lītus, -oris, *n.,* shore, coast, beach*

līvor, -vōris, *m.,* bluish coloring, bruise

locō (1), to place, locate, establish

Locrēnsēs, -um, *m. pl.,* the inhabitants of the town of Locri, the Locrians

locus, -ī, *m.,* place, position in society, family, rank, position; **locī, -ōrum,** *m. pl.,* passages of a book; **loca, -ōrum,** *n. pl.,* geographical places*

longē, *adv.,* far (away), (from) afar, at a distance, by far*

longissimē, *adv. superlative,* farthest

longitūdō, -dinis, *f.,* length

longus, -a, -um, *adj.,* long*

loquor, loquī, locūtus sum, to speak, talk* C8

lūbricātiō, -tiōnis, *f.,* work by lamplight, nocturnal study

Lūcānus, -ī, *m.,* Lucan, Roman poet

Lūcrētius, -ī, *m.,* Lucretius, Roman poet

luctus, -ūs, *m.,* grief, mourning

lūmen, -inis, *n.,* light, eye* C7

lūna, -ae, *f.,* moon, moonlight

lūnāris, -e, *adj.,* of or pertaining to the moon

lūsitō (1), to play

lūstrō (1), to survey; traverse; purify

lūx, lūcis, *f.,* light, life

M

mactō (1), to afflict, vex, sacrifice, slaughter; honor

macula, -ae, *f.,* spot, splotch, stain

madefaciō, -ere, madefēcī, madefactum, to soak, drench

māgālia, -ium, *n. pl.,* huts, hovels

magis, *adv.,* more, rather*

magister, magistrī, *m.,* teacher (male)* C3

magistrātus, -ūs, *m.,* office of a magistrate, magistracy, magistrate, officer, official* A8

magnificentia, -ae, *f.,* magnificence

magnificus, -a, -um, *adj.,* splendid

magnus, -a, -um, *adj.,* large, great, important*

maior, maius, *adj. comparative,* greater* C8

Māius, -ī, *m.,* May

male, *adv.,* badly, poorly

maleficium, -ī, *n.,* crime, offense; mischief, harm

malleolus, -ī, *m.,* small hammer, firebrand

mālō, mālle, māluī, —, to prefer*

malum, -ī, *n.,* evil, misfortune, trouble

malus, -a, -um, *adj.,* bad*

māne, *adv.,* early in the morning* C2

maneō, -ēre, mānsī, mānsum, to remain*

Manlianus, -a, -um, *adj.,* of Manlius

Mantua, -ae, *f.,* Mantua, Italy

manus, -ūs, *f.,* hand*

Mārcus Tullius Cicerō, -ōnis, *m.,* Marcus Tullius Cicero

mare, maris, *n.,* sea*

Marō, -ōnis, *m.,* Maro, Vergil's *nomen*

māter, mātris, *f.,* mother*

mātrimōnium, -ī, *n.,* marriage, wedlock; **in mātrimōnium dō, dare, dedī, datum,** to give in matrimony, to marry* C3

Matrona, -ae, *m.,* Marne river

mātūritās, -tātis, *f.,* ripeness, maturity

mātūrō (1), to hasten, hurry

maximē, *adv. superlative,* most, very, greatly, especially* C14

maximus, -a, -um, *adj. superlative,* greatest, largest; **maximus nātū,** oldest [by birth]*

medicus, -ī, *m.,* doctor

mediocris, -e, *adj.,* commonplace, mediocre, moderate, ordinary* A5

mediocritās, -tātis, *f.,* mean, moderation, keeping of a middle course

meditor (1), to meditate, design

medium, -ī, *n.,* the middle, midst, center*

medius, -a, -um, *adj.,* middle* C14

mēhercule, *interjection,* by Hercules!

mel, mellis, *n.,* honey

melior, melius, *adj. comparative,* better, superior, finer* C8

Melpomenē, -enēs, *f.,* Melpomene, one of the Muses

membrum, -ī, *n.,* limb, part

meminī, meminisse, + *gen.,* to remember, recall* A3

memor, -oris, *adj.* + *gen.,* remembering, mindful of (*usually of one's obligations*), unforgetting* A1

memoria, -ae, *f.,* memory; **memoriā teneō, -ēre, tenuī, tentum,** to remember, keep in mind*

memorō (1), to call to mind, state

mēns, mentis, *f.,* mind, spirit* C5

mēnsis, -is, *m.,* month

mercātor, -tōris, *m.,* merchant

meritum, -ī, *n.,* that which one deserves, due reward, service, meritorious action

merus, -a, -um, *adj.,* pure, unmixed; usually used of wine

mētior, mētīrī, mēnsus sum, to measure, estimate, value

metuō, -ere, metuī, metūtum, to fear, be afraid of, be afraid

metus, -ūs, *m.,* fear, anxiety, fright

meus, -a, -um, *possessive adj.,* my*

mīles, -itis, *m.,* soldier*

mīlia, -ium, *n. pl.,* thousands

mīlle, *adj.,* one thousand

minimē, *adv. superlative,* least, very little; no* C11

minimus, -a, -um, *adj. superlative,* smallest, least*

minister, -trī, *m.,* servant, agent, tool

minus, *adv. comparative,* not; less* C8 C11

mīrābilis, -e, *adj.,* wonderful, marvelous, wondrous

mīror (1), to marvel, be surprised at, wonder (at), admire, be amazed at* C13

mīrus, -a, -um, *adj.,* wonderful

misceō, -ēre, miscuī, mixtum, to mix, mingle, confuse, blend

miser, misera, miserum, *adj.,* wretched*

miserābilis, -e, *adj.,* miserable, wretched

misericordia, -ae, *f.,* compassion, pity

miseror (1), to pity, commiserate

mittō, -ere, mīsī, missum, to send*

mōbilis, -e, *adj.,* movable, changeable, inconstant, pliant

mōbilitās, -ātis, *f.,* mobility, activity, motion, speed

modo . . . modo . . . , at one time . . . at another . . . , now . . . now . . . * A2

modo, *adv.,* only, just now, recently

modus, -ī, *m.,* way, mode, method, manner, measure, meter, music, limit, rhythmic pattern; *in pl.* poetry* C10

moenia, -ium, *n. pl.,* ramparts, walls of a city

mōlēs, mōlis, *f.,* mass, burden, structure, construction, difficulty

molestus, -a, -um, *adj.,* troublesome, irksome, bothersome, annoying, distressing

mōlior, -īrī, molītus sum, to work, effect, make

molitus, -a, -um, *adj.,* milled, ground

mollēscō, -ere, to become soft

mollis, molle, *adj.,* effeminate, soft, gentle, graceful

moneō, -ēre, monuī, monitum, warn, advise

monīle, monīlis, *n.,* necklace

monimentum, -ī, *n.,* trophy, testimonial, memorial

mōns, montis, *m.,* mountain*

monstrum, -ī, *n.,* monster, prodigy, portent

Montioiicus, -a, -um, *adj.,* pertaining to William Blount (Lord Mountjoy)

Montioius, -ī, *m.,* William Blount (Lord Mountjoy)

monumentum, -ī, *n.,* monument, memorial

mora, -ae, *f.,* delay

morbus, -ī, *m.,* illness, sickness, disease, sickness of the mind, vice, fault* A10

mordeō, mordēre, momordī, morsum, to bite

morior, morī, mortuus sum, to die, perish* C12

moror (1), to stay for a long or short period, spend time, delay, hesitate, hinder* A9

mors, mortis, *f.,* death*

morsus, -ūs, *m.,* bite, biting, jaws, fangs

mortuus, -a, -um, *adj.,* dead, deceased

mōrum, -ī, *n.,* fruit of the mulberry tree

Morus, -ī, *m.,* Sir Thomas More

mōrus, -ī, *f.,* mulberry tree

mōs, mōris, *m.,* custom, habit, usage, rule, law; *pl.,* morals* C1

moveō, -ēre, mōvī, mōtum, to move*

mox, *adv.,* soon, presently*

mucrō, -ōnis, *m.,* tip, point of a sword

multiplex, -plicis, *adj.,* manifold, multiple

multitūdō, -ūdinis, *f.,* crowd, throng* C13

multum, *adv.,* much*

multus, -a, -um, *adj.,* much, many; **multum** + *partitive gen.,* a lot of

munditia, -ae, *f.,* neatness, cleanliness, elegance

mundus, -ī, *m.,* world, universe* C1

muniō, -īre, -īvī, -ītum, to fortify, (*of roads*) build

munitissimus, -a, -um, *adj.,* most guarded

mūnus, mūneris, *n.,* gift, ritual duty

murmur, -ris, *n.,* murmur, roar, rumble, whisper

mūrus, -ī, *m.,* wall, wall-fence, rampart*

Mūsa, -ae, *f.,* Muse, goddess of the arts

mūtō (1), to change*

mutuus, -a, -um, *adj.,* mutual, reciprocal

N

nam, *conj.,* for, in fact*

Nammēius, -ī, *m.,* Nammeius, a Helvetian leader

namque, *conj.,* indeed, for, because* A6

nārrō (1), to tell, relate, recount, report, narrate*

nāscor, nāscī, nātus sum, to be born, be produced* A9

nasus, -ī, *m.,* nose

nāsūtus, -a, -um, *adj.,* big-nosed

nātū maxima/minima, oldest/ youngest

nātūra, -ae, *f.,* nature, character* C14

nātus, -a, -um, *adj.,* born

nātus, -ī, *m.,* son

nauticus, -a, -um, *adj.,* nautical

nāvigātiō, -ōnis, *f.,* sea voyage

nāvis, -is, *f.,* ship*

–ne, a particle added to the first word of an interrogative sentence*

nē, *conj. + subjunctive,* in order not to, lest, that not, not to* C1

Neāpolitānī, -ōrum, *m. pl.,* inhabitants of the town of Naples, the Neapolitans

nec, *conj.,* and not, nor; **nec . . . nec . . . ,** neither . . . nor . . . * C4

necessārius, -ī, *m.,* relative, client

necesse, *indeclin. adj.,* necessary

nectar, nectaris, *n.,* nectar

nefārius, -a, -um, *adj.,* unspeakable, wicked

nefās (*indeclin.*), *n.,* a crime, a sacrilege, guilt, impiety, wrong, offense against divine law

neglegō, -ere, neglēxī, neglēctum, to neglect, disregard*

negō (1), to deny* C13

nēmō, *m.,* no one, nobody* C6

Neoptolemus, -ī, *m.,* Pyrrhus, son of Achilles

nepōs, -ōtis, *m.,* grandson, descendant

Neptūnus, -ī, *m.,* Neptune, god of the sea

neque = nec, and not; **neque . . . neque . . . ,** neither . . . nor . . . * A3

nēquīquam, *adv.,* in vain, to no purpose

nesciō, -īre, -īvī, -ītum, not to know* C11

nesciōquis, nesciōquid, *adj.,* someone or other, something or other

nescius, -a, -um, *adj.,* ignorant, unaware

neve, *adv.,* and not

nex, necis, *f.,* murder, death

niger, -gra, -grum, *adj.,* black, dark

nihil, *negative pronoun,* nothing*

nihilium, -ī, *n.,* nothing

nimbus, -ī, *m.,* rainstorm, (storm) cloud

nimium, *adv.,* too much, excessively, too, very

Ninus, -ī, *m.,* king of Assyria and second husband to Semiramis

nisi, *conj.,* if not, unless, but for, except* C12

niteō, nitēre, nituī, to shine, be radiant with beauty

niveus, -a, -um, *adj.,* snow-white, snowy, white

nōbilis, nōbile, *adj.,* noble, distinguished, known, of noble birth, remarkable

nōbilitās, -tātis, *f.,* nobility, nobles

nocēns, -entis, *adj.,* guilty, harmful

nocturnus, -a, -um, *adj.,* of the night, nocturnal, nightly

nōdus, -ī, *m.,* knot; fold, coil

nōlō, nōlle, nōluī, —, not to want, be unwilling* C7

nōmen, -inis, *n.,* name*

nōminō (1), to name, call, call by name

nōn, *negative adv.,* not*

nōn sōlum . . . , sed etiam . . . , not only . . . , but also . . . *

Nōnae, -ārum, *f. pl.,* Nones, either the fifth or seventh day of the month depending on the month

nōndum, *adv.,* not yet

nōnne, *interrogative adv.,* expects a positive answer

nōnnumquam, *adv.,* sometimes

Nōrēia, -ae, *f.,* principal town of the Norici

Nōricus, -a, -um, *adj.,* Noric

nōs, *personal pronoun,* we*

nōscō, -ere, nōvī, nōtum, to learn, recognize, get to know

noster, nostra, nostrum, *possessive adj.,* our*

notō (1), to indicate, note, mark

nōtus, -a, -um, *adj.,* well-known, familiar, notorious, known

novem, *indeclin. adj.,* nine

noviēns, *adv.,* nine times

novissimus, -a, -um, *adj.,* last, final

novus, -a, -um, *adj.,* new*

nox, noctis, *f.,* night*

nūbila, -ōrum, *n. pl.,* clouds, cloudiness

nūbilum, -ī, *n.,* cloud, cloudiness

nūbō, -ere, nūpsī, nūptum + *dat.,* to marry (*used of a woman marrying a man*)

nūdus, -a, -um, *adj.,* bare, naked

nūgae, -ārum, *f.,* trifles

nūllus, -a, -um, *adj.,* none; *as substantive,* **nūllus, -ī,** *m.,* no one, nobody*

num, *interrogative adv.,* expects a negative answer

nūmen, nūminis, *n.,* divinity, divine power, divine will

numerō (1), to number, count among* C13

numerus, -ī, *m.,* number, account, rhythm, meter* A2

numquam (variant, **nunquam**), *adv.,* never*

nunc, *adv.,* now*

nuntia, -ae, *f.,* messenger

nūntiō (1), to announce, speak

nuntius, -ī, *m.,* messenger, message

nūper, *adv.,* lately, recently, not long ago

nusquam, *adv.,* nowhere* C3

Nympha, -ae, *f.,* nymph, minor female divinity of the forests, water, etc.

O

ō, *interj.,* oh!

ob, *prep.* + *acc.,* on account of

obaerātus, -ī, *m.,* debtor

obdūrō (1), to persist

oblectātiō, -ōnis, *f.,* delight

oblinō, -ere, oblēvī, oblitum, to besmear, make dirty

oboleō, -ēre, oboluī, to smell of

oborior, oborīrī, obortus sum, to spring up, occur

obscūrus, -a, -um, *adj.,* covered, concealed, dark, obscure, dim

obsequium, -ī, *n.,* obedience

obsideō, -ēre, obsēdī, obsessum, to besiege; lie in wait for

obsolētus, -a, -um, *adj.,* worn out, shabby, ordinary

obstinātus, -a, -um, *adj.,* resolute, determined

obstipēscō, erc, obstipuī, to be dazed, stand agape, be amazed, be astonished

obstō, -āre, obstitī, obstātum, to stand in the way, block the path

obstrepō, -ere, obstrepuī, obstrepitum, to make a loud noise, roar, drown by louder noise

obticēscō, -ere, obticuī, to grow silent

obtineō, -ēre, obtinuī, obtentum, to hold, hold onto, obtain

occāsus, -ūs, *m.,* setting, fall; **occāsus solis,** setting of the sun, the West

occidō, occidere, occidī, occāsum, to fall, set

occīdō, -ere, occīdī, occīsum, to kill*

occupō (1), to occupy* C1

ōceānus, -ī, *m.,* ocean

oculus, -ī, *m.,* eye*

odī, odisse, *defective verb used only in the perfect tenses,* to hate

odium, -ī, *n.,* hatred, hate, grudge* C2

odor, -ōris, *m.,* scent, odor

oeconomus, -ī, *m.,* steward, household manager

offendō, -ere, offendī, offēnsum, to happen upon, offend, find, meet with, be offensive to, upset* C13

offensus, -a, -um, *adj.,* disliked, offensive, offended, displeased

offerō, offerre, obtulī, oblātum, to present, offer

olfaciō, olfacere, olfēcī, olfactum, to smell

ōlim, *adv.,* once upon a time, formerly, once, on an occasion, at some future date, someday

ōmen, ōminis, *n.,* sign, harbinger, portent, omen

omittō, -ere, omīsī, omissum, omit, pass over, pass by, let go, disregard

omnīnō, *adv.,* wholly, entirely, in all, altogether, in general, at all, generally

omnis, -e, *adj.,* each, every, all*

onus, oneris, *n.,* weight, burden, load* C9

opācus, -a, -um, *adj.,* dark, obscure, gloomy

operam dō, + *dat.,* to give care to, pay attention to (the study of)

opinor (1), to suppose

oportet, -ēre, oportuit, *impersonal,* to be proper, be necessary

oppidum, -ī, *n.,* town* C15

opportūnus, -a, -um, *adj.,* suitable, advantageous

opportūnitās, -tātis, *f.,* convenience, opportunity

opprimō, -ere, oppressī, oppressum, to overwhelm, oppress, suppress, crush*

oppōnō, -ere, opposuī, oppositum, to place against, place in front, put before, proffer

oppugnō (1), to attack

ops, opis, *f.,* aid, wealth, power; **opēs, opium,** *f. pl.,* resources, money

optimus, -a, -um, *adj.,* best* C8

optō (1), to desire, wish, choose, hope (for), wish for

opus, -eris, *n.,* work, deed, toil

opus est, is necessary

ora, -ae, *f.,* shore

ōrātiō, -ōnis, *f.,* speech, oration; **ōrātiōnem habeō,** to make a speech*

orbis, orbis, *m.,* circle, disc, globe, ring, fold, coil; earth; **orbis terrārum,** the earth, the world* C12

ōrdō, ōrdinis, *m.,* order, social class, class (in society), row, position* A9

Orgetorīx, -rigis, *m.,* Orgetorix, a rich Helvetian noble

orior, orīrī, ortus sum, + *abl.,* to be born of, be descended from, originate, arise, rise* A9

ōrnō (1), to adorn, decorate

ōrō (1), to ask, entreat, pray (for), plead, argue* C5

Orpheus, -ī, *m.,* Thracian singer who went to the Underworld

ōs, ōris, *n.,* mouth, face*

ōsculum, -ī, *n.,* kiss

ōtium, -ī, *n.,* leisure, free time* C7

P

pacīscor, -ī, pactus sum, to agree upon

pacō (1), to pacify

pactum, -ī, *n.,* pact, agreement

pāgus, -ī, *m.,* village

Palatium, -ī, *n.,* the Palatine (the hill immediately south of the Forum)

pallidus, -a, -um, *adj.,* pale, wan, pallid

pandus, -a, -um, *adj.,* curved, bent, bowed

Paphius, -a, -um, *adj.,* of or pertaining to the city of Paphos

Paphos, -ī, *m./f.,* child of Pygmalion

pār, paris, *adj.,* equal* A5

parcō, -ere, pepercī (parsī), —, + *dat.,* to spare somebody or something* C4

parēns, -rentis, *m./f.,* parent*

pareō, -ēre, paruī, + *dat.,* to obey

pariēs, -etis, *m.,* wall

pariter, *adv.,* equally, alike, side by side, at the same time, together

parō (1), to prepare, get ready, design, procure, get, buy*

parricidium, -ī, *n.,* murder, parricide

pars, partis, *f.,* part, section, side*

particeps, -cipis, *m.,* + *gen.,* participant in

partim, *adv.,* partly

partiō, -īre, -īvī, -ītum, to divide, distribute

partior, partīrī, partītus sum, to divide, distribute*

parum, *adv.,* slightly, too little, not

parvus, -a, -um, *adj.,* small, little*

passim, *adv.,* everywhere, all about

passus, -ūs, *m.,* step, pace, gait, stride

patefaciō, -ere, patefēcī, patefactum, to lay open, disclose

pateō, -ēre, patuī, —, to be open, be available, lie out in the open, be obvious, be accessible, extend, stretch out

pater, patris, *m.,* father*

patientia, -ae, *f.,* patience

patior, patī, passus sum, to endure, tolerate, suffer, allow, permit

patria, -ae, *f.,* fatherland, homeland*

patrimōnium, -ī, *n.,* inheritance

patrius, -a, -um, *adj.,* paternal, of a father, father's, ancestral

patrōna, -ae, *f.,* patroness, protectress

patrōnus, -ī, *m.,* lawyer, patron

paucī, -ae, -a, *adj.,* few*

paulātim, *adv.,* little by little, gradually

paulō, *adv.,* a little bit, to a small extent, shortly before, a little while ago* C6

paulō ante, *adv.,* a little while ago, shortly before

paulum, *adv.,* (a) little, slightly, somewhat

paulum, -ī, *n.,* a little bit

pauper, pauperis, *adj.,* poor*

pavidus, -a, -um, *adj.,* frightened, terrified, trembling, fearful

pāx, pācis, *f.,* pact, treaty, peace, quiet, repose*

peccātum, -ī, *n.,* sin

pectus, -oris, *n.,* chest, breast, heart*

pecūnia, -ae, *f.,* money

pecus, pecoris, *n.,* flock, herd, swarm, sheep

pelagus, -ī, *n.,* sea

Pēlīdēs, -ae, *m.,* descendant of Peleus, Achilles

pellis, -is, *f.,* skin, hide, pelt*

pellō, -ere, pepulī, pulsum, to push, drive back, rout

penātēs, -ium, *m. pl.,* household gods

pendeō, -ēre, pependī, — , to hang (*intransitive*), hang down*

penitus, *adv.,* deep, deeply, utterly, thoroughly

per, *prep. + acc.,* through, for the sake of*

peragō, -ere, perēgī, perāctum, to carry out, perform, accomplish, finish

percutiō, -ere, percussī, percussum, to strike through, beat, strike* C15

perdō, -ere, perdidī, perditum, to lose, waste, destroy, ruin* C3

peremō, -ere, perēmī, perēmptum, to kill

perennis, -e, *adj.,* lasting a long time, eternal, lasting throughout the year, lasting for many years, enduring

pereō, perīre, periī, peritum, to perish, die

perfacilis, -e, *adj.,* very easy

perfectus, -a, -um, *adj.,* perfect, complete

perferō, perferre, pertulī, perlātum, to endure, put up with

perficiō, -ere, perfēcī, perfectum, to finish, make

perfringō, -ere, perfrēgī, perfrāctum, to break down

perfundō, -ere, perfūdī, perfusum, to soak, drench, pour over, fill with

Pergama, -ōrum, *n. pl.,* (citadel of) Troy

pergō, -ere, perrēxī, perrēctum, to keep on, proceed, go forward

pergravis, -e, *adj.,* very weighty, very important

perhibeō, -ēre, perhibuī, perhibitum, to present, say

perīculum, -ī, *n.,* danger, peril, risk*

perinvītus, -a, -um, *adj.,* very unwilling

periūcundus, -a, -um, *adj.,* very pleasant

perlabor, perlābī, perlāpsus sum, to glide through

perlegō, -ere, perlēgī, perlēctum, to read through

permagnus, -a, -um, *adj.,* very great

permātūrēscō, -ere, permatūruī, to become fully ripe

permoveō, -ēre, permōvī, permōtum, to arouse, stir up, influence

permulceō, -ēre, permulsī, permulsum, to charm

perniciēs, -ēī, *f.,* destruction, ruin

perparcē, *adv.,* very stingily

perpaucī, -ae, -a, *adj.,* very few

perpetuus, -a, -um, *adj.,* continuous, permanent, everlasting

persaepe, *adv.,* very often

persequor, persequī, persecūtus sum, to follow persistently, go over, pursue, chase, follow all the way, accompany

persuādeō, -ēre, persuāsī, persuāsum, + *dat.,* to persuade, convince

pertimēscō, -ere, pertimuī, to become alarmed at, fear

pertineō, -ēre, pertinuī, pertentum, + *ad + acc.,* to relate to, pertain to, extend (to), reach (to)

pertrahō, -ere, pertrāxī, pertrāctum, to drag, entice, take by force

perturbō (1), to throw into confusion, disturb

pervagor (1), to wander through

perveniō, -īre, -vēnī, -ventum, to arrive, reach, come to* C9

pervolō (1), to fly through

pēs, pedis, *m.,* foot, step

pessimus, -a, -um, *adj. superlative,* worst*

pestis, -is, *f.,* plague, destruction

petītiō, -ōnis, *f.,* blow, attack

petō, -ere, petīvī, petītum, to seek, head for, go to, rush to, demand, entreat*

pharmacopōla, -ae, *f.,* pharmacy, drugstore

pharmacum, -ī, *n.,* medicine

Phoebus, -ī, *m.,* another name for Apollo

pictor, -tōris, *m.,* painter

pictūra, -ae, *f.,* picture, painting

pietās, pietātis, *f.,* loyalty, sense of duty, dutifulness to family and society

pila, -ae, *f.,* ball, sphere

pilula, -ae, *f.,* little ball, pill

pingō, -ere, pinxī, pictum, to paint, color

pīnus, -ūs, *f.,* pine

pius, -a, -um, *adj.,* loyal, devoted

placet, placēre, placuit, *impersonal,* it pleases, is pleasing

plācō (1), to placate, soothe, appease, calm

plangor, -oris, *n.,* beating, lamentation

plēbs, plēbis *or* **plēbēs, -eī,** *f.,* commoners, common people, the masses

plēnus, -a, -um, *adj.* + *gen.* or + *abl.,* full of, filled with*

pleurītis, -tidis, *f.,* pleurisy

plūma, -ae, *f.,* feather, plume

plumbum, -ī, *n.,* lead

plūrimum, *adv.,* most of all

plūrimus, -a, -um, *adj. superlative,* most, very much, very great*

plūs, *adv.,* more

plūs, plūris, *adj. comparative,* + *partitive gen.,* more, several*

poena, -ae, *f.,* punishment, penalty

poēta, -ae, *m.,* poet*

pollex, pollicis, *m.,* thumb

polliceor, pollicērī, pollicitus sum, to promise* A6

pompa, -ae, *f.,* retinue

pōmum, -ī, *n.,* fruit*

pōne, *adv.,* behind, after, from behind

pōnō, -ere, posuī, positum, to put, place, put down, lay aside*

pōns, pontis, *m.,* bridge* C4

pontifex, -ficis, *m.,* high priest, pontiff

pontus, -ī, *m.,* sea, waves

populus, -ī, *m.,* people, nation* C11

porta, -ae, *f.,* gate, door, opening, entrance, exit* C4

portō (1), to carry; to bring

portus, -ūs, *m.,* port, harbor

possum, posse, potuī, —, to be able, can*

post, *adv.,* afterward, subsequently

post, *prep.* + *acc.,* after, behind*

posteā, *adv.,* later on, afterward*

posterus, -a, -um, *adj.,* next, following, future, later

postquam, *conj.,* after, when*

postrēmus, -a, -um, *adj.,* last

potēns, potentis, *adj.,* powerful, able, potent* C7

potentia, -ae, *f.,* power, force* A4

potestās, -ātis, *f.,* command, control, power, authority* A4

potior, potīrī, potītus sum, + *gen.,* + *abl.,* to make oneself master of, take possession of, gain possession of, obtain

praebeō, -ēre, praebuī, praebitum, to offer, give, supply

praecēdō, -ere, praecessī, praecessum, to surpass, precede

praecellō, -ere, to excell

praeceptiō, -iōnis, *f.,* instruction

praeceptor, -ōris, *m.,* teacher

praecipiō, -ere, praecēpī, praeceptum, to order, admonish

praecipitō (1), to fall, sink

praeclārē, *adv.,* especially well, nobly, very well

praeclārus, -a, -um, *adj.,* famous, distinguished, excellent, very renowned*

praedīcō, -ere, praedīxī, praedictum, to predict, foretell

praedium, -ī, *n.,* estate, land

praemium, -ī, *n.,* reward, gift*

praemoneō, -ēre, praemonuī, praemonitum, to forewarn

praeparō (1), to prepare

praepōnō, -ere, praeposuī, praepositum, to put before, prefer

praesentia, -ae, *f.,* presence

praesēpe, -is, *n.,* stall, hive

praesertim, *adv.,* especially* C14

praesidium, -ī, *n.,* military escort, defense, guard, garrison, help, assistance, protection* A2

praestō, *adv.,* ready at hand, present

praestō, -āre, praestitī, praestātum *or* **praestitum,** +*dat.,* to make available, supply; fulfill, perform, offer; surpass, exceed, excel, outdo, show, provide* A1

praetereō, praeterīre, praeterīvī, praeteritum, to pass, go past

praeterquam, *conj.,* except that

praetexō, -ere, praetexuī, praetextum, to fringe, cloak

praetor, praetōris, *m.,* praetor

prandeō, -ēre, prandī, pransum, to lunch

prātum, -ī, *n.,* meadow

prāvum, -ī, *n.,* wrong, perverse act

precor (1), to beg, pray, entreat

premō, -ere, pressī, pressum, to press, follow closely, hug, squeeze, suppress, press hard, overcome

prīdie, *adv.,* the day before

prīmō, *adv.,* at first, in the beginning* C4

prīmum, *adv.,* first*

prīmus, -a, -um, *adj.,* first*

prīnceps, prīncipis, *adj.,* distinguished, first, first in time, leading, foremost

prīnceps, prīncipis, *m.,* leading citizen, leader, chief, most eminent, prince* A7

prīncipātus, -ī, *m.,* rule, leadership, chief command, first place

prīncipiō, *adv.,* in the first place

prior, prius, *adj. comparative,* before last, prior, earlier

prius, *adv.,* beforehand, previously, before, first

prīvātus, -a, -um, *adj.,* private, apart from the public sphere

prō, *prep.* + *abl.,* for, on behalf of, in proportion to*

probō (1), to approve, prove, show* C12

procella, -ae, *f.,* violent storm, gale, violent wind, storm, trouble

procul, *adv.,* far, far away*

proelium, -ī, *n.,* battle, combat, fight*

profectiō, -ōnis, *f.,* departure, a setting out

proficīscor, proficīscī, profectus sum, to set out, depart

profugus, -a, -um, *adj.,* exiled, an exile

prōgignō, -ere, prōgenuī, prōgenitum, to bring forth, bear

prohibeō, -ēre, prohibuī, prohibitum, to prevent, keep off, restrain, defend, keep away

prōlābor, -ī, prolāpsus sum, to fall, slide, perish

prōlēs, -is, *f.,* child, offspring

prōlixus, -a, -um, *adj.,* willing, copious

prōmereor, prōmerērī, prōmeritus sum, to deserve, earn

prōnuba, -ae, *f.,* matron of honor, bride's attendant

prope, *prep. + acc.,* near* C1

propemodum, *adv.,* almost

properātiō, -ōnis, *f.,* hasty departure

proprius, -a, -um, *adj.,* one's own

propter, *prep. + acc.,* because of, on account of*

proptereā quod, *conj.,* on account of which, for the very reason that

prosper, prospera, prosperum, *adj.,* fortunate, prosperous, favorable* C10

prosum, prodesse, profuī, *+ dat.,* to benefit

prōvincia, -ae, *f.,* province (territorial), any duty or sphere of activity (not territorial)

provocō (1), to provoke, call out, challenge

proximus, -a, -um, *adj. (+ dat.),* nearest, last, next, nearby, neighboring, closest, next to* C5

pruīnōsus, -a, -um, *adj.,* frosty

pūblicē, *adv.,* publicly, on behalf of the state, as a community

pūblicus, -a, -um, *adj.,* common, public, belonging to the state; **rēs pūblica,** state* C7

pudendus, -a, -um, *adj.,* shameful

pudor, -dōris, *m.,* sense of shame, shame

puella, -ae, *f.,* girl*

puer, puerī, *m.,* boy, boyhood*

puerīlis, puerīle, *adj.,* related to *puer;* boyish, childish, puerile; **puerīlis aetās,** boyhood

pulcher, pulchra, pulchrum, *adj.,* beautiful, nice, handsome, splendid, illustrious, noble*

pulchrē, *adv.,* beautifully

pullus, -a, -um, *adj.,* dingy, somber, drab-colored

pulsō (1), to beat repeatedly

pulvis, -veris, *m.,* dust, sand

pūmex, -icis, *m. (f.),* pumice stone

pūnctum, -ī, *n.,* vote

purgō (1), to cleanse, purify

purpureus, -a, -um, *adj.,* purple, crimson

putō (1), to think, consider, suppose, judge*

Pygmaliōn, -ōnis, *m.,* Pygmalion, legendary king of Cyprus

pyramis, -midis, *f.,* pyramid

Pȳramus, -ī, *m.,* Pyramus

Pȳrēnaeus, -a, -um, *adj.,* Pyrenees; **Pȳrēnaeī montēs,** Pyrenees Mountains, a mountain range between Spain and France

Pyrrha, -ae, *f.,* Pyrrha, woman's name

Pyrrhus, -ī, *m.,* Neoptolemus, son of Achilles

Q

quā, *adv.,* where

quadringentī, -ae, -a, *adj.,* four hundred

quaerō, -ere, quaesīvī, quaesītum, to look for, search, seek*

quaestiō, -ōnis, *f.,* question, dispute, investigation, trial, court, a seeking, judicial inquiry

quālis, quāle, *interrogative and relative pronoun,* what sort of, such as, as, of what sort, like, of such a sort* C7

quāliscumque, quālecumque, *adj.,* of whatever sort

quam, *interrogative adv. and exclamation particle,* how* C4

quam, *used with comparative words,* than, as* C6

quamdiū *or* **quam diū,** *interrogative adv.,* for how long a time* A9

quamquam, *conj.,* although* C12

quandō, *conj.,* when, since

quantum, *interrogative and relative adv.,* as much as, as much; how much, to what extent* C6

quantus, -a, -um, *interrogative and relative adj.,* how much, how great, so (much, great, many), as* C4

quārē, *conj.,* therefore, hence*

quattuor, *indeclin, adj.,* four

–que, *conj.,* and*

queō, quīre, quīvī (quiī), quītum, to be able, can

queror, -ī, questus sum, to complain, complain of

quī, quae, quod, *relative pronoun,* which, who, that*

quī, quae, quod?, *interrogative adj.,* which? what?*

quia, *conj.,* because* C12

quīcumque, quaecumque, quodcumque, whoever, whatever

quīdam, quaedam, quiddam, *indefinite pronoun;* **quīdam, quaedam, quoddam,** *indefinite adj.,* a certain, some* A7

quidem, *adv.,* indeed, in fact* C12

quiēscō, -ere, quiēvī, quiētum, to be quiet, rest

quīn, *adv.,* but that

quis, quid?, *interrogative pronoun,* who? what?*

quispiam, quaepiam, quippiam, *adj.,* some

quisquam, quicquam (quidquam), *indefinite pronoun (mainly in negative sentences)*, any, anybody* A9

quisque, quaeque, quidque, *pronoun*, each, each one, everybody

quisquis, quidquid (quicquid), *indefinite pronoun*, whoever, whatever

quīvīs, quaevīs, quodvīs, *adj.*, anyone you like, anything you like

quō, *adv.*, where

quōcumque, *conj.*, wherever, wheresoever, to whatever place

quod, *conj.*, the fact that, because* C12

quōminus, *conj.*, that not, from (after verbs of preventing)

quondam, *adv.*, once, formerly, at one time, at some time, sometimes, in the future

quoniam, *adv.*, since, because

quoque, *adv.*, also*

quōquō, *adv.*, wherever

quot, *adv.*, how many, as many as

quotīdiānus, -a, -um, *adj.*, daily; often spelled *cottīdiānus, -a, -um*

quotiēns, *exclamation,* how often

quotus, -a, -um, *adj.*, what number, how many

quum, see **cum**, *adv.*

R

radius, -ī, *m.*, rod, spoke, compass, ray of light

rādix, -dicis, *f.*, root, foot, base

rāmus, -ī, *m.*, branch

ratiō, -ōnis, *f.*, way, manner, account, transaction, business

raucus, -a, -um, *adj.*, hoarse, harsh

recēns, -entis, *adj.*, recent, fresh, new, late, modern

recipiō, -ere, recēpī, receptum, to receive, take back; **mē recipiō,** I retreat; **sē recipiō,** + *ad + acc.*, to withdraw, escape to, find refuge in* C4

reclūdō, -ere, reclusī, reclusum, to open, unsheathe

recōgnōscō, -ere, recōgnōvī, recōgnitum, to recall, recount, review

recondō, -ere, recondidī, reconditum, to close again

recreātus, -a, -um, *adj.*, restored to health

recreō (1), to recreate, restore, revive

rēctus, -a, -um, *adj.*, straight, right, correct, proper

reddō, -ere, reddidī, redditum, to render, make, give back, return, restore* C10

redeō, -īre, -īvī, -itum, to go back, return, rise, come in (*money*)* C13

redimīculum, -ī, *n.*, band, wreath, garland

reditiō, -ōnis, *f.*, return

redoleō, -ēre, redoluī, to be fragrant, smell (of)

redūcō, -ere, redūxī, reductum, to lead back

referō, referre, rettulī, relātum, to carry back, report, tell, bring back, withdraw* C13

rēgālis, -e, *adj.*, royal, regal

rēgīna, -ae, *f.*, queen*

Rēgīnī, -ōrum, *m. pl.*, inhabitants of the town of Regium, the Regians

regiō, -ōnis, *f.*, region, area

rēgius, -a, -um, *adj.*, royal, regal

rēgnātor, -ōris, *m.*, ruler, sovereign, lord

rēgnō (1), to reign, rule

regnum, -ī, *n.*, kingly government, royal power, kingdom, kingship, dominion, sovereignty, rule, authority

regō, regere, rēxī, rēctum, to rule, guide, direct

relēgō (1), to send away, banish

relevō (1), to relieve, ease

rel(l)igiō, -ōnis, *f.*, religion, sanctity, piety to the gods; *pl.*, religious observances, religious matters

religō (1), to tie back, fasten behind, untie

relinquō, -ere, relīquī, relictum, to leave behind, leave, abandon*

reliquus, -a, -um, *adj.*, the rest of, the remaining, left over; **reliquum facere,** to leave over* A10

remollēscō, -ere, to soften again

remoror (1), to linger, delay

removeō, -ēre, remōvī, remōtum, to move back, remove

reperiō, -īre, repperī, repertum, to find, discover

repleō, -ēre, replēvī, replētum, to fill, stuff

repōnō, -ere, reposuī, repositum, to lay to rest

reputō (1), to consider

requiēscō, -ere, requiēvī, requiētum, to rest

requīrō, -ere, requīsīvī, requīsītum, to try to find, inquire about, seek, look for, search, ask for

rēs, reī, *f.*, thing, matter*

rescindō, -ere, rescidī, rescissum, to cut down

resecō, -āre, resecuī, resectum, to cut back, prune, restrain

resideō, -ēre, resēdī, to stay behind, be left

respiciō, -ere, respexī, respectum, to look back, look at, look back at

respondeō, -ēre, -spondī, -spōnsum, to answer, sympathize with, agree with*

resupīnus, -a, -um, *adj.,* lying on one's back, supine

retractō (1), to handle, feel for a second time

retrō, *adv.,* backward

Reuchlinus, -ī, *m.,* Johann Reuchlin, German theologian and Hebrew scholar

revalēscō, -ere, revaluī, to recover

revellō, -ere, revellī, revulsum, to remove, tear away

reverentia, -ae, *f.,* shyness, modesty

revertor, revertī, reversus sum, to return

rēx, rēgis, *m.,* king*

Rhēnus, -ī, *m.,* the Rhine river

rhīnocerōs, -ōtis, *m.,* rhinoceros

Rhodanus, -ī, *m.,* the Rhone river

rictus, -ūs, *m.,* jaws, the opening of the jaws

rīdeō, -ēre, rīsī, rīsum, to laugh* C15

rigor, -gōris, *m.,* stiffness, rigidity

rīma, -ae, *f.,* crack, fissure

rīpa, -ae, *f.,* riverbank

rīte, *adv.,* rightly, properly

Roffa, -ae, *f.,* Rochester, England

Roffēnsis, -ē, *adj.,* of Rochester

rogō (1), to ask*

rogus, -ī, *m.,* funeral pyre

Rōma, -ae, *f.,* Rome*

Rōmānus, -a, -um, *adj.,* Roman, of Rome*

Romulus, -ī, *m.,* Romulus, the traditional founder of Rome

rosa, -ae, *f.,* rose

rubus, -ī, *m.,* bramble, prickly bush

rūmor, -ōris, *m.,* rumor

rumpō, -ere, rūpī, ruptum, to break, tear, split* C15

ruō, -ere, ruī, rutum, to destroy, ruin

rūpēs, -is, *f.,* rock, cliff, crag, rocky cliff

rūrsum *or* **rūrsus,** *adv.,* back, backward, on the other hand, then again, again

rūs, rūris, *n.,* countryside, country (district)*

S

sacculus, -ī, *m.,* little bag, wallet

sacellum, -ī, *n.,* shrine (classical Latin), chapel (later Latin)

sacer, sacra, sacrum, *adj.,* sacred, holy

sacerdōs, -dōtis, *m./f.,* priest(ess)

sacerdōtium, -ī, *n.,* priestly office, living, income

saeculum, -ī, *n.,* age, generation

saepe, *adv.,* often*

saepenumerō, *adv.,* often

saepiō, -īre, saepsī, saeptum, to hedge in, enclose

saevus, -a, -um, *adj.,* cruel, stern, fierce

sāl, salis, *m.,* salt, a quality that gives taste, wit; sea, brine* A5

salārium, -ī, *n.,* salary

saliō, -īre, saluī, saltum, to jump, leap

salum, -ī, *n.,* sea, swell (of the sea)

saltus, -ūs, *m.,* leap, bound, dancing

salūs, -ūtis, *f.,* health, welfare, safety; **salūtem dīcō,** + *dat.,* to greet (a customary way to begin a letter)* C3

salūtō (1), to greet, pay respects to* C11

salvus, -a, -um, *adj.,* safe, sound

sanctus, -a, -um, *adj.,* consecrated, inviolable, pure, sacred, holy, revered

sānē, *adv.,* of course

sanguineus, -a, -um, *adj.,* bloody, blood-red, bloodshot

sanguis, -inis, *m.,* blood*

saniēs, -ēī, *f.,* blood, gore

sapientia, -ae, *f.,* wisdom

sapienter, *adv.,* wisely

sapiō, -ere, sapīvī, to taste, understand, be wise

satis, *adv.,* enough, sufficiently* C6

satisfaciō, -ere, satisfēcī, satisfactum, to give satisfaction, give all that is required (*often with dat.*)

saxum, -ī, *n.,* stone, rock*

scaena, -ae, *f.,* stage, background

scandō, -ere, to climb over, mount, climb, ascend

scaphula, -ae, *f.,* little boat

scelerātus, -a, -um, *adj.,* wicked, accursed, impious, criminal, outlawed

scelestus, -a, -um, *adj.,* wicked* C10, wretched, unfortunate

scelus, sceleris, *n.,* crime, wrongdoing, affliction

schedula, -ae, *f.,* prescription

schola, -ae, *f.,* school

scientia, -ae, *f.,* knowledge

scīlicet, *adv.,* of course

scindō, -ere, scindī, scissum, to tear, cut, split, tear open

sciō, scīre, scīvī, scītum, to know*

scrībō, -ere, scrīpsī, scrīptum, to write* C3

scrīptum, -ī, *n.,* composition

scrīptūra, -ae, *f.,* scripture

sculpō, -ere, sculpsī, sculptum, to carve

sē, *acc. of the reflexive pronoun,* herself, himself, itself, themselves*

sēcēdō, -ēre, sēcessī, sēcessum, to withdraw, go away

sēcernō, -ere, sēcrēvī, sēcrētum, to separate, set apart

sēcessus, -ūs, *m.,* solitude, alcove, room

sēdecim, *indeclin. adj.,* sixteen

sector (1), to follow, pursue

secundus, -a, -um, *adj.,* favorable, second, following, fortunate, propitious* C6

sed, *conj.,* but*

sedeō, -ēre, sēdī, sessum, to sit (down), settle*

sēdēs, -is, *f.,* seat, abode, foundation, support, basis, house, dwelling* C15

sellula, -ae, *f.,* little bench, seat

semel, *adv.,* once* C10

sēmentis, -is, *f.,* sowing, planting

semper, *adv.,* always*

senātus, -ūs, *m.,* Roman Senate, senate, council of elders

senex, -is, *m.,* old man*

sensus, -ūs, *m.,* sense, feeling

sententia, -ae, *f.,* opinion, point of view, thought* C12

sentiō, -īre, sēnsī, sēnsum, to feel, notice, perceive, sense, know, understand*

septentriō, -ōnis, *m.,* seven stars comprising the Big Dipper; north

septimus, -a, -um, *adj.,* seventh

Sēquana, -ae, *m.,* Seine river

Sēquanī, -ōrum, *m. pl.,* Sequanians

Sēquānus, -a, -um, *adj.,* Sequanian

sequor, sequī, secūtus sum, to follow, come next*

seriēs, -ēī, *f.,* series, sequence, succession

sermō, sermōnis, *m.,* conversation, speech, gossip, talk

serpēns, -entis, *m. (f.),* serpent, snake

sērus, -a, -um, *adj.,* late, after the expected time

servō (1), to save, preserve*

servus, -ī, *m.,* slave, servant* C11

sēsē, *intensive form of reflexive pronoun* = sē

sēsquimēnsis, -is, *m.,* one and a half months (about six weeks)

seu, *conj.,* or, if; **seu . . . seu . . . ,** whether . . . or . . .

sevērus, -a, -um, *adj.,* serious, strict, severe*, austere

sī, *conj.,* if*

sībilus, -a, -um, *adj.,* hissing, whirring

Sibylla, -ae, *f.,* Sibyl, ancient Italian prophetess

sica, -ae, *f.,* dagger

sīc, *adv.,* in such a way, in this way, so, to such an extent* C15

siccō (1), to dry, dry up

sīdus, -eris, *n.,* constellation, star* C15

significō (1), to make known, signify, mean

signum, -ī, *n.,* sign, signal, token, mark

silēns, -entis, *adj.,* silent, quiet

silex, -icis, *m. (f.),* flint, rock, crag

silva, -ae, *f.,* forest*

similis, -e, *adj., + gen.* or + *dat.,* like, similar*

simplex, simplicis, *adj.,* simple, artless, plain

simul, *adv.,* at the same time, simultaneously, together*

simul atque, *conj.,* as soon as

simul . . . simul, *conj.,* not only . . . but at the same time

simulācrum, -ī, *n.,* image, statue, likeness, representation

simulō (1), to imitate, copy, represent

sīn, *conj.,* but if, if on the contrary

sine, *prep. + abl.,* without*

singulāris, -e, *adj.,* unique, exceptional, special, unparalleled, remarkable

singulī, -ae, -a, *adj.,* one apiece, one each (*a distributive*), one at a time, individual, each one, all these* A8

sinō, -ere, sīvī, situm, + *acc.* + *inf.,* to allow somebody to do something, permit* C2

sinuō (1), to fold, curve, twist, wind

Sirmiō, -ōnis, *f.,* Sirmio, island on Lake Garda in northern Italy

sitis, -is, *f.,* thirst

situs, -ūs, *m.,* neglect, decay, deterioration

situs, -ūs, *m.,* site, structure

sīve, *conj.,* or if; **sīve . . . sīve,** whether . . . or

sobrius, -a, -um, *adj.,* sober, moderate, sensible

socia, -ae, *f.,* partner

societās, -tātis, *f.,* association, bond, society, connection

socius, -ī, *m.,* associate, partner, ally* C13

sodālis, -is, *m.,* friend

sōl, sōlis, *m.,* sun; day* C1

sōlivagus, -a, -um, *adj.,* wandering alone, not gregarious, solitary

soleō, -ēre, solitus sum, + *inf.,* to be accustomed to, be used to*

sollemnis, -e, *adj.,* customary, solemn

sollers, -tis, *adj.,* skilled, expert

solum, -ī, *n.,* ground, soil, earth, land

sōlus, -a, -um, *adj.,* alone*

somnus, -ī, *m.,* sleep*

sonitus, -ūs, *m.,* sound, roar, noise, crash

sonō, sonāre, sonuī, sonitum, to (re)sound, roar

sonus, -ī, *m.,* sound, noise, roar

sordes, -dis, *f. (often pl.),* dirt, squalor, baseness

soror, -ōris, *f.,* sister*

sors, sortis, *f.,* lot (*in the literal sense of a lot one draws*), fate (*in the metaphorical sense of one's condition in life*), destiny, oracle, share, fortune* C12

spargō, -ere, sparsī, sparsum, to scatter, sprinkle

spatior (1), to walk about, walk

spatium, -ī, *n.*, space, period of time, span of life, interval, time

speciēs, -ēī, *f.*, appearance, sight, aspect

spectō (1), to watch, look at* C11

spēlunca, -ae, *f.*, cave, cavern, grotto*

spērō (1), to hope, hope for, expect* C12

spēs, speī, *f.*, hope, expectation* C12

spīra, -ae, *f.*, fold, coil, spire

splendidus, -a, -um, *adj.*, illustrious, distinguished, shining, splendid, magnificent

splendor, -ōris, *m.*, brilliance, splendor

spūmō (1), foam, froth, spray

squāmeus, -a, -um, *adj.*, scaly

Stator, -ōris, *m.*, the Stayer, Protector (a name given to Jupiter)

statua, -ae, *f.*, statue

statuō, -ere, statuī, statutum, to decide, set (up), found

stīpō (1), to stuff, crowd, stow

stō, -āre, stetī, statum, to stand*

strātum, -ī, *n.*, pavement, bed, coverlet, throw

strepitus, -ūs, *m.*, noise, uproar, clamor

strīdeō, -ēre *or* **stridō, -ere, stridī**, to hiss, whir, rustle, make a high-pitched sound, whistle, shriek

stringō, -ere, strinxī, strictum, to graze, unsheathe, draw

studium, -ī, *n.*, pursuit, activity to which one is devoted, study, literary occupation, zeal, eagerness* A7

stultē, *adv.*, foolishly

stupeō, -ēre, stupuī, to be amazed

suādeō, -ere, suāsī, suāsum, to persuade, convince

suāvis, -e, *adj.*, pleasant

sub, *prep. + abl.*, under* A8

subeō, -īre, subīvī, subītum, to go under, support, follow, approach, enter, undergo

subiciō, -ere, subiēcī, subiectum, to vanquish, bend, stoop

subinde, *adv.*, immediately after

subīrāscor, subīrāscī, subīrātus sum, to be rather angry

subitō, *adv.*, suddenly

submoveō, -ēre, submōvī, submōtum, to move away, remove, ward off, banish

subrigō, -ere, surrēxī, surrēctum, raise, rise

subsānnō (1), to mock, deride, insult by derisive gestures

subsellium, -ī, *n.*, seat, bench

subsīdō, -ere, subsēdī, to give way

subter, *adv.; prep. + acc.*, beneath, below

subvolvō, -ere, subvolvī, subvolūtum, to roll up

succēdō, -ere, successī, successum, *+ dat.*, to go under, advance, succeed, become a successor

succendō, -ere, succendī, succensum, to set fire to, light

sūdor, -ōris, *m.*, sweat

sufficiō, -ere, suffēcī, suffectum, to supply, suffuse

suffrāgor (1), to vote for, support

suī, sibi, sē, sē, *reflexive pronoun*, herself, himself, itself, themselves*

sulcus, -ī, *m.*, furrow, trench, ditch

sum, esse, fuī, to be*

summus, -a, -um, *adj.*, extreme, highest, utmost, supreme, at the top of, distinguished, top* A2

sūmō, -ere, sūmpsī, sūmptum, to take, take on, use*

sūmptus, -ūs, *m.*, expense, cost* A5

super, *adv.*, on the top, on the surface, above

superbia, -ae, *f.*, pride, arrogance

superbus, -a, -um, *adj.*, proud, haughty

superiōr, superiōris, *adj.*, more powerful, higher, former, above

superiora, -ium, *n. pl.*, the aforementioned, the foregoing

superō (1), to surpass, conquer, overcome, exceed, excel, outdo, surmount, survive

supersum, superesse, superfuī, *+ dat.*, to survive something, remain, be left over

superus, -a, -um, *adj.*, above, high; *as substantive*, god, divinity

suppetō, -ere, suppetīvī, suppetītum, to be available

suppleō, -ēre, supplēvī, supplētum, to fill up

supplicium, -ī, *n.*, punishment, penalty, supplication, execution

suprā, *prep. + acc.*, above, beyond

surgō, -ere, surrēxī, surrēctum, to rise (up)

suscipiō, -ere, suscēpī, susceptum, to undertake, take up

suscitō (1), to rouse, awaken

suspectus, -a, -um, *adj.*, suspected

suspendō, -ere, suspendī, suspēnsum, to hang up

suspēnsus, -a, -um, *adj.*, doubtful, anxious

suspiciō, -ere, suspexī, suspectum, to look up (at)

suspiciō, -ōnis, *f.*, suspicion, mistrust

suus, -a, -um, *possessive adj.*, his, her, its, their*

sylva, -ae, *f.*, forest, variant spelling of *silva, -ae*

T

tabella, -ae, *f.*, picture, painting; small board, panel; writing tablet

tabula, -ae, *f.*, board, plank, writing tablet, (votive) tablet; portrait, painting

taceō, -ēre, tacuī, tacitum, to be silent, keep quiet, silent* C11

taciturnitās, -tātis, *f.,* silence

tacitus, -a, -um, *adj.,* silent

taeter, -tra, -trum, *adj.,* loathsome, foul

tālis, tāle, *adj.,* such, such a* C13

tam, *adv.,* so, as, such, to that degree, to such a degree*

tamen, *conj.,* however, still, nevertheless*

tametsī, *conj.,* although

tamquam, *adv.,* as, as if, as though* C7

tandem, *adv.,* at last, at length, finally*

tangō, -ere, tetigī, tāctum, to touch, graze, reach*

tantopere, *adv.,* so greatly

tantum, *adv.,* only, so much, merely* A4

tantum, -ī, *n.* so much, this much, such great, so great

tantus, -a, -um, *adj.,* so great*

tardus, -a, -um, *adj.,* slow, late

Tarentīnī, -ōrum, *m. pl.,* inhabitants of Tarentum, the Tarentines

Tartareus, -a, -um, *adj.,* infernal, having to do with Tartarus

taurus, -ī, *m.,* bull, bullock, ox

tēctum, -ī, *n.,* roof, house, shelter, dwelling (by synecdoche)* A5

tēcum = cum tē, with you*

tegō, -ere, tēxī, tēctum, to cover, protect* A1

tellūs, -ūris, *f.,* land, earth, country, ground

tēlum, -ī, *n.,* weapon, spear, javelin* C15

temerē, *adv.,* hardly, heedlessly, without good cause, recklessly, rashly, hastily

temeritās, -ātis, *f.,* rashness, recklessness, whim, caprice, heedlessness

temperō (1), *ā(b) + abl.,* to refrain from, refrain, control

tempestīvus, -a, -um, *adj.,* timely, seasonable, ripe

templum, -ī, *n.,* temple, shrine, sanctuary*

temptō (1), to try, attempt, test*

tempus, -oris, *n.,* time*

tenāx, -ācis, *adj.,* tenacious, holding (to)

tendō, -ere, tetendī, tentum *or* **tēnsum,** to go, advance, strive, stretch, stretch out, extend, proceed

tenebrae, -ārum, *f. pl.,* shadows, darkness*

Tenedos, -ī, *f.,* small island near Troy

teneō, -ēre, tenuī, tentum, to hold; **memoriā teneō,** to remember, keep in mind*

tener, -era, -erum, *adj.,* tender, sensitive, fragile, delicate, weak

tenuis, -e, *adj.,* thin, tender, slender

tenus, *prep. + abl.,* to, up to, as far as

tepeō, -ēre, to be warm, tepid

ter, *adv.,* three times

teres, -etis, *adj.,* smooth, round

tergum, -ī, *n.,* back, body, rear

terra, -ae, *f.,* land*

terreō, -ēre, terruī, territum, to terrify, frighten

territō (1), to frighten, terrify, alarm

tertius, -a, -um, *adj.,* third* C6

testāmentum, -ī, *n.,* testimony, a witness's account; will

testūdō, -dinis, *f.,* shell of a tortoise, lyre

thalamus, -ī, *m.,* bedroom, marriage chamber

theātrum, -ī, *n.,* theatre

theologia, -ae, *f.,* theology

theologus, -ī, *m.,* theologian

Thisbē, -bēs, *f.,* Thisbe (a Greek name)

thymum, -ī, *n.,* thyme, a flowering plant

tigris, tigris/tigridis, *m./f.,* tiger

timeō, -ēre, timuī, —, to fear, be afraid, have cause to fear, be at risk from, dread, be anxious*

timidus, -a, -um, *adj.,* trembling, fearful

timor, -ōris, *m.,* fear*

tingō, -ere *or* **tinguō, -ere, tinxī, tinctum,** to wet, soak, dye, stain, tinge

tintinō (1), to ring, tingle

titulus, -ī, *m.,* title, degree

tollō, -ere, sustulī, sublātum, to lift up, raise, destroy, wipe out, lift, pick up, remove*

torpeō, torpēre, torpuī, to be numb, be stiff

torus, -ī, *m.,* (banqueting) couch, bed

tot, *indecl. adj.,* so many, in such numbers, as many* C7

totidem, *adv.,* the same number, so many

totiēns, *adv.,* so many times

tōtus, -a, -um, *adj.,* whole, entire, all* C11

tractō (1), to handle, manage

tractus, -ūs, *m.,* region

trādūcō, -ere, trādūxī, trāductum, to translate, transfer, bring across, lead over

trahō, -ere, trāxī, trāctum, to drag, draw* C7

tranquillitās, tranquillitātis, *f.,* calmness, quiet way of life, peace

tranquillus, -a, -um, *adj.,* quiet, tranquil, calm

trāns, *prep. + acc.,* across, through

trānseō, trānsīre, trānsiī, trānsitum, to go across, pass over, cross

trānsmittō, -mittere, -mīsī, -missum, to send over, hand over

trānsitus, -ūs, *m.,* a passage

tremebundus, -a, -um, *adj.,* trembling, quivering

tremō, -ere, -uī, to tremble, shake, quiver, shudder

trepidus, -a, -um, *adj.,* trembling, excited

trēs, tria, *numeral,* three* C6

tribūnal, -ālis, *n.,* platform

tribūnus, -ī, *m.* **plēbis,** tribune of the plebs

tribuō, -ere, tribuī, tribūtum, to grant, bestow, assign, give, attribute, allot* A3

trīduum, -ī, *n.,* period of three days

tristis, -e, *adj.,* sad* C6

Trōiānus, -a, -um, *adj.,* Trojan, of Troy

Trōius, -a, -um, *adj.,* Trojan, of Troy

trūcidō (1), to slaughter, butcher

truncus, -ī, *m.,* trunk, body, torso

trux, -cis, *adj.,* savage, grim, wild

tū, *personal pronoun,* you (sg.)*

tum, *adv.,* then, at that time*

tumultus, -ūs, *m.,* uproar, confusion, tumult, uprising, clamor*

tumulum, -ī, *n.,* grave, tomb

tumulus, -ī, *m.,* mound, hill

turbō (1), to confuse, shake, disturb

turgidus, -a, -um, *adj.,* swollen, turgid

turpis, -e, *adj.,* shameful, disgraceful* C11

turris, -is, *f.,* tower, turret* C13

tūs, tūris, *n.,* incense

tūtus, -a, -um, *adj.,* safe, secure* C4

tuus, -a, -um, *possessive adj.,* yours, your (sg.), of yours*

Tyrius, -a, -um, *adj.,* Tyrian, Carthaginian

Tyrrhēnus, -a, -um, *adj.,* Tyrrhenian, Etruscan

U

ūber, -eris, *adj.,* abounding in, plentiful, abundant

ubi?, *interrogative adv.,* where?* C7

ubi, *conj.,* when, where

ubīnam, *adv.,* where in the world?

ubīque, *adv.,* everywhere*

ulcīscor, ulcīscī, ultus sum, to take revenge, avenge, punish

ūllus, -a, -um, *adj.,* any*

ulna, -ae, *f.,* arm

ulterior, -ius, *adj.,* farther

ultimus, -a, -um, *adj.,* last, farthest, most remote

ultra, *prep. + acc.,* beyond

ululō (1), to howl, wail, shout, shriek

umbra, -ae, *f.,* shadow

umerus, -ī, *m.,* shoulder

umquam, *adv.,* ever*

ūnā, *adv.,* together, at the same time, along*

ūnanimus, -a, -um, *adj.,* of one mind, in accord

unda, -ae, *f.,* wave

unde, *adv.,* from where

ūndecim, *indecl. adj.,* eleven

undique, *adv.,* from all parts, from everywhere, on all sides, everywhere, from all directions* C14

unguentum, -ī, *n.,* ointment, perfume

ūniversus, -a, -um, *adj.,* all together; whole, entire

ūnus, ūna, ūnum, *adj.,* one* C7

ūnusquisque, ūnaquaeque, ūnumquidque, *pronoun,* each one, every one

urbanus, -a, -um, *adj.,* of the city, urban, refined, sophisticated, suave

urbs, urbis, *f.,* city (*usually the city of Rome*)*

urgeō, -ēre, ursī, to press (upon), push, make for

urna, -ae, *f.,* urn, pot

ūsque, *adv.,* right up, continuously, as far as one can go, constantly, continually, all the way; **ūsque ad,** up to* A7

ūsus, -ūs, *m.,* use, service, employment, need; **ūsū venīre,** to occur* A7

ut, utī, *conj., + indicative,* as, when, according to; *+ perfect indicative,* as soon as, when; *+ subjunctive,* in order to, so that, that, in the same way as* C2

uterque, utraque, utrumque, *adj. or pronoun,* each of the two, each, both

ūtilis, -e, *adj.,* useful* C7

ūtilitās, -ātis, *f.,* usefulness

utinam, *conj.,* would that!, I wish that, if only (a particle of wishing)* C1

ūtor, ūtī, ūsus sum, *+ abl.,* to use somebody or something; enjoy the friendship of, avail oneself of* C11

ūvidus, -a, -um, *adj.,* wet

V

vacuēfaciō, -ere, vacuēfēcī, vacuēfactum, to make empty, vacate

vacuus, -a, -um, *+ abl.,* empty of, empty, free, available* C4

vadum, -ī, *n.,* ford

vae, *interj., takes either the dat. or acc.,* alas, woe to!

vagor (1), to wander, roam

valeō, -ēre, valuī, valitum, *+ inf.,* to be able; be in good health; be of value, be strong, be able; **valēre ad,** to succeed at* C2

valētūdō, -ūdinis, *f.,* health, state of health* A10

vanus, -a, -um, *adj.,* empty, groundless, imaginary

vātēs, vātis, *m.,* prophet, bard, poet

–ve, *conj.,* or

vehemēns, vehementis, *adj.,* violent, vehement, earnest, enthusiastic* C5

vel, *adv.,* if you will, even, actually

vel, *conj.,* or*

vēlāmen, -minis, *n.,* veil, cloak, garment

vēlōx, -ōcis, *adj.,* swift, quick, rapid, fleet

vēlum, -ī, *n.,* sail, curtain

velut, *adv.,* just as

vēna, -ae, *f.,* vein, artery, blood vessel

venēnum, -ī, *n.,* poison, venom, drug*

veniō, -īre, vēnī, ventum, to come*

ventitō (1), to go often

ventus, -ī, *m.,* wind*

Venus, -eris, *f.,* goddess of love and beauty; love

Venusīnus, -a, -um, *adj.,* Venusian, from Venusia, Italy

venustus, -a, -um, *adj.,* charming

vēr, vēris, *n.,* spring

verbum, -ī, *n.,* word, speech, talk*

vērē, *adv.,* correctly, truly

vereor, verērī, veritus sum, to fear, respect, be afraid*

vergō, vergere, to slope, lie

vērō, *adv.,* in fact, truly; moreover (introducing a further argument)

versō (1), to turn*

versor (1), to be occupied in, be involved in, live, dwell, occupy oneself with, be engaged in, be busy (with)* C13

versus, -ūs, *m.,* line of writing, line of verse, verse, line (of poetry)* A8

vertex, -ticis, *m.,* peak, summit, head, top

vertō, -ere, vertī, versum, to turn, change

Verucloetius, -ī, *m.,* Verucloetius, a Helvetian leader

vērum, *conj.,* but

vērum, -ī, *n.,* truth, right, reality

vērus, -a, -um, *adj.,* well-founded, justifiable, true, real, genuine, honest*

Vestālis, -e, *adj.,* of or pertaining to Vesta, goddess of the hearth (fireplace)

vester, vestra, vestrum, *adj.,* yours (pl.), your, your own*

vestīgium, -(i)ī, *n.,* step, track, trace, footprint

vestīmentum, -ī, *n.,* garment, (pl.) clothes*

vestis, -is, *f.,* clothes, attire, cloth(ing), garment, robe* C2

vetus, veteris, *adj.,* long-established, old* C5

vetustus, -a, -um, *adj.,* old, ancient, former*

vexātiō, -ōnis, *f.,* harassing

via, -ae, *f.,* road*

vibrō (1), to quiver, vibrate, dart

vīcīnus, -a, -um, *adj.,* neighboring, nearby

vicis (*gen.*), **vicem,** *pl.* **vicēs, vicibus,** turn, alternation

victor, -ōris, *m.,* victor* C4

vīcus, -ī, *m.,* village

videō, -ēre, vīdī, vīsum, to see, (passive) seem*

vigeō, -ēre, viguī, to flourish, be strong, thrive

vigil, vigilis, *adj.,* wakeful, watchful, sleepless

vigilia, -ae, *f.,* night watch

vigiliae, -ārum, *f. pl.,* keeping awake, periods of keeping awake

vigilō (1), to be attentive

vincō, -ere, vīcī, victum, to conquer, defeat*

vinculum, -ī, *n.,* chain, fetter; *pl.,* prison*

vindicō (1), to punish

vīnum, -ī, *n.,* wine* C5

violēns, -entis, *adj.,* violent, vehement

vir, virī, *m.,* man*

virgō, -inis, *f.,* virgin, girl of marriageable age, maiden* A9

viridis, -e, *adj.,* green, fresh, young

virtūs, -ūtis, *f.,* virtue, courage, goodness, manliness, excellence* C5

vīs, vim, vī, *f. pl.,* **vīrēs, vīrium,** force, power, strength, violence; **prō vīribus,** with all one's might*

vīscus, -eris, *n.* (*usually pl.*), internal organs, vitals, bowels

vīsō, vīsere, vīsī, vīsum, to go and see, look at, visit

vīsus, -ūs, *m.,* sight, view, vision, aspect

vīta, -ae, *f.,* life*

vitālis, -e, *adj.,* vital, concerning life

vitiō (1), to impair, cause defects in

vitium, -ī, *n.,* vice, defect, moral failing, fault, flaw* C5

vītō (1), to avoid, evade, shun

vitta, -ae, *f.,* fillet, garland, band

vīvō, -ere, vīxī, vīctum, to live, be alive*

vīvus, -a, -um, *adj.,* alive, living, running, natural, lifelike

vix, *adv.,* hardly, scarcely, barely* C7

vixdum, *adv.,* hardly yet, barely

vocō (1), to call*

volēns, -entis, *adj.,* willing

volō, velle, voluī, —, to want, mean, signify, wish* C7

volō (1), to fly, flit, move with speed

volucris, -is, *f.,* bird

volūmen, -ūminis, *n.,* book, volume, fold, coil, roll* A8

voluntās, -tātis, *f.,* will, approval, desire; consent* C13

voluptās, -tātis, *f.,* pleasure, sexual pleasure

volvō, -ere, volvī, volūtum, to turn round, undergo* C14

vōs, *personal pronoun,* you (*pl.*)*

vōtīvus, -a, -um, *adj.,* votive, relating to a vow

vōtum, -ī, *n.,* prayer, vow, oath

vōx, vōcis, *f.,* voice, saying, word* C2

vulgāris, -e, *adj.,* common, ordinary

vulnerō (1), to wound, harm*

vulnus, -eris, *n.,* wound, deadly blow*

vultus, -ūs, *m.,* face, expression, countenance, aspect, complexion* C2

BIBLIOGRAPHY

WORKS CONSULTED

CAESAR

Harkness, Albert. *Caesar's Commentaries of the Gallic War*. Revised ed. New York, NY: Appleton and Company, 1886.

Kelsey, Francis W. *Caesar's Gallic Wars*. 8th ed. Norwood, MA: Plimpton Press, 1896.

CATULLUS

Dettmer, Helena. "Catullus Kisses: A Study in Passion," *Ars Lyrica*, Special Edition (1988), 71–82.

———. *Catullus: Love by the Numbers*. New York, NY: Peter Lang Publishers, 1997.

Garrison, Daniel H. *The Student's Catullus*. 2nd ed. Norman, Oklahoma and London, England: University of Oklahoma Press, 1995.

Lyne, R. O. A. M. *The Latin Love Poets*. Oxford: Oxford University Press, 1980.

———. "The Text of Catullus 107," *Hermes* 113 (1985), 498–500.

Pack, Roger. "Catullus, Carmen 5: Abacus or Finger-Counting?" *American Journal of Philology* 77 (1956), 47–51.

Quinn, Kenneth. *Catullus: The Poems*. 2nd ed., Reprint, New York, NY: St. Martin's Press, 1980.

CICERO

Craig, Christopher. "Three Simple Questions for Teaching Cicero's First Catilinarian." *Classical Journal* 88 (1993), 255–267.

Williams, Rose. *Cicero the Patriot*. Wauconda, IL: Bolchazy-Carducci Publishers, 2004.

HORACE

Lee, M. Owen. *Word, Sound, and Image in the Odes of Horace*. Ann Arbor, MI: University of Michigan, 1969.

LATIN DICTIONARIES

Lewis, Charlton T., and Charles Short. *A Latin Dictionary*. Oxford: Clarendon Press, 1879.

Oxford Latin Dictionary. Edited by P. G. W. Glare. Oxford: Clarendon Press, 1982.

LATIN GRAMMARS

Bennett, Charles E. *New Latin Grammar.* 1908. Reprint, Wauconda, IL: Bolchazy-Carducci Publishers, 1995.

Gildersleeve, Basil L., and Gonzalez Lodge. *Gildersleeve's Latin Grammar.* 3rd ed. 1895. Reprinted, Wauconda, IL: Bolchazy-Carducci Publishers, 2003.

Greenough, J. B., A. A. Howard, G. L. Kittredge, and B. L. D'Ooge. *Allen and Greenough's New Latin Grammar.* 1888. Reprint, New Rochelle, NY: Aristide D. Caratzas, 1998.

Woodcock, E. C. *A New Latin Syntax,* 1959. Reprinted, Wauconda, IL: Bolchazy-Carducci Publishers, 1987.

LATIN TEXTBOOKS

Horn, A., J. F. Gummere, and M. M. Forbes. *Using Latin 2.* Glenview, IL: Scott, Foresman, and Company, 1963.

Jenney, C., Jr., E. C. Baade, D. D. Coffin, and R. V. Scudder. *Second Year Latin.* Needham, MA: Prentice Hall, 1990.

Jenney, C., Jr., R. V. Scudder, and D. D. Coffin. *Third Year Latin.* Needham, MA: Prentice Hall, 1990.

Osburn, LeaAnn. *Beyond Latin One.* Elmhurst, IL: L and L Enterprises, 2000.

Palma, Ronald B., and David J. Perry. *Ecce Romani III.* 4th ed. Boston, MA: Pearson Prentice Hall, 2005.

Ullman, B. L., and A. I. Suskin. *Latin for Americans, Third Book.* Mission Hills, CA: Glencoe/McGraw Hill, 1990.

Ullman, B. L., C. Henderson Jr., and N. E. Henry. *Latin for Americans, Second Book.* New York, NY: The MacMillan Company, 1968.

LITERARY TERMS

Preminger, Alex, Frank J. Warnke, and O. B. Hardison. *The Princeton Handbook of Poetic Terms.* 1965. Reprint, Princeton, N.J.: University of Princeton Press, 1986.

Smith, Richard Upsher, Jr. *A Glossary of Terms of Terms in Grammar, Rhetoric, and Prosody for Readers of Latin and Greek: A Vade Mecum.* Mundelein, IL: Bolchazy-Carducci Publishers, 2011.

OVID

Allen, J. H. and W. F., J. B. Greenough, and H. N. Fowler. *Selections from Ovid, Chiefly the Metamorphoses.* Boston, MA: Ginn and Company, 1890.

Davis, Sally R. "Bringing Ovid into the AP Latin Classroom: Pygmalion," *Classical Journal* 90 (1995), 273–278.

VERGIL

Williams, R. D. *The Aeneid of Vergil, Books 1–6.* Basingstoke and London: St. Martin's Press, 1972.

Williams, Rose. *The Labors of Aeneas.* Wauconda, IL: Bolchazy-Carducci Publishers, 2003.

PHOTOGRAPHY CREDITS

LAST CENTURY OF THE ROMAN REPUBLIC ESSAY

Bust of Caesar (© 2012 Shutterstock Images LLC)

CHAPTER 1 CAESAR

Mantegna's Triumph of Caesar (Scala/Art Resource, NY)

Testudo Reenactment (© 2012 Shutterstock Images LLC)

Mourning Julius Caesar (© 2012 Shutterstock Images LLC)

Swiss Stamp: Chur Bimillennium (© 2012 Shutterstock Images LLC)

Lake Geneva (© 2012 Shutterstock Images LLC)

Trajan's Column (© 2012 Shutterstock Images LLC)

Forum of Julius Caesar (© 2012 Shutterstock Images LLC)

Tombstone of Roman *Imaginifer* (Wolfgang Sauber/ Wikimedia Commons)

CHAPTER 2 CATULLUS

Sappho Taking Notes from Cupid (National Trust Photo Library/Art Resource, NY)

Papyrus (© 2012 Photos.com)

Evangelist with Scroll (© 2012 Shutterstock Images LLC)

"Villa of Catullus," Sirmio (© 2012 Shutterstock Images LLC)

Statue of Sappho (Wikimedia Commons)

Lesbos (© 2012 Photos.com)

CHAPTER 3 CICERO

Fulvia's Visit to Cicero (Réunion des Musées Nationaux/Art Resource, NY)

Tusculum (Ad Meskens/Wikimedia Commons)

Roman Forum (© 2012 Shutterstock Images LLC)

Roman Road in Tall Aqibrin (Bernard Gagnon/Wikimedia Commons)

Bust of Cicero (© 2012 Shutterstock Images LLC)

Roman Forum and Curia (© 2012 Photos.com)

Curia Exterior, Rome (© 2012 Photos.com)

Curia Interior, Rome (Wikimedia Commons)

Roman Faesula (© 2012 Photos.com)

Zeno of Citium (© 2012 Shutterstock Images LLC)

Illuminated Cicero Manuscript (Erich Lessing/Art Resource, NY)

AUGUSTUS AND THE PRINCIPATE ESSAY

Colossal Statue of Augustus (Marie-Lan Nguyen, 2011/Wikimedia Commons)

Bust of Livia (Marie-Lan Nguyen, 2007/Wikimedia Commons)

Ara Pacis (© 2012 Shutterstock Images LLC)

Ephesus Gateway (© 2012 Shutterstock Images LLC)

Augustan Forum (© 2012 Shutterstock Images LLC)

CHAPTER 4 VERGIL

Illuminated *Aeneid* Manuscript (British Library/HIP/ Art Resource, NY)

Statue of Vergil, Los Angeles (© 2012 Shutterstock Images LLC)

Olympians on Pediment (© 2012 Shutterstock Images LLC)

Odysseus Sailing (© 2012 Photos.com)

Carthage (© 2012 Shutterstock Images LLC)

Laocoon Group (Yair Haklai/Wikimedia Commons)

Statue of Laocoon (© 2012 Shutterstock Images LLC)

The Trojan Horse (© 2012 Shutterstock Images LLC)

Venus and Anchises (Google Art Project/Wikimedia Commons)

Statue of Aeneas, Anchises, and Ascanius (Alphanidon/ Wikimedia Commons)

INDEX

Note: A reference to xvi or 192 indicates the main text, while xvi*p* or 192*p* indicates a picture or its caption.

imperfect subjunctive, formed from present active infinitive, 145

imperium maius, 225

impersonal verbs, 300, 563–564

    infinitive with, 330

    licet, 445

    with substantive clauses of result, 461–462

    use of infinitive with, 551

inceptive (inchoative) verbs, 448

indefinite pronouns and adjectives, 532–533

indefinite relatives, 533

indicative, in indirect statement, 568–569

indirect statements, questions, and commands

    distinguishing between them, 397

    indirect commands, 48, 542

        with *ut* omitted, 369

    indirect questions, 396–397, 541

        futurity in, 565

    indirect statement, 72–73

        infinitive in, 330, 551

        moods in, 568–570

infinitive

    complementary, 85–86, 98, 183

    in exclamations, 166

    future passive, 563

    historical, 246

    with impersonal verbs, 85–86, 551

    present active, used to form imperfect subjunctive, 145

    of purpose, 329, 552–553

    tenses of, in indirect statement, 553

    uses of, 551–552

        summarized, 330

Inquisition, 457

intensive pronoun *(ipse, ipsa, ipsum),* 35, 44, 122, 509

    syntax, 531

interrogative pronoun and adjective, 510

intransitive and transitive verbs, 538

invocation of the gods, characteristic of epic, 233, 239

Iris, 234

irony, 52, 165, 297, 490

irregular comparatives and superlatives, 115, 503

is, ea, id, 25, 35, 122

islands, usually feminine in Latin, 259, 336

iste, ista, istud, 508, 532

i-stem adjectives, 499

i-stem nouns, 51, 56, 303–304, 495–496

ita, as "tip-off" word for a result clause, 144–145

Iulus (Ascanius), 231, 272, 274, 276

J

James IV, of Scotland, 429

Jason, 351

Jerome, Saint, 414, 446, 466

John, King, 461*p*

Jonas, Jodocus, 436

Jubilee Year, 424

judge *(iūdex),* role of, 134

Judgment of Paris, 287*p*

Julia, daughter of Augustus, 228

Julia, daughter of Julius Caesar, 7, 128, 475

Julius II, Pope, 415

Juno, 229*p*, 234, 287*p*

Jupiter, 196, 234, 335

Juvenal, 308

K

Kalendae, Kalends, 69, 446

kiss, Latin words for, 356

Kore (Persephone), 328

L

Laeca, Marcus Porcius, 161, 170

Laelius, C., 206, 215*p*

land reform, 2–4

Landivar, *Rusticātiō Mexicāna,* 235

languages, Romance, 338*p*

Laocoon, 254, 260*p*, 263*p*, 265*p*

Larnaca, 211*p*

Latin

    as language of science, 410

    as a second (nonvernacular) language, 410–411

Latin-speaking world, map, xxxiv–xxxv

Latinus, 241

Latium, 241, 273

Latona (Leto), 335

laurel, sacred to Apollo, 343

Lavinia (person), 241

Lavinium (place), 241, 273

Leo X, Pope, 420

Lepidus, 222–223, 476

Lesbia, xxix, 78–79, 80, 92, 98, 118

Lesbos, 119*p*, 310, 343, 481

Leuconoe, 310, 320

    etymology of, 321

libertīnī, freedmen, 225*p*

Libya, 288

Licinius, 332

limping iamb (meter), 482–483

Linacre, Thomas, 444

literary present tense, 539

litotes, 52, 99, 158, 327, 371, 490

Livia Drusilla, 222*p*, 223

locative case, 138, 537

long vowels in Latin meter, 479

Longinus, *On the Sublime,* 132

Lord of the Rings (Tolkien), 235

Los Angeles Public Library, 231*p*

Louis IX, 435*p*

love in Horace, 312–314, 326

love poetry, 79–80

temporal clauses, 544
  with *cum*, 96
Tenedos, 254
tenses in indirect statement,
  72–73
Teutoberg Forest, Battle of, 227,
  478
Thames River, 431*p*
thanks, words for, 405
Thessaly, 129
thinking, Latin verbs expressing,
  69
Third Civil War, 476
Thisbe. *See* Pyramus and Thisbe
three, divine significance of, 401
Tiberius Caesar, 223, 228, 478
Tibullus, 80
tigress, 384*p*
time, Latin words related to, 324
tmesis, 259, 492
toga, 220*p*
Tolkien, J. R. R., 235
Tomis, 348, 365*p*
tot
  as "tip-off" word for a result
    clause, 144–145
  tot . . . quot, 216
totiēns . . . quotiēns, 216
Trajan's Column, 39*p*
transferred epithet, 120, 245, 278,
  296, 341, 492
transitive and intransitive verbs,
  538
trees, usually feminine in Latin,
  336
tribunes (civilian), 2–5
tribūnicia potestās, 225, 228, 477
tricolon, 177, 379, 464, 492
Triumvirate, First, 6–7, 11–12, 127,
  129, 475
Triumvirate, Second, 129,
  222–223, 476
trochee, 480
Trojan Horse, 254, 265*p*

Trojan War, 231, 254
Trojans, 229, 246
Troy, 78, 229*p*, 273, 351
  fall of, 254
Tullia, 129, 476
tum . . . cum, 216
Turkey, 138–139, 225*p*

U

ubi, unde, and *quō,* 175
Uffizi Gallery, 467*p*
Underworld, 233, 389*p*, 463–465
universities, medieval and
  Renaissance, 411, 415, 420,
  424
ŪNUS NAUTA rule, 35
ut
  with the indicative ('as'), 52,
    183, 197
  with the subjunctive (purpose),
    47–48

V

Valla, Lorenzo, 415, 417*p*, 418, 446
Varius, 309
Varus, Quintilius, 227
Vasari, Giorgio, 467*p*
vase painting, Attic, 265, 310*p*
Vatinius, 128
Venus, 227*p*, 231, 233–234, 246,
  275*p*, 287*p*, 312, 315, 390,
  400. *See also* Aphrodite.
Venus de Milo, 275*p*
Venus Genetrix, Temple of, 43*p*
Venusia (Venosa), 308, 329*p*, 469
verb conjugations
  regular, 510–515
  deponent, 515–518
  irregular
    eō, 521
    ferō, 525–527
    fīō, 527–528
    mālō, 524

nōlō, 523
possum, 520
sum, 519
volō, 522
gerunds and gerundives,
  528–529
verbal repetition, 101
verbs
  taking the dative case, 31
Vergil (Publius Vergilius Maro),
  xxix–xxx, xxxii, 78, 119, 226,
  229–235, 307*p*, 309, 414, 441,
  462, 463, 472, 476
  Aeneid, xxix–xxx, xxxii, 228,
    308, 350–351, 477
    meter of, 481
  Eclogues, 230, 351, 477
  friend of Horace, 308
  Georgics, 119*p*, 351, 477
  influence of, 235
Verona, 78, 80, 84, 230
Verres, 6, 127
Vestal Virgins, 342
  House of the Vestals, 181*p*
videō, passive means 'seem,' 64, 165
vīs (ambiguous noun and verb
  form), 64
vīs (noun), irregular declension of,
  206, 496
vocalization of prefixes, 465
volitive subjunctive, 540
vowel lengths in Latin meter, 479
Vulcan, 234

W

wall
  Latin words for, 201, 353
  in Pyramus and Thisbe story,
    352–353, 359
Washington, George, 468
wedding, features of Roman, 289
West Side Story, 349
Wilde, Oscar, 349
Williams, Rose, 235

wine, straining of, 322

wishes, and fear clauses, 398

word order

    complex, 358

    flexibility of, in Horace,
      310–311

    significant, xxix–xxxi, 267

Y

Yeats, W. B., 339*p*

yoke, sending a defeated army
     under, 69

Z

Zeno of Citium, 211*p*, 213

zeugma, 380, 492